EDITORIAL ADDRESS
Common Market Law Review
Europa Instituut, Hugo de Grootstraat 27,
Leyden, The Netherlands

Orders for subscriptions, advertisements and back issues should be sent either direct to the general distributor:

Academic Book Services Holland, P.O. Box 66, Groningen, The Netherlands
phone: (0)50-162329 telex: 53443

or to
Fred B. Rothman & Company, 57 Leuning Street, South Hackensack, New Jersey, N.J. 17606, U.S.A.
Hammicks - Sweet & Maxwell, 50 West Street, Farnham, Surrey, U.K.
Office International de Librairie, 30 Avenue Marnix, 1050-Bruxelles, Belgique.

Annual subscription price for Volume 13 (1976): Dfl. 125.00/ $ 52.00; single issue: Dfl. 32.00/ $ 13.25.

Originally published by A. W. Sijthhoff International Publishing Company in 1976

COMMON MARKET LAW REVIEW

Volume 13
1976

SPRINGER-SCIENCE+BUSINESS MEDIA, B.V

Published in Cooperation with the British Institute of International and Comparative Law and the Europa Instituut of the University of Leyden

Editorial Address

Common Market Law Review
Europa Instituut, Hugo de Grootstraat 27,
Leyden, The Netherlands

This Review may be cited as *13 C.M.L. Rev. 1976*

ISBN 978-94-015-2075-1 ISBN 978-94-015-3283-9 (eBook)
DOI 10.1007/978-94-015-3283-9

Originally published by A. W. Sijthhoff International Publishing Company in 1976

INDEX VOLUME XIII

I. SUBJECTS

II. CASE LAW

A. COURT OF JUSTICE OF THE EUROPEAN COMMUNITIES

B. NATIONAL COURTS OF THE MEMBER STATES

III. ARTICLES AND SHORTER ARTICLES

IV. LIST OF AUTHORS

Names of authors who have contributed to Volume XIII

V. LIST OF BOOKS REVIEWED

Author/Editor	Book Title	Reviewer	Pages
B. Börner and K. Carstens	*Die Aussenbeziehungen der Europäischen Gemeinschaft*	P. J. G. Kapteyn	443-444
J. Boulouis and R. M. Chevallier	*Grands arrêts de la Cour de Justice des Communautés Européennes*	K. Mortelmans	143-144
J. Rideau, R. M. Chevallier, J.-M. Rainaud, L. Balmond and A. Bailleux	*Droit Institutionnel des Communautés Européennes*	K. Mortelmans	143-144
Studienvereinigung Kartellrecht	*Neue Entwicklungen im EWG-Kartellrecht*	H. W. Wertheimer	445-447
A. von Geusau	*Energy in the European Communities*	R. Barents	444-445
H. P. Ipsen	*Europäischen Gemeinschaftsrecht*	J. A. Winter	555-556

TABLE OF CONTENTS

EDITORIAL COMMENTS ON EUROPEAN UNION

Already at the Paris Summit Meeting on 19-21 October, 1972, it was decided to request the institutions of the Community to draw up a report on the question of transforming, "before the end of the decade and with the fullest respect for the Treaties already signed, the whole complex of the relations of member States into a European Union". Another Summit conference in Paris on 9 and 10 December, 1974, repeated this request and invited Mr. Tindemans, Prime Minister of Belgium, to submit a "comprehensive report" to the Heads of Government before the end of 1975, "on the basis of the reports received from the institutions and of consultations which he is to have with the Governments and with a wide range of public opinion in the Community."

In the meantime the European Parliament, the Commission, the Court, and, using its newly required right of initiative, the Economic and Social Committee, have made their ideas known. It is now up to Mr. Tindemans to draw his conclusions from the reactions of the institutions and from the wide-ranging consultations he conducted over the past year in the various national capitals. His comprehensive report to the Heads of Government will not be available to the December Summit in Rome; but he should not be blamed for this delay. His task is far from easy. The whole idea of a European Union was born out of the clearly uncontrollable need of the assembled Heads of Governments to find something to cheer up their nations when the situation looks grim, or to divert their attention from the failures of the past. Nobody seems to have had any clear-conceived ideas about what was meant by the phrase "European Union", or, at any rate to have expressed such ideas at the Summit meeting, which, of course, facilitated reaching agreement as to the launching of the phrase.

But once it is necessary to elaborate the concept of a European Union, disagreement as to form and substance will appear, as Mr. Tindemans will have discovered when studying the notes he made of his visits to the capitals of the nine member States. Will he be able to bridge the gap between the desirable and the attainable? Or will he fall in to the trap of presenting something as a "European Union" that will not be unlike the new clothes of the emperor in Andersen's fairy-tale? It would be better to forget about a European Union, if it would only consist of dressing up what we have now. It does not make much sense to add new subjects of co-operation to the already rather long list, to further inflate the already top-heavy intergovernmental superstructure, to amend again the fairly complicated decision-making procedure, and to further reiterate the exhortations directed to the governments to apply the majority principle and to improve the co-ordination of national policies.

In a European Union that really deserves the name a satisfactory solution should be found for the problem of how to move from the rather easy stage of "passive" integration, *i.e.* the elimination of barriers to the free movement of the factors of production, to that of "active" integration, *i.e.* the implementation of common policies and action. The urgency of solving this problem should be stressed, because it is to be feared that "passive" integration will be mortally endangered in the absence of substantial progress in the field of "active" integration.

As the European Commission rightly observes in its report (para. 30), domestic and international economic and social developments and public demands lead to ever increasing interventions of national authorities in the national economy. Such interventions threaten the functioning and, in the long run, the continuing existence of the common market. In order to save the common market from withering away such interventions should not take place in a purely national framework, but in the framework of policies and actions developed and determined at the Union level. The existing co-ordination mechanisms have proved to be completely unsatisfactory to this end. Common rules for national policies should be adopted and enforced by the institutions of the Union. And these institutions should be given the necessary legal and financial instruments enabling them to influence directly certain structural and conjectural elements of economic and social development within the Union. (Cf. para. 34 of the Commission's report).

But how is one to find an adequate institutional structure capable of setting and enforcing such rules, and of handling such instruments in an effective and democratic way? On this point the European Commission is most explicit by proposing a kind of federal structure. A rather daring proposal, taking into account that one of the most influential Heads of Government, Chancellor Schmidt, is thinking in terms of expanding and strengthening the European Summit Council and the co-ordinating Council of Ministers of Foreign Affairs at the expense, one may expect, of the functions of the only embryonic element of a federal government in the existing Communities, the European Commission.

Nevertheless, as to the substantive and legal aspects of a European Union, the European Commission's report and, to a lesser extent, the opinion of the Economic and Social Committee, are worth consideration. It is interesting to note the priority that is given by the Commission to the realization of the Economic and Monetary Union as an essential element of a European Union. Studying this part of the report one gets the impression that the "monetarist" approach is gaining some ground in Brussels. Following the suggestion of the report of the Marjolin study group, the introduction of a European unit of account and official means of settlement is recommended. Much importance is attached to a gradually expanding Community budget as a means of influencing demand within the Union. Such an expansion of the budget is to be expected, if the proposals of the Commission are accepted that ask for the assignment to the Union of considerably more financial resources for the support of an active economic and social policy.

Unlike the European Commission, the European Parliament has not seized the opportunity of making a substantive contribution to the debate on a European Union. Its resolution is of an exhortatory nature, lacks any evidence of an earnest search for new solutions, and is largely devoted to the question of short-term improvements of the Parliament's own role in the decision-making process. One wonders whether this kind of a "report" to the Heads of Governments is the result of a sublime sense of realism, of want of time, or of political impotence. Anyhow, the resolution is rather sad reading for someone who believes that the real impetus for a European Union should come from parliamentary quarters.

The European Court's report deals mainly with the Rule of Law in a European Union. It contains a number of valuable suggestions for the improvement of judicial procedures to sustain it. We hope to publish in one of the forthcoming issue of this Review a contribution which will comment on these suggestions and on those concerning the same topic that are contained in the European Commission's report.

Editors' Note: since the time of writing of these Comments, the Tindemans Report has been presented to the Council. The Common Market Law Review will return to the subject of this Report in forthcoming Comments and articles.

THE EUROPEAN COOPERATION GROUPING

by

R. R. Drury*

I. INTRODUCTORY

(a) *Its Rôle in the EEC*

The European Cooperation Grouping (the Grouping) [1] is a new form of commercial association proposed by the Commission of the European Economic Community. The rôle that is envisaged for it can best be illustrated by means of a comparison with the proposed European Company.

The European Company Statute is aimed at providing a form of business entity that will facilitate long term cooperation between companies in different member States of the EEC. It seeks to assist in the development of permanent links between companies "whose activity is not confined to meeting purely local requirements".[2] Even with the proposed reduction in the minimum capital requirements announced by the Commission,[3] it is still obvious that this form of cooperation is restricted to large and medium-sized companies. Smaller businesses will not get a chance to participate. These two limiting factors of size of founder members and the semi-permanent nature of the link have been removed in the Commission's proposal for a European Cooperation Grouping.

The basic concept of the Grouping proposal is the promotion of cross-frontier cooperation between its members, rather than the pursuit

* Solicitor, Lecturer in Law, University of Durham.

1. See generally: P. Durand, "Vers un groupement européen d'intérêt économique?" J.C.P., ed. C.I. 1972, 10630; Pételaud, "Etude comparée de l'avant project d'un règlement portant création d'un groupement européen d'intérêt économique et de l'ordonnance du septembre 23, 1967 sur les groupements d'intérêt économique", (1972) Rev. Soc. 451; J.-P. Dubois and P. Guez, "Le groupement d'intérêt économique: jurisprudence française et projet européen", J.C.P., ed. C.I. 1970, 89021; J.-P. Dubois, "The economic interest group at Community level, the institutional context and political integration", 8 C.M.L. Rev. 1971, 168-183; Guyénot, "La vocation européenne des groupements d'intérêt économique comme instruments de coopération d'entreprises dans le marché commun", Gaz.Pal.Doct. July 28-29, 1971; Müller-Gugenberger: "Die Europäische Wirtschaftliche Interessengemeinschaft", *Aussenwirtschaftsdienst* (1972) 110.

2. Preamble to the proposed Statute for the European Company submitted by the Commission to the Council on June 20, 1970.

3. *The Times*, July 11, 1974,—Report on proceedings in the European Parliament; Bull. of the E.C., 5-1975, p. 22. The amended draft Regulation is contained in Suppl. 4/75, Bull. of the E.C.

13 C.M.L. Rev. 1976, 7-35

of profit as a business entity in its own right,[4] this latter being more the rôle envisaged for the European Company. The idea of assisting in the creation of an enlarged market, responsive as a unit to economic factors in the same way as national markets, is found in the Preamble to the draft Regulation establishing the Grouping, in terminology similar to that used in the European Company Statute. So too is a statement of the obstacle to cooperation presented by "legal, fiscal and psychological difficulties". Thereafter, the solutions to the problem of facilitating effective cooperation between entities subject to different national laws begin to diverge. The European Company is seen as a supra-national entity to make possible "the unimpeded formation and management of undertakings of European dimensions produced by regrouping the forces of national companies".[5] The Grouping, however, aims at producing "a vehicle for cooperation with a contractual basis" which will fulfil various functions for the members, to "facilitate the adaptation of their activities to the economic conditions of an enlarged market".[6] The members of the Grouping are autonomous profit-making entities, while the Grouping is there to provide joint facilities, or to provide a close or loose-knit structure enabling them to combine for a given purpose. Without wishing to obscure the true situation by a glib analogy, one could say that if the European Company can be viewed as a supra-national company, then the Grouping could be looked upon as a kind of supra-national partnership or joint venture.

(b) *Outline of Structure*

What then is the structure provided by the draft Regulation? It is a structure where flexibility is of the essence,—as the Commission's Information Memo states, "Indeed, the grouping is designed, above all, to allow for the conclusion of temporary combinations of interests, carried out under highly flexible procedures, and capable of rapid adaptation to the prevailing trends in the economic situation".

The concept is that two or more companies, firms or sole traders in any combination should enter into a contract to collaborate in a joint venture for a particular purpose and for a particular period of time. Registration of this contract, in one of the registries to be set up in the member States, confers a separate legal personality on the entity. The parties to this contract must come from at least two member States. The purpose, or object, of the enterprise is totally introverted, being the

4. Art. 2(1) of the draft Regulation, COM(73)2046, Dec. 21, 1973. Unless otherwise stated all subsequent references are to the draft Regulation.

5. See n.2.

6. Preamble to the draft Regulation.

provision of some form of service, administrative or practical, to the membership alone. For example, egg producers on the Franco-Belgian border might combine to run a packing station for their end products, and possibly to market them under one brand name. The members are jointly and severally liable for the debts of the Grouping. *Prima facie* every member has an equal say in the control of the Grouping, and it should be emphasised that they control the Grouping, and not the other way around. A Grouping cannot be the basis for the formation of a pyramidical multi-national enterprise, i.e. it cannot provide a management service for its members. Individual sovereignty, so to speak, remains unimpaired, the essence being to provide an EEC structure for the coordination of such part of the interests of the members as they think desirable. Consequently, because the provision of services to members is the rationale, the Regulation lays down that the Grouping shall be non profit-making. Thus the draftsmen of the Regulation clearly do not see it as an economic entity distinct from its members, even though it is a separate legal entity. Indeed, the insolvency of the Grouping itself is glaringly absent from the list of grounds for winding up. This view is reinforced by the provision [7] that any profits that do arise shall be taxed, not on the Grouping, but in the hands of the members. No capital for the Grouping can ever be obtained from the public; provision of this commodity, should it be required, is an entirely domestic concern between the members and their bankers.

What, then, about this vaunted flexibility that was mentioned earlier? The key to this is not in what the Regulation provides for, but in what it does not provide for. It contains a mere twenty Articles as compared with the European Company Statute's 284. Basically the Regulation states that the internal structure of the Grouping may be anything that the parties care to construct. One or two minimum internal requirements are laid down, such as that each member shall have at least one vote,[8] and that there shall be a manager, but for the most part the members can arrange the nature of their mutual relationship how they please. Some provisions are incorporated which apply unless the contract says otherwise, but these need not deter the ingenious draftsmen for a moment. However, when we come to the relationship of the Grouping with the outside world, the mandatory provisions do come thick and fast. The manager's authority to bind the Grouping is widely phrased; many facts have to be recorded at national registries, and identifying details must be placed on letter headings and the like. The weighting of the provisions of the Regulation in favour of third parties is nearly as obvious here as it has

7. Art. 20.
8. Art. 6(4).

been in other EEC products, such as the company law harmonisation Directives and the European Company Statute.

(c) *Function*

Having forged this instrument of cooperation, it is instructive next to look at the purposes to which its creators envisage it being put. Article 2 and the comment on this in the explanatory memorandum attached to the Regulation stress that the Grouping is not like any other firm or business. It must not seek to make profits for itself.[9] It is merely a means whereby its members in temporary combination seek to develop their own businesses and thereby increase their own profits. Transactions between members and the Grouping are not therefore on an arm's-length basis, but the services and facilities provided by it must be paid for at cost, and capital provided, in the main as it is required.

Article 2(2) limits the activities of a Grouping to the provision of services exclusively to its members, or the processing of goods, or the packaging of finished products exclusively for the purposes of its members. This latter type of activity is easily envisaged but the explanatory memorandum helps us to flesh out the legal bones by giving several examples of the former. Thus Groupings could be formed for providing to their members services such as the establishment of a common buying office (to combine orders and thus obtain better prices), or a common sales office (allowing joint marketing for producers of the same or similar products), or a wages calculation and payment department. The list goes on to include the cooperation of several firms to compete for one large contract, work being apportioned once the contract is obtained, or alternatively a common research and development department. All these things could of course be achieved fairly easily on a national scale if restrictive trade legislation would permit. It is in providing a vehicle for such cooperation on a trans-national scale that the Grouping breaks really new ground.

Most of the examples given are slanted towards giving to smaller firms the economies of scale enjoyed by their larger competitors. This would not of course preclude the large firms from using the vehicle provided, although whether they would wish to do so is another matter. Would, for example, the English and French participants in Concord have cared to unite in this way, even though projects of this sort are within the ambit of the scheme?

Also in Article 2 is a description of one operation that a Grouping may not perform. It may not exercise management functions in respect of the

9. Art. 2(1).

business of its members. Thus a Grouping could never be a type of holding company. If this prohibition were not there, then establishment of a Grouping devoted to providing management functions would be a very neat way of bringing about a *de facto* group of companies in a manner not only possibly disguised from the shareholders, but also not revealed in the shareholdings. Use of a Grouping in such a way would make it a commercialised vehicle in a way not wanted by the draftsmen of the Regulation, and perhaps bring it into disrespect. The Grouping is seen in a way as the instrument for the cooperation of its members and not for their domination.[10]

(d) *Origins*

Finally, before moving on to a more detailed discussion of the structure of the European Grouping, a few words must be said about the antecedents of this form of business association.

The obvious model for the European Grouping was the French *Groupement d'Intérêt Economique* (the G.I.E.).[11] This was introduced into French law by Ordonnance No. 67-821 of September 23, 1967, and has, since then, proved to be a succesful innovation. Both the G.I.E. and the European Grouping are in essence vehicles to provide a very flexible means whereby firms, companies and individuals can cooperate in a venture, and at the same time retain their individual independence. Enterprises can link up to pursue some economic objective in a manner that, within a broad framework, they can tailor to their individual needs. The basic structure of the G.I.E. is the same as that of its European fledgling. It is based on a written contract (the statutes), which, with fairly few limitations, organises the control infrastructure and the operation of management. Specific objects, the duration of cooperation, methods of voting and control, meetings and procedure, and the day-to-day management should all be provided for in the statutes. The G.I.E. acquires a separate legal personality once the statutes have been deposited with the local Registrar of the Commercial Court and the G.I.E. entered on the Commercial Register.

The G.I.E. is required to have at least two organs. Firstly there are the

10. Explanatory Memorandum, at p. 32.

11. See generally: Le Gall, *French Company law*, (London 1974), pp. 28-37; Guyon and Coquereau, *Le groupement d'intérêt économique, 2nd. ed. (Paris 1973); Durand (P.) and Latscha, Le groupement d'intérêt économique*, (Paris 1968); Guyénot, *Les contrats de groupements d'intérêt économique*, (Paris 1970); Guyénot, *Encyclopédie Dalloz—Sociétés*, 2nd. ed., Vol. I, Heading, *Groupement d'intérêt économique;* Lavabre, *Le groupement d'intérêt économique: une expérience de liberté contractuelle*, (Paris 1972); Lemeunier, *Pourquoi et comment constituer un groupement d'intérêt économique*, 2nd. ed. (Paris 1972).

directors (*administrateurs*), who undertake management of the G.I.E. These must be natural persons, but apart from this, there is a complete freedom to decide upon the number, powers and conditions of office of the directors. The other compulsory organ is that of the general meeting of the members. This meets and votes as and how the statutes provide, and its powers are also subject to any conditions imposed by the statutes. The ultimate power, including power to amend the statutes, lies with this general meeting.

The types of persons (natural and legal) who may form a G.I.E. are basically the same as those laid down in the draft Regulation, but without the latter's compulsory international element. Thus partnerships, companies and individuals can all participate. The vast majority of G.I.E.s have an all French membership, although there is a small but significant number which does possess an international element, and of course this internationalism is not restricted to European participation only. Grounds for dissolution parallel those for dissolution of the European Grouping and thus include fulfilment of the object, expiry of the stated term, death, dissolution, incapacity or bankruptcy of any of its members. Like the European Grouping, the members of a G.I.E. are jointly and severally liable for its debts, but the liability of any member for a debt of the G.I.E. can be circumscribed by agreement with the third party.[12]

The mode in which a G.I.E. is financed is on the same lines as that envisaged for the European Grouping. It can have its own capital, and an increasing number of them do; but if it is formed without capital, or if its capital is insufficient, it receives contributions from its members in cash or kind. A G.I.E. is able to borrow in its own right, but can only issue debentures or bonds if its membership is composed exclusively of companies which are themselves authorised to issue bonds.[13]

The similarities to, and hence the origins of, the European Grouping are thus obvious.[14] However, there are certain elements in the composition of the G.I.E. which have not been included in the Commission's draft Regulation, and there are also other more subtle differences. Among the latter is the object or purpose of the Grouping. To a large extent the wording of the draft Regulation and Article 1 of the Ordonnance of 1967 correspond on this point. Both require that the object shall be to facilitate or develop the business of their members and to improve or increase the results of such business. But then the draft Regulation

12. Art. 4 *Ordonnance* no. 67-821 of September 23, 1967.

13. The European Grouping however cannot issue debentures or invite investment by the public at all; Art. 8(3).

14. The G.I.E. does not seem to have any equivalent elsewhere. See de Juglart and Ippolito, *Droit Commercial*, Vol.2 (Paris 1970) No. 948 n.2 p. 711.

goes on expressly to prohibit the European Grouping from seeking to make any profits for itself. It further limits its activities to the provision of services for its members, or the processing of goods, or packaging exclusively for its members. The French legislation indicates that the G.I.E. does not give rise by itself to the seeking of profits, in so far as it must be an extension of the economic activities of its members, and not a vehicle to carry on a separate business, but it does not forbid profit making. The express prohibition in the draft Regulation is much more precise and ensures that the economic activity of the European Grouping is a very strictly collateral enterprise, even more of a 'service' to its members than that required of the G.I.E. Thus a G.I.E. could exercise a management function over its members to bring about a *de facto* group of enterprises in a way prohibited to the European Grouping.[15]

The French companies legislation of 1966 introduced as an option the possibility of a two-tier management structure, and it was obviously felt that this concept could be used to advantage in the structure of the G.I.E. Thus the statutes of a G.I.E. must provide for the appointment of one or more supervisors, (having similar powers to the supervisory board of a *société anonyme*) to exercise a permanent oversight of the management of the G.I.E. by the directors. This idea has not been included in the constitution of the European Grouping, possibly because the two-tier system is as yet alien to some member States.

Another difference is that a G.I.E. must make provision for the audit of its accounts [16] (by professionally qualified accountants if it has issued bonds). No requirement to this end is made of the European Grouping; doubtless the prohibition on issuing debentures etc., and the disparity between the accountancy professions in member States explains the omission.

The last major difference between the G.I.E. and the European Grouping arises in the matter of the liability of the Grouping for the acts of its directors. In the first place, there is the provision in Article 7(2) of the draft Regulation that where two or more managers are appointed, then, if the contract so requires, the European Grouping is only bound if they act jointly.[17] This is a novel addition to the French model, and not found in it in any way. Secondly, in a G.I.E., even where there are several directors, any director has full power to bind the G.I.E., but only by an act falling within its objects.[18] This limitation is thereby able to be a trap

15. Guyon and Coquereau, *op. cit.*, n. 11, at pp. 70-72, and de Juglart and Ippolito, *op. cit.*, n. 14, No. 957, p. 116.

16. Art. 10, *Ordonnance* No. 67-821 of Sept. 23, 1967.

17. See *infra* at p. 24. Note that no limitation in the statutes on the manager's powers is valid against third parties in the G.I.E., nor with this one exception about acting jointly, in the Grouping.

18. Art. 9 para. 2 *Ordonnance* No. 67-821 of Sept. 23, 1967.

for unwary third parties who will be deprived of the security of being able to sue the substantial participants in the G.I.E. The European Grouping, however, is a notable advance on this because the draft Regulation provides in Article 7(2) that the acts of a manager are binding on the Grouping as against third parties whether they are within the Grouping's stated objects or not. These provisions reflect the care taken by the Commission in Brussels to protect third party interests.

There are other minor differences of course, but in view of the very striking similarities, who can doubt the very strong French influence in the inauguration of this European Grouping project?

II. COMMENTARY

Having covered in outline the structure of the Grouping, it is now proposed to look in more detail at the provisions of the draft Regulation. This part will be divided into four sections each dealing with one aspect of the Grouping, namely: (a) Formation, (b) Organs and relations with third parties, (c) Relationship of members *inter se,* (d) Winding up and liquidation.

(a) *Formation*

A Grouping is formed by the creation of a contract between the potential members, and its registration at one of the national registries to be created pursuant to the Regulation.[19] Details of the contract must also be published in the "official journal for the publication of matters relating to companies in the State in which the Grouping has its head office".[20] This section therefore deals with the identity or qualifications of the members, the formation contract and its attendant formalities and the nature of the entity created. Linked generally to this is the question of the hierarchy of rules governing the Grouping.

Members

Who can form a Grouping? This is dealt with in Article 3. Two is obviously the minimum number and those two must be either companies, firms, or natural persons operating a business (sole traders), or a combination of these. The key factor behind this is that the parties must be related to at least two different member States, thus promoting multinational cooperation within the EEC. The Regulation has been subjected to a tightening up process because in the earlier draft it would have been

19. Art. 4(2).
20. Art. 19(1).

possible for companies formed and resident outside the Community to participate.[21]

If two companies or firms are the founder members, they must now be "established" under the laws of different member States. Established in this context presumably means formed, or possibly, as the explanatory memorandum puts it, "subject to the laws of". This is going to give rise to the dichotomy between the incorporation theory of recognition and the *siège réel* theory.[22] It does not seem that the EEC Draft Convention on the Mutual Recognition of Companies and Legal Persons will give any assistance in solving the problem. This convention is a somewhat unhappy marriage between the two theories, although with a little more emphasis on the incorporation theory. However, it just applies to recognition and does not provide a "European" method for linking companies and the like with any particular State. It can only be supposed that national courts will have recourse to the Court of Justice under Article 177 of the EEC Treaty for an authoritative ruling.

The companies and firms eligible for membership are defined with reference to Article 58 of the EEC Treaty.[23] Thus cooperative societies and other legal persons governed by public or private law are included, but all are subject to the *caveat* that excludes non profit-making concerns. With this *caveat* in mind, it may therefore be dependent upon the vicissitudes of English politics whether our nationalised industries are included within this definition or not. More seriously, difficulties could arise over whether the English partnership is within the definition, because under English law the partnership lacks legal personality.

The word "firm", while commonly applied in England to partnerships and some other forms of business association, is not a term of art. Therefore, although this word appears in the English "Authorised Version" of the Treaty it has no strictly definable meaning in English law.[24] Whatever meaning it does have in England can, on one inter-

21. P. Durand, *op. cit.*, n. 1, at 299. Also Guyon and Coquereau, *op. cit.*, n. 11, at p. 332.

22. See Schmitthoff, *European Company Law Texts*, (London 1974) pp. 44-45. For example, a company formed in Belgium but in fact operating south of the French border could on one theory form a valid Grouping with one or more French formed and based companies, but on the other theory the mixture would be too homogenous to qualify under Art. 3.

23. Art. 58 reads as follows: "'Companies or firms' means companies or firms constituted under civil or commercial law, including cooperative societies, and other legal persons governed by public or private law, save for those which are non-profit-making."

24. Wood, V.C. in a partnership case thought that the word "firm" meant both the name or style of a business undertaking and was also descriptive of the undertaking itself. *Churton v Douglas* (1859) 28 L.J. Ch. 841. More recent usage seems to have narrowed the meaning by excluding sole traders by implication. See R.S.C. 0.81 r.9. "An individual carrying on business within the jurisdiction in a name or style other than his own name, may be sued in that name or style, *as if it were the name of a firm*, and rules 2 to 8 shall . . . *apply*

pretation, be said to be further limited in Article 58 by the reference back of the words "other legal persons", to the initial phrase "companies or firms". Thus we find that only firms which are legal persons are within the definition. This is the view taken by Lipstein.[25] If adopted it would exclude the partnership. However, an alternative interpretation would be to say that the words "other legal persons" were put in merely to extend the category "companies or firms" to its furthest possible limits, before cutting it down to its true size by the limiting phrase at the end "save for those which are non profit-making". This latter being the more exact criterion which it was desired to express. When we look at the French version of the Treaty we find that the word *"sociétés"* is the word that has been translated into "companies or firms". The term *"sociétés"* under French law embraces the rough equivalent of the English partnership *(société en nom collectif* and *société en commandite simple)* as well as the public and private company (S.A. and S.A.R.L.). All of these entities enjoy legal personality *(la personnalité morale)*.[26] Therefore, the French version is more comprehensible in referring to *"les autres personnes morales"*. Under German law and Dutch law there are also partnerships which enjoy legal personality.[27]

In support of this interpretation one could argue that the draft Regulation is a facultative document promoting international cooperation not one basically conferring some privilege on a restricted class. The term "firm" would include partnerships in other member States and the stated intention of the Preamble of the draft Regulation is to facilitate cooperation, "particularly among small and medium-sized undertakings". In such circumstances to exclude English partnerships but include sole traders would surely be anomalous. In promoting cooperation between business enterprises one would have thought that the profit-making characteristic took precedence over the legal personality aspect where the wording was ambiguous, as it is here. One is left with the impression that the alternative words "or firms" included in the English version must mean the partnership, and that therefore the possession of legal personality is not decisive for the purposes of the Grouping Regulation.

The natural person who is eligible to participate in forming a Grouping is one who "operates an industrial, commercial, small craft or

---

as if he were a partner and the name in which he carries on business were the name of his firm." Author's emphasis.

25. Lipstein, *The Law of the E.E.C.*, (London 1974), p. 135.

26. But the term *sociétés* would also include the *société en participation* which because of its secret nature neither has nor needs legal personality. But, for the same reason, would not as such join a Grouping etc.

27. Lipstein, *loc. cit.* p. 135 n. 15.

agricultural undertaking".[28] Basically then only individuals who are businessmen, or sole traders in English parlance, are to be allowed to participate in a Grouping. However, the inclusion of the words "agricultural undertaking" should be noted. Farmers, while indubitably being businessmen in the broad sense, have often not been looked upon as "commercial men".[29] However, much will depend upon the interpretation given to the word "undertaking". The explanatory memorandum baulks at giving any sort of assistance here and contents itself with saying that if the expression was not defined in the Treaty of Rome, why should it be defined in the draft Regulation. As a final justification the draftsman adds [30] "Requests for its interpretation can always be made to the Court of Justice of the European Communities." It is thought that this approach will not give much solace to a French dairy farmer wanting to cooperate with various firms in a milk processing venture.

One last point on the characteristics of the potential members is contained in Article 3(2) where it is laid down that every member of a Grouping must be resident in a member State for tax purposes. This must be so otherwise the provisions for the taxation of any profits of the Grouping in the hands of its members [31] would be rendered nugatory, and a large loophole opened for abuse via EEC-formed Liechtenstein-resident companies.

It is interesting to examine the membership position of English-based Groupings in the light of section 434(1) Companies Act 1948. This section imposes a limit of twenty members on any "association . . . that has for its object the aquisition of gain by the . . . association . . . or by the individual members". While it cannot be the object of a Grouping to make profits on its own behalf, what are its members associating for except with a view of deriving some gain for themselves by cooperating in this manner? Thus under English law, which will apply if the Grouping is to have its head office in this country, a Grouping may only be entitled to have a maximum of twenty participants. However, the precedence of EEC Regulations over national provisions may provide a solution here.

The Formation Contract

Groupings are initiated by the potential members entering into a contract to cooperate as a Grouping for a fixed period. The fixed period

28. Art. 3(1)(b).

29. For example farming is not regarded as an *"acte de commerce"* under French law, *"exploitations agricoles et forestieres"* being dealt with by the civil law. See Ripert par Roblot, *Traité Elementaire de Droit Commercial,* 8th ed. (Paris 1974) pp. 107-110. But *cf.* the position under the Italian Code (Anc. art. 4 Co. Comp. art. 2135 C. Civ. of 1942).

30. Explanatory memorandum at p. 36.

31. Art. 20.

reflects the essentially temporary or loose nature of the cooperation envisaged. If desired, this term can be extended by unanimous resolution.[32] In addition to the term, the contract must also state the name of the Grouping, its object, and the identity of its members.[33] It must also designate its head office, which of course must be within the Community. The next step is the registration and filing of the contract in a register to be provided in the member State in which the head office is situated. Publication of the fact of registration and the name, object, membership and term of the Grouping must then take place in the official journal for publication of company notifications in the head office State.[34] Once registered, the Grouping becomes endowed with legal capacity.[35]

One difficulty that may arise over this contract lies in ascertaining its proper law. It will be necessary to determine the proper law to solve problems arising out of offer and acceptance in the constitutive contract, capacity of parties to enter it, interpretation, mistake, etc. One could apply Article 1(2) [36] as a solution to this problem and argue that choice of a particular State to be the head office of a Grouping is an effective express or implied choice of the proper law.[37] However, are the parties to the contract allowed by the Regulation to name a head office State for reasons of administrative convenience, while stipulating that their contract *per se* is to be governed by the law of another State? Article 1(2) seems to take this choice right out of the hands of the parties and make the selection of the head office State a compulsory selection of the proper law. But this interpretation does not fit well with the sentence in the Preamble which states that "a subsidiary law must be applicable in respect of any matter for which this Regulation or *the constitutive contract makes no provision.*[38]

Another possible interpretation would be that determination of the proper law is rendered unnecessary because Article 1(2) replaces all national choice of law rules in relation to a Grouping. If a problem arises in the court of a member State other than the head office State, which would normally require application of that court's conflict of laws rules,

32. Art. 6(3).

33. Art. 4(1). Thus the contract must be in writing although the draft Regulation does not so specify, unlike Art. 6 of the French *Ordonnance* creating the G.I.E.

34. In England this would be the *London Gazette;* and for Scotland the *Edinburgh Gazette.*

35. Art. 1(3).

36. Art. 1(2) reads as follows: "Where in respect of any matter no provision is made by this Regulation, the law applicable thereto shall be the law in force in the State where is situated the head office as specified by the contract forming the grouping".

37. An analogy can be drawn with the treatment of places of arbitration as selections of the proper law in English cases.

38. Author's emphasis.

it is possible to argue that the draft Regulation, being part of EEC law, has priority. The Regulation has specified that the law applicable to such matters shall be the law of the head office State (meaning presumably its domestic rules and excluding its conflict rules). Thus all choice of law provisions of the forum State are irrelevant. Both of these solutions to the problem of selection of the proper law have the signal merit of certainty. The former solution but not the latter works also in the unlikely event of an action being brought in a jurisdiction outside the confines of the EEC.

Generally then, it is felt that no independent choice of proper law is feasible on the wording of the Regulation as it stands. Such may have been the intention of its draftsmen but if so it accords ill with the hierarchy of rules envisaged in the Preamble and elsewhere. It is stressed that the Regulation and then the contract govern, albeit in their allotted spheres, thus giving the desired element of flexibility. Any other problems that arise are catered for by referring them to the law of the head office State.

Hierarchy of Rules

To amplify the point just made in the last section it is necessary to examine the hierarchy of rules which are applicable to questions arising about a Grouping.

First in order of precedence comes the Regulation itself. This contains many mandatory provisions, such as those relating to the constitution of the Grouping, and publicity requirements for its actions. Secondly there come the situations where the Regulation refers to the provisions of the contract itself. For example, Article 12 states that the contract may make provision for the resignation of members, and Article 8(1) refers the question of members' contributions in the first instance to the contract. Still other things are referred to the contract or the resolutions of the general meeting. Thus the terms upon which a Grouping may continue after one member dies or is wound up depends on any provisions for this in the contract, or failing this upon any laid down by the general meeting.

Third in this hierarchy of legal rules come the supplementary provisions of the Regulation. Thus in some cases matters are referred *prima facie* to the contract, but if that is silent they are governed by these supplementary provisions. For example, Article 11 says that unless the contract otherwise provides, a unanimous resolution shall be required for the admission of new members.

If a question arises to which the answer is not given by one of the above methods applied in order, then the law applicable is to be the law in force in the State where the head office of the Grouping is situated. Several examples of this are given in the body of this article.

Creation Formalities

The constitutive contract once formed must be registered and published.[39] Failure to comply with these formalities is penalised not by nullity, but by the contract's unenforceability against third parties.[40] Article 1(3) however makes registration alone necessary for the endowment of legal personality, and does not refer to publication at all, as does Article 4(3). What happens in the interim is a matter of conjecture.[41]

The difference between these provisions seems unnecessarily confusing. A simpler system might be one similar to the registration of companies in England whereby a Certificate of Incorporation is issued. This certificate could be issued after the publicity requirements have been complied with, and the date of the certificate made the official birth day of the Grouping, and thus the date upon which its legal personality commences. This could completely avoid problems over nullity if it were made conclusive evidence of the Grouping's valid constitution.[42] It would also provide useful evidence to third parties dealing with the Grouping that all formal requirements have been complied with. However it should be stated that the element of third party protection built into the Grouping's structure does seem quite adequate on this point. In practice though, it is likely that a copy of such a certificate would reassure third parties, especially in the early days of this venture when the Grouping will be a new European animal.

Legal Capacity/Personality

In order to overcome problems of definition in respect of the term "legal personality" the framers of the draft Regulation have just set out

39. Art. 4(2) which reads as follows: "The grouping shall be entered in a register designated for that purpose by the Member State where the head office is situated. The contract shall be filed at the time of registration; any subsequent amendments shall be filed also. The matters referred to in paragraph (1) above [the contents of the contract] shall be published in accordance with formalities to be adopted pursuant to Article 19 of this Regulation . . . ."

40. Art. 4(3) which reads as follows: "Failing completion of the formalities of registration and publication required by this Regulation the matters which should be published may not be relied upon against third parties, who may however themselves rely on such matters."

41. For an interesting French parallel see D. Bastian, "La situation des sociétés commerciales avant leur immatriculation au registre du commerce", in *Etudes de Droit Commercial—Henry Cabrillac,* (Paris, 1968) p. 23.

42. French reaction to such a suggestion may be at best uncertain if one looks at the favourable comments of jurists and the hostility shown in the French Parliament to the proposals of Art. 10 of the First Company Law Harmonisation Directive (No. 68/151 of March 9, 1968) for a judicial or administrative pre-constitution control of company formations. See Ripert par Roblot, *op. cit.*, n. 29, at pp. 568-570, and the bibliography there cited.

the legal capacity that the Grouping is to have and left it at that. Article 1(3) states that a Grouping shall "have the capacity to enjoy and be bound by rights and obligations, to make contracts, or accomplish other legal acts, and to sue and to be sued". This wide definition is culled from Article 7 of the Draft Convention on the Mutual Recognition of Companies and Legal Persons. The definition's function in Article 7 is to preserve a company's basic capacity or fact of existence while allowing member States to deny to a foreign company privileges not allowed to their own companies of a corresponding type.[43] With this in mind it can be said that the Regulation gives to the Grouping a basic right to exist as a legal person.

The problem therefore may be to decide whether national courts (and English courts in particular) will be sufficiently impressed by this description of the legal capacity of the Grouping to call it a corporation, and not merely treat it as a quasi-corporation.[44] Roxburgh J. defined quasi-corporations as "bodies different from the aggregate of the members e.g. a members club, and yet not corporations in the language of jurisprudence".[45] If a Grouping is established to be a corporation with a separate legal personality, then where England is the head office State, the English common law rules applicable to corporations can latch on to it.[46] If, on the other hand, it is held merely to be a quasi-corporation then it will become another candidate crying out for organisation under a general background statute.[47]

(b) *The Organs of the Grouping and its Relations with Third Parties*

The essential flexibility of this form of business association is ensured by providing that basically the organs and the internal regulations of the Grouping shall be determined by the contract.[48] With a few restrictions, therefore, the draftsmen of the contract can create the formal structure which most suits their members. However, the few restrictions that do exist are important ones, and consist of the institution of two organs, the

43. See G. K. Morse, "Mutual Recognition of Companies in England and the E.E.C." (1972) J.B.L.201.

44. It is interesting to note that the English courts are expressly denied the opportunity to call a trade union a corporation by the wording of s.2 Trade Union and Labour Relations Act 1974, despite the many attributes of incorporation possessed by a trade union under that Act.

45. *I.R.C. v Bew Estates Ltd.* (1956) 2 All E.R. 210 at p. 213.

46. For example the Rule in *Foss v Harbottle* (1843) I Hare 461 will apply.

47. Advocated by Wedderburn, "Corporate Personality and Social Policy", 28 M.L.R. 62.

48. Art. 6(1).

first a general meeting of members with very wide powers, and the second the compulsory creation of the office of manager which has wide powers to bind the Grouping.

The General Meeting

It is inherent in the concept of the Grouping that the ultimate power lies with the members in general meeting. It is this body that is assumed by the draftsmen of the Regulation to have the responsibility of directing the path the Grouping is to follow. The contract may, however, lay down any internal structure it likes, and may for instance provide that executive decisions of anything other than a fundamental nature shall be taken by a sub-committee of one or two powerful members, to whom the manager shall be solely responsible, or alternatively, by the president of the general meeting. Other members might thus be squeezed out of executive power.

It is always possible for a member suddenly to find himself in an oppressed minority. True, if he can gain the support of a quarter in number of the members, or of a manager, he can convene a general meeting.[49] But this may well not solve his problem, especially if it concerns the policy direction of the Grouping's activities which is favouring the majority members only. Therefore it becomes important to see whether we can define a Grouping as a legal personality or a corporation and apply to it, in England at any rate, conceptions such as fraud on the minority, which might be able to offer some protection in these circumstances.

We have said that ultimate power is vested in the members in general meeting. It is interesting therefore to see how that power is defined. Article 6(2) provides that "The widest powers to pass any resolution or execute or do any act or thing for the purpose of achieving the object of the grouping shall be vested in the members of the grouping in general meeting." How does this affect the Grouping's relations with third parties?

It is an extremely wide and general definition of power limited only by the boundaries of achieving the object of the Grouping. However, this built in limitation on the power of the members does mean that *ultra vires* is still a concept that we cannot forget. The general meeting lacks the power to do any act which is for a purpose outside the object of the Grouping. Necessarily this means also that they cannot ratify the act of a manager or of some other organ which is similarly outside this object. Third parties, however, are protected when they deal with a manager even if his acts fall outside the Grouping's object.[50] But the same does not

49. Art. 6(5).

50. Art. 7 and see *infra* p. 25.

apply if the general meeting enters into an *ultra vires* contract, either under the direct signature of each of its members, or by authorising some other organ, such as the chairman of the general meeting to sign or seal such a document. This would be outside the terms of the third party protection provisions which apply only to managers. It seems strange that after having resolved the *ultra vires* problem in relation to companies by its Directive of March 9, 1968,[51] the European Commission should then sponsor the creation of a business entity subject to just the kind of difficulties they were trying to abolish. It would have been better if the draft Regulation had utilised some blanket phrase such as the Directive's "Acts done by the organs of the company" to prevent third parties falling into the *ultra vires* trap.

The Manager

Every Grouping must contain at least one other organ apart from the general meeting. This organ is the office of manager and it can be held only by one or more natural persons. Thus a company can never manage a Grouping.[52] The manager is appointed either by the contract itself, or by the general meeting if nothing is said in the contract. It is another expression of the ideal of flexibility in that nothing is laid down in the Regulation about what powers the manager is to have. The explanatory memorandum says that the manager's powers can be laid down in the contract or specified in a resolution of the general meeting. If, however, the manager's powers and authority are not fully specified in the contract or by resolution, some problems may arise in the manager/members relationship, especially since the Grouping is a novel entity to most of the member States. Some means will have to be found of elucidating the "normal" or "usual" authority of the manager, perhaps by analogy with that of a managing director of a company. The French G.I.E. legislation being similarly mute on this point affords us no assistance.[53] The importance of the search lies in the fact that a manager will be liable to the members if he exceeds his authority.

There must, however, be one limitation on the authority of the manager, as between himself and the members. If the individual goes completely outside his mandate or rôle as manager of that particular Grouping, then, vis-à-vis the members, he cannot claim that he had authority. Thus if the manager of a Grouping instituted to negotiate the export sales of its members, contracts out the Grouping's services to a

51. Directive No. 68/151.

52. Art. 7(1).

53. Guyon and Coquereau, *op. cit.*, n. 11, at p. 204 say that if nothing is specified in the contract the *administrateur* has all the powers necessary to realise the object of that G.I.E., but admit that uncertainties could arise.

third party, then, whatever the position as regards the third party, the manager will be accountable to the members. His authority as far as the members are concerned must be limited at the outside by the authority and power of the general meeting. Therefore if he goes outside this he must be liable to the membership for his actions.

Next, the position of the manager as it affects third parties. It is in this area above all that the prevailing mood of solicitude for third parties' interests is most clearly demonstrated. Here too is found the one and only effective limitation on the powers of one individual manager.

Taking this latter point first, it is provided in Article 7(2) that where more than one manager is appointed, the contract may provide that the Grouping shall only be validly bound by the acts of the two or more managers when they are acting jointly. This fact must be registered and published in the same way as the other essentials of the contract, as must details of the names and addresses of the manager or managers. This is a very useful provision where two or more powerful firms link up in a Grouping, because management decisions can then be taken only with the concurrence of the manager/representative of each of the members. But it does mean that third parties must find out about the management situation of a Grouping before they deal with it—an unwelcome imposition, out of key with the usual pre-eminence of third party security.

The main point, however, is that subject to the above provisions on joint authority, the acts of a manager are binding on the Grouping so far as third parties are concerned, whether these acts are within the objects of the Grouping or not. This presumably corresponds, in the minds of the Regulation's draftsmen, to the first part of Article 9 of the Directive of March 9, 1968. There it is stated that acts done by the organs of a company bind it, even if those acts are outside the objects of the company. However, as has been pointed out above, if there are other organs of a Grouping and not just a manager, this provision does not cover them.

Article 7(2) of the Regulation goes on to provide that no limitation on the manager's powers, other than the obligation to act jointly, shall be capable of affecting third parties, even if such limitations are published. Consequently a provision limiting a manager's power to borrow in excess of say DM 10,000 for the purposes of the Grouping, while it may expose the manager to liability to the members for its breach, cannot in any way affect the liability of the Grouping to repay any sums borrowed, whether in excess the of limit or not. This provision corresponds closely to the terms of Article 9(2) of the First Directive mentioned above, by which limits on the powers of the organs of a company cannot be relied on as against third parties. However this provision in the draft Regulation is susceptible to just the same criticism as before. Other organs can be created and their authority does not fall within this provision.

It is suggested that there is one limitation on the authority of the manager with regard to third parties. This would be where the manager does an act completely outside his capacity as manager. The acts of a manager *qua* manager, are certainly binding, but whether other acts are is more difficult of resolution. The position can be illustrated with the aid of two examples.

In the first example, the manager of a Grouping set up to provide a computerised wages service to members, sells computer time a rival firm. Here the action of the manager would be completely outside the object of the Grouping, and yet it is an act done broadly in the capacity of manager of the Grouping, and as such the Grouping would be bound to fulfil the contract, although no doubt dismiss the manager. In the second example the manager of a Grouping instituted for research purposes sells incorrect information to a third party concerning investment prospects in one of the Grouping's corporate members. Here the manager could by no stretch of the imagination be said to be acting in his capacity as manager of that Grouping. If a third party suffers loss, then no recourse would surely lie against the Grouping. The "acts of a manager" bind the Grouping, but surely only the acts of the individual as a manager.

Protection of Third Parties Generally

In addition to the protection mentioned above, there are several provisions in the draft Regulation which have in view the protection of third party interests.

Firstly, there are the publicity requirements. Thc major facts about the Grouping must be registered in the head office State, and published in the official journal for company publicity in that State.[54] The contract is also filed in the register. Any later amendments must likewise be registered and published. Member States must allow the public to have access to this register and to all the filed documents including of course the contract.

The second string to the publicity requirements is one corresponding to Article 4 of the March 9, 1968 First Directive and to s. 9(7) of the European Communities Act 1972 which gave effect to it in England. Thus on letters and orders issued by the Grouping the following must be printed: the name of the Grouping and the appellation "European Cooperation Grouping"; the Grouping's registration number and name of its register (e.g. No. 1274 London Register); and the place where the Grouping has its head office. The purpose of these provisions is self-evident.

54. Arts. 4 and 19.

Another most important point which has the effect of protecting third parties is the liability provision. This is dealt with in Article 9 and provides that members shall be jointly and severally liable out of their own property for the Grouping's debts. This parallels an English partnership's liability in the case of tort. There is no question of the Grouping having limited liability. However a creditor cannot just proceed directly against an individual member. He must first make "a written demand for payment" to the Grouping and not be paid.[55] A written demand would just be a letter or the like; proceedings of any kind are not necessary. This procedure will enable a third party dealing with a Grouping with substantial members to have confidence that its debts will be met, whatever the state of the Grouping's own coffers.

Lastly, an outsider, perhaps a creditor, may apply to the court (and here is presumably meant the court of the head office State, and not the Court of Justice) for a winding up order for a Grouping whose object or business is *ultra vires*.[56] An applicant must prove a "legitimate interest" in order to succeed.

(c) *Relationship of Members Inter Se*

It is in this area above all that the partnership aspects of the Grouping come to the fore. This is partly true of the way in which the Grouping is financed, although this does more reflect the fact that the Grouping is not really envisaged as a separate economic entity. It is much more true of the other areas dealt with in this section, concerning liability, the admission of members and their expulsion or withdrawal.

Finance and Taxation

It is in the funding of the Grouping that its particular and individual nature stands out. Because it is not seen as having a separate economic existence, being there to provide facilities or services to its cooperating members, it therefore does not need to have a capital as such. Because its members can be made liable for its debts it does not need to have the creditor guarantee fund which gives an economic existence and creditworthiness to the ordinary corporation. Therefore the financing of the Grouping is made a personal thing between its (usually corporate) members. It is they who make the contributions[57] for the foundation and maintenance of the Grouping, and who make good any deficits, either in the proportions specified in the contract, or if that is silent, then in equal

55. Art. 9(2).

56. *i.e.* outside the terms allowed by Art. 2.

57. Contributions need not be in cash—they can take the form of provision of goods or services, including know—how.

shares. While the issue of debentures or invitations to the public to contribute are specifically prohibited,[58] it is still open to a Grouping to arrange a private loan to itself from third parties, and, for example to issue loan notes.

The draftsmen of the Regulation may well have intended that only enough capital should be put into the Grouping at the beginning to set it going. After that the remaining finance, including possibly staff salaries, would be drawn from members as and when required, or more probably in the form of a regular fixed subscription. However, while this may be the situation at the outset, it is hard to imagine managers of Groupings not wishing to have some working capital available. Therefore it is likely that we shall see Groupings establishing reserve funds and the like. Recent surveys in France by the *Bureau des Fusions et Regroupements d'Entreprises* have indicated that approximately thirty two per cent of French G.I.E.s now have their own capital.[59] It is likely that European Groupings, if established, will follow this trend.

If incidental profits are made, then the Regulation provides [60] that these are to be taxed in the hands of the members. It is uncertain as yet what this will mean. Either it means that for a Grouping with its head office in say Belgium, profits distributed to international members will be regarded as arising in Belgium and thus be taxed there regardless of the *siège* or residence of the member. This would mean that double tax conventions would have to be invoked when the remaining profits finally got home. Alternatively, it may mean that profits from the Belgian centred Grouping will be distributed to the members, and then each individual member will be assessed to tax on these in its home country. If this is the correct interpretation it will involve disparity in the treatment of members until such time as all taxation provisions in the EEC are harmonised.

Liability

The Grouping is not given the benefits of limited liability. Its members are to be jointly and severally liable out of their own property for its debts.[61] The general structure of liability has been dealt with above.[62] It remains only to say that if any individual member is sued for a debt of the Grouping, he can claim *pro rata* from the other members their share of the damages.

58. Art. 8(3).

59. See Goddard, Samuels and Groves, "Getting together in Europe", *Accountancy* September 1973 at 37.

60. Art. 20.

61. Art. 9(1).

62. See under Protection of Third Parties Generally at pp. 25-26 *supra*.

New Members

There are two ways in which a potential member may join an existing Grouping. Firstly by being adopted as a new member by a resolution of the general meeting.[63] Secondly by an assignment of the rights of an existing member.[64] Either way, the personalised or partnership nature of the Grouping is emphasized by the fact that, unless the contract specifies otherwise, the sanction of a unanimous resolution of the general meeting is required. Because this would involve amending the contract, such a resolution must be notified to the registry in the head office State, and publicised in the same way as the other information in accordance with Article 4(2).

Article 8 makes assignment of a member's rights possible, but only so, subject either to a unanimous resolution or to such resolution as is specified in the contract. The liability of an approved assignee for the debts of the Grouping would be the same as that of the assignor, subject to any contrary arrangement between the two. The liability of a new member admitted under Article 11 is total, that is, he is liable for all the debts of the Grouping whenever incurred. Of course, as the explanatory memorandum points out, this is the public position vis-à-vis third parties; the members of the Grouping may come to any arrangement of indemnity that they wish with the newcomer.

Withdrawal or Expulsion of Members.

Withdrawal from membership of a Grouping is only possible if the contract lays down exact terms and conditions for such an operation.[65] The Grouping can also expel any member who is "regularly in breach of his obligations".[66] Regard for the integrity of the institution that they have created has led the draftsmen to allow expulsion. Compare this to the English partnership where the close personal cooperation element is also paramount, but wilful and persistent breaches of the partnership agreement are only grounds for a dissolution, and application to the court is necessary. An earlier draft of the Regulation also required application to a court, but this has been dropped. The second ground for expulsion is where a member's "conduct disturbs the smooth running of the grouping". This phrase is vague in the extreme, and even the authors of the explanatory memorandum are at a loss to define it. They merely suggest that if national courts find difficulty in giving it a meaning they should apply to the Court of Justice for a ruling. Decisions on expulsion on either ground are to be made in accordance with the provisions of the

63. Art. 11(1).
64. Art. 8(2).
65. Art. 12(1).
66. Art. 12(2).

contract, or if this is silent, then unanimity among the remaining members is required.

This respect for the integrity of the Grouping is further illustrated by the provisions of Article 12(3) which are to the effect that if a member resigns or is expelled then the Grouping carries on. It does this either on such terms as are laid down in the contract or upon such as are provided by the general meeting. An outgoing member is responsible for all debts which have accrued prior to his departure, and is liable for them for a period of five years commencing on the date of publication of his departure.[67] This applies even where a member assigns his rights to another.

(d) *Winding up and Liquidation*

This section deals with the various ways in which the life of a Grouping may be brought to an end. Thus it may be declared a nullity, be automatically wound up, or its winding up may be ordered by a competent court. Details of liquidation will be dealt with somewhat briefly, and will be followed by comments on the provisions for limitations of actions.

Nullity

The contract forming a Grouping may be declared void. To protect third parties, Article 5 provides that for this a judicial decision is necessary. However, we are not told which court is to make this judicial decision, or according to which law it is to be made. The explanatory memorandum says that the general rule is that the subsidiary law should be applicable, although this is not apparent from the operative part of the Regulation. Even if the subsidiary law is applicable, and assuming that its function here is a compulsory choice of law, we are still left with the problem of deciding which court can make the decision.

Once a Grouping is declared void, it must be wound up, and the judgement must be published in the relevant official journal. Where a third party is acting in good faith, without knowledge of the nullity of the constitutive contract, then the Grouping can only rely on the nullity as from the date of such publication. However this limitation is not operative if it can be proved that the third party knew of the nullity at the time when they entered into contractual relations with the Grouping.

67. Art. 15(2).

Winding Up

The grounds stipulated in the Regulation upon which a Grouping shall be wound up are not remarkable. It is the ground which is not there that at first sight seems remarkable. Insolvency of the Grouping itself is not a ground for winding up. However, when one remembers that the Grouping is not conceived of as having any separate economic existence, and that its debts are met directly by its membership, the omission becomes understandable.

Automatic winding-up is to ensue if the Grouping attains its object, if its stated term expires, if the members pass a resolution to that effect, if the number of members falls below two,[68] or if all the members become subject to the law of one member State. Winding-up also ensues, but only where the contract does not provide to the contrary, on various other grounds including the death, winding up, bankruptcy or insolvency of any member, any consequences related thereto, or on a member's abandonment of his business or of his residence in the EEC for tax purposes.[69]

As has already been mentioned, where a Grouping's object, or its business, is outside the terms of Article 2, the court, on the application of any person who proves a legitimate interest, can order a winding-up.[70] Also, the court can order a winding-up on "just and equitable grounds" under Article 14(2). The explanatory memorandum states that this concept exists in the legal systems of most member States.[71] This is therefore the prime, and indeed the only remedy, other than resignation, which the Regulation provides for the succour of an oppressed minority.

Liquidation

Provisions are laid down in Articles 16 and 17 for the liquidation of any Grouping that is to be wound up. *Prima facie* the liquidator is the manager (or managers) for the time being. Any member aggrieved by this may apply to the court for appointment by the court of another liquidator. The usual process of liquidation is followed whereby assets are sold, debts paid, and any surplus distributed to members either as the contract dictates, or in equal shares. The fact of winding-up and the name or names of the liquidator must be registered and published by the machinery referred to elsewhere. When all is completed the liquidator must register and publish in like manner the fact of liquidation.

68. Art. 13(1).
69. Art. 13(2),—in this case the Grouping has 6 months to rectify the position.
70. Art. 14(1).
71. *Cf. "justes motifs"* under French law.

Limitation

The final provision to be dealt with is that of Article 18 [72] which concerns limitation. The period of limitation specified is five years from the date upon which the completion of the liquidation of the Grouping is published in the relevant official journal, whenever the right of action accrued. This limitation period applies to any action by the Grouping against any of its members for breach of the constitutive contract. It also applies to any action against a Grouping, either by a member, or more particularly by a third party. It is most important to note that this limitation provision does not seem to apply to actions by a third party against one of the members of the Grouping, in circumstances where he has previously made to the Grouping an unsatisfied written demand for payment under Article 9(2). Thus if the relevant national limitation period has expired, a creditor is forced back on the prospect of sueing the Grouping itself and hoping that in some way he can be subrogated to the Grouping's rights against its members—which have the benefit of the apparently long limitation period under Article 18.

However, many problems arise when one seeks to discover the scope of this provision and the interaction (if any) between it and the laws of member States. It could be argued for instance that this provision really only applies to claims that are made by and against the Grouping while it is in liquidation, the argument being that until a Grouping goes into liquidation no definite term can be set on the period of limitation. However, the fact that all Groupings must be formed for a fixed (if extendable) period of time does weaken this aspect of the argument. What weakens it more is that neither the wording of the Regulation itself, nor such light as the explanatory memorandum sheds on this point, show any intention to circumscribe the effect of the provision in this way. We are left then with a situation where a debt incurred by the Grouping at the beginning of a ten year fixed term, will remain enforceable against the Grouping for at least fifteen years, or longer if the Grouping decides to extend the term. This is the most likely outcome on a straight interpretation of the wording.

There is one other possible interpretation that will have the effect (if such is desirable) of cutting down such a long period of limitation. That is to say that the Regulation is there to provide a maximum period of limitation only. Therefore, if under the provisions of the applicable national law (for example the law of the head office State) a limitation period would keep alive a right of action until after the period provided

72. Art. 18(1) "Rights of action against a grouping, or by a grouping against one of its members in connection with the performance of the contract forming the grouping, shall be barred five years after the publication of the completion of the liquidation of the grouping."

in the Regulation, then it shall be cut down to five years from publication of the liquidation. On the other hand, if the provisions of the applicable national law prescribe a shorter limitation period, say three years from accrual of the right of action, then this shall stand. One can argue that although the Regulation cuts off the right of action at a date five years after the publication of the liquidation, it does not of necessity say that such a right is kept alive until that time. Therefore if such a right is barred earlier under any applicable national law, the Regulation does not operate to revive it. While you cannot have two periods of limitation in respect of the same right of action, you can have one provision cutting down the effect of the other. It will therefore act as a long-stop to the provisions of the various national laws. Strength is given to this argument by the fact that the Regulation's period is of rigid application. It cannot be extended or deferred by questions of fraud or disability, (unlike some national limitation provisions,) and thus it is well qualified to perform its long-stop rôle.

III. CONCLUSION

Having commented at some length on the details of the draft Regulation, it remains finally to consider the overall necessity for such an entity as is proposed. Is there any evidence to show that there is a crying need for this form of cooperation, or that it has a fair chance of succeeding once established?

The means of cooperation provided by the Grouping is intended to be used especially by small and medium-sized undertakings. Whether there is really any need for cross-frontier cooperation between such businesses is problematical. In the United Kingdom small firms contribute about one fifth of the Gross National Product.[73] Taking the manufacturing industry as an example, British small firms in the mid 1960's played a smaller rôle than those in any of the other EEC countries. It is probable therefore that small firms do account for a very significant percentage of the output of the Community.

To gain some insight into the problem we can look at the situation in England by way of example. It is evident from the Bolton Committee's Report that the position of the small firm is declining in Britain. There are many reasons for this, but two of those given are particularly relevant here. Firstly, "Improved travel and communications have affected the relative competitiveness of small firms adversely because markets have changed rapidly from local to national and are fast becoming international . . . we conclude that small firms are less well placed than larger ones to benefit from expanding international trade".[74] And secondly the

73. The Bolton Committee's Report on Small Firms (Cmnd. 4811) (1972) para 8:2.
74. *Ibid.* para. 7:10.

Report stated that "we consider that lack of access to economies in large scale marketing may be the most important single reason why the competitive strength of the larger firm has improved over the last fifty years".[75] Entry into the EEC it was said will exacerbate these trends and larger firms will be able to take opportunities to expand, to some extent at the expense of small businesses. It was noted also that the position of the small firm in the Netherlands declined after the formation of the EEC because of a tendency to larger scale production, mergers, takeovers and also the increased size of the market.[76]

It could be argued, therefore, that in order to preserve the possible advantages, in terms of competition, product choice etc., of having a variegated business community, there is a need to strengthen the position of small firms generally, without impairing their autonomy. The Bolton Committee in discussing leniency of application of Restrictive Trade Practices legislation to small firms, said "What we have in mind is that the competitive weakness of small firms in many industries could be remedied by permitting them to combine in small groups offering some of the advantages in product rationalisation and purchasing for example, which a merger might produce but within which they could retain their independent status".[77] This sort of combination on an international as well as on a national scale could give groups of small firms something more like parity of market power with larger companies and thus help to stimulate effective competition.

If there is a need to strengthen small firms, is the Grouping the best way to do it? Are there not already sufficient methods available? The fact that there are in existence other possible methods of actual combination is readily apparent.[78] Contractual associations, the use of joint holding companies, or joint operating subsidiaries are all ways that are currently in use. If mere international expansion is required, then the formation or acquisition of a foreign subsidiary will suffice. But these methods would be beyond the capital horizons of many small firms and sole traders. The unit created would in many cases be of a permanent or semi-permanent nature, and the independence of small firms may be threatened by their involvement in such an enterprise. Therefore, while larger businesses can use these other available methods succesfully it is reasonable to assume that a new method of cooperation is required to pass on the advantages of combination to smaller firms.

The loose-knit structure of the Grouping may be what is required, but

75. *Id.* para. 7:13.
76. *Id.* para. 9:33.
77. *Id.* para. 9:33.
78. For a summary of these methods see Lutter, "A European Contractual Group Company", 9 C.M.L.Rev. 1972, 53.

it is to be a Community-wide institution. It is instructive, therefore, to look at the criticisms levelled at that other Community institution, the proposed European Company, and see to what extent they apply to the Grouping. Common criticisms [79] include non-uniform interpretation, pre-existing viable alternatives, taxation and workers' participation.

Only the first of these will really affect the Grouping concept. One criticism is levelled at the difficulty of filling in gaps in the European Company Statute by applying general principles common to the laws of the member States. This, however valid in relation to the European Company, does not apply to the Grouping, because no such gap-filler is created by the draft Regulation. Another criticism is that disparity arises because points not covered by the Statute are to be governed by the law of the head office State of the European Company. This criticism though must apply even more so to the Grouping, for with less provided for in the draft Regulation, correspondingly more must fall to be decided by the head office State of the Grouping. Differences might arise, some of which could be damaging.[80] However, this may only result, in years to come, in the choice of one state to be host to many Groupings because of favourable laws covering those matters not governed by the draft Regulation. There is no evidence that the favoured position of the State of Delaware in the U.S.A. has significantly hampered corporate life in that country. It is also pointed out by some critics of the European Company that uniform interpretation of the Statute may be thwarted by non-reference of points by national courts under Article 177. This too is a valid criticism, especially in view of the number of times that the draftsmen of the Grouping Regulation specifically mention that detailed difficulties can be cleared up in this way. However, there are some indications that resistance to making a reference is lessening in some countries.[81] Also this is a question relating to the existence of the legal order of the EEC; it is a general problem and not one specifically referable to the Grouping.

The other criticisms are not so pertinent. Other methods of cooperation do exist, but as mentioned above these are often not financially feasible for small firms and fairly permanent in nature, so that they would not permit combination for just one project or one contract. The

79. See Hood, "The European Company Proposal", 22 I.C.L.Q. 1973, 434-461; Mann, "The European Company", 19 I.C.L.Q. 1970, 468; and Lutter, *op. cit.*, n. 78.

80. See *supra*, pp. 18-19.

81. See Bebr, "How supreme is Community Law in the National Courts?" 11 C.M.L.Rev. 1974, 3; and Simon, "Enforcement by French Courts of European Community Law", 90 L.Q.R. 1974, 467; also *Van Duyn v The Home Office* (1974) 3 All E.R. 178; *E.M.I. v C.B.S. The Times*, March 4, 1975. But see *H. P. Bulmer Ltd. v J. Bollinger S.A.* (1974) 2 All E.R. 1226.

fact that the Grouping is not intended to be a profit-making entity reduces greatly in importance the taxation difficulties which are very germane to the European Company. Workers participation too should not be a difficulty. Problems of forcing co-determination on unwilling states will not really arise.

One indication of the chances of success of the Grouping can be gained by looking at the G.I.E. in France. It was established in 1967 and in February 1970 a conference was able to decide that the initial stages of its development had been a success. Despite some criticisms G.I.E.s have continued to flourish and some have taken on an international aspect. For example, SNIAS, Deutsche Airbus GmbH and Fokker have joined in a G.I.E. to facilitate management and control on the European Airbus programme, and the insurance risk of Euratom is shared between 115 companies throughout Europe by means of an international G.I.E.[82] Critics have argued that it is doubtful if the G.I.E. as such is suitable as an instrument of Community industrial policy; its creation against a background of French law may mean that it is not adaptable to a wider scenario. However, the draft Regulation has done a reasonable job of translating the idea into a Community-wide context.

Overall, the project for a European Cooperation Grouping is a very interesting one, worthy of success. There are still difficulties to be overcome of course, and many of these have been referred to in this article. Wider problems too may arise, such as reconciliation of the concentration tendencies of the Grouping project with the principle of free competition founded on Articles 85 and 86 of the EEC Treaty. However one can argue that promoting methods of cooperation, such as the Grouping, and establishing a policy of free competition, are just two, not necessarily incompatible expressions of the EEC's wish to promote a healthy economic climate. One could for instance suggest that better cooperation via the Grouping, between small and medium sized enterprises enables them to compete better with their larger rivals, and thus helps to prevent the latter from achieving or abusing a dominant market position. Alternatively one could say that the provision of machinery for international selling or buying organisations can just as easily promote as prevent, restrict or distort inter-state competition within the EEC.

The problems with the Grouping, while admittedly complex, do not appear to be insuperable. Its comparative simplicity of form, its cheapness, and above all its flexibility are all strong elements in favour of the Grouping's acceptance.

82. See Goddard, Samuels and Groves, *op.cit.*, n. 59, at p. 39.

INDUSTRIAL PROPERTY, THE CENTRAFARM JUDGMENTS

by

E. A. van Nieuwenhoven Helbach*

1. With the two Centrafarm judgments, of which one [1] relates to parallel imports of trade marked products, the other [2] to parallel imports of patented products, an evolution would appear to be concluded the origin of which goes back to the *Grundig/Consten* judgment.[3] What was previously considered impossible, in particular by students of industrial property law, and as a rule was therefore emphatically disputed by them, now seems to have been put beyond doubt. It is not possible, by pleading the territorial effect of national industrial property rights, to oppose the movement of products governed by those rights from one member State to the other if those products have been put on the market in the member State from which they come by the holder of those rights or with his consent. At least, that is the tenor of recital 11 of the trade mark judgment (*Winthrop/Centrafarm*) as well as of recital 12 of the patent judgment (*Sterling Drug/Centrafarm*). What are we to think of all this? Is it really true that the holder of national industrial property rights acquired within the Community is barred from relying in any way on those rights in order to prevent the importation of products governed by those rights which have been put on the market elsewhere within the common market by him or with his consent? Have the judgments in question really resulted in a definite delimitation of the fields of application of national property rights on the one hand and of the rules of the Treaty relating to the free movement of goods and competition within the Community on the other hand? And above all: is the result thus obtained satisfactory, not only from the point of view of cartel law, but also as viewed against the background of the interests which are served by the national laws relating to industrial property?

In order to be able to answer these and similar questions, we have to trace the lines along which the conception of the Court has evolved, lines which, apart from the *Grundig/Consten* judgment as their starting-point and the two recently delivered *Centrafarm* judgments, are marked

* Visiting Professor of Law at the University of Utrecht; legal practitioner, The Hague.

1. Judgment of October 30, 1974, Case No. 16/74, (1974) Rec. 1183; 2 C.M.L.R. 480.

2. Judgment of October 31, 1974, Case No. 15/74, (1974) Rec. 1147; 2 C.M.L.R. 480.

3. Judgment of July 13, 1966, Case No. 56/64 and Case No. 58/64, 12 Rec. 429; (1966) C.M.L.R. 418; 4 C.M.L. Rev., 209.

13 C.M.L. Rev. 1976, 37-59

by four other judgments: *Parke Davis*,[4] *Sirena*,[5] *Deutsche Grammophon*,[6] and *Café Hag*.[7] Indeed, in all these judgments, though not always in the same form, nor always in relation to rights of the same kind, the central question was whether by reliance upon a national industrial property right the importation by a third party of products governed by such a right from one member State into the other can be prevented.

2. First of all, it is characteristic of the evolution of the Court's conception that in the statement of reasons of its judgments the emphasis has shifted from the rules of competition of the Treaty to those relating to the free movement of goods. First it was held in the *Grundig/Consten* Case that Article 36 cannot limit the field of application of Article 85; subsequently, in the *Parke Davis* Case, with a view to determining the scope of the rules of competition of the Treaty, Article 36 was applied analogically; thereafter, in the *Sirena* Case, a principle also capable of being applied in the field of competition was derived from Article 36, while finally, first in the *Deutsche Grammophon* Case, but then also in the *Café Hag* Case and in the two *Centrafarm* judgments, the exercise of the national industrial property right was examined with direct reference to Article 36. In the last phase of development the slight difference of approach was further to be detected in that recital 8 of the *Deutsche Grammophon* Case referred to the principles defined in the title relating to the free movement of goods, whilst in recital 8 of the *Café Hag* Case—and in the identically worded recital 6 of the *Centrafarm/Winthrop* judgment and recital 7 of the *Centrafarm/Sterling Drug* judgment respectively—the exercise of the industrial property right was examined with reference to the text of the article itself. Naturally this shift of the emphasis is connected with the different character of the facts of the case which the Court had to successively judge, but it cannot be altogether accounted for by this. Indeed, when in the *Deutsche Grammophon* Case the Court first directly examined the compatibility of exercise of an industrial property right with Article 36 of the Treaty, it was not the first time that the Court was faced with a case where the exercise of the right was *not* based on an agreement between undertakings. The Court had previously met with a similar situation in the *Parke Davis* Case, and on that occasion it did not go beyond the

4. Judgment of February, 1968, Case No. 24/67, 14 Rec. 81; (1968) C.M.L.R. 47; 6 C.M.L. Rev., 129.

5. Judgment of February 18, 1971, Case No. 40/70, 17 Rec. 69; (1971) C.M.L.R. 260; 9 C.M.L. Rev., 83.

6. Judgment of June 8, 1971, Case No. 78/70, 17 Rec. 487; (1971) C.M.L.R. 631; 9 C.M.L. Rev., 87.

7. Judgment of July 3, 1974, Case No. 192/73, (1974) Rec. 731; (1974) 2 C.M.L.R. 427, 11 C.M.L. Rev., 395 (case-note); 387-394 comment by W. Alexander.

statement that a patent in itself, apart from any agreement, does not show the features required in Article 85, namely, one of the three categories there referred to and for that reason—as stated expressly in ground 6—*the exercise* of the rights arising from a patent is not *in itself* governed by the rules of competition. Moreover, another feature characteristic of the initial conception of the Court is the way in which in the *Grundig/Consten* Case it rejected the invocation by Consten of the original acquisition of their right to the Gint trade mark. Instead of invoking Article 36, the Court established a link with Article 85 by reference to the consideration that Consten had been enabled by the agreement with Grundig to acquire the original right invoked by them.

3. When one asks oneself what value is to be attached to this shift of the emphasis, it is natural to consider this to be merely that it has thus become clear that the exercise of industrial property rights, even apart from those cases in which it is the object, means, or consequence of an agreement between undertakings or occurs in the context of the abuse of a dominant position, falls within the field of application of the Treaty and can therefore be examined with reference to the Treaty. Anything more than this, and in particular the development of another reference criterion going beyond the one contained in Articles 85 and 86, need not be seen in it. Indeed, the same elements which would render impermissible, according to Article 85, the exercise of an industrial property right linked to an agreement between undertakings, and according to Article 86 the exercise of an industrial property right linked to a dominant position—to wit that such an exercise affects inter member State trade unfavourably and distorts competition—are also found in Article 36 as the elements on which it depends whether a restriction on the free movement of goods is impermissible. In other words: the provisions of Articles 85 and 86 on the one hand and those of Article 36 on the other hand are linked with each other; they lay down the same norms with regard to related domains. The question is merely when the exercise of an industrial property right can be said to affect inter-state trade and to distort competition. When arguing in this way, however, one runs the risk of failing to appreciate that Article 36 says more than that restrictions on the movement of goods must not constitute either a means of arbitrary discrimination or a disguised restriction on trade between member States. In its first paragraph Article 36 also says that only those restrictions on the movement of goods are permitted which are justified on grounds of protection of industrial and commercial property, and it is open to question whether the latter does not amount to a supplementary condition, which has the consequence that Article 36 makes more exacting demands on the exercise of industrial property rights than do

the rules of competition of the Treaty. This question will be further discussed in section eight.

4. A second point on which the train of thought of the Court shows an evolution concerns the distinction between on the one hand the existence and on the other hand the exercise of industrial property rights. This distinction is already to be found, but without any statement of reasons, in the *Grundig/Consten* judgment, where the Court, with a view to refuting the invocation of Articles 36 and 222 of the Treaty, held that the prohibition of the use of national trade mark rights in order to oppose parallel imports restricts the exercise of those rights, without affecting them in their existence. The statement of reasons, still lacking in this judgment, follows, at least partly, in the *Parke Davis* and *Sirena* judgments, in which the distinction is repeated and elaborated, with an analogical reliance upon Article 36, with reference to the rights arising from a patent and to trade mark rights. These rights are not affected in their existence by the rules of competition of the Treaty, because they are based on a legal status conferred by the state. They may, however, be affected in their exercise by the rules of competition of the Treaty, the criterion being whether the exercise of the right is the object, means, or consequence of an agreement between undertakings prohibited under Article 85 or helps to create a dominant position, which is abused contrary to Article 86. That this did not yet constitute the full reasons, however, appears from the *Deutsche Grammophon* judgment, in which the Court had to deal with the exercise of a right which was not based on an agreement between undertakings or on a dominant position and to which the criterion developed in the *Parke Davis* and *Sirena* Cases consequently could not be applied. Nevertheless, in this case the Court again draws the distinction and develops that distinction solely on the basis of Article 36 in the sense that this article does permit restrictions on the free movement of goods which are justified on grounds of protection of industrial and commercial property, but only for such restrictions as find their justification "in the safeguarding of the rights forming the specific object of this property". What the Court means by the latter it then reveals in the *Café Hag* and *Centrafarm* judgments; first in the *Café Hag* Case indirectly through the statement of what are the abuses against which the trade mark legislation still does protect the holder of the right, and subsequently in the two Centrafarm judgments by the definition as to what is the specific object of commercial property with regard to trade marks and of industrial property with regard to patents.

5. If we consider this evolution, it would appear to be the manifestation of the Court's endeavour to make it plain where the line of demarcation

lies between the existence and the exercise of industrial property rights, and thus to mark the boundary of the area governed by the rules of the Treaty. This endeavour is quite understandable, because the distinction between existence and exercise of an exclusive right in reality is not by any means as clear as it seems to be terminologically, so that the line of demarcation between the two is not in the least obvious. It may even be seriously asked whether a line of demarcation can be drawn at all between the existence and the exercise of an exclusive right. An exclusive right does not exist for its own sake, but in order to be exercised and, viewed in this light, any restriction on the exercise of the right also affects it in its existence. Leaving this aside for the moment, it cannot be said that the Court has been successful in its endeavour to clarify the situation. This is particularly true with regard to the consequences which in its later judgments, beginning with the *Deutsche Grammophon* judgment, the Court attached to the distinction between the existence and the exercise of industrial property rights. Up to this judgment, *i.e.* during the period in which, as we saw, the Court only examined the exercise of industrial property rights with reference to the rules of competition of the Treaty, the situation appeared to be clear. At that time it was held that industrial property rights not only are not prejudiced in their existence, but that their exercise as such was also not affected by the rules of competition of the Treaty. Conflict with those rules only arose if the exercise of the rights involved an additional circumstance in the form of an agreement between undertakings or the abuse of a dominant position, in consequence of which the trade between member States would be restricted and competition within the common market would be distorted. In consequence, the boundary between existence and exercise of the right did not have to be determined at that time; the only relevant point for a possible conflict with the rules of competition of the Treaty was what the situation was *beyond* that boundary. The only thing that mattered was whether the exercise of the industrial property right was or was not linked with an agreement between undertakings or the abuse of a dominant position, which might give rise to restrictions on inter-state trade and to distortion of competition. This clarity, however, disappeared when the Court, in the *Deutsche Grammophon* judgment, again made the distinction between existence and exercise of industrial property right in a case where the exercise of the right was based neither on an agreement between undertakings nor on the abuse of a dominant position. Thus, the additional circumstance which, according to the *Parke Davis* and *Sirena* judgments, had functioned *beyond* the boundary between existence and exercise of the industrial property right, *i.e.* in the area of the *exercise* of the right, as a landmark for the application of the competition rules of the Treaty, was eliminated, and the boundary between the mere existence and the exercise of the right became important. In fact, it was then a matter of the exercise of the right *as such*. Considering that the Court had derived the distinction in question from Article 36 of the Treaty and had taken it, by way of an initial analogical application of this provision, as the basis of its interpretation of the rules of competition of the Treaty, it was to be expected that for the examination of the exercise of industrial property rights the Court should wish to adhere to the criterion that the exercise of the right distorted competition and restricted inter-state trade. The Court in fact did so, but the reasons it gave for the application of this criterion in the *Deutsche Grammophon* Case, and also in the later judgments, raise the question whether the Court in so doing really respected the distinction between existence and exercise of the exclusive right which it had chosen as the starting-point for its examination.

When in the *Deutsche Grammophon* and *Café Hag* Cases the Court says that the important thing is the protection of the rights forming the specific object of the industrial and commercial property, and subsequently, in the two *Centrafarm* judgments, indicates what in its view is the specific object of commercial and industrial property respectively, or—as the Court also formulates it—what is the "essential exclusive right" arising from this property, does not this mean that the Court shifts the line of demarcation between permissible and non-permissible exercise of the right to *this* side of the boundary between existence and exercise of the industrial property rights? Does it not affect these rights in their existence after all? This question will be discussed again in section eight.

6. The third point on which the conception of the Court shows a marked evolution concerns the cause of the tension between the industrial property rights on the one hand and the provisions of the Treaty on the other hand. In the *Parke Davis* case the Court indicates the national character of the protection of industrial property and the differences between the respective national legislation as the cause. Failing unification within the framework of the Community, these two factors are thought to cause the obstacles to the free movement of goods and competition within the common market which the Treaty wishes to avoid. In the *Sirena* judgment this opinion is further developed, in that there (in recital 4) it is solely the national character of the protection of industrial property that is mentioned as the cause of the said obstacles. The Court thus shows that it has meanwhile come to recognize (rightly) that the said obstacles are not removed by the elimination of existing differences between the national legislations so long as these legislations keep their national character.

Finally the Court moved a step further in the *Café Hag* judgment and in the two *Centrafarm* judgments by stating in these judgments why and in what respect in its opinion the national character of industrial property legislation is responsible for these obstacles. According to recital 12 of the *Café Hag* judgment the territorial delimitation of the national (trade mark) legislation entails that the exclusiveness of the trade mark right too has a territorial effect, while in the two *Centrafarm* judgments the cause is stated to be the existence in the national legislation of provisions according to which the industrial property right concerned is not exhausted by marketing in a country other than that to which the right applies under the national legislation.

7. What is striking in the evolution of the Court's conception of the cause of the tension between the industrial property rights and the provisions of the Treaty is the change in the argumentation by means of which the Court has pinpointed the national character of legislation relating to industrial property as the cause of this tension. When in recital 12 of the *Café Hag* judgment the Court speaks of the exclusiveness of the subjective trade mark right, which may result from the territorial delimitation of the national legislations, an exclusiveness which the holder of the trade mark may invoke to bar parallel imports, the Court would seem to assign territorial effect to the subjective trade mark right and to infer from this that such rights can also be exhausted only territorially. Not a trace of this train of thought, however, is to be found again in the two *Centrafarm* judgments, which on this point are almost identically phrased. It is true that in these judgments too the territorial exhaustion of the industrial property rights is regarded as the real cause of the tension between those rights and the rules of the Treaty, but here the territorial effect of the exhaustion is assumed solely on the ground of relevant provisions in the national legislation. This change in the Court's argumentation would appear to amount to an ultimate rejection of the territoriality principle as the basis for the exhaustion of industrial property rights. Nor is the Court alone in taking this view. It has repeatedly been argued that the territorial exhaustion of industrial property rights cannot be inferred from the territoriality principle—in itself a term which admits of a variety of interpretations and which consequently is by no means clear. In connection with industrial property rights the territoriality principle implies no more than that these rights are governed by the law of the territory where they find their basis, and apply only within that territory. However, this does not by any means imply that facts which have occurred outside the said territory could not affect the position of those rights within that territory.[8] Nor

8. Apart from Wertheimer in *Gewerbliche Schutzrechte im EGW-Kartelrecht*, 1970, p.

does this imply that there can never be any question of territorial exhaustion of industrial property rights. It only means that the scope of the exhaustion of industrial property rights is a matter of substantive law and accordingly must be judged by reference to the national law in question. That the Court also takes this view appears from the reference to the provisions of the national legislation in rectical 9 of the *Centrafarm* trade mark judgment and in recital 10 of the *Centrafarm* patent judgment. At most one might ask whether in the Court's view territorial restriction of the exhaustion of industrial property rights can only be assumed if it is expressly provided for in the national law, or if this is not the case, whether the restriction arises from the nature of the industrial property right in question. Indeed, just as in several countries it has been inferred by the case-law relating to trade mark rights from the nature of those rights that they are not exhausted territorially, but universally,[9] so it is at least conceivable that from the nature of the patent right it may be inferred that it can only be exhausted territorially. This question too will be referred to again later under section eight.

8. It is evident that the three above-mentioned lines along which the conception of the Court has developed come together at one point: the delimination between the field of application of the Treaty and that of the national legislation relating to industrial and commercial property. It is also evident that the three questions which have been raised above, each in connection with one of those three lines of development, converge on one central question, *viz.* how the Court ultimately drew this line of demarcation. As to that, it appears to have become clear, particularly through the decisions in the two *Centrafarm* judgments, that the Court does uphold in words, though not in practice, its thesis that the

177 *et seq.*, see for this the very detailed discussion—including references to a good deal of literature—by Koppensteiner, 1971 ADW, p. 357 *et seq.*, and further recently Cohen Jehoram in his discussion of the *Centrafarm* judgments in 1975 SEW, p. 351 *et seq.*

9. The Netherlands: HR December 14, 1956 *(Grundig)* 1962 N.J., No. 242; Belgium: Cass. May 23, 1945 *(Email-Diamant)*, 1949 Ing. Cons. 37; Germany: BGH January 22, 1964 *(Maja)*, 1964 GRUR Int., 202, BGH February 2, 1973 *(Cinzano)*, 1973 GRUR Int. 562; Sweden: HG October 17, 1967 *(Polycolor)*, 1968 GRUR Int., 22; Switzerland: BG Oct. 4, 1960 *(Philips)*, 1961 GRUR Int. 294; Austria: OGH November 30, 1970 *(Agfa)*, 1971 GRUR Int. 90; France: Cass. April 17, 1969 *(Körting)*, 1970 RIPIA, 5; Italy: C.d.C. March 18, 1958 *(His Master's Voice)*, 1958 GRUR Int. 580. It is to be noted that the two last decisions have been variously interpreted. For the present Benelux law, see further the Common Commentary of the Governments on Article 13 sub A, last para.: "The court, however, will only consider the utilization of the trade mark by successive sellers of the products which have been put on the market within the Benelux area or beyond by the trade mark holder or his licensee as an infringement of the right under the trade mark of the holder or the licensee who has put the trade mark on the products if the products have undergone a change ..."

Treaty does not affect the existence, but solely, under certain circumstances, the exercise of industrial property rights. If the Court ultimately bases its scrutiny of the exercise of industrial property rights entirely on Article 36 of the Treaty, and if in so doing the Court adopts the criterion whether this exercise does or does not do justice to that which in its view constitutes the specific object of industrial or commercial property, then the Court no longer accepts the existence of these rights as such. Rather the Court weighs up these rights; it distinguishes between what is and what is not in its view essential to them, and it thus affects them in their existence. This is further beyond doubt if one considers the decision of the Court in the *Centrafarm* patent jugdment in the light of the grounds by virtue of which the *Hoge Raad* had formed the opinion that "putting on the market" in Article 30 of the National Patents Act means putting on the market in the Kingdom of the Netherlands.[10] Putting on the market is one of the rights—and next to that of manufacture undoubtedly the most important right—which are conferred on the holder by the Netherlands legislation for the protection of the object of industrial property. If this right is restricted as much as has been done in the *Centrafarm* (patent) judgment, the right itself, in its very existence, is impaired.

Indeed, this can hardly be avoided, because, as already observed above, no sensible distinction can be made between the existence and exercise of an exclusive right, which is after all primarily—according to many people even solely—the right to prevent others from carrying out certain acts. Exercise of such a right is always the enforcement of the right of exclusion, the very thing of which the right consists. This is not, however, to say that the Court, in ultimately disregarding the distinction between the existence and exercise of industrial and commercial property rights, derived by it from Article 36 of the Treaty, has applied this provision improperly. As already observed above in section three, Article 36 lays down more than merely that the restrictions on the free movement of goods safeguarded in Articles 30-34, restrictions made for the protection of certain interests, such as industrial and commercial property, must not constitute either a means of arbitrary discrimination or a disguised restriction on inter-state trade. Article 36 lays down primarily—indeed in its very first sentence—that only *those* restrictions are precluded from the prohibitions in Articles 30–34 which are *justified* for the protection of the interests referred to in the latter. It is this term"justified" in the first sentence of Article 36 which accounts for the jurisprudence of the Court and at the same time makes it acceptable. The context in which this term is used in the first sentence of Article 36 entails

10. HR March 1, 1974 N.J. No. 329.

that for the application of this provision more is required than the establishing of the existence of a causal link between the restriction and protection of industrial or commercial property. What is also required is the *making of a value judgment* about this restriction; a value judgment in which the interests involved in the protection of industrial and commercial property must be weighed against the interests for the projection and promotion of which the Treaty was concluded. If one further bears in mind that the free movement of goods within the common market is a fundamental principle of the Treaty and that it is *this very* principle that is being thwarted by the territorial delimitation of industrial and commercial property rights, one may accept the fact that the Court did not regard the use of those rights for opposing parallel imports as justified for the protection of industrial and commercial property. When considered in this way, the provision in the second sentence of Article 36 automatically appears in another light. This provision does *not* contain a criterion for judging the exercise of industrial or commercial property rights which cannot be affected in their existence, but indicates when in each case restrictions arising from the existence of national industrial or commercial property rights for the protection of the object of that property are not justified.[11] A consequence of all this, which is important from a Community point of view, is that the boundary between the field of application of the Treaty and that of the national legislation relating to industrial and commercial property is determined by Community law on the basis of Community principles and not for each individual member State according to the relevant national law. In fact, were the latter the case the consequence would be unacceptable for the Community, namely, the conclusion that industrial and commercial property rights are not affected by the rules of the Treaty in their existence, but only in their exercise. The existence of these rights, as well as the scope of their existence, is indeed regulated *by* and laid down *in* the relative national legislation.[12] Thus it is clear that the answer to the question that was raised, and left open, in the conclusion of section seven in connection with the third line in the evolution of the Court's conception has lost its importance. Even if according to the national law it should already follow from the nature of the relative industrial property right that it can only be exhausted territorially, the Court would still be at liberty to examine the consequence of this with reference to the Community interest in a free movement of goods within the common market.

11. In the same sense recital 9 of the *Deutsche Grammophon* Case, where the definition of the second sentence of Article 36 is called a "more precise statement" of the content of the first sentence.

12. The same result was already reached, though by a different method, by Wertheimer in *EGW-Kartelrecht,* 1973, p. 118 *et seq.*

9. It now remains to ascertain what criteria the Court has so far applied in judging whether restrictions for the protection of industrial and commercial property were or were not justified, and further what can be inferred from these criteria for the future. Although the beginnings of a formulation of these criteria are already given in the *Deutsche Grammophon* Case, where the last paragraph of recital 11 refers to "the rights forming the specific object of this property", a definition of what is the specific object of industrial and commercial property respectively is not found until the two *Centrafarm* judgments. In the *Café Hag* Case the Court had already ventured on an attempt at an elaboration by indicating in recital 10 of that jugdment what belongs "in any case" to the said specific object, but this did not as yet amount to a concrete definition of this specific object.

According to the *Centrafarm* trade mark judgment, which should be examined first in order to gain a good insight into the Court's train of thought, the specific object of commercial property is "to ensure to the holder of the trade mark the exclusive right to utilize the mark for the first putting into circulation of a product, and to protect him thus against competitors who would take advantage of the position and reputation of the mark by selling products improperly bearing the mark". If this is considered as a definition of what the subjective right to a trade mark essentially implies, all sorts of objections might of course be raised against it. To mention just a few: the definition is based on the juxtaposition of *positives Benutzungsrecht* and *negatives Verbotsrecht* familiar from German legal literature, while it is at the least questionable whether the former right exists independently alongside the latter; [13] the right of exclusion of the holder of the mark concerns any use of the mark to distinguish his products, and not merely its use for the first putting into circulation of the products. The position and the reputation of the mark may be abused in many more ways than by the sale of products improperly bearing the mark, such as by the mention of the mark in comparative advertisements for another party's products offered under his own mark. To argue in this way, however, is to take a wrong view of the Court's task. The latter did not consist in pinpointing the essential substance of the subjective trade mark right in a definition, but in laying down the criterion by reference to which the rights arising from the subjective trade mark right could be examined for compatibility with the principles of the Treaty, in particular those relating to the free movement of goods. For the accomplishment of this task the Court did not need to consider the rights arising from the subjective trade mark right in their totality.

13. For all this, see in detail Schluep, *Das Markenrecht als subjektives Recht*, p. 213 *et seq.*

Because the Court had already established before—recital 12 of the *Café Hag* judgment—that the obstacles to the free movement of goods created by the subjective trade mark right result from the territorial delimitation of the exclusiveness of the right, it sufficed for the Court to devote its attention to this aspect. How the Court did this can be inferred from the definition given. The Court asked itself to what extent, if the free movement of goods is to be safeguarded, the holder of the trade mark ought to be able to enforce his right of exclusion if products bearing his mark are imported into a member State where he is entitled to this mark, and for this purpose it distinguished between two states of affairs. If the imported products have been labelled with the mark by the holder himself or with his consent and thus been put on the market, he cannot oppose the importation and the further sale of the trade marked products. If, on the contrary, the products have not been labelled with his mark by him or with his consent and thus been put on the market, he can indeed oppose their importation and further sale. By thus making the power of the trade mark holder to enforce his right dependent on whether the trade marked products do or do not originate from him or his licensee, without making a distinction as to the place where the trade marked products have been put on the market, the Court has deprived the subjective trade mark right of its territorial character, at least so far as its exhaustion is concerned, and has introduced a kind of universality principle.[14] Products which have been put on the market by the holder or with his consent (and consequently lawfully) under his mark in any place within the Community are regarded throughout the Community as lawfully put on the market. This interpretation of the definition of the specific object of commercial property given by the Court implies of course that the emphasis is placed on the use of the mark for "the first" putting into circulation of a product. It is precisely through the introduction of the priority element, without any territorial restriction, that the territorial element is discarded, at least with respect to the exhaustion of the trade mark right.

10. From the point of view of trade mark law the result reached by the Court is not astounding. By denying to the trade mark holder the right to take proceedings against the importation of products which have been put on the market by him or with his consent in another country under the same mark the Court does full justice to the function of the mark which is to distinguish the products originating from the holder or his licensee(s). These products do not improperly bear the mark; thus, no

14. For the application of the universality principle by the *Deutsche Reichsgericht*, see Riehle, *Markenrecht und Parallelimport*, p. 16 *et seq.*; Möschel, *Die rechtliche Behandlung der Paralleleinfuhr von Markenwaren innerhalb der EWG*, p. 25 *et seq.*

advantage is taken of the reputation of the mark. The view of the Court therefore is is in agreement with the one which had already been arrived at before in various countries, including member States, by the legislature or the national courts.[15] The criterion developed by the Court is moreover of great importance for a proper understanding of the previously delivered *Café Hag* judgment, which aroused anxiety among many people, in particular because of the view of the Court that the indication of the origin of a trade marked product is indeed useful, but that "consumers may be informed about this by other means than those by which the principle of the free movement of goods is infringed". This statement aroused the fear that also in cases where there is not the slightest link between parallel marks belonging to different holders in different member States the Court will regard the proceedings of one holder against the importation of products which have been put on the market by the other holder in another member State under his parallel mark as incompatible with the principle of the free movement of goods, and consequently impermissible.[16] However, it may be inferred from the very definition which the Court has given of the specific object of commercial property in the *Centrafarm* (trade mark) judgment that this fear is unfounded. At first sight it may appear otherwise, because on the basis of the definition of the specific object given by the Court one would be inclined to expect that in the *Café Hag* case the Court would have considered the action taken by Van Zuylen, the holder of the Café Hag trade mark in Belgium and Luxembourg, against the importation into those countries of coffee under the Hag trade mark by Hag AG from Germany to be permissible. Indeed, it was found that there was not the slightest link between Van Zuylen and Hag AG, the holder of the Hag trade mark in Germany, so that not only could Article 85 of the Treaty not be applied, but it was also out of the question that the coffee imported into Luxembourg by Hag AG had been put on the market by or with the consent of Van Zuylen.However, in this case there was a special circumstance, to wit that the German Hag trade mark of Hag AG and the Belgian and Luxembourg trade marks of Van Zuylen have "the same origin", as the Court repeatedly states in the judgment concerned. The Hag trade marks in Belgium and Luxembourg, too, had originally belonged to Hag AG, and it was only owing to an extraneous factor, namely, Belgian legislative measures concerning the confiscation of enemy property, that the rights to the Hag trade marks in Belgium and Luxembourg had ultimately fallen into the hands of Van Zuylen. In the

15. See n. 9.

16. See, *inter alia*, Mann, "Industrial Property and the E.E.C. Treaty", 1975, I.C.L.Q., 24; Ladas, 1974 IIC, 302 *et seq.*, Mak 1975 GRUR Int. 118 *et seq.*; Kemp 11 C.M.L. Rev. 1974, 360 *et seq.*

light of the conclusions reached by the Court in the *Centrafarm* (trade mark) judgment with regard to the specific object of commercial property, it is evident that this common origin is to be looked upon as the reason why the Court nevertheless considered the action of Van Zuylen as incompatible with the rules of the Treaty. Indeed, common origin of identical trade marks belonging to different holders in different member States implies that originally one and the same mark was in the hands of the same holder in all member States. According to the court's conception of the specific object of commercial property, this entailed that the original holder had the exclusive right to utilize the mark in question for the first putting into circulation of his product in one of the member States, but that he subsequently had to accept that the product thus put on the market in the member State concerned was also further sold under the mark in the other member States. It is then only natural that if through an extraneous factor [17] the said mark passes in one or more member States from the hands of the original holder into those of a third party, the situation such as it applied to the original holder cannot be altered. The exercise of parallel rights, which the original holder (Hag AG) had to tolerate before the occurrence of the extraneous factor (expropriation in Belgium and Luxembourg) in the one member State where he was entitled to the mark (Germany) with respect to the goods which had first been put on the market in other member States (Belgium, Luxembourg) where he was also entitled to the mark, he was still required to accept after the occurrence of the extraneous factor. Similarly, the new acquirer of the mark, Van Zuylen, had to accept in the member States where he had become the holder (Belgium and Luxembourg) in consequence of the occurrence of this extraneous factor, the exercise of parallel rights with regard to goods first put on the market under the mark by the holder in another member State (Germany).[18] If it were otherwise, the occurrence of the extraneous factor would have the curious consequence that both the rights of the original holder in the member State or States where he remains the holder and the rights of the third party in the member State or States where the latter becomes the

17. In this context it should be borne in mind that the unity from the point of view of trade mark law can be broken down against the will, or at least without the cooperation, of the trade mark holder in other cases besides that of confiscation of enemy property. For this, see Johannes, 1975 GRUR Int., 111 *et seq.*, who mentions nationalization and bankruptcy as other possibilities.

18. The views of Brinkmann, 1974 MA, 382 and Röttger 1974 GRUR, 574, to the effect that by virtue of the Café Hag judgment Hag AG was henceforth permitted to import coffee under the Hag trade mark into Belgium and Luxembourg, but Van Zuylen was to refrain from importing coffee under this trade mark into Germany and into other countries where Hag AG has corresponding rights to the Hag trade mark, are incorrect. On this, see Johannes, *loc. cit.*, n. 17, at p. 114; Schwab, 1975 GRUR Int. 75 *et seq.*

holder assume a wider scope than they had before. Hence in my opinion it cannot be doubted that in the train of thought followed by the Court in the *Café Hag* judgment the common origin of the litigious trade marks constitutes the decisive element.[19] Common origin of trade marks forms the line of demarcation between those cases where the influence of the exercise of the rights to corresponding trade marks belonging in different member States to different holders is justified, and those where it is not. With regard to the common origin of trade marks, the Court considered that there was at first no question of prevention of the free movement of goods by the exercise of the trade mark rights, and that this prevention was induced by the extraneous factor. In the absence of common origin of the trade marks, on the contrary, the possibility of hindrance of the free movement of goods was given from the start as the natural consequence of the juxtaposition of those trade marks. That is why in the former case the prevention does not, but in the latter case does have to be accepted. It is also in this light that the above-mentioned recital 14 in the *Café Hag* judgment about the possibility of informing consumers about the origin of the goods by other means than the trade mark, must be considered. This ground is clearly only to be understood in the context of the common origin of the trade marks.

11. From the above it will have become evident that in my opinion the end point has been reached in the case-law of the Court relating to the exercise of trade mark rights, so that no further—in the sense of more far-reaching—developments are to be expected. It is true that some more refinements may be expected on the results now reached. Thus, I am inclined to think that it has not yet been adequately expressed in the definition of the specific object of commercial property that the trade mark holder can indeed oppose the importation into one member State of goods put on the market under his trade mark by him or with his consent in another member State if in the meantime, through third parties, a change has been made in the composition of those goods. In this sense see the provision of Article 13 subsection A, last paragraph, of the Benelux Trade Marks Act.

12. The foregoing, however, does not mean that the result which the Court has reached in the *Café Hag* Case may be called satisfactory and therefore is to be welcomed. The contrary is true, and this is no doubt also the reason for the fear already referred to, namely, that on a further occasion the Court will repeat the decision given in the *Café Hag*

19. In the same sense also Baardman 1975 SEW 208-211, at 211, Von Gamm, 1975 GRUR Int., 190 *in fine*, and Schwab *op. cit.*, n. 18, at p. 77.

judgment in a case where the identical or similar marks were originally acquired in different member States by different holders and consequently do not have a common origin. Of course the result is clearly unsatisfactory from the point of view of trade mark law, *i.e.* in the light of the interests which are served by the protection of the trade mark as an object of commercial property. Those interests are on the one hand the interest which the holder of the trade mark has in making his product known to (recognizable by) the consumers among the multitude of products with which they are confronted and, on the other hand, the interest which the prospective buyers of the product have in being able to rely upon the trade mark of the holder and thus not to be deceived when buying his product. So long as the holder of the trade mark in virtue of his exclusive right can prevent anyone else from utilizing his mark or a mark corresponding to it for products of the same kind, both interests are protected and they receive equal attention. Then only the holder's product bears his mark and consequently only *his* product is individualized by that trade mark, and the consumer who wishes to receive the product of the holder may safely rely upon the latter's mark, without the risk of being deceived. If, however, the Court requires the holders of marks having the same origin to accept, throughout the common market the utilization of the other's trade mark alongside his own, then in end effect both the above-mentioned interests are deprived of any protection in cases where the trade marks have a common origin. As appears from recital 14 of the *Café Hag* judgment, the Court indeed realized that in this way not only the interest of the trade mark holder, but also that of the consumers is sacrificed to the interest of the free movement of goods, but it saw no reason in this for taking a different decision, since it held that other means were available for informing consumers as to the origin of products offered for sale under the same trade mark by different trade mark holders. However, in this way the decision cannot be justified from the point of view of *trade mark law.* In particular the fact that for the consumer the trade mark also indicates other, and even much more important, details of the products than their origin is disregarded. All sorts of different qualities of a product may induce the consumer to choose a particular product having a particular origin (which in any case is often not specifically known to him). And frequently one consumer will be influenced by quite different qualities in his choice of a particular product than another. It is not possible to bring home all those details to every consumer in a more simple and adequate way than by means of the trade mark so that they are grasped by him as it were automatically when confronted by the multitude of impressions which assail him in the buying situation, *e.g.* in a supermarket. Indeed, so long as the trade mark of the holder individualizes his product, and solely *his* product, the consumer may associate with that mark in perfect confidence all the practical experiences which he has gained with the product offered for sale to him under that mark and which induce him to buy the same product again the next time. The trade mark then functions for the consumer as the symbol of those experiences and of the qualities of the product which have evoked them. However, it is not the objections on the point of trade mark law to the Court's decision which may or can determine a final opinion as to the merits of this decision. Indeed, as already stated. Article 36 of the treaty provides for examination of the justification for restrictions on the free movement of goods which result from national industrial and commercial property rights by weighing up the interests served by the said rights against the interest of the free movement of goods within the common market. Ultimately, therefore, the decisive factor is whether the Court has properly carried out this weighing-up operation with regard to national rights to trade marks having a common origin. When judged by this standard, in my opinion three objections arise with regard to the *Café Hag* judgment.

The first is that the Court, in examining the exercise of the right relating to trade marks having a common origin, has accepted the possibility of the public's being deceived as to the origin of the goods put on the market in the Community by different trade mark holders under the same mark, and thus has introduced a possibility of distortion of competition which is contrary to the purpose of the Treaty. This is an objection which cannot be eliminated in the way recently attempted by Johannes.[20] If the hundred thousand Germans visiting the Belgian coast in summer are actually offered, under the Hag trade mark, coffee of a quality different from that to which they are accustomed in Germany and should they consequently be disappointed, this can hardly warrant a decision which has the consequence that many more Germans run the risk of being disappointed because in their own country coffee of a quality to which they are not accustomed there is offered for sale to them under the Hag trade mark.[21]

The second objection that can be advanced against the *Café Hag* decision is founded on the fact that this decision was given in a case where the trade mark holder in one member State imported his product

20. Johannes, *op. cit.*, n. 17, p. 113.

21. The reliance upon the argument of "greatly increased human mobility in present-day Europe" first used by Advocate General Dutheillet de Lamothe fails to convince for another reason as well. So long as Europe is still made up of nations, each with its own territory and own national character, it would not appear plausible that the consumer who, *outside* his own country, comes across a trade mark, which is also utilized *in* his own country in both cases expects the products to have the same quality under this trade mark. Is he not more likely to bear in mind the saying "different men, different ways"?

directly into a member State where instead of him another was entitled to the same trade mark. No such far-reaching decision was necessary to ensure the free movement of the trade marked goods within the common market. The Court could have confined itself to holding that the trade mark holder in one member State cannot oppose the importation into the latter of the goods which have been put on the market by or with the consent of the party entitled in another member State to the same trade mark, in the latter State. By not doing so, the Court failed to weigh up fairly the interests on both sides.

The final objection that can be raised against the *Café Hag* decision is that it attaches value to the common origin of the litigious trade marks in a case where this origin had been broken down long before the entry into force of the Treaty by an extraneous factor over which the original trade mark holder had no control. That the Court should regard obstacles to the free movement of goods which have become possible through the exercise of industrial or commercial property rights that have got into different hands *after* the entry into force of the Treaty as not justified for the protection of industrial or commercial property, is understandable in the light of the objectives of the Treaty. In fact, these are cases in which the possibility of obstructing the free movement of goods by the exercise of the rights in question did not yet exist at the time of the entry into force of the Treaty, this possibility only arising *afterwards,* so that it was in consequence contrary to the objectives of the Treaty. Such a situation, however, did not present itself in the *Café Hag* Case, because there the extraneous factor that was responsible for the fact that the trade mark rights concerned got into different hands had manifested itself long before the entry into force of the Treaty, while in those days the restriction on the free movement of goods that had thus become possible was not prohibited. It is specifically this latter objection which makes the decision in the *Café Hag* Case unacceptable, even apart from its defects from the point of view of pure trade mark law.

13. After all that has already been said above about the Centrafarm trade mark judgment no detailed discussion of the highly similar *Centrafarm* patent judgment is necessary. Again, in the definition in recital 9 of this judgment of what constitutes the specific object of industrial property in respect of patents, the Court, by introducing the priority element without any territorial delimitation—"the *first* putting into circulation of industrial products", deprived the subjective patent right of its territorial character, at least as regards its exhaustion. Any objections that could otherwise be raised against the definition given, as *e.g.* in respect of the legal basis for patent protection, which certainly does not consist solely or primarily in the recompense for the creative

effort of the inventor,[22] do not alter this fact. Special attention should be devoted to the elaboration, or at least the beginnings of an elaboration, which the Court gave in recital 11 to the practical application of this definition, by comparing the two opposing situations in which respectively the patentee can and in which he cannot take proceedings against parallel imports of products coming under his patent into the country of importation. On one side, where proceedings *are* possible, the Court places the situation already dealt with in the *Parke Davis* Case and the situations where parallel patents were acquired and are still in the hands of patentees independent of each other, while on the other side, where proceedings are not possible, is placed the situation where products are imported which have been put on the market in another member State, where the patentee holds a parallel patent, by him or with his consent under that parallel patent. It would appear evident that in the former cases the parallel import can be opposed, but not in the latter case. It is much less obvious, at least at first sight, what the solution must be in those cases which fall in-between the two extremes. First of all we may think of the case where parallel patents—*i.e.* more or less identical patents for the same invention—which at first were in the hands of the same patentee in different member States later got into different hands in consequence of an extraneous factor—not by virtue of an agreement, for in that case Article 85 would apply. Is it also possible in that case for the patentee in one Member State to oppose the importation of products falling under the patent there if they have been put on the market in another member State by the patentee holding the parallel patent there? It would seem to me that such a situation is comparable with the one that was settled in respect of trade mark rights in the *Café Hag* judgment. One might say that here the patents have the same origin and that consequently for this case the same line of reasoning applies as that which accounts for the decision in the *Café Hag* Case.[23] Besides, it appears significant to me in this context that in recital 11 of the *Centrafarm* (patent) judgment the Court expressly speaks of "original holder". Another intermediate case is that where for an invention no patent has been acquired in one of the member States for reasons different from those in the *Parke Davis* Case. One may think of the possibility that in one or more member States no patent application has been filed for the invention, with a view to saving

22. For the legal ground of the patent protection, see, *inter alia*, Monnet 1965 GRUR Int., 302 *et seq.*; Was 1965 GRUR Int., 609 *et seq.*

23. In this context I assume that the patents in question have got into different hands only *after* the entry into force of the Treaty. In the contrary case the holder of the patent in one member State will indeed be able to prevent the importation into that State of products falling under that patent which have been put on the market in another member State by or with the consent of the patentee there.

expense, or a patent has indeed been applied for in a member State, but has not been granted on account of an irremediable omission committed there in the procedure of grant. Can the products manufactured and/or put on the market by third parties in the patent-free country then be barred in the other member States, where a patent *has* been acquired? In my opinion this question must be answered in the affirmative. In those other member States the patentee himself was not the first to put into circulation the products manufactured and put on the market by third parties in the patent-free country, and according to the Court's definition of the specific object of industrial property with respect to patents he can exclude third parties, by virtue of his right, from doing so. However, in my view the same does not hold true if the patentee himself should manufacture and put on the market the invented product in the patent-free country, and subsequently third parties should import that product into other member States, where the patentee does have patent protection. In my opinion the patentee cannot take proceedings against such importation, because he has already put those products on the market in a member State. It is true that this putting on the market has not taken place in a member State where a patent protects the product, but this makes no difference so long as the first putting into circulation took place within the Community. Otherwise the patentee, by keeping one member State "patent-free" and producing there, would still be able to partition the common market with his parallel patents in the other member States. This would be contrary to the Court's definition of the specific object of industrial property in respect of patents, a definition by which precisely the exhaustion of the subjective patent right has been deprived of its territorial effect, because this is not compatible with the principle of the free movement of goods. It seems to me that a similar conclusion will have to be reached in the case where, for one reason or another, such as the expiration of the legal duration, delay in paying the fee due, or nullification on grounds to be invoked in one member State only, the duration of the patent terminates at an earlier date in a given member State than do the patents granted for the same invention to the same patentee in the other member States. According to the Court's definition of the specific object of industrial property the patentee will be able to prevent importation by third parties from the territory that has become patent-free when the products concerned have been manufactured and put on the market there by third parties, but he will have to tolerate the importation of products which have been put on the market in the patent-free territory by him or with his consent. Finally a remark has to be made about the case where for the same invention patent protection has not been granted in all member States to the same patentee to the same extent. This case may easily arise for a number of reasons. First of all, the differences between the national legislations, including the conditions regarding the grant of patents, entail that the formulation and the form of the claims on which a patent is granted for the invention in the different member States will vary rather appreciably. This may make a great deal of difference, because ultimately the substance of the claims primarily determines the scope of the protection granted. Moreover, the possibility can by no means be excluded that more or less identically worded claims will be interpreted in a markedly different way in one country than in another, according to whether the court is accustomed to heed the letter of the text rather than the essence of the invention. Nevertheless, such differences will in general not create problems with regard to the application of Article 36 to parallel imports, because in recital 14 of the *Centrafarm* patent judgment the Court has put a very wide interpretation upon the term parallel imports. If the patents granted in the different member States relate to essentially the same invention, the products put on the market by or on behalf of the patentee in one member State and protected by the patent granted there will be permitted to be freely imported into and sold in the other member States. It is only when a product is not protected in one member State by the patent granted there, but *is* protected in another member State, where patent protection of a much wider scope has been acquired, that the patentee will indeed be enabled to oppose in the latter member State the importation and sale of products manufactured and put on the market by third parties in the first member State.

14. Considering the conclusions which the Court had reached earlier, in the *Deutsche Grammophon* judgment, in respect of rights akin to copyright, the opinion given by it in the *Centrafarm* patent judgment on the relation between national patent rights and the provisions of the Treaty is hardly surprising. Those conclusions already raised the presumption that the Court would not make any distinction between the various industrial property rights in judging their relation to the rules of the Treaty, in particular those concerning the free movement of goods, even though in recital 7 of the *Sirena* judgment the Court for a moment had given the impression that it might at least be prepared to make more exacting demands on the exercise of trade mark rights than on that of other industrial property rights. For students of industrial property law the equal treatment of, in particular, trade mark rights and patents is

24. This applies also if in various other member States, perhaps to different degrees, patent protection has been acquired with a wider scope than in the member State from which the goods are imported. In that case the patentee is at liberty, in any member State where he has acquired patent protection with a wider scope, to apply this patent protection in order to oppose the said importation.

undoubtedly not obvious, because patents by their nature are tied down much more to the territory in which and for which they have been granted than are trade mark rights. Case-law, such as that in respect of trade mark rights, which states that these rights are not exhausted territorially, is to my knowledge not to be found in respect of patents, nor are theories such as those on which Koch and Froschmaier based the universal exhaustion of patents very convincing. However, a discussion about this question, interesting though it may be from the theoretical point of view, will be unprofitable in practice, because in the two *Centrafarm* judgments the Court in fact lumped together patents and trade mark rights, something which the first sentence of Article 36 of the Treaty makes possible. One may only wonder whether it makes any difference for the appraisal of parallel imports of patented products whether the patentee himself also produces in the member State into which the product is imported, so that he does not exercise his patent rights there as a commercial monopoly. Of course this fact does not change or reduce the effect of the exercise of the right on the free movement of goods, but it can be defended that in this case the obstruction must be justified on grounds of protection of industrial property. Indeed, it may be alleged, as the Danish government has done in its comments on the *Centrafarm* patent case, that if the patentee cannot oppose, in the member State where he produces the products, the importation of these products put on the market elsewhere in the common market by him or with his consent, then he is not assured in the importing country of the real exclusive position which he needs to reap back the effort and expense invested in the creation and development of the invention. We shall have to wait and see how the Court is going to judge this case. That opinions about it may differ is evident from the remarks of the Commission in the *Fourth Report on Competition Policy*, pp. 21-22, about "the question whether the licensor should be able by contract to prohibit licensees from making direct imports into territories he wishes to reserve to himself". In this case the question is essentially the same, only the context being different: not that of Article 36, but that of Article 85 of the Treaty. In this connection a complication is of course created by the fact that the Commission may give exemption in respect of application of Article 85, but not in respect of application of Article 36. In view of this the question asked by the Danish government calls for a "black or white" solution, because the in-between solution represented by exemption is not available.

15. A final question to which the two *Centrafarm* judgments give rise is whether there is still any point in continuing the efforts, undertaken and in part already completed, to accomplish unification of industrial prop-

erty law within the common market. Is it still necessary, now that the Convention on the Grant of European Patents has been concluded, to bring about a Community Patents Convention as well? And if a really efficient instrument for obtaining trade mark protection on a European scale is not yet available in the Convention of Madrid or in The Trade Mark Registration Treaty, is it not much better to supplement and perfect those existing agreements rather than to try once again to bring about a convention on European trade mark law? It must indeed be admitted that not *all* the disparities that may be produced in the free movement of goods by the exercise of industrial property rights have yet been eliminated by the case-law of the Court. There still remain those disparities which are either due to a difference between the possibilities of protection offered by the national laws or which tend to arise when in different countries different parties apply for and acquire rights for the same object of industrial property independently of each other. These disparities can indeed only be eliminated by unification of law, but then exclusively if at the same time the national laws are rendered inoperative, so that no national rights can be acquired alongside European rights for the same object of industrial property. It is, however, open to question whether the latter is really desirable. As is only to be expected, the acquisition of industrial property rights on a European scale will entail considerable expense, and this will tend to especially discourage smaller undertakings from developing new products, including new trade marked products. It will then be only the very big undertakings that will be able to afford the luxury of developing new products, and this is not a result that is in conformity with the objectives of the Treaty, because the possibilities of competition are thus restricted instead of being widened.

16. The fact that the above observations have only been devoted to the importance of the *Centrafarm* judgments for the application of industrial property law does not mean that no important decisions have been given in those judgments on other points as well. A discussion of these matters, however, would exceed the scope of the present article as well as the capacities of its author. They will, however, no doubt be further discussed by more competent writers in this review.

The Hague, August, 1975

ABUSE OF A DOMINANT POSITION IN ARTICLE 86; THE PROBLEM OF CAUSALITY AND SOME APPLICATIONS

by

P. Vogelenzang*

Note on the intention of this paper

The purpose of the present paper is to develop certain concepts with regard to the meaning of "abuse" in the expression "abuse of a dominant position", which is the main element of Article 86 of the EEC Treaty.

For the purpose of this paper the term dominant position will be considered defined in the manner set forth by the European Commission in the *Continental Can* Decision: "Enterprises are in a dominant position when it is possible for them to take independent lines of conduct and this enables them to act without much regard for competitors, buyers or suppliers. This is the case when, because of their share of the market, or because of their share of the market together with their access to technical knowledge, raw materials or capital, they can determine prices or control production or distribution for a substantial part of the product concerned".[1]

The main focus of inquiry will be the implications arising from the requirement that the abuse be an "abuse *of a dominant position*". This phrase is held by some to imply that it is not just any abuse that is condemned, but that there has to be a "causal relation" between the dominant position and the abuse. By way of preparation we will also have to discuss some other aspects of "abuse".

The practical implications of the concept of abuse to be developed in this way shall be shown by two examples. The first example covers the question in how far *unfair competition by major companies* comes under the purview of Article 86 of the EEC Treaty.

A second example covers the problem of *artificial product differentiation* caused by large-scale advertising.

My conclusion will be that both forms of market behaviour are covered by Article 86. I do realize that that conclusion may be surprising to many readers, but still I do think it has considerable support both in the text of Article 86 and the case-law of the European Commission and the Court of Justice.

* Legal practitioner, Amsterdam.

1. Case No. IV/26.811, Continental Can, 1972 O.J. L 7, under II A 3.

13 C.M.L. Rev. 1976. 61-78

SECTION 1. WHAT IS MARKET BEHAVIOUR, AND WHOM OR WHAT IS ARTICLE 86 MEANT TO PROTECT?

In Section 2 we shall inquire whether, in order to fall under Article 86, market behaviour should show any kind of relation to the dominant position of its perpetrator. We first have to solve some preliminary problems.

a. *What is market behaviour?*

In the *Continental Can* proceedings before the Court of Justice [2] the plaintiffs claimed that Article 86 only covered behaviour with effect on the particular market. The Court of Justice implicitly, in Consideration 21, admitted that claim, but said that requirement was fulfilled whenever the behaviour was apt to influence the market conditions (even if it was not behaviour on that market itself). A takeover bid thus may constitute behaviour on the market where the acquired company formerly operated.

It should also be noted that according to the Court of Justice Article 86 of the EEC Treaty covers abuses with effect on one market by way of a dominant position on another market (Cases No. 6 and 7/73—*ICI-CSC*).[3] No identity of markets is required. Market behaviour is any behaviour affecting any market.

b. *What is the nature of the interests which Articles 85 and 86 are meant to protect?* [4]

Before the Court of Justice formulated its position on this question in the *Continental Can* decision, one could distinguish two conflicting schools of thought. A narrow view was advocated by Professor R. Joliet, the broader position was taken by Professor E. J. Mestmäcker.

Professor Joliet presented his view on Article 86 in a very thorough study comparing the American concept of monopolization with the

2. Case No. 6/72, *Europemballage Corporation et Continental Can Company Inc. contre Commission des Communautés Européennes,* (1973) Rec. 215 *et seq.*

3. Joint cases No. 6 and 7/73: *Instituto Chemioterapico Italiano SpA. et Commercial Solvents Corporation contre Commission des Communautés Européennes,* (1974) Rec. 223 *et seq.*

4. The following discussion is, as said, nothing but a preliminary note to establish a frame of reference to proceed from in our discussion of the 'causal relation' between dominance and abuse. For a more thorough investigation see Cardon de Lichtbuer and Herbert, *Evolution recente de la notion d'abus de position dominante*(Document de travail Contre de Recherches Interdisciplinaires Droit-Economie, Louvain).

EEC concept of the dominant position.[5] He distinguished two methods of dealing with market power.

The first method was to attack the *creation, maintenance* or *expansion* of market power, in order to preserve competitive structures; the second method was government control over and regulation of its *exercise.* Although Joliet admitted that the methods did not necessarily exclude each other, he concluded that Article 86 was only meant to regulate the exercise of monopolistic market power *vis-à-vis* consumers (and purchasers and suppliers), but did not cover exclusionary practices directed against (potential) competitors.

Joliet's conclusion was reached after a thorough but rather isolated examination of the structure and wording of Article 86. Professor Joliet did not place Article 86 in the wider context of the system of the EEC Treaty and did not want to attribute much importance to Article 3f of the EEC Treaty, "the institution of a system ensuring that competition in the common market is not distorted".

The broader view was taken by Professor Mestmäcker.[6] He considered Articles 3f, 85 and 86 as parts of one system, and therefore refused to interpret Article 86 in an isolated manner. The general goal of undistorted competition being one of the EEC Treaty's pillars, he considered it mandatory that Article 86 should be considered as one of the instruments to further that goal. The concrete way to protect competition being the protection of competitors, he concluded that Article 86 ought be made to serve, next to the protection of consumers which does directly follow from the text of Article 86, the protection of both competition and competitors. Herbert and Cardon de Lichtbuer have pointed out how in the long run the narrow interpretation of Professor Joliet is bound to defeat the very purpose accepted by him: the protection of consumers. If exclusionary practices are not checked under the EEC Treaty, in the long run the consumers will be confronted with fewer and fewer alternatives to choose from.

Furthermore, if monopolization is allowed to go on unchecked, so that the necessity of control of daily business behaviour by way of Article 86 becomes ever-increasing, this will defeat the system of free competition which is the philosophy behind the EEC Treaty: instead there may be the necessity of increasing regulation of industry.

If one wants to effectively protect consumers, without having to fall back on regulation of industry, it is necessary to protect the competitive

5. Joliet, *Monopolisation and Abuse of Dominant Position,* (Collection Scientifique de la Faculté de Droit de l'Université de Liège, No. 31, 1970).

6. Mestmäcker, "Die Beurteilung von Unternehmungszusammenschlüssen nach Artikel 86 des Vertrages über die Europäische Wirtschaftsgemeinschaft" in *Probleme des Europäischen Rechts, Festschrift für Walter Hallstein,* (Frankfurt am Main, 1966), p. 322 *et seq.*

structure itself; and to protect competition, it is necessary to protect competitors. A parallel necessity exists for other market participants who may become the victims of abusive practices, for instance buyers of intermediate products and suppliers of raw materials. They as well are part of the market structure and their disappearance may in the long run also damage consumers.

In the *Continental Can* decision the Court of Justice rejected arguments based on Joliet's narrow view and adopted Mestmäcker's theory of the systematic interpretation of Articles 3f, 85 and 86 taken as a whole. "On different levels Articles 85 and 86 pursue the same purpose of *maintaining workable competition in the Common market*" (consideration 25, stress supplied).

In the *ICHI-Zoja* Case the Court of Justice sustained the Commission's use of Article 86 against CSC-ICHI, who had refused to supply Zoja whom it had formerly supplied in the context of the CSC-ICHI's decision to enter the market for Zoja's product, and in the *GEMA* Decision [7] the European Commission moved to protect the interests of members-suppliers of a copyright-organization against that organization.

We may therefore safely conclude that the interpretation of Mestmäcker is the accepted one, and that therefore Article 86 does not only protect consumers, but also other market participants, and the competitive structure itself.

As a result we may define "abuse" in Article 86 of the EEC Treaty as "market behaviour damaging either consumers, the competitive process, or other market participants". Such abuse, if bearing the specific relationship with the dominant position to be discussed in the next section, would then be the prohibited "abuse of a dominant position" of Article 86.

However, the following complication arises: the freedom to compete of any company, *including dominant ones,* must be recognised as one of the interests to be protected by the EEC Treaty. Competition is the fight for the consumer's dollar. If a large company obtains an order to the detriment of a smaller competitor such cannot be held *per se* to be undesirable under the EEC Treaty merely because of the fact that the smaller company, is indeed, "damaged".

The freedom to compete of one company must be balanced against the interest other companies have not to be hurt. This balancing must be done against the background of what is needed for *workable competition.* Workable competition means the structure and behaviour needed to make the market function properly, perceived from the traditional

7. J.O. 1972, L 166.

economic criteria of factor-allocation and need-satisfaction. Such additional balancing has as its ultimate purpose the ideal of "workable competition", and therefore is only to apply where the interests of several individual market participants are at stake. It would not be right to also require a balancing between the freedom to compete of a particular firm on one hand and the proper functioning of competition processes on the other; doing so we would bypass our goal, since the latter has to prevail anyhow. If there is damage to competitive processes, there is no *additional* requirement that the damage be undue; in the hierarchy of values involved here, with workable competition as the supreme value, *any* damage to workable competition is undue, whereas damage caused by one market participant to another may only be considered undue after an evaluation in the light of that supreme value.

We need a normative element: that only *undue* infliction of damage is to be prohibited. This additional normative element was explicitly acknowledged by the Court of Justice in its second decision in Case No. 127/73, *re BRT/Sabam/Fonior.*[8]

In this case the Court of Justice instructed a national court that had formulated a preliminary question on the problem as to how far certain conditions imposed by a nation-wide copyright organization (Sabam) might violate Article 86 of the EEC Treaty, through the imposition of unfair conditions, as follows: "that in order to judge (the unfairness of the conditions) it is necessary to take into account all interests involved in order to obtain the equilibrium between maximum freedom for the authors, composers and publishers to dispose of their work and the efficient management of their rights by an enterprise, membership of which is for them in practice unavoidable." [9]

The unavoidability of membership here was based on the impossibility for the members of effectively managing their outputs individually: centralized management is considered mandatory for this particular market, the market for copyrights on musical creations, to be able to function.

The Court of Justice has acknowledged here that a balance must be struck between the effective management of the copyrights and the market freedom of the members. A limitation of that freedom is not considered an abuse in itself, but only when it cannot be justified in terms of more efficient management, i.e. a more efficient operation of the market mechanism. Only such a justifiable limitation of freedom becomes *undue,* and is an abuse.

8. Case 127/73: *Belgische Radio en Televisie et Sociêté Belge des Acteurs, Compositeurs et Editeurs contre S.V. Sabam et N.V. Fonior,* (1974) Rec. 313 *et seq.*

9. *Loc. cit.*, consideration 8 at p. 316.

Generalizing from here we may say that market behaviour can never be abusive when such behaviour is actually necessary for a proper functioning of the market, and thus forms a necessary element of workable competition. Only if this necessity is lacking, the damage to other market participants becomes indue.

We can now extend our formula for abuse to: "market behaviour damaging competitive processes, or unduly damaging consumers or other market participants".

SECTION 2. THE QUESTION OF THE "CAUSAL RELATION" BETWEEN THE DOMINANT POSITION AND ITS ABUSE

The expression "abuse" in Article 86 of the EEC Treaty is qualified by the requirement that it shall be an abuse "of a dominant position". The syntax of the expression "abuse of a dominant position" makes it likely that it will not do to merely establish, that there is a) an abuse and b) a dominant position; an additional link between the two may have to be established.

The purpose of this section is to evaluate what could be the nature of such a link.

In order to develop the proper set of distinctions, it is useful to conceptualize abuse as 1) an *act* with 2) certain *undesirable consequences.*

We then derive two kinds of "abuse of a dominant position": [9a]

1) In the first place, those cases in which *the act itself can only be performed by someone in a dominant position.* An example is monopolistic pricing which, of course, can only be done by a monopolist, someone who has the *power* to impose inequitable prices.

2) In the second place we have those cases where the act complained of can be performed by anyone: it is only that *the effect would not occur if the enterprise were not dominant.*

An example is refusal to sell in a monopolistic situation. Anybody has the power to refuse to sell anything, you do not need a dominant position for that; but if a monopolist refuses, this can have a detrimental effect on the prospective buyer (See Case *ICI-Zoja*).

Within the second category we can conceive of another distinction.

(*a*) We have those cases where the dominant position was the *conditio*

9a. Mestmäcker, *Europäisches Wettbewerberecht* (München 1974) The same criterium, and distinction, is made also by Mestmäcker, at p. 388:

"Der wichtigste Anhaltspunkt is daraus zu entnehmen, ob eine Verhaltensweise einem einzelnen Unternehmen bei Vorherrschen von Wettbewerb unmöglich wäre oder andere Unternehmen dadurch in einer Weise behindert oder benachteiligt werden, wie es bei wirksamem Wettbewerb ausgeschlossen wäre."

sine qua non of the harmful effect; *no* harmful effect would have occured, if there had not been a dominant position.
(*b*) And we have cases where the harmful effect would have come about anyhow, even without the culprit being dominant, but where the harmful effect was *strengthened* by the circumstance that he was indeed dominant.

This last situation is well conceivable in cases of patent violation, boycott, industrial espionage and other forms of unfair competition. When powerful companies avail themselves of such techniques, the effect on their competitors and the market is likely to be more substantial than it would be in the case of smaller companies.

3) Finally, we can distinguish such cases of abuse as do not have any connection, either in their performance or in their effects, with the dominant position.

Under 2.b. we mentioned patent violation, boycott, industrial espionage and other forms of unfair competition. Of course, as the case may be, it may be found that actually the dominant position of the culprit did not reinforce the impact of these activities on the victims or the market. Where no such impact is found, category *(a)* applies. Here I could also think of rather far-fetched activities, like the kidnapping of the manager of a successful competitor. The meaning of this category lies not so much in the practical examples that can be given, as well as an indication of the fact that one should always be aware that certain abuses may have no connection whatsoever with a dominant position.

We have thus distinguished four modalities:

1) connection dominance-act ("causal relation")
2) a) connection dominance-effect (*"conditio sine qua non"*)
   b) connection dominance-effect ("worsening effect")
3) no connection.

From the top to the bottom of this list there is a certain order of decreasing consensus regarding their sufficiency as a link under Article 86 of the EEC Treaty. Everybody will agree that the "causal relation" provides a sufficient link between abuse and dominant position; that the *"conditio sine qua non"* suffices some people might doubt; this doubt will grow at the "worsening effect", and even fewer people will defend the proposition that there need not be a link at all. We will therefore have to find out which varieties we can accept, and which ones not.

In our search for an answer we first turn to the examples given in Article 86 of the EEC Treaty itself. Any categories containing one or more of these examples must of necessity constitute a link acceptable under Article 86.

Example (a):

Directly or indirectly imposing unfair purchase or selling prices or other unfair trading conditions.

This one comes under 1, "causal relation". It will only be possible for a company to impose unfair conditions on a client if the client, who will be motivated by the unfairness to look for a fairer supplier, cannot succeed there. In that case the supplier has a dominant position *vis-à-vis* the client, and the criterium of the "causal relation" is fulfilled.

Example (b):

Limiting production, markets or technical development to the prejudice of consumers.

The "limiting" here is the act; the prejudice to consumers is the effect. The act of "limiting" itself does not require a dominant position; the function of the dominance here is only that it causes or compounds the *prejudice* to the consumers. This example falls within category 2, although it is open to discussion whether both of the two sub-categories apply; 2a does certainly apply.

Example (c):

Applying dissimilar conditions to equivalent transactions with other trading parties, thereby placing them at a competitive disadvantage.

The ability to set prices arbitrarily rather than have them dictated by anonymous forces of the market constitutes market power. The difference between the lowest and the highest price charged for identical performance by one particular company gives a measure of the freedom enjoyed by that firm in its price policy.

Thus it may be argued that the very *act* of price discrimination cannot be performed without a dominant position; this would bring us under category 1.

On the other hand, an appraisal of real-life markets will teach us that many companies enjoy some freedom to set their prices, and that it would not be functional to view all of them as occupants of dominant positions. I would indeed prefer to say that price discrimination can also be exercised by non-dominant companies, and that only the effect is determined by the dominance; the placing of competitors at a competitive disadvantage. The effect, the competitive disadvantage, bears a specific relation to the dominant position; without the dominant position, the price discrimination would have less impact, and could not have brought about a competitive disadvantage. So we come under category 2 again, and the applicability of 2b is arguable.

Example (d):

Making the conclusion of contract subject to acceptance by the other parties of supplementary obligations which, by their nature or according to commercial usage, have no connection with the subject of such contracts.

Here as under example (a) we meet the phenomenon of imposition of conditions against the wishes of the other party. The same conclusions as under (a) apply.

We may conclude that the examples of Article 86 of the EEC Treaty contain cases of both category 1 and category 2. Whether, within category 2, any of the examples also fall under 2b cannot be said for sure. But it must be clear that Article 86 potentially covers cases where only the effect of the abuse, and not the act, is dependent upon a dominant position.

We must now turn to the major decision on Article 86, the judgment of the Court of Justice in the *Continental Can* decision. The decision is, for our purposes, most interesting, but rather less helpful.

The European Commission prohibited a merger on the ground that it constituted an abuse of dominant position under Article 86 of the EEC Treaty. In its appeal against the decision before the Court of Justice, the plaintiff, among many other arguments, argued that a merger could not possibly constitute an abuse of a dominant position:

> "Article 86 requires that there at least be *a causal connection* between the dominant position. In this sense Continental Can could be charged with violation of Article 86 only if it can be established that it *used* the allegedly *dominant position* of J.L.W. in the Federal Republic at Germany *to buy the T.D.V. stock* in the Netherlands." (My italics) [10]

If we translate this argument into the terms of our classification, we see that Continental Can claims that the relation postulated by Article 86 requires that the act of abuse, in this case the merger, can only be performed because of the circumstance of J.L.W.'s dominant position.

The reader should note that Continental Can did not argue simply that there should be *some* link, between the abuse and the dominant position, but also specified the exact nature of that link: it would only be satisfied with the "causal relation" of no. 1 of our classification. Let us see how the Court of Justice reacted to this particular stand.

The Court of Justice first considered the role and meaning of the system of Articles 85 and 86 of the EEC Treaty seen in the context of the Treaty as a whole. Those articles must, in the Court of Justice's reasoning, be seen as a closed system, as a result of which it is unthinkable that Article 86 should allow something that so fundamentally violates the spirit of Article 85 as does the monopolization of a market. Since monopolization, even if it appeared in the form of a cartel could not,

10. *Op. cit.* n. 2, at p. 225.

even under the text of Article 85, paragraph 3 of the EEC Treaty, be exempted, *a fortiori* one should reject the even more fundamental tightening of the market structure that is brought about by a merger.

The plaintiff's appeal to the necessity of a "causal relation" was not considered by the Court of Justice on its own merits, but was brushed away on ground of the general considerations, expounded above:

> "If Article 86 of the EEC Treaty is so construed, the question raised by plaintiffs as to the causal connection that should, in their opinion, exist between the dominant position and the abuse thereof is not material, since the strengthening of the position held by one enterprise can be an abuse and prohibited under Article 86 of the EEC Treaty *regardless of the methods and means used to attain it,* provided it has the effects described above." [11]

I find this formula of the Court of Justice rather cryptic. The only thing made clear beyond doubt is that, in the case of mergers, the "causal relation" stipulated by Continental Can is not mandatory. The formula does not say if the "causal relation" may still be required for abuses outside the field of mergers, and if, generally, the Court of Justice has made a statement about the necessity or lack thereof of any kind of link, or just about the "causal relation".

The Court of Justice has made some kind of statement about the link between abuse and dominant position implied in Article 86 of the EEC Treaty. I find it very difficult to see why whatever we may conclude it has said would not be valid for other cases that hinge on the interpretation of Article 86. I would therefore claim that the pronouncement of the Court of Justice is relevant for the general application of Article 86, for it would be unacceptable to give the same wording a different meaning for mergers on the one hand, and other abuses on the other hand.

Now what did the Court of Justice say? Let us first take a minimalistic approach. Continental Can explicitly claimed that only the "causal relation", our category 1, would be sufficient. Obviously, the Court of Justice has rejected that particular thesis, so that we may rest assured that, if it requires any link at all, link 2a will suffice.

When we closely read the Court of Justice's consideration number 27 and the previous observations, it is striking how little the Court of Justice is interested in the dominant position from which the acquisition is performed. The Court of Justice is only interested in the degree of dominance afterwards, as created by the merger, and in consideration number 29 goes as far as to suggest that a certain degree of dominance may *in itself* constitute an abuse.

For the Court of Justice, the initial dominant position is of no

11. *Ibid.*, p. 248, consideration 27.

particular interest. It is referred to, from time to time, because of the fact that Article 86 of the EEC Treaty appears to require such an initial dominant position, but it does not play any role in the Court of Justice's analysis of the legal and the factual situation, and, given the Court of Justice's stress on the all-importance of the final effect on competition of the merger, could as well, or, in the logic of the Court of Justice's reasoning, probably even better have been dropped.

The Court of Justice's reference to an initial dominant position appears to be no more than some kind of lip-service, and by implication no weight whatsoever is given to a possible requirement of a link between the initial dominance and the ultimate effects of the merger on competition. In the logic of the judgment this link is absent. It could only be introduced there by some artificial logical caprioles. The new entity created by the merger has dynamics of its own; the size, let alone the dominance of the component parts, is a question of the past. Whether consciously or not, the Court of Justice decided it could dispense with a link. Our appraisal of the *Continental Can* decision thus leaves us to conclude that the Court of Justice, at least for mergers, is not interested in any of our links. For mergers, it chose category 3, and I wonder whether there is any reason to assume that it would adopt a different position with any other kind of abuse.

Two other abuse cases have little new to offer to us. *General Motors* [12] is a special case of example a of Article 86 of the EEC Treaty: monopolistic pricing. The *ICI-CSC* case was a monopolistic refusal to sell; the harm came about by reason of the fact that victim could buy nowhere else, and category 2a applies.

The evidence from the examples of Article 86 of the EEC Treaty and the Court of Justice's *Continental Can* judgment do corroborate each other to such an extent that we may quietly accept the links of 1 and 2a. Category 2b more or less rests in limbo, and we must now take a closer look at it.

The basic distinction between 2a and 2b was, as we already saw, that whereas under 2a the relevant undesired effect of the abuse would not have *come about* if there had been no dominant position, under 2b that undesired effect would merely by *strengthened* by the presence of a dominant position, such effect being *already there* even without dominance. Under 2a the dominant position had both a quantitative and a qualitative impact, under 2b only the quantitative impact would be there.

I submit that against the background of the policy which is the fundament of Article 86 of the EEC Treaty, the distinction between 2a and 2b is not particularly relevant. If one wants to combat the harm

12. *General Motors Continental*, 1975 O.J. L 29/14.

arising from dominant positions, it does not really make that much difference whether the harmful impact arises or is just strengthened by the circumstance that the act originated from a dominant position; in both cases the harm, in such quantity as it occurs, is the result of the presence of a dominant position.

When acts that are harmful in themselves become much more so when perpetrated from a dominant position, it makes, at least to me, perfect sense to treat such acts as part of the field of problems created by the existence of dominant positions. Our conclusion is therefore that the logical difference that exists between 2a and 2b does not, in the light of the objects of Article 86 of the EEC Treaty, warrant the exclusion of the latter category.

The last category, 3, no link between abuse and dominant position, may be seen to be supported by the Court of Justice's judgment in *Continental Can.* Such an interpretation would stretch the text of Article 86 of the EEC Treaty rather far, by interpreting away the "of" in "abuse of a dominant position". I can imagine the Court of Justice reconsidering its stance here, but I refrain from any prediction. The further discussion will be based on a rejection of the "no-link" approach, while accepting the other links; however, even if the no-link approach would prevail, this would not invalidate the substance of the conclusions that are to follow.

SECTION 3. SOME APPLICATIONS

We have now developed a definition of "abuse of a dominant position" which runs:

> "market behaviour damaging competitive processes, or unduly damaging consumers or other market participants, which either could not be perpetrated without the dominant position, or would not harm, or not harm to the same extent, if not perpetrated from a dominant position."

We must now check in how far this definition fits the two specific problems mentioned in the introductory section, unfair competition, and artificial product differentiation.

1. Artificial product differentiation

a) Nature of the problem

For American authors *concentration,* i.e. the number of firms operating within a given market, and their respective market shares, is not the only dimension of market structure. Two other dimensions acknowledged by them are *product differentiation* and *entry barriers*.[13]

Product differentiation means the tendency of purchasers in certain markets to perceive the outputs of the several sellers as different, even if they are essentially identical in terms of the needs they serve.

Such perceived difference may be based on genuine variance in the quality of the products, but also merely on an image of the product instilled in the public, which often comes about through massive advertising compaigns. If a market has product differentiation, one buyer may prefer brand A, and another swear by brand B. If prices of brand A and brand B are more or less identical, one purchaser will buy A, and another B, and will, *even if* their favourite brand is subject to price raises, which the other brand does not have, stick to their favourite. It will be clear that this tendency to be faithful will vary with each purchaser, and with each brand. The market where purchasers, as a whole, show great fidelity even in the case of heavy price increases (relative to the other products in the market) is said to have strong product differentiation, and markets where buyers switch over with any relative change in price, none.

The more faithful his buyers are, the stronger will be the position of a producer. Such a producer will have a certain degree of freedom in setting his prices; indeed, if nobody were ever to change to his competitor's products, he would have the position of a monopolist. In a product differentiated market at least some of the producers have market power which they would not have without the product differentiation. It is nowadays accepted by most economists that, at least for consumer products, the great majority of real-life markets has product differentiation, with the market power of the producers implied in it.

It was already said that product differentiation could be based on genuine differences between the products as well as by a public image artfully created by advertising, creating a mere illusion regarding the product's separate identity. Massive advertising over an extended period of time can ingrain certain brand preferences unrelated to any special quality of the product involved, and as a result it may become well-nigh impossible for any outsider with a competing product to lure away a sufficient number of customers to make his new establishment operate successfully. The new competitor could only remedy this situation by investing huge amounts of money in advertising campaigns to break the fidelity to established brands, and this again would make it impossible for many years to operate profitably.

Our discussion of product differentiation through advertising has now

13. Cf. Joe S. Bain, *Industrial Organisation*, 2nd ed. (NY 1968), p. 225 *et seq.*, 255 *et seq.* Much on the following discussion on entry barriers and product differentiation is derived from this book.

brought us to our third element of market structure: *entry barriers.* The product differentiation brought about by massive advertising creates difficulties for outsiders to penetrate into the market; these difficulties constitute the entry barriers by which outsiders are confronted.

The barrier of entry into a given product market can be defined as the degree to which a potential entrant may expect, over a considerable period of time, to operate less profitably than the firms already established.

As long as the profit margins on the particular market remain lower than the quantity defined here, it will be unattractive for the outsider to enter that market, and the existing companies will remain shielded from outside competition.

One may distinguish three sources of barriers to entry:

1) product differentiation advantages over potential entrant companies;
2) absolute cost advantages over potential entrant companies;
3) economies of scale enjoyed by established large-scale companies.

The source in 3 cannot, in as far as I can see, possibly lead to a charge of improperly influencing the market structure, the source in 2 may very well do so in case of price discrimination by the seller of raw materials in collusion with the firm involved; but the source in 1 is the one that particularly concerns us here for the case where the product differentiation has been brought about by the active behaviour, in the form of a massive advertising, of the established companies, who, by doing so, deliberately influenced the structure of the market.

It is now clear from the *Continental Can* decision that companies who influence the degree of concentration on a market by way of a merger in principle are within the scope of Article 86 of the EEC Treaty. We have also seen that there are possibilities for companies to actively influence by their behaviour the two other dimensions of market structure: entry barriers and product differentiation. Such influence may be exercised by way of massive advertising. It would be interesting to find out whether this particular form of changing the structure of a market, to the detriment of competitive processes, could also come under Article 86 of the EEC Treaty.

b) An example: The American breakfast cereals industry

The Federal Trade Commission is a federal agency *inter alia* charged with the enforcement of the American antitrust laws. In addition, it was granted upon its creation special powers (under Article 1 paragraph 5 of the FTC Act) to combat "unfair trade practices".

The original idea behind this section was to create the possibility of attacking behaviour which, although violating the spirit of the traditional body of antitrust laws, could not be combatted under those laws because of gaps in their formal structure.[14] It was a mandate by Congress to fill gaps in the same manner as, according to many, the Court of Justice did when it decided to fill up what otherwise would have constituted a gap between Articles 85 and 86 of the EEC Treaty.

Under this paragraph 5 the FTC has now proceeded against the major American producers of breakfast cereals.[15] These producers are accused of having built up their brand names by way of exaggerated publicity campaigns, while pretènding, contrary to the truth, that essential differences existed between the various products.

The FTC insists that a considerable degree of artificial product differentiation has resulted, accompanied by almost unsurmountable entry barriers for new comers.

By their advertising the producers are said to have built up, and to maintain, a collective dominant position which outsiders are no longer able to challenge.

The case is still pending, and the outcome uncertain. The complaint does, however, show, that an authoritative body as the FTC considers advertising-induced advertising as a problem properly to be dealt with within the context of antitrust enforcement.

c) Applicability of Article 86 of the EEC Treaty

In order to find out whether artificial product differentiation fits our definition of abuse of dominant position, we must now start asking the various questions suggested by that definition.

Is the behaviour market behaviour? I have little doubt that advertising is intended to have an impact on the market. What is the harm done, and to whom, or what, is it done? Artificial entry barriers eliminate potential competitors. This elimination makes it easier for the established companies to maintain, without challenge, their shared monopoly. The harm done is thus: damage to competitive processes.

14. *Cf.* Areeda, *Antitrust analysis,* (Boston 1967), p. 33, sub (b).

15. Reference currently unknown to the author.

A parallel case occurred in the market for household detergent in England. In 1966 the Monopolies Commission, pursuant to Section 9 of the Monopolies and Restrictive Practices (inquiry and control) Act 1948, presented to Parliament the report "Household Detergents". In this report (par. 94) it was submitted "that their (Unilever and Proctor & Gamble's) advertising matter is more concerned with advertising unprovable qualities and building up a 'brand image' than with informing the public about the practical attributes of the product and how the best use can be made of it; (. . .) that as a result, not only does the public have to pay for costs for which it obtains no benefit but also, at least as regards powders, newcomers to the industry are deterred by the high cost of entry."

Amongst other things, the Monopolies Commission recommended: "The Board of Trade should encourage the two companies to agree that at least a 40% reduction in selling expenses should accompany the price reduction."

Finally (last but not least), what is the nature of the link between the abusive behaviour and the dominant position? The huge advertising budget may be seen as an aspect of dominance, which is then used to build up or expand the degree of product differentiation. Under this reasoning the dominant position is the necessary condition for the behaviour, and modality 1, the causal relation, applies. I would, however, prefer to see the situation in the context of link 2. In the breakfast cereals case it was the existing dominant position of the established firms which created the very environment in which it was possible for them to use advertising as an effective menas of protecting their dominance.

Had their market position been weaker it is likely that, in the face of non-product-differentiation competition (by which is meant outsiders claiming that their products, while as good as the established products, are yet cheaper) their attempts at product differentiation would be less effective. The degree of dominance of the established company may influence the effectiveness with which its advertising stimulates and maintains product differentiation.

Summing it all up, we must conclude that massive advertising directed at the creation of artificial product differentiation may, if perpetrated by an already dominant company, come under Article 86 of the EEC Treaty. Of course, it will be difficult to show that massive advertising does indeed lead to artificial product differentiation; this is, however, no reason to hesitate in cases where the artificiality is obvious.

I want to add that, if advertising by dominant companies is untruthful or obnoxious to such a degree that it can be considered to constitute unfair competition, it may come under Article 86 of the EEC Treaty by way of that latter category, which I will proceed to discuss now.

2. Unfair competition

What is the nature of the link between unfair competition and dominant position? By definition unfair competition is harmful to competitors, even if there is no dominance. Therefore we can generally say that if there is any link, it has to be the "worsening effect" of 2b. Unfair competition is abuse of dominant position only in those cases where the harmful impact on the competitors is strenthened by the circumstance that the culprit enjoys a dominant position.

This indicates that not every act of unfair competition in the context of a dominant position will fit our definition of abuse. Only when the facts of the case warrant the conclusion that the dominance has indeed had a worsening effect, should Article 86 of the EEC Treaty apply. Still, I think, this worsening effect will be inevitable in many cases. Is there anything unnatural about the inclusion of unfair competition under

EEC rules of antitrust? Let us try to evaluate how the two fields are related.

The EEC Treaty created a role for the Community administration in the proper functioning of competitive processes. In the earlier years the cartel policy of the European Commission showed a strong tendency to see antitrust as a means to the end of the creation of an integrated European market. In recent years, however, the proper functioning of competition has more and more become an end in itself.

The functioning of the market by way of competitive processes should be seen as a function of the individual market behaviour of all those who participate in the market. For the purpose of protecting the *market mechanism,* antitrust law creates norms to regulate the methods by which the participants in the market compete. Such norms are also formulated in the law of unfair competition, with the purpose of protecting the *individual participants.*

Both sets of norms therefore regulate the same thing: the competitive behaviour of entrepreneurs.

The market policy of any entrepreneur always has the purpose either of improving or of utilizing his position on the market. Industrial espionage, exclusive distributorships, price-cutting, price discrimination and price-fixing are but different tactics with the purpose of strengthening and exploiting market power. Antitrust and the law of unfair competition both have the objective of containing such tactics in as far as they are considered undesirable.

Given these parallels, we can now proceed with the differences. Antitrust law is primarily the basis for a government policy to ensure an optimal functioning of the market mechanism. Antitrust law primarily protects competition, not competitors. The law of unfair competition, in contradistinction, creates norms to regulate relations between individual competitors. Competitors are protected against each other, without reference to the global functioning of the market.

Antitrust and the law of unfair competition thus have the same subject matter i.e., the market behaviour of companies, but adopt a different approach; the one is to protect competition, the other to protect competitors. As we have already concluded, in the general context of Articles 3f, 85 and 86, that these articles do protect both competition and market participants, we see that there is nothing in the nature of unfair competition that would bar the use of Article 86 of the EEC Treaty against it.

SECTION 4. LEGAL POLICY

Is it desirable, from the point of view of legal policy, to extend the body of norms to be policed by the European Commission, beyond its traditional horizon? The European Commission already is confronted with a problem of very limited resources while dealing with traditional antitrust matters. One might argue, that the enforcement of fair competition added to the current tasks, might cause a bottleneck problem.

The author feels that in such a point of view the European Commission is seen too strongly as the enforcer of cartel *law*, rather than an organ conducting an antitrust *policy*.[16] If we stress the policy aspect the incorporation of unfair competition into Article 86 of the EEC Treaty does not, in the first place, mean that the European Commission will suffer a greater case load, but rather that it will obtain a more spacious legal framework within which to formulate its policy. Given the number of cases which its manpower can handle, the European Commission will now be able to select that number from a larger group.[17]

16. G. J. Linssen, "De rol van de Commissie bij de toepassing van het Europese mededingingsrecht" in: *Europees Kartelrecht anno 1973*(Deventer 1974), 8p.), p. 33 *et seq.*

17. The reader should note that the possibility of action before national courts under Art. 86 was not made a subject of discussion here. The reason for this is with respect to unfair competition that such actions are already possible under national laws of unfair competition, and thus would be nothing new; whereas, with regard to massive advertising, the damage will be so diffuse and impersonal that it is unlikely that damages will ever be awarded.

MEASURES HAVING AN EFFECT EQUIVALENT TO QUANTITATIVE RESTRICTIONS

by

A. W. H. Meij and J. A. Winter*

INTRODUCTION

Articles 30 and 34 of the EEC Treaty not only prohibit all quantitative restrictions but also all measures having an effect equivalent to quantitative restrictions in intra-Community trade.

In recent months the Court of Justice of the European Communities has rendered a number of decisions which throw new light on the meaning of the hitherto not entirely clear notion of measures having an effect equivalent to quantitative restrictions. In the *Dassonville* Case this notion was given a very wide scope. It was found to include "all trading rules enacted by member States which are capable of hindering, directly or indirectly, actually or potentially, intra-Community trade".[1] Barring the application of safeguard clauses, this definition seems wide enough to encompass in principle a great many measures taken by the member States in the area commonly regarded as the "reserved domain" of the member States.

In this article an attempt will be made to analyse the rule formulated by the Court of Justice in the light of the conclusions reached by the Commission and legal writers in the discussion on the scope of the concept of measures having an equivalent effect to quantitative restrictions prior to the Court's judgment in the *Dassonville* Case.

I. THE ELIMINATION OF OBSTACLES TO INTRA-COMMUNITY TRADE

The free movement of goods within the Community requires the elimination as between member States not only of customs duties and charges having an equivalent effect (Articles 12 *et seq.*) but also of quantitative restrictions on interstate trade and all measures having equivalent effect (Articles 30 *et seq.*). Within the Community of the Six customs duties on exports and charges having equivalent effect as well as quantitative restrictions on exports and measures having an equivalent effect were

* Lecturers in the Law of the European Communities, University of Groningen.

1. Case 8/74, *Procureur du Roi* v. *B. and G. Dassonville,* (1974) E.C.R., 837 *et seq;* 12 C.M.L.Rev. 1975, 413-415.

13 C.M.L. Rev. 1976, 79-104

abolished by the end of the first stage of the transitional period, *i.e.* December 31, 1961 (Articles 16 and 34).

Furthermore, the member States dismantled their customs duties on imports and quantitative restrictions on imports well before the end of the transitional period.[2] Upon the expiry of this period, the prohibition relating to charges of an effect equivalent to customs duties on imports (Article 13) and measures of an effect equivalent to quantitative restrictions (Artcile 30) became fully effective for those charges and measures the elimination of which had not previously been ordered by the Commission on the basis of a timetable determined by means of Directives (Articles 13, para. 2 and 33, para. 7).

As far as agricultural products are concerned, each Council regulation adopted in the course of the transitional period for the establishment of a common organization of agricultural markets incorporates *i.a.* the prohibition on quantitative restrictions and measures having equivalent' effect as far as trade in the relevant agricultural products is concerned. Regulations for the establishment of market organizations adopted after January 1, 1970, in general no longer mention explicitly the prohibition on quantitative restrictions and measures of equivalent effect.[3] At the end of the transitional period all quantitative restrictions and measures having equivalent effect were forbidden, with the exception of (a) systems of minimum prices falling under Article 44, (b) quantitative restrictions and measures having equivalent effect forming part of national market organizations not replaced by a common organization of agricultural markets, and (c) quantitative restrictions and measures falling under the "public policy reservation clause" of Article 36 or some other escape clause of the Treaty.[4]

2. See Council Decision No. 66/532 of July 26, 1966, J.O. p. 2971/1966 and the Acceleration Decisions of May 12, 1960, J.O. p. 1217/1966 and of May 15, 1962, J.O. p. 1284/1962.

3. See Ehlermann, in von der Groeben, Boeckh, Thiesing, *Kommentar zum EWG-Vertrag* (Baden-Baden 1974), Vol. I, p. 251; only Council Reg. No. 816/70 (wine), J.O. 1970, L 99/1, still incorporates the prohibition explicitly.

4. Recently, however, the Court has declared, that after the expiration of the transitional period quota systems forming part of a national organization of an agricultural market which has not been replaced by a common organization of the market in question, are no longer permissible. See Case 48/74 *Charmasson* v. *French Republic,* (1974) E.C.R. 1383. This judgment also casts some doubts on the possibility of allowing the maintenance of systems of minimum prices pursuant to Art. 44 of the EEC Treaty. See also Paulin and Forman in 12 C.M.L.Rev. 1975, 399 *et seq.*

II. THE DEFINITION OF MEASURES HAVING AN EFFECT EQUIVALENT TO QUANTITATIVE RESTRICTIONS

1. *General considerations*

Quantitative restrictions on imports and exports include all legislative or administrative rules or practices limiting the importation or exportation of one or more products according to quantitative criteria (number, weight, value). In their most extreme form such restrictions amount to prohibitions on imports or exports.[5]

The prohibition of measures of an equivalent effect to quantitative restrictions constitutes a necessary complement to the ban on straightforward restrictions on imports or exports (familiarly known as quotas). The Treaty does not define the concept and neither can any useful information be inferred from the corresponding rules in other economic treaties.[6] It is clear that, in order to be covered by the concept, there must be a measure of a member State which has restrictive effects on inter-state trade similar to those produced by quantitative restrictions, as described above. However, in a common market the range of state measures liable to affect inter-state trade is virtually unlimited. If every state measure having the effect of limiting or hindering the free flow of goods were to be covered by the concept of measures having an effect equivalent to quantitative restrictions, the member States would be left with very little power to regulate commerce or even to conduct economic policies of their own. Since the effects of commercial regulations and economic policy measures (*e.g.* price regulations, taxation policy, etc.) cannot be confined to purely domestic economic operations, the continued exercise of powers reserved to the member States would be jeopardized and would come to depend on the existence of escape clauses and the scope attributed to them. However, escape clauses such as Articles 36 and 108-109, are to be interpreted in a restrictive manner. Moreover, the whole Treaty is based on the idea that member States have not relinquished the power to take measures which can properly be qualified as measures of economic policy. If the exercise of these powers interferes with the functioning of the common market, and prevents the attainment of the Community's objectives, the member States shall, in co-operation with the Community institutions, coordinate their economic policies (*Cf. e.g.* Articles 2, 6, 103, 145).

5. See generally, for the definition of quantitative restrictions, Ehlermann, *op. cit.* (note 3) at p. 253, with further references.

6. The ECSC Treaty and the Euratom Treaty do not contain a similar prohibition. Art. XI of GATT prohibits quotas and other measures, but fails to give a further definition of such measures. See also Graf, *Der Begriff Massnahmen gleicher Wirkung wie mengenmässigen Beschränkungen im EWG-Vertrag,* (Hamburg, 1972), p. 59 *et seq.*

As a result of these considerations, a measure having restrictive effects on trade but which has been taken by a member State in the exercise of reserved powers cannot be caught by Articles 30 *et seq.* The problem remains, however, as to how the extent of the "reserved domain" is to be defined.

The difficulty in finding criteria allowing a satisfactory delimitation between State measures restricting trade which are forbidden under Article 30 *et seq.* and those which are not caught by these Articles is caused by the ambiguity of the term "free movement of goods".[7] This concept could be taken to mean that member States are prohibited only from promulgating rules designed exclusively to regulate imports or exports. If a wider interpretation is adopted, the concept would also involve limitations on the freedom of the member States to enact any rules which may affect interstate trade, even if these measures apply equally to purely domestic commercial operations. It is the latter broad concept of freedom which has been embraced in U.S. constitutional law. By virtue of the interstate commerce clause, the law-making powers of the several States are greatly restricted since the States are prevented from adopting measures which, though they may be indiscriminately applicable to purely domestic activities and to border-crossing activities, are apt to improperly burden interstate commerce. In the Community, the view that the objective of free movement of goods only deprives the member States of the power to enact measures containing an element of discrimination against foreign goods, is held by a minority of legal writers only. The wider interpretation which places more substantial limitations on the freedom of member States to regulate matters liable to affect intra-Community trade seems to be gaining ground. It fits in with the principle of Community solidarity as expressed in Article 5 of the Treaty because it makes it possible to condemn all measures which are contrary to the objectives of the Community, and which have not been taken in the area indisputably reserved to the member States.

2. *The definition of the concept proposed by the Commission*

Until 1967 the Commission had avoided giving a general definition of what State regulations constitute measures of an effect equivalent to quantitative restrictions. Its action in this field had been limited to issuing three directives based on Article 33, para. 7, addressing specific situa-

7. See Kapteyn and VerLoren van Themaat, *Introduction to the Law of the European Communities*, (London, Deventer, Alphen 1973), pp. 193-194, 203.

tions.[8] In rather cautious and pragmatic replies to parliamentary questions asked by Mr. Deringer in March and May 1967,[9] the Commission described a number of measures which it considered to constitute measures of equivalent effect to quantitative restrictions,[10] and it defined the measures falling under the concept as "all laws, administrative provisions and administrative practices which hinder imports or exports which could otherwise take place, including those provisions and practices which make importation or exportation more difficult or costly than the disposal of domestic production".[11] It was added, however, "that provisions which are equally applicable to domestic and imported products do not as a rule constitute measures having an effect equivalent to quantitative restrictions". This addition seems to indicate that the Commission has neither adopted the very broad concept of "free movement of goods" (which totally precludes member States from adopting provisions affecting inter-state trade), nor the narrow notion according to which member States have only relinquished the power to make rules relating exclusively to inter-state trade.

The Commission has further clarified its position in two Directives of December 1969.[12] It was in Directive No. 70/50 that the Commission elaborated the dichotomy between measures which discriminate against imports and measures which are equally applicable to domestic and imported products. As far as the category of measures discriminating against imports is concerned, Directive No. 70/50 abolishes measures which hinder imports which could otherwise take place, including measures which make importation more difficult or costly than the disposal of domestic production (Article 2, para. 1). It prohibits in particular measures which make imports or the disposal of imported products subject to a condition—other than a formality—which is required in respect of imported products only, or a condition differing from that required for domestic products and more difficult to satisfy. Equally, it covers, in particular, measures which favour domestic prod-

8. Dir. No. 64/486 of July 28, 1964, J.O. p. 2253/1964 (import calender); Dir. No. 66/682 of November 7, 1966, J.O. p. 3745/1966 (imports only allowed if an equivalent quantity of nationally produced goods are purchased); Dir. No. 66/683 of November 7, 1966, J.O. p. 3748/1966 (obligation to include home-produced materials in products otherwise likely to be made entirely from imported goods).

9. Written questions No. 118 of December 8, 1966, J.O. pp. 122 and 301/1967 and No. 64 of May 11, 1966, J.O. 1967, No. 169/11.

10. Question No. 118.

11. Question No. 64.

12. Dir. No. 70/32 of December 17, 1969, J.O. 1970, L 13/1 (prohibition of discrimination regarding government purchases); Dir. No. 70/50 of December 22, 1969, J.O. 1970, L 13/29 (abolition of measures which have an effect equivalent to quantitative restrictions on imports and are not covered by other Treaty provisions).

ucts or grant them a preference, other than an aid (Article 2, para. 2). Paragraph 3 of Article 2 lists a large number of examples of measures discriminating against imported products.

As far as measures applying equally to domestic and imported products are concerned, Article 3 of the Directive condemns measures governing the marketing of products which deal, in particular, with the shape, size, weight, composition, presentation, identification or putting up, where the restrictive effect of such measures on the free movement of goods exceeds the effects intrinsic to trade rules. The Commission thus wishes to apply a proportionality test to rules which are indiscriminately applicable to imports and domestic products. They are to be regarded as measures having equivalent effect if their restrictive effects on the free movement of goods are out of proportion to their purpose, or if the same objective can be attained by other means which are less of a hindrance to trade.

3. *The views of legal writers*

In recognizing that under certain circumstances measures which are equally applicable to imported goods and domestic products come under the scope of Article 30 of the EEC Treaty, the Commission takes a middle position in the discussion between legal writers on the scope of the concept of measures of an effect equivalent to quantitative restrictions.

(*a*) Some authors have defended the view that Articles 30 *et seq.* only encompass measures discriminating against imports.[13] Therefore, measures which are equally applicable to the disposal of imported and domestic products can not be prohibited as measures falling under Article 30 *et seq.* The main argument adduced in support of this restrictive interpretation is the alleged need to respect the sphere of reserved powers for the member States to regulate trade. In this conception Articles 100 *et seq.* are meant to circumscribe and to protect the sphere of the member States' reserved domain.

(*b*) Although Steindorff has also argued that discrimination is an essential criterion for distinguishing between measures having equivalent effect to quantitative restrictions and other State measures not falling

13. See in particular Graf, *Der Begriff "Massnahmen gleicher Wirkung wie mengenmässigen Einfuhrbeschränkungen im EWG-Vertrag"* (Hamburg 1972). This view was first defended by Seidel in (1967) N.J.W. 2081 *et seq.* Meier in Ehle-Meier, *EWG-Warenverkehr*, pp. 106, 112 and 127 *et seq.*, takes an even more restrictive stand in that measures which do not actually affect the importation of foreign goods in a technical sense, but only place them in an unfavourable position when they are offered for sale on the market, are not measures having an effect equivalent to quantitative restrictions.

under Article 30 *et seq.*, his view is more flexible in the sense that he favours a wide definition of the notion of discrimination.[14] Thus a State measure could be said to discriminate against imports not only if imported goods are subjected to conditions different from those applying to the disposal of national goods, but also in cases where imported and domestic goods are formally treated in the same manner, in spite of vast differences in the conditions under which they have been produced. Measures which in a formal sense apply equally to domestic and imported products could result in instances of *material* discrimination and come under the prohibition of Article 30 if they are tailored to the conditions governing domestic production and would consequently hinder the importation of foreign goods.

(*c*) The view that all measures restricting inter-state trade, in so far as they are not regulated by other Treaty provisions, come under the prohibition of Article 30 *et seq.* has been defended by authors such as VerLoren van Themaat [15] and Waelbroeck.[16] They argue that the only decisive criterion for comprising a measure under the scope of Article 30 *et seq.* is its restrictive effect on the free movement of goods. Any measure burdening, restricting or preventing the free flow of goods is incompatible with Article 30.

Restrictions on the free movement of goods can only be legitimate if the conditions justifying a derogation from the prohibition by virtue of Article 36 are satisfied.

In support of this thesis, its proponents point to the wide formulation of Article 30, which makes no mention of discrimination. The Community is based on a customs union (Article 9). To the measures necessary to achieve the free movement of goods are added provisions prescribing the abolition of obstacles to freedom of movement for persons, services and capital. These provisions generally distinguish between the abolition of discriminatory State measures (Articles 48, 52, 60, 68) and the abolition of restrictions (Article 67, possibly Article 48). Since Article 30 does not set forth a similar dinstinction, this provision must be taken to apply to all measures restricting intra-Community trade and not merely to measures discriminating against imports.[17]

Article 36 seems to confirm the correctness of this view. The public

14. *Der Gleichheitssatz im Wirtschaftsrecht des Gemeinsamen Marktes* (1965), p. 14; see also his contribution in *Dienstfreiheit und Versicherungsaufsicht im Gemeinsamen Markt*, 1971, p. 79 *et seq.*

15. See his article entitled "Bevat art. 30 van het EEG-Verdrag slechts een non-discriminatiebeginsel ten aanzien van invoerbeperkingen," 15 SEW 1967, 632 *et seq.; cf.* also his comments on Dirs. Nos. 70/32 and 70/50 in 18 SEW 1970, 258 *et seq.*

16. See Mégret-Louis-Vignes-Waelbroeck, *Le droit de la Communauté économique européenne*, Vol. I, p. 100 *et seq.*

17. VerLoren van Themaat, 15 SEW 1967, at 635-636.

policy grounds justifying import and export prohibitions are precisely the grounds which, in most cases, prompt national authorities to lay down rules governing the marketing of goods, irrespective of their origin. As a matter of principle, these trading rules contain restrictions which apply indiscriminately to the disposal of home-made products and to imported products.

If only measures discriminating against imported products could fall under the prohibition of Article 30, hardly any measure would come under the scope of this provision, since the bulk of these measures belong to the "equally applicable" category. If these provisions are not covered by Article 30, they are not prohibited, and there would have been no need to provide for their exemption from the prohibition of Article 30 under Article 36.[18]

Article 37 para. 1, prescribes the abolition of discrimination regarding the conditions under which goods falling under a State monopoly of a commercial policy are produced or marketed. By virtue of paragraph 2 of this Article, the member States are ordered to refrain not only from introducing any new measures involving discrimination but also from adopting new measures restricting "the scope of the Articles dealing with the abolition of customs duties and quantitative restrictions between States". The latter prohibition would be superfluous if the prohibition of Article 30 only related to measures discriminating against imported goods.[19]

4. *Critical analysis of these views*

a. The narrow view, which limits the scope of measures of an effect equivalent to quantitative restrictions to measures involving discrimination against imported products, is contrary to the tendency of the Court to interpret the concept broadly (see below, Ch. III). It also finds scant support in the Treaty. It may be true that the prohibition of customs duties and charges of equivalent effect, as well as that of quantitative restrictions and measures of equivalent effect are to be regarded primarily as a manifestation of the principle of non-discrimination. This does not mean, however, that such obstacles to intra-Community trade need not to be removed if the element of discrimination is lacking, *e.g.* in cases where a charge is levied on a product which is not manufactured in the country of importation.[20] It would also seem incorrect to consider Article 100 as a provision limiting the scope of the prohibition of

18. Idem, at 638.

19. Idem, at 640.

20. Béraud, "Les mesures d'effet equivalent au sens des articles 30 et suivants du Traité de Rome", 4 Rev. trim. dr. Europ. 1968, 265-292, at 286. See also *e.g.* Case 24/68, *Comm.* v.

measures of an effect equivalent to quantitative restrictions. Such a view is hardly reconcilable with the prevailing opinion that Article 100 only provides for approximation of measures that are not in themselves prohibited by the Treaty rules on the establishment of the common market.[21] Furthermore, the arguments developed by VerLoren van Themaat with regard to the Articles 36 and 37 are difficult to refute.

b. It should be pointed out that the scope of the prohibition of Article 30 could be extended by having recourse not to mere instances of formal discrimination (unequal treatment of equal situations) but also to cases of "material" discrimination (equal treatment of unequal situations). The Court found a case of material discrimination to exist in a judgment of 1963 [22] but, to our knowledge, it has not repeated the broad definition of discrimination propounded in that ruling. In fact, the application of this wide concept of discrimination appears extremely problematical.[23] It would require complicated evaluations of all relevant factors and circumstances determining the economic and commercial position of foreign economic agents as compared with those operating within the member State which enacts the allegedly discriminatory rules. To a certain extent, there would invariably be a case for considering the situation in which goods in other countries are produced as dissimilar to the situation in the country of importation, since conditions of production and sale are nowhere identical. However, it would undoubtedly go too far to make differentiated treatment with regard to the disposal of home-made goods and foreign goods an obligatory feature of every State measure regulating the marketing of goods on the national territory. The Treaty rests on the assumption that specialization and optimum allocation of factors of production ought to be promoted on the basis of existing conditions governing economic activities in the member States, subject to elimination of discrimination based on nationality and possible distortions due to the existence of divergent economic regulations in the member States. The conditions which will of themselves ensure the most rational distribution of production at the highest level of produc-

---

Italy, 15 *Recueil* 1969, 201 and Cases 2 and 3/69, *Sociaal Fonds voor Diamantarbeiders* v. *Brachfeld,* 15 *Recueil* 1969, 222. The charges complained of were qualified as charges having an equivalent effect to customs duties, even if they had no discriminatory or protective effects.

21. See *e.g.* Adv. Gen. Trabucchi in his submissions in the *Dassonville* Case, (1974) E.C.R., 858; Ulmer, "Zum Verbot mittelbaren Einfuhrbeschränkungen im EWG-Vertrag", 19 A.W.D. 1973, 349-361, at 357, with further references. See for a contrary view, Ehlermann, "Die Bedeutung des Artikels 36 EWGV für die Freiheit des Warenverkehrs", 8 EuR 1973, 1-17, at 5.

22. Case 13/63, *Italy* v. *Commission of the EEC,* 9 *Recueil* 1963, 335 *et seq.*

23. Ulmer, *loc. cit.* (note 21), at 354.

tivity (*Cf.* Article 2 of the ECSC Treaty) do not presume that all competitive advantages of economic operators are levelled off by way of an obligation to differentiate measures according to the more-or-less favourable conditions under which production takes place in the various member States.

c. For VerLoren van Themaat and Waelbroeck, the conclusive criterion lies in the trade-restricting effect of the measures.[24] In this view, however, the scope of Article 30 is so large that it threatens to deprive the member State of the authority to regulate domestic commercial matters. Since measures taken in the area of the reserved domain and pursuing legitimate goals cannot be distinguished from other, less unobjectionable, State regulations, an excessive appeal to the derogations under Article 36 may be expected to be the result. The need for a wide interpretation of Article 36 would depend, at least to some extent, on the limits imposed on the scope of Article 30 by other Treaty provisions. It follows from the Treaty system that Article 30 does not apply to trade-restricting measures involving financial burdens on imports. Such measures are governed by special Treaty provisions (Article 9 *et seq.* and 95 *et seq.*[25]). Likewise Article 37, relating to State monopolies of a commercial character, regulates a special case of restrictions on trade. Furthermore Article 92 relating to State aids should be regarded as a *lex specialis* in respect to Article 30. Restrictions on imports resulting from the grant of aids to national enterprises, which are authorized under Article 92, paras. 2 and 3, are therefore not covered by the prohibition of Article 30.[26] It has been maintained that Article 100 sets limits to the application of Article 30 to State measures which interfere with the free movement of goods.[27] Since obstacles to intra-Community trade resulting from such measures "as directly affect the establishment or functioning of the common market" are to be removed by way of approximation of laws, so runs the argument, such State measures could not already be covered by the prohibition of Article 30. The better view seems to be, however, that Article 100 cannot be regarded as a provision restricting the scope of the basic provisions on the establishment of the common market. Approximation of laws is only possible and necessary to the extent that the domestic provisions in question are not in themselves prohibited by the Treaty. It constitutes an auxiliary instrument for use in

24. See *supra*, notes 15 and 16.

25. *Cf.* Ehlermann in Von der Groeben, Boeckh, Thiesing, at 258. See also *e.g.* Case 7/68, *Commission* v. *Italy*, 14 *Recueil* 1968, 633 *et seq;* Case 29/72, *Marimex* v. *Italian Fiscal Administration*, 18 *Recueil* 1972, 1309 *et seq.*

26. *Cf.* Art. 2, para. 2 of Dir. No. 70/50.

27. *Supra*, note 21.

cases where the liberalization measures of the Treaty are insufficient to establish the four freedoms of the common market and the system of undistorted competition required by the Treaty.[28] This approximation of laws may be called for in cases where derogations from the prohibition of Article 30 are justified by virtue of Article 36.

Is the scope of Article 30 limited by Articles 103 *et seq.*? Underlying these provisions is the assumption that the member States have retained their powers in the field of conjunctural and general economic policies. However, it is obvious that the member States are just as little entitled, in the exercise of these reserved powers, to introduce new customs duties or similar charges to rectify the balance of payments position, as they are authorized to resort to other methods conflicting with provisions on the establishment of the common market. In Case 6/69 concerning the French preferential rediscount rates for export transactions,[29] the Court rejected the French contention that there were no restrictions in the Treaty on the exercise of the power to take measures in the monetary field.

The Court and the Commission did not dispute that discount policy belongs to the area where the member States have retained primary responsibility. However, they rejected the idea that reserved powers in the economic and monetary fields could have any strict significance. The Court ruled that the exercise of these powers does not permit the taking of unilateral measures which the Treaty prohibits. The preferential rediscount rates amounted to State aids and could not be countenanced on the basis of Article 92. Likewise, it may be submitted that, as a matter of principle, economic policy measures, such as *e.g.* price regulations, could not enjoy absolute immunity with regard to the application of Article 30.

The conclusion must, therefore, be that in the absence of important limitations on the scope of Article 30 to be derived from other Treaty provisions, the Treaty's escape clauses are to be heavily relied on if it is felt that member States ought to be authorized to lay down trading rules and to conduct their economic policies. Some relief might be afforded on the basis of safeguard provisions such as Articles 108, 109, 115, 223, 224. Their application is restricted, however, to exceptional circumstances. In this respect the potentialities of Article 36 are more promising.

Nevertheless, it is clear that the grounds mentioned in Article 36 fail to

28. *"Die Vorschrift hat (daher) typisch lückenfüllenden, bzw. ergänzenden Charakter. Bezogen auf die Einfuhrbeschränkungen setzt die in Art. 100 vorgesehene Rechtsanglei-chung da ein, wo das Verbot des Art. 30 am Vorbehalt des Art. 36, satz 1, scheitert"*(Ulmer, *op. cit.*, n. 21, at 357).

29. Case 6/69, *Commission* v. *French Republic,* 15 *Recueil* 1969, 523 *et seq;* 7 C.M.L.Rev. 1970, 479-489.

leave enough discretion to the member States to implement "necessary" measures of marketing, conjunctural and general economic policies, which, in many cases, will inevitably have effects on intra-Community trade. It follows from the Court's case law that Article 36 is to be interpreted restrictively.[30] Moreover, contrary to Article 226,[31] Article 36 only allows derogations from the prohibitions of Articles 30 *et seq.* in respect of measures pursuing goals of a non-economic nature.[32] It is clear, therefore, that regulations of the member States concerning *e.g.* industrial standards or weights and measures can only with considerable difficulty be brought under the public policy reservations of Article 36.

d. The Commission's view [33] (*per se* prohibition for measures discriminating against foreign imports, and a more flexible approach with reference to trade measures indiscriminately applicable to national and foreign products) has also invited criticism. It is not easy to distinguish between measures involving formal discrimination, to which the *per se* prohibition applies, and measures applicable equally to domestic and imported products. In Article 2, para. 3, of Directive No. 70/50 the Commission has listed a number of measures which it regards as measures "other than those applicable equally to domestic or imported products". It has been correctly pointed out, however, that the same discriminatory results in respect of foreign goods can also be reached in the form of measures applicable equally to domestic or imported products.[34] This may often be a question of legislative technique. Thus prescriptions regarding designations of origin of quality wines in the language of the country of origin may be regarded as measures applicable equally to foreign goods or domestic goods, but the country in question may in fact as well be considered to discriminate against foreign wines, if it excludes the use of its own language on the labels affixed to bottles of foreign wines.[35]

Moreover, in cases where there is no national production of a particular product, there could be no question of a *per se* prohibition. A measure regulating the disposal of the goods in question on the national

30. See Case 7/68, *Commission* v. *Italy,* 14 *Recueil* 1968, 633 *et seq;* Case 13/68, *Salgoil* v. *Italian Ministry for Foreign Trade,* 14 *Recueil* 1968, 679 *et seq;* Case 29/72, *Marimex* v. *Italian Fiscal Administration,* 18 *Recueil* 1972, 1309 *et seq.*

31. *Cf.* Art. 135 of the Act of Accession.

32. See Case 7/61, *Commission of the EEC* v. *Italian Republic,* 7 *Recueil* 1961, 633 *et seq.*

33. With minor variations this view corresponds to the thesis defended by Ehlermann (in Van der Groeben, Boeck, Thiesing, p. 247 *et seq.;* and in 8 EuR 1975, 1 *et seq.),* Béraud (in 4 Rev. trim. dr. europ. 1968, 265 *et seq.*) and Ulmer (in 19 A.W.D. 1973, 349 *et seq.*).

34. Ulmer, *op. cit.,* n. 21, at 351.

35. *Ibid.;* see also VerLoren van Themaat in 18 SEW 1970, 258.

market could be drafted in such a way that it would be necessary to regard it as one applying equally to domestic and imported products. In this field there is no provision similar to Article 95, para. 2, which prohibits discrimination against foreign products affording indirect protection to other domestic products. Why should the *per se* prohibition not apply in such a case of restrictive regulation?

Furthermore, there is one category of measures discriminating against imported goods that should not be covered by the *per se* prohibition. These are, according to paragraph 3 of the preamble to the Directive, read in conjunction with Article 2, para. 2, the normal formalities to which imports are subjected. Apart from normal customs clearance formalities, the Commission apparently recognizes the need for formally different rules with regard to imported goods (which are *e.g.* subject to quality controls that have already been effected at an earlier stage of the production process for the domestic goods). These should not be regarded as falling under the *per se* prohibition. Article 2, para. 2, provides that the Directive covers measures which make imports or the disposal at any marketing stage of imported products subject to a condition differing from that required for domestic products *and more difficult to satisfy*. Thus, in certain cases, there may be different conditions imposed with regard to national and foreign goods, but this inequality in treatment does not entail a prohibition of these measures to the extent that the foreign goods can as easily satisfy the particular conditions applicable to them as the national goods can fulfil the requirements laid down in respect of national production.

With regard to measures equally applicable to domestic and imported products, the Commission applies a more flexible test. Such measures are not condemned by Article 30 if their restrictive effects on the free movement of goods are not out of proportion to their purpose, or if the same objective cannot be attained by other means which are less of a hindrance to trade. In fact, this proportionality test is also expressed in the second sentence of Article 36 which provides that the prohibitions or restrictions on imports and exports exempted from Article 30 shall not constitute a means of arbitrary discrimination or a disguised restriction on trade between the member States. Thus, the Commission does not use the criteria laid down in Aticle 36, second sentence, to determine whether a measure coming under the prohibition of Article 30 qualifies for an exemption under Article 36 or does not so qualify. It rather applies these criteria to find out whether the measures ought to be brought under Article 30 at all. If it is found that the effect of the measure in question is out of proportion to its purpose and that Article 30 must therefore apply, to what avail can Article 36 still be applicable, the criteria for allowing or disallowing the exemption of Article 36 already having been incorporated in Article 30? The result of this approach seems to be that if a measure is brought under Article 30 in this manner, it can never qualify for an exemption under Article 36. Conversely, if a measure does not fall under Article 30 because it is not disproportionate, Article 36 need no longer be applied. According to this approach, a situation in which a measure falls under Article 30 but is exempted under Article 36 can never occur. The latter situation seems, however, to be the one envisaged by the Treaty.

III. CASE LAW

1. *General*

It was not until December 15, 1971 that the Court had an opportunity to interpret the concept of measures of an effect equivalent to quantitative restrictions. On that date it gave a preliminary ruling on the question of whether the expression quantitative restrictions and measures having an equivalent effect in Articles 30-34 of the Treaty and in Regulations Nos. 2513/69 [36] and 159/66 [37] includes national legislative provisions which prohibit imports without a licence, combined with a system of general exemptions or with the practice that licences applied for are always granted ("*toute licence accordée*"). This system could possibly have been regarded as a formality in the sense of Article 2, para. 2 of Directive No. 70/50, and would therefore not be covered by the prohibition of Article 30 as defined in the Directive. However, the Court, without referring to the Directive, held that apart from the exceptions laid down in Community Law itself, Articles 30-34 of the Treaty prevent the application in intra-Community relations of any national legislation whereby, albeit in a purely formal way, the requirement of import or export licences or any similar device is maintained.[38]

This judgment illustrates the Court's disinclination towards the whittling-down of the basic prohibition of measures liable to hinder inter-state trade.

The same trend appears from the Court's pronouncements with regard to the permissibility of restrictions on the free movement of goods resulting from the exercise of industrial and commercial property rights. According to Article 36, the protection of industrial and commercial property constitutes one of the grounds justifying a derogation from the provision of Articles 30 to 34. Obviously, national provisions allowing owners of such rights to prevent the importation of goods covered by

36. J.O. 1969, L 318.

37. J.O. 1966, No. 192.

38. Cases 51-54/71, *International Fruit Co. et al.* v. *Produktschap voor Groenten en Fruit*, 17 *Recueil* 1971, 1107; 9 C.M.L.Rev. 1972, 488-491.

their exclusive rights, are liable to restrict the free flow of goods within the Community. The Court has stated that while the Treaty does not affect the *existence* of the protective rights conferred by the national legislation of a member State, the *exercise* of these rights may fall under the prohibitions of the Treaty. Article 36 permits prohibitions or restrictions on the free movement of goods justified by the need to protect industrial an commercial property, but this justification is only deemed to exist if the prohibitions and restrictions are necessary to preserve rights constituting the specific subject matter of such property.[39] Thus it would be contrary to Articles 30-36 of the Treaty, if the rights resulting from industrial and commercial property were to be used to prevent the importation of products marketed in another member State by the owner of the protected right himself, or, with his consent, by third parties.[40]

The Court, in these decisions, has not referred to Directive No. 70/50. It is possible to regard its decision in the Cases 51-54/71, as an implied rejection of the rule laid down in Article 2, para. 2 of the Directive, which exempts customs formalities from the prohibition of Article 30. The Directive provides valuable information as to the sort of measures falling under Article 30. However, it cannot modify the Treaty or restrain jurisprudential evolution of the concept of measures having equivalent effect. Therefore, the adoption by the Court of different or additional criteria concerning the scope of Article 30 may be useful and entirely justified.[41]

2. *The application of Directive No. 70/50 by the Court.*

a. *Measures not applicable equally to domestic and imported products*

According to Article 2, para. 2 of Directive No. 70/50, measures having equivalent effect, other than those applicable equally to domestic and imported products, include measures which make imports or the disposal, at any marketing stage, of imported products subject to a condition which is required in respect of imported products only, or a

39. Case 78/70, *DGG* v. *Metro*, 17 *Recueil* 1971, 500 *et seq;* 9 C.M.L.Rev. 1972, 92. This case concerned a right akin to copyright. The Court has subsequently confirmed this ruling with regard to trademark and patent rights: see the *Centrafarm* Cases, Case 15/74, (1974) E.C.R., 1162, 11 C.M.L.Rev. 1975, 263; Case 16/74, (1974) E.C.R., 1194; 11 C.M.L.Rev. 1975, 268; See also Case 192/73 *Van Zuylen* v. *HAG*, (1974) E.C.R. 743; 11 C.M.L.Rev. 1974, 396; also van Nieuwenhoven Helbach, *supra*, pp. 37 *et seq.*

40. Commission Reply to Written Question No. 344/71 (Vredeling), J.O. 1972, C 53/1.

41. See generally for the character and contents of Directives Nos. 70/32 and 70/50, VerLoren van Themaat in 18 SEW 1970, 258 *et seq.*

condition different from that required for domestic products and more difficult to satisfy.[42]

In a case referred to the Court under Article 177 for a preliminary ruling on the question of whether phytosanitary inspections at the German frontier, which imports of apples from France were required to undergo, must be regarded as measures having an effect equivalent to quantitative restrictions, the Court found that the phytosanitary inspections in question only concerned importations of plant products and that similar domestic products, such as apples, were not subject to comparable compulsory examinations for the purpose of distribution.[43] These inspections thus amounted to a condition which is required in respect of imported products only, within the meaning of Article 2, para. 2 of Directive No. 70/50. In this Case, Article 36 was invoked by the German Government to justify the phytosanitary inspections. On the other hand, the importers of apples complained that the obligatory inspection of the imported foreign apples constituted "arbitrary discrimination" within the meaning of the second sentence of Article 36, because apples produced in the Federal Republic were not subject to a similar requirement of inspection when despatched within the country. The Court acknowledged that there might be a case of arbitrary discrimination if the different treatment of imported products was not matched by effective measures in order to prevent the distribution of contaminated domestic products, and if there was a risk of harmful organisms spreading if no inspection were held on importation.

It appears from this case that the test of discrimination applied with regard to the question whether there is a measure of equivalent effect in the sense of Article 2, para. 2 of the Directive will be followed by an enquiry into the possibility of allowing a derogation from the prohibition of Article 30. This is only possible if the measures are objectively justified on one of the grounds listed in Article 36. It would seem that the measures are only justified if the imports effectively constitute a threat to public morality *etc.*,if the measures are appropriate to counteract this threat and if the same protection cannot be achieved by measures which are less of a hindrance to trade within the Community.[44]

Among the measures other than those applicable equally to domestic and imported products, the Commission has also listed a number of

42. The second alternative is rather confusing because a condition different from that required for domestic products could be equated with a condition which is required in respect of imported products only.

43. Case 4/75, *REWE* v. *Director of the Landwirtschaftskammer*, Judgment of July 8, 1975, not yet published; *infra*, pp. 125-127 (annotation).

44. See Ehlermann, "Die Bedeutung des Artikels 36 EWGV für die Freiheit des Warenverkehrs", 8 EuR 1973, 1-17, at 14, 15.

measures which favour domestic products (Article 2, para. 2) and, especially as regards designations of origin, measures which "confine names which are not indicative of origin or source to domestic products only" (Article 2, para. 3(s) of Directive No. 70/50). This means that real designations of origin reserved to domestic products would not constitute measures having equivalent effect. It does not seem correct, however, to use the grounds for derogation laid down in Article 36 to deprive measures having equivalent effect of their character. In our opinion, the system laid down in Articles 30 to 36 supports the view that any designations of origin constitute measures having equivalent effect, and that only genuine designations meet the conditions of Article 36, allowing an exemption from the prohibition of Article 30.

In an action under Article 169 against the Federal Republic [45] the Commission asked the Court, to declare that by reserving the appellations *"Sekt"* and *"Weinbrand"* (sparkling wines and spirits obtained by distilling wines) to domestic products and the appellation *"Prädikatssekt"* to wines produced in Germany from a fixed minimum proportion of German grapes, the Federal Republic had violated its obligations under the Treaty, especially Article 30 and Article 12 para. 2 (b) of Regulation No. 816/70 of the Council of April 18, 1970. The Commission complained that by the new German Law on wine products of July 14, 1971 (BGBI I, 893) the Federal Government attempted to transform the generic appellations *Sekt* and *Weinbrand* into indirect indications of origin. Corresponding imported products were no longer entitled to take advantage of the well-known designations *Sekt* and *Weinbrand,* but were compelled to employ less attractive designations, such as *Schaumwein, Branntwein aus Wein* etc. This would favour domestic production to the detriment of imported goods and would thus constitute measures of an effect equivalent to quantitative restrictions, which could not be justified on grounds relating to the protection of industrial or commercial property within the meaning of Article 36.

The Court examined whether the appellations in dispute are among the names indicative of origin or source, which Article 2, para. 3 (s) by implication withdraws from the scope of Article 30 of the Treaty. Such names must safeguard the interest of the producers against unfair competition and also protect consumers against misleading information. These appellations only fulfil their specific purpose if the product which they describe does in fact possess qualities and characteristics which are due to the fact that it originated in a specific geographical area; as regards indications of origin in particular, the geographical area must

45. Case 12/74, *Commission of the E.C.* v. *Federal Republic of Germany,* (1975) E.C.R., 181 *et seq; infra,* pp. 121-124 (annotation).

confer on it a specific quality and specific characteristics of such a nature as to distinguish it from all other products (para. 7).[46]

The approach suggested by the Commission in Article 2, para. 3 (s) and followed by the Court in this case, pre-empts the application of Article 36. If it is found that a member State has enacted measures confining names which are not indicative of origin or source to domestic products only, and that such measures are to be qualified as measures having equivalent effect, an investigation as to whether such measures could nevertheless be tolerated on one of the grounds of Article 36 is obviously pointless. The conclusion that these measures fit the description given in Article 2, para. 3 (s) of the Directive seems to exclude the possibility that they could equally be regarded as measures aiming at the protection of national industrial and commercial property or as measures justified on other grounds such as the protection of public policy or public health. This is also confirmed by the fact that the Court's treatment of the defences based on Article 36 virtually amounts to an application of the same criteria as were used to qualify the German legislation as a measure of equivalent effect in the sense of the Directive. If the conditions governing exemption from the prohibition of Article 30 are used to determine whether State measures are covered at all by the prohibition of Article 30, this inconsistency can hardly be avoided. Yet, Article 5 of the Commission's Directive expressly specifies that the Directive shall apply without prejudice to the application, in particular, of Article 36 of the EEC Treaty!

b. *Measures applicable equally to domestic and imported products*

In a judgment of April 30, 1974, *Sacchi* v. *TeleBiella*,[47] the Court pronounced on the applicability of the prohibition of measures of equivalent effect in regard of trading rules, applying equally to imported products and to domestic goods. It considered that trade in materials, sound recordings, films *etc.* used for the diffusion of television signals, is subject to the rules relating to the free movements of goods. The fact that an undertaking of a member State has an exclusive right to transmit advertisements by television is not as such incompatible with the free movement of products, the marketing of which such advertisements are intended to promote. It would, however, be different if the exclusive right were used to favour within the Community particular trade channels or commercial operators in relation to others. Referring explicitly to Article 3 of Directive No. 70/50 the Court stated that measures governing the marketing of products, where their restrictive effect exceeds

46. *Cf.* the concept of the "specific purpose" of commercial and industrial property rights in the *DGG* case, *supra*, n. 39.

47. Case 155/73, (1974) E.C.R., 409 *et seq.*

the effects intrinsic to trade rules, are capable of constituting measures having an effect equivalent to quantitative restrictions. This judgment proves that the Court rejects the narrow view of the scope of measures of equivalent effect held by authors such as Meier and Graf and applies—at least in this case—the criteria laid down in the Directive in regard of measures applicable equally to domestic and imported products.

3. *Toward a wider definition—The Dassonville Formula*

In its judgment in the *Dassonville* Case,[48] rendered a few weeks after the *Sacchi* Judgment, the Court held that "all trading rules enacted by member States which are capable of hindering, directly or indirectly, actually or potentially, intra-Community trade are to be considered as measures having an effect equivalent to quantitative restrictions" (para. 5). Practically the same formula was used in the *Galli* Case and the *Van Haaster* Case decided a few months later (see below). The Court has certainly meant to confirm that the qualification of State measures as measures of equivalent effect to quantitative restrictions does not depend on the furnishing of proof that it *effectively* restricts intra-Community trade.[49] Did the Court also intend to indicate that it regards as measures having equivalent effect any trading rules which are equally applicable to domestic and imported products, without any further qualification in the sense of Article 3 of Directive No. 70/50? Paragraph 5 of the judgment is couched in the widest possible terms. Contrary to the judgment in the *Sacchi* Case it does not mention the requirement that in order to come under the prohibition of Article 30, the national measures must have restrictive effects out of proportion to their purpose.

It is to be noted, however, that in the following paragraphs the Court further qualifies its general formula: "In the absence of a Community system guaranteeing for consumers the authenticity of a product's designation of origin, if a member State takes measures to prevent unfair practices in this connexion, it is, however, subject to the condition that these measures should be reasonable and that the means of proof

48. See note 1, *supra*.

49. In particular, the British Government had argued that the prohibition of Art. 30 should be subject, for its application, to the condition that there should actually be a quantitative reduction in the movement of goods, and not a mere potential reduction. The rejection by the Court of this plea for some sort of *de minimis* rule is entirely in line with its case law on the subject of customs duties and charges of equivalent effect (*cf.* cases 2-3/69, *Sociaal Fonds voor Diamantarbeiders* v. *Brachfeld a.o.* 15 *Recueil* 1969, 222, and also with case 47/69, *French Republic* v. *Commission*, 16 *Recueil* 1970, 487 *et seq.*). It is only in the field of competition law that the Court has accepted that restrictive agreements which do not noticeably affect competition and inter-state trade escape from being prohibited (see Case 5/69, *Völk* v. *Vervaecke*, 15 *Recueil* 1969, 295 *et seq.*

required should not act as a hindrance to trade between member States and should, in consequence, be accessible to all Community nationals" (para. 6). Moreover, in paragraphs 7 and 8 it stated that "even without having to examine whether or not such measures are covered by Article 36, they must not, in any case, by virtue of the principle expressed in the second sentence of that Article, constitute a means of arbitrary discrimination or a disguised restriction on trade between member States. That may be the case with formalities, required by a member State for the purpose of proving the origin of a product, which only direct importers are really in a position to satisfy without facing serious difficulties".

If the member States are entitled to enact trading rules which may hinder intra-Community trade, provided that these rules are reasonable, does this imply that these rules do not come under the prohibition of Article 30, or does it mean that they fall under Article 30 but may qualify for an exemption under Article 36 if they are reasonable?

The distinction is important. If all trading rules which hinder intra-Community trade are prohibited under Article 30, trading rules not aimed at pursuing the objectives enumerated in Article 36 would be incompatible with the Treaty without the possibility of exemption under Article 36. However, reasonable trading rules which do pursue the goals mentioned in Article 36 would escape prohibition, regardless of whether they are covered by Article 30 and exempt under Article 36, or not caught by Article 30 in the first place.

It is difficult to argue that the Court has applied the criteria suggested by the Commission in Article 3 of Directive No. 70/50. The approach is different and the terminology is different. Moreover the Court does not interpret the criteria of Article 36, second sentence in the same manner as the Commission. The latter uses the proportionality test, derived from Article 36, second sentence, with reference to discriminatory treatment of imported products as compared with national products. The Court condemns another form of discrimination, *viz.* discrimination between those among the State's residents who are direct importers and those who are not.

It is not unlikely that the Court wished to dissociate itself from the formula which Article 3 of the Directive lays down in regard of measures applying equally to domestic and imported products. In that case, all trading rules fitting its definition come under the prohibition of Article 30, and the test of reasonableness is used to determine whether Article 36 applies. Reliance on Article 36 must be disallowed in any event if the rules constitute a means of arbitrary discrimination or a disguised restriction on trade. If this can be established without examining the question whether the measure is justified on one of the grounds listed in Article 36, first sentence, the measure cannot be qualified as reasonable.

This is what happened in the *Dassonville* Case. Paragraphs 7 and 8 of the judgment suggest that if the Belgian rules had not contravened the principle expressed in the second sentence of Article 36, it would have been necessary to examine whether these rules were covered by Article 36, first sentence. This tallies with our impression that the Court has meant to qualify all trading rules hindering intra-Community trade as measures coming under the prohibition of Article 30, from which derogations can be permitted if the measures are reasonable in the sense that they satisfy the conditions laid down in Article 36.

If the Court had wished to limit the implications of its very wide definition of measures of equivalent effect, it might possibly have made a qualifying remark to the effect that its definition was confined to measures other than those applying equally to imported and domestic products. Indeed, in het *Dassonville* Case, the Commission and the Advocate General described the controversial trading rules as measures discriminating against the importation of goods. It was only as a subsidiary point, and essentially because the civil parties had held that the measures were equally applicable to imported and domestic products, that the Commission examined them from the angle of Article 3 of the Directive. However, one is led to wonder whether these trading rules could properly be said to belong to either of the two categories between which the Commission makes a distinction in Articles 2 and 3 of Directive No. 70/50. The Court has not gone into the distinction, and by pointing out in paragraph 7 that Article 36 could not apply if the limits set for a derogation under Article 36 are exceeded, it seems to have separated the problem of the qualification of a State regulation as a measure of equivalent effect in the sense of Article 30 from the problem as to when a measure is reasonable enough to satisfy the requirements for derogation from Article 30 on the grounds mentioned in Article 36.

4. *The Dassonville formula in areas pre-empted by Community systems*

In the *Van Haaster* Case, which concerned the legality of a Dutch production quota system for the cultivation of hyacinth bulbs, the Court used the same broad definition given in the *Dassonville* Case.[50] Here, however, the Court was faced with a situation in which a Community system applied, *i.e.* the common organization of the market in live trees and other plants, bulbs, *etc.*[51] The referring judge more particularly asked the Court whether a system limiting production, by forbidding the

50. Case 190/73, *Public Prosecutor* v. *Van Haaster,* Judgment of October 30, 1974, (1974) E.C.R. 1123 *et seq;* 12 C.M.L.Rev. 1975, 415-418.

51. Regulation No. 234/68, O.J. 1968, L 55/1.

cultivation of hyacinth bulbs to anyone other than the holders of annually granted cultivation licences for specific and limited areas, is compatible with the prohibition of quantitative restrictions or measures of equivalent effect in internal Community trade, laid down in Article 10 of Regulation No. 234/68.

The Court acknowledged the fact that the national system and the relevant Community provision relate to different stages of the economic process, *viz.* production and marketing, respectively. At first sight the Court thus seemed to follow the observations submitted by the Commission and the Dutch Government. However, unlike the latter, the Court stressed the need—in the absence of express provisions as to the compatibility of a national system restricting production with the market organization in question—to consider the prohibition of measures having equivalent effect in the light of the objects and purposes of the Regulation within the framework of the principles laid down by the Treaty itself. Apart from marketing rules, the market organization provided for in Regulation No. 234/68 also involves provisions concerning production. These provisions relate in particular to the introduction of common quality standards, which have the purpose of encouraging trade initiatives with a view to improving the quality of the products and of perfecting the organization of production. Accordingly, the Court found these quality standards, which have a restrictive effect on the production stage, to constitute an essential element for achieving the system of free commercial transactions under conditions of genuine competition, on which the market organization is based. "Such a system", according to the Court "excludes any national system of regulations which could impede directly or indirectly, actually or potentially, trade within the Community". A national regulation with the purpose of rationing production should therefore be considered a measure having equivalent effect (paras. 15-17).

Apparently the Court's reasoning is based on the potential, indirect effect on trade of the national production quota system. In view of the conditions prevailing on the market in question, it might have been easier to consider the effect of the regulation of production as decisive, *viz.* similar to that of a quantitative restriction. This was submitted by the Advocate General, who pointed to the fact that the country in question produces 95% of the goods concerned. However, this might have been too direct an appreciation of the facts involved, which would not pertain to the Court's competence.

Obviously—as a consequence of the distinction made—a measure concerning the marketing of the products in question would have fallen without any doubt under the prohibition. In view of the existence of common rules on the subject concerned the concept of measures of equivalent effect has been broadened to include a national regulation of production. By following this line of reasoning the Court clearly kept aloof from the position taken by the Commission. The latter had observed—apparently on the basis of the conception developed in Directive No. 70/50—that many measures, despite their restrictive effect upon trade are not incompatible with Articles 30 to 34 of the Treaty, because they fall within the powers which the Treaty has implicitly or explicitly left to the member States. The disputed rules on production would count among such measures. Although a restrictive effect upon trade is inherent in many of these measures, particularly those relating to the quality of products, such measures would only have an effect equivalent to quantitative restrictions to the extent that they were unnecessary or disproportionate.

The Court, on the contrary, based its interpretation on the objects and purposes of the Community system involved, which led it to stress the pre-emptive character of the Regulation. In line with the ruling in the *Dassonville* Case (para. 6), the existence of a Community system in the present case was held to preclude the adoption of any further national rules liable to affect the scope of the Community system. The position of the Court in the *Van Haaster* Case seems to lead to the conclusion that the member States do not retain any power to adopt measures affecting intra-Community trade in areas pre-empted by a Community system pursuing the same objectives as the national rules concerned. This is in accordance with the frequently expressed principle that the supremacy of Community law precludes national measures from altering or touching upon the scope of Community provisions.[52]

On the other hand, as suggested by the *Dassonville* Judgment, in all areas where Community rules are lacking, member States remain competent to adopt reasonable trading rules in the sense of Article 36.

According to the *Van Haaster* Judgment it seems that the notion of trading rules should be understood in a broad sense. It should be kept in mind, however, that this case concerned a special situation in which the Court's general formula was qualified to cover production measures in the light of the objects and purposes of the applicable Community system. It remains to be seen therefore which other State regulations would come under the notion of trading rules and thus fit the Court's definition of measures of equivalent effect.

In its judgment in the *Galli* Case,[53] the Court found that the systems

52. See *e.g.* Case 74/69, *H.Z.A.* v. *Krohn,* 16 *Recueil* 1970, 451, as well as the cases mentioned by the Advocate General in his first Opinion on the *Van Haaster* case, (1974) E.C.R. 1140.

53. Case 31/74, (1975) E.C.R., 47 *et seq;* 12 C.M.L.Rev. 1975, 418-426, with note by VerLoren van Themaat.

laid down in Regulations No. 120/67 [54] and No. 136/66,[55] excluded any national system of regulation impeding directly or indirectly, actually or potentially, trade within the Community (para. 15). The formula used is strikingly similar to that used in the *Dassonville* Case. However, the Court has refrained from qualifying the national rules involved, which concerned a pricing system, as measures of equivalent effect. Although the national court referring the questions had specifically asked the Court whether these rules were compatible with Article 30, the Court confined itself to indicating that Article 30, among other Treaty provisions, was incorporated in the system embodied by the Regulation: indeed the Court's conclusion was entirely based on the exclusive character of the common organization of the market as such. Moreover it found that the unilateral intervention on the part of a member State in the movement of prices in the sector in question could not be justified by virtue of Article 103 of the Treaty. It held that Article 103 does not relate to those areas already subject to common rules such as the organization of agricultural markets. Although the Court thus admits that measures of conjunctural policy may affect interstate trade, it has, by founding its reasoning solely on the exclusive character of the Community system, avoided giving further qualifications of the concept of measures of equivalent effect. Although as appears from the *Dassonville* formula and the *Van Haaster* Case the Court apparently tends to a wider view than the Commission, it quite rightly hesitates to bring measures of conjunctural policy under the notion of "all trading rules", used in the *Dassonville* Case.

It is obvious that a decision to equate conjunctural policy measures with trading rules prohibited under Article 30, would have far-reaching consequences as far as the delimitation between the sphere of competence of the member States and the Community is concerned. A further definition of the concept of trading rules covered by Article 30 may be of great importance.

IV. CONCLUSIONS

The preceding analysis of the Court's case law shows that the prohibition of Article 30 also covers measures of a member State which do not discriminate against imports from other member States.

It has also become apparent that the application of Directive No. 70/50 of the Commission may lead to legal constructions which from the point of view of the Treaty system are less than satisfactory. Thus it seems unfortunate that the Commission tends to use the criteria laid down in

54. J.O. p. 2269/1967 (cereals).
55. J.O. p. 3025/1966 (oils and fats).

Article 36 to determine not whether a measure can be exempted from the prohibition of Article 30, but rather whether it should at all be qualified as a measure having an effect equivalent to quantitative restrictions within the meaning of Article 30. In such cases a finding that a measure falls under Article 30 implies that it cannot profit from an exemption by virtue of Article 36. Conversely, if a measure is found not to fall under Article 30, a derogation under Article 36 is no longer called for. The Treaty, so it seems, rather envisages a system whereby a measure falling under Article 30 can be exempted from this prohibition if it fulfils the conditions set forth in Article 36. The *Sekt* Case demonstrates that Article 36 is emptied of its substance and its meaning if no distinction is made between the problem of the qualification of State rules as measures of equivalent effect (Article 30) and the question under what circumstances member States may continue to apply such measures (Article 36).

In the *Dassonville* Case the Court has used terminology suggesting the possibility of an approach to measures applicable equally to domestic and imported goods deviating from that advocated by the Commission. The broad language in this Case could be taken to mean that all trading rules liable to impede intra-Community trade are covered by the prohibition of Article 30 and that such rules can only be maintained in force if they are reasonable, *i.e.* if they fulfil the requirements which, according to Article 36 justify a derogation from the prohibition of Article 30. The inherent difficulty in this approach which corresponds with the views of VerLoren van Themaat, is its potential curtailment of the scope of the "reserved" powers of the member States.

The adoption of Community rules relating to trading in goods has a pre-emptive effect on the authority of the member States to enact any further measures in the same area, even if such measures are only concerned with trade in an indirect way. In both the *Van Haaster* Case and the *Galli* Case the system introduced by common organizations of agricultural markets was held to preclude the adoption by member States of rules which, directly or indirectly, actually or potentially, could impede intra-Community trade. In the *Van Haaster* Case, the rules having this effect were qualified as measures having an effect equivalent to quantitative restrictions. However, in the *Galli* Case this qualification was not used to condemn the measures taken by the Italian Government. It was rather their incompatibility with the exclusive character of the agricultural regulations which caused them to be prohibited. One wonders whether the conclusion is warranted that the Court has avoided describing the price regulations of the Italian Government in terms of measures having equivalent effect because these measures pursued purposes of conjunctural policy (Article 103).

Obviously Article 30 should not be construed in such a way that it could gobble up, like some sort of octopus, the reserved powers of the member States. If our interpretation of the *Dassonville* Judgment is correct there is no possibility of exemption from the prohibition of Article 30 for trading rules not pursuing one of the objectives of Article 36. This results in a considerable reduction in the domain hitherto regarded as reserved to the member States. It would seem that rules which cannot properly be described as trading rules are not covered by the prohibition of Article 30. Rules which can be so described are covered by this provision, even if they are enacted under the guise of an exercise of reserved powers. The problem then becomes one of defining the concept of trading rules, without having recourse to criteria relating to the effects of the measures on intra-Community trade. In the case of trading rules such effects may be quite unintentional, whereas it may be among the declared aims of certain economic policy measures to dampen demand for consumer goods, be they home-made or foreign-produced, in order to combat inflation or to correct a balance of payments disequilibrium.

It may be hoped that the Court of Justice will further clarify its views on the scope of Article 30 and, in particular, that it will be given an opportunity to pronounce on the legal character, in the light of Article 30, of *e.g.* price regulations of the member States outside the framework of agricultural market organizations or other fields subject to common policies.

JOINT-SUBSIDIARIES; THE S.H.V.-CHEVRON CASE

by

G. J. Linssen *

The *SHV-Chevron* Decision of December 12, 1974, of the European Commission (OJ L38/75) is certain, in the near future, to draw much attention and comment because it is the first case where the Commission has given its opinion on the application of Articles 85 and 86 to the creation of joint subsidiaries.

The facts of the SHV-Chevron case

By an agreement of October 21, 1969, the Dutch firm Steenkolen Handels Vereniging (SHV), a company engaged in coal distribution, chain stores and transport,[1] and Chevron Oil Europe, Delaware, a member of the integrated international petroleum group Standard Oil of California, set up a jointly and equally owned subsidiary Calpam N.V., in the Netherlands, with its own subsidiaries in the other countries covered by the agreement.

The function of Calpam is to distribute paraffin oil, household fuel, industrial fuel, asphalt and marine fuels and lubricating oils in Belgium, the Netherlands, Luxemburg, Germany and Denmark, where both parent companies formerly had distribution networks but which have now been merged into Calpam. In Germany the agreement is applicable only to marine fuels and lubricating oils. It is not clear whether SHV sold other petroleum products in the countries mentioned and in particular whether SHV ever sold petroleum products in Germany other than those for marine uses.

The Calpam companies are supplied by Chevron under non-exclusive supply contracts. They determine their own prices, with the exception of asphalt the price of which is fixed by Chevron.

SHV and Chevron vested in the Calpam subsidiaries their distribution networks in the countries concerned and all assets related thereto for at least 50 years. As a consequence SHV disappeared as an independent company on the wholesale market for petroleum products. Both parties agreed not to compete with the other concerning the relevant products without the prior consent of the other party.

* Economic advisor, Brussels (formerly of Directorate General for Competition, Commission of the European Communities).

1. And in several other fields: trade in technical products, construction. The transport sector includes tanker-freight.

13 C.M.L. Rev. 1976, 105-119

The parent companies, at the request of the Commission, deleted a clause under which they agreed not to compete in respect of petroleum products not distributed by the Calpam subsidiaries, i.e. lubricating oil, diesel fuel and petrol in the Benelux area and Denmark. As a consequence there is no longer any clause restricting competition between SHV and Chevron in areas other than those covered by the Calpam joint subsidiaries.

The Commission's conclusion

The Commission came to the conclusion that the agreement brought about a real concentration between SHV and Chevron and their joint subsidiaries, confined to the distribution of the products specified by the agreement. For this reason Article 85 was not applicable, and negative clearance was granted. To understand this result, somewhat unexpected in the province of EEC-law, the case-law of the European Coal and Steel Community has to be examined. This is all the more justified in view of the fact that the Court of Justice in 1960 ruled that Articles 65 ECSC and 85 EEC are based on the same concepts,[2] and in view of the fact that both Treaties are now applied by a single Commission.

ECSC Treaty case-law

Article 66/1 ECSC states that any transaction which in itself or as a result of any action by any person or undertaking or a group of persons or undertakings within the Community, by some means of control directly or indirectly brings about a concentration between undertakings is subject to prior authorization. In its Decision No. 24/54 of May 6, 1954 [3] the High Authority of the ECSC defined the elements of control of an undertaking as rights or contracts which, either separately or jointly, and having regard to the considerations of fact and law involved, make it possible to determine how an undertaking shall operate as regards production, prices, investments, supplies, sales and appropriation of profits.

Examples include:

1. Ownership or the right to use all or part of the assets of an undertaking;
2. Rights or contracts which confer the power to influence the composition, voting or decisions of the organs of an undertaking;
3. Rights or contracts which enable any person, by himself or in association with others, to direct the business of an undertaking.

2. Case No. 13/60, Judgment of May 18, 1962, *Geitling, Mausegatt und Präsident* v. *H.A.*, 8 Rec. 1962, 165.

3. J.O. 345/54.

Furthermore a concentration is deemed to have been brought about if control of a firm is acquired by obtaining the right to determine the activities of the firm, more specifically by acquiring shares or assets, by leasing, or by interlocking directorates, *etc.*

How exactly the law has been applied is difficult to ascertain, because decisions of the High Authority and the Commission [4] were considered secret until March 28, 1974.[5] So we have to rely on other publications, such as the General Reports and Bulletins of the High Authority and the Commission. Also no judgment of the Court of Justice is available, as no appeal was laid against the decisions under Article 66, all being favourable for the participating firms, though sometimes only after modifications had been made.

The control concept calls for legal acts which "in themselves" ("*par elles-mêmes*") lead to a concentration. It is sufficient if the possibility exists for an undertaking to determine the essential questions of business management and to fix the general corporate policy of the controlled firm, whether or not the controlling firm in fact makes use of its powers or allows a degree of independence to the controlled firm.[6]

However, apart from the control of the dependent enterprise, a problem arises when several undertakings jointly control another firm or firms. Three aspects of this problem may be distinguished:

— the legal act founding the joint subsidiary;
— the collective determination of the corporate policy of the controlled firm;
— the ensuing restriction of competition between the mutually independent founders ("The group effect").[7]

It is the third aspect which requires special attention for the understanding of the *Calpam* case.

The High Authority did not at first consider that the joint formation of a company fell within the terms of Article 66, neither in theory, as regards the principles of the Treaty itself, nor in practice, as regards the effects on competition, which were indirect and negligible.[8] However, with the increasing economic importance of concentration, the High Authority had to reconsider the applicability of this rule. It authorized the formation of a joint subsidiary under Article 66 for the first time on

4. Since the establishment of a single Council and a single Commission of the European Communities, Merger Treaty of April 8, 1965.

5. First publication of a decision under Art. 66 ECSC, *Thyssen-Rheinstahl*, O.J. 1974 L 84/36.

6. H. Matthies: "Die Fusionskontrolle" (Art. 66 EGKS-V), in: Bernini, Jaeger, Matthies: *Kartellverbot und Fusionskontrolle in der Montanunion*, p. 100, 104; Mr. Matthies is a Legal Adviser in the Legal Service of the Commission.

7. *Ibid.*, p. 106.

8. 11th General Report, pt. 348.

September 27, 1961, when August Thyssen Hütte AG acquired a 50% holding in Stahlwerke Rasselstein AG, the other 50% being held by the firm Otto Wolff.[9] The High Authority considered that even if the joint control did not amount to a concentration between the controlling firms, there was bound to be some restriction of their production of the same products outside the enterprise under their joint control.

On April 25, 1962 the High Authority adopted a decision in the case of *Sidmar* of Brugge, an integrated steel-works founded by Cockeril-Ougrée (Belgium) and Arbed (Luxemburg), both of which continued their own production in the fields covered by Sidmar.[10]

In this decision the High Authority pursued the idea of a "group effect" and stated that it was inevitable that firms in the exercise of their joint control e.g. in fixing the prices of the undertaking under their control, would take into account their own prices for the same or similar products and very possibly agree all prices. As such a phenomenon is part and parcel of group control as such, it cannot reasonably—for practical purposes at any rate—be treated as an independent restriction of competition within the meaning of Article 65. In the second *Sidmar* decision of March 8, 1967,[11] it was held that notwithstanding the "group effect" the companies involved did not loose their freedom to act independently. If, however they were to bind themselves by mutual engagements and, in so doing, by agreement restrict competition, then Article 65 (1) would be applicable. This, in fact, they had done by creating a central bureau for the allocation of orders between Sidmar and its parent companies, and by fixing prices and profit-sharing.

Recently the Commission issued decisions in two comparable cases. On October 2, 1974 it published its decision in the *Manganese steel* case.[12] Three French companies had set up, together with Portugese interests, a company known as Eurominas to run a manganese steel plant in Portugal. Apparently no decision was given in respect of this aspect of the case; the reason may be that as it was a concentration outside the territory of the Common Market, it did not fall within the terms of Article 66 (1). The participating companies,[13] however, then sought approval for an agreement to sell Eurominas products for fifteen years exclusively through a selling agency (*Groupement Européen de Manganèse,* a *"groupement d'intérêt économique"*). The Commission considered that this exclusivity, and the fact that price-fixing of ferro-mangane-

9. 10th General Report, pt. 278.
10. 11th General Report, pt. 346-359.
11. O.J. 717/67.
12. Decision of October 2, 1974, O.J. 1974, L 286.
13. In the case of Eurominas: SNAP, CUA and Sofimelec, in that of GEM: SNAP, CUA and SOFREM; both Sofimelec and SOFREM are controlled by Ugine Kuhlmann.

se by the companies concerned would have an effect on the price-level of ferro-manganese produced by two participants (SNAP and CUA) sold within the Common Market, amounted to infringements of Article 66 (1).

The other recent case concerned *Solmer.* On July 25, 1973 the Commission authorized Usinor to take over half of the share capital of Solmer, hitherto a subsidiary of Sacilor for the joint development of a big steelplant near Marseilles.[14] The joint control of Solmer led to the co-ordination of investment and production of the two parent-groups with regard to the relevant products, but Usinor and Sacilor were to market independently their own products and those of Solmer, which they acquired at cost price. August Thyssen Hütte AG joined in later and the Commission approved its participation in Solmer (initially 5%, later not to exceed 25%).[15] In this case, also, the Commission considered Solmer to be a joint producing co-operative without its own selling organisation, and, with each group producing the greater part of its flat rolling steel output in its own plants, it could be assumed that the undertakings concerned in the relevant market would each pursue an independent pricing policy, although each group would naturally bear in mind its share in Solmer's output and regulate its own production accordingly. The Commission therefore approved first the concentration of the Usinor and Sacilor groups with Solmer, then that of August Thyssen Hütte with Solmer. Solmer is now concentrated with all the undertakings in the Usinor and Sacilor groups and with August Thyssen Hütte, but there is no concentration between the undertakings of the parent groups.[16]

On December 18, 1963, the High Authority applied the same theory to a merger in the distribution sector. Ferrostaal AG and Frank Haniel & Cie GmbH, wholesalers, had formed Eisenhandel Ferrostaal-Haniel GmbH for the sale of iron and steel products in a regional market (southern Germany). Ferrostaal and Haniel remained independent except in the field of activity of the joint subsidiary where, it was held, they had lost their economic independence and freedom of action and had amalgamated their financial risks.[17] The High Authority's decision to

14. Bull. EC 8/73, pt. 2112.

15. Decision of November 20, 1974, O.J. 1974, L 74.

16. It should be added that in other instances the High Authority and the Commission, while stating that certain cases came under Art. 66 (1) proceeded to authorize them under Art. 66 (2), taking account of the facts of the particular case and the law involved, but imposing conditions to secure that competition would not be impaired more than was indispensable. An example is the *Somosid* case, Decision of April 4, 1964, 12 Gen. Report, pt. 241-243 and Bull. ECSC No. 47, pp. 38-39. Some shareholders of the holding company were excluded from the membership of the management and administrative organs of Somosid.

17. 12th Gen. Report, pt. 250; Matthies, *op. cit.*, n. 6, at p. 94.

apply, on these grounds, Article 66 to a joint selling organisation seems more or less arbitrary. Normally, the cartel provision of Article 65 is applied to joint selling organisations, the assumption being that in such cases the companies involved do not lose their economic independence. The application of Article 66 to this case was no doubt founded on a thorough analysis of the case which made it clear that both parties did not intend to resume independent activity in the field covered by the concentration for a long time, but, due to the secrecy rule, we are not sufficiently informed. Had, for example, either of these undertakings activities outside the regional market? What were their activities other than those covered by the joint subsidiary? How did the takeover of Strassburger Stahlkontor GmbH by Ferrostaal-Haniel GmbH [18] fit into the scheme?

To summarise the "group effect" theory of the High Authority one may refer to its publication: *EGKS 1952–1962, Ereignisse, Grenzen, Perspektive* (Luxemburg 1963), where it is stated, at p. 375, that in the case of a joint subsidiary it is necessary to consider whether competition for its products will be eliminated not only as between the joint subsidiary and each controlling firm but also as between the firms themselves. It could hardly be imagined that firms which jointly manufacture and sell a product would compete with a joint subsidiary or among themselves for the same or comparable products. Such a restriction of competition is comparable with restrictions caught by Article 65(1) but which cannot be brought under that article because the joint venture as such would have had to be prohibited either at once or later, assuming that none of the criteria for authorization under Article 65 had been complied with. The High Authority therefore decided that this kind of restriction had to be considered as restrictions on competition which from their very nature form an integral part of the concentration process caught by Article 66, and have to be judged accordingly.

EEC Treaty case-law

Turning now to the EEC Treaty it should be noted that the Commission has reviewed some cases of central selling organisations under Article 85. It has, for example, decided that a sole distributorship given to a central selling agency by a group of producers and the engagement of the latter not to sell independently were restrictive of competition.[19] In these cases the producers of fertilizers refrained completely from selling independently in most markets, including the Common Market. (Because the

18. 13th Gen. Report, pt. 223, Decision of December 21, 1964.

19. Decisions of November 6, 1968 concerning *Cobelaz-Synthèse, Cobelaz-Cokeries and CFA*, J.O. L 276/68, and December 23, 1970 *Supexie*, J.O. 1971, L 10.

Commission objected to the exclusivity for deliveries into EEC markets other than the home market, the participants restricted the competence of the central selling agencies to home markets and third countries in order to obtain a negative clearance). This is in accordance with the decisions of the High Authority regarding central selling agencies in the fields of coal [20] and steel.[21] In all these cases the distribution activities of producing firms were completely amalgamated.

In the *Nederlandse Cement Handelmaatschappij NV* case [22] the Commission considered in great detail the problems of a central selling agency. NCH, a limited company under Dutch law had, according to its articles of association, as its object the sale of cement and other building materials. These articles did not contain any restriction of competition. However, NCH had concluded agreements with thirty-eight German cement producers according to which these producers were prevented from exporting into the Benelux area, either directly or indirectly, thus giving a sole distributorship to NCH. The Commission was of the opinion that these identical contracts between NCH and each of the German cement producers were not possible without a corresponding understanding between all the producers involved which had not been reduced to writing. This mutual understanding could be, but should not be compared to the "group effect" of concentrations resulting from the creation of joint subsidiaries. In any case the consequences are different. The uniform prices and sales conditions of NCH were an outcome of the mutual understanding between the cement producers and restrained them in their freedom to fix their own prices and conditions in the Benelux market. The same was true regarding the quantities offered in this market by the cement producers because NCH fixed the quotas. NCH's exclusivity reduced the producers' freedom to offer cement in the market involved. In this case it was held that Article 85 (1) applied, and Article 85 (3) did not; the producers' justifications failed to convince the Commission.

The "group effect" covers some of the restrictions on the freedom of action of parent companies which are indispensable for the realisation of a concentration. The restrictions exercised by NCH were the indispensable consequence of the activity of a central selling agency: it cannot sell homogeneous products at different prices and on different conditions of sale; it cannot avoid apportioning sales between suppliers and an exclusivity is almost unavoidable (the producers, when they sell directly, have to apply the same prices, etc. as the central selling agency, otherwise

20. Decisions *Geitling* and *Präsident* of March 20, 1963, J.O. 57/63.

21. Decisions *Walzstahlkontor-West, -Westfalen, -Nord, -Süd* of March 15, 1967, J.O. 1967, pp. 1373-1416.

22. Decision of December 23, 1971, J.O. 1972, L 22.

the system does not work). The adverse decision on the agreement involving the NCH central selling organisation means that the Commission must have considered this organisation to be the agent for the restriction of competition between the cement producers in a defined market in prices, sales conditions and quantities to be delivered, and not as a lasting concentration of limited scope between these producers and the central selling agency.

Summary

To sum up, the establishment of a company by several undertakings is a concentration if an economic and legal unit is created which cannot be dissolved or only at great cost, and which is controlled by the founder undertakings on a permanent basis. The resulting restrictions on the freedom of action of the controlling undertakings do not restrict competition in the sense of Article 65 ECSC or Article 85 EEC in so far as they are indispensable for the creation or the operation of the joint subsidiary. This concept usually applies to the distribution activities or the production of manufacturing companies but may be applied to distribution firms as well, if the permanence and irreversible character of the concentration has been established.

The SHV-Chevron case

If these criteria seem to be clear, their application is less so, especially in the case of concentrations in the distribution sector. A good example is the *SHV-Chevron* case.

In this case the first point to notice is that the parent companies did not merge; they remained independent. Only a part of their activities was merged, namely, the distribution activities of the two firms; this leaves open the question whether a central selling agency or a concentration in the form of a joint subsidiary had been created.

Secondly, the Commission considered that the agreement involved a lasting change in the structures of the companies involved and above all in that of SHV. This was the Commission's principal criterion. It is, however, to be noted that for Chevron and Standard Oil of California, as world-wide producers and distributors, no serious obstacles appeared to exist to the resumption of distribution of petroleum products in so small a geographic area. SHV, as an important trading and transport company, might also have been able to take up distribution of the products [23]

23. According to the 1974 General Report of SHV, with a total turnover of 6.294 guilders only 1.599 ml. related to the energy sector; so the distribution of petroleum products was not its principal activity, which was retailing with 3.733 ml. guilders.

again. Perhaps, but the Commission is silent on this point, the merger of the distribution networks diminished the number of retail outlets, in which case a dissolution of Calpam would have presented real difficulties for the companies involved. But, having regard to their importance and activities, these difficulties would not seem to be insurmountable. Failing any detailed indications on the problem we have to rely on the Commission's discernment.

Thirdly, SHV ceased to do business as an independent wholesale buyer of petroleum products. This argument is in accordance with the second point. SHV, however, did not lose touch with the market: as a transporter of petroleum products [24] and, jointly with other companies, holding exploration licences for the North Sea,[25] it might come into possession of crude oil (and it has complete freedom to sell this crude oil to any buyer of its choice).[26]

Consideration of these aspects of the case leads to the conclusion that the operation brought about a real concentration between SHV and Chevron and their joint subsidiaries, confined to the distribution of the products specified by the agreement. The distribution sides of the business of each of them was integrated into the new trading structure of the Calpam subsidiaries, formed for a period lasting until December 31, 2019, and this suggests the irreversible character of the merger of the assets concerned. This last argument seems to be controversial: it is not difficult to fix such a term of existence of a contract, since by mutual consent it can always be abrogated. But the Commission apparently was convinced that this was not the intention of the companies involved.

Thus, according to the principles developed earlier, a permanent

24. SHV has interests in the shipping line Nieveld Goudriaan and in LNG tanker-freights.

25. SHV also has interests in Deutsche PAM AG, petroleum, and in Dyas BV, together with Amoco Nederland and Gelsenberg, gas.

26. In which event one may wonder whether the agreement with Chevron would have to be re-examined. If Art. 85/3 is applied one may judge from the conditions and stipulations attached to a decision (Art. 8 of Regulation No. 17, O.J. 13/62) what view the Commission holds in such a situation, but no conditions and stipulations can legally be attached to a negative clearance and so we lack a condition in the decision which stipulates, *e.g.* that parties to the agreement have to notify to the Commission fundamental changes in their position as a producer or a distributor, especially if SHV becomes an oil producer for itself or jointly with others. See decision *Transocean Marine Paint Association* of November 21, 1973, O.J. 1974, L 19, stipulating that the cartel must inform the Commission, *inter alia,* of any change in the composition of membership, any links by way of common directors or managers between a member of the Association and any other company or firm in the paints sector or of any financial participation by a member of the Association in such outside companies or vice-versa including all changes in such links or participations already in existence. Compare also the *Somosid* Case, *supra,* n. 16, and judgment of the Court of Justice in the *Transocean* Case, No. 17/74 of October 23, 1974, 1974 Rec. 1063.

merger of assets leads to a concentration (in fact a partial concentration: *"eine echte Teilfusion"*).[27] This distinguishes the case from a central selling agency, where no participant disappears from the market, as SHV does as a buying and selling unit, and where all participants are required concert permanently about business policy, but retain their freedom of action and may retire at any moment from the cartel if they choose to do so.

Next, we have to consider the "group effect". This theory implies that the concentration process will include a certain degree of concertation between the parent companies as to their pricing or investment policy, subject to the requirement that the companies will not be bound by such concerted behaviour and will remain free to act otherwise. In the case of SHV and Chevron, each agreed not to compete with the other without prior consent of the other. This obligation exceeds the "group effect" and would appear to violate Article 85. The Commission, however, said that no appreciable restriction of competition in fact resulted and maintained a curious line of reasoning, which amounted to a mixture of concentration and cartel arguments.

With regard to SHV, the Commission stated that the agreement provided SHV with the assurance that the assets transferred by it to the joint subsidiaries would not lose in value as a result of competition by Chevron with the joint subsidiaries. *Quaere:* is the maintenance of the capital substance of an individual company a particular purpose of competition policy, or will competition decide upon the value of capital investment and the ensuing going concern?

With regard to Chevron, the Commission took the view that it had no industrial or commercial interests which could conceivably lead it to compete with its own 50% owned subsidiary. This clearly is the "group effect" argument which, in ECSC practice, was held to be the natural consequence of a concentration but which should not be converted into a legally binding commitment. Does the Commission intend to go further in EEC practice, by holding that such an obligation generally does not have an appreciable effect on competition?

On the other hand, the Commission was firm with regard to the undertaking made by SHV and Chevron not to compete in respect of petroleum products not distributed by the Calpam subsidiaries in the Benelux and Denmark; the Commission insisted that this agreement should be deleted.[28] However, this indicates that SHV had activities

27. Director General Dr. W. Schlieder at a conference at Innsbruck on February 13-15, 1975.

28. In the past the Commission has also objected to restrictions beyond the scope of the investigated agreement. See decision *Raymond-Nagoya* of June 9, 1972, O.J. 1972, L 143, where the Commission objected to a clause entitling Raymond to exclusive licences for

on the petroleum products market other than those covered by the agreement which, because it had disappeared as an independent wholesaler on that market as a result of the agreement, it had in fact put an end to (by tacit agreement?). Again, what about the possible activities of SHV in Germany not included in marine deliveries prior to the agreement? Because the decision is not clear as to the facts it is possible to think that SHV, in order to have the benefit of a close cooperation with a big oil company, in the present instance Chevron, had deliberately refrained from some of its former activities. Is such an act also covered by the "group effect" or is it a restriction of competition which is not be considered to be appreciable?

The Commission held that the clause providing that the price of asphalt was to be fixed by Chevron was not caught by Article 85 because this product was previously sold only by Chevron. We have, therefore, to assume that this means that SHV did not distribute asphalt and did not buy it from Chevron so that no change in competitive conditions in the market result. Is it, however, a normal consequence of a concentration process that one of the participants is prevented from having a say in a part of the activities of the joint subsidiary? In any event, the Commission's conclusion does not fit in with the "group effect" theory. From the moment that a product enters into the sphere of activity of a joint subsidiary an agreement on price-fixing by the parent companies (and the decision to leave the determination of a price to one of them is an agreement) goes beyond the principle of the "group effect" and would therefore seem liable to be caught by Article 85 (as in the *Manganese* case).

One particular element of the decision remains to be considered. The market shares of SHV and Chevron for the relevant products did not give either of them a dominant position so that the operation did not need to be investigated under Article 86. This is in accordance with the *Continental Can* doctrine laid down by the Commission [29] and the Court of Justice.[30]

---

patents and designs of Nagoya relating to innovations and designs outside the scope of Raymond engineering.

29. Decision of December 9, 1971 O.J. 1971, L 7/25, pt. II, 26: for an undertaking in a dominant position to reinforce that position by means of a merger with another undertaking with the consequence that competition ... is in practice eliminated for the products in question . . . constitutes behaviour which is incompatible with Art. 86; C.M.L.R. 1972, D 31.

30. Court of Justice, Case No. 6/72; Judgment of February 21, 1973, 1973 Rec. 215, pt. 26. There may therefore be abusive behaviour if an undertaking in a dominant position strengthens that position so that the degree of control achieved substantially obstructs competition, C.M.L.R. 1973, p. 225.

However, the paragraph of the *SHV-Chevron* decision dealing with this aspect of the case only refers to the dominant position of *one* of the parent companies and leaves open the question of the possibility of the creation of a dominant position through the establishment of the joint subsidiary. It has been concluded from the *Continental Can* judgment that if companies are not in a dominant position and if a concentration process between them and their subsidiary leads to a dominant position this may also amount to an abuse of a dominant position.[31] The Commission does not even allude to this interpretation of the Court's judgment, but no doubt it was unnecessary since Calpam's market share was unlikely to constitute a dominant position.

Conclusions on policy

It is proper to conclude that the Commission is continuing along the lines of thought of ECSC concentration policy by maintaining that a concentration which is not caught by Article 65 ECSC is not caught by Article 85 EEC. Indeed in the Memorandum on Concentrations [32] the Commission arrives at the conclusion that the application of Article 85 (3) in cases of concentration is legally impossible.[33] Thus the analysis of a case resulting in a conclusion that a concentration exists will exclude the question of the applicability of Article 85.

The SHV-Chevron case is clearly distinguishable from a cartel in the form of a central selling agency in that there is in that case a real modification in the organisation of business management and in property-relations, and not just a co-ordination of market behaviour on behalf of economically independent companies.[34]

It is notable that several forms of restrictions in the freedom of action of the parent companies are not attributed by the Commission to the "group effect" doctrine but are explained on the grounds that no appreciable restriction of competition is at stake. Director-General Schlieder [35] held furthermore that in the case where a new economic unit had been constituted, non-competition clauses between the parents are

31. Mestmäcker, *Europäisches Wettbewerbsrecht,* München 1974, p. 415-416. Court of Justice, Case No. 6/72, *supra,* n. 30, at pt. 28: In fact it may be regarded as abusive if an undertaking has a dominant position such that the objectives of the Treaty are frustrated *by a substantial change in the supply structure* seriously jeopardising the consumer's freedom of action in the market.

32. *The Problem of Concentration in the Common Market,* Series Competition no. 3, Brussels 1966, pt. II, C.

33. Contrary opinion: MM. Waelbroeck-Megret: *Le droit de la Communauté européenne IV, Concurrence,* Brussels 1972, p. 256-7.

34. *Ibid.,* p. 253.

35. See n. 27.

necessary components of the concentration process and therefore are to be accepted as "ancillary restraints". This is a clear statement which leaves much freedom to the Commission to determine which components are necessary and which are not. However, the Commission did not say this in the decision but treated these components as restrictions on competition, which is less convincing.

Furthermore, Dr. Schlieder went on to say that the decision presupposed, but does not say so explicitly, that the definition of the field of activity by the parent companies of a joint venture does not come under Article 85/1 for the reason that this is a line of business policy laid down by the management. This is in accordance with the *Christiani & Nielsen*[36] and *Kodak*[37] decisions. In *Christiani & Nielsen* it was held that the agreement between the parent company in Kopenhagen and the 100% subsidiary in The Hague amounted only to an allocation of tasks within an economic unit and that within such a unit a part, even if vested with legal personality, cannot compete with the parent company. In the *Kodak* case the parent company instructed the national subsidiaries to issue uniform selling conditions. In both cases the Commission issued a negative clearance; in the first case on the grounds that competition between parts of an economic unit is not possible and in the second case because there was no agreement between the Kodak companies, merely instructions from parent to subsidiaries. This kind of argument would have given a remarkable extension to the criteria of unity between parent companies and a joint subsidiary, but they are not used in the *Chevron* case. Anyhow, it is in the light of the "line of business policy" opinion (Dr. Schlieder) that such confusing elements have to be considered as the fact that Chevron, while no doubt selling in Hamburg City is, under the terms of its agreement with SHV, prevented from selling to ships in Hamburg Harbour. If Calpam were a one hundred percent subsidiary of Chevron, the instructions to Chevron Hamburg and Calpam Hamburg would form part of an apportionment of tasks within the group. After the *SHV-Chevron* decision it seems correct to presume that the "line of business policy" opinion holds, not only within the boundaries of one group, but even when several parent companies by agreement commit themselves not to compete with the joint subsidiary and apportion tasks, *e.g.* the fixing of a geographical area of common interest reserved to the joint subsidiary.

In any event Dr. Schlieder's comments indicate that the Commission intends not to impose the sanctions of Article 85 upon concentration

36. Decision of June 18, 1969, O.J. 1969, L 165/96; *cf.* the *Béguelin* judgment of the Court of November 25, 1972, Case No. 22/71, 17 Rec. 949, pt. 7-8.

37. Decision of June 30, 1970, O.J. 1970, L 147.

processes brought about by the establishment of joint subsidiaries. The rather confusing elements of the *SHV-Chevron* decision have to be considered in the same light. What is most confusing is that the reader and student of the Commission's policy is left in total obscurity with regard to the facts, and is reduced to conjecture as to how the general principles stated in the decision apply to these unknown facts. For example, why did SHV and Chevron wish to merge part of their activities? Was SHV in need of capital (in which case the failing company defence of anti-trust law might have applied)? Did SHV decide to concentrate on other sectors of activity (its retail sector, in particular, was in a bad state and it has continued its activities in the energy-field)?

Was its distribution network for petroleum products too small and did it have supply difficulties (Dr. Schlieder maintained that SHV no longer had access to safe supply sources, but surely one of the tasks of competition policy is to secure safe supplies, as the Commission insisted in the *Aardolie Belangen Gemeenschap* case in the Netherlands, reported in the press), *etc.?* With a greater knowledge of these different possibilities the understanding of the scope of the decision could have been strengthened. As it is, are we to conclude that the intentions of the participants are irrelevant, except as regard the permanence of the agreements? This would add to the impression that any concentration which does not constitute and outright abuse of (an already existing?) dominant position will be favoured by the Commission even if the restrictions on the participants go further than the "group effect" rule would seem to allow; alternatively that they will not even be considered to be infringements of Article 85 (1).

Finally, the decision continues the line of policy adopted by the Commission and laid down in its proposal for a regulation on the control of concentrations, which recommends the exemption from the requirement for prior notification to the Commission of those concentration operations where the turnover of the firm to be merged is less than 30 m. units of account,[38] the presumption being that the take-over of smaller firms does not in principle impair competitive conditions in the Common Market (and SHV by all standards was a small company in the energy market).

But the matter has been further complicated by the Commission's statement that it is prepared to include within the provisions for compulsory notification such cases as the formation of joint subsidiaries, if the turnover of the firms concerned is less than 30 m. u.a.[39] This was an

38. Proposal for a Regulation of the Council on the control of concentrations between undertakings, O.J. C 92/73, Art. 4(2).

39. Fourth Report on Competition Policy, April 1975, pt. 17.

answer to criticism in the European Parliament, especially from Dr. Patijn.

In its recently published Fourth Report the Commission added the argument that as in the *Agfa-Gevaert* and *Dunlop-Pirelli* operations the parent companies in the *Calpam* case took the form of holding-companies.[40] It continued that they thereby lost their economic independence on the markets concerned, since they could subsequently only act through their joint subsidiaries (note: but the parent companies determine the policy of a joint subsidiary!), which had been created "through transfers of assets" needed for their operation. It is important to note that in the Dutch version the part between quotation marks reads: "through an *irreversible* modification of the property of assets", which is more precise. To this should have been added: "and if the Commission has come to the conviction that this irreversible character is the lasting intention of the parties".

Finally, in this same Report [41] it would appear that the legal security in the sense of the predictable nature of the Commission's opinion, which is to be expected in cases involving concentration, has been lost with the words: "a uniform approach cannot be taken in all such cases. Having regard to all relevant aspects of each case it has to be decided from case to case whether there is in fact a concentration or a restrictive agreement".

40. As n. 39, pt. 41.
41. As n. 39, pt. 41.

CASE LAW

A. COURT OF JUSTICE

104. *Commission of the European Communities v. Federal Republic of Germany.* Case No. 12/74. Judgment of February 20, 1975.

Facts

The German law on vince products (*Weingesetz*) of July 14, 1971, and the implementing regulation of July 15, 1971, on sparkling wines and spirits obtained by distilling wine provide *inter alia*:
(a) for *sparkling wines*:
—that the appelation *"Sekt"* may only describe a home-produced sparkling wine satisfying the conditions of quality set out in the regulation, and may only be applied to quality foreign wines if German is an official language throughout the whole of the country of production; moreover, this appellation may be linked to the condition that a sparkling wine be produced from a minimum proportion of home-grown grapes.
—that the appellation *"Prädikatsekt"* may only describe a home-produced sparkling wine fulfilling the above-mentioned conditions and containing at least 60% of home-grown grapes.
(b) for *spirits obtained by distilling wine*:
—that the appellation *"Weinbrand"* may only be used for products entitled to the appellation "spirits obtained by distilling quality wine" and if German is an official language throughout the whole of the country of production.

As regards sparkling wines and spirits obtained by distilling foreign wines other than those coming from countries where German is the official language, other designations are applicable, such as "Schaumwein", *"Qualitätswein"*, or *"Qualitätschaumwein"* and *"Brantwein aus Wein"*.

By a letter of July 27, 1971, the Federal Republic of Germany sent the texts of the law and of the implementing regulations to the Commission.

By a letter of June 12, 1972, the Commission opened proceedings under Article 169 of the Treaty, at the end of which it concluded that the appellations in questions constituted measures having an effect equivalent to quantitative restrictions, within the meaning of Article 30 *et seq.*

After an exchange of communications between the Commission and the Federal Government, the Federal Government adhered to its view that the appellations did not contravene any rule of Community Law, the Commission then lodged an application with the Court of justice seeking a declaration that the Federal Republic had failed to fulfil its obligations under the Treaty, in particular under Article 30, and under Article 12 (2) (6) of Regulation No. 816/70 of the Council of April 18, 1970, by reserving the appellations "*Sekt*" and "*Weinbrand*" to the domestic product, and the appellation "*Prädikatssekt*" to wines produced within the country from a fixed minimum proportion of home-grown grapes.

13 C.M.L. Rev. 1976, 121-132

Submissions

The Advocate-General Warner held in his opinion:

That in reserving the name "*Prädikatssekt*" for sparkling wines produced with a specified proposition of home-grown grapes, the Federal Republic was in breach of its obligations. There was no indication that the name indicated to the German public a specifically German product; nor was the name a true indication of high quality wine, since the fixed proportion of 60% home-grown grapes could be of any variety provided that they were grown on German soil.

As to the reserving of the name "*Weinbrand*" to brandies produced in any country throughout which German is an official language, the Advocate-General considered that the Federal Republic was not in breach of its obligations. The Federal Republic had made good its assertion that, for the vast majority of German people, the appellation "*Weinbrand*" connotes a German product.

Judgment

The Common Market is based upon the free circulation of goods within the Community in order to ensure this freedom the Treaty prohibits, in particular by Articles 12 and 31, the introduction, as between member States, of new measures whose effect is directly or indirectly to create barriers to trade within the Community.

As regards *"Sekt"* and *"Prädikatssekt"* in particular, since the coming into force of Regulation No. 816/70, rules concerning the conditions of marketing of these products must be placed in a Community context.

Having regard to the prohibitions set out in the Treaty and in Regulation No. 816/70, it is necessary to consider whether the Federal Republic failed to fulfil its obligations under the EEC Treaty.

(1) *With regard to the appellations "Sekt" and "Weinbrand"*:

Directive No. 70/50/EEC, which is based on Article 33 (7) of the Treaty, states in Article 1 that its purpose is to abolish measures which have an effect equivalent to quantitative restrictions on imports, and sets out in Article 2 (3) the measures which must be regarded as prohibited. Under Article 2 (3) (5) it refers to measures which "confine names which are not indicative of origin or source to domestic products only".

The registered designations of origin and indirect indications of origin referred to in the Directive always describe a product coming from a specific geographical area.

These appellations are protected by law in order to safeguard producers against unfair competition and consumers against misleading information.

The appellations only fulfil their purpose if the products they describe does in fact possess qualities and characteristics which are due to the fact that it originated in a specific geographical area.

As regards indications of origin, in particular, the geographical area of origin of a product must confer on it a specific quality and specific characteristics of such a nature as to distinguish it from all other products.

An area of origin which is defined on the basis of the extent of national territory or a linguistic criterion cannot constitute a geographical area within the meaning referred to above, capable of justifying an indication of origin, particularly where the products in question may be produced from grapes of indeterminate origin.

The German Government further maintains that the products covered by the appellations "*Sekt*" and "*Weinbrand*" are clearly distinguished from all other products as a result of the particular method of manufacture used in Germany which confers on them a particular flavour.

In the case of wine products, the natural features of the area of origin, such as the quality of the grape, play an important role in determining their quality and characteristics.

The method of production used may play some part in determining the characteristics of a product, but it is not in itself a sufficient criterion, particularly in view of the fact that the method employed may be practised in other geographical areas.

The in provisions in the national regulation regarding sparkling wines, and in the law regarding wine products, the requirements of quality as to home-produced and foreign wines are effectively the same, nor does the law on wine products exclude the possibility that "*Weinbrand*" may be distilled from foreign wines.

In the light of these considerations it cannot be shown from the arguments of the defendant on the method of production used for "*Sekt*" and "*Weinbrand*" that, by reason of this method, the products have a quality and characteristics peculiar to them which render them typically German products.

Furthermore, the law in force until 1971 in the Federal Republic allowed, as regards "*Sekt*", and even as regards "*Weinbrand*", the use in German of these appellations as regards imported products, and this fact is not disputed by the defendants. These appellations were in fact applied to at least a part of the imported products, and there are indications that the quantity of products affected was increasing at the time of the entry into force of the legislation on vine products.

It must therefore be concluded that as the appellations "*Sekt*" and "*Weinbrand*" do not apply to products whose quality was essentially the result of their being restricted to a particular area of origin and as they could or should describe both imported goods and domestic production, such appellations were not, at the time of the entry into force of the legislation on vine products, capable of identifying the products in question as German, on the basis of their specific quality and characteristics.

This conclusion is not affected by evidence adduced by the Federal Government, on the basis of public opinion polls, that in the opinion of the German consumer the appellations "*Sekt*" and "*Weinbrand*" referred to the domestic product. By reason of the difficulties inherent in these types of inquiry, opinion polls are, by their very nature, incapable of producing results on the basis of which the facts in dispute may be objectively assessed.

(2) *With regard to the appellation "Prädikatssekt"*:

As regards this appellation, it cannot be accepted that the use of 60% of German grapes confers a particular flavour on the products in question.

Since the legislation on vine products does not define the grapes to be used in production of "*Prädikatssekt*" with reference to their specific character, but only on the basis of their national origin, the minimum percentage required does not necessarily imply that the product in question is actually of a special quality in comparison with "*Sekt*" and thus warrants the protection accorded to it.

The provision of the Treaty establishing the free movement of goods, in particular these of Article 30, prohibit, as between member States, quantitative restrictions on imports and all measures having equivalent effect.

Under the terms of Article 2 (3) (5) of Directive No. 75/50/EEC of the Commission, :measures which "confine names which are not indicative of origin or source to domestic products only" are to be regarded as prohibited within the meaning of Articles 30 *et seq.* of the Treaty.

By reserving these appellations to domestic production and by compelling the products of the other member States to employ appellations which are unknown to or less esteemed by the consumer, the legislation on vine products is calculated to favour the disposal of the domestic product on the German market to the detriment of the products of other member States.

Thus, this legislation on vine products involves measures having an effect equivalent to quantitative restrictions on imports within the meaning of the above-mentioned provisions; such measures, as regards imports of sparkling wines from third countries, are contrary to Article 12 (2) (6) of Regulation No. 816/70 of the Council.

For the purposes of this prohibition it is not necessary to show that such measures actually restrict imports of the products concerned but, in accordance with Article 2 (1) of the above-mentioned Directive, that they may merely "hinder imports which could otherwise take place".

The fact that the appellations "*Sekt*" and "*Weinbrand*" do not constitute indications of origin that the measures in dispute which are included in the legislation on vine products cannot be justified under Article 36 of the Treaty on the grounds of the protection of industrial and commercial property.

The Federal Republic maintains that, by referring to national rules on industrial and commercial property, Article 36 does not intend to refer to a specific system of legal protection of such property, but leaves to the member States the power to prepare and develop such a system, and that in this instance the system in force in the Federal Republic in the field of indications of origin, whilst still forming part of the law on competition, is in fact developing towards that of industrial and commercial property.

Such an unlimited development would run the risk of progressively restricting the scope of the Treaty.

Although the Treaty does not restrict the power of each member State to legislate in matters of indications or origin, they are nevertheless prohibited from introducing new measures of an arbitrary and unjustified nature whose effects are, for this reason, equivalent to quantitative restrictions.

This is precisely the case where a national legislature grants the protection provided for indications of origin to appellations which, at the time when such protection is granted, are merely generic in nature.

The assertion of the Federal Republic that the measures in dispute are justified on the grounds of public policy, within the meaning of Article 36 of the Treaty, in particular by reason of the need to protect producers against unfair competition and consumers against deception, could not be accepted.

Independently of any definition of the concept of public policy referred to in Article 36 of the Treaty, this provision could only derogate from Articles 30 to 34 to the extent necessary in order to ensure that producers and consumers are protected against fraudulent commercial practices.

Vine products of the same type may differ from each other by reason of their quality and certain of their characteristics. Nor has the defendant shown the reasons for which it has modified its earlier practice according to which, before the entry into force of the legislation on vine products, the designation of origin of at least some of the products in despite appeared on the labelling beside the generic appellation.

The Court ruled:

By reserving, in the law on vine products of July 14, 1971, and in the implementing regulation on sparkling wines and spirits obtained by distilling wine of July 15, 1971, the appellations "*Sekt*" and "*Weinbrand*" to domestic production and the appellation "*Prädikatssekt*" to wines produced in Germany from a fixed minimum proportion of German grapes, the Federal Republic of Germany has failed to fulfil its occupation under Article 30 of the Treaty and, as regards sparkling wine, under Article 12 (2) (6) of Regulation No. 816/70 of the Council of April 28, 1970.

105. *REWE Zentralfinanz GmbH, Köln,* v. Director of the *Landwirtschaftskammer, Bonn.* Case No. 4/75. Preliminary Ruling of May 27, 1975, on request of the First Chamber of the *Verwaltungsgericht, Köln.*

Facts

According to the German regulation of August 23, 1957, on measures for the prevention of the introduction of pathogenic organisms or pests which are dangerous to cultivated plants (*Pflanzenbeschauverordnung*), any person wishing to import certain fruits or vegetables into the Federal Republic must submit them to an official phytosanitary examination at the frontier. The requirement applied *inter alia* to prevent the introduction of San José Scale, a particularly dangerous and persistent pest.

On October 29, 1973, the firm REWE Zentralfinanz refused to submit a batch of apples to examination, with the result that permission to import was refused. REWE thereupon commenced contentious administrative proceedings contesting the legality of this decision, arguing in particular that a sanitary control of the type indicated was prohibited under Article 30 of the EEC Treaty since it amounted to a measure having an effect equivalent to quantitative restrictions on imports.

The German administrative court stayed proceedings and referred the following three questions to the Court of Justice for a preliminary ruling:

1. Do "quantitative restrictions on imports and all measures having equivalent effect" within the meaning of Article 30 of the EEC Treaty include the obligation to have plant products (here, apples) inspected on import, at the importer's expense, to see if they are carriers of certain harmful organisms, if refusal to allow the phytosanitary examination means that import of the goods will be prohibited?
2. Is the first sentence of Article 36 of the EEC Treaty to be interpreted in such a way as to make phytosanitary examinations imposed at the frontier under domestic law to prevent the introduction of San José Scale "justified" within the meaning of the first sentence of Article 36 even after the issue of the Council Directive of December 8, 1969, on the control of San José Scale?
3. Is the obligatory phytosanitary inspection on the importation of foreign apples "arbitrary discrimination" within the meaning of the second sentence of Article 5 of the EEC Treaty if apples produced in the Federal Republic of Germany are not subject to a similar requirement of inspection when despatched within the country?

Submissions

The advocate-General Reischl held in his opinion:

As regards the first question: the obligation to have plant products inspected on import from other Member States, in order to establish whether they are contaminated with certain harmful organisms, with the consequence that refusal to consent to the examination means that the import of the goods will be prohibited, is calculated, where no corresponding inspection are carried out where domestic products are marketed within the country, to make importation more difficult and costly and must therefore be considered, apart from the exceptions laid down in Community Law, as a measure having equivalent effect within the meaning of the EEC Treaty.

As regards the second question: such examinations may be justified within the meaning of Article 36 of the EEC Treaty where a serious risk exists of introducing the parasite without such protective measures, that is to say, where a danger to the state of health of the domestic plant is to be feared; in this connection account must be taken of the area of origin of the goods, the efficiency of the measures of control which are applied there, the reliability of the certificates of conformity with the phytosanitary regulations issued by the country of origin and, where applicable, of the seasonal variations of the risk. They may be justified even after the date by which the Member States were obliged to observe the minimum provisions laid down in the Council Directive of December 8, 1969, on the control of San José Scale.

As regards the third question: the compulsory phytosanitarry inspection of apples of foreign origin which takes place on the importation of this fruit from another Member State does not always amount to a means of arbitrary discrimination within the meaning of Article 36 because apples produced within the importing country are not subject, on despatch, to a similar compulsory inspection. The different treatment is permissible where the protection of the health of plants in a possible area of contamination within the national territory is ensured by adequate effective measures and where, on the basis of a reasonable assessment carried out in the light of the factors laid out under the answer to the second question, it may be assumed that the imported products present a greater risk of contamination and of introducing the parasite.

Judgment

....

In view of the interrelationship of the three questions it is necessary to consider them together.

Article 30 of the EEC Treaty prohibits quantitative restrictions on importations between Member States as well as all measures having an effect equivalent to quantitative restrictions.

In order to fall within the terms of this prohibition, it is sufficient if the measures in question are capable of hindering, directly or indirectly, actually or potentially, importations between member States.

According to Article 2, paragraph 2 of Directive No. 70/50/EEC of the Commission of December 22, 1969, measures having an equivalent effect are defined as those measures which subject the importation to a condition which is only imposed on imported products, or which subject them to a different condition, or one which is more difficult to satisfy, than that imposed on domestic products.

The phytosanitary controls in question are required only for the importation of vegetable produce, and similar national products, such as apples, are not obligatorily subjected to similar controls before they are marketed. These controls amount therefore to a condition imposed only on imported goods, in the meaning of Article 2, paragraph 2 of the above-mentioned Directive.

Moreover, in view of the delay which necessarily results from control operations, and of the supplementary transport costs which may also result for the importer, the controls in question are also likely to make importation more difficult and onerous.

It follows therefore that phytosanitary controls at the frontier to which vegetable produce, imported from another Member State, are subjected, amount to measures having an effect equivalent to quantitative restrictions on imports in the sense of Article 30 of the Treaty, and which are prohibited by the Article, apart from the exceptions permitted by Community Law.

According to the first sentence of Article 36 of the Treaty, Articles 30 to 34 are not applicable to those restrictions on imports and, consequently, those measures having an equivalent effect, which may be justified on grounds of the protection of plants.

The Directive No 69/466/EEC of the Council of December 8, 1969, lays down a number of measures concerning the San José Scale with the object of instituting certain common minimum measures in order to combat this pest.... These measures are, however, intended to complement, and not to replace, measures taken against the introduction of this organism in each Member State.

At the present stage of Community regulation of this matter, phytosanitary controls imposed by a Member State on the imports of vegetable products amount to import restrictions which are justified in terms the first sentence of Article 30 of the Treaty.

Such import restrictions are not, however, admissible if they amount to a means of arbitrary discrimination.

The fact of submitting vegetable produce imported from another Member State to a phytosanitary control, where domestic products are not subjected to a similar control, could constitute an arbitrary discrimination within the meaning of Article 36.

....

However, a differing treatment of imported and national products which is motivated by the necessity of preventing the propagation of a harmful organism should not be considered as constituting an arbitrary discrimination if effective measures are taken to prevent the marketing of contaminated national products, and if there is reason to believe, on the basis of past experience, that a risk of the propagation of the harmful organism would exist in the absence of the import controls.

....

The Court ruled:

1. The obligatory submission of imports of vegetable produce, originating in another Member State, to a phytosanitary control at the frontier, with the object of establishing whether the products in question are carriers of certain organisms which are harmful to plants, amounts to a measure having an effect equivalent to quantitative restrictions in the sense of Article 30 of the Treaty and prohibited by that Article, with the exception of the derogations provided for by Article 36;

2. The necessary supplementary or more rigorous measures foreseen by Article 11 of the Directive No. 69/466/EEC of the Council, permit Member States to carry out phytosanitary controls on imported products if effective measures have been taken to prevent the marketing of contamined national products, and if there are reasons to believe, on the basis of past experience, that a risk of the propagation of the organism would exist in the absence of controls at the time of importation.

B. FRENCH CASE LAW

Cour de Cassation (Ch. mixte), May 24, 1975
(Administration des Douanes v. *Société des Cafés Jacques Vabre et Société J. Wiegel & Cie.)*[1]

This decision of the French *Cour de Cassation* is a remarkable turning point as to the legal grounds for the supremacy of Community law in the French legal system.

Background and Facts of the Case

Briefly and generally stated the case concerned an importer's action for recovery of a consumption tax illegally imposed on imports of soluble coffee from Holland. In the importer's view the French customs code, modified subsequent to the entry into force of the EEC Treaty, was contrary to Article 95 of the Treaty. The lower courts, the *Tribunal de Paris* and the *Cour d'Appel,* in their respective decisions of January 8, 1971, and July 7, 1973, found for the importer and upheld the supremacy of this Treaty provision pursuant to Article 55 of the French constitution without making any reference to the *ENEL* ruling of the Court of Justice or to the nature of the Community legal order.

The French customs office appealed the decision of the court of appeal on two main grounds as far as the Community law is concerned. First, invoking the decision of the *Conseil d'Etat* in the *Semoule* case, it asserted that the lower court infringed the principle of separation of powers by refusing to apply a law absolutely binding on all French courts because the consumption tax pursuant to a law contrary to Article 95 was illegal. This is the traditional argument challenging the very existence of Article 55 of the constitution, which embodies a principle the *Conseil d'Etat* finds particularly difficult to accept—as its *Semoule* decision persuasively demonstrates.[2] Secondly, in the appellant's view the lower court infringed Article 55, as it recognized the supremacy of the Treaty without examining whether the condition of reciprocity required by this constitutional provision for the supremacy of an international treaty were actually met.

Opinion of the Procureur Général

Before the decision of the *Cour de Cassation* is presented and examined it may be helpful to a full understanding of it to outline first the illuminating and elaborate opinion of the *Procureur Général,* M. Touffait. The opinion concentrates, of course, on the overriding issue of the relation of the Treaty with a subsequent national law contrary to it and of the Competence of French courts to rule thereon. The strong determination of the *Procureur Général* to have these fundamental questions settled is evident throughout his opinion—and with good reason too, in view of the uncertainty prevailing as a result of the divergent views of the *Conseil d'Etat* on one hand and of the ordinary courts on the other.

His primary preoccupation concerns of course the stated view of the *Conseil d'Etat* on Article 55 that an examination of the relation of a treaty with a subsequent law constitutes a constitutional control which no French jurisdiction may exercise, a view which practically deprives Article 55 of any meaning at all. For this reason he advances counterarguments questioning the explicit views of the *commissaire du gouvernement,*

1. (1975) Recueil Dalloz, Jurisprudence, 497-507.
2. (1968) Recueil Dalloz, Jurisprudence, 285.

Mme. Questiaux, in the *Semoule* case, the leading case in which the *Conseil d'Etat* expressed this view.

Referring to the case law of the lower ordinary courts, the *Procureur Général* points out that in dealing with a conflict between two norms of a different hierarchical standing, they ensure the respect of the higher one certainly not by annulling the lower one, but simply by declaring it non-applicable. Could such an examination of compatibility of a law with a treaty really imply a constitutional control, inquires the *Procureur Général*? To demonstrate that it does not, he invokes the decision of the *Conseil Constitutionnel* (Constitutional Council) of January 15, 1975 which, in his view, is one, if not the, most important decision clarifying the scope and legal consequences of a constitutional control of laws. In this decision the Constitutional Council draws a neat distinction between a conflict of a law with the constitution and that between a law and an international treaty. Dealing with the compatibility of the law on the interruption of pregnancy with Article 2 of the European Human Rights Convention which, pursuant to Article 55 of the Constitution has a force superior to the law, the Constitutional Council decided that according to Article 61 of the Constitution it is only competent to rule on the compatibility of laws with the Constitution. This constitutional provision does not, however, in its view, imply that the Constitutional Council should also ensure the principle of supremacy of international treaties. Compared with a decision on the compatibility of laws with the Constitution, which has an absolute and definite effect, a decision on the supremacy of treaties over laws has an effect at the same time relative and contingent—relative because limited to the application of the treaties and contingent because subject to the principle of reciprocity.

The *Procureur Général* draws two significant conclusions from this reasoning of the Constitutional Council. First, a French court not only may, but must, in his view, recognize the supremacy of an international treaty over a subsequent national law contrary to it, otherwise it would commit a denial of justice. Secondly, in so doing the court does not review the constitutionality of that law, as it is merely concerned with the application of the treaty. Thus the prerogatives of the legislator are respected and preserved.

The second point concerns the meaning and scope of Article 55 of the Constitution. If this article intended international treaties to prevail over preceding law only, remarks the *Procureur Général*, it would have been sufficient if those treaties had been granted the force of law only. But this constitutional provision obviously does not, in his view, envisage only the supremacy of international treaties over preceding law. For solving such a conflict the principle of succession of laws in time would have been entirely adequate. He concludes that "... the notion of supremacy of a treaty over a law makes sense only in relation to a law subsequent to it because with regard to a preceding one the answer is clear". His preoccupation with the meaning and function of this constitutional provision should not lead to any hasty conclusions as to the legal basis for the supremacy of Community law. The characterization of the Community legal order which follows indicates already an entirely new approach to this problem.

The specific legal nature of the Community Treaty is this time fully recognized—this is the third revealing point of this remarkable opinion. Compared with traditional international treaties the notion and obligation as established by the EEC Treaty differ from and in the view of the *Procureur Général*, exceed those of traditional international treaties. This finding is then clearly reflected in his view as to the legal ground of supremacy of Community law—the fourth point to be noted.

The supremacy of Community law is based on the EEC Treaty itself. The objectives of the Treaty, the institutional structure and the powers granted for their pursuance are, in his view, formally reflected in the provisions of Articles 5 and 189 of the Treaty. These powers necessarily imply a corresponding limitation of State powers. In support of his view the

ENEL [3] and *Walt Wilhelm* [4] rulings of the Court are invoked and extensively cited, in itself already a remarkable innovation. The *Procureur Général* proposes therefore to base the supremacy either on Article 55 of the Constitution or on the EEC Treaty itself, and clearly prefers the latter alternative. Admitting that the supremacy of Article 95 of the Treaty could well be ensured on the basis of Article 55 of the Constitution, he categorically dismisses such a solution, stating significantly:

"... but personally, I ask you not to mention it, and to base your reasoning on the very nature of the legal order instituted by the Treaty of Rome". His explanation for this approach corresponds entirely to the reasoning of the *ENEL* ruling. If the supremacy of Community law were based on Article 55, reasons M. Touffait, it would imply that its supremacy in the French legal order is derived from and depends exclusively on the French constitutional provision—a solution which would have the most unfortunate consequences for the status of Community law, in those member States whose constitutions do not recognize the supremacy of international treaties. Such a solution of this conflict could provide a "not negligible" argument for the courts of those member States to deny on this ground the supremacy of Community law as done by the Italian Constitutional Court in the *ENEL* case in 1964 [5]. This consideration reinforces, in the opinion of M. Touffait, his resolute preference to establish the supremacy of Community Law on basis of the Treaty itself rather than on the constitutional provision, which certainly would have been sufficient to safeguard it but with undesirable implications.

The final point concerns the reciprocity clause of Article 55. Questioning the feasibility of applying it to multilateral treaties the *Procureur Général* seems to place this principle within the Community legal order. He points out that if a member State fails in its Treaty obligations another member State, "victim" of this failure, may bring an action before the Court pursuant to Article 170 of the Treaty instead of taking the law into its own hands. For this reason it seems the *Procureur Général* maintains—without unfortunately elaborating this view any further—that a failure to respect the reciprocity as required by Article 55 may no longer be invoked before a national court.

Reasoning and Decision of the Cour de Cassation

Following its *Procureur Général* the *Cour de Cassation* dismissed the appeal as unfounded. But compared with the opinion of the *Procureur Général* the *Cour de Cassation* slightly modified the emphasis of its reasoning.

First, as to the power of ordinary courts to rule on the conflict of a treaty with a subsequent law, the *Cour de Cassation* has simply exercised this power without making any pronouncements whatever.

Secondly, as to the grounds of supremacy of Community law the French supreme court is, compared with the view of its *Procureur Général,* less categoric. It still refers to Article 55 of the Constitution, even though in the most fleeting manner imaginable. But, and this is very important indeed, it also explicitly refers to and stresses at some length the independent legal order of the Community, which is integrated into the national legal order, its special character as a legal order directly applicable to individuals and binding on national courts. Because of the superior force of Community law, argues the *Cour de cassation,* the

3. Case No. 6/64, *Costa* v. *ENEL,* judgment of July 15, 1964, 10 Rec., 1158-1160; 1964 C.M.L.R. 455-456; 2 C.M.L. Rev. 1964-65, 197-198.

4. Case No. 14/68, *Walt Wilhelm and others* v. *Bundeskartellamt,* judgment of February 13, 1969, 15 Rec. 1969, 1-30; 1969, C.M.L.R. 100-121.

5. *Costa* v. *ENEL,* judgment of March 7, 1964, Foro It. 1964, I Col. 465; 1964 C.M.L.R. 435-436; 2 C.M.L. Rev. 1964-65, 224.

Court of Appeal did not exceed its powers when declaring Article 95 of the EEC Treaty applicable, thus excluding the subsequent French law.

Finally, as to the requirements of reciprocity required for the supremacy of an international treaty by Article 55, whose infringement was asserted by the appellant, the French supreme court, following its *Procureur Général*, ruled that a violation of this principle may not be invoked before a national court because within the Community legal order a failure of a member State to respect its obligations under the EEC Treaty is subject to an action pursuant to Article 170.

Critical Appraisal

The *Vabre* case is a true landmark decision as to the legal ground of supremacy of Community law in the French legal system. In this case the *Cour de Cassation* has largely and probably definitely abandoned the view of the *Ramel* case [6] in which it still based the supremacy of Community law exclusively on Article 55 of the Constitution, regarding the EEC Treaty as any other international treaty and failing to recognize the original and specific features of the Community legal order. Leaving aside its *Guerrini* decision[7] of January 7, 1972, which established the supremacy of a Community regulation on the basis of Article 189 of the Treaty, a decision at that time rightly hailed as a step forward, in the present *Vabre* case the *Cour de Cassation* breaks entirely new ground recognizing the finality and the distinct and specific character of the Community legal order.

However the *Cour de Cassation* has still hestitated to sever completely its link with this constitutional provision as strongly urged by the *Procureur Général* in upholding the supremacy of Community law. In a sense the French supreme court still timidly and unconspicuously invokes jointly not only Article 55 but also the legal character of the Community legal order as grounds of its supremacy. Its very reserved and almost passing reference to Article 55 of the Constitution is, however, quite significant for its new and approach which contrasts sharply with its subsequent elaborate characterization of the Community legal order. Still paying a reverence to this constitutional provision with possible undertones of an adieu, the French supreme court leaves no doubt as to the fact that it bases the supremacy of Community law primarily on the Treaty itself. However much it may be regretted that the high court has found it impossible to dispense with this constitutional provision altogether and base the supremacy of Community law even formally exclusively on the EEC Treaty, its reference to Article 55 may be plausibly explained. Being aware of the determined, almost obstinate refusal of the *Conseil d'Etat* to take cognizance of Article 55, let alone to apply it—because such an application, implying a control of the legislature by the judiciary would in its view be contrary to the principle of separation of powers—the *Cour de Cassation* appears anxious to demonstrate that Article 55 is a constitutional provision to be applied with all the consequences it may entail. The passing reference to Article 55 may be understood as implicitly challenging and criticizing the uncompromising position of the *Conseil d'Etat*. From the point of view of Community law this reference is not particularly disconcerting since the reasoning underlying the decision clearly marks a new stage of development favouring and re-enforcing the supremacy of Community law on the basis of its own inherent specificity and finality.

And this is also true for the meaning of the reciprocity clause of Article 55 according to which an international treaty enjoys supremacy in the French legal system if a State party to it recognizes it as well. The opinion of the *Cour de Cassation* that an infringement of this requirement may not be invoked before a French court may astonish at first. But this is

6. 90 Gazette du Palais, 344 (1970).
7. 9 Rev. Trim. de Dr. Europ., 1973, 133; (1972) Recueil Dalloz, I, 497.

merely a logical consequence of the supremacy of Community law as recognized by the *Cour de Cassation*. True, the supreme court is unusually brief on this point. But nevertheless, seen within the context of its reasoning the following consideration may have prompted the court to respect the inherent supremacy of Community law up to its ultimate logical consequence. The supremacy of international treaties pursuant to Article 55 of the constitution is based on reciprocity, it is a traditional international obligation. Nothing could have been easier for the supreme court than to ascertain that this condition was fulfilled since the Constitution of The Netherlands, from where the product was imported, also recognizes the supremacy of international treaties. But the *Cour de Cassation* does not seem to consider this requirement any longer as a constitutional one based on mutual State obligations but as a Community obligation of member States, as an obligation created by the Treaty and necessary for a uniform and unconditional supremacy of Community law.

The recognition of supremacy of Community law is, in the view of the French high court, a Community obligation of all member States; otherwise the court's reference to the infringement procedure pursuant to Article 170 could hardly be understood. It is a Community obligation which prevails as part of Community law over Article 55 of the Constitution. Puzzling remains, however, the reference of the *Cour de Cassation* to Article 170 of the Treaty only. Obviously its application presupposes the existence and infringement of a Community obligation as the high court rightly assumes. This restricted reference to Article 170 could perhaps be explained by the fact that the *Cour de Cassation* still considers this obligation within the Community legal order as being based on reciprocity. This obviously misconstrues the very foundation and nature of Community obligations of member States which is not based on reciprocity, as the high court seems to assume, but on solidarity, as the Court of Justice has ruled.[8] This false assumption leads the *Cour de Cassation* necessarily to an erroneous conclusion limiting the infringement procedure to Article 170. However, it seems incoherent to recognize the existence of a Community obligation and yet to limit its enforcement to an infringement procedure to be opened by a member State only, thus disregarding the power of the Commission, the true guardian of the Treaty, to initiate an infringement procedure pursuant to Article 169. The primary role of the Commission in enforcing Community obligations should have been considered as well. It is fairly obvious that the task of ensuring the respect of obligations by the member States rests primarily with the Commission and not with the individual member States, as amy be clearly deduced from Article 170 (2), according to which a member State must, prior to its action before the Court, submit the matter to the Commission. The Commission may not be by-passed in this procedure. Only if the Commission failed to give an opinion within three months may the member State proceed directly before the Court. Article 170 obviously does not exclude a possible rôle for the Commission, and is thus in a sense merely a complement to Article 169. This being so the omission of a reference to Article 169 is not easy to understand and explain. The respect of the supremacy of Community law by the member States is undoubtedly a Community obligation to be safeguarded by Articles 169 and 170. It is difficult to recognize such a Community obligation while limiting its enforcement to a secondary infringement procedure only.

Gerhard Bebr
(Member of the Legal
Service of the Commission of
the European Communities)

8. Case No. 39/72, *Commission* v. *Italy*, (1973) E.C.R. 101, 116; see also Cases No. 6 and 11/69, *Commission* v. *France*, 15 Recueil 1969, 523, 540.

SURVEY OF LITERATURE

I. *INTEGRATION, ECONOMIC AND POLITICAL*

Lord Gladwyn, "Western Europe's Collective Defense", 51 *International Affairs* 1975, 166-175.

G. G. Kaplan, "Legal aspects of aircraft finance in Europe", 9 J.W.T.L. 1975, 136-160.

E. Schulz, "Moskau und das Problem der Integration in Westeuropa", 30 E.A. 1975, 383-393.

O. Schwerin, "Die Solidarität der EG-Staaten in der KSZE", 30 E.A. 1975, 483-493.

Otto Suto, "The problem of relationship between Comecon and EEC in the European policy of security and cooperation", 27 *Studia Diplomatica* 1974, 765-779.

W. Wagner, "Eine Station auf einem langen Wege. Zur geschichtlichen Einordnung der Konferenz über Sicherheit und Zusammenarbeit in Europa", 30 E.A. 1975, 479-483.

W. Wallace, "Europa: the changing international context, Implications for British policy", 31 *The World Today* 1975, 177-214.

IV. *EUROPEAN COMMUNITIES*

A. COMMON SUBJECTS

1. *General*

L.Bianconi, "Vers un droit pénal communautaire", 1975 R.M.C. no. 181, 33-40.

A. Deringer, J. Sedemund, "Europäisches Gemeinschaftsrecht. Die Entwicklung bis Januar 1975 (continued from N.J.W. 1974, 1600) 28 N.J.W. 1975 482-486.

W. J. Feld, J. K. Wildgen, "National administration and European integration. Saboteurs at work?", 13 J. Comm. Mark. Studies 1975, 244-265.

W. Feld, J. W. Wildgen, "Electoral ambitions and European integration", 29 Int. Org. 1975, 447-468.

A. Fischer, "By the skin of our teeth: Gedanken zum Stand der europäischen Integration", 30 E.A. 1975, 95-103.

F. Gundersen, "Das Diskriminierungsverbot im EWG-Vertrag", 28 N.J.W. 1975, 472-476.
The author gives a personal view of Article 7. According to him, the discrimination prohibition is not directed to individual citizens, but has legal effects only for the member States and Community institutions.

E. Häckel, "Multinationale Konzerne—ein Motor der europäischen Integration?", 30 E.A. 1975, 277-289.

13 C.M.L.Rev. 1976, 133-142

N. Hansen, "Die europäische politische Zusammenarbeit bei den Vereinten Nationen. Die Neun suchen in New York Profil", 30 E.A. 1975, 493-501.

Analysis of the voting patterns of the nine member States in the framework of the U.N. The number of common votes is slowly increasing, but in view of the final objective—European unity—the situation is still far from satisfactory.

G. Maier, "Die Europäische Gemeinschaft im Uebergang", 21 *Recht der Internationalen Wirtschaft*/A.W.D. 1975, 65-68.

At the present stage of integration, according to the author, European integration shows signs of collapse as well as of further development. As examples he mentions economic and monetary policy, the decision-making process and the extension of the Community.

W. Much, J. C. Séché, "Les droits de l'étranger dans les Communautés européennes", 11 C.D.E. 1975, 251-280.

This article gives a well-documented picture of the position of foreigners in the European Communities. A clear distinction is made between the more favoured position of Community nationals, and that of nationals of third countries.

P. Pescatore, "L'intégration européenne: perspective nouvelle pour le pouvoir judiciaire", 90 J.T. 1975, no. 4908.

Text of a lecture given in Brussels in May, 1974. A discussion of various developments in Community law, including the areas of free movement of persons and goods and of agriculture. There is further discussion of the preliminary rulings procedure and of the action for failure to act, and, finally, the author expresses certain ideas regarding the influence of Community law.

P. Taylor, "The politics of the European Communities: the confederal phase", 27 *World Politics* 1975, 336-361.

R. S. Wood, "The diplomacy of the enlarged European Community", 137 *World Affairs* 1974, 3-23.

2. *Institutional*

M. Ayral, "La présidence du Conseil", 1975 R.M.C. no. 184, 163-167.

R. Bieber, M. Palmer, "Power at the top—the EC Council in theory and practice", *The World Today* 1975, 310-318.

The authors analyse the decision-making process of the European Communities. Since 1966 the special relationship between the Council and the Commission which is supposed to form the basis for Community decisions has functioned badly. Instead, certain new organs, such as the Committee of Permanent Representatives and the Summit Conference have been created, and have strengthened the position of the member States.

H. Deheyn, "Das Gipfeltreffen von Dublin", 30 E.A. 1975, 247-251.

F. Dehousse, "Réflexions à propos des élections européennes de demain", 1975, R.M.C. no. 182, 49-57.

U. Everling, "Die E.G. nach der zweiten Pariser Konferenz. Zu den Ergebnissen der Konferenz der Regierungschefs vom Dezember 1974", 30 E.A. 1975, 59-69.

A description of the development of the Communities between the two Paris Summits of 1972 and 1974. In 1972 the plan was formed to progress toward political union; but various circumstances have hindered this development. In analysing the final communiqué of the 1974 conference, the author concludes that this conference also has not been able to find a solution to the Community crisis.

G. Pridham, "Transnational partygroups in the European Parliament", 13 J. Comm. Mark. Studies 1975, 266-279.

The forming of political parties within the European Parliament is generally regarded as a central feature of the future development of a European federal parliament. This article poses two important questions in this context:

1. What political value these parties can have in a parliament whose function is still primarily advisory?
2. How far can these parties be compared with national political parties?

3. *Court of Justice*

A. Barav, "Considérations sur la spécificité du recours en carence en droit communautaire", 11 R.T.D.E. 1973, 53-71.

P. Gilsdorf, "Die Haftung der Gemeinschaft aus normativen Handeln auf dem Hintergrund der Rechtsprechung der Europäischen Gerichtshof", 10 EuR 1975, 73-113.

P. E. Goose, "Neuere Entwicklungen im Verfahrensrecht des Gerichtshofs", 10 EuR. 1975, 230-243.

H. Johannes, "Zum Kaffee Hag Urtel des Gerichtshofs der Europäischen Gemeinschaften", G.R.U.R. Int. 1975, 111-117.

J. Mertens de Wilmaars, "Procedurele aspecten van het prejudicieel beroep", 23 S.E.W. 1975, 78-98.

G. Püttner, "Der Schutz wohlerworbener Rechte im Gemeinschaftsrecht". 10 EuR. 1975, 218-229.

The author investigates the case-law of the Court of Justice with regard to the protection of acquired rights, and in particular in the case of unlawful administrative acts.

H. G. Schermers, "The law as it stands on the appeal for damages (Article 215(2) EEC)", L.I.E.I. 1975/1, 113-141.

Court of Justice Case no. 17/74, *Transocean Marine Paint v. Commission,* 23-10-74, with note by J. Temple Lang, 11 C.D.E. 1975, 280-292.

Court of Justice Case no. 41/74, *van Duyn v. Home Office,* 4-12-74; and Case no. 67/74 *Bonsignore v. Oberstadtdirektor Köln,* 26-2-75, with note by C. Tomuschat, 11 C.D.E. 1975, 292-310.

Court of Justice Case no. 2/74, *Reyners v. Belgian State,* 26-6-74, with comment by G. Nicolaysen, 10 EuR. 1975, 129-134.

Court of Justice, Case no. 192/73, *Van Zuylen Frères v. Hag A.G.*, with comment by D. C. Maday, 10 EuR. 1975, 134-142.

5. *Relationship between Community Law and National Law*

A. Barav, "Le commissaire du gouvernement près le Conseil d'Etat français et l'avocat général près la Cour de Justice des Communautés européennes", 26 Rev.int.dr.comp., 1974, 809-827.

P. Dagtoglou, "Der englische Richter und das Gemeinschaftsrecht: Ein Ruckblick auf die ersten zwei Jahre britischer Mitgliedschaft (1973 und 1974), 10 EuR. 1975, 247-266.

This article contains in particular a discussion of the approach to Article 177 by the British courts.

I. Davidson, "Sovereignty in the E.E.C.: The case of France", no. 259 *The Round Table* 1975, 235-243.

G. Fanico, "Adaptation and conflict between Italian law and Community law", 15 Rev.Dir.Eur. 1975, 15-35.

R. Riegel, "Zum Verhältnis zwischen gemeinschaftsrechtlicher und innerstaatlicher Gerichtsbarkeit", 28 N.J.W. 1975, 1049-1057.

An investigation of the relationship between the Community judges and the national judges with particular reference to the action for damages, the interpretation of Regulation 17, Article 9(3), and the preliminary rulings procedure. Particularly interesting is that part of the article devoted to the question of direct effects, especially with regard to directives and decisions addressed to member States. The author is of the opinion that even those provisions in these acts which do not produce direct effects should, after the expiration of an eventual time limit, be enforced by the national courts, so that conflicting national law may not be applied.

D. Sugarman, "Britain and the European Economic Community", 10 *Texas International Law Journal* 1975, no. 2, 279-320.

J. Taylor, "British membership of the European Communities: The question of parliamentary sovereignty", 10 *Government and Opposition* 1975, 278-293.

Franz Zehetner, "Zum Vorlagerecht nationaler Gerichte an den Gerichtshof der Europäischen Gemeinschaften (Article 177 Abs. 2 EWG-Vertrag)", 10 EuR. 1975, 113-128.

This article considers the question as to when a lower court has the right to refer a question of Community Law to the Court of Justice. The author discusses this problem from the standpoint of the principle of the unity of Community Law, and on this basis seeks a solution to the questions *e.g.* as to what is a "national court or tribunal", when an appeal against a decision to refer is possible, and as to whether the lower courts are bound by the interpretation of Community Law made by a higher court.

6. *Accession*

R. J. Harrison, "La renégociation anglaise et le Référendum du 5 juin", 1975, R.M.C. no. 185, 195-202.

J. J. Holst, "Norway's EEC referendum: Lessons and implications", 31 *The World Today*, 1975, 114-120.

J. Pinder, "Renegotiation: Britain's costly lesson?", 51 *International Affairs*, 1975, 153-166.

G. Smith, "The referendum and political change", 10 *Government and Opposition*, 1975, 294-305.

E. Wright, "The British referendum: The constitutional significance", 56 *The Parliamentarian* 1975, 151-159.

7. *Association*

G. Cheysson, "Europe and the Third World after Lomé", 31 *The World Today*, 1975, 232-240.

H. B. Krohn, "Das Abkommen von Lomé zwischen der Europäischen Gemeinschaft und den AKP-Staaten. Eine neue Phase der EG-Entwicklungshilfepolitik", 30 E.A. 1975, 177-189.

H. B. Krohn, "La Convention de Lomé entre la Communauté européenne et les pays ACP: Une étape importante dans les relations entre la Communauté et les pays en voie de développement", 1975 R.M.C. no. 183, 101-108.

N. Mousisis, "L'évolution économique de la Grèce depuis son association à la C.E.E.", 1975 R.M.C. no. 168, 258-268.

C. EUROPEAN ECONOMIC COMMUNITY

3. *Agriculture*

M. Broders, "La crise du marché de la viande bovine, origines et perspectives d'avenir", 1975 R.M.C. no. 185, 203-220.

A thorough analysis with a great deal of statistical material of the present crisis of the beef market in the European Communities, with suggestions as to solutions to this crisis.

Ian Smith, "Sugar markets in disarray", 9 J.W.T.L. 1975, 41-63.

4. *Free movement of persons; establishment and services*

Ch. Gavalda, "La libération de l'établissement et des prestations de services bancaires dans la CEE", 10 R.T.D.E. 1974, 695-708.

This article commences with a sketch of the situation regarding freedom of establishment and to provide services in the banking sector, and proceeds to a discussion, particularly with regard to France, of the effects of the Council directive of June 28, 1973, regarding these freedoms with respect to non-salaried activities in banks and other financial institutions. In spite of its limited scope of application, this directive may have a greater influence on the European banking sector than is admitted by some sceptics.

K. Winkel, "Der Ausbau der Freizügigkeit des Marktburgers durch die Rechtsprechung des Europäischen Gerichtshofs", 28 N.J.W. 1975, 1057-1061.

7. *Competition*

L. Focsaneanu, "La jurisprudence de la Cour de Justice des Communautés européennes en matière de concurrence (art. 85 et 86 du Traité de Rome), 1975 R.M.C. no. 184, 158-163; no. 185, 221-234; no. 186, 270-284.

T. Jones, "Droit antitrust américain et droit européen de la concurrence: Étude comparative", 1975 R.M.C. no. 181, 20-33.

H. G. Koppensteiner, "International enterprises under the antitrust law of the European Economic Community", 9 J.W.T.L., 1975, 287-318.

D. Thompson, "The competition policy of the European Community", 9 J.W.T.L. 1975, 63-79.

W. Vaughn, "Transnational policy program networks in the European Community: the example of European competition policy", 11 J. Comm. Mark. Studies, 1972/73, 36-60.

8. *Taxation*

H. Simonet, "Tax harmonisation and the Economic and Monetary Union", *Intertax* 1975-2, 40-46.

10. *Economic and monetary policy*

30 *Aussenwirtschaft* 1975, Heft I.

This edition is almost entirely devoted to the theme "The fight against inflation and European integration". After an introduction by R. Barre, P. van Bempt and C. Sommaruga discuss the problem of inflation in the context of the European Community and EFTA. Finally, two extreme cases, Italy and Germany, are compared by G. Pannoicini and M. Lahnstein respectively.

C. W. M. van Ballegooijen, "De rekeneenheden van de Europese Gemeenschappen", 23 S.E.W. 1975, 99-113.

Also published in 22 *Netherlands International Law Review* 1975, 51-69, under the title: "The Units of Account in Eurobonds".

R. Helkmann, "Probleme einer solidarischen Wirtschafts- und Währungspolitik der EG. Die Suche nach einem Koordinierungsinstrument", 30 E.A. 1975, 69-75.

E. S. Kirschen, "The American external seigniorage: Origin, cost to Europe and possible defenses", 5 *European Economic Review,* 1974, 355-378.

"External seigniorage" is the advantage enjoyed by a country which can impose the use of its currency on other, apparently independent, countries. This has been the case with the U.S. since 1960. Thus the EC countries were obliged to accept short-term interest on their 20 bill. dollar reserves, whereas in fact it amounts to long-term loans to the U.S. The loss of interest for the period 1970-72 amounts to almost 10 bill. dollars. The only remedy is the creation of a Community currency.

R. W. Russell, "L'engrenage collégial style and the crisis syndrome: Lessons from monetary policy in the European Community", 13 J. Comm. Mark. Studies 1975, 61-87.

D. Strasser, "Exécution des budgets des Communautés européennes (première partie), Les pouvoirs de la Commission et leurs limites", 1975 R.M.C. no. 185, 235-242.

An analysis of the executive power of the Commission with regard to the general EC budget, the "operational" ECSC budget (for intervention purposes), the European Development Fund and the resources of the Community. Finally, there is a discussion of the limits to this power imposed by the Council, the member States and the *ad hoc* committees.

P. VerLoren van Themaat, "Wirtschaftspolitische und rechtspolitische Aspekte einer Währungsunion mit unbefristeter Uebergangszeit", 10 EuR. 1975, 20-44.

The first part of this article discusses the notion of an EMu and of the necessity for its realisation. The second part investigates certain consequences in terms of legal policy, such as the distinction between the concepts of *Dauerordnung* and *Prozess-lenkung*, and the usefulness of such concepts in the realisation of the EMU; and also discusses the repartition of competences between the Community institutions and the member States. Finally, there is an investigation of the available legal instruments.

M. Zuleeg, "Die Währungspolitik im Lichte der Rechtsprechung des Europäischen Gerichtshof", 10 EuR. 1975, 196-218.

11. *Regional Policy*

P. Romus, "La création du Fonds européen de développement régional: Début de la politique régionale européenne?", 1975 R.M.C. no. 184, 149-153.

L. van Depoele, "Het Europees Fonds voor regionale ontwikkeling", 23 S.E.W. 1975, 387-395.

12. *Energy*

J. Carrié, "Les incidents de la crise énergétique sur l'économie de l'Europe et les Etats-Unis", 40 *Politique Etrangère* 1975, 85-99.

C. A. Ehrhardt, "Europa und Energiepolitik auf Chefebene", 26 *Aussenpolitik* 1975, 3-17.

V. Emmerich, " "Wettbewerbsordnung" für den europäischen Energiemarkt?", 21 *Recht der Internationalen Wirtschaft*/A.W.D. 1975, 8-14.

H. Simonet, "Energy and the future of Europe", 53 *Foreign Affairs* 1975, 450-464.

13. *Commercial policy*

R. Bieber, "Ansätze für ein europäisches Seehandelsrecht", 21 *Recht der Internationalen Wirtschaft* 1975, 73-78.

Certain initiatives on the part of the European Parliament and a recent decision of the Court of Justice (Case no. 167/73) have brought the notion of a common law regarding sea trade back into discussion. Certain activities in the framework of UNCTAD, and certain legislative initiatives in this respect in the Netherlands and

France call for a common Community stance. The author investigates the possibility of the French and Dutch initiatives preparing the way for similar Community initiatives.

F. F. Gundersen, "Die staatliche Handelsmonopole und die EWG", 139 Z.H.R. 1975, 1-19.
A thorough analysis of Article 37 EEC with reference to practice. Particularly interesting are the Nordic examples, which are considered also in the context of the treaties concluded by Norway with the European Communities.

16. *Company law—Bankruptcy law*

"Le statut des sociétés anonymes européennes", 18 *Les Annales du Marché Commun* 1975, no. 3, 18-23.

M. Lutter, "Die Entwicklung des Gesellschaftsrechts in Europa", 10 EuR. 1975, 44-73.
The first part of this article is devoted to a thorough discussion of the technique of harmonisation in the area of company law. With reference to examples, such as the right of co-management, the author shows that the objectives of the harmonisation go far beyond the protection of participants and third parties such as is foreseen in Article 54(3)g EEC. The second part analyses the specific problems which have arisen with regard to the directives regarding the capital, merger and structure of companies. The article is supplemented by a lengthy bibliography.

S. Suckow, "The European prospectus", 23 A.J.C.L. 1975, 50-68.
Discussion of the proposal for a directive, submitted by the Commission in September 1972, regarding the creation of a standard type of company prospectus for the member States.

17. *Recognition of Judgments*

L. S. Bartlett, "Full faith and credit comes to the Common Market: An analysis of the provisions of the Convention on jurisdiction and enforcement of judgments in civil and commercial matters", 24 I.C.L.Q. 1975, 44-60.

R. Geimer, "Einige Zweifelfragen zur Abgrenzung nach dem EWG Uebereinkommen vom 27.9.68", 21 *Recht der Internationalen Wirtschaft*/AWD 1975, 81-87.
This article discusses certain problems which arise from the point of view of German law with regard to the Convention of 1968 regarding the jurisdiction and enforcement of judgments in civil and commercial matters.

P. Jénard, "La Convention concernant la compétence judiciaire et l'exécution des décisions en matière civile et commerciale: Lignes directices", 11 R.T.D.E. 1975, 14-23.

11 R.T.D.E. 1975.
Almost the whole of this issue is devoted to articles on the subject of the Convention of 27.9.68 on jurisdiction and enforcement of judgments in civil and commercial matters. Articles by P. Jenard, M. Weser, P. Bellet and W. M. Hanschild derive from reports made at a colloquium organised in Brussels on the subject of the treaties which have been concluded between the EEC member States within the framework of Article 220 EEC.

R. A. Schütze, "Die Berücksichtigung der Rechtshängigkeit eines ausländischen Verfahrens nach dem EWG-Uebereinkommen über die gerichtliche Zuständigkeit und die Vollstreckung gerichtlicher Entscheidungen", 21 *Recht der Internationalen Wirtschaft/* AWD, 1975, 78-80.

18. *Industrial property*

Court of Justice, Case no. 15/74, and 16/74 *Centrafarm,* with note by B. Baardman, 23 S.E.W. 1975, 191-212.

H. Johannes, "Zum 'Kaffee Hag' Urteil des Gerichtshofes der Europäischen Gemeinschaften", G.R.U.R. Int. 1975, 111-118.

F. A. Mann, "Industrial property and the E.E.C. Treaty", 24 I.C.L.Q., 31-43.

E. Pakuscher, "Nichtigkeits- und Vorletzungsprozess im deutschen und europäischen Patentrecht", 21 *Recht der Internationalen Wirtschaft* 1975, 305-316.

The author, president of the *Bundespatentgericht,* considers that a European patents court must be created in order to provide a centralised and uniform legal protection of patents. This court should then be empowered to deal with nullity and violation actions. The German patent law should in the meantime be changed so that there is a single procedure for both nullity and violation actions.

I. Schwartz, "Zur Politik der Europäischen Kommission im Hinblick auf eine Europa-Marke", G.R.U.R. Int. 1975, 71-73.

B. Schwab, "Der freie Verkehr von Markenwaren im Lichte der Rechtsprechung des Gerichtshofes der Europäischen Gemeinschaften", G.R.U.R. Int. 1975, 73-78.

The author deals in particular with the HAG judgment. He does not agree with those writers who consider that this judgment, and also the Centrafarm judgment, are applicable also to trademarks which do not have a common origin. The Court of Justice is not able to go further than these two judgments, and it should also be borne in mind that the HAG judgment concerned a very exceptional state of affairs.

19. *External relations*

M. R. Behnam, "Development and structure of the generalized system of preferences", 9 J.W.T.L. 1975, 442-458.

J. A. Sieco, "The Atlantic alliance and the Arab challenge: The European perspective", 137 *World Affairs* 1975, 303-326.

L. Hurwitz, "The EEC in the United Nations. The voting behaviour of eight countries, 1948-1973", 13 J. Comm. Mark. Studies 1975, 224-243.

J. Klein, "L'Europe et les relations transatlantiques à l'heure de la négociation", 40 *Politique Etrangère* 1975, 59-85.

G. Marenco, "Bases juridiques communautaires de l'aide alimentaire aux pays en voie de développement", 10 C.D.E. 1975, 623-649.

E. Noël, "The external relations of the EEC and its internal problems", 10 Government and Opposition 1975, 159-166.

G. Pleuger, "Die Beziehungen zwischen der Europäischen Gemeinschaft und Kanada. Eine "special relationship"?", 30 E.A. 1975, 269-276.

20. *Environment policy*

B. J. Douwes, "Water als object van milieubeleid in de Europese Gemeenschappen", 23 S.E.W. 1975, 308-331.

VI. *COUNCIL OF EUROPE*

A. *General*

H. Winnik, "Chronique du Conseil de l'Europe", 17 *Les Problèmes de l'Europe* 1974, no. 66, 65-70.

B. *Human Rights*

R. Goy, "La ratification par la France de la Convention européenne des droits de l'homme", 22 *Netherlands International Law Review* 1975, 31-51.

Y. Coussirat-Coustère, "La réserve française à l'article 15 de la Convention européenne des droits de l'homme", 102 Journ.dr.intern. 1975, 269-293.

BOOK REVIEWS

Grands arrêts de la Cour de Justice des Communautés Européennes, Tome 1, J. Boulouis and R-M. Chevalier, Dalloz, 1974, 453 pp.

Droit Institutionnel des Communautés Européennes, J. Rideau, R-M. Chevallier, J-M. Rainaud, L. Balmond and A. Bailleux, Librairie Générale de Droit et de Jurisprudence, Paris, 1974, 541 pp.

The work by Boulouis and Chevallier contains passages from important judgments of the Court of Justice concerning institutional law, general characteristics of Community law, and judicial control. The second part, which will appear later, will deal with the substantive law of the Communities. Both parts appear in the series, well known in France, of *"grands arrêts".*

The relevant parts of the judgments are systematically classified. The most recent judgment cited (Case no. 8/73) dates from the beginning of 1973. Preceding the actual text of the judgment, references to many commentaries are given, not all of which, fortunately, are in French. A personal commentary, which is in part a digest of the annual chronicle made by Boulouis for the *Annuaire français de droit international,* places the judgment in question in the context of the development of Community Law. These commentaries contain references not only to other judgments of the Court of Justice, but also to important national case-law.

This collection of judgments invites comparison with that of Brinkhorst and Schermers, *Judicial Remedies in the European Communities,* but the French work covers a wider area and cites the judgments less fully. Both works have their individual merits, and the publication of the judgments of the Court of Justice in a well-known series of national case-law has the further advantage that in this way a wider public will be reached.

Consultation of the judgments is facilitated by the provision of a number of useful indexes which refer to a system of numbers. A small improvement could have been effected by further mentioning, next to the subject matter at the top of each page, the number of the judgment under discussion. This would further facilitate the looking-up of judgments. Altogether, however, a very worthwhile publication.

The work of Rideau, Chevallier, Rainaud, Balmond and Bailleux must, unfortunately, be less enthusiastically welcomed. This collection of texts concerning the sources of law, the institutions and the relationship between Community and national law has, to put it bluntly, been sloppily put together.

Preceded by an introductory note, which contains no more than a summary of the cited text, treaty articles, Community legislation and fragments from articles and publications follow each other in a rather arbitrary succession. An adequate explanation of the purpose of the work is not given. Proper indexes are also lacking, and the work thus becomes almost unapproachable, all the more so because the table of contents, due to a printing error, has in fact been numbered!

The collection also contains many errors and inaccuracies. To give just a few examples: the Summit Conference of Paris took place in October, 1972, not November (see page 107, and compare p. 29); the Resolution of the Council and the Representatives of Governments of the member States regarding the realisation by stages of the EMU, does not date from February 9, 1971, but from March 22, 1971 (see page 35); the chapter on the Court of Justice opens with the heading *"Contrôle des Organes Communautaires",* (see page 262) whereas what is clearly meant here is *"institutions".* The distinction between organs and institutions is of paramount importance *inter alia* for the initiation of the Article 175 EEC procedure. Further, the procedure regarding the management committees of the classical kind, such as that laid down in the first agricultural regulations (compare page 160), is falsely represented. According to the authors, the Commission may adopt the required

13 C.M.L. Rev. 1976, 143-144

measures, so long as the opinion of the management committee is favourable (see page 132). Clearly, the authors have confused this procedure with the so-called "procedure of a regulatory nature" which was adopted in subsequent regulations; but a text dealing with this procedure is not included.

Finally, the references to many cited documents are not given (see *e.g.* pages 35, 54, 123, 218). This is very irritating, since many texts are not quoted in full. The book does contain a bibliography of some 250 titles, but there are references to only twenty non-French publications.

K. Mortelmans,
Europa Instituut,
Leyden.

COMMON MARKET LAW REVIEW

AIMS

The Common Market Law Review is designed to function as a medium for the understanding and implementation of Community Law within the nine Member States, and for the dissemination of legal thinking on Community Law matters. It thus aims to meet the needs of both the academic and the practitioner.
For practical reasons, English is used as the language of communication.

EDITORIAL POLICY

The editors will consider for publication manuscripts by contributors from any country. Articles will be subjected to a review procedure. The author should ensure that the significance of his work will be apparent also to readers outside his specific expertise. Special terms and abbreviations should be clearly defined in the text or notes. Accepted manuscripts will be edited, if necessary, to improve the general effectiveness of communication.
If editing should be extensive, with a consequent danger of altering the meaning, the manuscript will be returned to the author for approval before type is set.

SUBMISSION OF MANUSCRIPTS

Manuscripts should be submitted, together with a covering letter, to one of the Editors. At the time the manuscript is submitted, written assurance must be given that the article has not been published, submitted or accepted elsewhere. The author will be notified of acceptance, rejection or need for revision within eight to twelve weeks.
Authors are requested to submit two copies of their manuscript, typed and double-spaced, together with a summary of the contents.
Manuscripts may range from 3,000 to 10,000 words.
The title of an article should start with a word useful in indexing and information retrieval. Short titles are invited for use as running heads.
The author should identify himself in print, with a short statement as to his current affiliation.
All references and notes should be numbered in a single sequence in the order in which they are cited in the text, and should be typed, single-spaced, on a separate sheet.

OFFPRINTS

The author will receive one free copy of the issue concerned and twenty-five offprints of his article. He may also order any quantity of additional offprints, with a minimum of 100 copies, at forty cents (Dfl. 0.40) per page per copy. This order must be submitted through the Executive Editor at the time of delivery of the corrected galley-proofs for print.

GPSR Compliance

The European Union's (EU) General Product Safety Regulation (GPSR) is a set of rules that requires consumer products to be safe and our obligations to ensure this.

If you have any concerns about our products, you can contact us on ProductSafety@springernature.com

In case Publisher is established outside the EU, the EU authorized representative is:

Springer Nature Customer Service Center GmbH
Europaplatz 3
69115 Heidelberg, Germany

Batch number: 10830943

Printed by Printforce, the Netherlands

EDITORIAL ADDRESS
Common Market Law Review
Europa Instituut, Hugo de Grootstraat 27,
Leyden, The Netherlands

Orders for subscriptions, advertisements and back issues should be sent either direct to the general distributor:

Academic Book Services Holland, P.O. Box 66, Groningen, The Netherlands
phone: (0)50-162329 telex: 53443

or to
Fred B. Rothman & Company, 57 Leuning Street, South Hackensack, New Jersey, N.J. 17606, U.S.A.
Hammicks - Sweet & Maxwell, 50 West Street, Farnham, Surrey, U.K.
Office International de Librairie, 30 Avenue Marnix, 1050-Bruxelles, Belgique.

Annual subscription price for Volume 13 (1976): Dfl. 125.00/ $ 52.00; single issue: Dfl. 32.00/ $ 13.25.

Originally published by A. W. Sijthhoff International Publishing Company in 1976

COMMON MARKET LAW REVIEW

Volume 13
1976

SPRINGER-SCIENCE+BUSINESS MEDIA, B.V

Published in Cooperation with the British Institute of International and Comparative Law and the Europa Instituut of the University of Leyden

Editorial Address

Common Market Law Review
Europa Instituut, Hugo de Grootstraat 27,
Leyden, The Netherlands

This Review may be cited as *13 C.M.L. Rev. 1976*

ISBN 978-94-015-2075-1 ISBN 978-94-015-3283-9 (eBook)
DOI 10.1007/978-94-015-3283-9

Originally published by A. W. Sijthhoff International Publishing Company in 1976

INDEX VOLUME XIII

I. SUBJECTS

II. CASE LAW

A. COURT OF JUSTICE OF THE EUROPEAN COMMUNITIES

B. NATIONAL COURTS OF THE MEMBER STATES

III. ARTICLES AND SHORTER ARTICLES

IV. LIST OF AUTHORS

Names of authors who have contributed to Volume XIII

V. LIST OF BOOKS REVIEWED

TABLE OF CONTENTS

EDITORIAL COMMENTS

How credible is Community Law?

The fact that for several years Italy disregarded the judgment of the Court of Justice given against it in December 1968 for imposing an export tax on art treasures, and that judgment against it had to be given again in July 1972, was serious.

The fact that the Council has not up to now followed the opinion of the Court of Justice on the "understanding on a local cost standard" [1] is more serious.

The fact that the four larger Member States (France, Germany, Italy and the United Kingdom) took part in negotiations together with the USA and Japan on an informal agreement to limit export credits which, shortly after the opinion of the Court of Justice was delivered, were concluded by a "consensus" which was acted upon by each of the participants "independently"—and that the Council has not up to now been in a position to assume a Community stance on this "consensus"; all this is even more serious. In fact, the gravity of the situation cannot be overestimated.

It must be admitted that any discipline imposed on export credits affects solidly-based economic, financial and political interests of the Member States. The temptation to retain a free hand is therefore great. The following argument in particular militates in favour of doing so: in the field of exports, not only are the Member States of the Community competing, but all exporting countries. It therefore appears illogical for the Community to impose restrictions on its Member States while other States enjoy complete freedom of action. In addition, national rules and practices in the field of export credits are diverse and complex. Evasions and breaches of agreements cannot therefore be excluded; in fact they are even probable. The mistrust felt by all the parties concerned is correspondingly marked.

Account must be taken of these facts in any attempt to regulate export credits. The Community has not been particularly successful in doing so in the past. Although small successes have been achieved in peripheral areas, there has been a complete failure to deal with the main issue, viz. the periods for which credit is granted and rates of interest. The decisive factor here was the objection referred to above that a world-wide

1. See Professor Maas's comment on the Court's Advisory Opinion at p. 379 *et seq.* of this issue.

problem could not be solved by obligations assumed solely by the "Six" or "Nine" of the Community.

No matter how obvious this objection appears at first sight, there are good reasons for refuting it. However, the question whether the approach chosen was correct at the time need not be answered here. It is certain that the negotiations with the Community's main competitor Japan and the USA, have recently yielded some results, however meagre. Nevertheless, the Council does not feel able to approve these results on behalf of the Community. This is because one Member State, France, refuses to consent to the adoption of a Community stance at the present stage of the efforts to ereate an economic and monetary union.

The conduct of the Member States which are parties to the "consensus", but above all France's refusal and the resultant inactivity on the part of the Council. have created a situation which from the political viewpoint is extremely serious.

Nothing less than the credibility of the Community legal system is at stake. Following the opinion delivered by the Court of Justice on the local costs issue, it is indisputable that the Community has *exclusive* competence in the field of export credits. Plans for economic and monetary union do not alter this fact in the least. The conduct of the Member States which are parties to the "consensus" therefore contravenes Community Law, in particular a leading decision by the Court of Justice. The Commission has drawn the logical consequence of this in deciding to proceed against those Member States on the basis of Article 169.[2]

The Council's attitude is, however, more serious than this contravention alone indicates. The effect of the "Luxembourg agreements" is glaringly obvious: although a qualified majority exists in favour of adopting a Community stance, the Council remains inactive because one Member State dissents.

Is it any wonder that astute observers of the Brussels scene see a connection between the Council's attitude to the "consensus" and the absence of the Community in Puerto Rico?[3]

2. See *Agence Europe* of July 22 and 23, 1976, at p. 4.
3. See *Agence Europe* of June 24, 1976, at p. 4.

DIRECT ELECTIONS TO THE EUROPEAN PARLIAMENT
(With special reference to the United Kingdom)

by

Michael Stewart*

The first two paragraphs of Article 138 of the Treaty of Rome required that the Assembly of the European Community should consist of 198 delegates (this being the number fixed after the accession of the U.K., Ireland and Denmark) "designated by the respective Parliaments from among their members in accordance with the procedure laid down by each Member State." One result of this was that all members carried a "dual mandate", *i.e.* were members both of their national Parliaments and of the European Assembly. A further result was that there was no election date for the Assembly as a whole; each national group in it was liable to be replaced, or re-elected, in accordance with the elections for the national Parliaments of each State. Under this arrangement the Assembly—or "European Parliament" as it has come, by courtesy, to be called—is a collection of national groups, each linked with its national Parliament, rather than a body of members responsible to the citizens of the Community as a whole: it is a *Parlement des Patries* rather than a *Parlement Européen*. This point, however, should not be over-stressed, since the strength of party organisation in the Assembly prevails over nationality. A British labour delegate, for example, finds himself, during the sittings of the Assembly, much more conscious of his membership of the Socialist Group than of a British national delegation. The national delegations are, in fact, concerned with travel arrangements and administrative tasks rather than with political work.

This arrangement was avowedly temporary. Paragraph 3 of Article 138 requires the Assembly to draw up proposals "for elections by direct universal suffrage in accordance with a uniform procedure in all Member States." It then requires the Council by a unanimous vote to "lay down the appropriate provisions which it shall recommend to Member States for adoption in accordance with their respective constitutional requirements." Notice how cautious this procedure is, full of respect for the

* Member of the United Kingdom Parliament and of the European Parliament; former Secretary of State for Foreign Affairs.

13 C.M.L. Rev. 1976, 283-299

wishes of each Member State. It was evidently not intended that there should be any imprudent rush into direct elections. Nor indeed was there a rush; despite the growing impatience of the Assembly, ministers did nothing. Recently, when it was suggested that Britain was "dragging her feet" over direct elections, Mr Callaghan was able to reply that it had taken the original six members of the Community seventeen years to get within reach of a workable plan.

It was during this quiescent period that several people, in various countries, considered whether direct elections could not be reached in accordance with the Treaty by some process more swift than that envisaged in paragraph 3 of Article 138. It will be convenient here to mention the present writer's plan which, though devised for Britain, could be applied, with minor adaptations, to any nation in the Community.

Under this plan Britain would have been divided into thirty-six European electoral areas. On polling day for a British Parliamentary election, the voter would see, on his ballot paper, first the names of the candidates for the ordinary British constituency in which he lived; then, the names of the candidates for the European electoral area of which his constituency formed part. When the newly elected Parliament assembled at Westminster it would contain the 635 members from the ordinary constituencies *plus* the thirty-six chosen by the European electoral areas: it would then, in order to conform to Article 138, pass a resolution declaring these thirty-six to be its choice for the European Assembly. They would be fully members both of the European Assembly and of the Westminster Parliament; but the chief difficulty of the "dual mandate" as we know it today would be resolved. Everyone would have known, from the start of the election, that these persons had a job to do in Europe; they would not be subject—as present members of the Assembly sometimes are—to the reproach that they were always bustling off to Europe and neglecting their constituents. Every British citizen would have a Member of Parliament from his own constituency to represent him at Westminster, and in addition a representative in the European Assembly.

The fact that these persons would be full members of the Westminster Parliament would ensure that the political parties would take a keen interest in their election. This, together with the fact that they would be elected at the same time as the Westminster Parliament, would ensure a reasonably high poll. The problem—always mentioned in any discussion of direct elections—of how to forge a link between members of the European Assembly and their national Parliaments, would be automatically solved. Moreover, they would be persons fully in touch with the political life of the country. It could well happen that a member, after serving for some years as one of these European-British members, might decide to stand for an ordinary British constituency; equally, there could be shifts in the opposite direction. An able young man or woman, nursing the legitimate ambition of becoming a Minister one day, would not need to fear—as in present circumstances, or under the plan now being considered by European governments, he well may—that by "going to Europe" he cuts himself off from a political career at home. These are considerable advantages; but it remains true that, under this or similar plans, there is still no one election date for the European Assembly—it would remain a *Parlement des Patries.*

It must, however, be realised that this plan may have been overtaken by events. The period of quiescence about direct elections ended, possibly in consequence of the enlargement of the Community. The Assembly approved the workmanlike proposals drafted by Mr. Patijn [1] for direct elections as envisaged in paragraph three of Article 138. Ministers at first gave their general approval, and we seemed to be on a straight course for direct elections to a *Parlement Européen* by 1978 or shortly thereafter. The subsequent disagreement at the meeting of the European Council in April, 1976 has created an uncertainty which will not be resolved until the further meeting in July of this year. If, by ill chance, agreement is not reached, and the prospect of direct elections on the Patijn basis fades, there may be a case for reviving my proposals. These proposals—with national variations of detail—could be adopted by any of the Nine at any time, without agreement from the rest: for they provide that the members of the European Parliament will be members of their national parliaments, chosen by those parliaments, and this is in conformity with the Treaty as it now stands. They have also the advantages of simplicity for the voter, the prospect of a good poll, a clear link between European and national parliaments, and reasonable career prospects for those who become members of the European Parliament. Nonetheless, they will still only produce a *Parlement des Patries*; they are only a second-best in comparison with the Patijn model, and in what follows I am assuming that agreement is in fact reached on something like the Patijn plan.

At Rome, the European Council decided, at least provisionally, that in the spring of 1978 seven of the nine countries would hold direct elections, and that Britain and Denmark would follow their example with as little delay as possible. Britain, indeed, did not rule out the possibility of reaching the 1978 target; but the Westminster Parliament will be heavily

1. See for the Resolution of the Assembly and the text of the draft Convention, O. J. 1975, C 32/15.

engaged, this year and next, with legislation concerning the devolution of powers to Scotland and Wales, and it was wise to give the warning that we may not be able to hold the necessary consultations and pass the legislation required for the holding of European direct elections within the time limit set.

Some voices in Britain have argued that since Article 138 requires the unanimous consent of the Council, Britain is not bound by treaty to hold direct elections. This argument can hardly stand examination. The requirement of unanimous consent certainly means that all the Nine must take great pains to meet each other's wishes in framing an agreed plan; but it would have been dishonest of Britain to have joined the Community with the intention of obstructing any and every plan for direct elections. Our clear obligation is to work in good faith for an agreed plan and to carry it out as soon as possible; and it was to this that the British Government committed itself at the Rome meeting.

Let us now examine the nature of the plans now under consideration and the problems which arise when they are put into effect.

First, as to the number and allocation of seats. When the European Council met in April of this year there were several proposals before it. The plan approved by the present European Parliament, following Mr. Patijn's draft, provided for 355 seats of which 269 (76%) would go to the four largest countries (Germany, Britain, Italy and france). A French proposal suggested a total of 284, with 237 (83%) for the large four; an Irish proposal was for 384 seats with 281 (73%) for the large four. Since these large four contain 88% of the population of the Nine, it is clear that all these plans accept that it is right to show some favour to smaller countries, though the French plan did this to a much less extent than the others. There is an argument of general principle in support of this special help to small countries; without such help they would fear that they would always be swamped by their larger partners. This principle is recognised in the composition of the United States Senate which gives equal representation to all States; and there are many comparable examples. In addition to this general principle there is a practical reason, concerned with the working of a parliament, for recognising the special claims of the smallest. If, for example, as under the French proposal, Luxembourg had only three members, there would be many committees and activities of the Parliament in which no Luxembourg member could take part, since no one can be in several places at once; and the group of three would be sadly overworked, trying to achieve between them expertise in the wide range of topics with which the Parliament deals. A larger group can organise and specialise, so if one group is five times as large as another it will exercise more than five times as much influence.

It should also be remembered that the Community will probably grow: in time Greece, Spain, Portugal and Turkey might adhere to it. This is an argument against adopting any figure substantially larger than that proposed by Mr. Patijn. It is also an argument—though this takes us beyond the subject of this article—for considering very carefully where the Parliament is to be sited, and what buildings will serve its purpose.

In April, however, France suddenly proposed that the directly-elected Parliament should, like the present Assembly, have only 198 seats, and that the national allocations should likewise be unchanged. This was surprising since—in contrast with the previous French view— it would show exceptional favour to the smaller countries. It was unattractive to Britain, partly because thirty-six seats for her would mean very large constituencies for each member to try to represent, and partly because the delicate task of allocating seats to England, Scotland, Wales and Northern Ireland would be made more difficult if the total were only thirty-six instead of sixty-seven. It is difficult to believe that agreement could be reached on the basis of this new French proposal; and we must hope that something resembling the Patijn proposals will survive the arguments which must now be conducted.

Once the numbers permitted for each State have been settled, there arises the problem of how each State's number is to be allocated among the regions and communities—and, in some States, one could use the word "nations" within that State. This is a problem for each State to settle by itself, but they must carry out the task with care lest local resentments should sour the whole project of European direct elections. In the United Kingdom the problem has been given a particular piquancy by the argument now proceeding about the future relations, and distribution of powers, between England, Scotland, Wales and Northern Ireland within the United Kingdom. In the present House of Commons, with 635 members, Scotland has seventy-one seats (11.2%), whereas Scottish voters make up 9.2% of the United Kingdom electorate; Wales has thirty-six seats (5.7%) while its voters form 5.0% of the United Kingdom electorate. This is in accordance with the principle mentioned above, of giving special advantage to minorities within a group, though the degree of advantage is not particularly large. Northern Ireland, on the other hand, whose voters are 2.6% of the United Kingdom electorate, has only twelve seats, making 1.9% of the total of 635. This apparent disfavour has been justified by the fact that—before the present troubles began—Northern Ireland managed her domestic affairs by herself, through her own Parliament, and only a small proportion of the laws passed at Westminster apply to Northern Ireland. This consideration, however, could not justify an underrepresentation of Northern Ireland when the

United Kingdom seats in the European Parliament were being shared out. On the other hand, it would not be acceptable to give Scotland and Wales a lesser proportion of the United Kingdom seats than the proportion they now hold of seats in the House of Commons. Probably the solution nearest to justice is to give England fifty-three, Scotland eight, Wales four and Northern Ireland two, out of a total of sixty-seven.

But immediately Scottish voices are raised. Is Scotland, with a population fifteen times that of Luxembourg, to have only eight seats to Luxembourg's six? Then answering voices come from Bavaria, from Brittany and who knows where else? Wisely, neither Mr. Patijn's proposals, nor any others likely to be considered by Ministers, touch on this problem; they regard it, correctly, as a problem for each State to solve by itself. Scotland and Wales must base their claims, not on comparison with Luxembourg or Denmark, but with the other parts of the United Kingdom. There are some Scots, though by no means a majority, who want their country to be independent, in the same relation to England as are Canada and Australia to the United Kingdom. If this were ever to happen, the whole allocation of seats would have to be considered afresh—if, indeed, such a Scotland wished to be, and were accepted as, a member of the Community. But the contingency is too unlikely to justify further speculation.

Second, as to the timing of the election. The plan put forward by the European Parliament asserts, as an ideal solution, that there should be a single polling-day for the election, throughout the Nine countries; but makes a concession whereby countries could have different polling-days, provided the whole process did not occupy more than three consecutive days. It might be wise to extend this concession and provide that the polling must take place within a prescribed week, leaving each country to pick the date within that week which it preferred. National habits about voting vary; in several countries there is a strong tradition and preference for voting on Sunday, whereas in Britain—and particularly in Scotland and Wales—this would be unwelcome. The objection is sometimes raised that if polling is spread over a week, the results of the election in some countries would be known while the campaign was still proceeding in others, and this might affect the way in which people cast their votes.

In what direction would the effect be? If the earlier results showed a swing to the Left, would this put heart into the Left and discourage the Right in the remaining countries? Or would it induce hesitant middle-of-the-road voters to move to the Right in order to moderate the result? These are interesting speculations, but one is tempted to ask, does it matter? In Britain we conduct the poll for the Westminster Parliament all in one day, but there is an obvious reason for this. A marked swing can result in a change of Government and there would be great inconvenience in a week of suspense with guesses as to the nature of the next Government varying from day to day as successive results were published. The same considerations apply to the election of national parliaments in each of the Nine countries, but they do not apply to the European Parliament. There is at present nothing we can call a European Government whose tenure of office depends on the composition of the European Parliament. In time, there may be such a European Government; but when we have progressed as far in European unity as that it will probably be easier to get agreement on a single day. Meanwhile, those who desire European unity should remember a word of caution which is valid both in this field and in many others—never press for uniformity just for uniformity's sake; if you do, you may well arouse national resentments and delay real progress. There is, moreover, a fairly simple solution to the problem posed in this paragraph. Have the vote, if you wish, on different days of the same week in different countries, but agree that there shall be no counting of votes or declaration of results until the last polling-day is over, after which counting and declaration can proceed simultaneously in all countries.

The mention which has just been made of uniformity brings us to a *third* problem. The plan drafted by Mr. Patijn and approved by the European Parliament provides that at the first direct elections of the European Parliament, timed for 1978, the election shall, in each country, be conducted according to that country's electoral laws. The Parliament is then charged with the task of drafting a plan for a uniform electoral system by 1980 at the latest; and a unanimous vote of the Council will then recommend to Member States the steps they should take to put such a plan into effect. This division of the task into two stages—direct elections first, and uniform electoral system later—is certainly wise. The argument about a uniform system is likely to be difficult and prolonged, and there would be no sense in delaying direct elections until agreement had been reached.

The first direct election, then, will be conducted under nine different electoral systems. How serious are the differences? In one respect all the systems are basically democratic; they all give the vote to all adult citizens. There are some national differences in the age at which a citizen is deemed to be adult for this purpose, the lowest being eighteen years, which prevails in the United Kingdom and several other countries. There would probably be no great difficulty in getting European agreement on the age of eighteen. It would be more difficult to fix a higher age: it would not be a good send-off for direct elections if in some countries younger citizens, considered fit to vote for their national parliaments, were denied a European vote. There are no doubt national differences in the arrangements to safeguard the voting rights of the sick, the elderly, those whose business requires them to travel, and those who have the misfortune to be in prison on polling day. There could be no objection in principle to harmonising these arrangements, but it would be a tiresome job in practice. Possibly, for these details, we could entrust the European Court of Justice—or some other body created for the purpose—with the task of reviewing the practice in each country, and with the power of giving or withholding a certificate approving these practices as democratic and in accordance with the spirit of the Community, even if they were not exactly identical. A more difficult problem arises with the laws which define bribery, corruption, and improper electoral practices and which control the amount of money which candidates may spend in an election campaign. We might begin by using the device of certification, as described above, and progress later to full uniformity. There is also the question of defining the persons qualified to stand for election. Mr. Patijn's draft contains a list of the kinds of person who would not be qualified, and the presumption is that anyone entitled to vote and not disqualified by this list, would be entitled to stand. Those disqualified are members of Governments and members or servants of Community institutions. So far as this list goes, however, there is nothing to prevent, for example, a British judge or civil servant from standing for election to the European Parliament. These people are not able to stand for election to the Parliament at Westminster, and it may be taken for granted that any legislation passed at Westminster to provide for the first direct European elections will likewise debar them; and the same may well be true of other countries in the Community. When the plan for a uniform electoral system is being drafted, some agreement will have to be reached on this. It is clear that an opponent of European unity could go on listing problems of this sort in an endeavour to prove that a uniform system was impossible. This is the case for establishing complete uniformity only in essentials, and and using the method of certification for details, possibly moving from certification to complete uniformity as and when agreement was reached.

There is one problem, a legacy of history, which is peculiar to the United Kingdom. Members of the House of Lords cannot become members of the House of Commons, nor vote at elections for the Commons, unless they first renounce their peerages. It has, however, been established that they can be members of the European Assembly in its present form. Presumably, British legislation will provide that they shall be able to vote, and stand for election, at the European direct elections.

Far more important, however, than any of these matters, is the prime and major difference between the electoral systems of the Nine, as they now stand. In the United Kingdom the whole country is divided into constituencies each of which returns one member to Westminster. In each constituency the candidate who gets most votes becomes the Member, whether he has an overall majority or not. In all other Community countries this "first past the post" principle is modified, to greater or lesser degree, by some approach to proportional representation—whether by list system, second ballot, alternative vote, multi-member constituencies *etc.* This is not the place to set out the whole argument for and against "first past the post" but it is fair to say that the British do not cling to it merely because they have always had it. There are serious considerations in its favour. It discourages an excessive proliferation of small parties and it usually, though not invariably, results in stable government. "Our system" said one observer "gives the effective power of government, for four or five years, to that party which the electorate dislikes least"—and this is no small advantage. A Conservative or Labour candidate in Britain fights his campaign in the knowledge that his party may win, and will then be expected to do what they have promised; they cannot push responsibility for failure onto obstinate partners in a coalition. Yet it is not only Britain that has a strong attachment to her own system. Will the Germans wish to abandon the system which was worked out so carefully after the War, and appears to serve them well? Electoral systems reflect, in fact, both the historical experience and the general attitude to government of peoples; and these are not uniform throughout the Community.

It is, of course, possible that each country could keep its own system for electing its national parliament, and adopt a compromise plan, whatever it might be, for the European elections. What is feared in Britain, and possibly in other countries as well, is that such a plan, once adopted, would prove infectious. Perhaps this fear is irrational; perhaps it could be allayed by a declaration, when the uniform plan comes to be adopted, to the effect that nothing in it should prejudice the right of each Member State to conduct elections to its own legislatures, national or local, as it saw fit.

Finally, on this question of electoral systems, we should notice one result of a uniform rule about who could vote and who could stand. It would presumably mean that, for example, an Englishman could stand in a French constituency, a Frenchman in Germany, and so on throughout the Community. Opponents of direct elections may try to frighten their fellow-countrymen with the horror of being represented by a "foreigner" but it will be a foolish argument. A native of one country, standing in another, would have no chance of election unless he knew that country well, had mastered its language and had earned the liking and trust of its people; and, if he possessed these qualifications, why should he not be elected?

A *fourth* problem arises when we consider the joint effect of two provisions of the Patijn plan: firstly, that the Parliament shall be elected for a fixed term of five years, with no provision for a dissolution before that term is complete, and, secondly, that the members shall vote on an "individual and personal basis" accepting "neither instructions nor any binding mandate." Most European constitutions provide a fixed term for the legislature, but this is usually qualified by provision for an earlier dissolution in exceptional circumstances and in conformity with a prescribed procedure. The British Constitution is furthest from the concept of a fixed term; there is a maximum of five years, but the Prime Minister can secure a dissolution at any time within that limit and, in fact, the average life-time of a British parliament is about four years.[2] The new European Parliament, on the other hand, would be like the United States Congress: its lifetime would be assured, whatever Ministers, or the electorate, might think about it. This is surely a wise provision. The Parliament has few powers at present, and will have an uphill struggle to increase them; if it lived under the shadow of possible dissolution at any time, it would make little progress.

The fixed term, however, means that European elections will not (except by occasional coincidence) occur at the same time as elections of national parliaments; and during the period between national and European elections, opinions may change. Thus there could arise, for example, a situation in which the majority of the House of Commons was Labour, but most of the British representatives in the European Parliament were Conservative. The reverse could, of course, occur, and similar situations could, and frequently would, arise in any of the nine countries. So long as the powers of the European Parliament remain small, there would be no great difficulty; but as those powers grow, there will be growing tension between the "national" and "European" members in each country, and the limitation on national sovereignty which membership of the European Community involves would be high-lighted. There seems to be no answer to this problem except to say that nations, and individuals, must learn to live with it. Indeed, the tension

2. Mr Macmillan, writing about the 1959 Election, argues that if a Prime Minister asks the Queen to dissolve Parliament before the five years are complete, the Queen may, constitutionally, refuse: that this is one of the very few matters on which the personal wish and judgment of the Sovereign can prevail. It is doubtful, however, whether this view would now command widespread agreement.

would have the useful result that political parties would fight the election with all the more vigour. The prohibition of instructions and mandates will certainly prevent a majority in a national Parliament requiring its European representatives to do its bidding.

This prohibition, and the insistence on "individual and personal" voting, might, if strictly interpreted, seem to forbid the formation of political parties in the new European Parliament. This could hardly have been Mr. Patijn's intention, nor the intention of the present European Parliament, when they endorsed his plan. The intention, presumably, was to protect members from being ordered about from outside, either by national Governments, or by their party organisations at home, and not to prevent them from forming their own groups and accepting group discipline. In fact, political parties in each country are already considering how to fight the forthcoming elections, and what their platforms or programmes for the election shall be. If representatives are elected as members of a political party, with the party organisation helping them, the electorate will expect them to act together and accept group decisions. It can, of course, be argued, that acceptance of the decisions of a group of which one is oneself a member—decisions which one has oneself helped to frame—are not "instructions" or "binding mandates", particularly since the only final sanction the group has against a rebellious member is to exclude him from the group; he remains a member of the Parliament. If at the next election, voters and party organisers refuse to help him, they are within their rights. Nonetheless, before final approval is given to rules governing the election to the European Parliament, it might be as well to revise the proposed wording, and put the legitimacy of parties in the Parliament beyond doubt.

Fifthly, the Patijn plan offers a simple solution to the oftdiscussed problem of the dual mandate. Membership of the European Parliament is to be compatible with membership of a national Parliament. The dual mandate will no longer be obligatory, as it is at present, but anyone will be able to take it on if he wishes, and—more importantly— if the voters are willing to elect him to both offices. How many members will wish to do this? The dual mandate is already felt to be onerous, except perhaps by British Lords and those others who do not have constituencies at home. If, at a meeting of a Committee of the European Parliament today, it is proposed, for some pressing reason, to hold extra meetings over and above the usual number, diaries are produced and heads are scratched while members wonder how they can fit it in. If we are thinking of the new European Parliament as a body vigorously asserting its rights and claiming more powers, we must realise that it cannot do so in this atmosphere; its members must be increasingly freed from other duties. It is probable, therefore, that the dual mandate, though not prohibited, will become increasingly rare.

So far, this article has examined legal and constitutional problems arising from the plans now being considered for direct elections. We must now look at certain practical problems which will face governments, candidates and voters, whatever the exact details of the plan finally adopted. *First*, there is the cost of the election. As to the public cost—that is to say the amount spent on printing ballot papers, employing polling officers, counting clerks *etc.*—this will be met at the first election by each national Government in accordance with its own laws and customs. At later elections, conducted according to a uniform method, the cost will presumably be met from Community funds. No great difficulties arise here. There remains, however, what may be called the candidates' costs *i.e.* the amounts spent by candidates, and the parties and individuals who support them, on fighting the campaign. In the United Kingdom the raising and use of funds for this purpose is regarded as a private matter. The law intervenes to prescribe a maximum expenditure for each candidate, to require the presentation of an accurate account of expenditure, and to prohibit the use of money in ways which amount to, or verge on, bribery. In Germany, and some other countries, there is help from public funds towards candidates' costs; and although, in time past, the British would have been startled at such a proposal, it is already in the arena of public discussion. It was natural that Mr Callaghan, as Treasurer of the Labour Party and accutely aware of its financial difficulties, should seize quickly on this point. The Conservative Party, likewise, is not free from financial anxiety, and for smaller groups and independent candidates the cost of a European election campaign might be prohibitive. An election in which no candidate could run a proper campaign would be a dispiriting exercise, and it would be unfair to the electors to ask them to take a decision when the issues had not been properly put before them. This last consideration needs to be emphasized, because it is the answer to those who contend that partisan campaigning ought not to be a charge on public funds. It is highly probable, therefore, that British legislation providing for direct elections to the European Parliament will contain provision for public help to candidates. This is one more field in which those who dislike the whole exercise will be able to marshal a host of detailed difficulties; but, though these will make the legislation lengthy and complicated, they will not make it impossible. The outward conservatism of the British Constitution—monarchy, Lords, *etc.*—often conceals from foreigners the startling capacity of the British to change their ideas and make innovations at short notice, once they see the necessity. The referendum was a striking illustration of this capacity.

Second, there is the task of delineating, on the map of the United Kingdom, the constituencies, which it may be convenient to call European Electoral Areas. The simplest way would be to have sixty-seven such areas, each returning one member, a bundle of existing Parliamentary constituencies. We already have machinery for dealing with the minutiae of boundaries, for deciding whether this street or the next should be the boundary of a constituency. A body charged with planning the European electoral areas would not be burdened with such details but would simply have to arrange constituencies in groups. On average, and subject to what has been said earlier about Scotland, Wales and Northern Ireland, each European area would contain nine or ten constituencies and an electorate of about 600,000. An alternative proposal is for larger European electoral areas, each returning several members. Wales and Northern Ireland, in this plan, could each be treated as one area. In Scotland the regions already created for local government, could each be one area; likewise, the English regions which are already officially in existence for socio-economic purposes. Such multi-member areas would facilitate—though they would not compel—the adoption of some form of proportional representation; but whether this is a recommendation or not depends on one's views about that electoral method.

Whichever plan is used, one result will follow. On the whole, though by no means invariably, European electoral areas are likely to be, in electioneering language, more "marginal" than the constituencies for the Westminster Parliament. We all know that the largest single factor, though not the only factor, influencing a citizen's vote, is his income and social class. In many Westminster constituencies there is such a preponderance of one class-and-income group that the seat can be regarded as "safe", for one party or another. The much larger European electoral areas will not be so homogeneous, and although some will be nearly "safe", in general candidates and party workers will find that they must be on their toes and not take success—or failure—for granted. This may well have the useful result of increasing the zest of the campaign and the size of the vote.

Even if single-member areas are established, it will not be easy for candidates to put themselves over to the electors, and the difficulty would be greatly increased if the decision was for multi-member areas with electorates of perhaps three million. Party organisations would have to think afresh and devise appropriate methods of campaigning; they might perhaps study how United States Congressmen and, still more, Senators, fight their vast constituencies. We should have to consider the part which local radio and regional television could play in making candidates and arguments known. Possibly the voters themselves, realising that they could not all hope to see the candidates, would pay more attention than they usually do in British parliamentary elections to the election addresses of candidates, and the other printed matter issued by parties.

These considerations lead to a *third* point, the selection of candidates by the parties. For party work in Britain, the vital organ is the constituency party. It is through these groups of zealots in each constituency that Parliamentary elections are fought and the ideas of the party put to the electorate. Constituency parties are already accustomed to acting together, in city, county, or regional organisations, to fight local elections. It should not be difficult for these parties, in each European election area, to act jointly for the selection of candidates and the running of the campaign. The greater "marginality" of the European campaign will enjoin extra care in the choice of candidates. A candidate who can win rousing cheers by preaching to the converted will not be enough; he—or she—must be the kind of person who can argue and persuade and influence those whose political allegiance is not fixed.

It is not, of course, necessary for candidates to be the choice of political parties, though those who seek to stand as independents in these large areas, will have a hard job on their hands. In the United Kingdom anyone who is not legally disqualified may stand if at least ten electors in the constituency will sign a paper nominating him; as a check on frivolous candidatures, he must put down a deposit of £150, which he loses if he gets less than one-eighth of the votes cast. There is no reason why the principles underlying these rules should not be applied to European elections, though the number of nominators required might reasonably be increased to fifty, or even one hundred.

The selection of candidates presents no problems that cannot be solved by commonsense and effective organisation. But once the machinery of selection is determined we come up against a *fourth* question— how many people, and of what kind and calibre, will there be who want to take on this European task? At this point we embark on a voyage into the unknown. For reasons given earlier, it is unlikely that more than a few would want, or receive, the dual mandate, and be national, as well as European, parliamentarians. Who will want to be a member solely of a parliament which has such small powers? If the powers remain small, it could be argued that the job will not be full-time; but if the member is not only to do the parliamentary work, but to keep in touch with his constituents, his party at home, and his national parliament, there will not be much time left in which to make himself a satisfying career in some other field.

Herr Brandt's decision to stand at the first direct elections is encouraging, and will enhance the Parliament's prestige; but it does not solve our problem. Ex-Chief Ministers are few in number. It may prove that most of those who stand will be people who have already become senior members of their national Parliaments and have reached an age where they will be content with a part-time occupation. Some elder statesmen are often useful members of any assembly; but 355 of them in one Parliament is not an attractive picture. Healthy assemblies contain a wide age-range, so that experience and impetuosity can work together.

Another possible supply of candidates could be found among those who have tried, unsuccessfully, to get into their national parliaments. This is not as depressing as it sounds: there is a large element of luck in democratic politics, and in all parties there are people who have not been chosen for winnable seats but would make better members than some who have been successful. There remains a further, and interesting possibility, that this new kind of election will attract a new kind of candidate. At most national elections, particularly in Britain, most candidates find it difficult to interest the electors in international affairs, unless, indeed, the international situation is critical or threatening. At direct elections for the European Parliament we shall have, for the first time, a contest in which the candidates are actually expected to talk about European matters, and even to range beyond Europe. There are, in all parties, those who firmly hold the party faith but whose chief interest has always been in world affairs; for these, direct elections offer an unprecedented opportunity.

If we succeed in holding elections at which there are able candidates and a high poll, we shall be faced with a *fifth* problem, of which some mention has already been made. Such candidates, once in the Parliament, are bound to press for greater powers than those of the present Assembly; and it will not be unreasonable for some of them, at least, to hope for increased scope for their talents. A full examination of this subject would go well beyond the limits of this article, but some suggestions can be made. Already, the Assembly has been granted a slight increase in its powers over the Budget, and if the British suggestion for an effective Public Accounts Committee is adopted, this will mark a further advance. The proposals made some time ago in the Vedel Report [3] for granting the Parliament powers of co-decision with the Council in certain fields, need to be examined afresh. The Tindemans Report [4] speaks of giving the parliament a right of "initiative". In a sense,

3. Bull. of the E.C. 1972, Suppl. 4.
4. Bull. of the E.C. 1976, Suppl. 1.

it has this already and one of its complaints is that it repeatedly puts forward ideas and proposals which get lost among the press of business in the Council and the Commission. What is needed—and this is suggested, though perhaps with insufficient emphasis, in the Tindemans Report—is the power to compel attention to its proposals. This might be achieved if the Parliament chose a group of its own members to go and argue with the Council and the Commission in the way that a small resolute group can argue and an Assembly of 355 cannot. In the language of seventeenth-century English politics, they would be "agitators"—persons whose job it was to get things done. The prospect of being entrusted with this task would provide members with that chance of using their talents which, in the Westminster Parliament, is provided to able back-benchers by the prospect of becoming a Minister.

There remains a *sixth* and last problem. How are members of the European Parliament to keep in touch with their national parliaments and with the political parties at home to which they belong? One of the reasons, in some countries, for hesitation about direct elections, has been the fear that a group of members of the European Parliament with the authority of direct election behind them, might become a rival to the group of members of the national parliament, of the same party, and that this might lead to strain and schism within the party. Some method of linking the European MPs, the national MPs, and the party, has to be found. As has already been argued, the dual mandate, though permissible, is not likely to be possible for most members; so this automatic link is not the answer. In Britain, of course, one could solve this problem on paper by putting the European Members of Parliament into the House of Lords where, like the Bishops, they would be ex-officio Peers, holding their places neither for life nor by inheritance, but during the period of their European office. This would not, however, bring them into contact with the real life of the Westminster Parliament and might embroil them in future arguments about the powers and position of the Lords in the British Constitution. Another solution is for national parliaments to establish committees of their own membership, and to co-opt the European Members to such committees.

Yet the real answer to this problem has to be supplied by the political parties. Even if the powers of the European Parliament increase, membership of it will not be as time-consuming as membership of a national parliament. Each European MP can properly be expected, by his party, to be active at home in party propaganda and research, to appear on platforms in his electoral area, together with the national Members of Parliament, and to explain to the electorate how the party's principles and beliefs are being promoted in Europe.

One aspect of the creation of a directly-elected European Parliament is institutional, the framing of the necessary laws and regulations. But men and women devote their lives and energies not to institutions for their own sake, but to what those institutions can do for human welfare. What kind of society best promotes human welfare is a question in dispute, and it is the function of parties to give expression to the differing views. The European Parliament will succeed insofar as the parties vigorously argue out the question "What kind of Europe do we want?". We see some signs of this already. If one sits down to re-read the Treaty of Rome as if one were reading it for the first time, one notices how deeply it was influenced by the market-economy philosophy as it flourished in the 1950's. Today, the emphasis is much more on deliberate planning; social justice and the "quality of life" have begun to rival free competition as the ideal of the Community. How this process will develop in the future we do not know, but it is this which the European Parliamentarians will have to determine.

April, 1976

Editors' Note: At the time of finally going to press, the European Council, meeting on July 12 and 13 in Brussels, had just reached a decision concerning the number and allocation of seats for the directly-elected European Parliament. The total number of seats will be 410, allocated between the Member States as follows: Italy, the United Kingdom, France and the Federal Republic, 81 seats each; 25 for the Netherlands, 24 for Belgium, 16 for Denmark, 15 for Ireland, and for Luxembourg, as before, 6 seats.

EXCHANGE RATE POLICY IN THE EUROPEAN COMMUNITIES *

by

C. J. Oort **

If ever we shall have a common European currency, I am sure it will carry the symbol of a serpent. For a new religion has invaded Europe: the cult of the snake. Its mystic origins are in the canyons of Luxemburg, its most faithful followers live across the Rhine and in the Rhine delta, but its most ardent prophets, recently turned heretics, were to be found in Gallia. A religous war is on: beware Brittania! A prime-minister of the Faith has recently relegated all heathens and heretics such as you to the status of second-rank citizens. When the true faith finally succeeds in subjugating these last remnants of heresy, the monster of Lock Ness has a strong case to serve as the model for our future money, for the European serpent is at least as elusive as your historical hoax! And if, in that distant future, we have not arrived at the cashless society, future Europeans will spin their coins, fully understanding the symbolism when they call their bets, according as the serpent comes up heads or tails.

Needless to say, I will speak to you today about the European "snake", the exchange rate arrangement among a number of countries, now reduced to Germany, the Benelux countries and Denmark, with Norway and Sweden as associated members. Just what is the "snake", what is the philosophy behind it and what are its prospects? Why is it considered important enough for Mr. Tindemans to make it the focus of the economic and financial paragraphs in his recent report to the Heads of State?

I propose to start off with a brief description of the "snake" mechanism, the purposes it was originally designed to serve, and its actual significance in today's very different monetary conditions in the world and in the European Community. I shall then move on to discuss the prospects and possibilities of monetary cooperation in the European Community as a whole such as I personally see them. I emphasize that I

* Text of an address delivered at the University of Edinburgh, Centre of European Governmental Studies, on May 11, 1976.

** Treasurer-General, Netherlands Ministry of Finance.

13 C.M.L. Rev. 1976, 301-314

speak entirely as a private person—or, if you prefer, as an ex-University professor—and not in my present capacity as a civil servant of the Dutch government. I value very highly the freedom of expression which in my country civil servants enjoy—a freedom which can be maintained only when others take it at its face value: as the expression of truly personal opinions, not necessarily related in any way to the official views of the government they serve.

1. *Origin and development of the "snake"*

The set of agreements, some of them of a formal and others of a quite informal nature that are usually referred to when we speak of the "snake" arrangement, really consists of four different elements. First, an agreement on exchange rate relationships among the currencies of the participating countries, the so-called "central cross-rates". For example, the agreed central rate relation between the DM and the Dfl. is now DM 1 equals Dfl. 1.04. Second, the obligation of participating countries to maintain the exchange rates of all "snake" currencies within the agreed band of 2¼% around the central rates by intervention in their domestic foreign exchange markets. For example, the Netherlands Bank would have to sell Deutschmarks for guilders when the value of the Deutschmark on the Amsterdam market threatens to rise above Dfl. 1.07, and buy Deutschmarks when their value threatens to fall below Dfl. 1.02. Third, agreed lines of credit among participating countries and rules for the settlements of the debts involved. Fourth the obligation of participating countries to coordinate their economic policies to the extent necessary for a smooth functioning of the arrangements.

I want to focus my address on the first element, the procedure and criteria for the determination and possible adjustment of the "central cross-rates". But first I would like to make a few general comments on the origin and the development of the "snake" as such.

We know that the "snake", such as it operates today, serves a very different purpose from the one it was originally intended to serve as recommended in the famous Werner report, submitted in October 1970. The idea of the Werner report was to approach European Economic and Monetary Union by stages. The coordination of economic policy would be gradually intensified and *pari passu* the margins of exchange rate fluctuation between the European currencies would be reduced, with a complete locking of the rates as the final goal, which was to be reached by 1980. We know now, wiser and sadder after many years of frustration with regard to Economic and Monetary Union, that at any rate the timing of the Werner report was not realistic. Personally, I have very little hope that we can achieve full monetary union even by 1990, for I believe that we shall need the escape hatch of exchange rate adjustment for a very long time to come. For all sorts of well-known political and economic reasons, our economies will not be locked on a parallel course until we are very much further advanced along the road of economic policy coordination, economic and social solidarity, and real interdependence in economic development and the growth of incomes. A premature locking of exchange rates, before our economies are definitely on a parallel course, would only end in disaster.

Does that mean we have to wait until the next century before we can do anything at all to improve the confused monetary relations in the Community? Of course it does not. I agree with those who have suggested that we might develop the idea of a European monetary unit, based on a basket of European currencies, to serve much the same purpose as the Eurodollar.[1] I have supported that approach on another occasion and I do not want to go into that now.[2] But there is yet another and perhaps more important area of monetary cooperation that we can and certainly should develop, namely the exchange rate system of the Community. We have to re-think the concepts which have been shaped for too long by the Wernerian vision of gradually narrower margins around gradually freezing parities. With that, I come back to the Werner report itself. It is only fair to recall that at that time we were living in a world dominated by dollar parities which were defended by intervention almost exclusively in dollars. In theory and in fact, the exchange rate relationships between European currencies and hence their margins of fluctuation were determined entirely by the relationship of each currency to the dollar. The Werner report proposed that the European countries would superimpose on this dollar-dominated system a set of rules which would enable them to contain the margins of fluctuation between their currencies within gradually narrower limits. The system was known as the "snake in the tunnel", the tunnel being the outer limits of fluctuation imposed by the relationship of each currency to the US dollar.

The monetary scene changed drastically and the "snake" became a very different reptile when the US dollar started to float in 1971. Among Eurocrats, the new situation was dubbed *"le serpent dans l'espace"*—the snake that escaped the constraints of the dollar tunnel. Instead of a device to gradually narrow the margins of fluctuation among the

1. See for example, G. Magnifico and J. Williamson, "European Monetary Integration" (London, Federal Trust for Education and Research, 1972).

2. Address at the University of Utrecht, May 1975, published in 13 C.M.L.Rev., 179-187.

European currencies, the "snake" became the instrument of a common float of the European currencies *vis-à-vis* the US dollar: a far more important function than was originally envisaged.

I shall not bore you with a description of the life and habits of the "snake", such as they developed in the past years, nor with the recurrent dramas of the entry and exit of individual countries, including succesful and unseccessful applications for associate membership. Rather, I would like to devote a few comments to what is certainly its most visible if not its most important aspect, namely the procedure for adjusting the "central cross-rates": the agreed exchange rate relationships between the currencies of the participating countries.

2. *Adjustment of central rates in the snake*

In the good old days, when countries still had official parities expressed either in gold or dollars, the central cross-rates were mechanically determined by these parities: when one dollar equals DM 2.67 and also equals Dfl. 2.78, the central cross-rate of the Deutschmark and the Dutch florin necessarily works out at DM1 against Dfl. 1.04. Decisions about the parity of a currency were at the same time decisions about the central cross-rates in the European context. Now that the European currencies no longer have a gold or dollar parity, central rates have become a matter for decision exclusively among the countries participating in the "snake" arrangement. A decision to adjust the central cross-rates implies a change in relative rates within the group, but does not necessarily affect the position of the "snake" as a whole *vis-à-vis* the rest of the world, in particular the US dollar. For example, a revaluation of the Deutschmark with respect to the other "snake" currencies might leave the Deutschmark-dollar rate largely unaffected, because the Deutschmark is clearly the dominating currency of the group. The value of the dollar on the exchange markets of the group would therefore be largely determined by the Deutschmark. Under these conditions, a revaluation of the Deutschmark would in reality work out as a depreciation of the other currencies of the group. The convential terminology of revaluation and devaluation has become very confusing indeed: in the example I just gave a *re*valuation of the Deutschmark works out in fact as a *de*valuation of the other snake currencies.

Why is this of interest to us? Because it has brought out into the open something that was far less obvious in the old days, namely that decisions about exchange rates are necessarily multilateral: one country's revaluation is per definition its partners' devaluation. Of course, this was always true in principle, but in the old days when one country changed its parity *vis-à-vis* the dollar and hence *vis-à-vis* the rest of the world, the decision could still be presented as affecting primarily the national interest of the country concerned and only in a more distant sense the international community. In the far smaller club of the "snake" countries this is no longer true: the devaluation of one is quite literally the same as a revaluation of the small group of other countries.

If I may be permitted to digress for one minute in order to illustrate the importance of these procedures with reference to recent events: It has been amply reported in the press that in the period before France left the "snake" on March 15, 1976, proposals were discussed to adjust the central rate of the French franc *vis-à-vis* the Deutschmark. During these discussions it appeared that both parties were willing to adjust the relationship between their currencies and they even agreed on the size of the adjustment, but neither wanted to present it as a change in the central rate of the national currency only. The idea of a revaluation was unpopular in Germany on account of its expected negative effects on German exports, and devaluation was as vehemently rejected by France for political reasons. Apparently, neither country saw it as a realistic possibility to explain to their citizens that the two measures were identical. Old concepts never die; one can only hope that they will fade away.

Under the circumstances, the obvious compromise was to split the difference: Germany would revalue to some extent and France would do the rest by devaluing its currency. I am convinced that it never entered the minds of the politicians that the decision to present the rate adjustment in this way simply could not be taken by the two countries alone, because it depended on the other partners allowing it. If the Benelux countries and the Scandinavians would stay with the Deutschmark, the operation would effectively constitute and would necessarily be regarded as a *de*valuation of the French franc. If, on the other hand, the smaller countries would stay with the French franc, the operation would be considered a Deutschmark *re*valuation. In the event, the whole compromise fell through, but it was an interesting lesson in political as contrasted to economic logic. One thing it did prove: adjustment of central rates within a small group is necessarily a matter of multilateral decision and procedures will have to be devised to take account of that fact.

It also, incidentally, provided additional support for the thesis I have long defended: that for precisely the kinds of political reasons that played a role in these recent events, declared parities or central cross-rates tend to be very sticky: they are seldom adjusted in time before an exchange crisis forces the authorities' hands. I may perhaps be permitted to quote from a paper which I had the great privilege and pleasure to present in 1974 before the joint meeting in Tokyo of the Per Jacobsson Foundation of the International Monetary Fund and the Japanese Federation of Bankers Associations.[3] I quote:

> "Why are countries reluctant to change their parities promptly? It is my conviction that this is basically due to the political asymmetry between positive action and non-action on parities. Governments are rarely criticized for not changing the par value, and when they are, it is easy to silence such criticism by appealing to the national interest that forbids open debate on such sensitive issues. A change of the par value, on the other hand, is a conscious, overt policy action that is unavoidably accompanied by all the trappings of a major public decision: comments in the press, complaints from groups that are injured, windfall profits and losses by "speculators" and traders, book gains or losses for the Central Bank or the Treasury, parliamentary debates, international repercussions, *etc.* Behind all this commotion are the very real facts that a parity change does hurt certain sectoral interests, particularly in the case of revaluation, and that a devaluation adds to cost-push inflation at home... Left to themselves, governments will continue to take delayed, discontinuous action on parities."...
>
> "My conclusion is that prompt adjustment of par values requires more than international consensus on the principle and active indoctrination of governments by the academic community. It requires a change in the political setting of the decision-making process. A radical way to achieve this would be to scrap the parity system altogether and accept a system of managed floating,"

That is what I wrote in 1974, and recent events have done nothing to change my opinion on these matters. In particular, and I quote from my paper again, I am still convinced that

> "the obligation to maintain exchange rates within the prescribed margins imposes a severe and often undesirable constraint on national monetary policy and, even more seriously, may lead countries to resort periodically, or even permanently, to direct exchange controls. I strongly believe that such direct exchange controls, however well-intended and however sincerely meant to affect only so-called disruptive capital flows, are in fact very harmful to the international financial system."

If my conclusion is correct that, at least for some time to come,

3. "Steps to International Monetary Order", The Per Jacobsson Foundation (Washington D.C., 1974).

managed floating under some international supervison may be prefeable to a system of stable but adjustable par values or central rates, what does this imply for the future of the "snake" and for European monetary cooperation in general?

3. *The future of European exchange rate arrangements*

The conventional wisdom among present "snake" members can be summarized in the following propositions. One: the "snake" arrangement is workable and credible only when adjustments of the central rates need not be large nor frequent. Two: as a consequence, the "snake" can be effective only among countries that are able and willing to submit to an effective coordination of their economic policies in the widest sense, and that are not too far apart in terms of wage and productivity developments. Three: the "snake" is an instrument of economic discipline and financial responsibility; there is no sense in "weakening" the arrangement in order to permit those countries to join which are now outside, *e.g.* by widening the margins or by allowing temporary floats outside the "snake".

I am very much afraid that the mythology of the "snake" and the doctrines associated with it are leading the European Community into a blind alley. It leads us to concentrate on the "snake", while monetary cooperation in the Community as a whole is suspended until a future time when present outsiders are in a position to join. It is my personal conviction that it may in fact be quite a while before all countries are on a sufficiently parallel economic course to permit present outsiders to join the "snake". If in the meantime we were to continue along present lines, I am afraid we shall witness a further slide towards a monetary division among Member States that grows deeper the longer the present situation lasts: "snake" members will strengthen their arrangement and widen the area of policy coordination, whereas the others may tend to fall back on nationally-oriented policies. The latter is the real danger of the present monetary vacuum in the Community: floating countries may start to abuse or may be accused of abusing their exchange rate freedom to the detriment of their partners. This might lead these partners to introduce restrictions on payments or even on trade with the obvious destructive consequences for the Community, both in economic *and* in political terms.

The present situation also carries the political implication of second-rate citizenship for the outsiders, a development which, even if it applies only to monetary matters, I strongly believe would be fatal for the Community. We must avoid that at all costs. We must create a framework for general monetary cooperation in the Community, including "snake" and "non-snake" members alike. But that surely does not imply that all arrangements must be identical for all groups of members. I can well imagine a Community in which some members will, at least for some time in the future, continue to exercise the option of floating their currency, while others accept a snake-type arrangement. What *is* essential, if we want to retain the monetary and hence also the economic cohesion of the Community, is that we have a general set of rules and mutual obligations with respect to our monetary behaviour, which we would *all* accept. Within that general set of rules, the "snake" would only be a special, tighter arrangement just as the Benelux "worm" was a special case within the European "snake".

I would propose, therefore, that we concentrate our attention in the Community on working out certain agreed "rules for floating". Such rules have been worked out in the framework of the IMF, but they have not been put into actual operation so far. There is every reason to do so in the European Community, which could serve as a pioneer and a testing ground for the world community. We could eventually even go a step further than the IMF both as to content and enforcement. In any case, it is very urgent that we devise effective rules for floating to govern the vulnerable relationships within the European Community.

4. *An Exchange Equalization Fund?*

Before going into the question of "rules for floating" I would like to briefly discuss another approach that has been suggested for dealing with the problem of exchange rate instability in the Community.[4] It has been proposed that the Community should set up an Exchange Equalization Fund, which would be charged with offsetting disruptive capital flows. Member countries would pool a part of their international monetary reserves and deposit certain amounts of their own currency in the Fund. The Fund would use these resources to intervene in the exchange markets, buying currencies of countries that are experiencing a temporary capital outflow and selling currencies of the countries to which the capital flow is directed. When the temporary disturbance is reversed, the Fund would reverse its original transactions.

The idea behind the Exchange Equalization Fund is that a country can generally cope on its own with temporary disturbances in its balance of payments to the extent that they are due to seasonal or even to cyclical

4. See, *e.g.*, "Economy Policy for the European Community", Sir Alec Cairncross *et. al.*, p. 43 *et seq.*

fluctuations in its foreign trade, but cannot do so with regard to large temporary capital flows. Since the early 'sixties, the international mobility of capital has become so large that a single country's reserves, including its international credit lines, may not be sufficient to permit it to offset large capital outflows by intervention in the foreign exchange market. If it does not want to take it on the exchange rate, by letting the rate depreciate temporarily, the country may be forced to impose restrictions on capital movements. The same holds, *mutatis mutandis,* for a country experiencing large capital inflows which it does not want to offset by buying up large amounts of foreign exchange. The proponents of the Fund argue that, if we want to avoid instability of the exchange rate as well as capital controls, we need the type of large temporary balance of payments assistance that would be provided for by a common Exchange Equalization Fund.

In commenting on this proposal, let me say first that I emphatically agree with the proposition that exchange controls are generally undesirable. Some are more harmful than others, but few can be so selective as to apply only to so-called disruptive capital flows, whatever they may be. I shall come back to this point in a minute. If I am right in this, it means that capital controls will almost always to some extent choke off legitimate capital movements. And even worse, they create an atmosphere in which the international business world is always uncertain as to whether restrictions will not be further tightened in the future. As I have said before, if anything is harmful to the process of economic integration, it is precisely these fears of exchange controls. They act as a serious disincentive to long-term ventures across national frontiers, whereas it is precisely such ventures that contribute to the convergence of economic development which in turn is the main prerequisite for economic and monetary union.

No quarrel at all, therefore, with the proposition that exchange controls should be avoided. But that does not lead me to support the idea of a European Exchange Equalization Fund. I am afraid it is *not* a very fruitful approach for several reasons. In the first place, it has emerged very clearly from the work of the so-called Committee of Twenty, set up in 1972 to prepare a comprehensive reform of the international monetary system, that it is impossible to formulate objective criteria which can identify disruptive capital flows in practice. Some verbal attempts have been made to define such criteria, *e.g.* by reference to the venerated Bretton Woods concept of fundamental disequilibrium, or to the more recent Franco-American invention, launched at Rambouillet, of "erratic" movements. The truth of the matter is that we simply do not have the operational tools to clearly and objectively identify a particular capital movement as "disruptive", speculative", "reversible" or whatever qualification one wishes to apply. Consequently, we would have to leave a large measure of discretionary judgement to the authorities of the Exchange Equalization Fund as to which capital flows they should offset by market intervention and which they should not. This would be asking a great deal in the way of relinquishing national autonomy in such an important area of economic policy. It is highly unlikely that countries would be willing to do so, in particular the so-called "strong" countries.

That brings me to the second objection against the idea of setting up a European Exchange Equalization Fund to deal with the problem of disruptive capital flows. The strong countries of the Community will inevitably consider the pooling of reserves as a more or less permanent and unconditional credit to the "weaker" members. They will therefore either reject the proposal outright—as in fact Germany and Holland have done—or they will demand an effective veto over the operations of the Fund which would severely curtail its effectiveness. In fact, any scheme that involves or is believed to involve unconditional credit for potentially long periods of time will *ipso facto* be highly suspicious in the eyes of the "strong" countries. They maintain—and I believe rightly so—that unconditional credit weakens the discipline that the balance of payments constraint imposes on individual countries and that credit should therefore be extended only on the basis of well-defined procedures such as those applied among "snake" countries. I would like to add as a footnote, but one I believe to be very important, that subjecting international credit to economic policy conditions may well be the only practical way of achieving at least some sort of effective coordination of economic policy in the European Community.

My final objection to the idea of a European Exchange Equalization Fund is that it separates two policy instruments that are very intimately related, namely, intervention in the foreign exchange markets and monetary policy. Countries influence international capital flows, particularly of short-term capital, primarily by their internal money market policies. By tightening the money market and hence driving up short-term interest rates, they attract foreign capital, and *vice versa*. Intervention in the exchange markets is generally used only as a second line of defense, which in any case can be succesful only when monetary policy does not frustrate it. Under those conditions, it would seem very inefficient, if not totally unworkable, to give all or part of the responsibility for intervention in the foreign exchange markets to a European Authority, while leaving the far more important say over monetary policy to the individual countries.

I have said too much already about the idea of a European Equalization Funds and the associated proposals for pooling international reserves of member countires. I now want to turn to what I consider a far more promising approach, namely, an initiative to apply certain rules for floating in the European context.

5. *Rules for floating*

Let me begin by recalling that the International Monetary Fund has agreed in principle on a set of rules for floating which involve positive as well as negative obligations of member countries, coupled with certain powers enabling the Fund to challenge the policies of member countries. The main elements of the scheme are the following, and I paraphrase the official language:

1. A country should smooth out fluctuations in the value of its exchange rate. It should not normally act aggressively, *i.e.* it should not depress the rate when it is falling or push up the rate when it is rising.
2. A country is allowed to act aggressively if in so doing it brings its exchange rate closer to a so-called "target zone of rates", which it has established with the concurrence of the Fund.
3. The Fund will consult with a member country and challenge its policies when its exchange rate has moved outside what the Fund considers a reasonable range, to an extent that the Fund considers likely to be harmful to the interests of members. But a member would not be asked to hold any particular rate against strong market pressure.

These are very ingenious rules indeed. They are a clever mixture of positive and negative commitments, supervised by the Fund that is given certain, albeit limited, powers in precisely those areas that are of greatest importance to the international community. The commitments are not excessively constraining on a floating country's freedom of action, for it retains the essential aspect of floating, namely that it is not forced to defend a parity value of its currency by positive action. Nor are the powers of the Fund more far-reaching than should be acceptable. So far, however, the rules have not been implemented by the IMF and I have some doutbs as to whether they will be in the near future, particularly with regard to the most important country with a floating currency, the United States. But I do believe that rules such as these could well be put into practice in the European framework.

A lot of work would still have to be done to make the IMF rules operational and suitable for application in the European Community. One thing we might want to investigate in particular are possibilities of putting more teeth into the commitments of member countries. It has been suggested, for example, that a country with a floating currency should in all cases be obliged to seek agreement on a target zone for its exchange rate; without such a target zone it would not be allowed to intervene in the foreign exchange market at all.[5] As a positive inducement, a country that does have a target zone and that intervenes to bring its exchange rate closer to the target might be eligible for the use of the credit mechanisms of the Community. Many other carrots and sticks with all sorts of procedural rules are conceivable and worth investigating. Many other questions will also have to be settled, such as the width of the target zone, the currencies in which a floating country may intervene, the rules for settlement of its intervention debts, *etc.* The aspect that intrigues me the most, however, is the procedure for setting and adjusting the target zones.

6. *Target zones for floating currencies*

One of the first points to be settled is how the target zone should be denominated: in some average value of "snake" currencies, in the European unit of account, in SDR's,[6] in dollars, or in terms of a trade-weighted average of rates, the so-called "effective rate"? It should be noted that whereas the first four are measured in absolute terms, the effective rate is necessarily expressed as an index number based on some reference period. My own preference would be for the effective rate, since it best represents a country's overall competitive position on the world market. If a country is able at all to state what its target zone is, it can do so only in terms of an effective exchange rate or something closely related to it (such as the SDR). Assuming that it is impossible in practice to prevent public knowledge of the target zones, the denomination in effective rates has the added advantage that it does not translate immediately into cross-rates for specific currencies. Hence, it does not as easily become a reference point for speculators, nor is it politically as difficult to change as rates in terms of specific currencies.

Assuming that a country is able and willing to state a target zone, what procedure should be followed (a) for gaining the approval of the European Community and (b) for adjusting it, when necessary. On the first point, it would be my feeling that the target zone as proposed by the country concerned should be accepted, unless a strong qualified majority of the other members, including the Commission, objects to it. The benefit of the doubt should, at least in the initial stages, be strongly in the

5. See J. Williamson, "The Future Exchange Rate Regime", *Quarterly Review of the Banca Nazionale del Lavorno,* June 1975, p. 127-143.

6. Special drawing rights of the International Monetary Fund.

proposing country's favour, but the Community should have a chance to object in case the target is manifestly unjustified by the underlying economic considerations, such as the international competitiveness of the country concerned.

In order to ensure that the targets continue to correspond to the changing economic reality, they should be periodically reviewed, say once every six months. In view of our experience that parities and central rates tend to be maintained until they are manifestly out of line and that adjustment then becomes a disturbing factor in the exchange markets—an experience that may well carry over to some extent to the more informal target zones—I would favour a procedure that establishes a *presumption* in favour of adjustment, with the possibility of blocking it by some qualified majority decision. The difficulty then is to find an appropriate objective indicator to trigger the adjustment, a problem that was extensively studied and discussed by the Committee of Twenty. Perhaps the most appropriate indicator would be some index of relative cost developments in the country concerned and in its major competitors, but I have come to despair of the possibility that we could ever agree on the appropriate indices. Under these conditions, we should perhaps return to the old idea of the crawling peg that used to be popular among academic economists but has very rarely been accepted by policy makers. Adjustment of the target zone would be a function of actual exchange rate behaviour in the period preceding the review. For example, the target zone would be adjusted downwards to the extend that the average of actual market rates in the period preceding the review had declined as compared to the average level in the period before the last review, provided the average is below the middle of the target zone. In other words, if actual market rates are declining from one period of reference to the next, the target zone is adjusted downwards as soon as market rates have for some time fallen below the middle of the target zone. The reverse would hold in case of a rise of market rates.

As I have said, the difference between this proposal and the automatic crawling peg is that the mechanism is only a presumption, that can be put aside by qualified majority decision. I believe that such a presumptive rule for the adjustment of target zones could provide a workable and an acceptable compromise between the need for some monetary rules of the game for the Community as a whole, including the floaters, and the need for sufficient flexibility to accommodate those countries that have decided to float their currency, presumably because they feel that their economic development will be different from that of their partners. Within these rules, the "snake" could continue to operate as it does today, providing a more tight system for those countries that are on a sufficiently parallel economic course to permit a more rigid exchange rate system between them. Time will show whether the Community will gravitate towards the "snake" system or to the looser arrangement of the target zones with presumptive rules for adjustment. Much will depend on our success in effectively coordinating our economic policies. But that is a different chapter of the story that began in 1959 with the first reductions in trade barriers and will, hopefully, end with full Economic and Monetary Union before this century is out.

THE LOME CONVENTION AND THE NEW INTERNATIONAL ECONOMIC ORDER

by

K. R. Simmonds*

1. *Introduction*

The Lomé Convention,[1] signed on February 28, 1975 in the capital of Togo between forty-six developing African, Caribbean and Pacific countries (the ACP States) [2] and the nine Member States of the European Community, has just, at the time of writing, come into effect, having received the necessary ratifications.[3] The Convention has generally been accorded a warm welcome in Europe and the words of M. Cheysson, the Commissioner with especial responsibility since 1973 for co-operation and development policy, community budgets and financial control, have been echoed by many subsequent commentators.

> "It is the first time that such a comprehensive approach to the problems of development has been agreed by industrialised countries with regard to such a large number of countries. It is unprecedented also because the whole of Black Africa has stood together. . . .

* Director of the British Institute of International and Comparative Law, London; Professor of International Law, University of London; President of the International Association of Legal Science.

1. Text in 12 C.M.L.Rev. 1975, 463-490. Hereafter referred to as "Convention".

2. The ACP States include (i) eighteen African and Malagasy States which were signatories to the Second Yaoundé Convention; (ii) twenty-two Commonwealth States—including (a) Mauritius, which had become associated with the Community under the Yaoundé Convention in January 1972; (b) in Africa—Kenya, Uganda, Tanzania (members of the East African Economic Community and signatories to the Arusha Agreement of 1969 with the Community), Botswana, The Gambia, Ghana, Lesotho, Malawi, Nigeria, Sierra Leone, Swaziland and Zambia, (c) in the Caribbean—Bahamas, Barbados, Grenada, Guyana, Jamaica, and Trinidad and Tobago, and (d) in the Pacific—Fiji, Tonga and Western Samoa; and (iii) a group of formerly non-associated and non-Commonwealth African countries—Ethiopia, Equatorial Guinea, Guinea, Guinea-Bissau, Liberia and the Sudan.

3. *Convention*, Art. 87. The ratification of all nine Member States of the Community and of two-thirds of the ACP signatories was required.

13 C.M.L. Rev. 1976, 315-334

.... we hope to have created a new pattern for the relationship between industrialised and developing countries."[4]

It is certain that the principal features and the major innovations of this ".... new style partnership between rich and poor countries"[5] will come in for very close scrutiny and criticism when the fourth UNCTAD Conference meets in Nairobi between May 5 and 28 next. The third UNCTAD Conference, held in Santiago de Chile in 1972, attempted to confine itself to a strictly narrow agenda, which was, in fact, largely disregarded. The provisional agenda adopted for UNCTAD IV[6] lists a total of 19 items, nine of which are substantive ones. Even a cursory glance at the list of substantive items, reproduced below, will indicate that both the style and the content of the Lomé Convention must inevitably figure largely in UNCTAD IV debates in these areas of discussion. As was the case during the final negotiations which preceded its signature, the Convention will equally inevitably be examined in the context of the latest assertions of new and fundamental State rights bearing on international trade and resource exploitation and against the ideological background of the UN General Assembly declarations on the *Establishment of a New International Economic Order*,[7] and on the *Charter of Economic Rights and Duties of States*.[8]

The substantive items listed for the provisional agenda of UNCTAD IV are as follows:

4. Claude Cheysson, "Europe and the Third World after Lomé", in 31 *The World Today* 1975, 232-239, at 235. *Cf.* John Pinder, "The Community's need for an active external economic policy", in 31 *The World Today* 1975, 368-375 at 375; and Gillian White, "The Lomé Convention—A Lawyer's View", in 1 E.L.J. 1976.

5. Carol Cosgrove-Twitchett, "From Association to Partnership", in *Europe and the World: The External Relations of the Common Market*, ed. Kenneth J. Twitchett (London: Europa, 1976) 121-150, at 121.

6. Report of the Trade and Development Board, October 28, 1975 (BR/75/39).

7. G.A. Resolution 3201-S VI (May 1, 1974): *cf.* Resolution 3202-S VI (1 May, 1974) on the accompanying "Programme of Action". Both Resolutions were adopted without vote but with a number of significant expressly stated reservations. The reservations (by the United States, Federal Republic of Germany, France, Japan and the United Kingdom) are reproduced in (1974) I.L.M. 744, 749, 753, 759 and 762.

8. G.A. Resolution 3281—XXIX (December 12, 1974), adopted by 120 votes to 6 (Belgium, Denmark, Federal Republic of Germany, Luxembourg, the United Kingdom, and the United States); Austria, Canada, France, Ireland, Israel, Italy, Japan, The Netherlands, Norway and Spain abstained. The Maldive Islands and South Africa were unrepresented. It will be observed that all nine Member States of the enlarged Community either voted against, or abstained from voting on, the Charter of Economic Rights and Duties of States. See in general: R.C.A. White, "A New International Economic Order", in 24 *International and Comparative Law Quarterly* 1975, 542-552.

8. Commodities
   - Action on commodities, including decisions on an integrated programme, in the light of the need for change in the world commodity economy.
9. Manufactures and semi-manufactures
   - Measures, including the elaboration of and decision on a comprehensive strategy to expand and diversify the export trade of the developing countries in manufactures and semi-manufactures, with a view to the attainment of the generally accepted goals for their accelerated industrial development.
10. Recent trends in international trade and development
    - Review and evaluation of progress made in the multilateral trade negotiations and other action and decisions taken at the international level.
    - Review of developments in the international monetary field.
11. Money and finance and transfer of real resources for development
    - Decisions on measures to alleviate the critical debt problems of many developing countries;
    - Measures to increase net capital flows to developing countries to meet their long-term external financing needs;
    - Measures to improve, on appropriate terms and conditions, the financial and monetary situation of developing countries, commensurate with their development needs and to facilitate and improve the financing of their exceptional deficits;
    - Review of requirements for evolving an international monetary system that would foster development and world trade, having particular regard to the interests of the developing countries.
12. Transfer of technology
    - Action to strengthen the technological capacity of developing countries.
    - Decisions on a code of conduct for the transfer of technology and, in the light of those decisions, a decision on the modalities for its establishment;
    - Action to be undertaken by UNCTAD with respect to the economic, commercial and development aspects of the international patent system in the context of the on-going revision of that system.
13. Least developed among developing countries, developing island countries and developing land-locked countries
    - Action on special measures in favour of these countries.
14. Economic co-operation among developing countries
    - Action to support, where appropriate, measures and initiatives

taken by the developing countries to strengthen economic co-operation among themselves.

15. Trade relations among countries having different economic and social systems
    - Multilateral action for expanding the trade and economic relations between countries with different economic and social systems, in particular action which would contribute to the development of developing countries.
16. Institutional issues
    - Recommendations on the future of UNCTAD, and decisions on future institutional arrangements within UNCTAD.

Certain political and legal aspects of the relationships between the Lomé Convention and Community development policy have been discussed by Eberhard Rhein in an earlier issue of this *Review*; [9] it is my purpose in this paper to draw attention to the features within the structure created by the Convention which bear particularly on the major issues on economic progress and social development that have emerged as between developed and developing States since the 1974 General Assembly debates. Can the Lomé Convention not only demonstrate an emphatic break with the "association" tradition established under the two Yaoundé Conventions of 1964 and 1969, but also make a positive contribution toward the achievement of a new international economic order based on consensus rather than confrontation?

2. *The Negotiations, 1973-75*

The most important stages in the preliminaries to the opening of the Lomé Convention negotiations were marked by the publication of the Commission's proposals in April 1973, and by the discussions at the meeting of OAU trade and planning ministers (at Abidjan) and OAU Heads of State (at Addis Ababa) in the following month. The Commission's proposals [10] on the institutional framework, on financial and technical assistance, on trade arrangements, and on a scheme to stabilise export earnings, were hardly unexpected, and, indeed, in some important respects were strongly indicative of a continuing faith in the basic premises of the Yaoundé formula and in the feasibility of developing them to fit the demands of a new Convention. The price stabilisation scheme appeared the most novel of the proposals at first sight, but a

9. Eberhard Rhein, "The Lomé Agreement: Political and Juridical Aspects of the Community Policy towards LDCs" in 12 C.M.L. Rev. 1975, 385-397.

10. See: Kenneth J. Twitchett, "The Yaoundé Association and the Enlarged European Community", in 12 *The World Today* 1974, 51-63.

comparable scheme had in fact been discussed (although not proceeded with) in the negotiations leading up to both the First and Second Yaoundé Conventions. For their part, although the African "associated" and "associable" States within OAU did not appear to achieve unity in principle on their approach to the future negotiations with the Community, there was in fact general agreement (initially dissented from only by two Francophone associated States – Senegal and the Ivory Coast) on their requirement of the acceptance of the principle of non-reciprocity with regard to trade preferences and on their insistence that Community aid should not be tied to trade concessions.[11] A greater cohesion [12] developed after the subsequent meeting of the trade and economic Ministers of the OAU and of the Commonwealth Caribbean States at Lagos in July 1973, and the personal contribution of General Gowon, the former Nigerian Head of State, was very considerable in achieving and consolidating agreement.

The negotiations were formally opened in Brussels on July 25 and 26, 1973, but the "concrete phase" of talks did not begin until the Ministerial Conference held on October 17 and 18 of that year. At that period, therefore, three sets of interrelated international negotiations were proceeding at the same time; these were (i) the EEC-ACP negotiations, (ii) the multilateral trade negotiations within GATT, and (iii) negotiations on the reform of the international monetary system within the framework of the IMF Committee of Twenty. Each of these sets of negotiations was concerned with a common basic objective – "the search for bargains and objectives by the developing countries from the more developed in order ... to place their economic and monetary relations on a footing of greater equality." [13]

Largely because of the distractions produced by the energy crisis within the Community [14] the negotiations from October 1973, until July 1974, failed to make substantial progress on a number of important matters, notably on "rules of origin", on the export earnings stabilisation scheme, and, not surprisingly, on the size of European Development Fund financing that would be required in order to support the financial and technical assistance sought by the ACP States. Other aspects of the Commission's proposals, with regard to the insistence on regional co-operation, the special effort agreed upon for the least developed ACP

11. See: Nicholas Hutton, "The Salience of Linkage in International Economic Negotiations", in 12 *Journal of Common Market Studies* 1974, 136-160.

12. On the significance of the geographical scope of the Lomé Convention, see Eberhard Rhein, *op cit.* n. 9, at 388-391.

13. Hutton, *op cit.* n. 11, at 136.

14. Carol Cosgrove-Twitchett, *op. cit.* n. 5, at 131-132.

States, and the strengthening of the active participation of the ACP signatories in the management of financial and technical co-operation and aid projects, seemed far less controversial but nonetheless were slow to crystallise into substantive negotiating positions between the parties. The major changes in the sugar policy, within the CAP framework, proposed by the Commission, attracted increasing attention during the early months of 1974, with the dramatic increase in world sugar prices and with the formal ending of the Commonwealth Sugar Agreement coming ever nearer.

A new impetus to the negotiations was urgently needed [15] and it was provided, at the initiative of the ACP States, by the convening of a ministerial meeting at Kingston, Jamaica, in July 1974. At the Kingston meeting three significant obstacles were overcome, although the Commission's earlier hopes that the negotiations could be concluded by July 31, 1974, were of course not to be realised. At Kingston the nine Community Member States (i) agreed that they would waive their requirement of reverse preferences and would further attempt to minimise obstacles to the free access of ACP goods to the Community market, (ii) conceded that the Stabex scheme should be substantially widened, and (iii) committed themselves to more positive action with regard to industrialisation in the ACP States. These concessions, and those emerging from subsequent negotiations in Dakar, Senegal, marked a turning point in the history of the negotiations as a whole, although it was not until the morning of February 1, 1975, that (after a difficult and tense ministerial conference at Brussels on January 13, 14 and 15, 1975) final agreement was reached and the final compromises settled. Even then, the overall agreement in principle had to be subjected to the outcome of further discussions (on the levels of 1975 sugar prices) affecting the content of what became Protocol No. 3 (on ACP sugar) to the eventual Lomé Convention. However, when the signing ceremony took place at Lomé on February 28, 1975, it was apparent to all concerned that the new Convention, particularly in regard to its field of application and to its policy and structural innovations, marked a fundamentally new point of departure in the Community's relationships

15. See: *Communication from the Commission to the Council on the Progress of the Negotiations with the African, Caribbean and Pacific States (Phases 1 and 2)*, Doc, VIII/230/74-E. This *Communication* (at p.2) stresses the "... remarkable level of cohesion and unity ..." achieved by the ACP States in their own negotiating positions and goes on to declare *(ibid.)* "As the Commission had always hoped, for both political and technical reasons, the Community is, in fact, dealing with a single negotiator representing the whole of the States in question."

with developing countries at a time when the international economic situation was going through a process of profound change.

3. *The Convention—Innovative Features*

(i) *The Institutions*

The *institutional and access provisions*[16] mark, clearly and unambiguously, a turning away from the associational framework established under the Yaoundé Conventions. This, as has been noted above,[17] was a central objective of the ACP countries during the negotiations. The preambular provisions stress the wish of all parties to establish "close and continuing co-operation, in a spirit of international solidarity" as between partners and on a "basis of complete equality". The agreement is designed to provide a structure within which the economic progress and social development of the forty-six ACP countries can be accelerated. There is also a significant reference, which harks back to the language of the General Assembly Resolution of 1974,[18] to the wish of the parties "to establish a new model for relations between developed and developing States, compatible with the aspirations of the international community towards a more just and more balanced economic order".

The Convention was to come into effect when ratified by the nine Member States of the enlarged Community, by two-thirds of the ACP countries, and after the receipt of the act of notification of the conclusion of the Convention by the Community.[19] It will expire on March 1, 1980, five years after the date of its signature.[20] The signatories are bound to enter into negotiations "in order to examine what provisions shall subsequently govern relations between the Community and its Member States and the ACP States" eighteen months before the end of this period.[21] Adhesion to the Convention is possible, following a simple procedure and subject to the agreement of the original signatories,[22] if

16. *Convention,* Title VII, Arts. 84-94.
17. See p. 319 *supra.*
18. See n. 7 *supra.*
19. The Convention came into force on 1 April, 1976, the first day of the second month following the date of deposit of the required instruments of ratification (see *Convention,* Art. 87 (i)).
20. *Convention,* Art. 91.
21. *Ibid.*
22. *Convention,* Arts. 88-90; note the prior consultation with, and approval of, the Council of Ministers required under Arts. 88 and 89 (1). The Council of Ministers also has the right to "be informed of any request made by *any State wishing to become a member of an economic grouping composed of ACP States*"(emphasis supplied).

the "economic structure and production" of the intending adherent States is comparable to those of the ACP countries.[23] In addition to Guinea-Bissau, which signed the Convention on May 16, 1975 (thus becoming the forty-sixth ACP signatory) the Community has already indicated that it will be willing to consider requests for adhesion from the former Portugese African dependencies as and when they achieve independent statehood.

The Convention co-operation institutions show some important changes, both of emphasis and of function, from the association institutions of the Yaoundé model.[24] The need for flexible arrangements to ensure a permanent dialogue between Community and ACP representatives was paramount. The Council of Ministers, Committee of Ambassadors and Consultative Assembly are likely in operation to resemble their Yaoundé predecessors (Council of Association, Committee of Association and Parliamentary Conference of Association) only very superficially. The Council of Ministers,[25] composed of, on the one hand, members of the Council of Ministers of the European Communities and members of the Commission of the European Communities, and on the other hand, members of the Government of each ACP State, has responsibility for broad policy decisions, for reviewing the operation and achievements of the Convention arrangements, and for taking such specific decisions as it is empowered to do by the Convention.[26] The division of the Council of Ministers into two groups required the Convention also to provide for the strict alternation of the Presidency of the Council between the groups [27] and for the procedure for reaching decisions to depend upon mutual agreement between the two groups.[28] Decisions are binding upon all contracting parties, who must take the necessary measures in order to implement them.[29]

The Committee of Ambassadors [30] has the responsibility, as did the Committee of Association under the Yaoundé Conventions, of ensuring the day-to-day operation of the Convention, of generally keeping under review the functioning of the Convention and the development of its objectives, and of supervising the work of committees, working groups

23. *Convention,* Art. 90, first para.

24. *Convention,* Title VI, Arts. 69-83.

25. *Convention,* Arts. 70-75.

26. See, for examples, the provisions of Arts. 17, 18, 21 ("Stabex") and 41, 48, 60 (financial and technical co-operation); and cf. Art. 73.

27. *Convention,* Art. 71.

28. *Convention,* Art. 73.

29. *Convention,* Art. 81, contains an elementary arbitration procedure for settling disputes on its implementation or interpretation.

30. *Convention,* Arts. 75-79.

and other bodies, whether standing or *ad hoc.* As with the Council of Ministers, the Committee of Ambassadors has representatives from each Member State of the Community, from the Commission, and from each ACP State.

The Consultative Assembly,[31] composed on a basis of parity of members of the European Parliament and of *representatives designated by the ACP States on the other,* reflects the lack of enthusiasm shown during the negotiations by the Commonwealth "associable" countries for the Parliamentary Conference of Association formula. The ACP States will accordingly include amongst their nominees here persons who come from many spheres of public life, as well as, inevitably, some parliamentarians.

(ii) *Trade and Commercial Co-operation*

The *provisions on trade and commercial co-operation* [32] lay stress on free access to the Community for almost all products from the ACP countries and on the non-reciprocity of trade obligations; the principle of free access for ACP products is not applied *ex principio* to goods covered by the common agricultural policy (CAP) [33] but the Convention provisions reflect the result of product by product negotiations here, with the principal problems relating to cut flowers, beef, maize, rice, citrus fruit and arrow root. At the end of the negotiations over 94% of ACP products subject to the CAP obtained exemptions from protective duties and free access to the Community. For the remaining 6% of such ACP products (on 1973 figures about 0.8% of total Community imports from the ACP groups) the Community has agreed to give preference to them over those from other countries. The Community has agreed to examine specific requests from the ACP countries for special arrangements for other farm produce as such countries diversify their economies and look for new consumer markets.

In spite, therefore, of the CAP difficulties, the Convention allows almost all ACP products to be admitted to the Community Member States free of customs duties or charges having similar effect and without being subject to quantitative restrictions. The Community has, in addition, considerably relaxed the *"rules of origin"* vis-à-vis imports from the ACP States.[34] In a separate Protocol [35] attached to the Convention there

31. *Convention,* Art. 80.
32. *Convention,* Title I, Arts. 1-15.
33. See Twitchett, *op. cit.* n. 5, pp. 135-136.
34. See: Doc. No. 388/74 (European Parliament) at p. 23.
35. *Protocol No. 1 concerning the definition of the concept of "originating products" and methods of administrative co-operation.*

is provision for the treatment of the ACP group as a single customs territory and for the treatment of imports as originating from ACP States (and as thus qualifying for duty-free entry) if the value added (for example, by processing) in the ACP States amounts to more than the low percentage of fifty per cent.

The absence of any requirement of reverse preferences, in favour of the Community, is one of the most important features of the entire Lomé Convention.[36] Reverse preferences, such as those provided for in the First and Second Yaoundé Conventions, have (almost irrespective of their economic impact) consistently been criticised as unfairly discriminatory within GATT and UNCTAD, and, most recently, were the subject of adverse provisions in the U.S. Trade Reform Act of 1974. The only obligation imposed upon the ACP signatories in the Convention is that of according Community Member States most-favoured-nation treatment; their relationships with other developing countries are excepted from this requirement.[37] In order to weaken the discrimination vis-à-vis other developing countries (for example, in Asia and in Latin America) which are not comprehended within the Lomé Convention, the Community has undertaken to extend its system of General Tariff Preferences, applicable to imports from all developing countries, which was established in 1971, at such date as the trade and commercial provisions of the Convention came into effect.[38]

(iii) *Stabilisation of Export Earnings*

The very important system of *stabilisation of export earnings* ("Stabex") was introduced into the Convention, as indicated above, after agreement had been reached at the Kingston Conference of July, 1974,[39] but such a scheme had been discussed, although not proceeded with, during the negotiations leading up to both the First and the Second Yaoundé Conventions. Recognising that the export of primary commodities is the principal source of foreign currency for most developing countries, the "Stabex" scheme adopted[40] is designed to afford some protection to the exporters of twelve primary products from the ACP

36. *Convention,* Art. 7 (1).

37. *Convention,* Art. 7 (2).

38. See: Regs. 2794-2800/71; J.O. 1971 L287, 289; and cf. Carol Cosgrove-Twitchett, "Towards a Community Development Policy" (Chap. 6) in *"Europe and the World: The External Relations of the Common Market"*(*op. cit.* n. 5) pp. 151-174, at 155-161, and *The Future Development of The European Community's Generalised Tariff Preferences* (Commission of the European Communities), Com (75) 17f, February 3, 1975.

39. See p. 320 *supra;* and see Twitchett, *op. cit.* n. 5, pp. 140-142.

40. *Convention,* Title II, Arts. 16-25, and see Rhein, *op. cit.* n. 9, pp. 392-393.

countries to the Community. The Commission's early proposals in 1973 were advanced by way of partial implementation of the undertaking contained in Protocol 22 of the Act of Accession and in order "to safeguard the interests of all countries concerned whose economies depend to a considerable extent on the exports of primary produce, and particularly of sugar".

For the first time, in the Lomé Convention, industrialised countries and countries which export raw materials have jointly established a system which guarantees to the latter a certain level of income by protecting them from price fluctuations due to market forces or the uncertainties of production. The list of products for initial inclusion within the "Stabex" scheme was the result of very hard bargaining but the Council of Ministers (of the Convention) has the power to recommend the inclusion of additional products at any time after the expiry of twelve months from the coming into force of the Convention.[41] The initial list of products [42] was drawn up in the light of (a) the importance of the product for the level of employment in the exporting country, (b) the deterioration in the terms of trade between the Community and the ACP State in question, (c) the level of development in the ACP group of States in general, and (d) the traditionally unstable character of income from the product concerned due to fluctuation in prices or in quantities produced. Twelve primary export products are covered by this scheme at the outset (groundnuts, cocoa, coffee, cotton, coconuts, palm and palm kernel products, hides and skins, wood products, bananas, tea, raw sisal and iron ore), together with a number of sub-products. "Stabex" offers a system of commodity-tied compensatory finance which does not directly interfere with the market in the product concerned. A total amount of 375 million u.a. has been provided to fund the stabilisation scheme for the duration of the Convention.[43] This sum is divided into five annual instalments of 75 millions u.a., with balances at the end of each year being carried over to the following year. Financial transfers from the "Stabex" fund to ACP States will be made when the actual export earnings from the product concerned drop by an agreed percentage in a given year as compared with the moving average of earnings from exports of the same product during the four preceding years.[44] This "activation threshold" is significantly lower in the case of the least

41. *Convention,* Art. 17 (3)
42. *Convention,* Art. 17 (1), (a) to (m).
43. *Convention,* Art. 18.
44. *Convention,* Arts. 17 and 19.

developed, landlocked or island ACP States [45] (thirty-four of the forty-six ACP signatories), as is the so-called "dependence threshold", the minimum percentage earnings of total export of a product in the year preceding the year of application of the scheme. Payments from the stabilisation fund, although negotiated as interest-free loans, are likely to become "non-reimbursable loans" and it is unlikely that the Convention obligation (imposed on all but the twenty-four least developed ACP countries [46]) to contribute toward the reconstitution of the stabilisation fund will be insisted upon.

(iv) *The Sugar Protocol*

The "Stabex" scheme is inseparably linked with the sugar question, which inevitably dominated the whole course of the negotiations leading up to the signature of the Lomé Convention[47] and the special arrangements for sugar that are contained in the Third Protocol to the Convention [48] have attracted almost as much attention as the provisions which establish the price stabilisation scheme for primary exports. The sugar arrangements, which are in principle valid for an indefinite period and will last for at least seven years (*i.e.* beyond the duration of the present Convention), involve the Community Member States in an undertaking to purchase and import at guaranteed prices cane sugar from certain ACP States. The producing countries, which include all three Member States of the East African Community, are allocated quotas to a maximum of 1.375 million metric tons annually. The guaranteed price is to be fixed annually between the contracting parties on the basis of prices applicable to the sugar production of the Community; the sugar from ACP producers will be offered initially on the Community market at freely negotiated prices and only if the guaranteed price is not reached will the CAP machinery intervene.[49]

As remarked above,[50] the signing of the Convention, and of the

45. *Convention,* Art. 24; cf. Art. 17 (1) and (2) and Art. 19 (2). The countries listed are: the Bahamas, Barbados, Botswana*, Burundi*, Central African Republic*, Chad*, Dahomey*, Equatorial Guinea, Ethiopia*, Fiji, the Gambia*, Grenada, Guinea*, Guinea-Bissau*, Jamaica, Lesotho*, Madagascar, Malawi*, Mali*, Mauritania*, Mauritius, Niger*, Rwanda*, Somalia*, Sudan*, Swaziland*, Tanzania*, Togo*, Tonga*, Trinidad and Tobago, Uganda*, Upper Volta*, Western Samoa* and Zambia.

46. *Convention,* Art. 21. The least developed ACP countries are indicated by an asterisk in the preceding footnote.

47. See pp. 318 *et seq. supra.*

48. And see *Convention,* Art. 25, containing the reciprocal Community/ACP undertakings.

49. See: Twitchett, *op. cit.* n. 5 pp. 137-138.

50. P. 320 *supra.*

Protocol on sugar, depended in the end upon the successful conclusion of an interim agreement between the United Kingdom and Commonwealth sugar producers. Given the ambiguous "promise" contained in Protocol 22 [51] to the Treaty of Accession and the somewhat muted approach to this question adopted by the British negotiating team during the final stages of the enlargement negotiations, the conclusion of this separate agreement was not easy. The dissatisfaction then expressed by certain of the Commonwealth sugar producers has not diminished during the past year, and, at the time of writing, the supply price to be re-negotiated, according to the terms of the Convention, by July 1, 1976, remains unsettled, with the current negotiations having reached deadlock. Because of the very considerable economic and social importance of this issue for so many of the ACP signatories the progress of this set of negotiations will be watched with great concern; continued acrimony here could well endanger the whole of the future operation of the Convention. As I have written elsewhere,[52] the secure long-term resolution of this issue is of critical importance if the developing countries who are primary producers of sugar are to come to grips with the basic problems of post-colonial economic fragmentation.

(v) *Industrial Co-operation*

The chapters of the Lomé Convention which are broadly concerned with industrial, technical and financial co-operation [53] between the Community and its partner ACP States all demonstrate, in a variety of ways, agreement between the signatories to devote a greater financial effort than in the past and to ensure better developing country participation and shared responsibility than was the case under the Yaoundé form of association.

The special chapter on industrial co-operation [54] was inserted into the Convention in response to a demand made by the ACP States at the ministerial meeting in Kingston, Jamaica, to which reference has been

51. Head III of this Protocol states, *inter alia:*
"... The Community will have as its firm purpose the safeguarding of the interests of all the countries referred to in this Protocol whose economics depend to a considerable extent on the export of primary products, and particularly of sugar.
The question of sugar will be settled within this framework, bearing in mind with regard to exports of sugar the importance of this product for the economies of several of these countries and of the Commonwealth countries in particular..."

52. See: K. R. Simmonds, "The Caribbean Economic Community: A New Venture in Regional Integration", in 23 *International and Comparative Law Quarterly* 1974, 453-458, at. 458.

53. *Convention*, Arts. 26-61.

54. *Convention*, Arts. 26-39.

made above. For that meeting the ACP States had prepared a wide-ranging memorandum [55] designed to secure "specific improvements in the general environment for industrial development". The terms eventually agreed upon are certainly less specific in their commitment of the Community than was hoped for but the provisions do cover the whole industrial field, including industrial infrastructures, the creation of new manufacturing enterprises, research and industrial studies, the transfer and adaptation of technology, special action programmes for small and medium sized enterprises, and programmes for the exchange of information on industrial promotion. The Community acknowledged its intention of making, in the Convention, a "... practical contribution to the rapid industrial development of the ACP States, with a view to achieving a better international division of labour" [56]. The implementation of the Convention provisions bearing on (i) co-operation between Community firms and ACP States, (ii) private sector investment and financing coming from within the Community, (iii) access to technological know-how, (iv) the transfer and *in situ* development of appropriate branches of technology, and (v) the training of national supervisory and managerial staff in the ACP States, will most certainly be scrutinised very carefully within UNCTAD, which, in its recent programme, has shown itself keenly aware of the weak bargaining position of the developing countries in the tranfer process.[57]

Although the provisions of the Lomé Convention here hardly seem adequately to reflect the fact that some of the ACP signatories showed themselves, during the negotiations, to be aware of the declining future importance to them of traditional financial co-operation, it must be assumed that much of the success or failure of this section of the Convention will in the end depend upon the operation of the two institutions which have been established to co-ordinate future industrial co-operation between the signatories. The Committee of Industrial Co-operation [58] has the task of following through the Convention "programme" of activities, dealing with problems as they arise and suggesting solutions. This Committee will also guide and supervise the work of the Centre for Industrial Development,[59] a functional body, to be managed jointly by the Community and the ACP States, which will

55. *Information Note,* 482/x/74-E (Commission), 8-9.

56. See: Doc. VIII/230/74-E (n. 15 *supra*), Annex I, and Carol Cosgrove-Twitchett, *op. cit.* n. 5, 142-145.

57. See: A. F. Ewing, "UNCTAD and the Transfer of Technology" in 10 *Journal of World Trade Law* 1976, 197-214.

58. *Convention,* Art. 35.

59. *Convention,* Art. 36.

gather and disseminate information on industrial affairs, provide research and support services, and organise and facilitate contacts between "... Community and ACP States' industrial policy-makers, promoters, and firms and financial institutions ...".[60] In turn, of course, the future development of this kind of co-operation must depend upon the general climate in which the continuing controversy, within the UN and a number of international as well as non-governmental agencies, on the control of foreign investment and the exercise, by the host country, of rights of "permanent sovereignty over economic activities",[61] develops in future years. In this connection, it is perhaps significant that the provisions in the Lomé Convention which relate to services, establishment, currency payments and capital movements,[62] are traditional in their form, embodying the principle of non-discrimination and committing the ACP States only to awarding equal treatment to all Community nationals and agencies. The ACP and the Community Member States are obliged to refrain from measures, such as the blocking of capital movements, which would be incompatible with their obligations generally under the Convention [63] and to avoid "as far as possible" taking discriminatory measures via-à-vis each other (or according more favourable treatment to Third States) in respect of foreign exchange transactions linked with investments and currency payments.[64] In view of the substantial variations on restrictions on foreign exchange existing currently within the ACP States, and bearing in mind the position adopted by the delegates of certain of these States during the debates in the General Assembly sessions in 1974 which led up to the adoption of the UN Charter of Economic Rights and Duties of States, the adequacy of these provisions for their purpose must be open to question.

(vi) *Financial and Technical Co-operation*

The seriousness of purpose of the Community in negotiating the Lomé Convention was nowhere more in question, and nowhere subject to more criticism, than on the fundamental question of how much financial aid could be made available to the ACP States under the agreement.[65] The negotiations from the early stages proceeded on two premises: (i) that the

60. *Ibid*, Art. 36 (c).

61. See: *Charter of Economic Rights and Duties of States* (n. 8 *supra*) Art. 2, and *Declaration on the Establishment of a New International Economic Order* (n. 7 *supra*) para. 4 (e).

62. *Convention*, Arts. 62-68.

63. *Convention*, Art. 65.

64. *Convention*, Art. 66.

65. See: Carol Cosgrove-Twitchett, *op. cit.* n. 5, 145-149.

countries already associated with the Community under the Second Yaoundé Convention (the associated African States and the Malagasy Republic) should be assured of retaining advantages already secured, and (ii) that the new signatories should be assured of equal treatment. This principle of parity (or solidarity) had necessarily to take account of special factors affecting the demography, geography or condition of economic development of the individual ACP signatories. At the Kingston ministerial meeting in 1974 the ACP States proposed an overall aid total of approximately 8,000 million u.a. It will be recalled that under the EEC Treaty (and during the period of operation of the Implementing Convention) the figure had been 581 million u.a. Under the first Yaoundé Convention the figure was 730 million u.a., and under the Second Yaoundé Convention the total sum made available was 918 million u.a. On this basis the Commission's original proposals in 1973 were based on a total figure of approximately 2,000 million u.a.[66]

The disparity between the ACP States' original demand and the Community's original response, aggravated by a general realisation of the consequences of the worsening world economic climate during the negotiations, produced much hard bargaining before a final compromise was reached. For the period of operation of the Lomé Convention the Community will provide total funds amounting to 3,390 million u.a. (*i.e.* 3.7 times the amount involved in the operation of the Second Yaoundé Convention).[67] Of this total 3,000 million u.a. will be made available from the European Development Fund (EDF) in the form of grants, "soft" loans, risk capital, and through the "Stabex" scheme. A further 390 million u.a. is available from the European Investment Bank (EIB) in the form of ordinary loans. The funds distributed by the European Development Fund will be financed, according to a proportionate scale, from a non-budgetary appropriation by contribution from the Member States of the Community.[68] It is significant that the grant element is dominant; approximately 80% of the EDF funds are to be allocated in this way. The terms on which the "soft" loans will be accorded (over 40 years, with 10 years deferral, and at 1% interest) now establish as a general rule the maxima, only infrequently available, under the Yaoundé formula. Even the interest on the ordinary loans available through the EIB will usually be accompanied by a subsidy which will reduce the effective rate to approximately 3%. The terms are, in fact,

66. See: Kenneth J. Twitchett, *op. cit.* n. 10, at p. 58.

67. *Convention,* Art. 42.

68. According to the scale: Belgium 6.25%, Denmark 2.4%, France 25.95%, Federal Republic of Germany 25.95%, Ireland 0.6%, Italy 12%, Luxembourg 0.2%, Netherlands 7.25% and United Kingdom 18.75%.

generous, even if the total funds available under the Convention may appear, in the light of the much larger number of recipients and the current world rates of inflation, less than satisfactory to many of the ACP signatories.[69]

As with the aid provided under the Yaoundé Conventions, the development aims of the Lomé Convention [70] are concerned with strengthening economic and social infrastructures in the ACP States, with rural development and training programmes, and with industrial development, market and sales promotion schemes. Particular emphasis is placed upon Community support for ACP regional and intra-regional co-operation schemes,[71] for specific aid to small and medium-sized firms, for small-scale development schemes (especially in the rural sector), and for special aid to the least-developed countries.[72] In this respect the Convention adopts a non-definitive list of the twenty-four least developed ACP States.

In general, the ACP States are given a much larger share in the management of this financial co-operation than was the case under the Yaoundé Conventions. They are free to define their own development progammes and are fully responsible for framing and formulating their requests for financing.[73] What the Convention does is to institute a framework within which a running dialogue between Community and ACP representatives can take place throughout the various stages of planning the aid, drawing up and appraising projects, preparing financing decisions, implementing the agreed projects and making a final evaluation of their results.[74] Here, certainly, the Lomé Convention is clearly characterised as a treaty of economic co-operation, attempting to organise systematically, on a basis of equal partnership, a growing economic interdependence between all its signatories. One feature of the Lomé scheme is perhaps typical of the new approach; the transfer of the functions of the Commission Representatives of the EDF (formerly held by the European financial institutions) to the central banks, or other public or semi-public national financial institutions of the ACP States. This is matched by a corresponding strengthening of the powers of the ACP national authorities as regards the implementation of financial and

69. See: Carol Cosgrove-Twitchett, *op. cit.* n. 5, 147.

70. *Convention,* Art. 46.

71. *Convention,* Art. 47 (1) (a).

72. *Convention,* Art. 48.

73. *Convention,* Art. 52.

74. *Convention,* Arts. 53-58. "Exceptional aid" measures (to deal with disaster or emergency situations), with an annual appropriation of 50 million u.a., are provided for in Art. 59.

technical co-operation and by a diminution in the administrative, financial and technical responsibilities of the Commission representatives.[75]

4. *The Convention in operation*

The new partners of the Community, in consequence of the signing of the Lomé Convention, include nearly all of independent black Africa and have a total population of some 268 million. Eighteen of the ACP signatories are, according to the current UN classification, amongst the poorest in the world. For the ACP States as a group the Community is at present [76] their most important commercial partner, taking some 54% of their exports and providing some 44% of their imports. The funds made available, through the EDF and the EIB, for the operation of the Convention, amount to about one-ninth of the aid provided by the Member States of the Community to developing countries as a whole. In scale and approach the Lomé Convention undoubtedly represents a very considerable achievement and it may well in time come to be seen as a landmark in the Community's movement toward the elaboration of a "common" development policy of a world-wide range.[77] It is also a Convention which clearly displays the equality of status between the contracting parties and in which the concept of co-operation between partners has displaced the Yaoundé concept of special treatment for formerly dependent colonial territories. Yet, although the association policy of the Community has now been transformed, and although the Lomé Convention marks a deliberate new beginning, there are still sufficient traces of the old style in the new Convention to raise the question of whether a truly satisfactory new formula has been achieved. It is unnecessary here to comment upon the erratic history and modest success of the Yaoundé formula of association, which was overtaken by the forces of political and economic change from its earliest days. The new priorities and needs which came to the fore during the negotiations leading up to the Lomé Convention have been to a substantial extent reflected in the innovative features of the Convention, upon which I have commented above. The Community has had, at the same time, the salutary experience of negotiating with developing countries from several regions acting together and with a single spokesman. Yet there is still much evidence of only ". . . a marginal consensus at the Community level

75. See generally, Protocol No. 2 to the Lomé Convention.
76. 1974 figures.
77. See: Eberhard Rhein, *op. cit.* n. 9, 394-397.

regarding external policy goals",[78] even though, as Eberhard Rhein has written, "... development policy is an inseparable part of today's external policy".[79] The Community is still searching for a convincing set of principles on which to base its external economic policy; although we are far from a coherent overall design, relationships with the less-developed countries will have in the future, within the Lomé Convention framework, at least a fair chance to proceed on an ordered and equitable, if even an interim, basis.[80]

The Convention, as has been noted above,[81] came formally into effect on April 1, 1976, although many of the trade co-operation provisions have in fact been applied unilaterally by the Community Member States since July 1, 1975. Exploratory talks on access to the Convention have been held with Sao Tomé and with Cape Verde; Surinam has now sent in an application for accession to the Convention.[82] In general, the Commission has indicated that it is in favour of admitting to membership any suitably qualified independent African State south of the Sahara, but that, with the exception of Papua New Guinea (which is a special case), the present Caribbean and Pacific area signatories are unlikely to be added to.

In addition to the current problems over the re-negotiation of the sugar supply prices, mentioned above,[83] there are reports of possible initial difficulties over the sufficiency of funding for the "Stabex" scheme, because of heavy losses last year [84] in certain sectors—notably leathers and hides, and wood—in Gabon and the Ivory Coast. The "Stabex" scheme is applicable retroactively to ACP exports for 1975, but, at the time of writing,[85] the dead-line for the receipt by the Community of requests for financial transfers for loss of earnings in 1975 has not been reached. On the eve of UNCTAD IV, therefore, there are many unresolved questions over the immediate application as well as the potential significance, of the Convention. Nevertheless, the large claim made by President Ortoli, in his speech on the occasion of the signature of the Convention, will certainly be in the minds of UNCTAD delegates when they assemble in Nairobi.

78. See: Carol Cosgrove-Twitchett, *op. cit.* n. 5, 174.

79. Eberhard Rhein, *op. cit.* n. 9, 397.

80. See: J. E. S. Fawcett, "UNCTAD IV: Another Bill of Rights?", in 32 *The World Today* 1976, 152-159.

81. P. 315 *supra*.

82. *"Europe"*, March 27, 1976, No. 1950 (new series) p. 7.

83. Pp. 326-327 *supra*.

84. *"Europe"*, April 1, 1976, No. 1953 (new series) p. 5.

85. April, 1976.

"... It is clear that the European Community does not regard the Lomé Convention simply as one instrument of development for the ACP States alone; it is also a fundamental component of comprehensive co-operation with all developing countries ...

The redefining of relations between rich and poor countries, between producers and consumers of raw materials, between industrialised economies and primary producer economies, is the vital issue of our time ..."[86]

86. Doc. IP (75) 41.

EEC-CMEA*: IS A MEANINGFUL RELATIONSHIP POSSIBLE?

by

Bernard R. Bot**

I. INTRODUCTION

For years the relationship between the EEC and the state-trading nations in eastern Europe has been strained. This state of affairs did not improve when, as of January 1, 1975, the EEC's common commercial policy replaced the last vestiges of bilateralism which till then had prevailed in east-west trade. Although the existing bilateral trade agreements between the EEC Member States and the east European States had automatically lapsed as of the above date, the vacuum had not been filled by a viable alternative; unless one wishes to call the autonomous EEC measures in respect of the state-trading nations a realistic solution.

To be sure, the fault did not lie with the EEC. The EEC Commission in particular had long been aware of the importance of a suitable replacement for the bilateral network of trade agreements, realising that eastern Europe had become of increasing importance to the individual EEC Member States for both political and economic reasons. The refusal of the east European countries, however, to recognize and deal with the EEC as such hampered the EEC's efforts to forge a common front and to arrive at an adequate solution.[1] This was clearly demonstrated when the long overdue draft of an EEC trade agreement, circulated by the EEC Commission prior to January 1, 1975 among the east European state-trading nations, was unanimously rejected by the latter. These countries objected categorically to the idea of separate negotiations between what they termed a powerful economic bloc, the EEC, and individual, economically weaker CMEA members.[2]

* Throughout this article the official abbreviation "CMEA" is used for the Council for Mutual Economic Assistance rather than "Comecon".

** The author is a member of the Dutch Foreign Service and the views expressed in this article do not necessarily reflect those of the institution to which he is attached.

1. 8th General Report (on the Activities of the E.C.) 1974, n. 452; Bull. of the E.C. 1974, no. 11, 1301; Sir Christopher Soames, "Europa in der Welt", 13 E.A. 1974, 425-426.

2. See Eberhard Schulz, "Moskau und das Problem der Integration in Westeuropa", 12 E.A. 1975, 385-386; Wolfgang Nicolai, "Realitäten und Möglichkeiten der ökonomischen Zusammenarbeit in Europa", 12 *Deutsche Aussenpolitik* (DDR) 1975, 1794.

13 C.M.L. Rev. 1976, 335-366

The alternative, on the other hand, of bloc-to-bloc negotiations did not seem a realistic solution either. Initially, the Community maintained the view that the CMEA was not a supranational body of the same stature as the EEC and that direct negotiations were consequently out of the question. Lately, however, the Community seems to have changed its mind. The original reluctance seems to have given way to the view that negotiations with the CMEA may be acceptable under certain conditions in order to put an end to the present stalemate. The Community's initial reluctance, nevertheless, remains understandable. The EEC is clearly different from such forms of regional cooperation as the CMEA. Agreements reached by the EEC bind the Member States under Article 228 of the Treaty of Rome, even though they are not themselves contracting parties, whereas the CMEA members have remained sovereign in such fields as trade and can conclude their own international trade agreements. But not only legal arguments have been invoked to reject such negotiations. Political motives also continue to play a significant role. The EEC considers that negotiations with the CMEA, representing its members in direct commercial affairs, may strengthen the Soviet Union's hand and lead to a further subordination of the smaller CMEA States. For it is no secret that the Soviet Union is pushing the idea of a united front in the CMEA mainly in order to get a firmer grip on, if not total control over, the foreign trade of its partners.

It is therefore understandable that the draft agreement concerning cooperation with the EEC, submitted in February, 1976 by Gerhard Weiss, the DDR's vice premier and president of the CMEA's executive committee, to premier Thorn of Luxemburg in his capacity as president of the EEC Council, was received with the necessary reserves. Although little is thusfar known about its precise contents [3], the CMEA proposal is reported to cover a wide range of topics. Apparently, it suggests the conclusion of agreements between the two economic organisations and/or their members on such divergent subjects as trade, environment, standardisation, economic forecasting, statistical cooperation, credit facilities, elimination of quantitative exchange controls, the normalisation of agricultural trade on a most-favoured-nation basis and a regular exchange of information on developments in the two economic groupings. The creation of a mixed commission is also envisaged. As a preliminary remark, it may be observed that the CMEA initiative must partly be seen as a propaganda move demonstrating the readiness of the east European countries to intensify cooperation in a number of fields of

3. *The Economist*, Feb. 21, 1976, at 64; *Frankfurter Allgemeine Zeitung*, Feb. 20 and 23, 1976; *Neues Deutschland* (DDR), Feb. 17, 1976.

economic activity as set forth in the Final Act of the Conference on Security and Cooperation in Europe, and partly as an expression of their wish to put commercial relations with the West once again on an official basis. But here some difficulties arise. The CMEA seems to advocate the conclusion of an "umbrella" agreement under which, notably, commercial relations will be dealt with bilaterally. But one of the principal EEC demands will undoubtedly be that the CMEA first recognize the EEC's exclusive competence in the field of trade before starting negotiations on a future cooperation. This implies that agreements on trade and related subjects can only be concluded between the EEC and the *individual* CMEA members, since the CMEA itself has no specific competence in this field. The CMEA's proposal, a return to fully bilateral trade agreements, would seriously weaken the EEC's integration efforts and therefore be unacceptable. For political reasons, however, the EEC may agree to conclude an "umbrella" agreement containing some of the suggestions advanced in the CMEA proposals.

It is nonetheless questionable whether direct negotiations on a number of issues between the EEC and the CMEA would succeed at all. The greatly differing structures of the two organisations, and the lack of common policies on many of these matters in both EEC and CMEA, might well prove to be an unsurmountable obstacle. For this reason too an "umbrella" agreement might therefore be envisaged more as a face-saving device than as a real solution, since the individual members of both organisations would have to work out the details at a later stage on a bilateral basis.

As far as industrial, economic and technical cooperation is concerned, it remains doubtful whether the individual EEC Member States would at this stage be willing to relinquish to the EEC the competences they still have in these fields. As will be shown, they have lately manifested an increasing interest in the conclusion of bilateral agreements with the east European countries on industrial, economic and technical cooperation. And this has been reciprocal. The CMEA member States were and still are experiencing the necessity to upgrade their own industry. To that end they needed a new framework in which to develop relations in such fields as industrial and technical cooperation which are, of course, narrowly linked to trade. The cooperation agreements in question apparently meet these needs, with their guaranties for long-term economic assistance, and are therefore of great interest to all parties concerned.

This development, however, evokes the question as to whether such agreements are contrary to the letter, if not to the spirit, of the Treaty of Rome; and if so, whether the Community should not eventually step in and take over this mushrooming practice. But is that feasible, or wise?

What would happen, for example, if the state-trading nations should stick to their refusal to deal with the EEC as far as these topics are concerned? Then a vicious circle, detrimental to all parties concerned, might well be created. It is questionable, furthermore, whether direct negotiations on issues concerning economic, industrial and technical cooperation between the EEC and the CMEA could at this point succeed at all.

Meanwhile, the Commission's attempts to forge a common EEC approach in the fields of trade *and* economic cooperation can only be applauded. A further postponement, for example, of the application of the common commercial policy towards the state-trading nations would have been undesirable and unrealistic. Undesirable because giving in to the wishes of the state-trading countries would have been interpreted as a sign of weakness; unrealistic because the non-implementation, long overdue anyway, of an obligation stemming from the EEC Treaty, would have further weakened the Common Market's unification process, already in jeopardy because of growing nationalist tendencies in the Member States.

Condemnations of the Member States' efforts, on the other hand, should not be made too hastily, certainly not before establishing that present forms of cooperation do violate the EEC Treaty. An honest appraisal therefore of all factors which have contributed to the present state of affairs may permit the drawing of new conclusions. To that end, the structures and competences of the EEC and the CMEA will be explored. This will be followed by an evaluation of the possibilities of future cooperation between these two organisations and/or their members.

II. THE GENESIS OF THE COMMON COMMERCIAL POLICY WITH REGARD TO THE STATE-TRADING NATIONS

For a better understanding of the present situation with regard to the east European state-trading nations, a brief review of the measures adopted over the years by the EEC in order to arrive at a common commercial policy will follow.

A. *Legal steps towards a common commercial policy*

The Treaty of Rome in its Article 113 provides that: "After the expiry of the transitional period, the common policy shall be based on uniformly established principles, particularly in regard to tariff amendments, to the conclusion of tariff and trade agreements, to the establishing of uniform practice as regards measures of liberalisation, to export policy and to commercial protective measures including measures to be taken in cases of dumping or subsidies".[4]

In the early stages of the Community's existence, the Council imposed upon the Member States the obligation to insert a so-called EEC clause into their tariff and trade agreements with third States.[5] Its purpose was twofold. On the one hand, this measure would enable the Community to guarantee a gradual adaptation of existing agreements to the evolving common commercial policy; on the other hand, third parties would be made aware of the future role of the EEC in commercial matters. The state-trading nations, however, refused from the beginning to accept such clauses, arguing that this would imply a recognition of the EEC, an organisation which they staunchly opposed for political and economic reasons. The first obstacle on the road towards a common commercial policy vis-à-vis the state-trading nations had therewith been established. Slightly over a year later, on October 9, 1961, the Council issued two other decisions dealing with the commercial policy. The first decision provided that tariff and trade agreements should not last beyond the end of the transitional period. Agreements without an EEC clause or a clause permitting denunciation within a year, should not exceed a one-year period. With regard to state-trading nations, no agreement should be concluded with effect beyond December 31, 1965.[6] The second decision introduced a consultation procedure for the conclusion of tariff and trade agreements or for changes in liberalisation vis-à-vis third States. In this way, conflicts with the existing rules of the common commercial policy could be avoided.[7]

As the end of the transitional period drew closer, it became apparent that the powers attributed to the Community under Article 113 could only be effectively wielded within the limits of a cohesive and clearly defined commercial policy. The Member States felt, however, that particularly in regard to the state-trading nations, insufficient progress towards completing such a policy had been made. Therefore, they argued, certain powers to negotiate and conclude bilateral trade agreements with east European States should remain for some time to come—*in concreto* till a cohesive commercial policy had been formulated—in national hands. This view finally resulted in the acceptance of

4. Quotes from the EEC Treaty in this article are based on the text found in *International Organisation and Integration,* (Sijthoff, Leyden and Kluwer, Deventer).

5. On July 20, 1960; see 4th General Report (on the Activities of the E.C.) 1961, no. 192.

6. Council Decision of Oct. 9, 1961, J.O. 1274/61, amended by Decision No. 65/572/EEC, J.O. 3275/65.

7. Council Decision of Oct. 9, 1961, J.O. 1273/61.

the well-known Council decision of December 16, 1969.[8] This decision, although confirming the general rule that in the future trade agreements could only be concluded by the Community, contained one notable derogation: for commercial agreements with state-trading nations. These could be concluded bilaterally until December 31, 1972, as a *provisional and exceptional rule,* apparently because the conditions for the opening of negotiations with the Commission were not yet fulfilled. In clear language this meant that since the state-trading nations refused to accept the Commission as a negotiating partner, the conclusion of bilateral agreements would remain possible at least until 1973.

At the same time, a number of conditions were laid down in order to involve the Community and to prevent clashes with the existing body of rules of the common commercial policy. Prior to the opening of bilateral negotiations, the Commission and the Member States were required to consult each other and reach conclusions which could serve as guidelines during the negotiations. The Council, furthermore, had to authorise in each particular case the opening of such negotiations. Finally, the initialled text of the agreement had to be submitted to the Commission and the other Member States for their tacit approval or, if necessary, for further deliberations. Thus it was hoped that this system of checks and balances would keep the powers of the Member States within acceptable limits.

The immediate reason for the above decision was an earlier Council ruling authorising France to conclude a so-called "umbrella" agreement with the Soviet Union for the period 1970-1974.[9] This agreement was to be implemented by means of yearly protocols which laid down the details of the commercial exchanges between the two countries, including the establishment of import-quotas. The advantage which France had thus received, could not be withheld from the other Member States; hence the ruling that although in principle only the Community could conclude trade agreements with third States after the transition period, the Member States retained a limited right to negotiate and conclude agreements with state-trading countries.

It was soon discovered, however, that the individual EEC Member States gave a fairly restrictive interpretation to the term "commercial negotiations". Negotiations that did not result in formal agreements, but which all the same implied the continued application of certain autonomous powers and notably of liberalisation measures, were not considered to fall under the above-mentioned decision. This meant a virtual

8. Council Decision No. 69/494/EEC of Dec. 16, 1969, J.O. 1969, L 326/39.
9. Council Decision No. 69/265/EEC, J.O. 1969, L 206/33.

exclusion of the Community well beyond 1975 and the non-application of the consultation and coordination clauses in regard to an important sector of the common commercial policy. To stop this gap, the Commission proposed new measures which were laid down in a Council decision of December 19, 1972.[10] Therewith the competences of the individual Member States in the field of commercial dealings with third States were definitely cut off, and transferred to the Community. In practice this meant that the Member States were only permitted to implement their long-term agreements with the state-trading countries up to December 31, 1974. As of that date all commercial dealings, including the conclusion of "umbrella" agreements, were forbidden.[11]

B. *Obstacles to the common commercial policy*

Why have the EEC Member States been so opposed to a transfer of their commercial powers to the Community? For a better understanding of the difficulties outlined above, the economic and political background of east-west trade over the past years must be sketched. At the outset it should be kept in mind that import quotas have traditionally been important mechanisms for regulating trade with eastern Europe. As such, their significance had been far greater than in commercial relations with other third States.

This factor, coupled with the great differences in systems of import quotas with regard to the east European countries which existed and still exist between the various EEC Member States, has contributed to the delay in the shaping of a common commercial policy of the Community. Some of the Member States had always carried on a fairly protectionist policy; others, such as the Benelux countries, had liberalised their trade to a considerable extent. When it came to negotiating advantageous trade deals with the east European countries, States of the first category were well aware of their strong bargaining position. They realized that in return for a further liberalisation they could obtain ample concessions. And why share these concessions with members of the second category who had already reaped their benefits at a much earlier stage? Consequently, the more protectionist members were hardly prepared to

10. Council Decision of Dec. 19, 1972, J.O. 1972, L 299/46; see further Schmidt, "Neues Gemeinschaftliches Aussenwirtschaftsrecht", 1973 A.W.D., 361-368.

11. See also the final declaration issued at the Paris Summit Conference of Oct. 21, 1972, in which the Community confirms its intention to carry on a common commercial policy vis-à-vis the east European state-trading nations, Bull. of the E.C. 1972, no. 10, 15; see further Council Decisions Nos. 74/34/EEC and 74/35/EEC of Dec. 6, 1973, O.J. 1974, L 30/1 and L 30/7, and Decision No. 74/482/EEC of Sept. 17, 1974, O.J. 1974, L 266/1.

consent to a common commercial policy towards the state-trading nations, and if at all, in a minimalistic spirit.

The countries which had already liberalised their commerce, on the other hand, balked at the prospect of a common regime more restrictive than the existing import regime; the result might be too protectionist for their taste. Paradoxically, on the basis of these opposing views, a common front was created against the ready implementation of the common commercial policy.[12]

But the opposition to a common policy was also fed by political considerations. Several Member States feared that the improvement of relations between the EEC and the state-trading countries might jeopardise their own efforts to strengthen bilateral relations with this category of States. Against this background the need to establish a common commercial policy, even if presumably only of a technical nature, was considered of secondary importance.

The Member States concerned preferred to explore the possibilities of upgrading their political relations with the east European countries, *inter alia* by means of bilateral trade agreements containing favourable conditions, trade representations, official and semi-official visits by high dignitaries under the guise of improving trade relations *etc.* The bigger EEC nations in particular feared that premature Community moves might oblige them to make undesirable sacrifices for what was in any case considered a rather doubtful aspect of European unity.

From the foregoing, the motives behind the delays in the realisation of the common commercial policy can easily be understood. It should furthermore be recalled that the reluctance of the EEC Member States found a grateful response in the individual state-trading nations which were opposed to the EEC mainly for political reasons, but also from fear that this powerful bloc might eventually be capable of imposing unfavourable trade conditions. This constant refusal by the Soviet Union and the other east European countries to recognise the EEC was, in turn, invoked by the EEC Member States as one of the arguments to continue bilateral trade relations. Therewith a vicious circle was created, whose consequences are still felt today.[13] And despite the recent CMEA proposal, it is by no means certain that a satisfactory solution for these commercial troubles will be reached soon.

12. *Europe* (Agence Internationale d'Information pour la Presse) Nov. 8, 1973, 4 and 5.

13. *Cf.* Sasse, "Kooperationsabkommen und EWG Handelspolitik, Parallelität oder Konflikt?", 20 E.A. 1975, 698.

C. *Towards a common trade agreement*

Provisionally, the last step towards the completion of a common commercial policy was taken when the Community offered to conclude common trade agreements with the individual east European countries. At a rather late stage, in November 1974, the Council approved an outline for a long-term, non-preferential, agreement between the Community and the above-mentioned States. The terms of the draft agreement circulated by the EEC Commission among the east European States provide for ample guarantees. Therewith the suspicion that the EEC would try to abuse its position of strength as an economic power bloc, has been adequately refuted.[14]

i. In the tariff sector, the Community would offer most-favoured-nation treatment, taking into account the usual exceptions. This concession could benefit those products which play an important role in the commercial exchange with the country in question. Generally, however, the tariff sector will not be very important given the low, or even zero, Community tariffs for the bulk of east European imports, which consist mainly of raw materials.[15]

ii. Import-quotas are a harder nut to crack, given the disparity in liberalisation between the EEC Member States. In the Benelux countries, France and Great Britain, import-quotas protect only a limited number of sensitive products, but in the Federal Republic of Germany protection is rather substantial even though many quotas have recently been enlarged. Only in Italy do quotas still protect a wide range of products.[16] It could be expected, however, that an agreement might be reached between the EEC Member States on this issue once the east bloc countries indicate willingness—*quod non* so far—to accept the Community's offer to negotiate.

iii. Farm products will certainly be of interest to the state-trading countries, but negotiations in this field promise to be difficult. The EEC may be willing to discuss certain exceptions to its common agricultural policy, but will be rather limited in its consessions both for international reasons and in regard to possible repercussions from third States.

iv. Given the intrinsically different economic structures of the EEC and the state-trading nations, protective measures such as safeguard mechanisms will certainly be included in such agreements. The institution of mixed commissions, furthermore, will be useful in order to supervise the

14. Bull. of the E.C. 1974, no. 5, 1201; Sasse, *op.cit.* n. 13.
15. *The Economist*, Aug. 30, 1975, 29.
16. Nicolai, *op.cit.* n.l, at 1792-1794.

proper execution of the agreements and to discuss future developments in the field of trade and cooperation.

What could the EEC hope to get in return for these concessions? Apart from certain guarantees for a satisfactory development of its exports, better access to east European markets would certainly have high priority. This would in particular imply direct contacts with end-users of western products, more information on economic planning and regular contacts with the east European decision-makers in the commercial field. It may be questioned, however, whether on the whole the EEC concessions would not be rather onesided, given that the nature of the concessions to be expected from the east European side is hard to define.

After the submission of the above draft agreement there was much speculation as to the possible reactions from the east European countries.[17] Many observers expected the Soviet Union and its allies to buckle down and accept the EEC as a negotiating partner. For the EEC, which is eastern Europe's main western trading partner, could not easily be ignored. On the other hand, a counter-move in the form of an offer to negotiate with a (*pro forma*) united CMEA, which would present itself as a partner of equal stature representing a formidable trade bloc, could not be excluded. If so, the most likely compromise was considered to be the negotiation of an "umbrella" agreement coupled with permission to the individual CMEA members to fill out the details with the EEC. To date, however, the CMEA's expressed willingness to envisage direct bloc-to-bloc negotiations, made possible by certain recent changes in its Statute,[18] remains coupled to the demand that trade talks take place on a bilateral basis, *i.e.* between the individual members of both organisations. This demand is unacceptable to the EEC.

Meanwhile, only the People's Republic of China has confirmed to the EEC that it is interested in negotiations on the basis of the Commission's proposals and both sides hope to come to terms about an agreement before the end of the year. China's interest is, of course, understandable, in the first place because it considers a strong and united Europe of vital importance to its own security, and secondly, in order to annoy the USSR.

D. *Evaluation*

In spite of the present difficulties in east-west trade negotiations, the

17. Bull. of the E.C. 1975, no. 5, 1201.
18. For the latest version consult 11 E.A. 1975, D 281.

exchange of goods has in no way been impeded. Contrary to many fears, the termination of bilateral trade agreements did not result in a situation of economic anarchy. The autonomous EEC measures, on the one hand, and bilateral cooperation agreements on the other, have provided the mechanisms which have secured an uninterrupted flow of goods. This can, with good right, be considered an advantage for the Community and its Member States in the coming negotiations with the CMEA and its members.

The autonomous measures comprise at present a common external tariff for all agricultural and industrial products,[19] guaranteeing a uniform approach by the nine Member States. They comprise, furthermore, harmonised regulations dealing with customs practices, and measures dealing with dumping and subventions.[20] On the export side, dealings with state-trading nations are free from any restraints.[21]

The Community's agricultural policy does not need much further comment, since it constitutes a fully autonomous system which has proved difficult to change even in bilateral negotiations with associated States. The state-trading nations should not, therefore, set their hopes too high when discussing their agricultural imports into the Community.

In regard to import-quotas, however, the Community has only been able to take note of the *status quo* by establishing a list of products which are *not* subject to such quotas.[22] Although it constitutes a modest step forward, it does not solve the issue of existing bilateral import quotas, which still differ considerably from one Member State to another, as we have seen. Changes in existing quotas have been made subject, however, to a procedure of consultation and coordination since March 27, 1975.[23] Import quotas have therefore been frozen at their present level and unilateral changes are in fact no longer possible. It seems unlikely, furthermore, that in this field much progress can be made in negotiations with the CMEA Member States. Certainly their demand for most-favoured-nation treatment can hardly be met.

Credits have become, next to import quotas, an important bargaining tool in negotiations with state-trading nations, since all of them are running deficits in their trade with the EEC. The EEC's exports to CMEA

19. Council Decision No. 950/68 of June 28, 1968, J.O. 1968, L 172/1.
20. Council Decision No. 459/68 of April 5, 1968, J.O. 1968, L 93/1.
21. Council Decision No. 2603/69 of Dec. 20, 1969, J.O. 1969, L 324/25.
22. Council Decision No. 109/70 of Dec. 19, 1969, J.O. 1970, L 19/1; see further the Commission's communications in O.J. 1975, L 124/1 and C 287/55.
23. Council Decision No. 75/210 of March 27, 1975, O.J. 1975, L 99/7; Council Decision No. 74/652 of Dec. 2, 1974, O.J. 1974, L 358/1.

countries increased by 41,5% in 1974, imports only by 23%.[24] In this field the Community has only managed to harmonise certain details of the official credit insurance policies of the Nine; but interests and other terms are still determined by and large by the Member States individually. The European Court recently stated that export credits also come under the Community's exclusive competence in the field of foreign commerce.[25] Many Member States, however, seem to fear at present that they stand more to lose than to gain from further integration in this particular field.[26] Credit facilities, as reputedly demanded by the CMEA in its recent proposals, are therefore not likely to be granted quickly by the EEC.

III. CMEA, A VIABLE PARTNER FOR THE EEC?

A. *The background*

The proposed CMEA-EEC agreement evokes several questions, notably concerning the consequences for the individual CMEA Member States.[27]

The extent to which the CMEA should control trade relations between the EEC and the east European countries, is a complex question which partly underlies the EEC's reluctance to deal with the CMEA as an equal partner.[28] The question arises as to how far the EEC should contribute to a further reduction of the limited autonomy which the state-trading nations (still) enjoy in foreign trade and other economic fields.[29] In fact, it is to be feared that an upgrading of the CMEA might lead to a further subordination of these countries to the Soviet Union, a tangible danger

24. *The Economist, op.cit.* n. 15.

25. Reference may be made to the important Advisory Opinion of the Court of Justice (1/75 of Nov. 11, 1975, O.J. 1975, C 268/18) on the basis of Art. 228 concerning export credits. According to the Court, this subject matter belongs to the exclusive competence of the Community which can therefore conclude agreements with third States concerning this matter, see further comment of H. Maas, *infra* p. 379; further, Council Directive No. 70/509/EEC of Oct. 27, 1970, J.O. 1970, L 254/1; Directive No. 70/510/EEC of Oct. 27, 1970, J.O. 1970, L 254/26; Decision of Dec. 16, 1970, J.O. 1970, L 284/59; Directive of Feb. 1, 1971, J.O. 1971, L 36/14.

26. *Cf.* Sasse, *op.cit.* n. 13.

27. Hans Herbert Götz, "Die Europäische Handelspolitik muss sich bewähren", *Frankfurter Allgemeine Zeitung,* Oct. 21, 1974, 12; Hans Bräker, "Osteuropa, die Europäische Gemeinschaft und das GATT", 19 E.A. 1973, 679; *Die Welt,* Aug. 18, 1973, 5.

28. A. van Goedland, "EEG-Comecon: een Vervolgroman?", (1975) *Internationale Spectator,* 280.

29. For a different opinion see Eberhard Schulz, *op.cit.* n. 2, at 383.

now that the latter is using its power as the main supplier of oil and a wide variety of raw materials to enforce integration—socialist style—to its own advantage and to get, essentially, an even firmer grip on the economies of its smaller partners.

The relationship between the two organisations, furthermore, has by no means crystallised. As stated earlier, in Soviet eyes closer cooperation is only interesting if therewith the EEC's common commercial policy can be sufficiently diluted.[30] This implies that bloc-to-bloc negotiations can only be successful if the former structure of bilateral commercial arrangements could somehow be restored, thereby weakening the EEC's integration process. The new CMEA proposals clearly point in this direction. In other words, it looks as if the Soviet Union is using the CMEA to dissuade the other east European countries from turning directly to the EEC.

Apart from these aspects, there is the "technical" question as to whether the CMEA is sophisticated enough to be expected to handle the commercial and/or economic interests of its members in an adequate way. From this perspective, the structure, evolution and competences of the organisation will be briefly reviewed.

B. *Planned Development: Integration or mere Coordination?*

i. *The objectives of the CMEA*

The meeting of Mr. Weiss, the vice premier of the German Democratic Republic and current president of the CMEA's executive committee, and Mr. Thorn, Luxemburg's premier and president of the EEC Council, in February 1976, highlighted the relationship between the EEC and the CMEA.[31] In fact, it was the closest contact between the two since Mr. Wellenstein, the European Commission's director-general for external relations and Mr. Moyseyenko, the head of the CMEA's foreign trade department, met a year earlier in Moscow,[32] and the first sign that the CMEA and its members were willing to extend recognition to the EEC, thereby paving the way towards official negotiations. The Weiss-Thorn meeting proved how anxiously Moscow and its allies want to secure a development along parallel lines—in a formal sense at least—

30. *Supra* p. 344; Juri Schischkow, "EWG Krise: Character, Ursachen, Tendenzen" 2 *Deutsche Aussenpolitik* (DDR) 1975, 212-226.
31. *Supra*, p. 336 *et seq.*
32. See *The Economist*, Aug. 30, 1975, 26; already in 1973, Mr. Fadeyev, the CMEA's Secretary-General, had made the first overtures to the Danish President of the Council of Ministers.

between the EEC and the CMEA.[33] The following may illustrate this thesis.

To start with, the CMEA was founded in 1949 primarily as a Soviet response to the Marshall Plan and its alleged violations of national sovereignty. Clearly again in response to the establishment of the EEC, in 1959 a statute was adopted which defines the economic aims of the organisation.[34] Article 1 of the Statute sets forth that the purpose of the CMEA is to promote "by uniting and co-ordinating the efforts of the Member States of the Council, the further intensification and improvement of the cooperation and development of socialist economic integration, the planned development of the national economies and the acceleration of the economic and technical progress and the raising of the level of industrialisation of those countries wit a less-developed industry, a continual growth in productivity, the gradual rapprochement and balancing of the level of economic development, together with a steady increase in the well-being of the peoples of the member countries of the Council".[35]

At first sight the economic and welfare objectives do not differ greatly from those enumerated in the Treaty of Rome.[36] Still, it is significant that the term "socialist economic integration" used for some time already by east European authors and politicians, has now also appeared in the latest version of the CMEA Statute.[37] But the concept of "planned development" is in fact all that points in the direction of "integration", although even that term smacks rather of the coordination of plans thus far practiced by the CMEA members than of an EEC-style integration which would permit concerted action. So it is far from clear what in practice the process of socialist economic integration entails and where the dividing line between mere coordination and the abandonment of certain elements of national sovereignty has to be drawn. The Statute in fact only talks in general terms of coordination of national plans, specialisation and cooperation.

33. *Cf.* A. van Goedland, *op.cit.* n. 28.

34. N. Faddejew, "Internationale Wirtschaftsorganisation sozialistischer Länder 1949-1974", I *Einheit* (SED Party journal) 1974, 20; Henry Schaefer, *Comecon and the Politics of Integration* (New York, 1972), Ch. 8; Alexander Uschakow, "Probleme der Wirtschaftsintegration im RWG", 3 *Aussenpolitik* 1972, 148-158.

35. This is an unofficial translation of the latest version of the CMEA Statute of June 21, 1974. For the complete German text see 11 E.A. 1975, D 282.

36. The Preamble and Article 2 of the EEC Treaty, for example.

37. Gerhard Brendel & Hans-Joachim Dubrowsky, "Der Aussenhandel der RWG Länder unter den Bedingungen der sozialistischen ökonomischen Integration", 6 *Deutsche Aussenpolitik* (DDR) 1974, 1321-1344; Kohlmey, *Vergesellschaftung und Integration im Sozialismus*, (Berlin, 1973).

Also the document "The Basic Principles of the International Socialist Division of Labour" of 1967 is rather opaque as far as a closer coordination of economic policies of its members is concerned, and certainly does not give any clear indication as to an advanced form of integration. In 1962 an attempt was undertaken by Khrushchev to remedy this shortcoming, albeit not in the interest of a greater economic upswing of the CMEA, but rather to get a better grip on the economies of the other member countries. He proposed the establishment of a "unified planning organ empowered to compile common plans for the whole CMEA area". The Rumanians, however, threw a spanner in the works precisely because they realized that such a plan threatened their national independence. Although Rumania was the most vocal member in its opposition, it is well known that other members also discreetly opposed such ideas. Such coordination as meanwhile exists is predominantly bilateral and, as far as can be ascertained, mainly restricted to external commercial relations and specialised forms of technical cooperation.

In July 1971, at the 26th Session of the CMEA, the twenty-year "Comprehensive Programme of Economic Integration"[38] was adopted, therewith opening a new chapter in the history of the socialist Commonwealth. This Programme enjoys the formal status of a multilateral treaty and aims at improving the coordination of national plans as well as the financial and currency systems. In a way it is meant as a theoretical blueprint of how the region's economies should complement each other, emphasising the general need for improved exchanges of scientific and technical information and the specific need to evolve a fuel and raw-materials policy.

However, the text makes abundantly clear that the promotion of coordination and integration in no sense means a change in the partners' traditional commitment to the principle of *state sovereignty*.[39] Therefore, the establishment of supranational organs is expressly precluded. The Programme merely endorses the setting up of "international economic associations", *i.e.* interstate entities, to direct and channel multilateral activities between economic trusts, enterprises, *etc.*

ii. *Obstacles to integration*

Two principal shortcomings, it would seem, have stymied the integration efforts of the CMEA planners. First, the rigidities of the national

38. Text in *Neues Deutschland* (DDR) of Aug. 7, 1971, no. 216; 20 E.A. 1971, D 479.

39. George Ginsburg, "The implications of the 20-year Comprehensive Programme of Economic Integration", Proceedings of the 67th Annual Meeting of the Am.Soc. of Int'l.L., 67 Am.J.Int'l.L. 1973, 48-55.

planning mechanisms directed by huge bureaucracies and, secondly, the lack of a unified system of domestic price formations. Internal and foreign trade prices often stand in no fixed relation to each other, whereas the exchange rates are not established in relation to purchasing power but mainly serve accounting purposes; hence their apparent lack of influence upon the direction or the volume of commercial exchanges with other countries. A more sophisticated plan coordination, coupled to a workable clearing system for multilateral payments would therefore seem the minimum conditions for further integration worthy of that name as well as for a common approach towards third States or international organisations such a the EEC.

It is not surprising, consequently, that so far socialist integration has had meagre results, if at least measured by EEC standards. The CMEA has only been instrumental in promoting the exchange of economic, scientific and technical information between its members and has stimulated, on a modest scale, specialisation in production, mainly in the field of transport, engineering and chemicals. Here the specialised CMEA agencies,[40] in particular, have contributed to a greater integration in certain industrial sectors where a closer coordination was necessary anyway, if only to prevent inefficient production. There has furthermore been a certain amount of cross-national investment, mainly in the raw materials sector. The International Investment Bank, founded in 1970, is in particular intended to promote such investments. But only since the energy crisis erupted have these investments, which particularly benefit the Soviet Union, taken on real significance. Thus, for example, the CMEA's so-called integration plan has obliged most east-European countries to help finance such joint construction programmes as the Orenburg pipeline which will carry natural gas westward from the Urals.[41] The forced credits paid by the Soviet Union's partners will be repaid only when the major deliveries of natural gas start. The situation is identical in regard to many other projects. As a general rule, however, the CMEA members still organise the bulk of their economic relations on a *bilateral basis,* which clearly delimits the perimeters of a future EEC-CMEA trade agreement.

iii. *Integration CMEA style*

It is apparent, on the other hand, that the long-term socialist concept of cross-national integration is often misunderstood by western obser-

40. Harald Zschiedrich, "Internationale Wirtschaftsvereinigungen der RWG Mitgliedsländer", 11 *Deutsche Aussenpolitik* (DDR) 1975, 1678-1687.

41. Brendel & Dubrowsky, *op.cit.* n. 37, at 1342.

vers. According to socialist authors, integration implies an harmonious accommodation of all economic activities in particular sectors and particular regions without sacrificing the component national interests.[42] Capitalist attempts at integration, they assert, on the contrary violate the inherent sovereign rights of the smaller and weaker nations, through the media of supranational organisations, which apply such "tricks and devices" as the rule of majority voting and weighed ballots. Needless to say, in the socialist view, the capitalistic monopolies are the main beneficiaries of such policies rather than the citizens of the Member States.[43]

Socialist integrational progress, furthermore, rests on the notion that the interstate organisations mentioned in the Comprehensive Programme will increasingly and quite naturally service the needs of the developing community. Therewith their functions and responsibilities will multiply and in turn lead to greater authority and power. As a consequence of this evolutionary process, new economic problems will increasingly be solved on an international rather than a national level.[44] In this context, particular consideration should be given to the fact that already two-thirds of the members' foreign trade takes place on an intra-bloc basis, which in itself may form a strong impetus towards further integration. The question as to whether some sort of supranational principle will not, perforce, have to be introduced eventually, does not, however, seem to have come up yet; at least not publicly. It remains to be seen, therefore, whether the overall CMEA concept of political consonance—translated into the imperative of unanimity—does not in the long run lead to serious delays in the integration process, certainly if it is compared to the progress realized by the EEC through such "devices" as supranationality and majority voting.

It would be unfair, on the other hand, to belittle the pace of progress and efforts that have so far been put towards forging a kind of "socialist economic integration". Certainly, a planned, organised approach based on central control over every little detail of the process slows down the speed of any major undertaking. And the rigidity of the procedural system precludes any rapid and spectacular success, but this does not mean that the impetus behind the project may not be very great. As such,

42. *Ibid.;* Karl Peuser, "Sozialistische Ökonomische Integration", 2 *Deutsche Aussenpolitik* (DDR) 1975, 181-190.

43. Fred Oelssner, "Ökonomische Integration und Internationale Beziehungen", 1 *Deutsche Aussenpolitik* (DDR) 1975, 37-40; Gerhard Huber, "Zur Wirtschafskooperation der RWG Länder mit kapitalistischen Industrieländern", 10 *Deutsche Aussenpolitik* (DDR) 1975, 1479-1494.

44. *Ibid.*

the CMEA's existing momentum may carry the Member States *in the long run* over the difficulties they are experiencing at the moment, towards a real form of integration, provided the will is there. There is little solace, however, in this long-term prospect for all those who would like to see a closer cooperation between the CMEA and the EEC in the more immediate future.

Even the existing procedural system prevents at present such a closer cooperation, as may be illustrated by the way recommendations are translated into norms binding the interested States. Recommendations usually relate to broad policy guidelines. They can only be implemented after having been adopted unanimously by the group of States concerned. Next, they have to be endorsed in accordance with the national legislations, by decisions of the governments concerned or of the "competent" authorities in those countries.[45] In other words: after "ratification" by the various interested Member States, the recommendation does nothing more than impose a duty to negotiate in good faith with other CMEA partners so as to arrive at an agreement on a particular subject. But when contrary interests are involved, who in last resort must decide which State has acted most in accordance with the substantive tenor of the orginal recommendation?[46] The answer is far from clear, even to a well-informed student of CMEA procedure. The real solution would lie, of course, in the adoption of a system of majority voting. This would permit mandatory directives which could be enforced under the threat of appropriate sanctions. It is not to be expected, however, that this concept will be adopted in the near future since it goes against the grain of present Communist convictions on the subject. Consequently, the hope for a meaningful and substantial cooperation between CMEA and EEC should, for the time being at least, be abandoned.

For the purposes of this article, furthermore, it is important to note that CMEA integration efforts have so far mainly been focused on the *technical* aspects of intertwining certain branches of the production apparatus. The foreign trade sector, however, apart from the coordination of the five-year plans between the CMEA Member States, has remained the exclusive prerogative of the sovereign national State.

Precisely because of the extensive national competences left to the individual CMEA Member States, it is doubtful whether the EEC could hope to see many of its claims realized in direct negotiations with the CMEA. It would seem more likely that supplementary agreements or

45. Art. 4 CMEA Statute, 11 E.A. 1975, D 284; *cf. International Organisation and Integration, op. cit.* n. 4, at 1029.

46. Ginsburg, *op.cit.* n. 39.

deals, implementing the broad guidelines laid down in an eventual "umbrella" agreement between EEC and CMEA, would have to be worked out with the individual CMEA members. As such the EEC is right in claiming that a meaningful trade agreement can basically only be concluded with the *individual* CMEA members. The same, of course, is true for cooperation agreements, given the greatly differing stages of economic development in the CMEA countries.

C. *The treaty-making power of the CMEA*

The foregoing demonstrates clearly how difficult the implementation of a trade agreement between the EEC and the CMEA would be, even if the two organisations were ever to come to terms about its conclusion. To be sure, it would hardly pose a problem to the EEC which in tariff and trade matters has adopted a rather uniform policy, while it is, furthermore, competent to conclude agreements in this area which bind its members. The CMEA's competence in this field, on the contrary, is rather hazy, quite apart from the fact that it does not even possess the rudiments of a common commercial policy.

To what extent does the CMEA possess treaty-making power? Although the Statute in its latest version, attributes to the CMEA the power to conclude international agreements with third States and international organisations,[47] it is not clear which substantive issues, if any, the CMEA is allowed to deal with. In view of the exclusive competence of the Member States in the foreign commercial sector, the CMEA's treaty-making power seems a rather hollow shell, a face-saving device at best. This treaty-making power probably has to be seen in the light of developing the so-called "mutually advantageous relations with countries of the capitalist world" and is best illustrated by the agreements concluded with Finland in 1973,[48] Iraq in 1974 and Mexico in 1975.[49]

47. Art. 3(2): "In accordance with this Statute, the CMEA . . .
b. can negotiate international agreements with member States of the Council, with other States and with international organisations". Art. 12: Contacts between the Council and international organisations.
"The CMEA can establish and maintain contacts with . . . international organisations.
The nature and the form of these contacts will be established by the Council according to an understanding with the . . . international organisations, in particular by concluding agreements with them".

48. Text in 5 E.A. 1974, D 99; for comment see Sorsa, "Finnland zwischen EWG und RWG", 14 E.A. 1974, 461.

49. Huber & Hübler, "Gemeinsame Integrationsplanung im RWG", 9 *Deutsche Aussenpolitik* (DDR) 1975, 1328.

These agreements are "umbrella" agreements under which Finland, respectively Iraq or Mexico have the possibility to conclude special agreements with the individual CMEA members in which the real issues are tackled. The role of the CMEA's secretariat during these negotiations was limited to the presidency of the sessions, while it was, furthermore, empowered to sign the agreements. The treaties' entry into force, however, was made dependent on the approval of the individual Member States. It was, furthermore, stipulated that all issues which may arise under these agreements are to be dealt with in the "mixed commission" which unites "representatives of Finland (or Iraq or Mexico) and of the CMEA Member States". In a special protocol it was determined that a representative of the secretariat will participate in the sessions of the mixed commission; in his absence, nonetheless, all decisions taken will be valid, which shows the paramount influence of the Member States within the CMEA.

These agreements are interesting because they could well be used as blueprints for a future CMEA-EEC agreement. As to the contents of such an agreement one may expect a catalogue of high sounding principles, partly taken over from the final act of the European Security Conference,[50] notably the second basket, and partly reiterating the noncommittal formulas found at present in the bilateral cooperation agreements. There may even be references to exchanges of information and technical cooperation, to the environment, standardisation and statistical cooperation, or to most-favoured-nation treatment in particular sectors. A mixed commission will undoubtedly be set up to supervise the implementation of the agreement. As to the substantial issues, however, it seems inevitable that the EEC would have to deal on a direct basis with the individual east European states. For, as explained earlier, the CMEA thusfar does not have the power to oblige its members to make concessions regarding foreign trade or industrial cooperation. As in the Finnish, Iraqi or Mexican case, therefore, the essentials would have to be worked out on a bilateral basis, that is to say, between the EEC and the east European country in question, and not, as the CMEA seems to expect, between the individual EEC countries and the individual CMEA countries. Precisely this demand, a return to fully bilateral trade negotiations and agreements, till now essential to Moscow and its allies, must be considered unacceptable to the EEC.

But before even arriving at this point, the CMEA and its Member States have to recognise the EEC as an organisation which represents its members in commercial dealings and related matters with third States.

50. *Cf.* A. van Goedland, *op.cit.* n. 28.

Thusfar most east European States have maintained a rather negative attitude towards the EEC. This they clearly demonstrated when they rejected the draft trade agreement submitted to them by the EEC Commission towards the end of 1974.[51] On the other hand, not too much attention should be paid to this purely formal attitude which is based on political considerations. With the exception of the Soviet Union, all east European countries have had contacts with the EEC in one form or another,[52] while Rumania has even entered into official contacts with the Community.[53] The recent changes in the CMEA Statute, furthermore, have facilitated the extension of recognition on the legal plane.[54] Also Mr. Wellenstein's visit to Moscow in 1975 and Mr. Weiss's contacts with premier Thorn in 1976 point in the direction of a gradually changing mood within the CMEA, although it is by no means clear whether the CMEA is prepared to recognize the EEC's competence in the commercial field.[55]

To a certain extent, of course, the reverse is also true. The EEC does not, for example, consider the CMEA capable of effectively representing its members in the field of commerce. Hence its official attitude, not modified to date, that trade agreements can only be concluded between the EEC and the individual east European countries and not with the CMEA in the name of its members.

IV. COOPERATION AGREEMENTS

A. *General*

Recent international economic developments have incited many countries to search for legal instruments other than the classical tariff and trade agreements to stimulate economic cooperation and the exchange

51. See n. 2, *supra;* but *cf.* the fact that Prime Minister Aldo Moro of Italy signed the final act of the European Conference on Security and Cooperation in his function as Prime Minister and in the name of the European Community, see Schwerin, "Die Solidarität der EG-Staaten in der KSZE", 15 E.A. 1975, 492.

52. Certain deals on agricultural imports between the EEC and east European countries have been concluded since 1964. Such agreements have been concluded with Bulgaria, Hungary, Poland, Rumania and Czechoslovakia, see *The Economist,* Aug. 30, 1975, 26.

53. Rumania, always the maverick, applied for a limited application of general preferences from the EEC side in a note addressed to the EEC on Jan. 31, 1972. As of 1974 Rumania has been granted this right, see Council Decisions Nos. 3500/73, 3506/73 and 3507/73 of Dec. 18, 1973, O.J. 1973, L 358/1, L 358/94, L 358/117 and L 358/124.

54. See ns. 35 and 47 *supra.*

55. *The Economist,* Aug. 30, 1975, 26; *ibid.,* Febr. 21, 1976, 64; *Frankfurter Allgemeine Zeitung,* Febr. 20 and 23, 1976.

of technical knowledge. The EEC Member States in particular have become increasingly inventive in finding new cooperation formulas, primarily to extend their relations with east European countries.[56] The success of these alternative solutions has strengthened their intention to further explore the possibilities inherent in these new instruments. Consequently, many economic and even commercial relations with east European States are nowadays channelled *via* bilateral cooperation agreements, chamber of commerce agreements, credit facilities and other instruments. Most significant of these new forms of cooperation, however, are the economic, industrial and technical cooperation agreements. These agreements have recently come under fire for being, in fact, disguised commercial treaties. References to most-favoured-nation treatment, the promotion of long-term contracts, clauses referring to *"sociétés-mixtes"*, the exchange of licences, know-how, the conclusion of compensation transactions for the delivery of complete factories, *etc.* have been cited as proof of the above allegation.[57]

Although there are indications that cooperation agreements in some instances are trying to circumvent the Community's prerogatives in the field of commerce, recent criticism against them seems not in all cases to be justified. Furthermore, in the absence of formal trade agreements between the EEC and the state-trading nations it may for all practical purposes be asked whether these agreements are not the only alternative which could have been devised in order to channel the increasing flow of goods and services to and from eastern Europe.

Although trade with the CMEA bloc is not yet very significant for the EEC as a whole,[58] interest is rapidly increasing. This becomes very clear if one takes a look at the trade expansion over the last decade when the Community's imports and exports from the CMEA increased almost twice as much as its total imports and exports. Yet trade with the CMEA accounts at present only for a small percentage of the EEC's total trade. For the CMEA, on the other hand, trade with the EEC makes up almost a quarter of its total trade. Certain EEC countries, such as Germany and Italy, are deeply involved in trade with the east European countries and would try to avoid a stagnation at almost any price. And ever since the state-trading nations indicated that they may have to reduce their trade with the West,[59] partly as a consequence of their own economic troubles,

56. Peter Knirsch, "Vom Ost-Westhandel zur Wirtschaftskooperation", 2 E.A. 1973, 67.
57. Sasse, *op.cit.* n. 13, at 700.
58. ECE Analytical Report on Industrial Cooperation among ECE countries (Geneva, 1973); Paul Bähr, "Handel und Händel zwischen Ost und West", 5 E.A. 1973, 177.
59. Gerhard Huber, *op.cit.* n. 43, at 1480.

and partly because of the Soviet Union's price increases for raw materials, many EEC Member States have refrained from adopting too principled an attitude on the subject of cooperation agreements.

B. *Implementation*

For that reason the scope of cooperation agreements may be briefly examined. Essentially, cooperation agreements were born out of the need to adapt the overall structure of economic relations between western and eastern Europe to the present state of technical and industrial development. The underlying philosophy was that an appropriate division of labour and a more rational exploitation of the economic opportunities would stimulate the industrial and technical evolution of the two economic groupings. As a result of intensified cooperation, the flow of goods and services between West and East would increase and long-term stability and growth would be guaranteed.

Studying the contents of the cooperation agreements which are supposed to bring about this miracle one cannot help but feel disappointed. In fact, those agreements appear to be, certainly as far as the "western" side is concerned, mere "umbrella" agreements, limited to declarations of intention concerning the promotion of economic, industrial and technical-scientific cooperation between firms in eastern and western Europe. Ample reference, furthermore, is made to the exchange of licences, know-how and scientific materials, to visits of experts and, of course, to the meetings of the mixed commissions.[60]

At best these agreements can be described as "promotional" instruments. It is, by and large, left to individual firms, enterprises and business organisations,[61] stimulated by the yearly meetings of the mixed commission, to implement the terms of the agreement. And references to direct *official* influence or powers are hard to find. It seems a fundamental misconception, therefore, to equate promotion and stimuli with official measures intended to enlarge or diminish the volume of trade (commonly referred to as commercial policy), and to say that cooperation agreements have in fact replaced trade agreements. Lest there be any misunderstanding: the national authorities of the EEC Member States will naturally remain interested in an increase of trade and stable economic relations with eastern Europe and will, consequently, continue to urge

60. For a list of cooperation agreements concluded between EEC Member States and east European countries, see Sasse, *op.cit.* n. 13, at 706.

61. Gerhard Huber, *op.cit.* n. 43 at 1484, mentions that in the framework of the official cooperation agreements 600 agreements have been concluded between East and West.

their national enterprises to greater activity. But it is unrealistic to believe that west European governments, even though they can create favourable conditions, have the power to force private firms into business deals with east European countries. As long, therefore, as the instruments used towards that purpose are not in evident contradiction to existing Community Law, it is hard to see why the Member States should not continue to use them.

According to the opponents of cooperation agreements, however, these instruments are essentially "trade agreements new style".[62] They lead to a further integration of the two systems which would not have been possible by means of the classical tariff and trade agreements. They intend to step up trade under the disguise of economic cooperation and should therefore be concluded by the Community.

Objections are made against cooperation between firms of EEC Member States and of east European countries on third markets (since it presumably has a bearing on the EEC export policy); the system of *"toute licence accordée"*, as far as products resulting from cooperation deals are concerned (EEC import policy); favourable credit terms (EEC export policy) and most-favoured-nation treatment, which is an exceptional measure anyway, not found in most cooperation agreements. Naturally, there can be no doubt that when purely commercial issues are touched upon, they should be delegated to the EEC. But it seems reasonable to admit, on the other hand, that in the absence of a fully elaborated common EEC commercial policy, the Member States should be allowed to continue to apply the above-cited measures in order to prevent a stagnation of their industrial and economic cooperation with eastern Europe (for the legal framework, see next paragraph). And once again, the real impetus for the realisation of these objectives has to come from the private, not from the official sector; this applies notably to such subjects as business cooperation on third markets, licenses and, in most cases, even to credits.

The yearly meetings of the mixed commissions are, furthermore, limited to such activities as the evaluation of cooperation efforts over the past period and the establishment of a working programme for the next year. As a rule such programmes are harmless, containing schedules for the exchange of delegations, technical symposia and other related subjects, and do not refer to official commercial measures. If direct commercial issues are brought up by the east European side, they are as a rule referred to the EEC by the west European party for a final decision.

62. Sasse, *op.cit.* n. 13, at 701.

For east European countries, with their central planning organisation, the situation is of course different.[63] They can engage themselves commercially and implement effectively the objectives laid down in the cooperation agreements. They have the power to force state enterprises into particular forms of cooperation with particular partners. The element of central power over foreign trade in most west European governments is, on the contrary, more limited.[64]

Subjects dealing with industrial and technical cooperation are not yet dealt with on a common basis. There is no reason, therefore, why the Community should control the conclusion of cooperation agreements simply because one of their consequences is to influence the flow of trade. All this would change, of course, if the Member States would relinquish their powers in the fields of economic and industrial cooperation and leave it to the EEC to deal with them in a centralised manner. It is, moreover, one thing to consult the EEC and to involve the Commission so as to avoid violations of Community Law, but it is quite another to act as if a cohesive common policy in these fields already existed, *quod non.* As such there is no reason why the Member States should not be allowed to continue to conclude bilateral cooperation agreements, always provided they do not infringe upon the Community's commercial powers. All this does not mean, of course, that a gradual involvement of the EEC would not be beneficial, or that efforts in that direction should not be made. Such an involvement could well be realised under an "umbrella" EEC-CMEA agreement, notably with respect to certain technical issues. But it simply is not realistic to demand that the Community completely take over at this point, with all the risks this entails for the smooth development of relations between western and eastern Europe.

C. *Legal Basis*

It should now be examined to what extent Article 113 could possibly encompass the subject matter commonly referred to as industrial and economic cooperation. Basically this boils down to the question of whether the term "common commercial policy" should be interpreted in a *restrictive* or in an *extensive* sense. It should moreover be kept in mind that Article 113 is generally understood to confer an *exclusive* competence on the Community which implies that the Member States have lost all competence in the fields covered by this Article.[65]

63. Huber, *op.cit.* n. 43.
64. See debates of the E.P. on the relations between the EEC and the east European countries and Comecon, Supp. n. 186, Feb. 1975, 106; Huber, *op.cit.* n. 43, at 1490.
65. Court of Justice, *op.cit.* n. 25.

Cooperation agreements as such are, understandably, not mentioned either in Article 113 or in the decision of December 16, 1969.[66] One will also look in vain for references to industrial cooperation, exchange of technical information, *etc.*, terms commonly found in bilateral cooperation agreements. Should these subjects nonetheless be brought under the nomer "commercial policy"?

The European Court has recently pronounced itself in favour of an extensive interpretation of Article 113, without specifically mentioning cooperation agreements.[67] It remains unclear all the same which elements found in cooperation agreements should be brought under an extensive interpretation and which not.

Still, from a strictly legal point of view the Court's approach seems justified; for not so much the limitative enumeration of subjects found in Article 113, as the general objectives of the Treaty of Rome, and notably those laid down in Article 110,[68] should be used as a yardstick. Under an extensive definition of commercial policy all official measures which are intended to influence positively or negatively the structure, composition and volume of *commercial* transactions with third States should *in principle* come under the Community's exclusive competence. Parting from an extensive definition, moreover, it should be of relative importance whether a common approach has already been worked out in respect of all details of the common commercial policy (almost impossible given the fluid nature of the above definition) or whether some aspects have so far only been covered incidentally. As such it should also be of relative importance whether or not the Member States are at present still wielding some of the powers belonging in principle to the Community. In other words, for the Community's external competence it is not essential whether or not there is internally a fully elaborated common policy, but rather whether there is full agreement on the scope of the Community's powers.

It should be observed at this point that the EEC Commission has long been aware of this problem. As early as 1972 it pointed out the need to provide the common commercial policy with new instruments and to enlarge its scope so as to enable it to match the new methods in the field of cooperation employed by the Member States in their dealings, *inter*

66. *Op.cit.* n. 8.
67. Court of Justice, *op.cit.* n. 25.
68. Art. 110: "By establishing a customs union between themselves, Member States aim to contribute, in the common interest, to the harmonious development of world trade, the progressive abolition of restrictions on international trade and the lowering of customs barriers"; *cf.* Ganshof van der Meersch, *Droit des Communautés Européennes* (Brussels, 1969), p. 921, no. 2295.

alia, with the state-trading nations. But in spite of the Court's abovementioned Opinion [69] and the Commission's well-intentioned efforts to arrive at a homogeneous commercial policy, its realisation in practice has been limited to the issues specifically mentioned in Article 113. In view of this—perhaps regrettable—situation, it looks as if bilateral cooperation agreements will continue to carry the day for some time to come. This does not mean that the Commission's efforts to work out an acceptable commercial policy (including elements now found in cooperation agreements) based on an extensive interpretation of Article 113, should not be continued. What is more: it should be accepted by the Member States, if only to prevent a gradual erosion of the Community's prerogatives in this field and a weakening of its prestige and effectivity.

There are, however, two obstacles which obstruct a speedy realisation of such a policy.

The *first* obstacle concerns a negotiating mandate for common cooperation agreements, which the Commission is not likely to receive from the Member States in the near future.[70] For it is evident that legal arguments alone will not sway the Member States in their conviction that cooperation agreements should, for the time being, be concluded on a bilateral basis instead of on a common basis. In the absence of a fully elaborated common commercial policy, particularly in such sensitive sectors as national industrial development and technical cooperation, it looks as if national powers will be jealously nurtured for some time to come.

The *second* obstacle has been created by the Council's decision of July 22, 1974 instituting a consultation procedure for bilateral cooperation agreements.[71] Not so much the consultation procedure itself, which is a laudable initiative, but rather the legal basis for this measure is worth examining. The Council's decision was based on Article 235; in other words, it was an *ad hoc* attribution of a competence to the Community, therewith rejecting the existence of an exclusive competence as far as cooperation agreements are concerned. Article 113 was only mentioned, it seems, in order to place the consultation procedure against the background of the common commercial policy. This decision may be invoked as proof by some Member States that the Community has officially acknowledged the fact that issues dealt with in cooperation agreements do *not* fall under the Community's exclusive competence.

69. *Op.cit.* n. 25.

70. Bot, "Negotiating Community Agreements: Procedure and Practice", 7 C.M.L.Rev. 1970, 292-295.

71. The Commission's proposal in O.J. 1973, C 106/22; the Council's Decision No. 74/393/EEC of July 22, 1974, in O.J. 1974, L 208/23.

The consultation procedure, it will be argued, is only intended to ensure that purely commercial elements will not inadvertently be included in those agreements. Therewith, in a sense, the Community would have gone back to a restrictive interpretation of Article 113. Therewith also the realisation of a comprehensive common commercial policy would have received a serious set-back.

Is there a way out of this dilemma? Two solutions seem possible, taking into account both the necessity for an extensive interpretation of Article 113, and the Member States' reluctance at this stage to hand over certain powers over vital sectors of their economies.

The *first* solution would be to *maintain* an *extensive* interpretation of Article 113, but to limit its *exclusiveness.* It could be argued that much of the subject matter dealt with in cooperation agreements should in principle fall under the scope of this Article, but that the Member States have retained some competences in this field. To be precise, issues which according to existing Community Law do clearly fall under the common commercial policy (tariffs, protective measures, levies, quotas, *etc.*) are the Community's exclusive competence;[72] but issues which have not yet been regulated are subject to a shared competence. This means that the Community has to share its competence with the Member States until a definite transfer of powers in these fields has taken place (*i.e.* commerce in wider sense covering the exchange of licences, industrial and technical cooperation, *etc.*).

Such a transfer could be considered to have taken place either when the Community has dealt with these issues exhaustively and adopted binding regulations of a *general* character or when it has dealt with them on an *ad hoc* basis, for example in common cooperation agreements.[73] But so long as this has not occurred, the Member States should be considered free to avail themselves of their remaining powers. This reasoning clearly parts from the view that basically the question of exclusivity or non-exclusivity is not so much based on Article 113 itself, as on the nature of the instruments in question. The danger inherent in this solution is that the Commission's role will, also in the future, remain rather limited; reference may, for example, be made to cooperation formulas in Community agreements with Jugoslavia (Article 7 [74]), Uruguay (Article 3 [75]), India (Article 6 [76]) and Brazil (Articles 3-5 [77]).

72. *Op.cit.* n. 25.
73. *Ibid.*
74. O.J. 1973, L 224/1.
75. O.J. 1973, L 338/ .
76. O.J. 1974, L 82/1.
77. O.J. 1974, L 102/23.

If one proceeds from this working hypothesis, it would at least be advisable for the Member States to include in their cooperation agreements a revision clause. This would enable them to terminate the agreement in question at short notice if newly-established Community Law should necessitate a speedy transfer of powers; for, as a general rule, care should be taken that the provisions of Article 5 of the Rome Treaty [78] are not invalidated.

Several Member States will undoubtedly be in favour of this interpretation. *Firstly,* because a large number of cooperation agreements has already been concluded under national aegis, often for periods as long as ten years with the possibility of tacit renewal. *Secondly,* because the formulation of a cohesive common policy on such sensitive issues as those presently dealt with in cooperation agreements cannot be expected to take place in the near future. *Thirdly,* because it is not clear whether the east European countries would accept the Community as a negotiating partner, particularly on this subject matter.

A *second* and more consistent solution would consist of an interpretation which holds that Article 113 *confers an exclusive* competence on the Community in all commercial matters, *extensively interpreted.* This view is also shared by the European Court in its earlier mentioned Advisory Opinion. From there on, however, a reasoning should be developed identical to the one underlying the Council's decision of December 16, 1969 (notably Article 9). Therewith the general rule of the Community's competence could be confirmed while a derogation—limited in time—could be envisaged as to certain issues not yet exhaustively regulated by Community Law. The argument could then be defended that so long as the conditions for the opening of negotiations with the Community have not been fulfilled, either because third parties refuse to deal with the Commission or because a common approach is still lacking, the Member States should retain a (non-autonomous) power to conclude bilateral cooperation agreements.

In adopting this solution, the Member States' rights would, of course, be much more restricted than under the first solution; for in principle the Community would be the competent institution to conclude cooperation agreements, and it would only be a matter of time, before it could fully exercise this competence. The second solution is consequently more in tune with the Community's overall unification concept, but much harder to realize in practice, given the understandable objections of the Mem-

78. Art. 5: "Member States ... shall take all appropriate measures to ensure the carrying out of the obligations of this Treaty and ... shall abstain from any measures which could jeopardize the attainment of the objectives of the Treaty".

ber States mentioned earlier. Still, it is the opinion of the present author that the second solution is in the long run inevitable if one ever wishes to arrive at an economic integration worthy of that name.

V. CONCLUSION

What does the future hold for relations between the EEC and the CMEA?

As regards trade relations, the EEC clearly prefers to come to terms with the individual CMEA Member States rather than with the CMEA as such. Its offer to negotiate, coupled with suggestions for a draft trade agreement submitted to the east European countries in 1974, clearly points that way.

With the possible exception of Rumania, however, the east European countries do not seem to welcome this idea. Meanwhile, the ensuing stalemate characterized by the EEC's autonomous commercial policy, might lead to haphazard commercial relations with eastern Europe. Although potentially risky to the Nine, this situation could be even more disadvantageous to eastern Europe in view of its heavy commercial involvement in western Europe. The Community's position is therefore relatively comfortable.

Is there an alternative to this predicament, apart from continued pressure on the individual CMEA members to accept the principle of separate commercial agreements with the EEC?

The conclusion of a so-called "umbrella" agreement proposed by the CMEA might be a solution. Many of the smaller CMEA members, it seems, are in principle interested in such an agreement. The CMEA countries, however, in an attempt to stress the symmetry between the two organisations, seem to be pressing for purely bilateral negotiations with the EEC Member States in order to work out the details of the "umbrella" agreement. In view of its advanced degree of commercial integration, the EEC's bargaining position appears strong enough to resist such pressure. The CMEA countries should therefore get accustomed to the idea of the Community, rather than its individual members as a partner on all commercial issues. Much would depend, of course, on the biggest partner, the Soviet Union, whose will has turned out to be paramount in almost all decisions concerning the CMEA's future course, all principles concerning unanimity and political consensus in that organisation notwithstanding.

But prior to such negotiations the CMEA and its members would have to accept the EEC as a negotiating partner, *i.e.* they would have to extend formal recognition to the EEC.

The situation is less simple in regard to cooperation agreements. For the Nine these are useful vehicles to develop their political and economic relations with eastern Europe. Many EEC Member States, therefore, consider the Commission's claims for greater influence in this sector a direct challenge to their freedom in a vital area of national foreign competences. Here indeed the question arises as to how far the Community's jurisdiction in external affairs can be stretched beyond purely commercial matters. Some Member States feel that Article 113 of the Treaty of Rome is limited to issues which have a *direct* bearing on trade and that the Community's competences should consequently be limited to those issues. Other Member States, however, consider that all issues *likely* to affect trade, *i.e.* much of the subject matter dealt with in cooperation agreements, should be brought under this Article and that the Community could justifiably claim a degree of jurisdiction in this field.

Still, the political and economic environment does not yet seem to be prepared for a complete transfer of powers to the Community. Or, to put it bluntly, most EEC Member States are still unwilling to relinquish their traditional roles to a supranational body in a sector so closely linked with their foreign policies. The lack of sufficient guarantees, and particularly of a cohesive common policy, the economic interests at stake and growing nationalist tendencies are among the factors which have contributed to this attitude.

The CMEA's views on this issue are not precisely known, but it may be safely assumed that, particularly in the field of cooperation, it will be interested in an "umbrella" cooperation agreement with the Community, possibly even in combination with an "umbrella" trade agreement, provided the details can be worked out with the Nine individually. There is no reason, however, why an EEC-CMEA agreement should not contain such issues as statistical cooperation, standardisation, the exchange of economic information and similar technical issues, since in this respect the EEC is certainly competent to speak in the name of its Member States.

Inter-tribal fighting for the favours of the east European markets, meanwhile, would only play into the hands of the CMEA countries. For the time being, therefore, a balance should be struck between the extreme individualism of some Member States and the overbearing claims of the Community. The acceptance of measures which gradually improve and render compulsory prior notification and coordination on cooperation agreements should be a first step towards this objective. The final result should be a common basis which permits a greater involvement of the Community. For, as Sir Christopher Soames recently put it, whatever we do, we can do it with greater hope of success if we act as a Community rather than if we march separated from each other, every one for himself.[79]

79. Soames, *op.cit.* n.l, at 428.

THE EXECUTION OF COMMUNITY FOOD AID TO DEVELOPING COUNTRIES

Introduction

Without being mentioned in any of the Community Treaties, the Community food aid policy has developed to considerable dimensions. Thus in answer to a written question posed by Lord Reay on April 3, 1975 the Commission gave a summary of all the food aid programmes including Member States' own cereal programmes, operated by the Community since they began in 1969.[1]

(in 1,000 metric tons)

	1969	1970	1971	1972	1973	1974	1975
1. Cereals							
Community programmes	301	337	353	414	464	580	643.5
National programmes	734	698	682	621	697	707	643.5
Total	1,035	1,035	1,035	1,035	1.161	1,287	1,287
2. Other products (Community programmes)							
- milk	-	127	-	60	13	55	55
- butteroil	-	37	-	15	-	45	45
- eggs	-	-	-	0.5	-	-	-
- sugar	-	-	-	6	6	6	-

From above table it can be seen that there has been a steady increase in the Community's share of the cereals food aid programmes which are carried out as part of the Community's and the Member States' obligations under the Food Aid Convention.[2] There has also been a rather more erratic progression on the Community's programmes for milk products.

1. Written question No. 48/75, O.J. 1975, C 170/28.
2. Council Decision of June 25, 1974 on the conclusion of the International Wheat Agreement, consisting of the Wheat Trade Convention and the Food Aid Convention, O.J. 1974, L 219/24.

13 C.M.L. Rev. 1976, 367-374

Accompanying this general increase in the amount of food aid given by the Community as such there has been an increase in recent years in the proportion of emergency food aid actions to normal food aid actions, *e.g.* the actions mounted in 1974 in favor of the African countries most affected by the drought. The total cost of food aid actions (excluding export refunds) for 1975 is estimated at 200 million units of account.

This increasing activity, some of which has required extremely quick decisions and execution, has strained the procedures of the Community to their limits, and brought into question the institutional balance between the Council (in food aid matters the dicision-making body) and the Commission (the executing body). This has led to the proposal and adoption of a number of remedies, involving in particular the delegation of substantial powers from the Council to the Commission. It is my purpose not to make a general description and critique of the Community's food aid procedures,[3] but rather to describe and to examine the recent changes in these procedures.

The proposals of the Commission

The problems of the Community's food aid procedures were squarely raised in a "Memorandum on the Food Aid Policy of the E.E.C." presented by the Commission to the Council on March 11, 1974.[4]

In this Memorandum the Commission recalled that food aid policy requires rapid and efficient procedures for its implementation. It demanded that the responsibilities within the Community for implementing food aid actions be re-allocated between the Council and the Commission. In the Commission's view, the existing procedures were not adapted to the requirements of efficient management, since not only the broad questions of principle but also the smallest details of food aid executions were subject to Council debate and approval.

In effect, these existing procedures consisted of two phases. First, the Council took a decision offering food aid to certain developing countries and international organisations. This decision permitted the opening of negotiations with the country concerned. Normally, such a decision would be implicit in the Council's acceptance of an annual food aid programme, but in case of emergency, it would be taken on an *ad hoc* basis as and when the emergency occurred. Secondly, the Council had

3. For such an account see Marenco, "Bases juridiques communautaires de l'aide alimentaire aux pays en voie de dėveloppement", (1974) C.D.E., 623-648.

4. Bull. of the E.C. 1974, no. 3, 1303-1313, esp. 1312, para. (iv), and 1313, para. (d).

also to approve the terms of every agreement, after its negotiations with the recipient country and international organisations, including such details as the nature of product, conditions of its distribution, the proposed use of counterpart funds.

As a result, several months might pass before the Council's decisions could be effectively implemented. In effect, after completing negotiations with the recipient country and international organisations concerned, it was necessary, according to the practice at the time, to bring the matter once again before the Council to obtain a decision authorizing the definitive conclusion of the agreement.

The Commission considered that it was necessary to adopt more flexible procedures with a view to improving working efficiency and shortening delays in the execution of the Community actions. It therefore proposed that in the future the Council should decide on the adoption of indicative medium-term and annual programmes, and on allocation of the Community's food aid among beneficiary countries and international organisations, as well as on basic conditions underlying the distribution of the Community's food aid. The Commission would act on behalf of the Community vis à vis beneficiary countries and international organisations as regards the definition of relevant rights and obligations concerning implementation of actions decided by the Council.

For discharging these functions it was proposed that the Commission should be assisted by a Committee of the type of a management committee, consisting of Member State experts on development and cooperation, familiar with agricultural and nutritional problems.

For emergency situations, especially those relating to natural disasters and conflicts, the Commission envisaged a two-stage procedure, whereby the Commission itself:

- would have authority to decide on the first, limited amounts of aid to be dispatched during the early days immediately following the disaster, if necessary by air transport; and
- would propose to the Council to take a decision—by an accelerated procedure—concerning the dispatch of the remaining quantities of food aid.

The decisions of the Council

Some powers of decision had already been delegated by the Council to Commission for the execution in emergency situations of the framework agreement between the Community and the Red Cross.[5] The Council

5. Council Decision of October 15, 1973, O.J. 1974, L 23/17.

were able to accept the Commission's proposals for emergency actions almost in their entirety, with certain significant reservations which had the effect of:

(a) excluding actions necessitated by war situations;

(b) keeping each emergency action within certain quantitative limits (5,000 tons of cereals and 500 tons of milk powder and butteroil);

(c) requiring the prior consultation of Member States by telex "with a view to any possible observations which might be made within a period of two working-days".

For normal actions however, the proposal that the Commission should "engage" the Community with regard to third countries proved too much for the Council to swallow. This reluctance stemmed partly from political reasons, despite the joint declaration of the presidents of the Council and of the Commission of April 30, 1974 on the decision making process of the Community which had declared that:

> "a greater responsibility should be entrusted to the Commission by the application of Article 155, fourth indent of the Treaty,[6] it being agreed that collaboration between the Commission and the competent national administrations would be assured by procedures deriving from those already applied within the Community for the management committees or other committees."

Of more interest, however, are the legal arguments which developed about the legitimacy of such an "engagement" procedure under the terms of the Treaty. On the one hand it was argued that:

(a) agreements for the supply of food aid by the Community to third countries are international agreements within the terms of Article 228 of the Treaty;

(b) Article 228 provides that such agreements are negotiated by the Commission and are concluded by the Council;

(c) this power to conclude international agreements cannot be delegated by the Council to the Commission under the terms of Article 155, paragraph 4, which only permits the attribution of newly created powers and not a proper delegation, in the sense of a transfer of power;

6. Article 155: "In order to ensure the proper functioning and development of the common market, the Commission shall: . . . "exercise the powers conferred on it by the Council for the implementation of the rules laid down by the latter".

(d) the appropriate case-law of the Court of Justice is therefore not *Köster*[7] but rather *Meroni*.[8]

On the other hand the following counter-arguments were developed–
(a) in the *Meroni* case the Court does not exclude delegation of powers as such by a Community institution, but rather defines the limits within which such a delegation should be exercised;
(b) it is the nature of the Community system that the general policy decisions should be taken by the Council and that the detailed decisions should be taken by the Commission acting under powers conferred by the Council, as is confirmed by the Court's judgement in the *Köster* case;
(c) there is nothing sacred about the conclusion of international agreements which excludes them from the application of the Council's general powers to delegate, provided that proper limits are put on the power delegated.

The legal arguments were not resolved in the debates within the Council's working group.[9] A solution did however emerge which, in one sense, gave to the Commission greater powers than it had originally requested. This solution involved the abandonment of the idea that the Commission should "engage" the Community by way of an agreement with the beneficiary countries or organisations, since there would be no "agreement" at all between the Community and the beneficiaries. As finally decided by the Council on April 14, 1975, the new procedure took the following form:
(a) prior adoption by the Council of food aid programmes in all the necessary detail;
(b) contacts between the Commission and the beneficiary countries and organisations included in the programmes to confirm their requirement for the aid decided and to regulate the details of its delivery; the Commission to send to the beneficiaries a letter in a standard form approved by the Council;
(c) after receipt of this letter and confirmation of its terms by the beneficiary, the Commission to proceed to the measures necessary for mobilization of the food aid and for its delivery.

7. Case 25/70, *Einfuhr- und Vorratsstelle für Getreide und Futtermittel v. Köster, Berodt & Co.* (Judgment of December 17, 1970) 16 *Recueil* 1970, 1161 *et seq.* In this case the Court authorized the procedure, widely used in the management of the common agricultural policy, of Commission decisions in association with management committees consisting of representatives of the Member States.

8. Cases 9/56 and 10/56, *Meroni & Co. v. High Authority* (Judgment of June 13, 1958), 4 *Recueil* 1958, 8 *et seq.* In this case the Court annulled a decision of the ECSC High Authority because of an irregular delegation of powers to a private body.

9. The *"ad hoc"* Food Aid group.

Provision was also made for Member States to be informed in advance by the Commission prior to the sending out of the letters referred to and for the examination of objections by any Member States within the Council's working group.

Discussion

Within their limits the new procedures appear to have worked reasonably well. The procedure for emergency actions has not so far been extensively used, chiefly because since the adoption of the Council's decision on August 14, 1975 many international food shortages have resulted from war situations.[10] The procedures for normal situations after some initial confusion over their date of entry into force [11] are now applied universally. The only exception to this general rule is the three-year agreement with the United Nations Relief Works Agency for Palestine refugees (UNRWA),[12] which expired in 1975 and is being renegotiated by the Commission with a view to conclusion by the Council.

Notwithstanding the practical success of these measures, certain doubts remain, both from the point of view of their strict conformity with the relevant case-law and of the risk they bring of confusing the distinct roles of the Council and of the Commission.

From the case-law of the Court of Justice two distinct limitations on the Council's power to delegate can be discerned. Firstly, a delegation of powers should be appreciated in a different light according as to whether in concerns well-defined powers of execution or a discretionary power which contains a wide freedom of appreciation and which is suitable to conducting a real economic policy.[13] Secondly, "procedural requirements are satisfied from the moment that the essential elements of the matter to be decided have been fixed in conformity with the procedure provided by (the Treaty article in question)".[14] Applying these criteria to the emergency procedure, it is difficult to find that the Council has regulated the essential elements or indeed given the Commission any guidelines for the exercise of its discretion, except in so far as a general aid policy can be discerned from the programmes which are decided at

10. *E.g.* Vietnam, Cyprus, Angola, the Middle East.

11. It was finally decided by the Council that the new procedure should be equally applied to unexecuted actions remaining over from programmes prior to 1975.

12. O.J. 1972, L 304/24.

13. *Meroni op.cit.* n. 8, 43.

14. *Köster op.cit.* n. 7, 1172.

the same time by the Council.[15] The Council has rather concentrated on the negative aspects of its delegation—the exclusion of war situations, the quantitative limitations and the obligation of prior consultation.

With regard to normal procedures the same criticism cannot really be applied since all that the Commission is authorized to do is follow certain standardized procedures in order to fix transport and other details with the beneficiaries. Indeed it is arguable whether in this case there is any delegation at all of a real power.

However, examination of the normal procedures does show the same concentration on negative aspects as the emergency procedures. This negative emphasis, with the Council almost taking back with one hand what is has given with the other, does run the risk of bringing about that confusion of the two institutions which is the second line of doubt about the new procedures. Under the normal procedure the Commission sends out standard form letters and conditions. If these are not acceptable to the beneficiaries to the extent that substantial changes are required, it is "understood" that the Commission will first examine these with the Council's working group. Similarly, if any Member State objects to the sending off of a letter to a beneficiary, within the ten days provided for "the question is to be examined within the competent working-group". Both these reserves can be criticized as subordinating the action of the Commission to the undefined control of a Council committee which has no recognized institutional role.[16] The same criticism cannot be made of that aspect of the emergency procedure which requires the prior consultation of the Member States for their observations. Given the time scale involved in an emergency action, discussion in the working-group is not feasible. One is nevertheless left with the impression that the Commission would be unwise to disregard the observations of Member States.

15. By contrast, the classic procedure was followed for the sale of skimmed-milk powder from public stocks for supply to developing countries, which all parties have been careful to assert not to be "food aid". Thus the Council fixed the essential elements in Regulation 155/75 (O.J. 1975, L 19/3), and the Commission fixed the detailed rules in Regulation 602/75 (O.J. 1975, L 63/18) and takes decision on each action with the advice of the management committee for milk and milk products.

16. In contrast to the Commission's management committees which are established by Council regulation and which have precisely powers and procedures. See Chr. Bertram, "Decision-Making in the E.E.C. The Management Committee Procedure", 5 C.M.L. Rev. 1967, 246.

Conclusion

It cannot be pretended that the criticisms of the strict legality of the procedures described, if founded, are any serious cause for concern. These procedures affect relations between the Council and the Commission and relations between the Community and the rest of the world.

Private rights are not affected directly, since they continue to be governed by the general and particular rules covering tenders for the mobilization of food aid actions which follow well-defined norms published as regulations in the Official Journal. The risk of a challenge to the procedures before the Court of Justice is therefore remote, and if such a challenge were mounted it is unlikely that the Court would hold any procedural irregularities to be sufficiently serious as to nullify the action in question.

The institutional confusion is however potentially more serious. It is in one sense symptomatic of the hesitant attitude of the Member States towards the position of the Commission in the field of external relations.[17] A practical result is that in their execution of food aid programmes the Commission are liable to political pressure from Member States. This is something that should be a cause for concern to all who regard the assertion of national interests over the Community interest as being damaging to the existing state and continuing development of the Community.

Richard Wainwright *
Brussels

17. An attitude which prompted the Commission to seek the opinion of the Court under Article 228 on the compatibility with the Treaty of a proposed OECD arrangement concerned with export credits and on the competence of the Community to conclude such an arrangement. Opinion of the Court of Justice 1/75, O.J. 1975, C 268/18. Report and comment by H. H. Maas, *infra*, pp. 375 *et seq.*

* Member of the Legal Service of the Commission of the European Communities.
The views expressed in this article are purely personal to the author.

CASE LAW

A. COURT OF JUSTICE

106. *Opinion 1/75* - Opinion of the Court given pursuant to Article 228 of the EEC Treaty of November 11, 1975.

On July 14, 1975, the Court of Justice received a request for an opinion submitted by the Commission of the European Communities pursuant to the second paragraph of Article 228 (1) of the Treaty establishing the EEC, according to which:

> "The Council, the Commission or a Member State may obtain beforehand the opinion of the Court of Justice as to whether an agreement envisaged is compatible with the provisions of this Treaty. Where the opinion of the Court of Justice is adverse, the agreement may enter into force only in accordance with Article 236".

Discussion

The question arising from the request for an opinion prompts the following considerations:

A. Admissibility of the request for an opinion

The second subparagraph of Article 228 (1) lays down that the Council, the Commission or a Member State may request the Court for an opinion as to the compatibility with the provisions of the Treaty of an agreement to be concluded with one or more third countries or with an international organization.

The formal designation of the agreement envisaged under international law is not of decisive importance in connexion with the admissibility of the request. In its reference to an "agreement", the second subparagraph of Article 228 (1) of the Treaty uses the expression in a general sense to indicate any undertaking entered into by entities subject to international law which has binding force, whatever its formal designation.

The Understanding in question fulfils these conditions. It contains a "standard", that is to say a rule of conduct, covering a specific field, determined by precise provisions, which is binding upon the participants. The very fact that the standard expressly provides that derogations shall take place only in exceptional cases and under strict conditions is sufficient evidence that the Understanding is such as to bind the contracting parties and therefore fulfils the conditions of the second subparagraph of Article 228 (1) of the Treaty.

Moreover, discussions concerning the substance of the agreement are at an end and the conclusion of the Understanding in the form of a resolution of the Council of the OECD is now envisaged.

At the same time, the "draft Report to the Council of the OECD concerning the Understanding on a Local Cost Standard" states that there only remains to be clarified "the form of the participation in the Understanding by the European Economic Community, whose decision on the subject is to be made very soon".

In view of these factors and bearing in mind the recommendation of the Commission concerning the "form" of the Community's participation in the Understanding in question, it cannot be doubted that the draft Understanding constitutes an agreement "envisaged"

13 C.M.L. Rev. 1976, 375-387

within the meaning of the second subparagraph of Article 228 (1) of the Treaty.

Moreover, the fact that the Commission raised the problem of the compatibility of this agreement with the provisions of the Treaty for the purpose of obtaining the opinion of the Court of Justice on the extent of the Community's powers to conclude the agreement envisaged cannot be sufficient of itself to render the request inadmissible with respect to the second subparagraph of Article 228 (1) aforementioned.

The compatibility of an agreement with the provisions of the Treaty must be assessed in the light of all the rules of the Treaty, that is to say, both those rules which determine the extent of the powers of the institutions of the Community and the substantive rules.

It is the purpose of the second subparagraph of Article 228 (1) to forestall complications which would result from legal disputes concerning the compatibility with the Treaty of international agreements binding upon the Community. In fact, a possible decision of the Court to the effect that such an agreement is, either by reason of its content or of the procedure adopted for its conclusion, incompatible with the provisions of the Treaty could not fail to provoke, not only in a Community context but also in that of international relations, serious difficulties and might give rise to adverse consequences for all interested parties, including third countries.

For the purpose of avoiding such complications the Treaty had recourse to the exceptional procedure of a prior reference to the Court of Justice for the purpose of elucidating, before the conclusion of the agreement, whether the latter is compatible with the Treaty. This procedure must therefore be open for all questions capable of submission for judicial consideration, either by the Court of Justice or possibly by national courts, in so far as such questions give rise to doubt either as to the substantive or formal validity of the agreement with regard to the Treaty.

The question whether the conclusion of a given agreement is within the power of the Community and whether, in a given case, such power has been exercised in conformity with the provisions of the Treaty is, in principle, a question which may be submitted to the Court of Justice, either directly, under Article 169 or Article 173 of the Treaty, or in accordance with the preliminary procedure, and it must therefore be admitted that the matter may be referred to the Court in accordance with the preliminary procedure of Article 228.

Similarly, the fact that discussions concerning the substance of the Understanding in question are now at an end cannot constitute a valid argument on which to base a finding that the request for an opinion is out of time, since the Treaty, by reason of the non-contentious character of the procedure contained in the second subparagraph of Article 228 (1), does not lay down a time-limit for the submission of such a request.

There is therefore no reason why the request for an opinion should not be admitted.

B. The reply to be given to the questions submitted

1. The existence of a Community power to conclude the OECD Understanding on a Local Cost Standard

Articles 112 and 113 of the Treaty must be borne in mind in formulating a reply to this question.

The first of these provisions provides that:

> "... Member States shall, before the end of the transitional period, progressively harmonize the systems whereby they grant aid for exports to third countries, to the extent necessary to ensure that competition between undertakings of the Community is not distorted."

Since there is no doubt that the grant of export credits falls within the system of aids granted by Member States for exports, it is already clear from Article 112 that the subject-matter of the standard laid down in the Understanding in question relates to a field in which the provisions of the Treaty recognize a Community power.

Furthermore, Article 113 of the Treaty lays down, in paragraphs (1) and (2), that:

> "... the common commercial policy shall be based on uniform principles, particularly in regard to ... export policy ...".

The field of the common commercial policy, and more particularly that of export policy, necessarily covers systems of aid for exports and more particularly measures concerning credits for the financing of local costs linked to export operations. In fact, such measures constitute an important element of commercial policy, that concept having the same content whether it is applied in the context of the international action of a State or to that of the Community.

Directives concerning credit insurance, adopted by the Council towards the end of 1970 and the beginning of 1971 expressly recognize the important role played by export credits in international trade, as a factor of commercial policy.

For these reasons the subject-matter covered by the standard contained in the Understanding in question, since it forms part not only of the sphere of the system of aids for exports laid down at Article 112 of the Treaty but also, in a more general way, of export policy and, by reason of that fact, of the sphere of the common commercial policy defined in Article 113 of the Treaty, falls within the ambit of the Community's powers.

In the course of the measures necessary to implement the principles laid down in the abovementioned provisions, particularly those covered by Article 113 of the Treaty, concerning the common commercial policy, the Community is empowered, pursuant to the powers which it possesses, not only to adopt internal rules of Community law, but also to conclude agreements with third countries pursuant to Article 113 (2) and Article 114 of the Treaty.

A commercial policy is in fact made up by the combination and interaction of internal and external measures, without priority being taken by one over the others. Sometimes agreements are concluded in execution of a policy fixed in advance, sometimes that policy is defined by the agreements themselves.

Such agreements may be outline agreements, the purpose of which is to lay down uniform principles. Such is the case with the Understanding on local costs: it does not have a specific content adapted to particular export credit transactions; it merely lays down a standard, sets out certain exceptions, provides, in exceptional circumstances, for derogations and, finally, lays down general provisions. Furthermore, the implementation of the export policy to be pursued within the framework of a common commercial policy does not necessarily find expression in the adoption of general and abstract rules of internal or Community law. The common commercial policy is above all the outcome of a progressive development based upon specific measures which may refer without distinction to "autonomous" and external aspects of that policy and which do not necessarily presuppose, by the fact that they are linked to the field of the common commercial policy, the existence of a large body of rules, but combine gradually to form that body.

2. The exclusive nature of the Community's powers

The reply to this question depends, on the one hand, on the objective of the Understanding in question and, on the other hand, on the manner in which the common commercial policy is conceived in the Treaty.

At Nos I and II the Understanding itself defines the transactions to which the common standard applies, and those which, on the other hand, are excluded from its field of application because they are directed to specifically military ends or because they have been entered into with developing countries.

It is to be understood from this definition that the subject-matter of the standard, and therefore of the Understanding, is one of those measures belonging to the common commercial policy prescribed by Article 113 of the Treaty.

Such a policy is conceived in that article in the context of the operation of the Common Market, for the defence of the common interests of the Community, within which the particular interests of the Member States must endeavour to adapt to each other.

Quite clearly, however, this conception is incompatible with the freedom to which the Member States could lay claim by invoking a concurrent power, so as to ensure that their own interests were separately satisfied in external relations, at the risk of compromising the effective defence of the common interests of the Community.

In fact any unilateral action on the part of the Member States would lead to disparities in the conditions for the grant of export credits, calculated to distort competition between undertakings of the various Member States in external markets. Such distortion can be eliminated only by means of a strict uniformity of credit conditions granted to undertakings in the Community, whatever their nationality.

It cannot therefore be accepted that, in a field such as that governed by the Understanding in question, which is covered by export policy and more generally by the common commercial policy, the Member States should exercise a power concurrent to that of the Community, in the Community sphere and in the international sphere. The provisions of Articles 113 and 114 concerning the conditions under which, according to the Treaty, agreements on commercial policy must be concluded show clearly that the exercise of concurrent powers by the Member States and the Community in this matter is impossible.

To accept that the contrary were true would amount to recognizing that, in relations with third countries, Member States may adopt positions which differ from those which the Community intends to adopt, and would thereby distort the institutional framework, call into question the mutual trust within the Community and prevent the latter from fulfilling its task in the defence of the common interest.

It is of little importance that the obligations and financial burdens inherent in the execution of the agreement envisaged are borne directly by the Member States. The "internal" and "external" measures adopted by the Community within the framework of the common commercial policy do not necessarily involve, in order to ensure their compatibility with the Treaty, a transfer to the institutions of the Community of the obligations and financial burdens which they may involve: such measures are solely concerned to substitute for the unilateral action of the Member States, in the field under consideration, a common action based upon uniform principles on behalf of the whole of the Community.

Similarly, in relation to products subject to the ECSC Treaty, it is of little importance to note that the power of the Member States to conclude the Understanding envisaged is safeguarded by Article 71 of that Treaty, according to which:

> "The powers of the Governments of Member States in matters of commercial policy shall not be affected by this Treaty . . ."

The matter under discussion has been referred to the Court pursuant to the second subparagraph of Article 228 (1) of the EEC Treaty. The opinion which it has been called upon to give therefore bears upon the problem of the compatibility of the agreement envisaged with the provisions of the EEC Treaty and will define the power of the Community to conclude that agreement solely in relation to those provisions.

Independently of the question whether, in view of the necessity of ensuring that international transactions to which the Communities are party should have as uniform a character as possible, Article 71 of the ECSC Treaty retains its former force following the entry into force of the EEC Treaty, that provision cannot in any event render inoperative Articles 113 and 114 of the EEC Treaty and affect the vesting of power in the Community for the negotiation and conclusion of international agreements in the realm of common commercial policy.

Accordingly, the Court gave the following opinion:

The Community has exclusive power to participate in the Understanding on a Local Cost Standard referred to in the request for an opinion.

The External Powers of the EEC with regard to Commercial Policy: Comment on Opinion 1/75

1. The EEC (hereafter referred to as the Community) is, according to the Treaty of Rome, empowered to conclude agreements with third states or with international organisations "...where provided for by the Treaty" (opening words of Article 228). Such Treaty provisions are Articles 111 (2) and 113 (commercial policy), Articles 229-231 (relations with other international organisations) and Article 238 (association with third countries).

The wording of Article 228, as reproduced above, should not, however, be too literally interpreted. Not only can the Council, where action of the Community appears necessary to attain, in the course of the operation of the Common market, one of the objectives of the Community, and the Treaty has not provided the necessary powers, take the appropriate measures (Article 235), which measures may also include the conclusion of an international agreement,[1] but, in particular, since the celebrated *ERTA* decision,[2] it is assumed that a Community power to conclude international agreements may also proceed from other Treaty provisions, and from actions of Community institutions within the framework of those provisions. According to the Court, each time the Community, with a view to implementing a Community policy envisaged by the Treaty, lays down common rules, whatever form these may take, the Member States are no longer empowered, acting individually or even collectively, to contract obligations towards third countries affecting these rules, but rather the Community is competent to do so. To the extent that such common rules come into being, the Community alone is in a position to assume and carry out contractual obligations towards third countries affecting the whole sphere of application of the Community legal system. One cannot, said the Court, in implementing the provisions of the Treaty, separate the category of measures internal to the Community from that of external relations.

2. When the Community intends to conclude an international agreement, the question may arise as to whether the agreement is compatible with the provisions of the Treaty. Both the question as to whether, by means of the agreement, an amplification or modification of the Treaty may be effected, and the question as to which institution is competent to conclude the agreement, may be disputed. For this reason, Article 228 (1) (ii) provides that an advisory opinion of the Court regarding the compatibility of the agreement with the Treaty may be requested before the agreement is finally concluded. The opinion that the Court issues on this question is binding in the sense that where it establishes the incompatibility of

1. *Cf.* E. Petersmann, "Auswärtige Gewalt (u.s.w.) der EWG", (1975) ZaöRVR, 215.

2. Case 22/70, 17 *Receuil* 1971, 263; 10 CMLR 1971, 335; 8 C.M.L.Rev. 1971, 392, with note by J. A. Winter, *ibid.*, 550 *et seq.*

the envisaged agreement with the Treaty, it cannot then be concluded, or at least cannot come into effect until the Treaty is revised under the conditions laid down in Article 236 in such a way that the incompatibility of the agreement is removed.

Up to 1975 no use was made of this possibility of avoiding legal uncertainty. The explanation for this may probably be found in the fact that in many cases where doubt has arisen as to the powers of the Community, the Community and the Member States have together concluded agreements, acting as one contracting party.[3] However, on July 14, 1975, the European Commission plucked up the courage to apply to the Court of Justice with a request for a decision concerning the compatibility with the EEC Treaty of the draft "Understanding on a local cost standard" drawn up under the auspices of the OECD.[4]

3. According to this Understanding, the participating governments agree, with regard to officially-supported contracts related to exports under credit terms, in principle not to finance or cover credit exceeding the total amount of payments to be received for the goods and services exported on completion of the exporter's contractual obligations (the so-called 100% rule). The Understanding was drawn up by the Group on Export Credits and Credit Guarantees of the OECD, in which Group, according to the normal procedure of the OECD, the Commission participated as well as the representatives of the Member States. Before the last phase of negotiations, on December 19, 1974, the Commission—in accordance with Article 113 (3) of the EEC Treaty—submitted a recommendation to the Council with the purpose of empowering the Commission to express the Community position within the OECD and to act on its behalf. In the course of the discussion of this recommendation, it became clear that the Commission considered that the matter in question was an exclusively Community affair, and that therefore only the Community as such should adopt the Understanding and thereby bind the Member States. It appeared that within the Council at least one Member State contested the competence of the Community, and that several others considered that the Member States could very well also participate in the Understanding side by side with the Community, and conclude it of their own accord. The chairman of the OECD Group who on February 11, 1975, was able to declare that "all delegations had given their approval to the draft Understanding", noted that in this respect there remained only to be clarified the form of the participation of the European Economic Community in the Understanding. The Commission's request to the Court then served to make this clarification possible. More specifically, the Commission posed the question as to whether "the Community has the power to conclude the said Understanding and, if so, whether that power is exclusive".

4. The Rules of Procedure of the Court provide for a special procedure in this respect (Articles 107-108). The Court gives the Council and the Member States the opportunity to submit their written comments within a time limit fixed by the President, it hears the opinions of all of the Advocates-General, and finally, sitting in the Judges' Council Chamber, delivers a reasoned opinion which shall be served on the Council, the Commission and the Member States. In the present case, the procedure was concluded on November 11, 1975, with the issue of the Advisory Opinion Number 1/75, which is

3. See in this respect "Wetgevingskroniek" in (1961) S.E.W. (Europa), 229; W. Alexander, "De associatie van Griekenland met de EEG", (1962) S.E.W. 514-5 and 527-8. *Cf.* more generally, J. J. Costonis, "The Treaty-making Power of the EEC", 5 C.M.L.Rev. 1967-68, 421 *et seq.*

4. For what follows, see Bull. of the E.C. 1975, no. 11, 2308.

published in the Official Journal 1975, C 268, pages 18-23.[5] A summarized version of the Opinion precedes this comment.

It appears from the Opinion that four of the Member States, as well as the Council, took advantage of the opportunity to submit observations. In judgments of the Court which contain preliminary rulings, such observations are normally reproduced, with mention of the government or institution which submitted them. In the Opinion of the Court, this is not the case, and one can therefore only guess as to who advanced what argument. One might be very curious to know what arguments were advanced by the Council, as that institution had found it impossible to reach a common standpoint. Assuming that the Court did not entirely of its own accord investigate the question of admissibility, it appears from the Opinion that four different arguments were advanced with the object of persuading the Court to declare the request inadmissible. These arguments will be dealt with first, and thereafter I shall go into the answer given by the Court to the actual questions posed.

5. According to Article 228 (1), the Court may be requested to issue an opinion as to the compatibility with the Treaty of an agreement which the Community envisages concluding with one or more third countries or with an international organisation. In this context the Court discusses two questions: was the present case concerned with an "agreement", and was the agreement "envisaged"?

(a) The draft Understanding elaborated by the OECD Group was to be implemented in the form of a resolution of the Council of the OECD. Such a resolution is binding on those members of the organisation which have adopted it—see Articles 5 and 6 of the Convention.[6] It should therefore be considered as an "agreement" in the sense of Article 228 EEC. The Court defines the term as "any undertaking entered into by entities subject to international law which has binding force, whatever its formal designation". The Court then considers whether the draft Understanding can be said to have binding force, and answers this question in the affirmative, because the Understanding contains a rule of conduct covering a specific field, determined by precise provisions providing that derogations shall take place only in exceptional cases and under strict conditions. With reference to the instant case, this argumentation is certainly adequate, but one may well ask whether the definition given by the Court of the term "agreement" is not rather too narrow. As I see it, it would be difficult to bring agreements which provide only for particular procedural rules under this definition; yet these can surely also give rise to questions as to their compatibility with the Treaty.

(b) The Court points out that, according to its authors, the draft Understanding was to enter into force in the form of a resolution of the Council of the OECD, and that, according to the draft report of the competent Group to that Council, the decision of the Community regarding the form of its participation in the draft Understanding was to be expected within the very near future. The Court concludes from this that there can be no question but that the draft Understanding constitutes an agreement "envisaged" in the sense of Article 228.

But envisaged by whom? Surely the Commission envisaged that the "agreement" should be concluded by the Community? This follows from its recommendation to the Council to empower it, the Commission, to express the Community standpoint. That the Member States also envisaged the conclusion of the agreement, either in their own names or by the Community, appears also to be beyond doubt. But is this sufficient? Should not the words

5. See also (1975) E.C.R., 1355. Citations are from this source.

6. See *International Organisation and Integration* (1968), pp. 1018 *et seq.*; U.N.T.S., Vol. 184, p. 41.

"envisaged agreement" be read as "the agreement envisaged by the Community?" In the present case there was no question of this, as is evident from the fact that the Council had not carried out the terms of the Commission's recommendation.

The resort to Article 228 thus appears in this case somewhat artificial. But it is clear that such an artifice can help to break through an impasse. Where, as in the present case, the Council cannot reach a decision as to the power to negotiate but, on the other hand, the Member States of their own accord do not move to conclude the envisaged agreement, then there is no other way of solving the problem. Any action under Article 169 can only be taken if it is the view of the Commission that a Member State can be reproached with something, and Article 173 can only help if the Council could be accused of acting beyond the scope of its powers, or in some other way in violation of the Treaty. The Treaty contains no general clause to solve conflicts of competence, and the Council has never yet attempted to put such a conflict to the test in another way. For this reason many directives and other measures are based on several Treaty provisions, such as Articles 43 and 100,[7] or one or another article together with Article 235.[8] This procedure frequently disguises differences of opinion regarding the proper voting procedure. In the past it was several times proposed that in case of doubt measures should be adopted under Article 43 i.e. by means of a qualified majority; any Member State which opposed this could then turn to the Court in order to find out whether it was in the right. But this suggestion was never followed up, not so much because this would have been in conflict with the so-called Luxembourg Accords, but because the Member States concerned which wished to abide by the unanimity procedure did not wish to run the risk of finding themselves in the wrong.

The above-named artifice is therefore rather to be applauded, and that precisely because it makes it possible to solve a difference of opinion concerning the repartition of competences between the Community and the Member States, and to break through the deadlock. One may, however, wonder whether such an application of Article 228 would have been permitted by the "authors of the Treaty", had they been able to foresee it.

6. This doubt also arises from the third question considered by the Court in the context of the admissibility of the request for an opinion. Apparently it has been held that in fact the request did not at all have the purpose of controlling the compatibility of the draft Understanding with the Treaty, but rather of obtaining a decision as to the competence of the Community to conclude the agreement at all. Clearly, it was hoped that the competence question would in this way be eliminated. The Court, however, did not follow this line of reasoning. It points out that the special procedure for a prior opinion of the Court of Justice is provided for precisely in order to forestall complications both within the Community and in relations with third countries as a result of legal disputes concerning the compatibility with the Treaty of international agreements which would also bind the Community. The question as to whether the conclusion of an agreement comes within the competence of the Community certainly falls among these questions.[9] This, in any case, is how I would summarize the more elaborate arguments of the Court. Any reference to

7. See *e.g.* Directive of June 26, 1975, concerning legal veterinary questions in the sphere of intra-Community trade in beef and pigs, J.O. 1964, 1971; *Cf.* "Wetgevingskroniek", (1964) S.E.W., 40-41.

8. See *e.g.* Reg. No. 302/68 of June 27, 1968, concerning the Community definition of the term "origin of goods", J.O. 1968 148/1. It can be concluded from Case 8/73, *Massey Fergusson v. H.Z.A. Bremerhaven,* that the resort to Article 235 was superfluous, 1973 *Receuil,* 897, at 907 (consideration 4).

9. *Cf.* R. M. Chevallier in *Les Novelles, Droit des Communautés Européennes, no. 1132.*

Article 107 (3) of the Rules of Procedure of the Court was left out. However, that provision states expressly that "the opinion may deal with either the compatibility of the envisaged agreement with the provisions of the EEC Treaty, or the power of the Community or one of the institutions to enter into that agreement".

7. The last obstacle raised in order to contest the admissibility of the request consisted in the argument that the discussions concerning the substance of the agreement were already at an end, and that the request was therefore submitted out of time. The Court dismisses this argument rather too facilely, stating that the Treaty provides for no time limit regarding the submission of a request. I would rather put it this way, that precisely because it was a matter here of controlling the compatibility of an "envisaged agreement", the fact that the substance of the agreement was already decided upon could not stand in the way of a request. A request is thus only excluded when an agreement has already been concluded by the Community.

8. After these preliminary skirmishes the Court proceeds to the more important questions posed, namely to whether the Community has the power to conclude the present agreement and, if so, whether this power is exclusive. That the reply to both questions is in the affirmative, is in itself not surprising. More interesting are the reasons advanced by the Court as a basis for its Opinion. Here, even more than with the question of the admissibility of the request, one can ill spare a summary of the observations of the Member States and of the Council. But instead one can only guess at the reasons why the Court advances particular arguments. One can, to a certain extent at least, find an answer in the literature relating to the common commercial policy.[10]

Under the first heading "The existence of a Community power to conclude the OECD understanding on a local cost standard", the Court discusses the question whether or not it is a matter here of commercial policy, and the question whether the Community, in the absence of autonomous Community rules of law, still is competent to conclude an agreement in the sphere of the common commercial policy. Under the second heading "The exclusive nature of the Community's powers" the Court indicates the elements on which the exclusive character of the Community powers are dependent.[11]

9. The draft Understanding is undoubtedly related to an area for which the Treaty recognises the Community as competent. This follows from Article 112, according to which, before the end of the transitional period, Member States shall progressively harmonise the systems whereby they grant aid for exports to third countries. That area forms part of the common commercial policy, as appears from the fact that export policy is expressly mentioned in Article 113. The action programme for the common commercial policy [12] also expressly mentions this subject matter, and the directives in the sphere of credit insurance [13] are, after the expiry of the transitional period, based by the Council both

10. See in particular M. d'Orville, "Die rechtlichen Grundlagen für die gemeinsame Zoll- und Handelspolitik der EWG" (Kölner Schriften zum Europarecht, Bd. 19, 1973) and W. Ernst and H. F. Besler in Groeben-Boeckh-Thiesing, Kommentar zum EWG-Vertrag (2nd edition, 1974), Articles 110-116; *cf.* also Kapteyn & VerLoren van Themaat, *Inleiding tot het recht van de Europese Gemeenschappen* (2nd edition 1974), pp. 366 *et seq.*

11. In what follows I have drawn on a paper written by P. J. G. Kapteyn entitled "The common commercial policy of the EEC: the delimitation of the Community's power and the Opinion of the European Court of Justice of 11 November 1975" which will appear shortly in the *Texas International Law Review.*

12. J.O. 1962, 2353.

13. J.O. 1970, L 254/1, and J.O. 1971 L 36/4 (not yet come into force).

on Article 112 and Article 113. In more general terms, the Court states that the notion of commercial policy has the same substance whether applied to the sphere of international commerce of a Member State or to that of the Community. In this context I will not go further into the implications of this statement.

Without saying it in so many words, the Court rejects the opinion of Ipsen [14] that Article 112 (harmonisation of aid to exports) does not in fact concern measures falling under commercial policy, but rather a subject matter which belongs under Article 92 *et seq.* The Court clearly leaves open the question as to whether Article 112 has any residual significance since the expiry of the transitional period, and in particular whether it perhaps in any way limits the powers of the Community.[15] I am rather of the opinion that the Community, since the end of the transitional period, can certainly go further in the regulation of aid to exports than is "necessary to avoid the distortion of competition between Community undertakings" (*i.e.* on the markets of third countries); this proceeds from the objectives of the commercial policy. Insofar as measures concerning aid to exports permitted in the context of the common commercial policy, have repercussions on the competitive balance in the Common Market, they can in any case be controlled under Article 93.[16]

10. Having concluded that the area of aids for exports in a general sense belongs to the export policy, and thus to the sphere of the common commercial policy, the Court goes thoroughly into the second question, namely the question of whether the exercise of external powers in this area must be proceded by the adoption of internal measures of Community Law. An answer in the affirmative, which may be drawn from the *ERTA* judgment, already mentioned above, is, according to the Court, not applicable to the sphere of the common commercial policy: "A commercial policy is in fact made up by the combination and interaction of internal and external measures, without priority being taken by one over the other. Sometimes agreements are concluded in execution of a policy fixed in advance, sometimes the policy is defined by the agreements themselves".

Anyone who has studied the development of the commercial policy of modern States in the industtrial age will readily support the correctness of this statement. Thus the Community's commercial policy is also the outcome of a progressive evolution "based upon specific measures which may refer without distinction to "autonomous" and external [17] aspects of that policy, and which do not necessarily presuppose, by the fact that they are linked to the field of the common commercial policy, the existence of a large body of rules, but combine gradually to form these rules". In other words it is not necessary that a system of "uniform principles" (such as may be derived from Article 113(1) [18] should first be established, which subsequently would form the basis for autonomous and/or conventional actions; Article 113 permits the Community to take any kind of measure of commercial policy. Rather one should interpret the "uniform principles" as forming a contrast to the "various principles" which might be distinguished in the commercial policies of the Member States, and which were the object of coordination, harmonisation and unification in the course of the transitional period.

11. The Community is thus competent to conclude agreements in the sphere of the common commercial policy with regard to a particular facet of that policy, even if in

14. H. Ipsen, *Europäisches Gemeinschaftsrecht* (1972), p. 824.
15. *Cf.* Kapteyn, *op. cit.* n. 11.
11. *Contra*, Ernst and Beseler, *op. cit.* n. 12, pp. 1437-1438.
17. The opposition of "autonomous" to external is not particularly satisfactory!
18. *Cf.* d'Orville, *op. cit.* n. 12, p. 26.

respect to that facet the Community has not as yet established any internal rules of Community Law. The creation, or rather the existence, of external powers is independent of the existence of such rules, and proceeds rather from the Treaty. This can already be concluded from the express words of the *ERTA* decision (sixteenth consideration). One may also find in that decision the answer to the question whether the Community alone is competent to exercise these external powers. In that judgment the Court declared that the Member States cannot enter into any engagements outside the framework of the Community institutions which might affect rules of Community Law, laiw down in order to realise the objectives of the Treaty, or which could prejudice them or be detrimental to their significance, and that the existence of a Community external authority excludes the possibility of a concurrent authority of the Member States (see twenty-second and thirty-first considerations). It was therefore only to be expected that the Court would make similar statements regarding the *external* powers of the Community in the sphere of the common commercial policy, which powers were brought into consideration by the Commission's question.

12. In its actual statement of opinion the Court limited itself to this point of external powers. But in the "discussion" of the questions the Court went further and considered also the *internal* powers with regard to the common commercial policy. The point of departure for the Court's argumentation is that the common commercial policy is conceived in the context of the operation of the common market, for the defence of the common interests of the Community, within which the particular interests of the Member States must endeavour to adapt to each other. The existence of a concurrent power of the Member States is "quite clearly" incompatible with this conception: 'Unilateral action on the part of the Member States would lead to disparities in the conditions for the grant of export credits, calculated [19] to distort competition between undertakings of the various Member States in external markets.... It cannot be accepted that in a field such as that governed by the Understanding in question, which is covered by export policy and more generally by the common commercial policy, the Member States should exercise a power concurrent to that of the Community in the Community sphere and in the international sphere... To accept the contrary would amount to recognising that, in relation with third countries, Member States may adopt positions which differ from these which the Community institutions adopt, and would thereby distort the institutional framework, call into question the mutual trust within the Community, and prevent the latter from fulfulling its task in defence of the common interest."

It would seem to appear from this that the conflict surrounding the exclusivity of Community powers in the sphere of commercial policy has been settled: where both conventional and autonomous measures are concerned, the Member States no longer possess any power to act of their own accord, even if the Community itself does not act. As Cartou [20] has expressed it: since the expiry of the transitional period, *"les organes communautaires sont les vêritables responsables—et même les seuls—de la politique commerciale avec les pays tiers".*

13. Yet there remains ground to question the correctness of such a far-reaching conclusion from the cited considerations contained in the Opinion. The most important ground for this is a semantic one. In paragraph 11 above I cited the *ERTA* case, in which the Court excludes the possibility of "a concurrent authority" of the Member States. The same

19. This word does not reflect the meaning of the text in the other languages. In French this passage reads: "... *disparités ... de nature à fausser la compétition*".

20. H. Cartou, *Organisations Européennes* (3rd edition 1971) p. 193.

adjective is used in the English text of the Opinion. However, in the French, German and Dutch texts of its Opinion, the Court does not make use of the same expression as in the *ERTA* case. In the latter case, the Court excludes the possibility of "concurrent authority",[21] in the former it speaks of the impossibility of "parallel" powers. By their very nature, parallel powers may be exercised at the same time in relation to the same subject matter; but they do not affect each other. That such parallel powers are inconceivable within the context of the common commercial policy is indeed *"de toute évidence"*. But is the same true of "concurrent" powers, in the sense employed in the literature, largely of German origin, on this matter? Where a Member State has a competence which competes with that of the Community, it is indeed justified in making use of that power, but only until such a time as the Community has made use of its powers with regard to the same subject-matter.[22] In other words, the national powers will be excluded or restricted—one might say, ousted— by the exercise of the Community powers, and not by their mere existence.[23] Is it not justified to suppose that, whereas the Court has certainly expressed a final opinion concerning the "parallel" powers, it has not yet done so with regard to the "concurrent" poers of the Member States? The validity of this argument may be better understood if one bears in mind that two Member States took the view in the Council that the participation of the Community in the draft Understanding did not of itself necessarily exclude that of the Member States, so that both could take part together in the conclusion of the agreement. This argument of the member States clearly amounted to one of the reasons for the submission of the request for an opinion. It is certainly my view that the Opinion should be read in this light, so that the question of the exclusion of "concurrent powers" is not yet finally decided.

A cautious interpretation is of particular importance for the sphere of the co-called autonomous commercial policy, but is also not without significance for that of the conventional commercial policy. Such an interpretation would for instance permit the Member States, to still independently establish rules governing the financing of export credits until such a time as the Community, by means of autonomous or conventional rules—as with the "envisaged" OECD rules—restricts or even nullifies this freedom. This interpretation would also allow Member States to conclude agreements with third countries, independently and of their own accord, until the Community removes or restricts their freedom to do so. This freedom has, for instance, been removed with regard to bilateral commercial agreements in the narrow sense of the term since January 1, 1973,[24] and has been restricted with regard to bilateral cooperation agreements with third countries, if only by means of the consultation procedure introduced in this regard.[25] Were one to adopt an extensive interpretation of the Court's Opinion, and on that basis refuse to

21. In French: *"compétence concurrente"*; in German: *"Konkurrierende Zuständigkeit"*; in Dutch: *"samenlopende bevoegdheid"*.

22. D'Orville, *op. cit.* n. 12, p. 98.

23. *Cf.* for the same phenomenon in other spheres, Cases Nos. 40/69, *HZA Hamburg v. Fa. P. Bollmann,* 16 *Receuil* 1970, 69, (1970) C.M.L.R., 141; 72/69, *HZA Bremerhaven v. Bremer Handelsgesellschaft,* 16 *Receuil* 1970, 427, (1970) C.M.L.R., 466; 22/70, *op. cit.* n. 2; 31/74, *Pubblico Ministero Italiano v. F. Galli,* (1975) E.C.R., 47, 12 C.M.L.Rev., 418, and annotation P. VerLoren van Themaat, 422; in the same sense, 65/75, *Pretore of Padua v. R. Tasca* (not yet published).

24. Council Decision of Dec. 16, 1969, J.O. 1969, L 326/39, and J.O. 1971, L 36/14. See also Council Decision of Dec. 19, 1972, J.O. 1972, L. 299/49.

25. Council Decision of July 22, 1974, O.J. 1974, L 208/23.

recognise the existence of concurrent powers in the final phase of the common market, then such cooperation agreements in the economic, industrial and technological sphere would already now be in conflict with the Treaty. I have no wish to draw such a conclusion, however much I find such agreements regrettable from the point of view of Community interests.[26]

14. At the end of the considerations preceding the actual statement of its Opinion, the Court also deals with some other arguments which were clearly advanced with a view to saving the existence of Member States' own powers alongside those of the Community.

(*a*) The first is a financial argument: the Member States must bear the financial consequences of the 100% rule, and therefore they must also be allowed to decide whether they wish to adopt the rule. The Court correctly treats this argument as irrelevant with regard to the question of compatibility with the Treaty. In order that internal and external measures adopted in the sphere of the common commercial policy be compatible with the Treaty, it is not necessary that the financial burdens proceeding from them be borne by the Community. This argument was in fact directed against the existence of a Community competence as such. For an agreement concluded by the Community is, according to Article 228 (2), binding on the Member States regardless of whether they make use of their own pretended "parallel powers" in order to conclude the agreement of their own accord.

(*b*) The last argument proceeded from the fact that the draft Understanding would also be applicable to export transactions involving the delivery of ECSC (steel!) products. The ECSC has, in fact, no common commercial policy—see Article 71 ECSC. How can the Community therefore act in place of the Member States? The Court pushes this argument aside by referring simply to the fact that its opinion was requested on the basis of and in relation to the EEC Treaty, and it expressly leaves open the question whether "... in view of the necessity of ensuring that international transactions, to which the Communities are a party, should have as uniform a character as possible, Article 71 of the ECSC Treaty retains its former force following the entry into force of the EEC Treaty ...", and states that "provision cannot in any event render inoperative Articles 113 and 114 of the EEC Treaty and affect the vesting of power in the Community ..." This statement is correct, but leaves unanswered the question as to whether the EEC, by means of the adoption of the draft Understanding, binds the Member States insofar as export credits for the delivery of ECSC products are concerned.

A positive answer to this question is very well defensible. It was given already in 1958 by Carstens,[27] who demonstrated that the EEC may certainly implicate ECSC products under the common commercial policy. Article 232 EEC forms no barrier to this argument, since no more is said here than that the provisions of the EEC Treaty do not affect those of the ECSC Treaty, in particular as regards the right and obligations of the Member States and the powers of the institutions. And, according to Carstens, this does not occur. Under the ECSC Treaty, the competence in matters of commercial policy rests with the Member States, but this competence is brought under the common commercial policy by the EEC Treaty. According to this view, the powers of the High Authority are not increased, since not this authority but the EEC institutions are competent. It is in itself interesting that the Court did not in so many words reject this argument.

H. H. Maas

26. Kapteyn, *op. cit.* n. 11, goes thoroughly into this question.

27. See K.W. Carstens in (1958) ZaöRV, 520-521; *cf.* Pescatore in *Les Novelles, Droit des Communautés Européennes, no. 1663.*

B. NATIONAL CASE LAW

THE ATTITUDE OF BRITISH COURTS TO COMMUNITY LAW– THE FIRST THREE YEARS

The authors have found some twenty reported cases [1] to the end of 1975 in which British courts have had the opportunity to consider the nature of Community Law and its effects, if any, on the issues before them.[2] These cases have been heard before a considerable span of the British judicial hierarchy, ranging from a National Insurance Commissioner, a Value Added Tax Tribunal, a Magistrates Court, a County Court, to the High Court (about half the cases), the Court of Appeal (on several occasions) and, on one occasion, the House of Lords. At the same time it is interesting to note that Mr. Justice Graham, a judge of the High Court, and the Master of the Rolls, Lord Denning (Court of Appeal), have each been involved in five of the cases: in other words, a mere two judges have decided, or been instrumental in deciding, half the total number of U.K. cases having Community Law aspects in the first three year period after accession. The one case which has so far come before the House of Lords with a Community Law element was the last to be decided in 1975 and is arguably the most important to date, even though what was said on the subject of Community Law is minimal and was not even directly relevant to the case concerned.

It is certainly not surprising that the majority of cases before the U.K. courts has been concerned with the Community's rules on competition and the free movement of goods. In particular, the difficult question of the relationship between the free movement of goods and the protection of industrial property rights has taken up a large amount of time of the Chancery Division of the High Court. However, the remaining cases have by no means covered all the other fields of Community Law. Leaving aside the cases which have concentrated on the legality of the Treaty of Accession or the European Communities Act 1972—the Act which has given effect to Community Law in the U.K.—whilst the Community rules on the free movement of workers and related social security provisions have been considered in two cases and one court was called upon to take into account a Community Directive on Value Added Tax, not a great deal more has come to light. The Common Agricultural Policy, for instance, has so far been left relatively untouched by the courts.

Again, the majority of the cases has involved requests for interlocutory injunctions. At the same time, an application has often been made by one or other of the parties for a request for a preliminary ruling from the Court of Justice. As a result, Article 177 EEC has

1. See the list at the end of this Article.

2. It should also be borne in mind that, besides the twenty cases to be considered in this Article, there have been several actions involving British litigants which have been the subject of direct proceedings before the Court of Justice, for example: Joined Cases 160, 161 and 170/73: *Miles Druce v. Commission* (1974) E.C.R. 281. Case 3/75, *Johnson & Firth Brown v. Commission* (1975) E.C.R. 1. Case 34/75, *Sirdar v. Commission*, removed by order of the Court of April 7, 1976, O.J. 1976, C 104/4. Case 109/75, *National Carbonising Company v. Commission* (1975) E.C.R., 1193.

13 C.M.L. Rev. 1976, 388-414

been analysed in several of the cases reported and in two [3] of them requests for preliminary rulings have, in fact, been made to the Court of Justice: one of these requests was introduced in the beginning of 1974, the other in 1975. Pursuant to the attitude which the House of Lords manifested on this question it is to be hoped that as of 1976 greater use will be made of this Article to ensure that all branches of Community Law are correctly applied in the U.K.

In describing and briefly analysing the U.K. cases having a Community Law element reference will first of all be made to those in which the very principle of accession was at stake. Subsequently a more detailed review will be given of those cases involving the concrete application of various aspects of Community law. Finally, consideration will be given to the several cases in which Article 177 EEC has been a major element involved.

I. *The constitutionality of accession*

It was perhaps to be expected that even before accession of the new Member States to the European Communities the attempt would be made to have the national courts declare such a step as unconstitutional. In the United Kingdim two [4] separate actions were introduced before the Court of Appeal, the first in 1971, somewhat prior to the signature of the Treaty of Accession, the second in 1972, after signature but before the passing of the European Communities Act 1972.[5]

However, before considering these two cases in rather more detail mention will be made of a case decided on March 7, 1975 before the Court of Session of Scotland, Outer House, which concerned the constitutionality of the European Communities Act 1972 itself. In *Gibson v. The Lord Advocate* [6] it was argued by the pursuer (Plaintiff) that immediately prior to the Act of Union of 1707 (between England and Scotland) Scottish subjects had exclusive rights of fishing in Scottish coastal waters; that the laws which conferred those exclusive rights were laws concerned with private rights which could not be altered by the Parliament of Great Britain except for "evident utility" of the subjects within Scotland under Article 18 of the Act of Union; that section 2 (1) of the 1972 Act had the effect of making Article 2 of Council Regulation 2147/70 part of United Kingdom domestic law with the result that the rights of Scottish subjects to fish in Scottish waters would become non-exclusive as from December 31, 1982, (Articles 100 to 103 of the Act of Accession); that this result was not for the evident utility of Scottish subjects and that therefore section 2 (1) of the 1972 Act was, to the extent of the alteration in question, contrary to Article 18 and therefore null and void.

3. On Feb. 12, 1976, Mr. J. G. Monroe, National Insurance Commissioner, submitted the U.K.'s third request for a preliminary ruling to the Court of Justice (case 17/76). In *Brack (deceased) against Insurance Officer* the questions for interpretation concern the meaning of "worker" in Regulation (EEC) No. 1408/71.

4. *The Times* newspaper of Sept. 28, 1972 also contains a reference to a third instance in a short article entitled "Treason alleged in writ over entry to Europe". It states that "Mr. *Bradford*... took out the writ under the Act of Settlement, 1701 ... It alleges that ... the Governement would be extending illegally the Royal prerogative of treaty making ...". It would seem the matter never reached the courts.

5. Similar questions also arose in Denmark, for instance, *Gronborg v. Prime Minister (1972)* C.M.L.R., 879 and *Tegen v. Prime Minister* (1973) C.M.L.R. 1, but not, it seems, in Ireland.

6. (1975) C.M.L.R., 563.

The relevant part of the judgment of Lord Keith held that "section 2 (1) of the 1972 Act apparently seeks to give effect to (Article 189 EEC) and I have no doubt that it has the effect of causing to be binding on individual subjects in Scotland such EEC regulations as are capable of being so binding.[7] Some EEC regulations, however, do not purport to impose any obligations upon individual citizens and I regard the particular regulation now under consideration as falling into this category. That regulation, in my view, operates in the field of public law. The obligations which it imposes are imposed on the Member States, not upon any individuals". Lord Keith therefore held that section 2 (1) of the 1972 Act and Article 2 of the Regulation did not effect any alteration in the private laws of Scotland.

Returning to the two English cases on the constitutionality of accession, in the first, *Blackburn v. Attorney-General,*[8] the Plaintiff had claimed in 1971 that the proposed signature of the Treaty of Rome committed the Government "to an irreversible partial surrender of the sovereignty of the Crown in Parliament [which] cannot be reconciled with the rule of law . . . that the . . . sovereignty of . . . Parliament cannot be fettered". It was also contended that the provisions of the Treaty whereby the United Kingdom could not withdraw from the Common Market without the consent of the other member countries were ultra vires both the Government and the Parliament: these provisions could, it was argued, be accepted only if a new constitution were adopted with the consent of the British people. In passing it is to be noted that even if an entirely new constitution was not in fact adopted, approval was at least given by the British people to continued membership of the Community pursuant to the U.K. referendum of June 5, 1975.

By the time of the decision in *McWhirter v. Attorney-General*[9] the Treaty of Accession had been signed but not yet implemented in the U.K. by Act of Parliament. In this case the Plaintiff relied on a further ground of complaint against the Executive's action, namely that it was not in conformity with the Bill of Rights (1688).

The Court of Appeal had no difficulty in dismissing both the *Blackburn* and *McWhirter* cases. In the *Blackburn* case, the Master of the Rolls (Lord Denning) quoted a passage from a decision of 1876 in which the following was said: "the Queen acted throughout the making of the Treaty and in relation to each and every of its stipulations in her sovereign character, and her own inherent authority; and, as in making the treaty, so in performing the treaty, she is beyond the control of municipal law, and her acts are not to be examined in her own courts". Lord Denning was equally emphatic in *McWhirter.* He held: "even though the Treaty of Rome (sic) has been signed, it has no effect, so far as these Courts are concerned, until it is made an Act of Parliament. Once it is implemented by an Act of Parliament these Courts must go to the Act of Parliament. Until that day comes, we take no notice of it." The Master of the Rolls then recalled what was said in a more recent case of 1937: ". . . the stipulations of a treaty duly ratified do not within the Empire, by virtue of the Treaty alone, have the force of law. If the national executive, the government of the day, decide to incur the obligations of a treaty which involve alteration of law they have to run the risk of obtaining the assent of Parliament to the necessary statute or statutes".

It was clear that neither action had any chance of success in the light of the strict dualist approach to treaties adopted by the U.K. courts: the courts do not give effect to a treaty but only apply the Act of Parliament which has implemented it (or some of its terms) into

7. It is to be noted that the direct effect of Community regulations is stated to depend on the European Communities Act rather than on the Community legal order itself, an idea which finds equal expression in several of the English cases which deal with this matter.

8. (1971) C.M.L.R., 784; 9 C.M.L. Rev. 1972, 94-95.

9. (1972) C.M.L.R., 882.

municipal law. Both cases, therefore, did no more than confirm the traditional constitutional roles of the executive, the legislative and the judiciary in connection with the conclusion, implementation and application of treaties in the UK.

In view of this it was, strictly speaking, unnecessary to consider either the effect Community Law might have on U.K. constitutional law *(Blackburn)* or even the compatibility of the Treaty of Accession with the Bill of Rights *(McWhirter)*. However, this did not prevent the Master of the Rolls [10]—at least in the *Blackburn* case—from taking the opportunity of expressing some ideas on the relationship between United Kingdom and Community Law.[11] On the one hand he appeared to agree with the Plaintiff that accession implies "a step which is irreversible. The sovereignty of these islands will henceforward be limited". At the same time, with regard to the sovereignty of Parliament and in particular to the concept that no Parliament can bind its successors, Lord Denning had the following to say: "We have all been brought up to believe that, in legal theory, one Parliament cannot bind another, and that no Act is irreversible. But legal theory does not always march alongside political reality. Take the Statute of Westminster 1931, which takes away the power of Parliament to legislate for the Dominions. Can anyone imagine that Parliament could or would reverse that statute? Take the Acts which have granted independence to the Dominions and territories overseas. Can anyone imagine that Parliament could or would reverse those laws and take away their independence? Most clearly not. Freedom once given cannot be taken away. Legal theory must give way to practical politics. It is as well to remember the remarks of Viscount Sankey L.C. in *British Coal Corporation v. The King* [12]: "the Imperial Parliament could, as a matter of abstract law, repeal or disregard Section 4 of the Statute of Westminster. But that is theory and has no relation to reality."

A question more immediate than the possible repeal of the European Communities Act, namely whether the U.K. courts would recognise a Community law having direct effect in the face of a conflicting subsequent Act of Parliament was, of course, not considered directly by the court nor has it, it seems, yet been considered by any court since then.[13] Lord

10. Neither was Lord Denning unduly concerned with the questionable *locus standi* of the Plaintiffs: Mr. Blackburn felt "very strongly" and "he thinks it important to clear the air"; Mr. McWhirter's action concerned a "matter of importance".

11. Neither the fact that the Court of Appeal was prepared to entertain the actions, nor that if the more general opinions of Lord Denning are left to one side, the decisions lose most of their interest, means that such opinions are other than *obiter dicta*. See also (1971) *Public Law*, 243; Bebr, (1971) *Europarecht*, 270.

12. (1935) A.C., 500, 520.

13. This is perhaps not surprising. See *British Railways Board v. Pickin* (1974) C.M.L.R., 208 where the House of Lords said: "the idea that a Court is entitled to disregard a provision in an Act of Parliament on any ground must seem strange and startling to anyone with knowledge of the history and law of our country. In earlier times many lawyers seemed to have believed that an Act could be disregarded in so far as it was contrary to the law of God or of nature or of natural justice but since the supremacy of Parliament was finally demonstrated by the Revolution of 1688 any such idea has been obsolete." In addition as regards the relationship between the Courts and the legislator in the UK the House of Lords said: "for a century or more both Parliament and the Courts have been careful not to act as to cause conflict between them. Any such investigation as [the appellant] sought could easily lead to such a conflict . . . but the whole trend of authority for over a century is clearly against permitting any such investigation."

Denning left the point open [14] and Salmon L.J. was careful to state that *"in the present state of the law,* Parliament can enact, amend and repeal any legislation it pleases". In the *Gibson* case Lord Keith also remained neutral. He referred to the situation where a domestic legislative act is found to be in conflict with a pre-existing EEC regulation, "a situation which it was maintained could arise in this country . . . and to be one with which the Court might have to deal by declaring the domestic legislative act to be void. It may well be that such a situation will arise but in my view it should be left to be considered if and when it does."

This question of conflict has, of course, been vigorously considered before and since by academic writers [15] and it is also reflected in the European Communities Act itself (section 2 (4)).[16]

II. *Specific cases of application*

A number of U.K. judgments reported for the years 1973 to 1975 tend to concentrate, in a practical and detailed manner, on the specific arguments based on Community Law put forward on behalf of the parties. In these cases the wider principles involved in the acceptance by the U.K. of a new legal order have tended to be considered, if at all, only in a subsidiary manner. A brief description of these cases will be given, first of all those which are concerned with a certain variety of Community aspects other than the rules on competition and industrial property rights and, subsequently, those which are mainly concerned with these latter matters.

The first case under the former heading, *Processed Vegetable Growers Association Ltd. v. The Commissioner of Customs and Excise,*[17] was heard by the Leeds Value Added Tax Tribunal on September 7, 1973 and involved the interpretation of the Community's second Value Added Tax Directive of 1967. The facts of the case were as follows. The Processed Vegetable Growers Association (PVGA) was established by the National Farmers Union (NFU), an organisation whose object is to promote the interests of farmers and, in particular, to act as a pressure group on the Government: the special activity of the PVGA was, in fact, to promote the interests of vegetable growers whose produce is processed. As the NFU is a much larger organisation than the PVGA an arrangement was entered into whereby certain employees of the PVGA were transferred to the payroll of the NFU so as to benefit from the accounts expertise and pension arrangements of the latter. The PVGA repaid the actual disbursements made in relation to the "transferred" men but did not pay any additional fee for the services rendered by the NFU. The Commissioner of Customs and Excise claimed that the reimbursement made by the PVGA was consideration for the supply by the NFU of services of its employees to the PVGA and was taxable at the applicable V.A.T. rate. The PVGA appealed against the Commissioner's decision to the Tribunal arguing that the relevant supply was not made by the NFU "in the course of a business" so as to make it a taxable supply under section 2 (2) of the Finance Act 1972 (which

14. *Cf.* Collins, "European Community Law in the United Kingdom" (1975), p. 18.

15. See, e.g. , Wade, "Sovereignty and the European Communities", (1972) L.Q.R., 1. Mitchell, Kuipers and Gall, "Constitutional aspects of the treaty and legislation relating to British membership", (1974) C.M.L.Rev., 134 and especially the authors listed at the foot of 136.

16. The relevant part reads: ". . . any enactment passed or *to be* passed . . . shall be construed and have effect subject to the foregoing provisions of this section . . .".

17. (1974) C.M.L.R., 113.

introduced V.A.T. in the U.K.). The Tribunal upheld this argument and decided that the agreements in question were only "domestic arrangements" and did not, therefore, constitute a "business" for the purposes of section 2 (2).

One of the arguments put forward by the Commissioners was that by virtue of the European Communities Act 1972 and the Treaty of Accession V.A.T. was to be imposed in the U.K. in accordance with the second Council Directive of 11 April 1967 and that this Directive did not require a supply to be made "in the course of business". Not surprisingly, the Tribunal was not convinced by this argument. First of all, and at all events, it held that there was no divergence between the provisions of the Directive and the Finance Act 1972 in so far as it was relevant to the case. It decided that although Article 2 of the Directive did not expressly require a taxable supply to be made "in the course of business" the definition of "taxable person" in Article 4 indicated that "taxable supplies" were supplies made in the course of "economic activity". The Tribunal then made the following very pertinent remarks: "the foregoing findings are not to be taken as an indication that we accept that the Second Directive is relevant on this appeal. If the Finance Acts do not, in any respect, correspond with the Second Directive, *prima facie* a liability for tax is to be determined on the basis of such Finance Acts unless and until an Act of Parliament is passed or an Order in Council [18] or other regulation is made under section 2 (2) of the European Communities Act 1972 which brings the laws of the United Kingdom into line with the Second Directive. The obligation undertaken by the United Kingdom under the Treaty of Accession, at least so far as taxation is concerned, is to bring its laws into line with Community law". In particular the Tribunal then held: "it would be astonishing if the Crown could levy tax in circumstances not authorised by Parliament on the basis of a Directive of the Council of the European Communities at a time when the United Kingdom was, under its treaty obligations, in default in relation to the imposition of that tax, by not giving relevant effect to that Directive. We do not accept that the words "in the course of a business" in section 2(2) of the Finance Act 1972 are to be ignored on the present appeal because that Act appears to have been passed in order to fulfil the obligation of the United Kingdom under the Treaty of Accession to introduce in the United Kingdom value added tax in accordance with the Second Directive, with the result that, to the extent that the Finance Act does not completely fulfil that obligation, the Second Directive overrides the Act by virtue of section 2 of the European Communities Act 1972. The Finance Act 1972 was passed before the European Communities Act and, in such circumstances, section 2 (2) of the latter Act envisages an Order in Council or regulations being made to bring United Kingdom law into line with Community Law to the extent that the United Kingdom is under an obligation so to do by the Treaty of Accession".

It is to be noted that as there was no question of any advantage to the individual under the Directive not being mirrored in the Finance Act, the possibility of the Directive (or at least the provision concerned) having a direct effect was not at issue.[19]

A second case involving the detailed interpretation of a Community provision in the U.K. occurred in July 1974 before another tribunal, in fact, a National Insurance

18. Bridge, "Community law and English Courts and Tribunals: General principles and Preliminary Rulings" (1975) *European Law Review*, 13, points out that this could only be done by an Act of Parliament because of the provisions of schedule 2 of the European Communities Act.

19. On the general question of direct applicability/effect, see, *infra*, pp. 404 *et seq.*, the *Van Duyn* case.

Commissioner. *Re a Holiday in Italy*[20] was concerned with the Community's social security provisions and, in particular, the meaning of the word "treatment" in Article 22 (2) of EEC Regulation 1408/71. Following a heart-attack, the claimant was incapable of work. Before the attack he had arranged a holiday in Italy and was medically advised that it would be beneficial to take it. He accordingly went on the holiday having been told at the local office of the Department of Health and Social Security that his benefit would not be affected by his going abroad. In fact he was refused benefit by the local insurance officer for the period during which he was wholly outside the United Kingdom. His appeals to the local tribunal and to the National Insurance Commissioner were dismissed.

In his judgment the Commissioner Mr. J. G. Monroe, considered whether, *inter alia,* there was not some relevant provision of Community Law which exempted the claimant from disqualification for benefit under the U.K. legislation. This legislation did not permit benefit to be continued where, although the claimant was suffering from incapacity which commenced before he left Britain, he was not so absent for the specific purpose of "being treated" for that incapacity inasmuch as he went abroad for the purpose of convalescence. In taking into account Article 22 of Regulation 1408/71 the Commissioner first of all considered the nature of regulations in general and then how he should interpret the particular regulation in question. On the former point he had the following to say: "by virtue of Article 189 of the EEC Treaty, generally known as the Treaty of Rome, referred to in Part I of Schedule 1 to the European Communities Act 1972, taken together with section 2 (1) of that Act [the regulation has] direct effect in the United Kingdom without further enactment". Whilst, therefore, the Commissioner, using the precise words of section 2 (1), recognised that a regulation has "direct effect without further enactment", he regarded this direct effect as a result, not of Article 189 EEC alone, but also of section 2 (1) of the European Communities Act.

In interpreting the particular regulation the Commissioner recognised that regulations are to be construed in a uniform manner throughout the Member States: his authority was not it seems, the case law of the Court of Justice itself but Lord Denning in the *Bulmer/Bollinger* case *(infra).* He then went on: 'one cannot assume that there is an exact coincidence between the meaning of the word "treatment" in the Community Regulation and the words "being treated" in [the domestic legislation]'. In support of this he looked to the French[21] text of the Regulation and noted that the word "treatment" read both *"soins"* and *"traitement".* Nevertheless he held that the treatment to which reference was made in the Community regulation and which would have entitled the claimant to benefit "did not comprehend the mere benefit of rest and change of air involved in a holiday abroad": he accordingly dismissed the claim for the sickness benefit. It does not appear from the judgment whether any Community case-law was considered to arrive at this decision.

In addition to the case of *Gibson v. The Lord Advocate (supra),* 1974 saw one further case in which a lower court in the U.K. was called upon to consider the more general aspects of Community Law. This case, *Regina v. Secchi,*[22] was heard on March 25, 1975 before the Metropolitan Magistrate, Marylebone and was concerned with the free movement of workers. Here the Defendant, an Italian national had, at the age of 18, left his architectural studies in Sardinia before completing them and then wandered about Europe doing work "such as washing up in restaurants" to pay his way. He entered the U.K. in October 1974 and subsequently did a little casual work. He was twice convicted of criminal offences and

20. (1975) C.M.L.R., 184.
21. It does not appear that the other language versions were considered.
22. (1975) C.M.L.R., 383.

recommended for deportation. At a subsequent hearing it was argued that deportation could not be recommended because the Defendant was a "worker" under Article 48 EEC and that his two convictions would not amount to the "personal conduct" under Article 3(1) EEC Directive 64/221 needed to justify deportation.

The judgment contains a number of comments which demonstrate a rather restrictive attitude towards the nature of the Community and its legal order. First of all, on a more general level, the Magistrate decided that the Treaty of Rome "has become part of English law by section 2 of the European Communities Act". Somewhat illogically he added that: "the effect of this is to make English law, both statute and common law, subordinate to Community Law, in those fields in which Community laws have been passed". The judge then considered the way in which English courts should deal with the impact of Community Law on English law. He pointed out that this had been dealt with at great length by the Master of the Rolls (Lord Denning) in the *Bulmer/Bollinger* case in which, in his view, the essential guidelines which English courts must follow had been laid down.

More particularly as to the meaning of a "worker", which he noted had not been defined in the Treaty, the Magistrate, after having considered a number of cases both before the Court of Justice and the courts of the Member States, felt satisfied that the "clue" was to be found in Part One of the Treaty, headed "Principles", and in particular Articles 1 and 2 whose terms explained the "economic" character of the Treaty. It followed for him that "not every national who in the course of his life may at different times have done a few hours, a few days or even a few weeks work can be regarded as someone whose freedom of movement within the Member States is necessary for the fulfilment of the task of the Community as set out in Article 2 EEC". The Magistrate, for himself, was equally satisfied that Directive 64/221 did not apply to the Defendant who, again, did not fall within the category of persons in Article 1. Although this would have sufficed to settle the issue he nonetheless went on to hold that notwithstanding the provisions of Article 3 (2) of the Directive which states that "previous criminal convictions shall not in themselves constitute grounds for making an expulsion order", the personal conduct of the Defendant, including his convictions, could form the basis of an expulsion order on grounds of public policy in compliance with the terms of Article 3(1).

For the sake of completeness, passing mention may be made of one further case cited in *The Times* newspaper of July 23, 1975 before the Winchester Magistrate involving the imposition of a fine on a farmer, *Mr. Price*, under national law, for the making of a false statement to obtain payment under the Dairy Herd Conversion Premium Regulations 1973, in turn made pursuant to EEC Regulation 1353/73. The latter Regulation was designed to encourage farmers engaged in producing and supplying milk or milk products to change to the production of meat. Of course, the separate problem of the recovery of any money paid on behalf of and its transfer back to the Community would remain, notwithstanding the imposition of a fine in a particular case.

Turning to the other group of cases under this heading, namely those involving the rules of competition and industrial property rights, the first—and which was in fact the first reported action before a U.K. court in which Community Law was considered in some detail—arose just before accession in November 1972. In *Lerose Ltd. and Another v. Hawick Jersey International Ltd.,*[23] heard before the High Court of Justice (Chancery Division), the Plaintiffs sought an interlocutory injunction to restrain the infringement of copyright by the Defendants in certain drawings for fabrics. The Defendants contended, as one of their arguments, that just as an agreement restricting them from making certain

23. (1973) C.M.L.R.. 83.

types of material could (once the U.K. joined the European Community) amount to an infraction of Article 85 EEC, so also could an undertaking offered by the Defendants to the Plaintiffs that they would not deal with such materials. The Defendants then submitted that an injunction granted by the court was to be regarded in the same way as such an undertaking and therefore should not be granted. However Whitford J. was far from impressed by this argument. He remarked: "I confess I find myself quite unable to see that *prima facie* the provisions of Article 85 can in any way affect the jurisdiction of the Court to grant injunctions against the breach of the statutory grants of rights such as I have to consider in the present case".

Reference was also made to Article 36 EEC which provides that Articles 30 to 34—prohibiting restrictions on imports and exports between Member States—shall not prevent such restrictions justified on the grounds of, *inter alia,* the protection of industrial and commercial property, provided they do not amount to an arbitrary discrimination or a disguised restriction on trade between Member States. On this aspect Whitford J. was equally emphatic when he held that the Plaintiffs' exercise of their copyright did not contravene the Treaty. He said: "nothing has been suggested before me in connection with the facts of this particular case which could even begin to suggest that . . . the Plaintiffs are using those provisions (of the Copyright Act 1956) to bring about some arbitrary discrimination, some disguised restriction on trade. This is a very simple and straightforward case of alleged infringement of copyright".

On the dawn of accession, therefore, not only had the Court of Appeal considered the constitutionality of accession, but the High Court had also dealt with its first case involving Community Law provisions. A second soon followed! In *Minnesota Mining and Manufacturing Company and 3M United Kingdom Ltd. v. Geerpres Europe Ltd.,*[24] again heard before the Chancery Division of the High Court (in January 1973), it was the turn of Mr. Justice Graham to grant an interlocutory injunction to restrain the import into the U.K. of certain products in alleged infringement of the Plaintiffs' English patent. The goods in question had been obtained by the Defendants from a U.S. distributor who in turn had bought them from a U.S. manufacturer holding a licence from the Plaintiffs.

As one of their main points the Defendants argued that, although they would not contend that the provisions of the EEC Treaty did not specifically prevent the Court granting an injunction, nevertheless as a discretionary matter, it ought not to do so. They argued that Community Law, in the same way as United States law, was tending towards adopting, in cases relating to letters patent, the "doctrine of exhaustion". To Graham J. this doctrine meant that "once a patentee has sold or licensed someone else to sell a product for royalty in one country he has exhausted his rights and cannot thereafter prevent anyone else from buying up that article and selling in another country".

First of all, however, Graham J. considered the relevant Treaty Articles and held that the grant of the injunction was not contrary to any of their provisions.[25] He decided that Articles 30 to 34 EEC were not apposite to cover measures such as the grant of an interlocutory injunction to protect patent rights. And even if he were wrong on this: "Article 36 makes it specifically clear that [these] Articles do not preclude prohibitions or restrictions justified on the grounds of protection of industrial and commercial property, subject to the general proviso that they do not constitute means of arbitrary discrimination or disguised restriction on trade between Member States". In turning to Article 85 EEC he

24. (1973) C.M.L.R., 259.

25. Melville, (1973) *The Law Society's Gazette,* argues that the Court's views on Articles 36, 85 and 86 are *obiter dicta.*

noted that it was primarily concerned with agreements between undertakings and did not apply to the normal case of the grant by the court of any interlocutory injunction restraining infringement of letters patent, thereby confirming the previous *Lerose* decision on this point. As to Article 86 EEC he held that it only applied when a dominant position existed. That this was the proper view of the provisions of Articles 85 and 86 seemed to him clear from the *Parke, Davis* case.[26] Turning to the doctrine of exhaustion Graham J. had to decide whether this would affect the exercise of his discretion in granting or refusing the injunction. In this connection he was specifically referred to the *Deutsche Grammophon* case.[27] He held that where the Defendants imported into a Member State (U.K.) from a non-Member State (U.S.A.) patented goods obtained from an undertaking which obtained them from a licensee of the patentee in that non-Member State in breach of the U.K. licencee's monopoly right, this was distinguishable from the case *(Deutsche Grammophon)* where the patentee had himself sold the goods in question in one country and then tried to stop their import into another country by virtue of his patent in that second jurisdiction, attempting thereby to get round the provisions of a treaty such as the EEC Treaty.

The subsequent case of *Esso Petroleum Co. Ltd. v. Kingswood Motors (Addlestone) Ltd. and others* [28] (April, 1973) gave Mr. Justice Bridge, sitting in the High Court, Queen's Bench Division, the opportunity to consider in greater detail Article 85 EEC and its "extremely complex" implementing legislation, Regulation 17/62.

Briefly the facts of this case were as follows. The Defendants, garage owners, had agreed in 1969 with the Plaintiffs, suppliers of motor fuels, to operate the garage in a certain manner for five years (i.e. selling only the oil products of the Plaintiffs—a "solus tie agreement") and only to sell the garage on the condition that the purchasers entered into a similar agreement. At the time of the agreement the Defendants entered into a mortgage deed which was associated with the solus tie agreement giving collateral advantages to the Plaintiffs as mortgagees. Two years before the expiry of the solus tie agreement and with the purpose of defeating it the Defendants were taken over by another company and the outstanding mortgage debt repaid. The take-over company then acquired the land on which the garage stood and began to sell products other than the Plaintiffs'. The Plaintiffs sought interlocutory relief which was resisted by the Defendants on the grounds that the solus tie agreement was unenforceable as it was prohibited by Article 85 EEC.

On the various aspects of Community Law before him, Mr. Justice Bridge had the following points to make. First of all he said that the Treaty "became part of our domestic law in this country on January 1, 1973, and where it is in conflict with our domestic law the effect of the [European Communities] Act of 1972 is to require that the Community law shall prevail".[29] He then referred to the *first Brasserie de Haecht* case [30] "which clearly establishes that a solus agreement is potentially capable of being within the prohibition embodied in Article 85 (1) (2), though it is not within that prohibition *per se*. Whether it is or not depends on surrounding circumstances, not upon the terms of the individual

26. Case 24/67, (1968) E.C.R., 55; 6 C.M.L. Rev. 1967-68, 129-132, 217-222.
27. Case 78/70, 17 *Recueil* 1971, 487; 9 C.M.L. Rev. 1972, 87-93.
28. (1973) C.M.L.R., 665.
29. This sentence does not fully reflect the independent nature of the Community legal order, and this on two counts: first, by stating that Community Law is "part" of domestic law, and secondly, by asserting that the supremacy of Community Law follows from the European Communities Act and not Community Law itself.
30. Case 23/67 (1967) E.C.R. 407; 5 C.M.L. Rev. 1966-67, 478-480.

agreement considered in isolation". Bridge J. then considered Regulation 17 and in particular Article 9 (3), according to which, so long as the Commission has not initiated the procedures under the Regulation for the examination of the agreement in question (and the Commission had not, in fact, commenced such procedures in the case) "the authorities of the member States"—which Bridge J. took to include the courts of the Member States [31]—"shall remain competent to apply Article 85 (1)".

Turning then to the distinction between "old" (i.e. pre-1962 or, for the new Member States, pre-1973) and "new" agreements, Bridge J. held he was dealing with an "old" agreement because it was concluded in 1969. Basing himself on the 1970 *Bilger/Jehle* decision of the Court of Justice [32] he then concluded that because, as in that case, there was no question of goods crossing the border, so that no import or export among Member States in the sense of Article 4 (2) (1) of Regulation 17 was involved, the agreement was one exempt from notification to the Commission. The second question which then arose was whether an agreement, which was not subject to notification, was provisionally valid. Again the *Bilger/Jehle* decision was considered "although it is not expressed in the kind of language with which English lawyers are familiar and it may be that, the photocopy with which I was provided not being an official report of the case, the translation is imperfect".[33] Bridge J. concluded that "the national judge who has to consider in the interim period before there has been any declaration by the Commission the status of an agreement which is in the category of not notifiable, is entitled to assume that the agreement is valid and not struck down by the provisions of Article 85 (1) (ii)".[34] Bridge J. also found support for the provisional validity of the agreement in question "by a different route", namely in the *second Brasserie de Haecht* case [35] where it was said that "as far as old agreements are concerned, certainty of law as regards contracts requires that a court cannot . . . establish nullity until after the Commission had made a decision under [Regulation 17]." As Bridge J. was, in fact, faced with an "old" agreement he concluded that it would be considered as valid under Article 85 (1) at the trial of the action: accordingly he granted the interlocutory relief.

Two further cases were heard by Mr. Justice Graham in November 1973 in the Chancery Division of the High Court. The first, *Aero Zipp Fasteners Ltd. and Lightening Fasteners Ltd. v. Y.K.K. Fasteners (U.K.) Ltd.* [36] was a straightforward interlocutory proceeding for the amendment of pleadings in a patent infringement action whilst the second, which is considered below, and further under Part III, is of considerably more interest. The Defendants in the *Aero Zipp* case had simply claimed that "if the Defendants have infringed any valid claim of letters patent, the Plaintiffs are not entitled to the relief claimed by virtue of the provisions of Articles 85 and 86 of the Treaty of Rome." In reply to the Plaintiffs' application to have this pleading struck out as disclosing no reasonable defence, the Defendants gave evidence that a complaint of violation of Articles 85 and 86 had been lodged with the Commission against the second Plaintiffs' parent company and that the Commission had consequently initiated proceedings under Article 3 of Regulation 17.

31. But see now on this point, case 127/73 *B.R.T. v. SABAM* (1974) E.C.R. 313; 11 C.M.L. Rev. 1974, 341-347.

32. Case 43/69, 16 *Recueil,* 127.

33. There are still not authentic translations in English of all the cases decided by the Court of Justice.

34. However, see now on this the *second Brasserie de Haecht* case, Case 48/72 (1973) E.C.R., 77; 10 C.M.L. Rev. 1973, 309-311.

35. See n. 34 above.

36. (1973) C.M.L.R., 819.

This, it was argued, would not have been done unless the Commission had been satisfied that there was at least a *prima facie* case of infringement of Articles 85 and 86. The Defendants also maintained that they could not give further particulars regarding their defence until discovery of documents by the Plaintiffs.

In the light of this Graham J. held that the general terms in which the Defendants had pleaded Articles 85 and 86 were quite permissible in the first instance provided this was later followed by full particulars of the facts relied upon in support. He therefore ordered mutual discovery of documents and that the Defendants should then give further and better particulars after this discovery had taken place.

As a foot-note to this case it is interesting to read the succinct description of the relationship between Community and national law given by Mr. Justice Graham. "This country, ... to implement [the U.K.'s] obligations under [the EEC] Treaty, passed the European Communities Act 1972. This Act... enacted that relevant Common Market law should be applied in this country, and should, where there is a conflict, override English law." By using these words Graham J. appears to be recognizing that Community Law is distinct from, and not necessarily "a part of" English law. This is in marked contrast to certain previous and subsequent opinions of U.K. judges.

On November 27, 1973, Mr. Justice Graham was faced with a much more onerous task. The case of *Löwenbräu München and Another v. Grunhalle Lager International Ltd.*[37] is something of a landmark in English jurisprudence, being the first in which an English Court was asked to make a reference to the Court of Justice under Article 177 EEC. Whilst this important aspect will be considered more fully in the subsequent section, the following description is concerned only with the remaining issues of the case.

First of all the facts! The Plaintiff was a well-established Munich brewery which made an expensive high quality lager and sold it under the name "Löwenbräu". In Germany other brewers are allowed to use the name Löwenbräu but always accompanied by their own names and those of their respective breweries. The Defendants sold in England a cheaper lager called "Grunhalle Löwenbräu". The Plaintiffs thereupon brought an action for an interlocutory injunction to restrain alleged passing off. The Defendants argued that the Plaintiffs could not prevent others using the word "Löwenbräu" in Germany and that therefore they could not stop them (the Defendants) using the name on lager in England since that would amount to an arbitrary discrimination or a disguised restriction on trade between Member States under Article 36.

In coming to the conclusion that it would be proper to grant the injunction requested by the Plaintiffs Mr. Justice Graham directed his attention in particular to the scope of Articles 36, 85 and 86 EEC and the relevant case law of the Court of Justice on industrial property rights, namely *Grundig* (trade marks), *Parke, Davis* (patents), *Sirena* (trade marks) and *Deutsche Grammophon* (copyright).[38] In his view the important principle to be derived from these cases was that though the general protection afforded by industrial property rights, such as prevention of passing off, infringements of patents and trade marks and infringement of copyright, was preserved by the Treaty, nevertheless the exercise of such rights, by making use of and relying on the territorial effect of the national legislation in several Member States, might in certain circumstances be contrary to the basic principle of ensuring free movement of goods within the Community. Such circumstances, he noted, would exist if the industrial property right was the subject of an agreement, decision or

37. (1974) C.M.L.R., 1.

38. *Grundig*, (1966) E.C.R., 229, 4 C.M.L. Rev. 1966-67, 209-220; *Parke Davis, op.cit.* n. 26; *Sirena*, 17 *Recueil* 1971, 69; *Deutsche Grammophon, op.cit.* n. 27.

concerted practice prohibited by Article 85 or the subject of a dominant position prohibited by Article 86. Such circumstances would also exist if the industrial property owner had already "exhausted his rights",[39] as had happened in the *Deutsche Grammophon* case and to which Graham J. made especial reference: "there the owner of the copyright in the records had through a subsidiary company released them in France for free circulation and was held thereby to have exhausted his rights of protection in all Member States. He could not therefore sue in Germany in respect of records so released in France and then imported into Germany". Mr. Justice Graham then applied these principles to the case before him and held that the Plaintiffs were not doing otherwise than properly exerting their common law trade mark rights against a wrongdoer in England. There was no exhaustion of rights in Germany which the Defendants could rely on to excuse passing off in England and nothing proved which would be contrary to Articles 85 or 86 or would amount to an arbitrary discrimination or disguised restriction in trade between Member States, which would fall within the proviso of Article 36. Accordingly, Graham J. granted to the Plaintiffs the injunction they sought. Of course, had, for instance, the Plaintiffs put parcels of their lager onto the market in Germany and then tried to sue in England in respect of those same parcels when imported into the U.K., the position, according to the judgment, might have been otherwise.

The next case to be considered, *Application des Gaz S.A. v. Falks Veritas Ltd.,*[40] a decision of May 22, 1974, was in fact the first case after the accession of the U.K. in which the Court of Appeal (Civil Division) had to consider a question of Community Law. The proceedings were again of an interlocutory nature dealing with a request for the amendment of pleadings so as to include a defence based on the EEC Treaty. In addition to the specific issues involved, the case gave Lord Denning, three years after the *Blackburn* case, the opportunity to make some general comments regarding the impact of the Treaty of Rome on English law. In fact, as we shall see below, the Court of Appeal handed down a second decision on the same day in which Lord Denning went considerably further and which, to date, has caused the greatest amount of comment amongst the reported U.K. cases involving Community Law.

In the *Application des Gaz* case, the Plaintiffs, a French company, held the copyright in an industrial design of a camping gas container while the Defendants, a British company, produced and marketed a gas container of a different shape under a patent licence from the Plaintiffs. In 1970 the Defendants began to make containers of the same shape as those of the Plaintiffs although the latter had granted to another English company an exclusive concession to make and sell its Gaz products in the U.K., including the distinctive containers. The Defendants alleged that to stop it marketing its new (copied) containers, the Plaintiffs, through their English concessionaires, approached the wholesale firms which handle camping equipment (and which had until then handled the products of both Plaintiffs and Defendants) and threatened to cut off supplies of the Plaintiffs' product unless the wholesalers agreed to cease to handle the Defendants' products. The Plaintiffs then sought an injunction against the Defendants claiming that the latter's containers infringed the Plaintiffs' copyright in the original design. The Defendants lodged their defence in 1972 but subsequently the Treaty of Rome became applicable in England. As a result the Defendants sought to amend their defence by alleging that the Plaintiffs, together with their English concessionnaires, had abused their dominant position by bringing pressure to

39. The "doctrine of exhaustion" had already been considered by Graham J. in the earlier *Minnesota Mining* decision, *op.cit.* n. 24.

40. (1974) C.M.L.R., 75.

bear on the wholesalers and had engaged in a concerted practice by seeking to enforce their alleged copyright so as to prevent or restrict competition within the Common Market, in breach of Articles 86 and 85 resprectively. These amendments were allowed at first instance and the Plaintiffs then appealed to the Court of Appeal.

First of all Lord Denning accepted as a general proposition that where a civil action was brought in an English court before the entry into force of the Treaty of Rome, EEC law should not be applied retroactively, but instead the case should be decided according to the law as it existed when the action was begun. However, as the Plaintiffs in the present case were claiming an injunction which would affect the Defendants' future conduct, the applicable law would be the law as it stood at the date of the trial, which would include EEC law.

Lord Denning then turned to the Treaty of Rome itself: "I was greatly impressed with the impact which it will have on our law. In any transaction which contains a European element, we must look to the Treaty . . . for the Treaty is part of our law. It is equal in force to any statute".[41]

As to Articles 85 and 86 "they make a great change in the law of England, as well as Europe". Not only that but they "are framed in a style very different from an English statute. They state general principles. They lay down broad policies. But they do not go into detail. The words and phrases are not defined . . . Much is left unsaid. So much, indeed, that a great deal has to be filled in by the . . . European Court". Applying the rulings of the Court on Articles 85 and 86 to the case, Lord Denning considered it arguable that to enforce the copyright against the Defendants might impede the free movement of the Defendants' tins within the Community. On the specific question of the breach of Article 86, Lord Denning again considered it arguable, on the basis of the *Commercial Solvents* ruling [42] of the Court of Justice, that the Plaintiffs, through their English concessionaires, were abusing a dominant position. Lord Denning then went on to consider the remedies available to persons injured by infringements of Articles 85 and 86 and, in this context, drew particular attention to the *B.R.T. v SABAM* ruling of the Court of Justice:[43] "that judgment of the European Court shows that Articles 85 and 86 create rights in private citizens which they can enforce in the national courts and which the national courts are bound to uphold . . . So we reach this important conclusion: Articles 85 and 86 are part of our law. They create new torts or wrongs. Their names are "undue restriction of competition within the Common Market", and "abuse of dominant position within the Common Market". Any infringement of those Articles can be dealt with by our courts".

In the light of the above Lord Denning concluded that the Defendants should be granted leave to amend their defence. They had raised points, he said, which if correct, would show that even if the Plaintiffs were in strict (English?) law entitled to the copyright they claimed, they should not be allowed to enforce it because they were infringing Articles 85 and 86 and should not be granted an injunction.

Stamp L.J. (with whom Roskill L.J. concurred in full) also agreed that leave should be given to amend and that therefore the appeal should be dismissed. In particular he held that pursuant to the European Communities Act "a defence based on the provisions of [the] Treaty is a defence in English law . . . [so that] the question whether . . . it ought to be allowed to be raised by amendment falls precisely as if the terms of the Treaty were contained in an enactment of the Parliament of the United Kingdom".

41. So much for the supremacy of Community Law!
42. Joined Cases 6 and 7/73, (1974) E.C.R., 223.
43. *Op.cit.* n. 31.

In the only case in this section to be heard in 1975 (but see the *EMI/CBS* case *infra*) it was again the turn of Mr. Justice Graham to decide, on March 19, 1975, a case involving Articles 30 to 36 and Article 85. In *Sirdar Ltd. v. Les Fils de Louis Mulliez and Orsay Knitting Wools Ltd.*[44] the Plaintiffs had sought an interlocutory injunction to restrain the Defendants from selling or dealing in knitting yarns under the name "Phildar" or any other name so close to "Sirdar" as to infringe the Plaintiffs' registered trade mark in this name. The Plaintiffs also relied on the Defendants' acts being a breach of a 1965 agreement between the parties, the effect of which was to confine the Plaintiffs and their mark to the U.K. and the Defendants and their mark to France. In fact the Commission had held this agreement void under Article 85 (1) EEC although the decision in question has been subsequently attacked before the Court of Justice.[45] At all events Graham J. felt he could decide the case without having to determine whether the agreement in question was in force or not. This was, he said, primarily a matter for the Court of Justice and as the decision was the subject of an appeal it would be better for the Court to decide on it. He had not been asked to refer the question of the validity of the agreement to the Court and he felt it would be wrong for him to do that of his own motion because such a reference would not be necessary for the decision of the present case. In fact, for himself he felt that even if the decision of the Commission were technically faulty, it was correct. At the end of the day he held that there were sufficient reasons in favour of the Defendants, as far as the balance of convenience was concerned, that the request for an interlocutory injunction should be dismissed.

III. *Article 177 of the EEC Treaty*

In the years 1973 to 1975 there have been ten reported decisions in the U.K. in which Article 177 EEC has been considered in some detail. Whereas in two of these, *Van Duyn* and *EMI/CBS (infra)*, the High Court in fact requested a preliminary ruling from the Court of Justice, in the remaining eight it was not considered necessary to do so. Although at the time (the middle of 1974) it was the *Bulmer/Bollinger* case which caused the greatest amount of interest and comment an analysis of what was said in all the judgments on the question presents a very much more accurate picture of the general attitude of U.K. courts to this particularly important article representing, as it does, one of the cornerstones of the Community's legal order.

Already in 1973, in the *Löwenbräu/Grunhalle* case *(supra)* the cross-motion of the Defendants had sought a reference to the Court of Justice. Mr. Justice Graham, it will be recalled, held that an interlocutory injunction should be granted in favour of the Plaintiffs although he did say that if he had felt that the Defendants were likely to have a good defence by virtue of Community Law, then the retention of flexibility in considering the grant of an interlocutory injunction would probably have prevented him granting one.

With regard to Article 177, counsel for the Plaintiffs had argued that at the interlocutory stage, before the facts had been established, no final decision was being given so that it could not be "necessary" to have the view of the Court of Justice before deciding whether an injunction should be granted pending trial.[46] He further argued that pursuant to the last

44. (1975) C.M.L.R., 378.
45. Case 34/75 removed by order of the Court of April 7, 1976.
46. On this aspect of the case see Collins, *op.cit.* n. 14, at p. 103. In particular he says that in English proceedings of an interlocutory character, only "very sparing use" should be made of the power to refer questions to the Court of Justice; *cf.* Jacobs "When to refer to the European Court", (1974) L.Q.R., 486, at 491-492.

sentence of Article 177 a court against whose decision there is no appeal is under a duty to refer but that that stage had not been reached. On the other hand, counsel for the Defendants contended that where any doubt arises and where a court would find assistance on any point of interpretation the "restrictive attitude" of the Plaintiffs' counsel should be rejected and the Court of Justice always consulted for guidance. On these conflicting views Mr. Justice Graham had the following to say: "I do not think that either view put before me by counsel is wholly correct. As I read the Treaty, references are not to be made unnecessarily, but on the other hand the power to refer is not confined only to courts whose decisions are final, or to any particular stage of the case ... If I felt in this case a need of guidance upon the interpretation of any article of the Treaty and that such guidance was necessary for my decision I have unfettered power to refer the matter to the EEC Court. Such appears to me to be the clear intention of the Treaty from its wording. If, however, I do not feel guidance is necessary and can come to a decision without it, there is no need for me to make a reference".

At the end of 1973, then, we are faced with what could be described as a guardedly open approach to preliminary rulings.

This case was followed on February 14, 1974 by *Van Duyn v. Home Office*,[47] the first reference by a British Court for a preliminary ruling, where the relatively open attitude of Mr. Justice Graham was confirmed by Mr. Justice Pennycuick, Vice-Chancellor of the Chancery Division of the High Court.

The facts of this case were as follows. Miss van Duyn, a Dutch national, had been engaged in the study and practice of Scientology in the Netherlands. Having been offered employment as a secretary in the college of the Church of Scientology she came to England with a view to taking up that employment. An Immigration Officer refused her leave to enter as the U.K. government regarded the activities of the Church of Scientology as contrary to public policy, although not illegal. The Plaintiff thereupon sought a declaration that she was entitled to enter and remain in the U.K. for the purpose of accepting the employment offered. There was no significant dispute between the parties on the facts and it was agreed that under English law Miss van Duyn had no right of entry.

As to Community Law it was argued that Article 48 (3) EEC embodied the right of free movement and that the proviso subjecting the right to national limitations justified on grounds of public policy or public security was to be read in the light of Article 3 of Directive 64/221, which provided that any such measures should be "based exclusively on the personal conduct of the individual concerned". The Home Office argued that neither article had "self-executing" effect and that in any case the refusal was based on the Plaintiff's personal conduct in that she had worked in a Scientology establishment in Amsterdam, had taken a course on Scientology, was a practising Scientologist and was intending to work at a Scientology establishment in the U.K.

The case consequently depended upon three questions of interpretation of Community Law: (a) Was Article 48 (3) directly applicable? (b) Was Article 3 of Directive 64/221 directly applicable? (c) Did the conduct attributed to Miss van Duyn amount to "personal conduct" within the meaning of Article 3 of the Directive? The Plaintiff requested that these questions should be referred to the Court of Justice under Article 177 (2) EEC since they were "relevant" and had been "raised" and there was genuine doubt as to whether the two Articles were directly applicable and whether her conduct amounted to "personal

47. (1974) C.M.L.R., 347. For the decision of the Court of Justice, see case 41/74 (1974) E.C.R., 1337; see also Simmonds, "Van Duyn v. The Home Office: the direct effectiveness of Directives", (1975) I.C.L.Q., 419.

conduct". She argued that any national court was entitled to make a reference at any stage of the proceedings: in the present case it was not premature to make a reference as soon as the initial pleadings were complete, the legal issues being clear. The Home Office, on the other hand, argued that a reference would be premature and, indeed, was unnecessary since all the existing national cases on similar matters had been decided by the national courts in question. National courts of first instance should, it maintained, be loath to refer for fear of overburdening the Court of Justice and because of delay and extra costs.

Turning to the judgment itself Mr. Justice Pennycuick stated, as the first main issue, that Article 48, when read in conjunction with the 1964 directive, raised a question of interpretation because the latter introduced the element of "personal conduct" in addition to the notion of "public policy" (Article 48 (3)). As to Article 177 – "the word "preliminary" is rather obscure" – it therefore seemed to the judge that a decision as to the meaning of the expression was necessary "in the full sense of the word" to enable him to give judgment. "Indeed, it would be quite impossible to give judgment without such a decision. That being so it seems to me that I ought certainly to exercise my discretion" to request a preliminary ruling.

With regard to the Home Office contention that the reference should be deferred until after the trial of the action, or at least after discovery, the judge held that "in general, issues of fact and issues of national law should be determined before a reference is made since the determination of those issues in a particular sense may make the reference, with the expense and delay involved, unnecessary". However, that was not, according to the judge, the case in the present action. As to the further contention that the national Court should not overburden "the already overburdened European Court" with a deluge of references, Mr. Justice Pennycuick doubted whether this was a legitimate consideration and, in any event, the issue seemed to him as one of the first importance upon which a reference was appropriate. The passage, in the judgment of Graham J. in the *Löwenbräu/Grunhalle* case *(supra)*, was then quoted and expressly adopted by Pennyquick J.

The second main issue, according the judgment, was the direct applicability of Article 48.[48] There again it was held that a reference could only be refused if it were "really clear" that Article 48 was not directly applicable: this, it was decided, was not the case.

Before now turning to the *Bulmer/Bollinger* decision, it is interesting to note what Lord Denning had already said with regard to Article 177 and the rôle of the Court of Justice in the *Application des Gaz* case, which was decided earlier on the same day. Speaking generally on the interpretation of Community Law he pointed out that "if you read through the Common Market Law Reports, you will find that case after case is referred to the Court which interprets them according to the "wording and spirit" of the Treaty. Every one of these cases is important to commercial men. The Court is moulding the Law of Europe into a single whole which every country of the nine must obey. The present case is a good illustration . . ." Nevertheless, with regard to Articles 85 and 86 he said that "any infringement can be dealt with by our English courts. It is for our courts to find the facts, to apply the law, and to use the remedies which we have available. If it should turn out, after finding the facts, that it is necessary to seek the opinion of the Court – on a point of interpretation of the Treaty – the English courts can refer that point to the European Court. But the eventual decision of the case is for our English courts. It is for us to give the judgment and to enforce it. It is a task worthy of our mettle".

Notwithstanding these remarks it became apparent in the following decision of the

48. *Cf.* the *Schorsch Meier* case *(infra)* where the direct effect of Article 106 was not even considered.

Court of Appeal, *H. P. Bulmer Ltd. and another v. J. Bollinger S.A.and another*[49] (May 22, 1974) that the open attitude of the High Court as represented in the previous two decisions (*Löwenbräu* and *Van Duyn*) was not fully shared by Lord Denning. The case has given rise to a great deal of criticism.[50] On the other hand the fear expressed that what was said might determine the future approach of English courts to the Article 177 procedure should be considerably reduced in the light of the subsequent *Miliangos* decision of the House of Lords *(infra).*

The facts of the *Bulmer/Bollinger* case can be briefly stated as follows. In 1970 the Defendants, French producers of champagne, brought an action for an injunction against the use by the Plaintiffs of the word "Champagne" as part of the terms "Champagne Cider" and "Champagne Perry". To counter this, the Plaintiffs brought the present action for a declaration that they were entitled to use the two expressions which, it was claimed, had been used in England for seventy to eighty years. In 1973 the Defendants amended their pleadings to the effect that the use of the word "Champagne" in connection with any beverage other than champagne would contravene EEC law, namely, Article 30 of Regulation 816/70 and Articles 6-8, 12 and 13 of Regulation 817/70. They then applied for two points of Community Law to be referred to the Court of Justice for a preliminary ruling: a) Whether . . . the use of the word "Champagne" in connection with any beverage other than champagne is a contravention of . . . the provisions of Community Law; b) whether a national court of a Member State should . . . refer to the Court of Justice such a question. Whitford J., sitting at first instance in the High Court,[51] had already recognised that the matter was "of some interest and importance". As to Article 177 he said that "the national Court is given a discretion: it may request a ruling from the Court of Justice . . . on a question relating to the interpretation of the Treaty if it comes to the conclusion that such a ruling is necessary to enable it to give judgment". But before giving his decision he made two remarks. On the one hand he said that, whatever answer were given by the Court of Justice in reply to a request, the Plaintiffs might be able to satisfy him that in the light of the domestic doctrine of "acquiescence" they could continue a practice which they asserted had been going on since the last century. Further on in the judgment, in reply to the contention that it may be necessary not merely to rely on one text, the English text, but to

49. (1974) C.M.L.R., 91.

50. Mitchell "Sed quis custodiet ipsos custodes", (1974) C.M.L.Rev., 351; Jacobs, *op.cit.* n. 46; Graupner, "Zur Anpassung des Rechts in Grossbritannien an das Recht der Europäischen Gemeinschaften", (1974) A.W.D., 261; the same, "References to the European Court according to Article 177 of the EEC Treaty", (1974) *Law Society's Gazette,* 1240; Collins, "Article 177 and interlocutory proceedings", (1974) I.C.L.Q., 840; the same, *European Community Law in the United Kingdom,* especially pp. 76-110; Dogtaglou, "Der Englisch Richter und die Gemeinschaft", (1975) EuR, 247, (At. 248 the title of the *Times Law Report* of this case is given as "Wither (rather than Whither) the Law of England"; this is, no doubt, a typographical error!); Bridge, *op.cit.,* n. 18. Note also the somewhat apologetic editorial in 11 C.M.L.Rev. 1974, 349; *cf.* Bebr, "Critical review of recent case-law of national courts", 11 C.M.L.Rev. 1974, 420, where it is said: ". . . the decision of the Court of Appeal is, from the point of view of Community Law, certainly satisfactory".

51. (1974) C.M.L.R., 97.

have a collation of all the foreign language texts, he said "I am not sure I would accept that".[52]

As to the grounds for his judgment, Whitford J. expressly noted that if it were necessary for a reference at some stage then it would be better to have it at that point so that when he came to make a final judgment he would have all the relevant law and could apply that to the facts as they emerged. But he was not satisfied that the question was one which could be satisfactorily posed or satisfactorily answered "in quite so much of a vacuum as counsel for the defendants suggest": the judge had, in fact, only been given a very brief view of the regulations in question. On the second question b) it appeared to him, from the cases cited, that there existed an established practice according to which each national court, when any question of a reference arose, considered in relation to the facts and the circumstances of the particular case whether a reference was or was not appropriate and that this was the procedure envisaged by Article 177. Consequently Whitford J. refused to refer either question and said that he would first try the whole case.

In view of the attitude of Whitford J., which is very much in line with those already described of Pennycuick J. and Graham J., it was perhaps unfortunate, although not surprising in the light of what he had said in the *Application des Gaz* case, that Lord Denning, on appeal of the case from the High Court, went into such detail in giving "his understanding"[53] of the words "necessary" and "may" in Article 177. However, it is to be noted that when Lord Denning gave his "guidelines" as to a) whether a decision is "necessary" and b) on the exercise of the discretion, he did qualify them with the following words: "it may not be out of place to draw attention to the way in which other national courts have dealt with (these two matters)".

On the former question as to whether a decision is necessary the Master of the Rolls made four points. In the first place he said that "the point must be conclusive" so that whichever way it is decided, it is conclusive of the case. Secondly, he held that if the same point "or substantially the same point" has already been decided by the Court of Justice in a previous case, it is not necessary for the English Court to decide it. The third point was that if the question is "reasonably clear and free from doubt" there is only need to apply it. On this point the controversial *Shell-Berre* decision of the French Conseil d'Etat was cited. Finally, Lord Denning noted that "as a rule you cannot tell whether it is necessary to decide a point until all the facts are ascertained. So in general it is best to decide the facts first".

Turning his attention to the exercise of the discretion involved in Article 177, Lord Denning went into even more detail and gave a total of six "guidelines" which the national courts had "taken into account". First, a ruling from the European Court may take "months and months . . . Meanwhile, the whole action in the English court is stayed . . . This may be unfortunate, especially in a case where an injunction is sought or there are other reasons for expedition". Lord Denning then suggested that the court should not be overloaded:[54] "so do

52. On this latter point see, however, the remarks of Lord Denning, *infra* p. 407; see also case 35/75, *Firma Matisa v. H.Z.A. Berlin* (1975) E.C.R., 1205, where it is said: "Although the . . . German version . . . is capable of giving (a particular) impression, a comparison with the other language versions shows . . ."

53. See the Commission reply to Written Question No. 25/75 by Mr. Bayerl on "Procedure under Article 177 of the EEC Treaty", O.J. No. C 161, 17.7.75, p. 13; *cf.* Bebr, *op.cit.* n. 50, at p. 420, who suggests that the decision, in its interpretation of Article 177, constitutes a binding precedent for lower English courts.

54. There would as yet seem to be little danger of this at the hands of British Judges!

not put too much to them. They cannot split up into divisions of three of five judges".[55] Thirdly, the question should be clearly formulated. "In fairness to (the Court of Justice) it is desirable to find the facts and state them clearly before referring the question". In the fourth place "unless the point is really difficult and important, it would seem better for the English judge to decide it himself. For in so doing, much delay and expense will be saved". (This point has been the subject of particularly strong criticism). The fifth and sixth considerations to which reference was made were, respectively, the expense to the parties in getting a ruling and the wishes of the parties. As to the latter it was said: "if both parties want the point to be referred . . ., the English court should have regard to their wishes, but it should not give them undue weight". On the other hand "the English court should hesitate before making a reference against the wishes of one of the parties, seeing the expense and delay which it involves".

Clearly each of the above considerations may be of relevance with regard to Article 177: what makes them less acceptable is the manner in which they are expressed. The emphasis on every occasion is that questions of interpretation should be decided by the English judge unless this is unavoidable. At the same time, there is a noticeable reluctance to acknowledge that in the absence of a Community appeal procedure the success of Article 177 and the uniform application of Community Law depends on a spirit of close co-operation between the Court of Justice and all the courts of each Member State.

This restrictive attitude of Lord Denning showed itself with equal force in other parts of the judgment. Thus when dealing with the impact of the Treaty on English law, the Master of the Rolls expanded on what he had already touched upon in the *Application des Gaz* case in the following way. "The Treaty concerns only those matters which have a European element; that is to say, matters which affect people or property in the nine (sic) countries of the Common Market besides ourselves. The Treaty does not touch any of the matters which concern solely the mainland of England [56] and the people in it". Then on a more positive note, he proclaimed: "when we come to matters with a European element, the Treaty is like an incoming tide. It flows into the estuaries and up the river. It cannot be held back". However, to dispel any fears (or hopes!) that what was involved was a new legal order, he continued: "Parliament has decided that the Treaty is henceforward to be part of our law. It is equal in force to any statute. The governing provision is section 2 (1) of the European Communities Act 1972". Again the statement: "the supreme tribunal for interpreting the Treaty is the European Court" is immediately qualified by the words "our Parliament has so decided [by] section 3 of the European Communities Act 1972".[57] Finally Lord Denning felt that "short of the House of Lords, no other English court is bound to refer a question". To him this meant that the judges of the Court of Appeal have complete discretion.[58]

Having in effect suggested to the lower courts that they should be wary of entering into a dialogue with the Court of Justice, the Master of the Rolls was, of course, bound to tell them—which he did, and in rather more detail than in the *Application de Gaz* case—how they should interpret Community Law. What must they do? "They must follow the European pattern. No longer must they examine the words in meticulous detail.[59] No

55. This is no longer the case. See Commission reply, *supra* n. 53.
56. Not surprisingly Mitchell, *op.cit.* n. 50, 353 was quick to point out this slip.
57. As Mitchell, *loc.cit.*, at 352, rightly points out: "The place of the European Court depends on the new legal order . . . Section 3 is essentially secondary". However that it "was perhaps just as well" to have the section remains debatable.
58. Even when leave to appeal to the House of Lords is necessary?
59. *Cf.* the word "necessary" in Article 177!

longer must they argue about the precise grammatical sense. They must look to the purpose or intent. They must not confine themselves to the English text. They must consider, if need be, all the authentic texts, of which there are now eight.[60] They must divine the spirit of the Treaty and gain inspiration from it. If they find a gap, they must fill it as best they can . . .".

Before considering what has happened in the U.K. since the *Bulmer/Bollinger* decision, it should be mentioned that Lord Justice Stephenson gave a considerably shorter and somewhat more cautious judgment than Lord Denning. In particular he said that if Whitford J. had intended to refuse *ever* to request a ruling he would have been wrong. "It is too early to say whether it will become necessary and whether he should request a ruling. . .". He also expressly said that nothing he said was intended to doubt the decision of Mr. Justice Pennycuick in the *Van Duyn* case. On the question of "guidelines" to lower courts, Stephenson L.J. said that these should be few and closely related to the basic requirement that the decision of the question raised must be necessary at the time the reference is requested to enable the court to give judgment at the end of the case. The Court "should bear in mind the other considerations which the Master of Rolls has set out, but beyond that I would not go to guide the court of trial". It should also be pointed out that Lord Justice Stamp adopted the judgment of Stephenson L.J. as if it were his own "because I would be reluctant to express any views which might be said to go outside the confines of this case".

One final point considered in detail by Lord Stephenson was Order 114, rules 1 to 6 of the Supreme Court, which deal with the procedure to be followed in respect of references to the Court of Justice.[61] "Perhaps by an oversight, Order 114, rule 6, which deals with appeals, does not deal with *refusals* to make an order to the European Court. By order 114, rule 6, an appeal lies without leave against an order referring, but that special provision cannot offend the general power of the judge or this court to grant leave against a refusal to make such an order".

The judgment of Lord Denning was subsequently taken into account in two later decisions of lower courts. In *re a Holiday in Italy* (supra) reference was expressly made to what had been said by him in connection with the uniform construction of regulations. In addition, although not specifically referring to the *Bulmer/Bollinger* case in this connection, the National Insurance Commissioner was particularly emphatic on the question of a possible reference to the Court of Justice. "In my judgment, as this decision of the Commissioner may be set aside by an order of certionari made by the High Court on the ground of an error in point of law, . . . in giving it I do not constitute a tribunal against whose decision there is no juridical remedy under English law, even though an application for an order of certiorari cannot be made without the leave of the High Court. In my judgment, therefore, I am not bound to refer the question of the interpretation of these regulations to the European Court for a preliminary decision and in this case I do not do so, but shall proceed to decide it myself".

In the *Secchi* case *(supra)* the Metropolitan Magistrate, Marylebone relied more directly on Lord Denning's guidelines: "the extent of this subordination [of English law to Community Law] and the proper way in which English courts should deal with the impact

60. The authors would point out that Article 160 of the Act of Accession states that the Treaties shall be authentic in the Danish, English and Irish languages, (as well in Dutch, French, German and Italian), therefore only *seven* texts. Irish is not an authentic language in respect of acts of the institutions (Article 155).

61. Graupner, *op.cit.* n. 50, deals in more detail with these procedures; see also Jacobs and Durand, *References to the European Court* (1975), at p. 165.

of Community Law on English law were dealt with at great length by the Master of the Rolls in his judgment in *Bulmer v. Bollinger* ... which provides the essential guidelines which English courts must follow". He then drew the consequences from what Lord Denning had said in a manner as concise as in the previous case "the Master of the Rolls in the *Bulmer* case gave clear guidance as to how English courts should proceed in the absence of... definitions. They must look to the purpose and intent with which particular words are used in the Treaty and these, he pointed out, are to be found in the general wording and spirit of the Treaty which lays down general principles and expresses aims and purposes. Lord Denning went on to say that the courts must divine the spirit of the Treaty and gain inspiration from it. If they found a gap they must fill it as best they can. In view of this very clear guidance given by Lord Denning, I do not feel it necessary to refer the interpretation of the word "worker", or for that matter anything else in the Treaty or Directive 64/221 to the Court of Justice at Luxembourg for a ruling under Article 177. ... My task is the application of the relevant Community Law which is for the national courts, not the Community Court, to do, as Lord Denning said ...".

It is clear that these two lower courts, post *Bulmer/Bollinger*, did not reflect the openness of the three High Court judges previously. On the contrary, the impression is gained that the national courts should try to apply Community Law without calling upon the assistance of the Court of Justice.

Between these two decisions, the Court of Appeal was again seized of a case with an important Community element. In *Schorsch Meier GmbH v. Hennin*,[62] decided on November 26, 1974, the Master of the Rolls, on this occasion sitting with Lord Justice Lawton and Mr. Justice Foster, himself took the opportunity to put into practice what he had said in the *Bulmer/Bollinger* case. He decided a point of Community Law without making a reference to the Court of Justice, notwithstanding that that Court had never itself considered the point and notwithstanding that "it may be doubted" that the Article in question meant what Lord Denning considered it to mean.[63]

The facts of the case can be summarised as follows. The Plaintiffs, Schorsch Meier GmbH, were motor manufacturers established in Munich. The Defendant, Mr. A. R. Hennin, lived in England and was engaged in the motor car trade. In 1970 and 1971 he ordered spare parts from the Plaintiffs. The company invoiced the goods to him, giving the price in Deutschmarks, and despatched them to him in England. In February 1972 the company rendered an account of the outstanding payments, for 3756.03 DM, for goods sold and delivered, at that time equivalent to £ 452. Sterling was subsequently devalued and in July 1973 the company issued a summons in the West London County Court for 3756.03 DM, then equivalent to £ 641. It was submitted that the rule of English law by which an English court can give judgment only in sterling was incompatible with Article 106 EEC. The County Court Judge refused to accept the argument or to give judgment in Deutschmarks. The Plaintiffs appealed to the Court of Appeal.

In his judgment Lord Denning first of all considered English law apart from the Treaty. He recalled what he had said in the *Havana* case[64] that "if there is one thing clear in our law, it is that [a] claim must be made in sterling and the judgment given in sterling". However since then, according to the Master of Rolls, things had changed: "Sterling floats in the wind. It changes like a weathercock with every gust that blows. This change compels us to think again about our rules." Very astutely, Lord Denning then held that because the

62. (1975) C.M.L.R., 20.
63. See (1975) L.Q.R., 162.
64. *In Re United Railways of Havana and Regla Warehouses Ltd.*, (1961) A.C., 1007.

previous rule was basically procedural and because the reason for that procedure had ceased to exist "we are at liberty to discard the rule itself". Accordingly, he held that when the money of account and the money of payment is a foreign currency the English Courts have power to give judgment in that foreign currency. But in addition to amending a rule which had existed for several hundred years in England, the Master of Rolls directed his attention to Community Law and held that: "the purpose of Article 106—or one of its purposes—is to ensure that the creditor in one Member State shall receive payment for his goods in his own currency—if it is the currency of the contract—without any impediment or restriction by reason of changes in the rate of exchange. The English Courts would be acting contrary to the spirit and intent of the Treaty if they made a German creditor accept payment in depreciated sterling".[65]

On the other aspects of the Treaty, and in particular Article 177, Lord Denning ruled again that by statute the Treaty of Rome is "part of the Law of England". Referring to the *Van Gend en Loos* and *De Costa* cases, he pointed out that it creates rights and obligations, not only between Member States themselves, but also between citizens and the Member States, and between the ordinary citizens themselves. He went on: "the national courts can enforce those rights and obligations themselves". And citing the *"Champagne"* and *Application des Gaz* cases, he said: "whenever the Treaty is prayed in aid, the English courts can themselves interpret it, subject always to the European Court, if asked, having the last word". Turning then to Article 106, he held that it was not necessary to examine the words in meticulous detail but rather to look at the purpose or intent (again the *"Champagne"* case was quoted).

It is not surprising, in the light of his equation of the Treaty of Rome with a statute, that Lord Denning did not consider the direct effect or otherwise of Article 106.

The next case which arose with an Article 177 element, *DDSA Pharmaceuticals Ltd. v. Farbwerke Hoechst A.G. and the Comptroller General of Patents*[66] was heard by Whitford J. on 24 June 1975 before the High Court (Chancery Division). Involved was a clause in a compulsory licence which prohibited the export of material by the licensee or the sale of such material to third parties who, to the knowledge of the licensee, might export the licensed material.

The Plaintiffs argued that this clause constituted a fetter upon the free movement of goods and, inasmuch as it was arguable that the licence was an agreement between two parties, was in breach of Article 85. They accordingly sought a reference to the Court of Justice. Whitford J. held that the application for a request was premature although he accepted that a stage might emerge at which it became apparent that a reference would be desirable. However at that stage it was said that: "quite clearly this is not a case where there has been or could be any agreement between the parties as to what questions ought to be referred". Nor did the judge consider that he had sufficient material before him so that he could himself decide what, if any, questions should be sent forward.

The two final decisions in this section are, perhaps, the most important decided in the U.K. during the period in question. In one the High Court, after the Denning "guidelines" had been given, nevertheless sought a preliminary ruling. Subsequently, in the most recent case, the House of Lords took Lord Denning to task for having interpreted Article 106 EEC without asking for guidance from the Court of Justice.

65. But see the reply of the Commission to Written Question No. 705/74 of Mr. Glinne on "Application of Article 106 of the Treaty by the Court of Appeal in London", O.J. 1975, C 170/10, where in particular it is said that: "Article 106 of the Treaty has nothing to do with creditors receiving payment in a strong currency rather than an unstable currency".

66. (1975) C.M.L.R., 50.

In the case before the High Court, Mr. Justice Graham, putting into practice the positive approach he had demonstrated in earlier cases, became the second (and only other)[67] judge in the U.K. to request the Court of Justice for a preliminary ruling. This he did on March 13, 1975 in the case of *E.M.I. Records Ltd. v. C.B.S. United Kingdom Ltd.*[68]

The facts, briefly stated, were as follows. The Plaintiffs, an English company, owned the rights in the trade mark "Columbia" in the U.K. and in other countries including all the Member States. The Defendants were the English subsidiary of an American company who owned the same mark in the United States. Originally the mark was in the same hands in both the U.K. and the U.S.A. but the two present owners were unrelated. The Defendants imported gramophone records bearing the mark "Columbia" from the U.S.A. into Britain. The Plaintiffs sought an interlocutory injunction to restrain infringement of their trade mark "Columbia" in the U.K. by the sale of records made by the Defendants and bearing that mark. The Defendants resisted on two grounds, one of which was that it was necessary to seek a preliminary ruling from the Court of Justice under Article 177.

Turning to the Community Law aspects involved, Graham J. first of all referred to what he had said in the *Löwenbräu München* case on the principles underlying the relevant cases of the Court of Justice, in particular with respect to the doctrine of "exhaustion of rights". He concluded: "the Common Market, so far at any rate as free circulation of goods is concerned, is treated by the EEC Court as being one and indivisible and free circulation is expressed to be of fundamental importance and should only be hindered if there is some interest which the Community recognizes as overriding".

He then pointed out that since 1973 there had been further developments in this area, namely the *Café Hag*[69] and *Centrafarm*[70] cases. As to the former, the judge noted that its facts had been unusual and unlikely to occur again frequently, if at all. He recalled that the Court of Justice had held that it was incompatible with the Community provisions on free circulation of goods to prohibit trading in one Member State (Luxembourg) of a product which lawfully bore a trade mark in another Member State (Germany) for the sole reason that an identical mark (Hag), sharing the same origin, existed in that State. On this, Graham J. then stated that it "appears to go a long way in restricting the exercise of industrial property rights and at first sight may be thought to be inconsistent with the provisions of Article 36, preserving prohibitions justified on the ground of the protection of such property, and with Article 222. Indeed, since the decision there has been considerable public criticism of its soundness". In dealing with the *Centrafarm* case on the other hand, Graham J. pointed out that the Court of Justice would prevent carving up the market into units by exploitation of the territorial effect of property rights whilst the primary monopoly rights of preventing imitation and uncertainty of origin would be preserved, so far as compatible with the principle of maintenance of free circulation of goods lawfully on the market.

Directing his attention to Article 177, Graham J. came to the conclusion that in the light of these recent developments the point at issue was not a simple one! At all events: "I am certainly not prepared to class it as falling within the principle of *'acte clair'*—see *Bulmer v. Bollinger*— because Common Market law at the moment is ... so far as industrial

67. But see n. 3, *supra*.

68. (1975) C.M.L.R., 285; see judgment of June 15, 1976 (not yet published).

69. Case 192/73 (1974) E.C.R., 731.

70. Cases 15 and 16/74 (1974) E.C.R., 1147; 12 C.M.L. Rev. 1975, 261-266, 267-268, and see E. A. van Nieuwenhoven Helbach, "Industrial Property, the Centrafarm Judgments", 13 C.M.L. Rev. 1976, 37-59.

property is concerned in a formative stage and the conflict between national territorial rights and the doctrine of the free circulation of goods has not yet been fully worked out. Decisions, sometimes even inconsistent or illogical, may well perhaps be given by the various courts concerned until such times as wider Common Market rights displace existing national rights". Applying this to the case before him, Graham J. said that if the Defendants succeeded in establishing their argument (based on the *Café Hag* case) they would have a complete defence; if they failed, the Plaintiffs would succeed on the facts admitted. He continued: "it is unnecessary for further facts to be found on title and infringement. Faced with this dilemma ... it is 'necessary' for me, within the meaning of Article 177, to have a ruling on this point from the EEC Court before I am in a position to give final judgment in the action.[71] I do not consider that what is necessary within the meaning of Article 177 must be limited to an interlocutory decision before the Court. So to limit it would make the section largely nugatory in practice. From a practical point of view ... time and expense will be *saved* by the matter being referred now, rather than at the trial. This is really a fight for entry into the whole of the Common Market, and that is why there are parallel actions in Denmark and Germany (references were in fact also made in both these cases [72]). In such cases it seems to me that the sooner the matter is clarified by the EEC Court, the better. Unfortunately there is as yet no central court of appeal which is in a position to reconcile conflicting decisions emanating from different countries of the Community. Different decisions by the three countries concerned in the present case would lead to chaotic results and this shows the logical necessity for such a court ... It seems to me, therefore, essential, in the meantime to do anything which can be done to make it less likely that such an unfortunate position will occur and this can best be done by a reference as quickly as possible".

In this way Graham J. has taken up a position rather different from that of the Court of Appeal in the *Bulmer/Bollinger* case as regards Article 177: his remarks draw attention to some of the more compelling reasons in favour of cooperating with the Court of Justice.

The final case, *Miliangos v. George Frank (Textiles) Ltd.*[73] (November 1975), was concerned with the instability which had overtaken the pound sterling in recent times. The House of Lords, on the basis of English law alone, held that payment of foreign currency debts (in the case Swiss francs) could be made in foreign currency. It will be recalled that in the *Schorsch Meier* decision *(supra)* the Court of Appeal had come to a simular conclusion, although in doing so it had also relied upon Article 106 EEC.

On Article 106, Lord Wilberforce, who gave the leading judgment in the *Miliangos* case, had the following to say. "Although Switzerland is not an EEC member, the argument unanimously accepted by the Court of Appeal in *Schorsch Meier* was invoked by the respondent in this appeal. It cannot therefore be passed over in silence, *all the less since there is a risk that it may be quoted as a precedent.* There are two reasons for dealing with it here with restraint ... (secondly) the issue of the applicability and interpretation of Article 106, if it were to be considered by this House, would necessitate a reference to the European Court under Article 177 of the Treaty. But nevertheless I feel bound to say that I entertain the strongest reservations concerning the use made by the Court of Appeal of Article 106 in the present context ... *Any other court in which such issues arise would be*

71. It is to be noted that according to the wording of Article 177 it is the decision on a question of interpretation which should be "necessary" and not the request to the Court of Justice for a ruling.

72. Cases 86/75 and 96/75, judgments of June 15, 1976 (not yet published).

73. (1975) 3. W.L.R., 758.

well advised to refer them to the European Court for clarification". Lord Simon of Glaisdale and Lord Cross of Chelsea expressly agreed with Lord Wilberforce on this point whilst the other two Lordships agreed more generally on what had been said.

The weight to be attached by the U.K. courts to this advice cannot be overestimated.

Conclusions

Even if the number of U.K. cases involving Community Law has been small and their scope relatively limited, and even if the House of Lords (which plays a particularly important rôle in the U.K. judicial system) has not yet had the occasion to consider the Community legal order in any depth, it is still interesting to note the extremely detailed yet practical and, at all events, open way in which the U.K. judges have treated the Community Law elements with which they have been faced. Judges do not seem to have been unduly wary of taking into account, interpreting and applying Community Law, on the basis of arguments put forward by Counsel for both Plaintiffs and Defendants—which the latter have done in an extremely active fashion.

At the same time, it must be said that in cases where real doubts as to the meaning of Community provisions have arisen the courts have, in general, shown marked reluctance to seek the opinion of the Court of Justice, albeit stating in full why they did not feel this was necessary.[74] But a cautious approach in the first few years is certainly understandable.

On the other hand, the idea expressed at one stage that the Court of Appeal should act as a filter to determine which cases should be referred does not seem to have gained general favour. Both references to date have, in fact, been from the High Court.[75] Again, in the light of the judgments so far handed down it would not appear that the question as to which courts are to be recognised as final courts in the U.K. in the terms of Article 177 (3) EEC should play an unduly important role in practice. The House of Lords has already accepted that it may be obliged to make a reference. Other courts will, no doubt, especially after the *Miliangos* judgment, seek a ruling whenever they feel this is "necessary" (interpreted flexibly) to decide the case whether their decisions are at an interlocutory stage, are subject to judicial review or appeal is subject to leave being given.

But whereas they have not been inactive it cannot be said that U.K. courts have shown an attitude towards Community Law, which, in any way, reflects the dynamic approach of the Court of Justice.[76] Whilst the negotiation and signature of the Treaty of Accession has been an issue before the courts, the fundamental rather than immediate implications of the European Communities Act itself have not yet given rise to profound reflection. Thus it has been pursuant to this Act (in particular section 2 (1)) rather than the independent nature of the Community legal order, which applies as such in nine Member States, that the direct

74. Bridge. *op.cit.* n. 18 refers to an "ultra-cautious approach" and an "unjustifiably complacent attitude". In the years 1973 to 1975, whereas two requests for preliminary rulings were submitted by U.K. courts, the total number of cases decided by the Court pursuant to requests for preliminary rulings was 139 of which 16 came from France, 68 from Germany and 14 from Italy.

75. A close reading of the more recent cases also gives the impression that the lower courts would not be unduly worried by any doctrine of stare decisis if they felt a reference under Article 177 was necessary.

76. In addition to what is said below this is also regrettable because it is particularly via the Article 177 procedure that national legislation, practice and personalities have an influence on the Community legal order.

effect of Community Law has been recognized. The further question which then arises, namely what happens when an Act of Parliament is passed which conflicts with existing Community Law having direct effect, has as yet hardly been considered by the U.K. courts. In other words how does one reconcile the irreconcilables, the Sovereignty of Parliament and the Supremacy of Community Law. The problem is certain to present itself, as it has done in the other Member States, however much attempts may be made to reconcile divergent provisions. It is to be hoped that a greater degree of cooperation will be established with the Court of Justice (via the Article 177 procedure) for it to be able to assist the U.K. courts in their whole approach to Community Law and, in particular, to this fundamental question.

John Forman
Trevor Stevens**
Brussels

Chronological list of Cases

Case	*Court or Tribunal*	*Date*	
1. Blackburn v. Attorney-General	C.A.	1971	
2. McWhirter v. Attorney-General	C.A.	1972	
3. Lerose v. Hawick Jersey	Ch. D.	1972	
4. Minnesota Mining and Manufacturing v. Geerpres	Ch.D.	1973	January
5. Esso Petroleum v. Kingswood Motors	Q.B.D.		April
6. Processed Vegetable Growers Case	Tribunal		September
7. Aero Zipp Fasteners Case	Ch.D.		November
8. Löwenbräu München Case	Ch.D.		November
9. Van Duyn v. Home Office*	Ch. D.	1974	February
10. Application des Gaz Case	C.A.		May
11. Bulmer v. Bollinger	C.A.		May
12. Re a Holiday in Italy	Tribunal		July
13. Schorsch Meier v. Hennin	C.A.		November
14. Gibson v. Lord Advocate	Scotland	1975	March
15. EMI v. C.B.S.*	Ch. D.		March
16. Sirdar v. Mulliez	Ch. D.		March
17. R. v. Secchi	Magistrate		March
18. The DDSA Pharmaceuticals Case	Ch. D.		June
19. The Price Case	Magistrate		July
20. Miliangos v. George Frank (Textiles)	H.L.		November
Brack v. Insurance Officer*	Tribunal	1976	February

* Followed by a request for a preliminary ruling.

** The opinions expressed in this Article are personal to the authors.

SURVEY OF UNITED STATES LITERATURE RELATING TO THE EUROPEAN COMMUNITY 1970-1975 *

Note: This survey covers both articles written in legal and academic periodicals and books published in the United States from January 1970 through July 1975. If an article appeared simultaneously in a European publication, it was included in this survey unless its European counterpart was also published in English. Likewise, in the case of a book published both in the United States and in Europe, only if its European edition appeared in a language other than English was it included in this survey.

a. *List of Subjects*

* Prepared by Jon E. Hayden, 3rd year student at the University of Michigan Law School, Ann Arbor, U.S.A.

13 C.M.L. Rev. 1976, 415-442

15. European Investment Bank
16. Company law—Bankruptcy law
17. Recognition of Judgments
18. Industrial property
19. External relations
20. Environment policy

D. EURATOM

V. EFTA

VI. COUNCIL OF EUROPE
a. General
b. Human Rights

b. *List of abbreviations*

A.B.A.J.	American Bar Association Journal
A.C.Q.	Atlantic Community Quarterly
A.J.C.L.	American Journal of Comparative Law
A.J.I.L.	American Journal of International Law
Ala. L. Rev.	Alabama Law Review
Am. Bankr. L.J.	American Bankruptcy Law Journal
Am. Bus. L.J.	American Business Law Journal
Am. Econ. Rev.	American Economic Review
Am. Pol. Sci. Rev.	American Political Science Review
Antitrust Bull.	Antitrust Bulletin
Bus. Lawyer	Business Lawyer
Calif. W. Int'l L.J.	California Western International Law Journal
Case W. Res. J. Int'l L.	Case Western Reserve Journal of International Law
Colum. J. of Transnat'l L.	Columbia Journal of Transnational Law
Colum. L. Rev.	Columbia Law Review
Cornell Int'l L.J.	Cornell International Law Journal
Creighton L. Rev.	Creighton Law Review
De Paul L. Rev.	De Paul Law Review
Fordham L. Rev.	Fordham Law Review
Ga. J. Int'l & Comp. L.	Georgia Journal of International and Comparative Law
Harv. Int'l L.J.	Harvard International Law Journal
Hastings L.J.	Hastings Law Journal
Int'l Lawyer	International Lawyer
Int'l Org.	International Organization
J. Conflict Resolution	Journal of Conflict Resolution
J. Int'l Affairs	Journal of International Affairs
J. Int'l L. & Econ.	Journal of International Law and Economics
J. Pat. Off. Soc'y	Journal of Patent Office Society
Law & Contemp. Prob.	Law and Contemporary Problems
Law & Policy in Int'l Bus.	Law and Policy in International Business
Md. L. Rev.	Maryland Law Review
Mich. L. Rev.	Michigan Law Review
Natural Resources J.	Natural Resources Journal
N.Y.U. J. Int'l & Pol.	New York University Journal of International Law and Politics
Q. Rev. of Econ. & Bus.	Quarterly Review of Economics and Business

Record	Record of the Association of the Bar of the City of New York
Rev. of Econ. & Statistics	Review of Economics and Statistics
San Diego L. Rev.	San Diego Law Review
S. Cal. L. Rev.	Southern California Law Review
Stan. L. Rev.	Stanford Law Review
Sw. U. L. Rev.	Southwestern University Law Review
Texas Int'l L.F.	Texas International Law Forum
Texas Int'l L.J.	Texas International Law Journal
Trademark Rep.	Trademark Reporter
Tul. L. Rev.	Tulane Law Review
U. Chi. L. Rev.	University of Chicago Law Review
Va. J. Int'l L.	Virginia Journal of International Law
Vand. Int'l	Vanderbilt International
Vand. J. of Transnat'l L.	Vanderbilt Journal of Transnational Law
Va. Q. Rev.	Virginia Quarterly Review
Vill. L. Rev.	Villanova Law Review

ARTICLES

I. *INTEGRATION, ECONOMIC AND POLITICAL*

G. Agnelli, "Economic Relations Across the Atlantic: An Agenda for Cooperation", 11 *A.C.Q.* 1973, 79-92.

Discussion of major problem areas in the economic relations between Europe and the United States, monetary relations (international liquidity, the balance-of-payments adjustment process), trade relations (the charge of "discrimination" against American trade, agriculture, non-tariff distortions, and the avoidance of market disruption), of investment relations and of proposals for their reform.

N.D. Aitken, "Effect of the EEC and EFTA on European Trade: A Temporal Cross-Section Analysis", 63 *Am. Econ. Rev.* 1973, 881.

R. Albrecht-Carrié, "North Sea Triangle", 17 *Orbis* 1974, 1306-1325.

Historical account of relations between the countries of the "North Sea Triangle", United Kingdom, France, and Germany, and of what these relations have meant, and will mean, for the development of a united Europe.

H.R. Alker, Jr., "Integration Logics: A Review, Extension, and Critique", 24 *Int'l Org.* 1970, 869-914.

G. Ball, "Parochialism in Europe: 'Creeping Guallism' in America", 11 *A.C.Q.* 1973, 161-170.

R. Ball, "The Common Market Is Still Good News", 10 *A.C.Q.* 1972, 27-41.

Discussion of some of the ramifications of the enlargement of the EEC, particularly as relates to United States-European relations.

C.G. Bare, "Trade Policy and Atlantic Partnerships: Prospects for new Negotiations", 17 *Orbis* 1974, 1280-1305.

As the author states: "This article seeks to explore the drift of Atlantic relations as affected by the formation and development of the European Community; to examine the emergence of two specific trade irritants—agricultural restrictions and the growth of preferential agreements; to trace the movement toward, and national attitudes on, a new round of multilateral trade negotiations; and to evaluate the prospects for liberalization of industrial tariffs, agricultural restrictions, non-tariff barriers and preferences."

K. Birrenbach, "United States and Western Europe: Partners or Rivals?", 17 *Orbis* 1973, 405-414.

Analysis of the changing economic and political relationships between Europe and the United States, especially in the area of United States trade relations with the expanded EEC and of security. The author sees a shift in power in favor of the Soviet Union, with a resultant increase in the danger of Soviet hegemony in Europe, undiminished by the Nixon doctrine of dêtente.

W. Brandt, "European Union Is Germany's Hope", 12 *A.C.Q.* 1974, 76-80.

J. Chace, "The Concert of Europe", 52 *Foreign Affairs* 1973, 96-108.

General discussion of United States-European relations, beginning with a comparison to the period ten years earlier, and concentrating on relations in the early 1970s and the future, with emphasis on the military and economic spheres.

C. Clark and S. Welch, "Western European Trade as a Measure of Integration: Untangling the Interpretations", 16 *J. Conflict Resolution* 1972, 363-382.

Technical analysis of the relationship between trade statistics and the integrative behavior and tendencies in Western Europe. Contradictory conclusions reached by various analysts of trade data, concerning the tendencies toward integration, may result from the emphasis on different aspects of supranational integration.

K.A. Dahlberg, "Regional Integration: The Neo-Functional Versus a Configurative Approach", 24 *Int'l Org.* 1970, 122-128.

R. Dahrendorf, "The Common Market, the U.S.A. and Japan", 9 *A.C.Q.* 1971, 61-68.

R.B. Du Boff, "1973: The Year of Europe", 25 *Monthly Review* 1974, 22.

B. France, "Washington's New Look at the European Community", 8 *A.C.Q.* 1970, 242-250.

Outline of the shift in United States opinion of the EEC, as the latter has become a stronger economic force in world affairs. Discussion of the impact of British entry and of the effect of the Common Agricultural Policy on United States farm exports.

C. Gasteyger, "Europe and America at the Crossroads", 10 *A.C.Q.* 1972, 154-166.

C. Gasteyger, "Europe Cool to U.S. Suggestions on Revitalized Charter", 11 *A.C.Q.* 1973, 319-321.

T. Geiger, "Toward a World of Trade Blocks?", 9 *A.C.Q.* 1971-72, 426-437.

Examination of the development of the world economic system in the direction of what the author considers a system of four or five giant preferential trading blocs.

Criticism of the developing system is coupled with an analysis of those European Community and United States policies contributing to bloc formation.

M.A. Goldberg, "Determinants of U.S. Direct Investment in the EEC: Comment", 62 *Am. Econ. Rev.* 1972, 692-699.

J.O. Goldsborough, "France, the European Crisis and the Alliance", 52 *Foreign Affairs* 1974, 538-555.

Analysis of the status of the Atlantic Alliance at the end of 1973, the year which the author sees as the most significant for Europe since 1963, in that it demonstrated the necessity for political union. Examination also of the integral roles of the Germans and the French in the movement toward union, with the latter offering a form of "Europeanism", an attempt to make Europe distinct from, but not alienated from, America.

E.B. Haas, "The Study of Regional Integration: Reflections on the Joy and Anguish of Pretheorizing", 24 *Int'l Org.* 1970, 607-646.

Broad survey of regional integration theory, with an evaluation of the several "schools" of integration study active in the field in the last fifteen years, and of their contributions in the way of "generalizations of empirically-founded truths about integration".

F.M. Haywood, "Continuities and Discontinuities Between Studies of National and International Political Integration: Some Implications for Future Research", 24 *Int'l Org.* 1970, 917-941.

J.W. Holmes, "The Illusion of Europe", 12 *A.C.Q.* 1974, 327-340.

R. Howe, "The European Challenge", 9 *A.C.Q.* 1971, 344-352.

R. Inglehart, "Public Opinion and Regional Integration", 24 *Int'l Org.* 1970, 764-795.

R. Inglehart, "The New Europeans: Inward or Outward-Looking?", 24 *Int'l Org.* 1970, 129-139.

Conclusions about public attitudes developing in recent years towards the nature of European unification and its relation to other forms of internalism. Based on survey data gathered from samples of youths in West Germany, France, the Netherlands, and the United Kingdom in 1964-65.

M.W. Janis, "Development of European Regional Law of the Sea", 1 *Ocean Development and International Law* 1973, 275-289.

Survey of those steps taken by the Common market towards a regional law of the sea (e.g., the Common Fisheries Policy, and the Commission decision to apply the Rome Treaty to the continental shelf), an approach which the author sees as more practical than attempts to achieve a global policy for the oceans and as more desirable than the extension of national maritime jurisdiction.

K. Kaiser, "Europe and America: A Critical Phase", 52 *Foreign Affairs* 1974, 725-741.

Examination of the crisis of European integration and of European-American relations, the inability to approach and solve in common those problems, as accentuated by the energy crisis, which affect both the EEC and the United States.

W. Kaltefleiter, "Europe and the Nixon Doctrine: A German Point of View", 17 *Orbis* 1973, 75-94.

Analysis of the weakened state of the Atlantic Alliance, with special emphasis on the German response to the Nixon doctrine and on how their response reflects the domestic policy-making structure and party configurations within Germany.

H.H. Kerr, Jr., "Changing Attitudes Through International Participation: European Parliamentarians and Integration", 27 *Int'l Org,* 1973. 1973, 45-83.

Interviews with French and German members of the European Parliament, when compared with a group of their colleagues from the national parliaments, indicate that, while the delegates had extended their knowledge and expertise in regard to European matters, their basic attitudes towards the process of European integration had not changed as a result of their experience in the Parliament; the delegates were neither more favorable nor less hostile to the process as a whole. Various explanations are offered, with the overall conclusion being that the European Parliament will assume a more important role in the integrative process only when its powers are substantially increased.

W.L. Kohl and W. Taubman, "American Policy Toward Europe: The Next Phase", 17 *Orbis* 1973, 51-74.

J. Laloy, "Does Europe Have a Future?", 51 *Foreign Affairs* 1972, 154-166.

J.M. Leddy, "The United States, the European Community, and Prospects for a New World Economic order", 37 *Law & Contemp. Prob.* 1972, 235-246.

Brief survey of world monetary and trade relations and the need for reform, with particular emphasis on relàtions between the United States and the EEC. Discusses the nature of United States policy towards a united Europe, especially as regards the EEC's Common Agricultural Policy.

R.J. Lieber, "Interest Groups and Political Integration: British Entry into Europe", 66 *Am. Pol. Sci. Rev.* 1972, 53-67.

L.N. Lindberg, "Political Integration as a Multidimensional Phenomenon Requiring Multivariate Measurement", 24 *Int'l Org.* 1970, 649-731.

R.C. Macridis, "What Kind of Europe?", 49 *Va. Q. Rev.* 1973, 183-195.

Assessment of the internal relations of the European Community at the time of the 1972 Paris Summit, focusing on the problem of political, as opposed to economic, cooperation.

R. McGeehan and S.J. Warnecke, "Europe's Foreign Policies: Economics, Politics, or Both?", 17 *Orbis* 1974, 1251-1279.

Analysis of United States-EEC relations, the nature of the Community policy-formulating process as relates to external relations, the importance of economic policy in this process.

L.A. Manson, "The EEC Patent Union and Political Integration", 12 *Colum. J. of Transnat'l L.* 1973, 342-358.

E.L. Morse, "Why the Malaise?", 51 *Foreign Affairs* 1973, 367-379.

Criticism of the Community's perceived inability to act with a "single voice" over its own destiny, despite the many recent occasions to do so. Several problems are identified, including the intrusion of electoral politics into foreign policy, the expansion of the EEC, the inflationary spiral and labor unrest, and intra-European political jealousy.

C.G. Nelson, "European Integration: Trade Data and Measurement Problems", 28 *Int'l Org.* 1974, 399-433.

Technical economic analysis concerning the implications of recent trade data for trends in European political integration. After determining that EEC members' trade preferences for one another have increased only modestly since the establishment of the Common Market, as opposed to a greater rise in intragroup trade preferences among other groups of Western industrialized countries, the author concludes that little integration has actually occurred.

J. Newhouse, "Stuck Fast", 51 *Foreign Affairs* 1973, 353-366.

Discussion of the proposition that only an external catalyst is likely to foster greater political unity and integration within the European Community, a catalyst which is unlikely to be provided by British accession, or from either the United States or the Soviet Union, both of whose attitudes towards Europe may not be conducive to further unification.

J.S. Nye, "Comparing Common Markets: A Revised Neo-Functionalist Model", 24 *Int'l Org.* 1970, 796-835.

D.J. Puchala, "Domestic Politics and Regional Harmonization in the European Communities", 27 *World Politics* 1975, 496-520.

Examination of what happens after EEC decisions are reached, respecting the execution (or non-execution) of EEC programs, based on research into national attempts to implement directives in the fields of regional aid, pharmaceutical marketing, investment control, and fiscal harmonization. Emphasis is placed on the politics involved in regional implementation, with the evidence indicating that the ability of a Member State to contribute to European integration depends fundamentally upon its government's ability to act politically in its domestic arena.

D.J. Puchala, "International Transactions and Regional Integration", 24 *Int'l Org.* 1970, 732-763.

Assessment of transactional analysis as applied to the regional integration problem, from both the theoretical and the empirical standpoint. The descriptive potential of transactional analysis is illustrated with data from Western Europe.

"Regional Economic Integration and GATT: The Effects of the EEC-EFTA Agreements on International Trade", 6 *Law & Policy in Int'l Bus.* 1974, 207-235.

S.A. Resnick and E.M. Truman, "The Distribution of West European Trade Under Alternative Tariff Policies", 56 *Rev. of Econ. & Statistics* 1974, 83-91.

Analysis of the impact on the trade patterns of Western Europe of the Dillon and Kennedy Rounds of tariff reductions, of the creation of the EEC and EFTA, and of the enlargement of the EEC. Based upon the simulation of an econometric model estimated for 1953 to 1968 of bilateral trade flows for ten Western European countries.

S.A. Riesenfeld, "Legal Systems of Regional Economic Integration", 22 *A.J.C.L.* 1974, 415-443.

General comparative analysis of the various legal structures of regional economic integration, including identification of those legal factors necessary for, or at least conducive to, successful operation of such integrative schemes. The EEC, LAFTA, and the Andean Group are discussed.

W.P. Rogers, "Our Permanent Interests in Europe", 10 *A.C.Q.* 1972, 21-26.

D. Rusk, "Perspectives on European Unification", 37 *Law & Contemp. Prob.* 1972, 221-227.

A.E. Scaperlanda and L.J. Mauer, "The Determinants of U.S. Direct Investment in the EEC: Reply", 62 *Am. Econ. Rev.* 1972, 700-704.

W. Scheel, "Europe on the Move", 4 *Foreign Policy* 1971, 62-76.

S.A. Scheingold, "Domestic and International Consequences of Regional Integration", 24 *Int'l Org.* 1970, 978-1002.

Calls for a broadening of the study of regional integration to include research expressly concerned with the consequences of integration, and particularly with the question of the difference it makes whether or not such regional entities are created.

P.C. Schmitter, "A Revised Theory of Regional Integration", 24 *Int'l Org.* 1970, 836-868.

T. Sommer, "Community Is Working", 51 *Foreign Affairs* 1973, 747-760.

Optimistic appraisal of the Community's development, as the "Davignon phase" progresses, marked, as the author sees it, by the systematic cooperation of governments on a widening range of questions—a Europe of "dynamic pragmatism."

P. Taylor, "Britain, the Common Market, and the Forces of History", 16 *Orbis* 1972, 743-759.

R. Vernon, "Rogue Elephant in the Forest—An Appraisal of Transatlantic Relations", 51 *Foreign Affairs* 1973, 573-587.

Analysis of the shift taking place in relations between the United States and Western Europe, especially in regard to the economic sphere. The United States' negotiating position with Europe is seen as far from dissipated, however, and room for compromise remains.

"Western European Sovereignty and American Export and Trade Controls", 9 *Colum. J. of Transnat'l L.* 1970, 109-139.

Working from the proposition that American influence on European trade policies may lead to a confrontation over trade restrictions, the author proceeds to examine the United States export and trade control system, its extraterritorial effect (as evidenced by the American *President Lines* case, the *Moeus v. Ahlers, North German Lloyd* case, the *Fruehauf* case, and the *Sud-Aviation* affair), what the European states might do to nullify this effect, and the possible United States response.

E. Wistrich, "Way to a European Government", 12 *A.C.Q.* 1974, 213-218.

Z., "The Year of Europe?", 52 *Foreign Affairs* 1974, 237-248.
Analysis of the perceived deterioration of relations between the United States and Europe as a result of the events of the 1973 Middle East crisis, and of what must be done to salvage the Atlantic Alliance.

II. *INTEGRATION, GENERAL LEGAL ASPECTS*

G. L. Bustin, "Financing the European Economic Community: Autonomy and the Problem of Parliamentary Control", 13 *Harv. Int'l L.J.* 1972, 481-500.
Examination of two measures designed to strike a new balance between national/ supranational jurisdiction within the EEC: the 1970 Council decision concerning financing for the EEC, and the proposed amendment to Article 203 of the EEC Treaty, revising the budgetary procedures of the Community in the direction of greater participation by the European Parliament.

K. Lipstein, "Some Practical Comparative Law: The Interpretation of Multi-Lingual Treaties with Special Regard to the EEC Treaties", 48 *Tul. L. Rev.* 1974, 907-915.

III. *INTEGRATION, TECHNOLOGICAL ASPECTS*

H.R. Nau, "Practice of Interdependence in the Research and Development Sector: Fast Reactor Cooperation in Western Europe", 26 *Int'l Org.* 1972, 499-526.
Examination of the prominence of political considerations, in relation to scientific and commercial interests, in determining the nature and extent of coordinated activity between national and Community programs in the field of atomic research.

IV. *EUROPEAN COMMUNITIES*

A. *COMMON SUBJECTS*

1. *General*

D.F. Cavers, "Common Market's Draft Conflicts Convention on Obligations: Some Preventive Law Aspects", 48 *S. Cal. L. Rev.* 1975, 603-626.
Analysis of the 1972 draft of the EEC's choice-of-law convention, with emphasis on the contract provisions bearing most directly on the concept of "preventive law."

D.F. Cavers, "Legislative Choice of Law: Some European Examples", 44 *S. Cal. L. Rev.* 1971, 340-361.
Examination of several codes and conventions (actual and proposed) that have emerged in Europe during the past thirty years, in regard to choice of law questions. Emphasis is placed on those provisions relating to contractual and non-contractual (tort) obligations, as found in Italy, France, the Benelux, and Portugal. Discussion also of the Hague Draft Convention of the Law Applicable to Traffic Accidents.

R.D. Hansen, "European Integration: Forward March, Parade Rest, or Dismissed?" [Review article], 27 *Int'l Org.* 1973, 225-254.
Review of *Europe's Would-Be Polity* (Lindberg and Scheingold) and *Regional Integration, Theory and Research* (*ibid.*, as editors), with the following areas used as the focus of discussion: the major weaknesses in previous regional integration theory;

and the prospects for eventual European union, especially since the Hague Summit of December 1969, and in light of recent significant trends in the international system and environment.

L. Scheinman and W. Feld, "The European Economic Community and National Civil Servants of the Member States", 26 *Int'l Org.* 1972, 121-136.

K.A. Smith, "The European Economic Community and National Civil Servants of the Member States: Reply", 27 *Int'l Org.* 1973, 563-568.

P. Taylor, "The Politics of the European Communities: The Confederal Phase", 27 *World Politics* 1975, 336-360.

Discussion of the main features of the style of politics found in the "confederal" phase of integration since 1969, in relations between Member States of the European Community. This phase has been marked by the oscillation of the various governments between the competing claims of national sentiment and greater European integration.

2. *Institutional*

P.N. Brush, "Permanence of Powers: Commission of the European Communities v. France", 4 *Calif. W. Int'l L.J.* 1973, 43-60.

Analysis of the nature of Euratom and its subsidiary institution, the Supply Agency of the European Atomic Energy Community, followed by a discussion of *Commission v. France* (Case 7/71), in which the permanent competence of the Supply Agency was challenged. The case is discussed with a view to its impact upon the emerging "constitutional" nature of the Communities *i.e.,* upon the preemptive power of the institutions of the Communities, in relation to the power of the Member States.

3. *Court of Justice*

P.J.G. Kapteyn, "'Domestic' Law Effect of Rules of International Law Within the European Community System of Law and the Question of Self-Executing Character of GATT Rules", 8 *Int'l Lawyer* 1974, 74-82.

Examination of *International Fruit Co.* cases (21-24/72), generally in respect to the relationship of the EEC and its legal order to the international law system, and more specifically as regards the weakening domestic juridical character of GATT provisions.

G.S. Murray, "Casenote, Case 48/69 (*Dyestuffs* cases)", 13 *Va. J. Int'l L.* 1973, 375-383.

S.A. Riesengeld, "The Doctrine of Self-Executing Treaties and Community Law: A Pioneer decision of the Court of Justice of the European Community", 67 *A.J.I.L.* 1973, 504-508.

Analysis of *International Fruit Co.* cases (21-24/72).

H.G. Schermers, "The European Court of Justice: Promoter of European Integration", 22 *A.J.C.L.* 1974, 444-464.

Analysis of the Court's institutional and legislative roles—its relations to other Community institutions, and to the national courts, and its status as a legislator, by way of interpretation of Community Law, with special emphasis on its efforts in the areas of competition law, admissibility of individual appeals, protection of human rights, prescription (statutes of limitation), and clarification of time limits.

5. *Relationship between Community Law and National Law*

"Common Market: Council Regulations: Regulations Take Precedence over Provisions of Member States' Constitutions", 7 *Vand. J. of Transnat'l L.* 1974, 487-493.

W.J. Feld, "Legal Dimensions of British Entry into the European Community", 37 *Law & Contemp. Prob.* 1972, 247-264.

Examination of British entry into the EEC, the nature of the Community accession procedure, the modifications to be brought about by the accession, and the problems posed for British ratification by the concept of parliamentary sovereignty. Analysis also of the likely influences of common law practice on the Community court and, in greater detail, of the corresponding impact of Community Law on the British legal system.

"French Conseil d'Etat and Article 177 of the Treaty of Rome: A Case Analysis", 12 *Va. J. Int'l L.* 1972, 377-389.

Discussion of four cases decided by the French *Conseil d'Etat* to determine the *Conseil's* attitude towards the legitimacy of the European Court of Justice's jurisdiction over Community-related matters. The author concludes that the *Conseil,* influenced greatly by political considerations and the constraints of its past practice, exhibits a consistent unwillingness to refer cases to the European Court pursuant to Article 177.

"Jurisdiction: the EEC Convention on Jurisdiction of Courts and Enforcement of Judgments: Effects on British Common Law Principles", 6 *Vand. J. of Transnat'l L.* 1973, 633-641.

P.J. Kozyris, "National and Supranational Law in the EEC on the Eve of British Entry", 37 *Law & Contemp. prob.* 1972, 286-305.

After an introductory examination of the Rome Treaty and its status as "more than a traditional international agreement and less than a federal constitution," the author discusses the source, form, and content of Community Law and its relation to national law of the Member States. He concludes with a short analysis of the impact of British entry on the Community legal system, and of the Community upon the British legal system.

T.M. Lane, "Legal Implications of British Entry into the Common Market", 37 *Law & Contemp. Prob.* 1972, 359-375.

Beginning with a brief survey of the procedure whereby Community Law becomes British law and the resultant effects on parliamentary sovereignty, the author proceeds to a more detailed analysis of the antitrust implications of British entry, by means of a comparison of british statutory and EEC Treaty and case-law.

S.S. Malawer, "American Banking in the Channel Islands and the United Kingdom in the 1970s: Membership in the EEC and the Finance Act 1972", 7 *Int'l Lawyer* 1973, 423-439.

Examination of several issues affecting the type of corporate tax system to be developed in the United Kingdom and the Channel Islands, including the status of the Channel Islands as tax havens which are exempt from the operation of most of the

Rome Treaty provisions, the emerging harmonization of community corporate tax laws, and the United Kingdom Finance Act of 1972.

N.I. Miller, "Some Tax Implications of British Entry into the Common Market", 37 *Law & Contemp. Prob.* 1972, 265-285.

Analysis of the EEC's value added tax system and how it would be implemented in Britain, as well as the reform of the corporation tax necessitated by British entry into the Community, and the new policies created to stimulate industrial development in certain areas of Great Britain.

J.G. White, "Effect of the Common Market on British Law", 59 *A.B.A.J.* 1973, 620-624.

6. *Adhesion*

P. Bareau, "The European Common Market: A View from Britain", 9 *A.C.Q.* 1971, 310-319.

B.L. Crowe, "British Entry into the Common Market: A British View", 37 *Law & Contemp. Prob.* 1972, 228-234.

A. Douglas-Home, "Britain's Future Lies in Europe", 8 *A.C.Q.* 1970, 76-78.

C. *EUROPEAN ECONOMIC COMMUNITY*

1. *General*

"Expansion of the Common Market A Symposium", 37 *Law & Contemp. prob.* 1972, 219-391 [specific articles also included in this Survey].

W. Feld, "Political Aspects of Transnational Business Collaboration in the Common Market", 24 *Int'l Org.* 1970, 209-238.

Examination of the nature and pattern of transnational business collaboration in the EEC, and specifically of the major objectives pursued by firms involved in such collaboration, and of the effect that these firms might have on the political integration process in Europe.

G. Ginsburgs, "Implications of the 20-Year Comprehensive Programme of Economic Integration", 67 *A.J.I.L.: Proceedings* 1973, 48-55.

B. Goodwin, "Common Market Twenty-First Century (with an international Franchising Assit)", 3 *Vand. Int'l* 1970, 75-89.

C. Gordon, "Plus ça Change: The Future of the European Community", 26 *Int'l Org.* 1972, 691-697.

Analysis of the 1972 disagreement over the location of a proposed political secretariat, a matter which the author sees fundamentally as a disagreement over the political structure of Europe, not simply a matter of political consultation.

A. Grosser, "Europe: Community of Malaise", 15 *Foreign Policy* 1974, 169-182.

Examination of the differences between the three major countries of the European Community, Britain, France, and Germany, which preclude the establishment of a *directoire à trois* by the three, in their relations with the other Member States.

"Horizontal Integration of the Common Market Economy: Recent Decisions and Communications by the Commission of the European Communities", 6 *Texas Int'l L.F.* 1971, 259.

S.J. Koch, "Local Impact of the European Economic Community: The Economic and Social Ties of Alsace with West Germany", 28 *Int'l Org.* 1974, 153-178.

Analysis of the impact of the EEC on the French border region of Alsace, by means of an examination of its economic and social transactions with West Germany since 1960. The data indicate a considerable growth in economic contacts, which was not matched either by Alsatian economic integration with France, or by growth of social ties with Germany.

"Treaty of Rome: Individual Rights: Articles 31 and 32 (1) Held Directly Applicable to Private Parties", 4 *N.Y.U. J. Int'l L. & Pol.* 1971, 134-143.

M. Waelbroeck, "Recent Developments and Future prospects of the Common Market", 1 *Ga. J. Int'l & Comp. L.* 1970, 1-18.

Discussion of the extent to which the purposes that the authors of the Rome Treaty set out to achieve had been attained by the end of the transitional period on 31 December 1969. Specific examination of the area of imports and exports (duties, quantitative restrictions, etc.), movement of persons, capital movement, antitrust law, and commercial policy.

2. *Customs Union*

A.S. Golbert, "Customs Union Theory v. Practice", 4 *Sw. U. L. Rev.* 1972, 250-284.

A.J. Yeats, "Effective Tariff Protection in United States, the European Economic Community, and Japan", 14 *Q. Rev. of Econ. & Bus.* 1974, 41.

3. *Agriculture*

P. Malve, "A European Approach to Agricultural Cooperation", 10 *A.C.Q.* 1972, 203-214.

Examination of the necessity and possibility for United States-EEC cooperation in the area of agriculture.

J.J. Norton, "Heart of the Matter: U.K. and the EEC, the Problem of Agriculture", 6 *Texas Int'l L.F.* 1971, 221.

J.A. Schnittker, "Reflections on Trade and Agriculture", 9 *A.C.Q.* 1971, 362-376.

4. *Free Movement of Persons; Establishment and Services*

"Free Movement of Labor in the E.E.C.", 8 *Texas Int'l L.J.* 1973, 375-402.

6. *Transport*

D.S. Collinson, "Economic Regulation of Transport Under the Common Transport Policy of the European Communities", 24 *Stan. L. Rev.* 1972, 221-346.

As the author indicates, this extensive article "(1) summarizes the most important provisions of the transport titles of the Paris and Rome Treaties; (2) provides a broad outline of the stages of Community action on the CTP [Common Transport Policy]; (3) describes relevant portions of the Member States' national provisions respecting transportation regulation; (4) examines in greater detail Community action respecting (i) rate discrimination, (ii) control of rate levels, (iii) bilateral quota restrictions on international road transport, and (iv) control of transport capacity; and (5) identifies obstacles to agreement on the CTP and appraises the prospects for future progress."

D.S. Collinson, "Rhine Regime in Transition: Relations Between the European Communities and the Central Commission for Rhine Navigation", 72 *Colum. L. Rev.* 1972, 485-517.

7. *Competition*

'Abuse of a Dominant Position by Acquisition in the Common Market: The Continental Can Cases", 12 *Colum. J. of Transnat'l L.* 1973, 359-386.

H. Adler, Jr. and M.J. Belman, "Antimerger Enforcement in Europe—Trends and Prospects", 8 *J. Int'l L. & Econ.* 1973, 31.

H. Adler, Jr. and M.J. Belman, "Comment: The EEC's Proposal for a Regulation on the Control of Concentrations Between Undertakings", 8 *J. Int'l L. & Econ.* 1973, 267-275.

Analysis of the substantive content of the proposed regulation, with a focus on the Commission's use of Articles 235 and 3 (f) to circumvent the limitations of Article 86.

J.D. Allen III, "Present Status of Exclusive Patent Licensing Agreements in Relation to the Rules of Competition of the EEC, as Indicated by Four Recent Decisions of the EEC Commission", 19 *Antitrust Bull.* 1974, 81-133.

"Antitrust and International Law as Viewed from the United States and the European Common Market" (Thiesing, Turner, Ellis, Rahl), 25 *Record* 1970, 206.

"Antitrust Law: Enforcement Provisions: Commission of the European Communities Imposed Fines for the First Time to Penalize Anti-Competitive Activities Violating Article 85 (1) of the Treaty of Rome", 3 *N.Y.U. J. Int'l L. & Pol.* 1970, 174-192.

"Antitrust: Article 86 of the EEC Treaty Applies to Certain Changes in Internal Corporate Structure", 6 *Vand. J. of Transnat'l L.* 1973, 669-677.

"Antitrust—E.E.C. Treaty: Acquisition and Merger of Enterprise by Firm Holding a Dominant Position Within Common Market with Effect of Eliminating Actual or Potential Competition in a Substantial Part of the Community Violates Article 86 of the E.E.C. Treaty", 5 *Vand. J. of Transnat,l L.* 1972, 525.

"Antitrust Law: Article 86 of the Treaty of Rome", 10 *Texas Int'l L.J.* 1975, 185.

"Assaulting Transnational Mergers Through the Potential Competition Theory: The United States and European Economic Community Experience", 8 *Ga. L. Rev.* 1974, 650-679.

Comprehensive analysis of the concept of potential competition in anti-merger litigation in the transnational setting, with emphasis on the United states experience under the Clayton Act, but with a final section on EEC use of the concept (especially in the *Continental Can* case).

R. Callman, "Law of Unfair Competition in the Member States of the European Economic Community", 7 *Int'l Lawyer* 1973, 855-866.

C. Canenbley, "Price Discrimination and EEC Cartel Law: A Review of the Kodak Decision of the Commission of the European Communities", 17 *Antitrust Bull.* 1972, 269-281.

"Common Market: Antitrust: Interpretation of Concerted Practices Within Meaning of Article 85: Extraterritorial Jurisdiction of European Commission", 14 *Harv. Int'l L.J.* 1973, 621.

"Common Market Antitrust Law: Jurisdiction: Limitations Imposed by Article 85 (1) of the Treaty of Rome", 6 *Cornell Int'l L.J.* 1973, 163-185.

Discussion of the requirements for the application of Article 85(1), as regards the "domestic effects" clause and the interstate trade clause. Particular emphasis on the *Dyestuffs* case.

"Common Market: Antitrust—Use of Article 86 to Ivalidate Mergers: Europemballage and Continental Can Co. v. Commission, Court of Justice of the European Communities", 15 *Harv. Int'l L.J.* 1974, 333-349.

"Common Market Merger Policy: Sources and Development", 14 *Va. J. Int'l L.* 1974, 501-534.

"Continental Can: New Strength for Common Market Antitrust", 11 *San Diego L. Rev.* 1973, 227-534.

"Control of Concentrations Betwee Undertakings: A Proposal for a Regulation (EEC) of the Council, the Commission of the European Communities", 19 *Antitrust Bull.* 1974, 65-79.

"Control of Concentrations in the European Economic Community: Evolving Restrictions on the Urge to Merge", 19 *Vill. L. Rev.* 1974, 420-469.

A. Deringer, "Current Trends of EEC Competition Policy", 8 *J. Int'l L. & Econ.* 1973, 203-221.

"Developments in Common Market Competition Policy: The Quinine (International Quinine Cartel, 2 CCH. Comm. Mkt. Rep. ¶9313) and Dyestuffs (Dyestuffs Cartel, 2 CCH Comm. Mkt. Rep. ¶9314) Cases", 2 *Law & Policy in Int'l Bus.* 1970, 259-283.

Analysis of the *Quinine* and *Dyestuffs* cases in light of two conflicting EEC competition policies: the aim of the Common Market to encourage the development of larger firms, to compete more effectively in the world market; and the desire to break up existing cartels and barriers which distort trade among the Member States.

J. Dietz, "Enforcement of Anti-Trust Laws in the EEC", 6 *Int'l Lawyer* 1972, 742-770.

In the wake of the *Continental Can* case, the author attempts to show that in fact a vigorous enforcement policy has not generally been adopted by the EEC. Moreover, he stresses that "true extraterritorial application" of Articles 85 and 86 is rare.

"EEC Antitrust: An Exercise in Prior Restraint", 7 *Law & Policy in Int'l Bus.* 1975, 143-172.
Examination of the 1973 Proposed Concentration Regulation: its main features in light of existing competition law, and its prospects for enactment. Particular emphasis is placed on an analysis of its prior notification procedure.

"EEC Antitrust: Continental Can Company Held To Be in Violation of Article 86 of the Treaty of Rome", 5 *N.Y.U. J. Int'l L. & Pol.* 1972, 357-377.
The author takes issue with both the "strict constructionists" of Article 86 and the position taken by the Commission in the *Continental Can* case, preferring instead that Article 86 be described as designed to control market behavior and not market structure, but with market behavior defined broadly to include both the internal and external workings of a corporation. Highly critical also of the Commission's attempts to prove dominant position, with the choice of the relevant geographic and product markets being "unrealistic and misleading."

"Emergence of a Common Marlet Merger Control Policy: The Aftermath of Continental Can: The Proposed EEC Merger Control Regulation", 7 *Cornell Int'l L.J.* 1974, 131-147.
Historical approach to the formulation of EEC policy with regard to mergers and concentrations, with emphasis on the *Continental Can* case and the subsequent proposed merger control regulation. The Author feels that the inadequacies of Article 86 in dealing with the growth of large scale concentration may in large part be resolved by the proposed regulation, which provides greater legal certainty for Commission intervention in this area, and the legal machinery necessary for more effective action against concentrations.

"European Economic Community Antitrust Law: The Continental Can Decision: Forerunner of a New European Antimerger Policy?", 47 *Tul. L. Rev.* 1973, 829-851.

E.A. Forcione, "Intra-Enterprise Conspiracy Under the Anti-Trust Regulations of the Common Market", 25 *Bus. Lawyer* 1970, 1419-1440.

B.E. Hawk, "Antitrust in the EEC: the First Decade", 41 *Fordham L. Rev.* 1972, 229-292.
Comprehensive summary of EEC antitrust law, with emphasis on developments in 1973.

P.W. Heil and G. Vorbrugg, "Anti-Trust Law in West Germany: Recent Developments in German and Common Market Regulation", 8 *Int'l Lawyer* 1974, 349-386.
Detailed examination of German antitrust legislation enacted in 1973, involving new concerted practices prohibition, resale price maintenance rules, and controls over the abuse and achievement of market power; followed by a brief look at recent EEC merger control activities (*Continental Can* and the Proposed EEC Regulation for the Control of Mergers).

J.D. Hurwitz, "Impact of the Continental Can Case on Combinations and Concentrations Within the Common Market", 25 *Hastings L.J.* 1974, 469-517.

"International Law: Antitrust Law of the EEC: the Purchase of a Dutch Concern by a United States-Owned German Subsidiary Constitutes an Abuse of its Dominant Position in Violation of Article 86 of the Treaty of Rome", 8 *Texas Int'l L.J.* 1973, 95-102.

"International Law: Competition Law of the EEC: A Parent and its Subsidiary Are Not Competing Enterprises Under Article 85 (1) Unless the Subsidiary Is Capable of Taking an Economic Measure Independent of the Parent", 6 *Texas Int'l L.F.* 1970, 148.

"International law: Competition Law of the EEC: The Exercise of an Industrial Property Right To Partition Markets Within the EEC Is Violative of the Basic Policy Providing for Free Movement of Goods Embodied in the Treaty of Rome", 7 *Texas Int'l L.J.* 1972, 516.

"International Organisations: Concerted Practices: Jurisdiction: Commission of the European Communities May Find Concerted Practices Even in the Absence of Agreement, and Is Competent To Fine a Non-EEC Corporation Which Produces Effects Within Common Market Through Its Subsidiaries", 13 *Va. J. Int'l L.* 1973, 375-383.

A.P. Jaquemin, "Application to Foreign Firms of European Rules on Competition", 19 *Antitrust Bull.* 1974, 157-179.

R.T. Jones, "Primer on Production and Dominant Positions Under E.E.C. Competition law", 7 *Int'l Lawyer* 1973, 612-634.

Comprehensive examination of EEC competition policy, written with American antitrust lawyers in mind.

H.T. King, Jr., "Comments on Acquisitions and Mergers in the Common Market", 37 *Law & Contemp. Prob.* 1972, 341-350.

Brief discussion of the tax aspects of acquisitions and mergers in the EEC, with some consideration of the corporate legal aspects of the problem, under present and proposed laws.

J. Kamp, "Antitrust in the Common Market: The American Way?", 12 *Am. Bus. L.J.* 1974, 145-164.

J.B. Koback, jr., "Three Approaches to the Bureaucratic Dilemma: The Administration and Enforcement of the Antitrust Laws of the United States, France, and the Common market", 23 *Ala. L. Rev.* 1970, 43-97.

S.P. Ladas, "Assignment of Trademarks and Antitrust Law: The Sirena (Sirena S.r.l. v. Eda GmbH (1971) 10 Comm. Mkt. rep. 260) Case of the Court of Justice of the European communities", 62 *trademark Rep.* 1972, 566-580.

J. Loyette, "Dominant Size and Merger Under Article 86 of the Rome Treaty", 27 *Bus. Lawyer* 1972, 531-541.

Discussion of the position taken by the Commission concerning Article 86 in its *GEMA* decision (2 June 1971) and in its complaint filed in the *Continental Can* case. in the latter case, particular issue is taken with the Commission's definitions of "dominant position," which are considered "incomplete" and "superficial." Also outlines the Berkhouwer report before the European Parliament.

S.S. Malawer, "Rule of Reason Under Article 85(1) of the Treaty of Rome and Vertical Distributorship Agreements in European Economic Community Antitrust Case law", 33 *md. L. Rev.* 1973, 265-288.

P. Mathijsen, "State Aids, State Monopolies, and Public Enterprises in the Common Market", 37 *Law & Contemp. Prob.* 1972, 376-391.

Examination of the Community rules of competition which apply to Member States, specifically as relate to the regulation of state aid programs, state monopolies, and public enterprises. (Articles 37, 90, 92, 93.)

T.O. Moss, "European Community Still Has No Competition Policy", 16 *Antitrust Bull.* 1971, 443-449.

"Patent Licensing Agreements and Anti-Trust in the EEC: Recent Decisions of the EEC Commission", 49 *Notre Dame Lawyer* 1973, 392-409.

"Price Fixing in the European Economic Community: Litmus Test for International Cartels", 5 *Law & Policy in int'l Bus.* 1973, 971-998.

W. Schlieder, "Recent Antitrust Developments in the European Economic Community", 27 *Record* 1972, 212-220.

W.F. Schwartz and E.W. Wellman, Jr., "Rule of Reason in EEC Antitrust: Efficiency Enhancement Through Integration by Agreement Among Competitors", 12 *Va. J. Int'l L.* 1972, 192-210.

The authors argue that, while Article 85 requires a detailed factual appraisal of the efficiency enhancement achieved by arrangements between competitors, such an appraisal has not been undertaken by the Commission. Rather, various political and economic reasons may explain the behavior of the Commission in this area, most notably, a concern to provide small EEC firms with a way to cooperate in order to meet the competition of larger rivals while at the same time preserving their separate identities and limiting their operations to their home countries.

R.S. Singley, "Casenote on the Continental Can Case", 12 *Colum. J. of Transnat'l L.* 1973, 359-386.

S. Timberg, "Antitrust in the Common Market: Innovation and Surprise", 37 *Law & Contemp. Prob.* 1972, 329-340.

General review of the history and legal development of Common Market antitrust policy, with some comparison of substantive EEC antitrust law to the American experience, and with analysis of antitrust enforcement procedures and recent case developments.

J. Treeck, "Joint Research Ventures and Antitrust Law in the United States, Germany and the European Economic Community", 3 *N.Y.U. J. Int'l L. & Pol.* 1970, 18-55.

"Uniform Pricing in Concentrated Markets: Is Conscious Parallelism Prohibited by Article 85(1) of the Treaty of Rome?", 7 *Cornell Int'l L.J.* 1974, 113-130.

This note takes the position that anticompetitive intent should be an essential element to establish Article 85 (1) violations, and that a distinction should therefore be made between "conscious parallelism" and "concerted practices." The EEC is seen as not making this distinction, imposing instead strict liability for noncompetitive effects in concentrated markets—a position which the author feels is inconsistent with the Rome Treaty. A short analysis of United States practice is provided to show the viability of drawing the aforementioned distinction.

G.A. Zaphirion, "Rule of Reason and Double Jeopardy in European Antitrust Law", 6 *Texas Int'l L.F.* 1970, 1.

8. *Taxation*

U. Anshutz, "Harmonization of Direct Taxes in the European Economic Community", 13 *Harv. Int.'l L.J.* 1972, 1-58.

A comprehensive examination of the legal and economic bases for harmonization of direct taxes in the EEC, as well as specific analysis of projected harmonization measures and their stages of implementation.

G. Brosio, "National Tax Hindrances to Crossborder Concentration in the European Economic Community", 11 *Harv. Int'l L.J.* 1970, 311-357.

In a detailed analysis, the author determines that crossborder business concentrations, by way of mergers, are still effectively ruled out within the EEC, by limitations resulting from the tax and corporate laws of virtually all Member States. Beyond these technical difficulties, however, he stresses that until closer political integration occurs in the EEC, and the right and burden to control crossborder concentration expansion of European industry is removed from national to Community-wide authority, such expansion is unlikely to occur to a large extent, especially when it is felt by the national governments that the ensuing multinational concerns would impose their own plans and policies on the governments themselves.

"Taxation of Crossborder Concentrations in the EEC", 9 *Texas Int'l L.J.* 1974, 313.

W.B. Taylor, "U.S. Tax Treaties and Common Market Corporate Tax Systems", 28 *Tax Lawyer* 1974, 73.

9. *Harmonization of Legislation*

D. Berger, "Harmonization of Company Law Under the Common Market Treaty", 4 *Creighton L. Rev.* 1970-71, 205-234.

I.E. Schwartz, "Creating a Common Market for Insurance: Harmonization of EEC Insurance Legislation", 18 *Antitrust Bull.* 1973, 103-116.

G. Winter, "Regulation of Insurance in the European Economic Community", 9 *Forum* 1973, 123-154.

10. *Economic and Monetary Policy*

W.J. Feld, "The Enlargement of the European Community and Atlantic Relations: Economic and Monetary Implications", 10 *A.C.Q.* 1972, 215-225.

11. *Regional Policy*

W.J. Feld, "Subnational Regionalism and the European Community", 18 *Orbis* 1975, 1176-1192.

Examination of the existing and potential role of subnational regionalism (*i.e.*, the movement towards safeguarding of the particular traits and identities—historical, cultural, ethnic, *etc.*— of territorial units exceeding the limits of municipalities and villages) in the development of the European Community, especially as a means for a more rational distribution of political power within the Community. Results of a series of interviews with the political elites of such regions indicate varying attitudes towards the concept of a "Europe of Regions." Some discussion also of the response of the Community institutions to regional-national and regional-Community matters.

12. *Energy Policy*

H. Simonet, "Energy and the Future of Europe", 53 *Foreign Affairs* 1975, 450-463.

After surveying the events and activities in the year-and-a-half following the onset of the October 1973 energy crisis, including the establishment of the Energy Coordinating Group, the International Energy Agency, and the European Community loan system to aid Member States with balance-of-payments deficits, the author stresses the need for a Community energy policy, a policy which he now sees as capable of being developed.

13. *Commercial Policy*

W.J. Feld, "Trade Between the U.S. and the European Community: Differing Expectations in a Changing Power Relationship", 28 *J. Int'l Affairs* 1974, 7-24.

A short summary of the historical development of United States-European Community trade is followed by a discussion of the still unresolved problems in this trade relationship, as well as by proposals for their resolution. Economic policy, as affecting this trade relationship, is viewed as an inseparable part of the "changing power relationship" between the United States, the European Community, and the "Communist bloc."

D.B. Fowler, "EEC Enlargement and United States Farm Exports: Prospects for the Coming Negotiations", 13 *Va. J. Int'l L.* 1972, 192-224.

Examination of the EEC's Common Agricultural Policy in light of the GATT rules pertaining to preferential trade agreements and customs unions. After discussing the impact of the EEC on United States farm exports, the author concludes with a series of recommendations for the United States in its approach to the problems of international trade discriminiation in general and agricultural trade distortion in particular.

R.T. Jones, "Practical Aspects of Commercial Agency and Distribution Agreements in the European Community", 6 *Int'l Lawyer* 1972, 107-127.

After a brief outline of the various methods by which an enterprise located outside the EEC might seek to market its products within the Community, the author analyzes in depth the nature of the agency and distribution agreements commonly used, including the basic elements of such agreements and the features of domestic law of the Member States regarding agencies and distributorships.

J.J. Norton, "Common Commercial Policy of the EEC: Developments in the Final Stage", 6 *Vand. J. of Transnat'l L.* 1972, 44.

J.J. Norton, "Doing Business and the U.S. Commercial Treaties: The Case with the Member States of the EEC", 5 *Case W. Res. J. Int'l L.* 1972, 4-34.

J.J. Norton, "Renegotiability of United States Bilateral Commercial Treaties with the Member States of the European Economic Community", 8 *Texas Int'l L.J.* 1973, 299-373.

J.C. Tuttle, "Emerging Dimensions in International Trade Law and the Desirability of a Non-Tariff Commercial Treaty with the EEC", 5 *Int'l Lawyer* 1971, 722-737.

"United States Response to Common Market Trade Preferences and the Legality of the Import Surcharge", 39 *U. Chi. l. Rev.* 1971, 177-243.

Detailed examination of the nature and history of EEC preferential trade agreements, and the principal United States responses thereto. Analysis also of the policy and legal questions raised by the 1971 import surcharge imposed by the United States, including the question of the constitutionality of the surcharge.

16. *Company Law-Bankruptcy Law*

"Common Market Responds to 'The American Challenge': The Proposal for a European Company", 45 *S. Cal. L.Rev.* 1972, 1168-1183.

C. Dalton, "Proposals for the Unification of Corporation Law Within the European Economic Community: Effect on the British Company", 7 *N.Y.U. J. Int'l L. & Pol.* 1974, 59-102.

B. D. Forrow, "The Multinational Corporation in the Enlarged European Community", 37 *Law & Contemp. Prob.* 1972, 306-317.

Beginning with a discussion of the definition of a multinational corporation and of the nature of some attacks by United States labor on such corporations after 1970, the author describes briefly the effects of the enlarged European Community on American business—effects which he sees as being largely insubstantial.

J. P. Griffin, "Power of Host Countries over the Multinational: Lifting the Veil in the European Economic Community and the United States", 6 *Law & Policy in Int'l Bus.* 1974, 375-435.

W. C. Hillman, "American Lawyer Looks at the Common Market Bankruptcy Convention", 48 *Am. Bankr. L.J.* 1974, 369.

J. J. Norton "A Cheshire Cat Affair: The European-Type Company and Its Meaning for the American Enterprise in the European Community", 6 *Cornell Int'l L.J.* 1973, 111-136.

The author starts with an historical analysis of the development of the European Company, leading up to the 1970 Draft Regulation of the Commission, which is outlined in detail. He does not foresee any short-term advantages for American business as a result of the development of the European Company, a development which even on the European side would be of interest largely only to mediumsized firms wishing to expand within the EEC market.In the long-run, he sees the European Company becoming competitive with American multinational corporations, through the gradual extension of formal controls and the evolution of a more fully coordinated EEC policy towards such corporations, while "truly competitive" European economies of scale are being fostered.

"Proposed Statute for a European Company", 10 *Texas Int'l L.J.* 1975, 90.

E. Stein, "Conflict-of-Laws Rules by Treaty: Recognition of Companies in a Regional Market", 68 *Mich. L. Rev.* 1970, 1327-1354.

Starting with the premise that uniform conflict-of-laws rules respecting recognition of companies by Member States may be desirable for the realization of a Common Market, the author proceeds to examine the divergent national bases for recognition and the 1968 Convention on the Mutual Recognition of Companies and Legal Persons, the latter being some advancement towards greater uniformity, but basically failing to ensure true uniform treatment and legal certainty in the practice of recognition.

E. Stein, "Harmonization of European Company Laws", 37 *Law & Contemp. Prob.* 1972, 318-328.

The author identifies and analyzes two separate but closely related processes in the area of company law: the national company law reform process, which is described for each Member State of the Six; and the transnational coordination process, which aims at building a legal framework for multi-state European business.

P. M. Storm, "New Impulse Towards a European Company", 26 *Bus. Lawyer* 1971, 1443.

S. Suckow, "European Prospectus", 23 *A.J.C.L.* 1975, 50-68.

17. *Recognition of Judgments*

B. M. Carl, "Common Market Judgments Convention—Its Threats and Challenge to Americans", 8 *Int'l Lawyer* 1974, 446-451.

A brief survey of jurisdictional concepts in the civil law is followed by criticism of the 1973 Judgments Convention of the EEC, which is seen as maintaining, and in some cases extending, the "excessive" grounds of jurisdiction found in many of the Member States, as against persons domiciled outside the Common Market.

18. *Industrial Property*

W. Alexander, "Market Divisions Within the European Common Market by Means of Trademarks Belonging to an International Group of Companies", 61 *Trademark Rep.* 1971, 14-27.

M. Arrigucci, "Impact of European Economic Community Regulations on Italian Trademark Licensing", 63 *Trademark Rep.* 1973, 13-23.

M. Arrigucci and F. de Benedetti, "National Trademark Rights and EEC Jurisprudence: From Coexistence to Conflict", 65 *Trademark Rep.* 1975, 11-33.

"EEC Patent Union and Political Integration", 12 *Colum. J. of Transnat'l L.* 1973, 342-358.

S. Jecies, "International Market Division on the Basis of Industrial Property Rights", 7 *Int'l Lawyer* 1973, 838-854.

R. T. Jones, "Fundamentals of International Licensing Agreements and Their Application in the European Community", 7 *Int'l Lawyer* 1973, 78-115.

Extensive analysis of international licensing agreements, with discussion of the tax aspects of such agreements, of the basic elements of a licensing contract, and of United States and EEC competition law as it relates to the licensing area. Included also is a detailed checklist for the drafting of licensing agreements.

D. C. Maday, "Hag and the Negram Decisions of the European Court of Justice", 65 *Trademark Rep.* 1975, 34-42.

R. C. Newman, "Progress Toward a European Patent", 5 *N.Y.U. J. Int'l L. & Pol.* 1972, 449-484.

Historical examination of the background and development of the Convention Establishing a European System for the Grant of Patents and the Convention Relating to a European Patent for the Common Market, followed by a more detailed analysis of the substantive patent law and procedural provisions contained in the two Conventions, as well as of the place of the Conventions within existing international law.

J. G. Semmes, "Protection of Inventions and Know-How in the Common Market", 37 *Law & Contemp. Prob.* 1972, 351-358.

Brief survey of patent rights in Europe, presenting the disadvantages of the old system and the characteristics of the New European Patent, plus a more thorough discussion of the licensing of industrial rights—including a section on the drafting of licensing agreements.

H. C. Wegner and F. E. Miller, "Negram: The Common Market-Wide Exhaustion of Patent Rights Through Territorial Licenses", 57 *J. Pat. Off. Soc'y* 1975, 46.

19. *External Relations*

D. S. Collinson, "Foreign Relations Powers of the European Communities: A Comment on Commission v. Council [No. 22/70]", 23 *Stan. L. Rev.* 1971, 956-972.

W. Hager, "Mediterranean: A European Mare Nostrum?", 18 *Orbis* 1974, 231-251.

Extensive discussion of the Community's relations with non-Member States bordering on the Mediterranean, with emphasis on European economic interests in the region, and the problem of European security.

J. J. Norton, "Treaty-Making Power of the European Economic Community: A Constitutional Crisis Facing the EEC", 7 *Int'l Lawyer* 1973, 589-611.

Analysis of the scope of the exclusive treaty-making competence of the EEC, as advocated by the Council, the Commission, and the Court of Justice, respectively. From an examination of Articles 238 and 113 of the Treaty of Rome, and the 1971 decision of *Commission v. Council* (Case 22/70), the author concludes that the Council's restrictive interpretation of the Community's competence in this area has no legal basis.

20. *Environment Policy*

W. E. Burhenne and T. J. Schoenbaum, "European Community and Management of the Environment: A Dilemma", 13 *Natural Resources J.* 1973, 494-503.

D. *EURATOM*

D. Smith, "European Atomic Energy Community (Euratom): The Limits of Supranationalism", 1 *Calif. W. Int'l L.J.* 1970, 33-59.

VI. *COUNCIL OF EUROPE*

b. *Human Rights*

"Application of Article 50 of the European Convention for the Protection of Human Rights and Fundamental Freedoms: The Vagrancy Cases and the Ringeisen Case", 7 *N.Y.U. J. Int'l L. & Pol.* 1974, 177-189.

K. Boyle and H. Hannum, "Individual Applications Under the European Convention on Human Rights and the Concept of Administrative Practice: The Donnelly Case", 68 *A.J.I.L.* 1974, 440-453.

Examination of the *Donnelly* case and the individual application procedures of the European Convention on Human Rights, with the conclusion that the status of the individual applicant under the Convention has been strengthened.

T. C. Daintith and A. B. Wilkinson, "Bail and the Convention: British Reflections on the Neumeister and Wemhoff Cases", 18 *A.J.C.L.*1970, 326-342.

Examination of the *Wemhoff* and *Neumeister* decisions of the European Court of Human Rights, which were concerned with the rights to liberty and to fair trial (especially in regard to pretrial release against financial guarantees), as enunciated particularly by Articles 5(3) and 6(1) of the European Convention on Human Rights. The British bail system is analyzed with these cases in mind.

K. Doehring, "Non-Discrimination and Equal Treatment Under the European Human Rights Convention and the West German Constitution, with Particular Reference to Discrimination Against Aliens", 18 *A.J.C.L.* 1970, 305-325.

O. Espersen, "Denmark and the European Convention on Human Rights", 18 *A.J.C.L.* 1970, 293-304.

"Human Rights: The European Convention and Its National Application", 18 *A. J.C.L.* 1970, 233-366 [specific articles in this Survey].

A. A. Khol, "The Influence of the Human Rights Convention on Austrian Law", 18 *A.J.C.L.* 1970, 237-258.

R. Linke, "Influence of the European Convention on Human Rights on National European Criminal Proceedings", 21 *De Paul L. Rev.* 1971, 397-420.

S. MacBride, "European Court of Human Rights", 3 *N.Y.U. J. Int'l L. & Pol.* 1970, 1-17.

Discussion of the European Convention and its institutions, with suggestions for reform. European experience is compared with recent trends in the United States, Latin America, and Asia.

P. Pescatore "Fundamental Rights and Freedoms in the System of the European Communities", 18 *A.J.C.L.* 1970, 343-351.

Analysis of the means available in the European Community for the construction of an adequate system of controls of Community action in the area of human rights, controls which should not require resort either to international law beyond the sphere of the Community treaties (e.g., the European Convention on Human Rights) or to the law of national constitutions, in order to be effective.

E. Rauch, "The Compatibility of the Detention of Terrorists Order (Northern Ireland) with the European Convention for the Protection of Human Rights", 6 *N.Y.U. J. Int'l L. & Pol.* 1973, 1-7.

A. H. Robertson, "The European Convention on Human Rights: Educational Aspects", 18 *A.J.C.L.* 1970, 352-366.

Stressing the need for individual knowledge and understanding of the international protection of human rights, the author discusses the present situation as concerns education on human rights in general, and more particularly in regard to the European Convention. Calls for a program of education to operate at three levels: at the general level, to increase community awareness; at the academic level, to train lawyers, administrators, legislators; and at the level of the legal profession, to increase awareness of the rights and remedies available to clients.

E. Schwelb, "The International Protection of Human Rights: A Survey of Recent Literature", 24 *Int'l Org.* 1970, 74-92.

J. Velu, "Article 6 of the European Convention on Human Rights in Belgian Law", 18 *A.J.C.L.* 1970, 259-292.

BOOKS APPEARED

Note: Books on the Euro-Dollar market are included under IV.C.10—Economic and Monetary Policy

I. *INTEGRATION, ECONOMIC AND POLITICAL*

Albinsks, H. S., and Pettit, L. K., *European Political Processes.* (Allyn and Bacon, Boston 1971).

Bech, R. H. et al, *The Changing Structure of Europe.* Economic, Social and Political Trends. (University of Minnesota Press, Minneapolis 1970), 286 pp.

Brooke, M. Z., and Remmers, H. L., eds., *The Multinational Company in Europe: Some Key Problems.* (University of Michigan Press, Ann Arbor 1974).

Charlton, S. E. M., *The French Left and European Integration.* The Social Science Foundation and Graduate School of International Studies, University of Denver, Colorado, Monograph Series in World Affairs, Vol. 9, No. 4 (University of Denver 1972).

Cobb, R. W., and Elder, C., *International Community: Regional and Global Study.* (Holt, Rinehart & Winston, New York 1970), 160 pp.

Deutsch, K. W., *Political Community at the International Level.* (Anchor Books, Hamden, Connecticut 1970).

Dogan, M., and Rose, R., *European Politics.* (Little, Brown & Company, Boston 1971).

Jordan, R. S., ed., *Europe and the Superpowers.* (Allyn and Bacon, Boston 1971).

Lichtheim, G., *Europe in the Twentieth Century.* (Praeger, New York 1972).

Lieber, R. J., *British Politics and European Unity.* (University of California Press, Berkeley 1970).

Lindberg, L. N., and Scheingold, S. A., eds., *Integration: Theory and Research.* (Originally published in *International Organization,* Autumn 1970). (Cambridge, Mass. 1971).

Malmgren, H. B., *International Economic Peacekeeping in Phase II.* Published for the Atlantic Council of the United States, Quadrangle Books. (New York Times, New York 1972), 267 pp.

Nye, J. S., *Peace in Parts.* Integration and Conflict in Regional Organization. (Little, Brown & Company, Boston 1971), 210 pp.

Shonfield, S. A., *Europe: Journey to an Unknown Destination.* (International Arts and Sciences Press, White Plains, New York 1974), 98 pp.

Strauss, F. J., *Challenge and Response: A Programme for Europe.* (Atheneum, New York 1970), 175 pp.

Vernon, R., ed., *Big Business and the State: Changing Relations in Western Europe.* (Harvard University Press, Cambridge, Mass. 1974).

Weil, G. L., *The Benelux Nations; the Politics of Small-Country Democracies.* (Holt, Rinehart & Winston, New York 1970).

II. *INTEGRATION, GENERAL LEGAL ASPECTS*

Scheingold, S.A., *The Law in Political Integration.* The Evolution and Integrative Implications of Regional Legal Processes in the European Community. (Harvard University, Center for International Affairs, Occasional Papers in International Affairs, no. 27, Cambridge, Mass. 1971), 63 pp.

III. *INTEGRATION, TECHNOLOGICAL ASPECTS*

The Technology Gap: U.S. and France. Prepared by the Atlantic Institute. (Praeger Special Studies in International Economics and Development, New York 1970).

IV. *EUROPEAN COMMUNITIES*

A. *COMMON SUBJECTS*

1. *General*

Armstrong, J. A., *The European Administrative Elite.* (Princeton University Press, Princeton 1973).

Bliss, H., *The Political Development of the European Community; a Documentary Collection.* (Blaisdell Pub. Co., Waltham, Mass. c1970).

Davidson, I., *Britain and the Making of Europe.* (St. Martin's Press, New York 1972), 150 pp.

Heopli, N. L., ed., *The Common Market.* (H. W. Wilson, New York 1975).

Holt, S., *Six European States; the Countries of the European Community and Their Political Systems.* (Taplinger Pub. Co., New York 1970), 414 pp.

Lindberg, L. N., and Scheingold, S. A., *Europe's Would-Be Polity: Patterns of Change in the European Community.* (Prentice-Hall, Englewood Cliffs, New Jersey 1970), 314 pp.

Mowat, R. C., *Creating the European Community.* (Barnes and Noble, New York 1973).

C. *EUROPEAN ECONOMIC COMMUNITY*

3. *Agriculture*

Andrews, A., *Agriculture and the Common Market.* (Iowa State University Press, Ames 1973), 183 pp.
Rogers, S. J., and Davey, B. H., *The Common Agricultural Policy and Britain.* (D. C. Heath, Lexington 1973), 158 pp.

7. *Competition*

Feld, W. J., *Transnational Business Collaboration Among Common Market Countries.* Its Implications for Political Integration. (Praeger, New York 1970), 139 pp.
Rahl, J. A., *Common Market and American Antitrust.* Overlap and Conflict. (McGraw-Hill, New York 1970), 476 pp.

8. *Taxation*

Von Steinaecker, M., *Domestic Taxation and Foreign Trade.* The U.S.-European Border Tax Dispute. Praeger Special Studies in International Economic and Development. (New York 1973), 183 pp.

10. *Economic and Monetary Policy*

Barbash, J., *Trade Unions and National Economic Policy.* (Johns Hopkins Press, Baltimore 1972).
Cairncross, A. *et al, Economic Policy for the European Community: The Way Forward.* (Holmes & Meier, New York 1975).
Corden, W. M., *Monetary Integration.* Essays in International Finance, no. 93. (Princeton University 1971), 38 pp.
Friedrich, K., *A Quantitative Framework for the Euro-Dollar System.* Princeton Studies in International Finance, no. 26. (Princeton University 1970), 39 pp.
Hodgman, D. R., *National Monetary Policies and International Monetary Cooperation.* (Little, Brown & Company, Boston 1974).
Krause, L., et al, *European Monetary Unification and Its Meaning for the U.S.* (The Brookings Institution, Washington 1973), 322 pp.
Little, J. S., *Euro-Dollars: The Money-Market Gypsies.* (Harper & Row, New York 1975).
Magnifico, G., *European Monetary Unification.* (Wiley, New York 1973).
Marston, R. C., *American Monetary Policy and the Structure of the Eurodollar Market.* Princeton Studies in International Finance, no. 34. (Princeton University 1974).
Mayer, H. W., *Some Theoretical Problems Relating to the Euro-Dollar Market.* Princeton Essays in International Finance, no 79. (Princeton University 1970), 37 pp.
Prochnow, H. V., ed., *The Eurodollar.* (Rand McNally, Chicago 1970), 418 pp.
Scott, I. O., *The Euro-Dollar Market and Its Public Policy Implications.* (U.S. Government Printing Office, Washington 1970), 39 pp.

13. *Commercial Policy*

Kreinin, M. E., *Trade Relations of the EEC: An Empirical Investigation.* (Praeger, New York 1974).

Zartmann, I. W., *The Politics of Trade Negotiations Between Africa and the European Community.* (Princeton University Press, Princeton 1971).

16. *Company Law—Bankruptcy Law*

Stein, E., *Harmonization of European Company Law.* National Reform and Transnational Cooperation. (Bobbs-Merrill, Indianapolis 1971), 558 pp.

18. *Industrial Property*

Mello, X. de, *Trademarks and European Competition.* The effects of the Common Market Rules of Competition on trademark protection in the Western European countries. (Commerce Clearing House, New York 1972).

19. *External Relations*

France, B., *A Short Chronicle of United States-European Community Relations.* (European Community Information Service, Washington 1973).
Kaiser, K., *Europe and the United States: The Future of the Relationship.* (Columbia Books, Washington 1973).
Mally, G., ed., *The European Community in Perspective.* The new Europe and the United States—Partners or Rivals? (D. C. Heath, Lexington 1973), 349 pp.

VI. *COUNCIL OF EUROPE*

b. *Human Rights*

Haas, E. B., *Human Rights and International Action.* The case of freedom of association. (Stanford, California 1970).
Sohn, L. B., and Buergenthal, C., *International Protection of Human Rights.* Contemporary Legal Education Series. (The Bobbs-Merrill Company, Inc., New York 1973), 1395 pp.

BOOK REVIEWS

Die Aussenbeziehungen der Europäischen Gemeinschaft, Kölner Schriften zum Europarecht, Band 25, Carl Heymans Verlag K.G., D.M. 27.—

Students of European law should be greatly indebted to the Cologne Institute for the Law of the European Communities and its two directors, Karl Carstens and Bodo Börner, for publishing this excellent series of contributions to the knowledge of European law. The 25th volume on *the external relations of the European Community* contains five papers submitted to a colloquium of the Wissenschaftliche Gesellschaft für Europarecht held in Bad Ems in April 1974.

The first paper, by Robert Fischer, deals with *the extent of the Community's power to conclude trade and association agreements.* In both matters he firmly adheres to a broad interpretation of these powers. He states, for instance, that all measures relating specifically to external trade fall under the head of common commercial policy (p. 6). External trade is here to be understood as the exchange of goods and services (p. 8). Fischer even goes so far as to consider international transport as a matter to which the Treaty rules on the common commercial policy in principle apply (p. 12), an opinion which seems not to be in line with the reasoning of the European Court of Justice in its famous *ERTA* decision (March 31, 1971, 17 *Recueil* 1971, 263), in which it sought to found the Community's powers in this field on the general system of the Treaty and its Chapter on Transport, irrespective of the articles on the common commercial policy. Fischer's contribution is especially valuable because of its frequent use of materials contained in secondary Community Law and in the many agreements already concluded by the Community with third countries.

Christoph Sasse's paper on *co-operation agreements and the Community's common commercial policy* is to my knowledge the first profound legal analysis of the question to what extent this new kind of agreement on economic and industrial co-operation between individual Member States and third countries (especially those who practice state-trading) is covered by the Treaty rules on the common commercial policy. This kind of economic co-operation is threatening to empty the principle of a common commercial policy *vis-à-vis* Eastern Europe and the Soviet Union of much of its meaning. Like Fischer, or even more so, Sasse is inclined to adopt a broad definition of the concept of the common commercial policy. In his view, it relates to all measures taken with the purpose of influencing the exchange of goods, including that of payments and services, irrespective of the question whether such influence is direct of indirect, or whether the measures applied are specific or unspecific (p. 41). No wonder he reaches the conclusion that economic co-operation as envisaged in the said agreements is a matter which comes within the definition of the common commercial policy. In this context he severely criticizes the procedure concerning the conclusion of co-operation agreements established by the Council's 1974 decision (O.J. 1974, L 208/23). By providing only for mutual consultation instead of requiring an authorization for concluding such agreements, this decision seems to suggest that the Member States dispose of an autonomous power in this field.

The three remaining papers, by Eberhard Grabitz, Bernhard Schloh and Gottfried Zieger all concern *the position of the Community and its organs in international organizations.* They offer the reader a wealth of interesting facts and valuable comments on the ways and means by which the Community participates in the activities of a great number of world-wide and regional organizations. One must be grateful to the authors for their extensive research into a field that was hitherto nearly inaccessible due to lack of sufficient information.

P.J.G.K.

F. A. M. Alting von Geusau, ed., *Energy in the European Communities.* John F. Kennedy Institute, series no. 9, Tilburg, 1975, xix and 213 pp.

This book is one of the first in describing some aspects of the post-crisis approach to energy policies, thereby concentrating especially on the role of energy in the European Community. It is the outcome of an international colloquium organized by the John F. Kennedy Institute on "Energy Planning in the European Communities", from May 29 to June 1, 1974. The final report of this colloquium is published in Appendix 3 at the end of the book.

It should first of all be mentioned that the book is very well prepared, with a list of abbreviations and a glossary of technical terms which may be helpful for the non-technical reader. The same applies for the appendices at the end of the book concerning the elasticities of demand and supply and the uranium-enrichment technology, and the well-prepared list of authors and subjects.

The book itself is divided into three parts. In Part I the European energy situation is discussed, in Part II several alternatives to oil imported from OPEC countries are presented, and in Part III attention is paid to some policy issues.

Part I begins with an introductory chapter by the editor concerning the changing energy situation in the European Communities. In chapter II, Adelman and Frijs discuss the situation on the world market and the monopoly of OPEC. One of their interesting conclusions is that the destruction of the OPEC monopoly by supply substitution is a myth. Although over-capacity cannot be avoided, a break-up of the cartel is very unlikely because of the very strong political ties between the oil-producing countries.In chapter III,Leardini gives a very clear analysis of the role of electric energy in the Common market, with some interesting conclusions at the end of his contribution. In particular, his conclusion that the trend towards nuclear energy is likely to be irreversible may cause some discussion. But his further conclusion that psychological means of convincing the population to reduce the energy demand will only be efficient in the short term is perhaps too pessimistic, for most countries do not as yet have any major experience in the use of thes techniques.

Part II of the book begins with a chapter in which Odell, in his own unconventional manner, sketches an alternative strategy for complete independence of outside resources. He presents his analysis as a choice between two other policy options: a policy aimed at the establishment of special relationships with the oil-producing countries, and the nuclear power option. In my opinion, his contribution is the most interesting in this book.

In chapters V, VI and VII, by Schmitt, Grenon and Gumpol respectively, three other alternatives to oil imported from OPEC are discussed. The authors reach more or less the same conclusion, that the possibilities of substituting coal, nuclear energy and oil imported from the USSR for OPEC oil are very limited.

Of Part III, the most interesting chapter is the concluding one, written by the editor, in which he analyses the present—almost nonexistent—Community policy in energy matters. Nearly two years after this colloquium, his conclusion that a common European policy is less likely than ever to emerge in the future, is still a vivid reality.

Two final remarkts can be made about this book. First, it is a pity that hardly any attention is paid to the Washington Energy Conference of February, 1974, and to the follow-up of this conference in the negotiations in the framework of the Energy Coordinating Group, and in the birth of the International Energy Agency, at the moment of the completion of the book. The rather disappointing role of the European Commission reaffirms the pessimistic conclusions about a European energy policy. But, on the other hand, it cannot be denied that there is at least a certain common policy, on an Atlantic scale, for the safeguarding of oil supplies by means of a common oil-sharing scheme. In the second place, something could have been said about the origins and functioning of OPEC from the point of view of the members of that organisation. The book lacks a contribution which seeks for possibilities of cooperation with the oil-producing countries. Further, it would have been worth mentioning that OPEC is responsible for the oil price increases, but that the oil embargo was not brought about by OPEC as such, but by the Arab oil-producing countries. But these remarks are only minor criticisms of a carefully-edited work which gives fresh insight into a totally new problem area.

R. Barents
Europa Instituut

Neue Entwicklungen im EWG-Kartellrecht. Editor: Studienvereinigung Kartellrecht, Carl Heymanns Verlag, Köln, 1975, 208 pages.

This book which came from the press in 1975 contains the text of the reports presented and a résumé of the discussions held during a seminar organized in October 1973 by the editor of the book, the *Studienvereinigung Kartellrecht.*

At regular intervals these kinds of seminars are held—the previous one took place in 1970—in order to keep those who are interested, but not capable of following the day by day events, informed on the latest developments in the field of EEC competition law. The papers presented are therefore designed to give an account of those recent developments.

It was no doubt an excellent idea of the organizers to ask the Director General for Competition of the European Commission, Mr. Schlieder, to give his evaluation of the actual situation. Nobody but he would be better qualified to do this job. Unfortunately, however, Mr. Schlieder had not prepared a written statement, so that the text of his paper is missing in the present book. A fifteen page account of the discussions following his presentation gives a sketchy impression of the ideas Mr. Schlieder had brought forward. When going through the items Mr. Schlieder had touched upon at that time, such as merger control, licensing agreements, selective distribution systems, and investment agreements, one perceives that even today the European Commission is still grappling with the same issues.

The Advocate-General Trabucchi presented his views about the "new" and the "old" in the field of competition in the EEG. He gives an account of the competition cases the European Court has dealt with. One is struck by the eulogy he showers on the Court. Not a word is spent on the strange capers this venerable institution cut in the *Haecht II* case, where it reversed completely its previous opinions. It is presumed that this unrelented approval of all these performances of the Court is not completely shared by his fellow Advocates-General, since their submissions in this domain of law were more than once at variance with the subsequent rulings of the Court. In any case, this paper contains an objective and impartial account of the developments at that time. Taken from that angle, it served perfectly the purpose of conveying truthful information to those who wanted to know more about competition law as it stood in October 1973.

Mr. de Richemont's paper concerning Article 86 EEC and merger control can hardly be put into this category. Many commentaries have been written on the *Continental Can* case, and Mr. de Richemont's account is one of them. Everybody is, of course, entitled to his own views. However, at a colloquium such as this, designed to convey objective information to its participants, an attempt should at least be made to do justice to that aim.

When one reads, however, that through the *Continental Can* decision the Court had implicitly introduced a preventive merger control (pp. 58 and 64) and that from now on a new area is manifesting itself completely fraught with dirigism and supervision (p. 72) one could hardly say that a detached view of the *Continental Can* ruling is taken. One wonders why the draft regulation on merger control of July 1973 was not submitted to a short analysis. It might have afforded insight in to the limited conclusions the European Commission itself had drawn from the *Continental Can* case.

Mr. Sölter, an economist and director of the Competition department of the German Federation of Industries, gave an exposé of the various transformations through which the concept of competition is passing. In this paper that transgresses the boundaries of EEC competition law itself he develops a number of ideas which he was to enlarge upon later on in his book *"Der unvollständige Wettbewerbsbegriff"* (the imperfect concept of competition), Verlagsgesellschaft Recht und Wirtschaft, Heidelberg 1975. The general theme thereof is that transparency of market conditions is a prerequisite for true competition based on performance. The entrepreneurs should be entitled to an exchange of all the data that constitute the elements of what he calls an "all parameter" competition since competition is not limited to price competition only. According to this view a prohibition of concerted practices designed to exchange that kind of information would be contrary to the elementary principles of the concept of competition (p. 88).

Leaving the merits of this view aside, it would at least have been useful to remind the reader that this viewpoint collides head-on with the judgments of the European Court. So in the *Vereniging van Cementhandelaren* case of October 17, 1972 (Case 8/72, 1972 *Receuil*, 977), where an agreement concerning suggested prices was at stake. Here the Court felt that although the suggested prices themselves did hardly restrain the conduct of the parties, the fact that such an agreement enabled all the participants to predict fairly accurately the competitor's price policies, was enough to establish the presence of a restriction of competition. Moreover, in the *Dyestuffs* case of July 14, 1972 (Case 48/69, 1972 *Recueil*, 662) the European Court held that by the announcement of their future prices the enterprises indulged in concerted practices which created an artificial market transparency. Thus their conduct eliminated temporarily price competition. Apparently, according to the Court, some measure of uncertainty and risk is inherent to the concept of dynamic competition. It is to be regretted that the reader of the book is deprived of that kind of information.

Mr. Cawthra, Deputy Director of the Confederation of British Industry, gave a British view on European competition policy. He confronts British pragmatism with the EEC credo in competition as a means of achieving an integrated common market. The major part of his paper is devoted to British competition policy and especially to the valium and librium case which was under scrutiny just at that time. His exposition of British and European policies is mainly descriptive and some conclusions as to their differences in approach are drawn.

Mr. Joiliet, by now professor at the University of Liège, read a paper on concerted practices. Apparantly he was not too content with it, since, even before its publication in the present book, he re-issued—according to his own words—a completely redrafted article on the same subject in the *Cahiers de Droit Européen* 1974, pp. 251-287. His exposition is a fine example of thorough scholarly research. The emphasis placed on the reciprocal nature of this kind of arrangement in order to distinguish it from parallel action and market leadership, and the warning that one should not confuse market conduct which only could constitute the proof of the existence of a concerted practice and the concerted practice itself, should be recalled.

Finally Prof. Waelbroeck from the University of Brussels came forward with a paper on industrial property rights and the EEC. He seemed to be quite satisfied with it since before the book appeared he published a French—practically unchanged—version of it in the *Revue de Droit Intellectuel/L'Ingénieur Conseil* 1973 (12) pp. 157-174. In his presentation he emerges as an advocate of the "reward theory" as propounded by Koch and Froschmaier ten years ago. This theory holds that an owner of an industrial property right is not entitled to reap twice a reward for his exclusive right. Consequently the owner of such a right cannot oppose the importation of a product brought on the market abroad under his parallel right by himself or with his consent. Unfortunately, however, Waelbroeck attempts to demonstrate the correctness of this theory with the example of the *Deutsche Grammophon* case, where the German owner of the exclusive right in his homeland just did not possess a parallel right in France from where the products were imported into Germany.

The greatest flaw of this article is, however,—the author cannot be blamed for it—that in the middle of 1975 when reviewing this domain of law one cannot refrain from drawing into the discussion the two *Centrafarm* judgments and the *Hag* ruling of the Court, various decisions of the Commission such as those on *Advokaat Zwarte Kip*, on *Sirdar-Phildar*, and on *Kabelmetal*, as well as one of the opinions of the Commission referring to the Community Patent-Convention, issued on April 4, 1974.

In this article, dating from 1973, Waelbroeck speculated on future developments which are flatly contradicted by subsequent events. We know now more than we did in 1973 and one would do injustice to Waelbroeck to be harsh with him for his predictions.

In his inaugural speech reprinted in the book (pp. 7-11) the chairman of the *Studienvereinigung* mentioned the giant strides with which EEC competition law had progressed since 1970 when the previous seminar had taken place. It is, however, clear to everyone that these developments have not stopped at 1973. Conscious thereof the Studienvereinigung has organised a new seminar also entitled *"Neue Entwicklungen im EWG-Kartellrecht"* in June 1975. An account of this conference can be found in GRUR Int. 1975 (8/9) pp. 310-312. All these events lead to the conclusion that the present book entitled *"Neue Entwicklungen im EWG-Kartellrecht"* contains an account of developments that at the date of its publication in 1975 were not so new anymore.

H. W. Wertheimer

COMMON MARKET LAW REVIEW

AIMS

The Common Market Law Review is designed to function as a medium for the understanding and implementation of Community Law within the nine Member States, and for the dissemination of legal thinking on Community Law matters. It thus aims to meet the needs of both the academic and the practitioner.
For practical reasons, English is used as the language of communication.

EDITORIAL POLICY

The editors will consider for publication manuscripts by contributors from any country. Articles will be subjected to a review procedure. The author should ensure that the significance of his work will be apparent also to readers outside his specific expertise. Special terms and abbreviations should be clearly defined in the text or notes. Accepted manuscripts will be edited, if necessary, to improve the general effectiveness of communication.
If editing should be extensive, with a consequent danger of altering the meaning, the manuscript will be returned to the author for approval before type is set.

SUBMISSION OF MANUSCRIPTS

Manuscripts should be submitted, together with a covering letter, to one of the Editors. At the time the manuscript is submitted, written assurance must be given that the article has not been published, submitted or accepted elsewhere. The author will be notified of acceptance, rejection or need for revision within eight to twelve weeks.
Authors are requested to submit two copies of their manuscript, typed and double-spaced, together with a summary of the contents.
Manuscripts may range from 3,000 to 10,000 words.
The title of an article should start with a word useful in indexing and information retrieval. Short titles are invited for use as running heads.
The author should identify himself in print, with a short statement as to his current affiliation.
All references and notes should be numbered in a single sequence in the order in which they are cited in the text, and should be typed, single-spaced, on a separate sheet.

OFFPRINTS

The author will receive one free copy of the issue concerned and twenty-five offprints of his article. He may also order any quantity of additional offprints, with a minimum of 100 copies, at forty cents (Dfl. 0.40) per page per copy. This order must be submitted through the Executive Editor at the time of delivery of the corrected galley-proofs for print.

GPSR Compliance

The European Union's (EU) General Product Safety Regulation (GPSR) is a set of rules that requires consumer products to be safe and our obligations to ensure this.

If you have any concerns about our products, you can contact us on ProductSafety@springernature.com

In case Publisher is established outside the EU, the EU authorized representative is:

Springer Nature Customer Service Center GmbH
Europaplatz 3
69115 Heidelberg, Germany

Batch number: 10830943

Printed by Printforce, the Netherlands

EDITORIAL ADDRESS
Common Market Law Review
Europa Instituut, Hugo de Grootstraat 27,
Leyden, The Netherlands

Orders for subscriptions, advertisements and back issues should be sent either direct to the general distributor:

Academic Book Services Holland, P.O. Box 66, Groningen, The Netherlands
phone: (0)50-162329 telex: 53443

or to
Fred B. Rothman & Company, 57 Leuning Street, South Hackensack, New Jersey, N.J. 17606, U.S.A.
Hammicks - Sweet & Maxwell, 50 West Street, Farnham, Surrey, U.K.
Office International de Librairie, 30 Avenue Marnix, 1050-Bruxelles, Belgique.

Annual subscription price for Volume 13 (1976): Dfl. 125.00/ $ 52.00; single issue: Dfl. 32.00/ $ 13.25.

Originally published by A. W. Sijthhoff International Publishing Company in 1976

COMMON MARKET LAW REVIEW

Volume 13
1976

SPRINGER-SCIENCE+BUSINESS MEDIA, B.V

Published in Cooperation with the British Institute of International and Comparative Law and the Europa Instituut of the University of Leyden

Editorial Address

Common Market Law Review
Europa Instituut, Hugo de Grootstraat 27,
Leyden, The Netherlands

This Review may be cited as *13 C.M.L. Rev. 1976*

ISBN 978-94-015-2075-1 ISBN 978-94-015-3283-9 (eBook)
DOI 10.1007/978-94-015-3283-9

INDEX VOLUME XIII

I. SUBJECTS

II. CASE LAW

A. COURT OF JUSTICE OF THE EUROPEAN COMMUNITIES

B. NATIONAL COURTS OF THE MEMBER STATES

III. ARTICLES AND SHORTER ARTICLES

IV. LIST OF AUTHORS

Names of authors who have contributed to Volume XIII

V. LIST OF BOOKS REVIEWED

TABLE OF CONTENTS

EDITORIAL COMMENTS

How many swallows are needed to make a summer?

Even if the agreement on the direct elections to the European Parliament may be thought to belie the cries of the disintegration and collapse of the Community, it constitutes only one battle won. The danger remains very real that the public and the Member States will be tempted to loose confidence in the Community's potentialities. Its lack of authority and, in particular, its inability to play a decisive role in overcoming the economic crisis and monetary disturbances may well give certain Member States, who appear to have coped succesfully with their economic problems under their own steam, the idea that the threat of disintegration is not such an awful prospect after all. Other Member States, whose economic plight has not been lessened to an appreciable extent by the efforts of the Community, may be led to believe that, on balance, membership of the Community is of little advantage to them and that a further degeneration of the Community would not really matter. Failure of the Community in the months ahead to achieve substantial successes in respect of the big economic and social issues is therefore liable to add fuel to the feelings of scepticism and indifference. The prospect of increased democracy in the Community's decisionmaking process can hardly be a cure for the rampant disillusionment.

Whether the current political and psychological deadlock can be broken by new efforts to coordinate economic policies is anybody's guess. The believers are not in need of conversion, but the nonbelievers are unlikely to place much faith in the Community's programmes and policies if these lack teeth and run aground as soon as it comes to implementing them. Nevertheless, it might be termed progress if agreement on the principles and the direction of coordinated economic policy measures is reached and if not only the Member States and the institutions but also both sides of industry pledge their support. In this respect, the outcome of the Tripartite Conference, held at Luxembourg on June 24, and the Fourth Medium-Term Economic Policy Programme, soon to be approved by the Council and the Member States, may herald a positive development.

The Tripartite Conference, attended by representatives of the Commission, the Governments and the social partners, was able to reach a consensus on a large part of the proposals presented by the Commission in a document entitled "The re-introduction of full employment and stability in the Community". Not surprisingly, agreement on the major objectives (*i.e.* a return to full employment by 1980, achievement of an annual growth rate of 4,5% to 5% and reduction of inflation to a level of 4% to 5% by 1980) was less difficult to reach than a consensus on strategy. At the end of the day, most participants were pleased with the results, although several major trade unions in France, Belgium and Italy were unable to subscribe to the conclusions of the Conference. On behalf of the Commission, Mr. Haferkamp labelled the joint declaration "a major step forward towards social peace and an important move in the direction of a certain convergence in the economic and social policies of the Member States". Still, even if all parties concerned have promised to act in their own field of responsibility and in accordance with their own commitments, one wonders if this is good enough. With regard to the rather crucial issue of the necessary moderation of wage claims to be observed by workers and the strict discipline in the matter of prices expected from employers, the Conference had to content itself with the formula: "Only a joint effort by all parties to adapt the pattern incomes of all types to the economic data, going hand in hand with moderation in the field of prices, will make it possible to set up once again the conditions for an economic situation characterized by an improved balance and a higher degree of equity".

The Commission's draft of a Fourth Medium Term Economic Policy Programme reflects the objectives put forward at the Tripartite Conference and must be seen as the framework for a Community strategy in the economic field between 1976 and 1980. The Commission points out that severe constraints continue to weigh on Community action, *viz.* the excessive structural disparities within the Community, the varying degree of economic and social consensus amongst the Member States and the inclination of Member States to give different priorities to major economic policy objectives. At present the necessary political and institutional basis for Community action capable of overcoming these obstacles does not yet exist. However, achieving the objectives of the Programme would help establish this basis. To this end the Member States should endorse a Community strategy consisting of quantitative guidelines which constitute medium-term points of reference with respect to the employment situation, growth, price stability and external balance. The draft spells out the relative priority of the objectives (a return to full employment being the prime objective) and the overall and specific policies necessary for their attainment. Regarding the apparent contradiction between the pursuit of macro-economic equilibria and the achievement of more qualitative objectives, the Commission observes that full employment based on sustained growth in conditions of stability and respect for the constraints imposed by macro-economic equilibria, is a necessary condition for social progress and a better achievement of other qualitative objectives. Among the measures necessary to implement the guidelines, a policy-mix calculated to bring about a significant increase in productive investment ranks high. This will require some painful adjustments in the distribution of incomes and in the trend of public finance. It is, however, regrettable that in the discussion on the Programme no attention was given to the qualitative conclusions of the so-called Maldague report on "Inflation Problems" which was submitted to the Commission on March 6, 1976. The Report has received only a limited circulation, no doubt because the analysis of the origins of structural inflation in the Community and the measures proposed to direct the Community towards a new kind of economic system are of too progressive a character in the present social and political climate.

Even if the programme is of an indicative nature only it is the yardstick against which Member States' economic performance should be measured periodically. It could be implemented by legally binding acts decided on in the context of the periodic examination of the economic situation in the Community provided for in the Council's Decision of February 18, 1974, on "the attainment of a high degree of convergence of the economic policies of the Member States of the EEC". (O.J. L 63/16). The Commission has already indicated that it will make proposals aimed at checking the expansion of money supplies and budgetary deficits. More effective use should be made of the mechanisms for the grant of loans and other forms of Community support for Member States which appear to be getting off course. But the credit must be made available on tough conditions, perhaps linking tranches of a loan to fulfilment of interim economic and monetary objectives.[1]

The European Trade Union Confederation has pointed out that the Governments must concentrate first and foremost on eliminating the current disorganisation in the monetary system. Without efforts in that direction there is a risk that any actions regarding economic expansion, investment and employment may lose their effectiveness. The draft Programme hardly touches upon this problem. It seems resigned to suspending further monetary co-operation within the Community until all countries are on a sufficiently parallel economic course to join the "currency snake". In a previous issue of this Review, Mr. Oort, the Dutch Treasurer-General, has outlined the dangers of such an approach.[2] The Dutch presidency of the Council is currently promoting a scheme, no doubt inspired by Mr. Oort's ideas, to create a framework for monetary co-operation in the Community which would include "snake" and "non-snake" members alike. This plan may be a far cry from the ideas laid

1. Europe, Sept. 30, 1976, no. 2062.
2. 13 C. M. L. Rev. 1976, 301-314.

down in the E.M.U. Resolution of March 22, 1971. However, it seeks to implement the concept of "adequate parallelism", of progress in the economic field and in the area of monetary co-operation. The plan deserves to be studied. The attainment of a high degree of convergence of economic policies can hardly be a realistic proposition if the Member States fail to organize their monetary interdependence.

THE TINDEMANS REPORT– RETROSPECT AND PROSPECT
(or, Round and About the Tindemans Report)

by

J. D. B. Mitchell*

I. INTRODUCTION–THE BACKGROUND

It is too easy, in certain ways, for anyone who is outside the processes of government to criticize the *Tindemans Report.*[1] Any such who writes on it has to remember two things. First that he, the writer, neither toured the capitals, nor has sat in the European Councils. Thus he cannot judge either the pressures or prejudices that were brought to bear (or sensed), nor the feeling induced at the time of writing the Report of what were the likely limits of acceptability, or of how big a jump it was sensible to propose. The second is the extreme contrast between the circumstances which led up to the *Spaak Report* and those that lay at the origin of *Tindemans.* In the first case, the Governments of the Six declared their belief that the time was ripe for a new advance, and determined the broad objectives. The report of the Intergovernmental Committee was to constitute the preparatory work. If it were sound it was condemned to success. For Prime Minister Tindemans the scene was fundamentally different.

At the Paris Summit of October 1972, the Heads of State or Government had requested the Institutions of the Community to draw up a report, before the end of 1975, on the subject of European Union.[2] There were already ambiguities. The precise meaning of the phrase of the Communiqué "with the fullest respect for the Treaties already signed", was by no means clear, unless it was one way of writing in protections in advance against any re-emergence of the idea of a "*Directoire*", which was feared. Nor had the phrase "whole complex of the relations of the Member States" any greater precision. Little had happened from that date up to the date of the Paris Summit of 1974. That was understandable. Apart from the energy crisis, there was, of course, re-negotiation. In his statement in Luxembourg on April 1, 1974, Mr. Callaghan had said:

* Salvesen Professor of European Institutions, University of Edinburgh.

1. Perhaps for the sake of brevity one may, without disrespect, hereafter simply refer to the Report as *Tindemans.*

2. Cmnd. 5109, Bull. of the E.C., 1972, No. 10, para. 16.

13 C.M.L. Rev. 1976, 455-484

"Then we are concerned at another phrase from the Paris Summit Communiqué—at the intention there stated of transforming the whole complex of the relations of Member States into a European Union by 1980. What does this mean?... It seems to us to imply a change which is quite unrealistic and not desired by our peoples".[3] When all allowance is made for the circumstances in which that statement was made, there was little likelihood that work on European Union would go ahead with fervour. Uncertainty there was in any event. The Communiqué of December 1974 underlines this, in saying "they [the Heads of Government] consider that the time has come for the Nine to agree as soon as possible on an overall concept of European Union". Though the objective remained, it had no precision, and the Belgian Prime Minister was asked to submit a "comprehensive report".[4]

Two further citations indicate something of the atmosphere in which Prime Minister Tindemans had to work. In the Foreign Secretary's six-monthly report on *Developments in the EEC for April-October 1975* it was briefly said that Ministers had explained the views of the Government to M. Tindemans, and welcomed the opportunity "to discuss with him without commitment".[5] What these views were is made clear in the *Report on Renegotiations.* Two passages are worth citing. First, "But the Government have established that there is no agreement in the Community on what European Union means beyond a general aspiration to closer co-operation... that closer co-operation is desirable and must be pursued in a pragmatic way, but... there is no wide support for moves towards a centralised federal state". The second runs: "The Government do not accept any commitment to any sort of federal state in Europe... All member states agree that future institutional developments must conform to political decisions of the Governments and Parliaments of member states. The consent of the United Kingdom Parliament would be sought before any institutional developments of major importance."[6] Doubtless these statements must be construed in strictly political terms, and they may well be simply the consequences of an internal political situation. They are cited simply to underline the difficulties facing the Belgian Prime Minister, and then only as samples. Views not very different would have been expressed elsewhere. It is, though, worth stressing the emphasis on simple co-operation, and the deep-rooted opposition to anything that could be designated "federal", a concept

3. Cmnd. 5593 para. 7—See now Mr. Hattersley's explanation of this remark (1975-76) H.L.P., Q. 1.
4. Cmnd. 5830, p. 5. Bull. of the E.C., 1974, No. 12, 1104, para. 13.
5. Cmnd. 6349, para. 69.
6. Cmnd. 6003, para. 130 and 132.

which had come to be regarded as a dangerous one in government circles in the United Kingdom.[7]

Thus the contrast with the situation at Messina is sharp. In that case the Ministers knew what they wanted, and all that they desired were the structural lines on the basis of which they could make progress. Even those lines could be predicted. Implicitly, they were expected to emerge as adaptations of established techniques. In the present case, terminology indicated uncertainty of purpose and aim. In the White Paper on Re-negotiation the Government remarked (and perhaps realistically) that the report "should enable member governments to define what their purpose is". Possibly even the idea of European Union had receded once there appeared to be agreement on direct elections. Intervening events between the commissioning of the report and its presentation were no more helpful. The accentuation of the recession, in the prevailing political conditions, had the effect of intensifying economic nationalism, an effect as much observable in the United Kingdom as elsewhere.[8] Thus, for example, pressures for import controls came from many quarters and those who had lost in the referendum, and who remained discontented with the outcome of re-negotiations, could find ready means to continue the debate, and, in an uneasy internal political situation, could carry weight.

It was, then, in any event unrealistic to believe that *Tindemans* could amount to a new grand design. A tour of Europe would indicate other political difficulties as great as those sketched above. Even at the level chosen – of proposing limited or short-term solutions – it was inevitably affected by the run of events during its period of gestation.

II. THE REPORT IN SUMMARY

A. *Analysis and Method of Reform*

Against that background what did the Report propose? First there was analysis, with the conclusion *"L'Europe d'aujourd'hui est celle du quotidien, elle semble avoir perdu son parfum d'aventure".* The *Spierenburg Report* put it more bluntly. The failure to meet a series of crises had, it said, "given the impression that the integration process, is past its peak

7. There is a curious permanency about this antithesis: see (1975-76) H.L.P. 277, The House of Lords Select Committee on the European Communities Report on *Tindemans.*

8. There is little need to document this. It relates, as President Ortoli remarked (and the remark was not original), to the circumstance that "the gaps between us are wider now than when the crisis began". (European Parliament Debates Feb. 10, 1976, Annex 199, p. 60).

rather than making new, if laborious, progress. . . . The repeated claim that the "point of no return" has been reached does not appear to be based on fact".[9] As both imply, there were two related underlying causes. The change of generations, with an emphasis on current problems (rather than those of the past), has been allowed too little effect (though it did receive oblique notice in the penultimate paragraph of the October 1972 Communiqué). Hence, the *Spierenburg Report* emphasised that governments, if they should wish for progress in the making of Europe, cannot rely on any automatic process, but must make deliberate choices. The limit has been reached of the doctrine of *faits créateurs*. In view of what follows, this emphasis on governments should be noted, though *Spierenburg* adds that what was true of them was also true of parliaments and parties, of the whole political apparatus. These two causes are related. The sense of need, which appeared in the referendum result, fails to have its impact on the apparatus. Hence, the decline in the authority of the Communities risks producing an even sharper decline in the sense of their legitimacy.

All of this becomes encapsulated in what Mr. van der Stoel has called the stagnation and ineffectiveness of the Council.[10] Even when one accepts the limitations imposed by the conditions in which *Tindemans* was written, and those which exist (and will dominate its implementation), the proposals which it contains must be judged by their capacity to prevail over, or even survive, those conditions. One can accept the need to remedy the discontinuities which exist between external appearances and internal realities, just as one can accept that economic and monetary evolution lies at the heart of future internal developments, but then one is brought up against the *Marjolin Report:*[11] "The fact is that at no time did governments really try to face together the difficult circumstances". It is not intellectual pleasure, but the facts which drive one back to

9. *The Advisory Committee on European Union* (appointed by the Dutch Minister of Foreign Affairs) para. 2.1.10. For personal convenience (or because of personal deficiencies) citations from that Report will be from the English version. The first issued texts of the *Tindemans* indicated that only the French and Dutch text were authoritative and citation will be from the former. The three basic causes of decline emphasized in *Spierenburg* were:
"a) the Community structure has not proved to have enough vitality to acquire its own political authority over the years;
b) the creation of an administrative structure is lagging behind economic integration and even impeding it;
c) the positive aspects generally speaking date from the earlier period and are now being jeopardized by the failures and shortcomings of more recent years." para. 2.1.10.

10. Debates of the European Parliament, July 7, 1976.

11. Report of the Study Group on Economic and Monetary Union 1980 (Brussels, 1973).

institutional frameworks. Therein lay one of the dilemmas of *Tindemans.* Accepting the need for institutional change, but fearing the immediate unacceptability of change, there runs through the report a method—first change practices and then incorporate the new habits in a text. The method is typically elaborated in the proposals relating to common external policy. Practices of political co-operation have developed—now, therefore, Paragraph 11 of the Copenhagen *Report on Political Co-operation* [12] can become a protocol. That pattern underlines the whole proposed development. At the outset, *Tindemans* states: *"lorsque le processus d'édification de l'Union aura acquis son dynamisme propre, il conviendra alors de consacrer dans un texte juridique l'ensemble des modifications apportées progressivement à la construction européenne."* The method is, it seems, to be applied not merely in the field of high politics but also in matters which are strictly legal. The question remains, by what means is that dynamism to be found?

B. *The Policies*

This choice of method had, of course, its consequences on substance, particularly in relation to institutional change, since it imposed limitations on what could be proposed. Institutions should never be separated from discussion of their function, since function should determine shape. Rightly, therefore, *Tindemans* moves first to the policy content of the Union; while admitting that it was for the European Council to decide the general direction and content of European Union, *Tindemans* outlines proposals. In relation to the rest of the world the need is emphasised for a common external policy, especially in four areas; the emerging world economic order, relations with the United States, security and defence, and crises in the areas immediately around Europe. Within these proposals lies the idea of a single decision-making centre which would deal both with matters within the Treaties and with political co-operation (and within which there would be a move towards majority decision). The whole would be supported by a political engagement of the Member States to conduct, in agreed fields related to the Union, a common external policy. Internally the choices were perhaps predictable (they coincide in broad outline with those in *Spierenburg* and in the Commission's Memorandum and none of the lists surprises). First, there is economic and monetary policy (with its two-level snake), and, among sectoral policies, energy and research. Under the heading of Social and Regional Policies, particular emphasis is put upon conditions

12. Cmnd. 5432. Bull. of the E.C., 1973, No. 9, para. 1281.

of employment broadly conceived. The heading "Citizens' Europe" covers the protection of fundamental rights [13] and those of consumers and the protection of the environment, as well as improvements in the condition of movement and a proposal for a European Foundation in the field of education. The detail with which proposals are made under each head varies, but the broad outline suffices to show the social (and thus political) impact of many.

C. *Institutional Change*

Thus, finally, the Report turns to institutional proposals, and the tendency to rely on practice leading to amendment is again apparent. For the Parliament there is proposed *"une faculté d'initiative"*, consisting of an undertaking by the Council to consider specific resolutions addressed to it, which would ripen into a true right of initiative, and when ripe would be incorporated in a Treaty amendment. From the start of the whole process, the Parliament should be able to debate all matters within the scope of the Union, and at least once a year hold a debate on the "state of the Union" to which should be invited, as participants, a number of prominent political figures. The Court is briefly dealt with. There should be opened up a direct right of challenge by individuals of acts of the institutions where a breach of fundamental rights is alleged. Thereafter, once the Union has acquired its own dynamism, the jurisdiction of the Court should be looked at on the lines proposed by the Court itself in its Memorandum.[13a] (These included protection against failures of national jurisdictions to use Article 177 correctly, and the suggestion of the extension of Article 41 (E.C.S.C.) over the whole system, and perhaps some form of full judicial review of legislation.)

The essence of *Tindemans* in this section lies, as was to be expected, in the passages dealing with the Council and Commission. The emphasis is put on the European Council, transforming it, in effect, into the real motor (though when acting within the Treaties their rules are to be observed). It is to produce clear directives to the other organs, indicating even the time-scale for compliance. Its meetings are to be prepared by the Council in the form of the Foreign Ministers. As has been seen, that body would cover both fields, but the theme is repeated—that at this higher level, too, the distinction between meetings for political co-operation and others should be abandoned (without prejudice to the Treaty rules). By directive of the European Council, the Foreign Ministers

13. See *e.g.* Point IV A 1 in regard to fundamental rights.
13a. Bull. of the E.C., 1975, Supp. 7, at pp. 17-21.

should co-ordinate the activities of the specialised councils. As was to be expected, there is an invocation to majority decision-taking, both in Treaty matters, and in those in the agreed sectors of common external policy. To promote continuity and to strengthen the dialogue with the Parliament, the Presidency of the European Council and of the Council should be extended to one year. Both bodies should charge the Commission, particular countries or individuals with specific tasks ranging from studies to negotiations. (Earlier, and in a sense as a concrete example of this technique, *Tindemans* had proposed that the European Council should delegate to one of its members the task of initiating a joint consideration of the relationships between the Union and the United States.)

For the Commission, the Report expresses the wish to conserve its powers of initiative. At the same time the Report proposes, through the use of Article 155 (E.E.C.), an increase in its delegated powers, suggesting that both the Council and the Commission should report to the European Council on the possible scope of such delegation, now and in the future. Other proposals have greater political content. The Commission should be strengthened by having its President designated by the European Council, and he should go before the Parliament and seek confirmation there. The President should himself choose his colleagues in consultation with the Council. No mention is made, curiously, of the term of office of the President. As an interim measure it is suggested that the next President should be thus designated in mid-1976, that he should present himself to the Parliament, and have some voice in the choice of his colleagues. The first element of this proposal was, in some degree, acted on in Brussels in July 1976, when it seems that the Heads of Government, informed of the proposed appointment of Mr. Jenkins to the Commission, affirmed that they "intend to support his appointment in due course, under the provisions laid down in the Treaty, as President". The third element met also with some acceptance, since, it seems, the designated President was to be consulted on his colleagues, though Mr. Callaghan has said firmly that the final choice of the other British Commissioner is his.

In conclusion, the Report makes some operational proposals, which are not without legal and political significance; all are aimed at decongesting the machine. First, it is proposed to give a genuine power of decision, by delegation from the Council, to the Permanent Representatives when consensus is apparent there. Second, to increase the delegation of powers of execution by clarifying in the basic decisions the body or person which should carry it out and allowing that body the necessary discretion. Thus, in particular, there would be a decongestion towards the Permanent Representatives on the one hand and the Commission on the other. In areas not of Community competence the enhanced Presidency of the Council should itself receive powers in regard to the day-to-day application of policies which had been jointly agreed upon.

A summary was asked for, and it is to be hoped that this one (of a Report, which is itself brief) does no essential injustice to that Report. It does help to bring out certain major lines, for despite the appearance of detail, the changes advocated in the Report could have major effects.

III. COMMENT

Comment must focus on the institutional shape. Improvement in the decision-making process is essential even for present purposes, and is even more so if further tasks are to be assumed. The areas of policy upon which the Report concentrates provoke, in any event, little controversy, once the concept of a two-speed Europe had been explained by M. Tindemans, and seem no longer to be in the debate.[14] The other elements are, for the most part, necessary prolongations of what exists. Even the special emphasis upon *L'Europe des citoyens,* and upon social aspects of industry, is only a reflection of changing patterns of thought, which are already having their impact in the Community. The resolution on the Social Action Programme,[15] the directive on mass dismissals,[16] the green paper on employee participation [17] are sufficient evidence of that. It might also be said that the method of change and the structural changes which are proposed are also rooted in the past. The 1972 Summit noted that political co-operation "had begun well and should be still further improved"; [18] that of 1974 had urged delegation and a strengthening of the role of the Permanent Representatives. History, though, also demonstrates the weakness of that method; it has the superficial attraction of being pleasing to the pragmatists, but precisely for that reason co-operation tends to become optional. On the one hand, there is the example of the debate about participation in "extra-Community summits" of the Rambouillet type, a debate which does not seem to have been resolved at the European Council in July 1976, and on the other hand, there is the example of the Opinion of the Court under Article 228 of the EEC

14. Indeed, the ideas of "serpentology" are once again being challenged, as shown by Dr. C. J. Oort in the last issue of this journal, 13 C.M.L. Rev., 1976, 301 *et seq.*

15. O.J. 1974, C 13.

16. Dir. No. 75/129, O.J. 1975, L 48.

17. Bull. of the E.C. 1975, Supp. 8.

18. Cmnd. 5109; Bull. of the E.C. 1972, No. 10, para. 14.

Treaty.[19] Indeed, in its report the Commission underlines the limits to what *has* been achieved.[20] Admittedly, the field of external relations (except in the area of commercial policy) is one difficult to regulate by a legal text. Moreover, the Community is not now, nor will be the Union at its birth, equipped for the task of assuming full responsibility. Even the stage at which an obligation to consult could be transformed into an obligation to arrive at common policies cannot easily be predicted. Nevertheless, it seems desirable that a legal text should go further than the protocol proposed by *Tindemans,* and at least express clearly the objective of attaining the stage of a common policy.

Politically, such a text seems essential, if the idea of European Union is to retain any credibility. Other reasons of detail support this view. First, the existence of such a text would limit the tendency to construe narrowly such external powers as already exist, particularly in the fields of commercial policy, since the existence of that text would remove much of the attraction of that tendency. It would block an escape route. Secondly, the fact that no full transfer of powers is possible has its inevitable consequences on the institutions. If, as both *Tindemans* and the Commission suggest, the distinction between ministerial meetings concerned with political co-operation and those concerned with Treaty matters should go, and there should be a single decision-making body, it will be important that the mode of operation should be specifically regulated. Otherwise the risk will exist that the more formal Community procedures will be eroded. While the background which has been sketched makes it understandable why *Tindemans* should have adopted the method which it did of attaining the desired goal, that method must, it seems, be rejected, or at least modified.

In parenthesis, it should be said that doubts about the method chosen—of a move from practice to amendment—are general and not limited to this instance. It may seem paradoxical for a British lawyer to criticise a method which could be said to be analogous to evolution by constitutional conventions. Yet, in broad terms, conventions have been successful in helping the politically strong to increase strength and not for the politically weak to gain strength.[21]

That choice of method had its effect on what is said about structures.

19. Advisory Opinion No. 1/75, (1975) E.C.R., 1355 - demonstrating the need for a framework if progress is to be maintained; for report see 13 C.M.L.Rev. 1976, 375 *et seq.*, and comment by H. H. Maas at pp. 379 *et seq.*

20. Bull. of the E.C. 1975, Supp. 9, para. 65. In effect, it has been a co-operation of reaction to situations and not a dynamic co-operation.

21. For the analogies, see Mitchell *Constitutional Law* (2nd Ed.), 38-39. The limitations to this technique of evolution pointed out there may be important here.

In effect what is proposed is simply an extension and intensification of what exists. Indeed the only Treaty amendments specifically mentioned are in relation to the extension of the Presidency of the Council to one year, and in regard to the nomination of the President and Members of the Commission. Two questions arise. First, whether even at this stage a new structure should be proposed. Second, whether even if the answer to that question is "no", as much weight should be placed upon the European Council as it is in *Tindemans.* The first question is not argued in *Tindemans,* but the proposals therein are supported by the impression gained in consultations that *"L'Union Européenne peut et doit s'édifier sur les bases institutionnelles déjà acceptées par les Etats membres dans le cadre des traités existants".* Again, the background which has been sketched would suggest that that impression was deep. For its part, the Commission, rejecting a narrow interpretation of the phrase "fullest respect for the Treaties" in the 1972 Summit, debates this question and concludes strongly in favour of a new structure. The arguments deployed in favour of that choice are attractive. It is difficult to see how the traditional timetable of stages could work well in this field, and there is strength in the argument that political forces are most likely to develop within a structure which is definitive. In part, this difference in choice was governed by the fact that the perspective of *Tindemans* was short-term, and that of the Commission was long-term. But *Tindemans* does not stand alone; the *Spierenburg Report,* looking even beyond the 1980's, concluded that it would be unrealistic to propose radical political changes at a time when Member States would continue to function as recognisable national entities.[22] The answer need not be in terms of black and white. Intermediate solutions have been proposed, modifying existing structures and proposing a creation by stages with, from the outset, a "Resident Council" to carry through the building of the union.[23] Such solutions are open to the objections raised by the Commission,[24] and, moreover, probably present as great a political shock as does the Commission's preferred solution, and thus gain little and would lose some of the certainty of the Commission scheme. Though optimism might push to the maximalist solution, realism forces the conclusion that, for the moment, the basic structural choice made in *Tindemans* was

22. Para. 1:2:3, as indeed does the Commission when it speaks in its Memorandum of concurrent powers, and of the reserved powers of the States.

23. Chapman, *The Road to European Union.* It may be noted that that author also holds the view that no quick jump is possible, and avoids defining the time span of the stages of evolution.

24. Bull. of the E.C., 1975, Supp. 9, para. 94.

the correct one, even if the method of change, where change is needed, is open to doubt.

The second question therefore remains, but must be enlarged to include the issue of whether, even if the basic structure should remain as it is, the right modifications have been made. The key to the proposals is the European Council. There have already been changes since the name was first adopted. Meetings have become more frequent than was envisaged in 1974. The reasons are mixed; the run of events (which required meetings at that level), the enduring weakness in the way in which the normal machine worked, and a continuing need that politicians of the highest order should be involved. Nevertheless, what is now proposed is a fundamental change. The European Council becomes the primary organ for maintaining dynamism and progress, determining not merely global issues, but also, it seems, matters of much greater detail; the decisions it will take will also specify the organ which is to implement them, which implies a degree of precision in the decision. Although it is said that the presence of the Commission in the Council would guarantee observance of the Treaty rules, in practice it would seem that the Commission's right of initiative would be diminished, and not, as it should be, enhanced. Moreover, under the system, such initiative as there was would, it seems, in practice come from the Council (composed of Foreign Ministers) charged with preparing the meetings of the European Council. Those European Councils, such as Dublin, where the ground had been well prepared, have had a different degree of success from others, and in the Dublin preparation the Commission had played its part. Thus, there is a risk of overturning the structure.

This did not appear to be the intent of the Paris Summit. Two separate problems were involved there. The practical need for meetings at the highest level had given rise to the meetings designated those of Heads of State and Government, which necessarily moved the meetings outside the institutional structure in terms of Article 2 of the Merger Treaty. The difficulty lay in the duality of the role of one Head of State who combined both functions in different degrees. Once it was accepted by President Giscard d'Estaing that it was possible to meet as Head of Government,[25] there was no Community reason why the Council should not itself meet, composed of the effective Heads of Government, and that

25. Meanwhile, M. Pompidou foresaw the necessity of accepting the role of Head of Government—*Le Noeud Gordien*, 65 *et seq.* If internally this were true, then external practice would also have to recognise it. It is curious that the House of Lords Select Committee on the European Communities perceives none of these problems. It uses [(1975-76) H.L.P., 277 para. 40] the terms "Heads of State" and "Heads of Government" as interchangeable.

problem could find a solution. The other problems which were the effective cause of continuing the European Council were the need for a nexus with political co-operation, the failure of the Copenhagen "fire-side" technique and the irrationality of meeting apparently distinctly to discuss matters which were essentially interrelated. This second series of problems is capable of solution, even in accepting the immediate steps proposed in *Tindemans* in regard to external policy. The name European Council, created to solve this second line of problems, has tended to obscure the real links which exist with the established institutional structure and thus to threaten distortion.

It is that risk which appears in the passages in *Tindemans* dealing with the European Council. The Report appears to be torn by conflicting desires, both of which are in themselves laudable, but which in unresolved conflict can become injurious. There is the desire both to engage politically major political figures in the European construction, and also to conserve the role of the Commission, to which the Report refers frequently. The proposal to confide particular studies to individuals or bodies chosen *ad hoc* (which corresponds with the first desire) can, in abstract terms, be helpful. In particular it can serve, in one form, to secure that political engagement which is needed and which is lacking. Yet, in this particular setting it works uneasily. The report thus commanded is accepted, or even simply commended, as a basis for action; then the right of initiative of the Commission may well be excluded or becomes formal. Even if the report be rejected, or put on one side, it remains a political fact which can have the effect of excluding certain options. It is not merely the Commission which would be affected. If the decision-making process starts at the top, then there are obvious consequences for the Parliament's right to propose amendments. The right may remain but its reality changes. It must, moreover, be remembered that thus composed the members are, paradoxically, those who have the heaviest burdens and pre-occupations in the domestic political scene. Of this there is evidence in the recent European Councils in general, and of the discussions therein of direct elections in particular. Its members may also be those in some ways least "responsible". The fact that successful criticism of a Head of Government will bring about the fall of a Government affects attitudes. The proposition is true in general terms; in the case of France it is, of course, one, the application of which is complicated by the accepted double nature of the Presidency. In the case of the Federal Republic it is reinforced by the special rules governing the Chancellorship.

The Council in its various forms is itself touched by the distinctive establishment of the European Councils. There is established a full hierarchy. The European Council itself and a subordinate level, the Council of Foreign Ministers having its own functions, but also charged with co-ordinating the specialised Councils. Thus composed it is formally elevated, and those differently composed are placed at a lower level. The Agricultural Council, because of its speciality and peculiarity may well not fit into this hierarchy. In such a situation there is a serious risk that once the European Council has become a "normal" part of the machinery, and a part not restricted to major issues (variously defined) but also involved in running that machine, it would, as the *Vedel Report* feared, in fact slow down decision-making.[26] If there is a higher instance which meets with regularity, the natural tendency is to resort and defer to it. One of the major problems of political structures is the tendency to involuntary centralisation. The same objection affects the formal elevation of the Council composed of the Foreign Ministers. Whatever current practices may be, that becomes entrenched, with consequences for patterns of work.

It thus follows that the European Council fits uneasily into the democratic structures of the Community or of the Union. Each of its members can claim a democratic legitimacy which is quite independent of the Union, and it is that other legitimacy which will pre-occupy each, however strong the sentiment of each may be for the ultimate construction of Europe. The immediate will thus tend to prevail. Thus, the European Council will be the last body to be largely influenced by the European Parliament. If it fits uneasily into the democratic structures, it fits no more easily, in its condition of half-in and half-out of the system, into the legal structures. Without elaboration, it suffices to give brief examples. The nature of its decisions remains obscure; are they susceptible of juridical attack? What consequences do they have for the classification of expenditure as obligatory or non-obligatory? That question has already arisen in the context of the Regional Fund. It is probably true that the law can be strong enough to prevent major distortions of the Treaties.[27] It is, though, undesirable that such conflicts between the political and legal orders or structures should arise more frequently than they need to, either at the constitutional or at the working level. Without greater clarity, problems could arise at both levels. It must be admitted that the proposals in *Tindemans* for much greater precision in decisions would help in this respect, even though such proposals would, on the other side, tend to pre-empt the normal

26. Bull. of the E.C. 1972, Supp. 4, 81.

27. Consider e.g. case 7/71, *Commission v. France*, 17 *Recueil*, 1003, or at a much lower level, Case 43/75, *Defrenne v. SABENA*, (1976) E.C.R., 455, in *attendu* 57.

machinery.[28] Such a change in precision would, again, be welcome since difficulties arise at the moment not merely from substance, but also from form.

The difficulties may be practical, but they are, nevertheless, significant. Perhaps as an aftermath of the Copenhagen "fire-side" concept, Communiqués have stopped. There are internal reports, there are reports to national Parliaments, but information tends to stop at too low a level of precision or certainty. Mr. Callaghan, reporting on the last European Council said: "I am placing in the Library of the House copies of the Statements agreed by the European Council on direct elections, fisheries, the Tindemans Report and international terrorism." [29] Yet interest does not stop at the House. The form of decision reflects upon its context. It is clear from what Mr. Callaghan said in the debate just referred to that, despite apparent certainty, a number of major issues on direct elections remained unresolved at the July meeting. Such doubts affect all aspects of responsibility. Hence it is arguable that in its style of work, the European Council, conceived for different purposes, can only fulfil its role with difficulty. Because of its origins, elements of informality endure. They are in part welcome, but in part not so. It is evident, for example, over the question of the number of seats in the European Parliament, that at two successive European Councils formulae were appearing, or produced, at the last moment. Such habits do not necessarily help decision or the coherence of a range of decisions. Equally, the secretariat of the Council, reinforced from the staff of the Presidency, has also to serve the European Council. This is reasonable, and the present tasks may suffice. It could hardly suffice were there to be, as is proposed in the field of political co-operation, a delegation of genuine power to the Presidency. Almost of necessity, a political secretariat attached to the European Council would arise, and old quarrels would be reopened.

The emphasis on the European Council is understandable. The desire to secure the political engagement of the Heads of Government which

28. It is always comforting to find respectable support. The House of Lords Committee, referred to above, adopts something of the same attitude, para. 43. Its main objections are, however, to the operation of the European Council in regard to Political Co-operation. The objections are either peculiarly technical, turning on staff costs incurred in respect of non-Treaty or marginal functions. More seriously, it raises the argument that on the Political Co-operation side "the representative of each Member State would be exercising in effect his country's treaty-making powers. Unless there were a fresh Act of Parliament of the same kind as the European Communities Act it would be contrary to constitutional practice for the United Kingdom to be committed to accepting international obligations towards other Member States of which Her Majesty's Government of the day might not approve." para. 43. This view might be difficult to sustain.

29. 915 H.C. Deb., at 653.

motivates it cannot be objected to. It may also be explained as a logical prolongation of the equally attractive idea of producing, at a lower level, a single decision-making centre straddling political co-operation and Community affairs. Yet, on reflection, the losses which could arise seem greater than the gains that could be won. There is no guarantee that the European Councils will prove to be an effective way of unblocking decisions, or at least of doing so rapidly. There seems little reason to suppose that, not being bound even by rules which are disregarded, there would be any greater tendency to majority decisions. Indeed, at this level, the tendency is to seek consensus.[30] Thus the normal working of institutions will not necessarily improve; in practical terms, it is likely to go on as before. Tied, of course, to the greater role of the European Council, is the proposal to extend the Presidency to a year. If one falls, so does the other. Certainly, there should be hesitancy about accepting this greater role, at least otherwise than on the basis of a specific text. Otherwise, the risk of degeneration would be substantial.

The real problem is not to invent new organs. The European Councils are no doubt here to stay, as indeed the Commission Report admits, but the escape from difficulty does not necessarily lie in burdening yet more heavily those who are heavily burdened. The European Councils should stay, but should stay to deal with an appropriate level of politics, or of crises, which was part of the original intent. Thus the problem remains of whether anything can otherwise be done to improve the normal working of the institutions. That part of the Report dealing with the Parliament has not been discussed. There is a group of propositions; the investiture of the President, but not of the Commission as a whole;[31] the acceptance by the Council of an obligation to debate resolutions of the Parliament, with the intent that in time this should become a genuine right of initiative;[32] acceptance of the right of the Parliament to debate, as from now all matters falling within the competence of the Union. To these must be added the proposed debate on the State of the Union. The Report is brief on these matters, which are of uneven weight. To that

30. Again, on such questions it is frequently pleasant to cry in aid the words of practitioners; hence, one cites Mr. Michael Stewart in the Debates of the European Parliament April 7, 1976, Annex no. 202 at p. 90.

31. On this point the *Spierenburg Report* para. 12:3:3 follows the *Vedel Report* in stipulating a phased development; only in an advanced phase would the President nominate his colleagues, and then jointly with the Governments, and only in a third phase would there be an investiture.

32. *Vedel* did not propose a formal initiative. *Spierenburg* was silent, but might well have agreed with that view. The Commission, though in a different setting, tentatively accepts an initiative, but with restrictions related to any new expenditure.

general rule there is one exception. There could be a political/psychological problem of the President of the Commission, nominated by the European Council, later appearing in full independence before that same body. His strength is enhanced in that situation when he owes his place in the scheme of things not just to nomination but also, even if subsidiarily, to another source of legitimacy. In contrast, the range of debate is scarcely now confined to the narrow view of the Treaties. Some of these proposals would certainly require elaboration and a timetable for change, such as that relating to the enhanced role of Parliament in the formation of the Commission. This brevity may partly be due to the weight placed upon the European Council. In any of its normal formulations it is difficult for the Parliament to bring weight to bear upon the Council; it is even more difficult for it to do so upon the European Councils. These matters will, however, be held over until the next section which turns upon a possible role of the European Parliament in the whole construction.

This article is mainly concerned with the political processes, but, by way of parenthesis, something should be said of the Court. For that body *Tindemans* would re-create in new fields the existing heads of jurisdiction, create a new direct action for a challenge based on fundamental rights, and recommends at a later stage a re-examination of the system. For its part, the Court, as was to be expected, was restrained in its Memorandum, equally concerned with the preservation of what exists and the extension of present techniques to the content of the Union. The emphasis in both *Tindemans* and the Memorandum on fundamental rights [32a] is understandable, as is the wish expressed by the Court for a general declaration and not a specific charter. Two points made by the Court are particularly relevant here. First, that at the technical level of drafting, when the experts are deadlocked, there could be the possibility of nominating a mediator to evolve the definitive text, a concept which could certainly help. On the other hand, the Court emphasised the difficulties which would arise "should the States forming the European Union agree to measures without indicating their specific legal form, as a result of informal undertakings which only become public when those undertakings are performed." Hence, a plea that all decisions which could affect individuals be taken in appropriate legal form and published. This comment by the Court, read against the background of its past achievements, underlines some of the arguments earlier advanced here.

32a. Bull. of the E.C., 1976, Supp. 5.

IV. THEORIES OF POLITICAL RESPONSIBILITY AND THE CONSTRUCTION OF THE UNION

Returning to political structures, the starting point must be the remark that, fortunately, there is now, even granted the present institutional shape, more reason than ever to elaborate upon this question of concepts of political responsibility. Direct elections are agreed upon, and there is also, perhaps, a general acceptance of the fact that it is the second election which will be much more important than the first. Whether or not the Communities, and thus also the Union, will strike roots will depend upon the second election. A relative lack of interest of the electors in the first occasion could be understood and accepted. It could not be in the second. Should interest not be awakened by then, the European Parliament would fall into disrepute and it would be difficult to resist the tendency for national parliaments to attempt to assert increasing control over the European activities of their own Governments. Thus, in the relatively short period between now and the second elections (one can assume a period of roughly seven years), the European Parliament has to define its role and make its mark. Unfortunately, as has already been suggested by their analysis, the *Tindemans* proposals are finally not helpful to the parliamentary processes at either level—the European or the national—and that is perhaps the major criticism which may be made of them. To say that is not to assert that democratic assemblies can be the means of building Europe. The history of the Consultative Assembly of the Council of Europe disproves any such proposition. It is merely to assert that, in Europe, the detachment of the decision-making process from democratic elements will, at a certain point, endanger the whole structure.

Certain assumptions (which represent expectations and not necessarily hopes) should be stated before advancing too far into the argument. First, that the Commission's longer-term proposals will not find favour in the near future. Hence the short- or medium-term period during which, with or without adaptation, existing institutions will stand, remains critical for building the legitimacy of the European Parliament and of the decision-making process itself (though what follows is also valid in principle even if those proposals of the Commission should find favour). Second, from what has been said, it may well be that the enhancement of the European Council will also not find favour. Apart from anything that has already been said, there still exist fears (perhaps renewed) that that process would lead to a *"Directoire"*. Thus we will be left with a bi-cephalous Government of Europe. Should the opposite be true, and the role of European Council be substantially enhanced, then what follows has increased validity. That enhancement by itself decreases total parliamentary control. To change the anatomical metaphor, there will be one arm of that Government (the Council structure) greatly increased in strength at the cost of the other (the Commission), and the stronger arm is, as has been shown, more removed from parliamentary processes at both levels. Hence, if things are left as they are, then the European Parliament will be left with inadequate means to deal with the weaker arm and few to deal with the stronger. In one sense there is no cause for distress. When the situation is examined scientifically, there is no absolute reason why one should not live with a bi-cephalous system of government, any less well than with any other system, provided that concepts are adjusted to take account of the situation that exists. There is no need to assume that "The European Government" must grow out of either the Commission or the Council, or even to assume that it must exist on a single plane.

Account must be taken not merely of the Council/Commission relationship, but also of the whole political conditions in which the Parliament, as well as the other institutions, will probably exist. Doubtless, in some form, European political parties will come into being. With what coherence they will exist is another question. The determination of a common programme (even at the level of greater generality which it would have at the European level) for a European Socialist Party embracing the parties of the present German Chancellor, that of the present British Prime Minister and that of M. Mitterand (to limit the spectrum) will, it seems, make the efforts of M. Mitterand to the same end on the domestic front appear too easy an apprenticeship. Other major political groupings are unlikely to be more coherent. In a situation in which real power was exercised by the Parliament these coalitions would be fragile. On the other hand, there will exist coalitions or groupings which will face the Parliament. Politically the Commission will, one hopes, remain pluri-polar, drawn from a diversity of political backgrounds (and will include some members drawn from none). Although *Tindemans* speaks only of *"tenant compte de la rêpartition nationale"*, either diversity of political outlook must be taken to be subsumed within that *rêpartition* or allowance must otherwise be made for it. The Council will share the same mixed nature. It is improbable that all nine Governments will, at any one time, be of the same political persuasion. Thus, parties which will be more of coalitions than any existing party at the national level (all of which are to a greater or lesser degree coalitions), and the nature of the coalition will be more complex, embracing not merely differences of view, but differences of approach. These coalitions will face two different coalitions, one chosen (in principle for a period of years) because of particular attributes of its members, but not specifically to represent a particular political party, and the other body, the Council, the political composition of which depends on the chances of national politics, and one member of which, the President of France (if one assumes the continuance of the 1974 rules about the composition of the European Council), need not have a secure majority support in the Assembly.[33]

One other major assumption must be made. Member States are going to remain prominent on the political scene for some time to come, and certainly over the critical years that lie just ahead. They are not going to wither away rapidly, and if they did even more problems would arise than exist today. This is accepted in *Spierenburg,* if, for the sake of argument, one classes that in the "minimalist" group. It is similarly accepted by the Commission, which, for contrast, can be called "maximalist". Their continued existence will of necessity involve legislative activity at the national (and also, perhaps, sub-national) level, if the over-centralisation which the Commission in its Memorandum fears is to be avoided. That activity is implicit in the broader range of powers proposed in *Tindemans,* though the problems posed by that range are not clearly presented, perhaps because to do so would be to go into too much detail. It follows from that situation that frontiers (except in terms of competences) between the European and national political levels will be dangerous, breeding misunderstandings and misconceptions. Political activity will be mixed, yet the participant parties will not be identical at the two levels; parliamentary behaviour will, because of history, differ between the two levels. Yet the whole will be part of a joint endeavour. Thus frontiers (again, one must underline, with the exception of competences) would injure the endeavour. Moreover, such frontiers would not correspond with the other forms of Community activity. The Community is moving to styles of mixed or indirect administration.[34] This will be repeated. It cannot be said too often, in order to remove either the fear or the incubus of simple (or unexamined) ideas of federalism, for there are antitheses between the two concepts. The new legal order, which of course departs from so called federal patterns, has to be matched or balanced by an equally novel political structure. These considerations

33. Arguments flowing from that possibility remain hypothetical, and go into too much detail to be developed here.

34. Consider *e.g.* the political problems of national attempts at counterinflationary legislation and the conflict with Community Law which underlie cases like, Case 31/74, *Galli* (1976) E.C.R., 47, 12 C.M.L. Rev. 1975, 418 *et seq.;* or Case 60/75, *Russo* (1976) E.C.R., 45. There is a range of problems: consider too Case 23/75 *Rey Soda v. Cassa Conguaglio Zucchero* (1975) E.C.R., 1279 in this light.

imply a connexion of some form between the different levels of parliamentary activity. Such a conclusion is, above all, reinforced by any contemplation of the development of monetary union, itself dependent upon the convergence of economies, with the obvious significance of making apparent, in an era when economics and politics are so intertwined, why convergence is needed and where it leads. The example is at the extreme, but there is no single political advance or policy advocated in *Tindemans* which does not make the same demands on mutual comprehension. These demands must, above all, be met by the parliamentary processes. If these are inadequate, as a whole, even success of the European Councils would lead to failure. The resultant spurt of Community or Union activity would, unless suitable steps are taken, be likely to provoke such hostility as to destroy the potential gains. These are the problems and assumptions.

If the remainder of the argument had to be summarised, the heads of argument would read something like this; (a) There is a desire to return to some classical form of representative government. (b) The conditions in which, and for which, that classical form existed (if it ever did) no longer obtain. (c) Hence, that desire must be resisted and an alternative form of parliamentary activity which surmounts or circumvents the difficulties inherent in the classical form (but which nevertheless can be called democratic) must be sought.

The first head can be clearly illustrated by the Commission Memorandum.[35] When discussing possible structures, and the creation of its preferred "Second model" of a European Government, which is to be a collegiate body independent of the national governments, the Memorandum hinges the whole of its relationship with the legislature on the procedure for nominating the executive, and the premiss that it must be thus created. The first system the Memorandum imagines is nomination by the elected chamber which it asserts is "very similar to the constitutional practice of several Member States". The proposition would have been more true had it referred to theory and not practice; but, leaving that on one side, the emphasis indicates the desire to return to old days and old ways. The second system (which is preferred in the Memorandum) hinges on the right of censure, but it is said to lack legitimacy because the "government" would not be nominated by the legislature. There is no attempt to seek alternative sources of legitimacy not of a government, but of a system of government. It is the latter that matters. Yet one condition for the working of the classical model was the existence of a single "government", a condition which will not soon be

35. *Op. cit.* n. 24.

attained, even on the Commission's own terms. A second condition which must be remarked, is that of party structures.[36]

There should be no need to underline their significance in the "real" constitutions. M. Duverger has done it with admirable brevity.[37] A practising politician did it more succinctly still. Mr. Richard Crossman wrote: "Parliamentary control becomes a fiction with the disappearance of that solid centre of independent and independent-minded members", adding: "So long as parties were little more than electoral caucuses, the responsibility of the Minister to Parliament was an important check on bureaucratic incompetence." [38] A yet more notable practitioner remarks *"Dans un régime de partis multiples, où les majorités sont les majorités de co-alition, l'Assemblée nationale est par nature un foyer de division et instabilité".*[39] In the political conditions which are predictable within the European Parliament, and within the Union, the classical theory is unlikely to be able to avoid instability or to provide effective government. There are real changes, too often underrated, involved in attempts to translate theories which once had validity in national systems (but probably have it no longer) onto the supra-national level in circumstances in which the Union will have to struggle for its existence. There are other changes which matter as much, notably the high technical content of government at the European level (including a high economic content, even if that must be given a human face). The classical theory flourished (if it ever did) in a less complex age. But to revert, effective government will matter greatly, for there will be little temptation (even when the real limitations on the capacities of national governments to control their own destinies by themselves are accepted) to exchange a system based on them, with all its relative inefficiencies and out-dated as it may be, for a system which is more remote, and which is incapable of operating effectively, particularly on the level at which deficiences are currently felt. The relative remoteness of the system will be compensated by efficiency, provided that that larger system can have its own legitimacy.

The attainment of that legitimacy seems, then, to require the abandonment of classical theories of responsibility. That thought should not be shocking. The British would have a different idea of geography if the meridian did not run through Greenwich, but the world would be the same. Words or figures can mystify. After all, the Basic Law of the Federal Republic (in what were, at the end of the day, easier circum-

36. *Ibid.*, para. 103.
37. *Institutions Politiques*, Vol. 1, Part I, Chap. II.
38. Introduction to Bagehot's *English Constitution* (Fontana Edition) pp. 43-45.
39. G. Pompidou, *Le Noeud Gordien*, at p. 65-66.

stances for establishing "a government", though it may not have seemed so at the time) moved away from the pure theory.[40] Again, M. Pompidou, in reflecting on experience, argues, when contemplating the choice between a pure presidential system and a return to old ways, for the avoidance of both.[41]

In the situation which faces Europe, one may be more logical than M. Pompidou would have liked, or else one can accept some illogicality by retaining the nominal or ultimate existence of Article 144 (E.E.C.), but in principle accepting a theory of an "irresponsible executive" (the word "irresponsible" being obviously used in its technical sense).

What is meant by such a theory? A simplified answer is clear. The European Parliament becomes not merely the forum wherein power is exercised (which it scarcely is as yet) but, furthermore, by sharing independently in the exercise of power, it can conduct a continuous and efficient dialogue with those who also hold power. If one only accepts this as the basis on which one constructs a system of government, then the origin or mode of formation of each participating organ in the process becomes immaterial. Each participant can emerge independently of the others, and be independent of the other participants in continuity, yet functionally they are all interlocked. The emphasis is on the working relationship. M. Tindemans has put it, "the legislative and executive functions in the original structure are exercised in a delicate balance between the Council and the Commission", adding, "we must review the system and consider whether it is effective enough to exercise Community power."[42] One can follow that line of enquiry, and say that in that review, all that is needed is to discover a different perspective which conserves the heart of the original structure but makes the structure tripartite. To achieve that, all that is necessary is to stop thinking that the motion of censure is, or could be, corner-stone, and to look critically at the concept of responsibility as, in the realities in prospect, it could exist.

Obviously the motion of censure can never be such a corner-stone under the bi-cephalous system, because one head, the Council, escapes the axe. In the shape of the European Council it is yet further from the axe. Thus one constructs a parliamentary activity, properly called

40. Consider *e.g.* Arts. 54-69 of the Basic Law. History played its part no doubt in formulating them, and so did modern thought.

41. *Op. cit.* n. 39: *"En somme, notre système, précisément parce qu'il est bâtard est peut-être plus simple qu'un système logique. Les "coniards" sont souvent plus intelligents que les chiens de pure race!"* He underlines at p. 64 his reluctance to accept *"le retour au régime d'Assemblée"*, a regime which some still think of as classical.

42. European Parliament Debates July 9, 1975, Annex 193, p. 128.

democratic, which accepts that bringing about the downfall of a government is not necessarily the triumph of democracy, but rather that the continuous exercise of effective and rational influence on the legislative and executive powers may be such a triumph. To adopt such a theory is not only to accept the reality of the situation of Council and Commission and provide means to make it work, but also to move towards solutions of a number of problems present or proximate. It will, for example, be more easily possible to retain the principle of the collegiality of the Commission and avoid the easy temptation of accepting the individual responsibility of Commissioners (which is something different from the dominance of particular Commissioners in particular fields), the acceptance of which would be dangerous.[43] It will be possible to exercise on that basis an appropriate control over the Council (even in the form of the European Council), and finally, despite first appearances, confer a genuine democratic legitimacy on the system. With all its shortcomings, the American system, which incorporates this principle, cannot be classed as undemocratic, though what is here urged is not simply an importation of the American model.

The attractiveness of the idea (which may seem aberrant, but is not) lies in two circumstances. First, that it is not intrinsically strange to the Member States. In modern constitutions there are, as has been seen, moves in that direction. Second, and more importantly, it is entirely consistent with hopeful developments in the Communities. The start is made with the idea of co-decision advanced by the *Vedel Committee* in a passage which indicates how supple the mechanisms can be.[44] The matter is carried further by the Joint Declaration of the Institutions establishing the concertation procedure,[45] which, it is true, is only a first step in the direction of co-decision and one which was not found to be entirely satisfactory by the Parliament.[46] Yet all that is required is to push forward with co-decision. Correspondingly, the second budgetary Treaty [47] can be analysed in the same terms. Against the background of the established conciliation procedure, the power there admitted of the Parliament to reject *en bloc* can be regarded as in this line of co-decision. The right thus to reject has been admitted *ad interim*. As the President of the Parliament said, it is a right only to be used in full seriousness and for

43. If one looks at the legal system, *e.g.* the significance of Art. 169 (EEC) then obviously, for those purposes the maintenance of collegiality matters, but there are many other reasons for maintaining it.
44. *Op. cit.* n. 26, at 38-49.
45. O.J. 1975, C 89/1.
46. See European Parliament Debates Feb. 19, 1975, Annex 186, pp. 141 *et seq.*
47. The essentials of that Treaty are given in 12 C.M.L. Rev. 1975, 312.

weighty and clear reasons.[48] It is on such a basis of the acceptance of its true responsibilities that the Parliament will build itself and enrich the system. Because of the history of the Community budget and of its limited nature (in contrast to that of national budgets) it might be argued that it is an exaggeration to say that this provision, since the rejection of the budget has none of the consequences of a successful motion of censure, is equally in line with the theory of an irresponsible executive. Probably the contrary argument is true, but at very least there is coherence.

The key lies then in co-decision. It must, moreover, be emphasised that the theory of the irresponsible executive as an extension or facet of co-decision preserves the institutional balance. The debate is triangular and does not exclude the Commission. So, as the *Spierenburg Report* demonstrates, the consequence of Article 149 is that, provided the Commission retains its role within the co-decision process, the essential institutional balance is conserved. That Report, in order to break deadlocks, goes further than the *Vedel Report* in one respect.[49] It proposes, by the inverse procedure, that in appropriate cases the amendments of the Parliament should stand, unless overruled unanimously by the Council, provided always that the Commission were prepared to incorporate the amendments made by the Parliament in its proposals. That extension is sound, but on one condition.

Spierenburg explicitly assumes the continuing political responsibility of the Commission to the Parliament, but it is arguable that this is neither necessary nor desirable. Already there are cases relating to the role of the Commission as guardian of the Treaties in which political responsibility is inappropriate (the decision whether or not to commence proceeedings under Article 169 is an example) and it could well be that the decision of the Commission on this point should be regarded as falling into the same category. Indeed, the vote of censure would add nothing. It would not achieve the purpose of the Parliament in securing the adoption by the Commission of the amendment proposed by the former. This particular case could, therefore, even be an instance which helps to demonstrate the coherence of the concept of technical irresponsibility carried through logically with the structures of the Treaties. (The coherence of course neglects Article 149, but the whole argument is that that Article lacks the political significance often attributed to it.) What acceptance of the theory does is to intensify the debate between the institutions. There are obvious advantages and disadvantages. The most obvious advantage is

48. European Parliament Debates Dec. 9, 1974, Annex 184, p. 3.
49. Para. 12:4:2.

that by avoiding the word responsibility a richer relationship between Council and Parliament would be developed and the realities of that situation would not be lost in secrecy, as is the debate on the budgetary conciliation procedure.

It is true that the conciliation procedure and its evolution is only concerned with legislative acts; but, since the execution of policies requires such acts, its influence is much broader. It is true also that as far as the Parliament is concerned it has a passive quality, unless a full power of initiative be given. It seems doubtful that that power should be given, in any precise terms. It can and does, of course, exist in other systems in which the theory of the irresponsible executive is accepted. In the setting of the Communities or of European Union, it probably should not be accepted, for three reasons; the complexity and technicality of European legislation, the need to conserve, in the interest of maintaining the place of the Commission, and the fact that its exercise would require a duplication of technical staff which would unbalance or distort the Parliament. The absence of that right, granted the evolution of co-decision, can become of little significance, since by virtue of that evolution the Parliament is in a significant bargaining position.

The risk, of course, is of creating more blockages when the need is to unblock. It is a partial answer, but an unsatisfactory one, to say that the risk of blockage continuing under a system which admits the dominance of European Councils is certainly as great. A more satisfactory answer is that if the probable working of the system is examined, then the bargaining process in fact holds out good possibilities for unblocking. The Council or European Council would be met with genuine counter-forces, and thus be forced to act by modern variants of withholding supplies, though the precise technique is inappropriate in European terms. Thus there could be an amelioration of the voting situation in the Council, by bringing forces to bear which encourage less rigidity, and this could, at least, help to justify abstentions. Governments would have an excuse for correct behaviour. In the predictable political circumstances, the composition of the Parliament and of parties within it could, moreover, well produce conditions which would be likely to unblock. It is precisely in circumstances of coalition against coalition (which is the predictable situation) that problems could be resolved. That there are such risks could not finally be denied, but against them three primary advantages must be weighed. First, this is the one method which can realistically bring the Council or the European Council properly within the system. It by-passes the problems of making these bodies responsible by substituting something different, which is workable. At the extreme, it might produce the one condition upon which the general predominance of the European Councils could be safely admitted. Second, it is the one method which would not merely force the Parliament to accept its responsibilities,[50] but would also make it an attractive body to candidates, without opening up the risks of *Gouvernement d'assemblée.* Thus it overcomes the real problem that the European Parliament is, in broad terms, the one Parliament which affords its members little political future. In the situation envisaged, as experience elsewhere demonstrates, leaders in such a legislature or Parliament become figures of political eminence in their own right. Third, it is a method which does not injure what is essential in the Council/Commission relationship and would help to restore an appropriate balance between those bodies, giving to the whole structure, at the same time, a democratic legitimacy.

As set out briefly here, the theory or the method may seem blunt. In fact, as has already been said, there are many ways of reaching the desired ends, and many forms of the co-decision process can be imagined, with variants between basic regulations and implementing regulations. Levels of co-decision can also be contemplated, ranging from a full right of co-decision to suspensive vetoes, in either case a decision being capable of being over-ruled (granted certain conditions). Indeed, these techniques could work in either direction, for or against the Council. In any of its forms, a true right of co-decision may require for its effective use the adoption of other techniques, in particular those of hearings, but these techniques would themselves open up the process of decision-making. That opening-up is important, so that it can be clearly seen where the defects lie.

By itself this change could do much for the European Parliament; what it would not do is solve the problem of parliamentarism on the European scale. That problem which exists now will become much more acute with the evolution to European Union. Essentially, that is the problem of the linkage between the two levels. There are possibilities of connecting the two levels envisaged in both the *Spierenburg* and *Vedel Reports,*[51] but these do not suffice.

It must be assumed that if the European Parliament becomes as heavily charged as it would be, the dual mandate, even if allowed, would in practice be unworkable, with the consequent separation of levels. What then is needed is that the European Parliament become bi-cameral. The second chamber should be nominated or elected by national

50. It cannot be said that either of the attempts of move a vote of censure have enhanced the reputation of the Parliament, and the second demonstrated the risks of degrading such votes when they are the only effective weapons left to the Parliament.

51. *Op. cit.*, ns. 9 and 26, at para. 12:4:4 and p. 70 respectively.

parliaments. In this non-directly-elected Chamber, the dual mandate could well be obligatory, since that Chamber should be regarded not as the Chamber of the States, but as a Chamber of the national Parliaments. In brief, any analogy with the *Bundestag* should not be pushed too far. The Commission, which saw the need for bi-cameralism, chose the title *Chambre des Etats,* but the name is false in the model here envisaged. Here the States, as such, have their full place (admittedly lacking in the Commission model) in the Council, but are brought within a control system.

Moreover, if the specific purpose, which is to relate the two Parliamentary levels to each other, be recognised, then divisions of functions between the two Chambers, and even the composition of this Second Chamber (if the Dutch will forgive the phrase), become sufficiently clear. The prime function is as a connecting link, bringing some domestic considerations to bear upon European legislation, and, much more importantly, carrying principles and explanations back to the national forum. Thus, the essence of the process of co-decision, which is political on the European scale, should be left with the First (elected) Chamber. Paradoxically, much of the activity of the Second Chamber would be concerned with two main areas, economic affairs and social policies, since it is in those areas that explanation will be most needed. If there is to be any convergence of economies, it is in that field that there will be most need for communication to explain objectives. If one looks at the heads proposed in *Tindemans* under "Social and Regional Policies", it is clear that while there could be general agreement on objectives, each particular proposal (many of which would need to be implemented, in part at least, in national legislation) would encounter entrenched historical attitudes. Hence, it would follow that the members of the European Second Chamber should predominantly come from the lower houses of national parliaments, either because it is there that national budgets will be argued, or because it is there that entrenched attitudes would be most sharply felt. It follows, then, that in such fields the Second Chamber would be concerned with principle.

In no sense would this Second Chamber duplicate the work of the First, and its membership could be much smaller. There is even one other function which could, indirectly, be performed by such a Chamber. It is to be hoped that the First Chamber become essentially political. To build up too strong a range of consultative bodies beside the European Parliament would be wrong. Such a construction, by diffusion, will simply weaken political development, and would congest the decision-making process. All that such bodies could do, could be done effectively by the European Parliament, through specialised committees using appropriate techniques. One such body, in particular, should be avoided, a Committee of the Regions. Nevertheless, there is a place for the expression of regional views. It would be possible for any Member State which so wished to arrange its delegation to the Second Chamber to allow for such voices and, in that way, it could also serve as a corrective to any imbalance which could emerge from the distribution of seats in the First Chamber.

V. CONCLUSION

What then does one conclude? It may seem that one has moved from *Tindemans* to purely personal views and abandoned the Report. Even to the extent that that is true, it is in itself a recognition of the virtue of the Report. It is precisely because its author accepted the challenge of circumstance, and was thus forced to produce a pragmatic rather than a doctrinal Report, that the Report itself forces its readers back to considerations of principles and structures. By analysis, the Report sharpens the sense of crisis, and by highlighting certain essential policy areas, which do involve at least changes of emphasis, it evokes consideration of the sort of political processes or machinery which will be required if results are to be attained harmoniously. By indicating firmly one way out of the difficulties, the Report forces thought about whether that is the best or only way. If one major purpose was to re-open the debate, then its author should be well content, and because of the way he did it that debate will, of necessity, be practical. The House of Lords Committee, it seems, drew the wrong conclusion. Being confident "that M. Tindemans was writing as a convinced Federalist", it nevertheless commented: "The Tindemans Report seeks a middle way between Federalists and those who desire co-operation by pragmatic means." [52] The phrase, it seems, misconstrues, by over-simplification, the nature of the debate. It is not one between "Federalists" and those who seek simple co-operation. It is about the sort of machinery, which, in the difficult circumstances which face Europe, could produce the functional results which are necessary, and to achieve which the partner States first undertook the joint enterprise. A distinction must be drawn between constitutional aims or morality, on the one hand, the fundamentals of a genuine rule of law and of democracy for example, and constitutional theories as to the means appropriate for achieving results, on the other. The first must dominate. The second must be adaptable to the factual

52. (1975-76) H.L.P. 277, para. 3.

conditions in which they operate. To that extent they are subservient. It does not help to impose theories derived from other circumstances. It is silly to put such weight on ambiguous words such as "Federal" and its derivatives.

It is too early to write a constitutional theory of Europe, though the material on which such a rationalisation could be based is steadily emerging. What is evident is that the nature of that "constitution" will be complex, because of the circumstances in which the polity is being created. It will involve not merely indirect intervention from the European level of government, but also the combined intervention of all branches of Government at two (or more) levels in ways which are novel. The debate is not about theories or attitudes; it is about how, consistently with very basic principles, Europe can be made governable in the conditions, political and institutional, in which it must live. It is only if it is governable that one can ensure practical results for those who live below the level of government.[53] *Tindemans* chose a mechanism to achieve that. Compromises were forced on it by circumstances. That fact enlivens the debate because it evokes criticism. But the Report did not lose sight of the fact that it was about government on a large scale to produce practical results. It leaves no doubt that European Union is a highly political concept in form and content. It is an inadequate response to say that "over the last ten years there has been too much talk about structures and not enough talk about getting on with the job",[54] when the analysis in *Tindemans* and in other reports discussed here demonstrate that it is structural failures which have impeded the attainment of results. One can doubt whether the solution proposed is satisfactory. It is for that

53. Mr. Hattersly, in his evidence before that Committee, did underline the priority need for "making the Community a realistic proposition for ordinary people". That need dictates improved efficiency in decision taking, with obvious consequences on governments. One minor point may illustrate this. In view of what has just been said on constitutional theories, though the House of Lords Committee did not pick it up, there are clear "constitutional" problems in British Constitutional theory in delegating decision-taking powers to the Permanent Representatives, they not being Ministers. Yet, in the different situations, other theories are needed, and such a delegation could fit well into the parliamentary scheme here sketched. The need to look at the real situation which is likely to exist and not to look simply at past models is underlined by reading the evidence in (1975-76) H.L.P. 119-i on Direct Elections, *e.g.* Q. 14 (Lord Bessborough).

54. Mr. Hattersley, see Q. 5 in his evidence to that Committee. He added later, at Q. 7, "I do not think it is possible to abandon the Luxembourg compromise". It may perhaps be said that at the highest levels of government "counting heads" is not always the best solution when discontent will linger. What has been here proposed could take much of the sting out of such adherence to the Luxembourg compromise. See: Minutes of Evidence to the House of Lords Select Committee comsidering Tindemans, not yet published.

reason, since criticism alone is unhelpful, that the attempt has been made here to sketch an alternative parliamentary system which could, it seems, help to solve problems. What one cannot deny is that the Report has effectively re-opened the debate in real terms, by stating what results are needed and on that basis seeking the means to attain the ends.

THE APPLICATION OF RULES OF PUBLIC INTERNATIONAL LAW WITHIN COMMUNITY LAW

by

Karl Matthias Meessen *

A. PUBLIC INTERNATIONAL LAW GOVERNING THE LEGAL RELATIONS BETWEEN THE COMMUNITY AND THIRD STATES

For more than a decade the relationship between Community Law and national law has been the object of careful and enlightening studies. Since the main issues, such as the problems of direct applicability and of priority of Community Law, are about to be settled, the attention of European lawyers is by now shifting to the analysis of the relation between Community Law and public international law (henceforth: international law) which had been neglected so far.

The European treaties have, of course, been concluded according to the rules of international law. But the legal order which was erected soon emancipated from its origins. Community Law, governing the legal relations between the Community itself, Member States and individuals, has aptly been denominated a "law of integration".[1] It is modelled according to a pattern of its own. In contrast to both international law and constitutional law of federal states it is not a static, but a highly dynamic legal system: A sectoral economic union on its way towards closer political union. Thus inside Community Law rules of international law (and of federalist constitutional law) are only applicable insofar as they happen to coincide with principles of Community Law, which means that they hardly are of any help in solving legal problems. After some early innocent references to international law, the Court of Justice corrected its position in the famous *Van Gend & Loos* and *Costa/ENEL* cases.[2] Since then it has avoided open references to international law. In the recent *Van Duyn* case, however, it attempted to justify a somewhat restrictive interpretation of the freedom of movement under Community

* Dr. iur., Professor of Public Law, International Law and European Law, University of Augsburg.

1. Pescatore, *Le droit de l'intégration*, 1972.

2. Case 26/62, *van Gend & Loos*, Feb. 5, 1963, 9 *Recueil* 1963, 1, at 23; Case 6/64, Costa/ENEL, July 15, 1964, 10 *Recueil* 1964, 1141, at 1158; for a more complete account of the early jurisprudence (and literature) see Meessen, "Der räumliche Anwendungsbereich des EWG-Kartellrechts und das allgemeine Völkerrecht", 8 EuR. 1973, 18-38, at 28 *et seq.*

13 C.M.L. Rev.,1976, 485-501

Law by referring to an alleged principle of international law.[3] This rather ill-conceived allusion to international law [4] must be regarded as the exception that proves the rule of non-applicability of international law as far as the legal relations within the Community are concerned.

International law does, however, govern the legal relations between the Community and third states and, in this respect, it certainly deserves the growing interest of European lawyers. The Community finds itself in an extensive network of treaty commitments *vis-à-vis* third states. The subjects of these treaty commitments are rather technical. They concern tariffs, preferences, cooperation, restrictive practices, *etc.* But these technical matters possibly are of greater practical importance than the usual international law issues of war and peace.

A German importer (and the German tax authorities) might like to know whether a certain heading of the Community's Common Customs Tariff is invalid, because it is contrary to a GATT Consolidating Agreement between the Community and Switzerland.[5] Is Italy entitled to apply a pre-war legislative decree and levy a duty on veterinary tests on certain imported products after the Association Agreement of Yaoundé has entered into force?[6] Does the 1972 Treaty between the Community and Switzerland entitle the Commission's officials in charge of antitrust matters to investigate the files of a Swiss company with the clandestine assistance of one of the company's employees, or would such measure be forbidden by general international law?[7]

The following discussion of these matters, which is limited to the law and practice under the EEC Treaty, will focus the attention on three problems:

(1) Which rules of international law are binding on the Community? To what extent and on what legal basis is the Community bound to respect treaties concluded by one or more of its Member States with third states?

(2) Under which conditions are rules of international law directly applicable by the Court of Justice and/or the courts of Member States?

(3) Which rules are to be applied in case of a conflict between rules of international law and rules of Community Law?

3. Case 41/74, *van Duyn*, Dec. 4, 1974, (1974) E.C.R., 1337, at 1351.

4. For a critical remark see Simmonds, "Van Duyn v. Home Office: The direct effectiveness of directives", 24 I.C.L.Q. 1975, 419-437, at 437.

5. See Case 9/73, *Schlüter*, Oct. 24, 1973, (1973) E.C.R., 1135.

6. See Case 87/75, *Bresciani*, Feb. 5, (1976) E.C.R., 129.

7. See *Hoffman-La Roche* Case, Written Questions No. 54/75, O.J. 1975 C 161/15 and No. 152/75, O.J. 1975 C 209/14.

B. RULES OF INTERNATIONAL LAW BINDING UPON THE COMMUNITY

1. *General international law*

General international law may be regarded as consisting of international customary law and of the "general principles of law recognised by civilized nations" according to Article 38 (1) (c) of the Statute of the International Court of Justice. Except for a few rules of *ius cogens* (the peremptory character of which will continue to be disputed) general international law constitutes *ius dispositivum.* Thus, the Member States were entitled to abrogate rules of general international law and they did do so by forming an international organisation which in some of its functions and with its long-term aim of integration has little in common with international organisations of the traditional type. But this right could only be exercised by the Member States as among themselves. Any attempt to abrogate rules of general international law as against third states could be regarded by those states as *res inter alios acta* and would be invalid on the level of international law. Thus general international law is binding upon the Community as far as it concerns the legal relations between the Community and third states and to the extent that it pertains to subjects of international law which are not states.[8] For example, the rules of general international law concerning the jurisdiction of states will have to be respected by the Community *vis-à-vis* third states. In the *Dyestuffs* case the Community violated the territorial integrity of Switzerland when it served the statement of complaint by mailing it directly to the headquarters of the companies in Switzerland. The Court of Justice did not deny the binding character of the relevant rules of international law, though in contrast to the Commission and to the Advocate General, it carefully avoided a positive statement to that effect.[9] In the recent decision in the *Fisheries* case the Court expressly admitted that the Community would have to respect all the rules of general international law limiting the jurisdiction of states in relation to the high seas.[10]

8. Meessen, *loc. cit.*, note 2, at 31-32.

9. Case 52/69, *CIBA-Geigy*, July 14, 1972, 18 *Recueil* 1972, 787, at 826 (Commission at 797 *et seq.*, 806, Advocate General, at 692 *et seq.*).

10. Joined Cases 3, 4, 6/76, *Kramer et al.*, July 14, 1976, consideration 14, not yet published.

2. *Treaties concluded by the Community*

As a subject of international law the Community is entitled to conclude agreements with third states. On the plane of Community Law, this right is confirmed by Articles 113 and 238 of the EEC Treaty. Treaties with third states are binding upon the Community if they are binding under general international law. This statement which may seem to amount to a truism does, however, underline that the entry into force of international agreements is exclusively regulated by international law: Failures to comply with the rules of Community Law concerning the conclusion of treaties could only be invoked to the extent that third states would be entitled to invoke their domestic constitutional law, *i.e.* they could hardly be invoked at all.[10a] Furthermore, the interpretation of treaties between the Community and third states would have to follow the rules of international law only. The favourite principle of interpretation under Community Law, the *"effet utile"* principle, may not be applied, or rather it has to be boiled down into the traditional principle of teleological interpretation. The "usefulness" of any line of interpretation would have to be judged from the point of view of all the parties to the treaty and not only under the aspect of the Community's policy of integration.

The Community has, in fact, concluded many international agreements. Among the more important are the association agreements with Mediterranean and African states, the agreements on the establishment of a free trade area with those EFTA countries which did not join the Community, and a number of preference and cooperation agreements with various countries of the world.[11] The Court had to deal with tariff agreements in the *Interfood* and *Schlüter* cases and with association agreements in the *Schröder, Haegeman II* and *Bresciani* cases.[12] The internationally binding effect of the treaties had not been disputed.

3. *Treaties with third states concluded by one or more Member States*

If the number of treaties concluded by the Community is by now a rather impressive one, the treaty commitments of each Member State exceed

10a. Bleckmann, *Europarecht,* (1976), at p. 227.

11. For a survey of the treaty practice see E. U. Petersmann, "Auswärtige Gewalt, Völkerrechtspraxis und Völkerrechtsbindungen der Europäischen Wirtschaftsgemeinschaft", 35 Zeit A.O.R.V. 1975, 213-281, at 219 *et seq.*

12. Case 92/71, *Interfood,* April 26, 1972, 18 *Recueil* 1972, 231; Case 9/73, *Schlüter,* Oct. 24, 1973, (1973) E.C.R., 1135; Case 40/72, *Schröder,* Feb. 7, 1973, (1973) E.C.R., 125; Case 181/73, *Haegeman II,* April 30, 1974, (1974) E.C.R., 449; Case 87/75, *Bresciani,* Feb. 5, 1976, (1976) E.C.R., 129.

the Community's commitments in quantity and in variety. Are any of these treaties binding upon the Community? This question pertains not only to the binding character of old treaty commitments, such as the Convention of Mannheim of 1868 on the legal régime of the Rhine [13] or as the Charter of the United Nations of 1945,[14] but also to new obligations which the Member States may have incurred in accordance with Community Law after the entry into force of the European treaties. An example for the latter type of treaty commitments is provided by the *Fisheries* case:[15] The Convention on Fishing in the North-Atlantic was originally concluded in 1963; under the terms of the *AETR* judgment,[16] the treaty-making power in the field of fisheries policy was transferred to the Community as of 1970; the relevant obligation to fix quotas was imposed upon the Member State at an even later date, but again in conformity with Community Law, since the Community had not yet completely exercised the competences conferred upon it under Community Law. Such treaty commitments may be regarded as binding either by virtue of international law or by virtue of Community Law. We shall first discuss the matter on the plane of international law.

The formation of international organisations of the type of the European Community is a new phenomenon in the history of international relations. Hence, general international law is unlikely to contain any rules as regards the succession to treaty commitments of the Member States by the Community. This view is confirmed by Article 234 of the EEC Treaty. The provision that treaty commitments of Member States *vis-à-vis* third states "shall not be affected" excludes any attempt on the part of the Community to have the rules of state succession concerning unions of states applied to its own formation. The non-application of these rules must be regarded as operating in two directions: the treaty commitments of the Member States are neither cancelled nor are they automatically transferred to the Community.[17] But international law,

13. Rittstieg, *Rheinschiffahrt und Gemeinsamer Markt*, (1971); Zuleeg, "EWG-Vertrag und Rheinregime", in *Verkehr und Gemeinschaftsrecht*, (1972), 25-44; Meissner, *Das Recht der Europäischen Wirtschaftsgemeinschaft im Verhältnis zur Rheinschiffahrtsakte von Mannheim*, (1973).

14. As regards the Community's participation in applying sanctions against Rhodesia under the U.N. Charter, see Kuyper, "The EEC and the Implementation of General International Legal Rules", 12 C.M.L.Rev. 1975, 231-244.

15. Joined Cases 3, 4, 6/76, *loc. cit.*, note 10.

16. Case 22/70, *AETR*, March 31, 1971, 17 *Recueil* 1971, 263; see also Opinion 1/75, *OECD*, Nov. 11, 1975., (1975) E.C.R., 1355, 13 C.M.L. Rev. 1976, 375 *et seq.*

17. Usually only the aspect of non-cancellation is taken account of: O'Connell, *International Law*, (2nd ed., 1970), vol. 1, at p. 367; E. U. Petersmann, in von der Groeben/von Boeckh/Thiesing, *Kommentar zum EWG-Vertrag*, (2nd ed., 1974), Art. 234, vol. 2, at p. 738.

being based on the consent of states, would always permit an individual transfer of treaty rights and obligations by the consent of all the states and other subjects of international law in question. An individual transfer of commitments has in part taken place as regards the General Agreement on Tariffs and Trade, as has been correctly elaborated by the Court in the *International Fruit* case.[18] In an earlier case it had already referred to explanatory notes by the "Committee for the Nomenclature" acting under the supervision of the "Council for Cooperation in the Field of Customs" in order to support a certain interpretation of rules of Community Law.[19] Only the Member States, not the Community, are contracting parties of the GATT and of the agreement providing the legal basis for the institutions which were just mentioned. A confirmation of the *International Fruit* case may be found in the *Schlüter* case in which the Court had to deal with a tariff agreement concluded by the Community and Switzerland within the framework of GATT.[20] The reasoning used in these cases is applicable to various other treaties, especially to multilateral conventions in the implementation of which the Community has actively participated. Most treaty commitments, however, have not been individually transferred to the Community and would therefore not be binding upon the Community on the international plane.

As regards the plane of Community Law, it has been argued that treaty commitments which may not be invalidated unilaterally should be regarded as binding not only on the Member States concerned, but also on the Community itself by virtue of an internal obligation under Community Law.[21] Is this view in conformity with Article 234? The Community takes notice of the continuous existence of the treaty commitments of its Member States (para. 1). At the same time it urges their adaptation to its own needs (para. 2). It is the long-term perspective which gives a clue to the interpretation of these two provisions. The wide scope of the Community's treaty-making power[22] suggests that the Community is ultimately destined to take over the control of the complete range of treaty commitments *vis-à-vis* third states in its field of activity. For the transitory period (which may last long) Article 234 could

18. Joined Cases 21-24/72, *International Fruit*, Dec. 12, 1972, 18 *Recueil* 1972, 1219.

19. Case 14/70, *Deutsche Bakels*, Dec. 8, 1970, 16 *Recueil* 1970, 1001, at 1010.

20. Case 9/73, *loc. cit.* note 5; see also Case 38/75, *Nederlandse Spoorwegen*, Nov. 19, 1975, (1975) E.C.R., 1439.

21. Zuleeg, *op. cit.* note 13, at 30; E. U. Petersmann, *loc. cit.*, note 17.

22. For the exclusive character of the Community's competences see the *OECD* Opinion, *loc. cit.*, note 16; as regards certain qualifications during a transitory period see the *Fisheries* case, *loc. cit.*, note 10.

perhaps be described as providing for a régime of intended parallelism. The obligations of Member States as against third states and inside the Community exist parallel to each other. The gap between the two is not bridged by an indirect order of priority in favour of international law, but by flexible obligations of fair play binding on the Community (and on the Member States). On the one hand the Community is free to create additional "incompatibilities" according to Article 234 para. 2, for instance by enacting regulations providing for a policy not in line with the commitments of Member States. On the other hand, it would not be allowed to impose its policy on the Member States concerned by all the means available under the EEC Treaty. The wording of Article 234 does not cover treaties which Member States have concluded after the entry into force of the EEC Treaty, but in conformity with its rules on the treaty-making power. The concept of intended parallelism, however, appears to offer an adequate solution of this problem as well. Both groups of treaties should therefore be treated alike. The internal acceptance of treaty commitments would, as on the plane of international law, have to be proved individually.

Article 119 of the EEC Treaty, which contains an obligation to grant "equal pay without discrimination based on sex", has been interpreted in a recent decision of the Court by reference to ILO Convention No. 100.[23] Such a reference could be construed as an obligation of the Community to respect treaty commitments of Member States by virtue of an individual rule of Community Law.

The occasional influx of treaty commitments into Community Law is also demonstrated by two recent decisions concerning the application of fundamental rights *qua* "general principles common to the laws of the Member States". In the *Nold* case the Court referred to the European Convention on Human Rights to which all the Member States are contracting parties, since France had ratified it just a couple of days before the Court's decision.[24] In the *Rutili* case the Court based its decision not only on the Convention itself, but also on an additional protocol which actually had not been ratified by all the Member States.[25] The Court was right in not giving too much weight to the number of Member States bound by a treaty. This number constitutes just one factor in the very complex process of ascertaining general principles of

23. Case 43/75, *Defrenne II*, April 8, 1976, consideration 20, (1976) E.C.R., 455; see also Advocate General, in Case 80/70, *Defrenne I*, May 25, 1971, 17 *Recueil* 1971, 445, at 456.

24. Case 4/73, *Nold*, May 14, 1974, (1974) E.C.R., 491, at 507.

25. Case 36/75, *Rutili*, Oct. 28, 1975, (1975) E.C.R., 1219, at 1232. For a somewhat restrictive interpretation of the *Rutili* decision see Advocate General Trabucchi, in case 118/75, *Watson*, July 7, 1976, not yet published.

Community Law.[26] In respect to human rights, the adoption of a standard below the standard which all the Member States have accepted for themselves does not appear to be admissible. In this field, even obligations which have been incurred, but by several Member States only, may be regarded as designating the minimum standard of protection under Community Law, because any restriction of the exercise of public power outside a state is welcome even to those states which do not accept such restrictions for their own actions.

Apart from Article 119 and the general principles of law, there may be other rules of Community Law which incorporate obligations incurred by Member States *vis-à-vis* third states. In the absence of such a provision, the régime of intended parallelism described above will come into operation. Thus in the *Fisheries* case the Court rightly acknowledged that the Netherlands, being competent to conclude the Fisheries Convention, is also entitled to provide for its implementation.[27]

C. THE DIRECT APPLICABILITY OF BINDING RULES OF INTERNATIONAL LAW

The notion of direct applicability, no matter whether it has been used to describe the possible effect of international law within national law, of Community Law within national law, or of international law within Community Law, always stands for a considerable amount of confusion. It therefore appears to be appropriate to define its meaning for the purposes of this article: a rule is considered to be directly applicable within a certain legal order, whenever the courts set up under this legal order are entitled (and bound) to apply the rule without having to wait for any executory legislation. It has to be ascertained whether the rule is addressed to the legislative organs or to the judiciary.[28] Of course, addressing a rule to the judiciary presupposes that administrative authorities and/or individuals whose conduct may be regulated by the rule should rather follow the rule in order to avoid loosing their case when it is brought before court.

Courts will always look for advice to their own legal order as to which

26. For a discussion of the Court's role in ascertaining general principles of Community Law see Meessen, "Zur Theorie allgemeiner Rechtsgrundsätze des internationalen Rechts: Der Nachweis allgemeiner Rechtsgrundsätze des Europäischen Gemeinschaftsrecht", 17 *Jahrbuch für Internationales Recht* 1974, 283-306.

27. Joined Cases 3, 4, 6/76, *loc. cit.*, note 10, consideration 17.

28. For a similar view see Pescatore, *L'ordre juridique des Communautés Européennes, Etude des sources du droit communautaire,* (2nd ed., 1973), at p. 210.

rules they have to apply. Hence, the problem of direct applicability must be approached by first examining the court's legal order. In the present context three different solutions are offered. Community Law, being the legal order of the Court of Justice, could prohibit the direct applicability of any rule of international law; it could provide for the direct applicability even of those rules of international law which under international law are not supposed to be directly applicable; or it could just leave it to the relevant rule of international law itself whether it is meant to be applied directly or not. Which alternative has Community Law opted for?

As regards treaties concluded by the Community itself, Article 228 para. 2 may provide for an answer. It reads: "Agreements concluded under these conditions shall be binding on the institutions of the Community and on Member States". The term "these conditions" refers to the rules of Community Law concerning the attribution of the treaty making power to the Community (as against the Member States), the distribution of functions among the Community's institutions, and the procedure to be followed by these institutions. A violation of these rules, which will not be discussed in this article,[29] could lead to the non-applicability of the treaty in question on the plane of Community Law, whereas, on the plane of international law, the treaty would normally enter into force all the same.[30] If all the relevant rules of Community Law have been observed, the treaty provisions are binding "on the institutions of the Community and on Member States". The Court of Justice, being one of the institutions of the Community, belongs to the potential addressees of treaty rules. It appears to follow that Community Law has in Article 228 opted for the third alternative as outlined above: it is left to the relevant rules of international law whether they are to be applied directly or not.

Rules of international treaty law may be directed only against the contracting parties, which may then be bound to enact some implementing legislation, or they may at the same time be addressed to the courts of the contracting parties. In the latter case they are said to be "self-executing".[31] Whether a treaty is self-executing or not is exclusively a

29. But see the three leading decisions of the Court, viz. the *AETR* case, *loc. cit.*, note 16, the *OECD* Opinion (*loc. cit.*, note 16), and the *Fisheries* case, *loc. cit.*, note 10. See also Hermann, Das Abschlussverfahren völkerrechtlicher Verträge der Europäischen Wirtschaftsgemeinschaft, 1973; Die Aussenbeziehungen der Europäischen Gemeinschaft, Wissenschaftliches Kolloquium am 4. und 5. April, 1974, in Bad Ems (1975).

30. See above under B 2.

31. For a helpful analysis, see Zuleeg, "Die innerstaatliche Anwendbarkeit völkerrechtlicher Verträge am Beispiel des GATT und der Europäischen Sozialcharta", 35 Zeit. A.O.R.V. 1975, 341-363 with further references.

matter of treaty interpretation according to the rules of international law. Of course, in practice some criteria have been developed to which reference is made regularly: If, for instance, the treaty provision is formulated in very vague terms it is usually not designed to be applied by the courts directly. But since many rules of national law are worded rather vaguely, and still have to be applied by the courts, it is perfectly conceivable that a treaty provision, despite its vagueness, must be applied directly.[32] A second criterion which may, however, not be considered to be conclusive either, is indicated by the question whether the treaty itself provides for a procedure of settlement of disputes which may arise in the course of application of the treaty. If so, the treaty is rather unlikely to be directly applicable, since its applicability before national courts would provide for another, more effective, system of enforcement. The Court of Justice used this line of reasoning in respect to the GATT.[33]

The question of direct applicability has to be examined according to the rules of interpretation of international law only. Any blend of international law and Community Law criteria would be at odds with Article 228 para. 2 which demands nothing less and nothing more than the complete performance of the international agreement. Its general idea, obviously, is to avoid any divergence between the obligations under international law and those under Community Law. Of course, it may happen that a treaty concluded between the Community and third states contains specific references to Community Law and may therefore have to be interpreted in the light of such references. Article 2 of the Association Agreement of Yaoundé of 1963 may serve as an example. It refers to Articles 12 *et seq.* of the EEC Treaty (containing rules on the elimination of customs duties).[34] The Court held that Article 2 of the Agreement is, because of its similarity to Article 12 of the EEC Treaty, to be applied directly within the Community, though corresponding provisions of the Agreement could not be regarded as being directly applicable in the Associated States.[35] Under the rules of interpretation of international law, the Court had in fact to take account of the particular circumstances of the case instead of sticking to the traditional international law criterion of reciprocity of rights and obligations.

Summing up, it is submitted that a treaty concluded by the Community is directly applicable under three conditions:

32. See, for example, the application of a rather vague rule on the protection of private property contained in the German-AmericanTreaty on Friendship, Commerce and Navigation by the German *Bundesgerichtshof,* in 26 *Entscheidungen in Zivilsachen,* 200.

33. Joined Cases 21-24/72, *loc. cit.,* note 18, at 1227-1228.

34. See also Petersmann, *loc. cit.,* note 11, at 270.

35. Case 87/75, *loc. cit.,* note 6, consideration 25.

(1) The treaty is binding upon the Community under international law;
(2) The treaty has been concluded in conformity with the rules of Community Law on the treaty-making power, *etc.;*
(3) The treaty clause in question is self-executing according to the rules of interpretation of international law.

As regards treaties which have not been concluded by the Community, but which are binding upon it by virtue of rules of international law, and as regards general international law, the EEC Treaty does not contain any specific rules dealing with the question of direct applicability. But the concept of complete performance of international obligations would also apply in respect of these internationally binding commitments. Perhaps Article 228 para. 2 should be applied by way of an analogy. Article 228 para. 2 would, however, not be applicable as to treaties which are only binding on the Community by virtue of a rule of Community Law, such as Article 119, or a general principle of law. The direct applicability has to be determined by interpretation of the specific rule of Community Law which incorporates the treaty commitment of Member States.

Is it possible to reconcile the above conclusion with the attitude of the Court, especially as it has been laid down in the *International Fruit* case?[36]

The Court uses neither the term "direct applicability" nor the term "self-executing character", but it examines whether the relevant rule of international law is "capable of creating rights of which interested parties may avail themselves in a court of law".[37] The meaning of this phrase may not easily be established. Whereas Kapteyn regards this formulation as equivalent to the term "self-executing",[38] Millarg and Schermers blame the Court for introducing an additional (and unwarranted) condition for the application of international law within Community Law.[39]

If taken literally, the Court's formulation suggests that there is a distinction to be made between rules which are directly applicable within the meaning of the above definition and rules which can be invoked by individuals. Such a distinction would be relevant if under international law one and the same rule may be directly applicable, but

36. Joined Cases 21-24/72, *loc. cit.*, note 18.

37. *Id.* at 1228; English translation quoted according to Schermers, "Community Law and international law", 12 C.M.L.Rev. 1975, 77-90, at 80.

38. Kapteyn, "The 'Domestic' Law Effect of Rules of International Law within the European Community System of Law and the Question of the Self-Executing Character of GATT Rules", 8 *The International Lawyer* 1974, 74-82, at 76.

39. Millarg, Annotation to the *International Fruit* case, 8 EuR. 1973, 148-155, at 152; Schermers, *loc. cit.*, note 37.

not available to individuals, and if the court under its own procedural law is to apply only rules of this kind. It is open to doubt whether these two conditions will very often be fulfilled. In the first place, the contracting parties are free to provide for any different degree of the binding force of treaty clauses, but it is not very likely that they would choose that the treaty be applied directly, but not be invoked by individuals, because then the courts would rarely have an opportunity to apply the clause at all. In the second place, procedural law may require a plaintiff to have a legally protected interest in the matter.[40] In the cases decided so far—all of them were brought before the Court of Justice under Article 177—the national courts have apparently never raised any questions under this aspect of national procedural law. Thus it must be assumed that the above requirement had always been met. Forming two groups of rules of international law, viz. rules which are not available to individuals and rules which are available, would, in this connotation, be of an academic interest only.

Perhaps it is the perspective of national courts which prompted the Court of Justice to postulate this requirement. If so, it would not be so much the question of whether an individual is entitled to invoke a certain rule of international law, as whether it is to be applied only by the Court of Justice or by the courts of Member States as well. Rules of Community Law which are not directly applicable by the courts of Member States could still be applied by the Court of Justice, for instance in an action under Article 169 of the EEC Treaty. But the problem of direct applicability of rules of international law before the courts of Member States is of a different character. It should be approached systematically. The national court would consult the national legal order as to whether a certain rule of international law binding on the Community should be applied directly or not. In national law, the general rules concerning the applicability of Community Law, in Germany Article 24 of the Constitution, would be applicable[41] and would, probably in all the Member States, refer the question of direct applicability to Community Law. Community Law expressly provides that rules of international law are binding upon Member States (Article 228 para. 2). Thus it leaves the ultimate decision to international law itself. Under international law, a self-executing clause is to be applied by any court which may have jurisdiction within the legal order of the contracting party. Since the Community is the contracting party and since the national courts of

40. See for instance Art. 173 para. 2 of the EEC Treaty or para. 42 II *Verwaltungsgerichtsordnung* (German statute on procedure before administrative courts).
41. Bleckmann, *loc. cit.*, note 10a, at p. 98.

Member States which apply Community Law form part of its legal order, international law does not distinguish between direct applicability before the Court of Justice and before national courts. This attitude is, as has been shown, respected by both Community Law and national law of Member States.

The Court of Justice has, correctly, been interpreted as applying the standards developed under Community Law in order to ascertain whether a certain provision contained in an international treaty is directly applicable or not.[42] The standards of international law and of Community Law may happen to coincide. But the Court's approach could generally not be accepted: the standards of international law have to be applied for the reasons outlined above.

Finally there is a procedural matter which should be mentioned in this context. Under Article 177 of the EEC Treaty the Court of Justice can only be asked "to give preliminary rulings concerning:... (b) the validity and interpretation of acts of the institutions of the Community". The wording of this provision led to the assumption that international law may only be applied in so far as it relates to the validity and/or interpretation of acts of the institutions of the Community and that it may not itself be the object of questions submitted by a national court.[43] In a very pragmatic, but persuasive, manner the Court has pointed out that the acceptance of an international treaty amounts to an "act performed by an institution of the Community" and that such treaties may be the object of a request for interpretation under Article 177 para. 1b.[44]

D. THE ORDER OF PRIORITY BETWEEN INTERNATIONAL LAW AND COMMUNITY LAW

If a rule of general international law or of international treaty law is directly applicable within Community Law, it may happen that a rule of Community Law contains a contrary stipulation. Which rule is to be followed? Does there exist any order of priority between international law and Community Law?

From the point of view of international law, international law prevails

42. Millarg, *loc. cit.*, note 39.

43. Daig, in von der Groeben/von Boeckh/Thiesing, *Kommentar zum EWG-Vertrag*, 2nd ed., 1974, Art. 177, vol. 2, at p. 266.

44. Case 181/73, *Haegemann II, loc. cit.*, note 12, at 460; confirmed in Case 87/75, *Bresciani, loc. cit.*, note 6. For the traditional position see Pleadings of the Advocate General in the *Haegeman II* Case, *id.*, at 473.

over any other legal order. But it would be unrealistic to assume that the other legal orders which usually dispose of far more effective sanctions would automatically accept such demand for primacy. An *a priori* assumption of primacy of international law would be premature. The reaction of the "other legal order", in this context of Community Law, has to be examined.

In respect of international treaty law one would be inclined to apply Article 228 para. 2 once more. On the one hand, it could be argued that this provision stipulates the applicability of international treaties by all the institutions of the Community and by the Member States without deciding upon the question of priority.[45] On the other hand, the wording would also cover an interpretation to the effect that the binding character of agreements implies a rank superior to any legislative acts.

The latter interpretation would be in conformity with the jurisprudence of the Court of Justice. On several occasions the Court has had to examine the validity of legal acts of the Community which were alleged to be contrary to earlier treaty commitments of the Community. The Court made it clear that such acts would be declared invalid if a violation of international law could be established. But, for varying reasons, the Court did not yet have an opportunity to effectuate its intention. In the *International Fruit* case, Article XI of the GATT was held to be not directly applicable.[46] So was Article II of the GATT in the *Schlüter* case.[47] In the *Haegeman II* case enactments of the Council and of the Commission were held to be in conformity with the Association Agreement with Greece.[48] In the *Nederlandse Spoorwegen* case also the Community's acts were regarded to be in conformity with tariff regulations to which the Community had given its consent within the framework of the GATT.[49]

The Court's interpretation should be accepted, not because it is based on particularly convincing reasoning, but because it is about to develop into customary law.[50] Since the issue appears to be more or less settled, the reservations as regards the reasoning shall be summarised in a few points:

(1) The *lex posterior* rule may not make much sense on first sight, but it

45. Bülow, "Die Anwendung des Gemeinschaftsrechts im Verhältnis zu Drittländern", in *Einführung in die Rechtsfragen der Europäischen Integration,* (2nd. ed., 1972), 52-61, at 55.

46. Joined Cases 21-24/72, *loc. cit.,* note 18, at 1229.

47. Case 9/73, *loc. cit.,* note 12, at 1157.

48. Case 181/73, *loc. cit.,* note 12, at 460 *et seq.*

49. Case 38/75, *loc. cit.,* note 20, at 1450.

50. Bleckmann, *loc. cit.,* note 10a, at p. 96.

does if, as happens quite often, the binding character of treaty commitments cannot be clearly established because of violations of the treaty by the other party. The enactment of a statute might then help to clarify the situation, but only if its validity cannot be challenged by reference to the treaty.

(2) If the *lex posterior* rule is abrogated, the Council of Ministers would by giving its consent to an international agreement bind itself for the future, no matter by which political forces it will then be dominated and no matter what its rules of procedure (abandonment of the Luxembourg unanimity rule?) will be like.

(3) Third states would be in a stronger position than the Community, because most of them (if not all of them) would be able to enact legislation contrary to their treaty commitments.

(4) Finally, an argument which was originally advanced by the Advocate General in the *International Fruit* case [51] should be mentioned. The Community could not on the one hand demand primacy for its law in relation to the national law of Member States and on the other hand refuse primacy to international law. If this were so, no federal state which stipulates the primacy of federal law over state law would be entitled to apply the *lex posterior* rule *vis-à-vis* international treaty law.[52]

The only valid reason appears to consist in the Community's attitude of openness towards third countries. This attitude is reflected by some provisions of the EEC Treaty, such as Article 234, and especially by the way in which the Community has conducted its external relations. This notion would sum up the author's reasoning in an earlier article where the primacy of general international law as against secondary Community Law was asserted.[53] As regards general international law there is not even a provision of the kind of Article 228 para. 2 which might be interpreted as regulating the order of priority. But the Court would certainly not want to attribute a lower status to general international law than to international treaty law. Furthermore, at least one of the reservations outlined above would not apply to general international law. By incurring treaty obligations the institutions of the Community could, as was pointed out, bind themselves in an excessive manner for the future. Such a danger would not exist in the case of general international law. General international law is binding upon the Community anyway, and its contents is hardly open to the Community's influence. It may be

51. Joined Cases 21-24/72, *loc. cit.*, note 18, at 1235.

52. Meessen, *loc. cit.*, note 2, at 34; Bleckmann, *loc. cit.*, note 10a, at p. 94; but see Schermers, *loc. cit.*, note 37, at 84.

53. Meessen, *loc. cit.*, note 2, at 32-33; similarly, Petersmann, *loc. cit.*, note 11, at 273-274.

added that the European Treaties forming the basis of Community Law would prevail over both general international law and international treaty law.[54] Finally, the rank of international commitments of Member States which are binding upon the Community by virtue of a rule of Community Law (Article 119 of the EEC Treaty, general principle of Community Law, *etc.*) is determined by such a rule. The order of priority among the various sources of Community Law should, however, not be discussed here.

The rank of international law within Community Law could then be established as follows. The first priority is attributed to the law of the EEC Treaty itself which would, of course, be interpreted in such a way as not to violate any rules of international law *vis-à-vis* third states. Primary Community Law is followed by the rules of international law binding upon the Community. These rules are regarded as prevailing over rules of secondary Community Law such as regulations of the Council, *etc.*, no matter whether they have been enacted before or after the entry into force of the rule of international law. This order of priority may lead to a peculiar situation in those Member States which, as for instance Germany, apply the *lex posterior* rule to international treaty law. An international treaty binding upon the Community would, because of the primacy of Community Law, be regarded as prevailing over later statutory law, whereas provisions of a treaty binding on such Member States only could be abrogated internally.

E. TECHNIQUES OF HARMONISATION

Some readers might miss a reference to the traditional concepts of the relation between international law and national law, such as the monist and the dualist doctrines. To take any of these theories as a starting point for the discussion would have amounted to a *petitio principii.* But it may now be examined whether the individual conclusions that were reached can be expressed in terms of monism or dualism.

The monist doctrine would correspond to the notions of complete performance of international law and to the Community's attitude of openness as outlined above. But it would neither cover the notion of intended parallelism between Community Law and treaties concluded by Member States, nor be able to explain the possible divergence of Community Law and international law in the case of treaties which enter into force on the plane of international law, but not, for instance because

54. Meessen, *id.* at 34; Bleckmann, *loc. cit.*, note 10a, at p. 96.

of the violation of procedural rules, on the plane of Community Law. The dualist concept would in its extreme version certainly be at odds with the multitude of interactions between the two legal orders. Combining aspects of both theories would be more realistic, but it would hardly promote understanding of the legal situation.

The theory of harmonisation,[55] however, might express both the necessity of thinking in terms of two different legal orders and the need to arrive at concordant practical solutions. Instead of proposing a more specific overall theory of the application of international law within Community Law, we would, therefore, prefer to regard our own contribution as a discussion of some "techniques of harmonisation".

55. O'Connell, *loc. cit.*, note 17, at p. 43 *et seq.*

CASE LAW

A. COURT OF JUSTICE

SURVEY OF CURRENT CASE LAW OF THE COURT OF JUSTICE

In 1975, the European Court of Justice issued 78 rulings, 11 of which concerned direct actions, 45 were cases sent for preliminary rulings by national courts and 22 concerned disputes between officials and the European institutions. These figures, as well as those of the new cases which faced the Court in 1975, show a considerable increase in the overall number of cases in comparison with previous years. in addition, a strong increase in the number of cases referred for preliminary rulings is discernible, while there is a clear drop in the number of appeals from officials.

This survey includes all decisions rendered by the Court of Justice in 1975, except decisions in disputes between Community institutions and their officials and rulings of the President of the Court by way of summary procedure.

For the classification of subject-matter, see the previous survey in 12 *Common Market Law Review* 1975, page 101 *et seq.*

IV. *JUDICIAL REMEDIES*

(51) Case Nos. 72/74, *Union Syndicale—Service public européen, Brussels, and others* v. *Council.* Judgment of March 18, 1975, (1975) E.C.R., 401.
See also Cases Nos. 175/73 and 18/74, 12 C.M.L.Rev. 1975, 104 no. (12).

The trade unions of EC officials applied by means of Article 173 para. 2, for nullification of a Decision of the Council regarding official's salaries.

The Court held that the application was inadmissible, because in the system of forms of actions laid down by the Treaty, natural or legal persons to whom Article 173 refers and to whom the disputed measure is not addressed, may only claim that that measure is of individual concern to them, if it affects them by reason of certain attributes which are differentiated from all other persons and by virtue of these factors distinguishes them individually just as in the case of the person addressed. In this context, an organisation founded for the protection of the collective interests of a category of persons cannot be considered as being directly and individually concerned by a measure affecting the general interest of that category.

Furthermore, the court indicated to the trade unions the way of participating in the proceedings foreseen in Article 37 of the Statute of the Court, *i.e.* by way of intervention.

(52) Case No. 100/74, *Société C.A.M. SA* v. *Commission.* Judgment of November 18, 1975, (1975) E.C.R., 1393.

The contested Community measure in this case was a regulation, and the Court found it necessary to consider the true scope and character of the measure in relation to the requirements of Article 173 relating to the admissibility of applications for annulment. The Court held that the Commission regulation, by denying to a class of traders the benefit of an increase in the amount of refunds for specific exports which had been awarded by a previous Council regulation, and which had been granted to those whose applications for advance fixing had been made at a later date, did directly concern the said traders. Moreover, the contested measure, even though it was one of a number of provisions having a legislative function, individually concerned the traders in that it affected their legal position because of a factual situation which differentiated them from all other persons and distinguished them individually just as in the case of the person addressed. The Court therefore declared that the application was admissible.

However, on the substance of the case, the applicants failed in their application. The Court held that even if they were able to rely upon vested rights or legitimate expectation in the continuation of increases in the amount of refund, as laid down by the earlier Council regulation, they could not take advantage of those rights as regarded that part of the refund which could not have been foreseen at the time of the advance fixing of the amount.

(53) Case No. 99/74, *Société des Grands Moulins des Antilles* v. *Commission.* Judgment of November 26, 1975, (1975) E.C.R., 1531.

The applicant company, established in the French Overseas Departments, requested compensation under Article 215 (2) for the damage occasioned to it by the implied refusal of the Commission to pay the export refunds due to it under Regulation No. 120/67 and implementing regulations, concerning the common organisation of the market in cereals.

In its judgment, the Court first re-stated the principle that the action for damages provided for in Articles 178 and 215 of the Treaty was included as an independent form of action with a particular purpose to fulfil within the system of legal remedies, and subject to conditions on its use arising out of its specific aim. But in this instance the Community measures in question left no doubt that the payment or refusal of payment of export refunds were a matter for the national authorities, and the refusal by the Community to pay a debt which may be owed by a Member State under Community Law is not a matter involving the non-contractual liability of the Community. Moreover, for an action involving non-contractual responsibility to lie, it is necessary that an injury arising from the act or omission of the Community be capable of adversely affecting the applicant. Since the question of the legality of the refusal of payment was for the national courts to decide, the Court declared the application inadmissible.

See also *infra,* nos. (69), (72) and (81).

V. *CUSTOMS UNION*

(54) Case No. 12/74, *Commission* v. *Federal Republic of Western Germany.* Judgment of February 20, 1975, (1975) E.C.R., 181.

The German law on wine products *("Weingesetz")* provides *inter alia* that the appellation "Sekt" may only describe a *home-produced* sparkling wine which satisfies certain conditions or a sparkling wine produced in a country where German is an official language through out the whole country. Wine produced elswhere may be described as "Sekt" on the condition that it is produced from a minimum proportion of home-grown grapes. The use of the appellation *"Prädikatssekt"* is tied to similar conditions.

These rules were considered by the Commission as a measure which has an effect equivalent to a quantitative restriction. The German government did not agree with this view, and the Commission started before the Court an action on the basis of Article 169 of the EEC Treaty.

The Court held *inter alia* that, as regards indications of origin, the geographical origin of a product must confer on it a specific quality and specific characteristics of such a nature as to distinguish it from all other products. An area of origin which is defined on the basis of the extent of national territory or a linguistic criterion cannot constitute an area within this meaning capable of justifying an indication of origin. As the indication of origin in this case was not justified, the rules of the *Weingesetz* are to be considered as a measure having an equivalent effect to quantitative restrictions.

Article 36 of the EEC Treaty does not provide a justification for this measure of equivalent effect, because this provision could only derogate from Articles 30 to 34 to the extent to which such derogation proves to be necessary in order to ensure that the producer and consumers are protected against fraudulent commercial practices.

The Court concluded that the Federal Republic had failed to fulfil its obligations under the EEC Treaty.

(55) Case No. 63/74, *SpA W. Cadsky, Bolzano* v. *Instituto Nazionale per il Commercio Estero, Rome.* Preliminary ruling of February 26, 1975 on request of the *Tribunale di Bolzano;* (1975) E.C.R., 281.

The applicant, an exporter of Italian vegetables, was required to pay to the ICE a charge relating to quality control of the exported products and consequently to the affixing of national export stamp.

In the applicant's view, the charge was prohibited by Article 16 of the Treaty, so he claimed repayment of the sum paid. The *Tribunale di Bolzano* stayed the proceedings and referred a series of questions under Article 177 EEC.

The Court ruled *inter alia* that any pecuniary charge, whatever its designation and mode of application, which is imposed unilaterally on domestic goods by reason of the fact that they cross a frontier and which is not a customs duty in a strict sense, constitutes a charge having equivalent effect, even if it is not imposed for the benefit of the State. The Court, however, held it not impossible that in certain circumstances a specific service actually rendered may form the consideration for a possible proportional payment for the service in question, but this may only apply in specific cases which cannot lead to the circumvention of the provisions of the Treaty.

(56) Case No. 92/74 *Melkproduktenmaatschappij G. van den Bergh B.V., Nijmegen* v. *Produktschap voor Zuivel, Rijswijk.* Preliminary ruling of May 15, 1975 on request of the *College van Beroep voor het Bedrijfsleven;* (1975) E.C.R., 599.

The applicant claimed the granting of the aid for skimmed milk and skimmed milk powder for use as feed, as laid down in Regulation No. 986/68. The *Produktschap* refused to pay, for the reason that the fat content of the products exceeded the maximum laid down in the Regulation. The applicant considered that a certain amount of phosphatides has to be deducted from the fat content in order to obtain the pure fat content as referred to in the Regulation.

On this question the Court ruled, that the fat content referred to in the Regulation must be interpreted as including fat-like substances such as phosphatides, insofar as those substances are not extracted when applying the methods of analysis in current use.

(57) Case No. 91/74, *Hamburger Import-Kompanie GmbH, Winsen/Luhe* v. *Hauptzollamt Hamburg-Ericus.* Preliminary ruling of June 10, 1975 on request of the *Bundesfinanzhof;* (1975) E.C.R., 643.

Imports of concentrated orange juice are free of levies if their value per 100 kg is higher than D.M. 109,80. The applicant had bought a large quantity of concentrated orange juice. According to his contract, the value per 100 kg of this quantity was 109,89 D.M. It appeared, however, to the customs authorities that the content of the bottles was more than contracted, with the consequence that the price per 100 kg was 105,73 D.M., so they charged the applicant a levy. The applicant appealed and the *Bundesfinanzhof* stayed the proceedings in order to refer a question to the Court of Justice.

The Court ruled, *inter alia,* that when an excess of total weight of the goods is the foreseeable consequence of the obligation to guarantee the agreed minimum weight per unit, it cannot be considered as being the supply of an additional quantity "without further charge" by the vendor, in accordance with trade usage, but must be taken into consideration for the determination of the value of the goods for customs purposes.

(58) Case No. 94/74, *SpA Industria Gomma Articola Vari, Abbiategrasso* v. *Ente Nazionale per la Cellulosa e per la Carta, Rome.* Preliminary ruling of June 18, 1975 on request of the *Pretore di Trieste,* (1975) E.C.R., 699.

ENCC charged IGAV a levy on imports of paper and cardboard. The levy must, according to Italian legislation, be paid by the national producers and importers of paper and cellulose and is intended for the financing of research activity for the benefit of national undertakings which produce cellulose and paper. IGAV contested the compatibility of the levy with Article 13 para 2 of the EEC Treaty. The *Pretore* stayed the proceedings and referred a series of questions on this matter to the Court.

The Court ruled *inter alia,* referring to its judgment of June 19, 1973 (Case No. 77/72, (1973) E.C.R. 611), that the fact that a duty is levied by an independent institution governed by public law rather than levied by the State itself, and is used by that institution for purpose intended by the relevant legislation, involves no difference with regard to the possible definition of that fiscal charge as a charge having an effect equivalent to customs duties. Furthermore, the Court ruled that Article 13 para 2 of the Treaty is to be considered as directly applicable from the end of the transitional period *i.e.* from January 1, 1970, and not from July 1, 1968, being the date of realisation of the total abolition of customs duties and quantitative restrictions.

Finally, the Court ruled that the activities of an institution of a public nature, even if autonomous, do not fall under Articles 85 and 86, but under special provisions, *i.e.* Articles 90, 92 to 94, 101 and 102, and 37 of the EEC Treaty, at least to the extent that its interventions take place in the public interest and are devoid of a commercial character.

(59) Case No. 4/75, *REWE Zendtralfinanz* v. *Landwirtschaftskammer.* Preliminary ruling of July 8, 1975 (1975) E.C.R., 843; on request of the *Verwaltungsgericht,* Köln;

In October 1973 the firm REWE Zendtralfinanz had refused to submit a consignment of apples coming from France to a health inspection at the German frontier, with the result that permission to import the fruit was refused. The *Verwaltungsgericht* of Köln referred a number of questions to the Court concerning the compatibility of such inspections with Article 30 and concerning the interpretation of Article 36.

The Court ruled that health inspections of vegetable produce imported from another Member State do amount to measures of an effect equivalent to quantitative restrictions prohibited by Article 30, but subject to the derogations laid down in Article 36. The Court further ruled that any necessary additional or stricter provisions within the meaning of Article 11 of the Council Directive No. 69/466 concerning the control of the pest known as St. Jose Scale, would allow the Member States to carry out health inspections of imported produce, provided that effective measures were also taken to prevent the marketing of contaminated national produce and provided that there is reason to believe that in the absence of such control there exists the risk that the harmful organism may spread.

(60) Case No. 21/75, *Firma I. Schroeder KG* v. *Oberstadtdirektor der Stadt Köln*. Preliminary ruling of July 9, 1975, on request of the *Verwaltungsgericht* Köln; (1975) E.C.R., 905.

In this case the Court was asked to give a preliminary ruling as to the compatibility of charges imposed in connection with the health inspection of meat imported into the Federal Republic from a non-member country with the provisions of Regulation No. 121/67 on the common organisation of the market in pigmeat, and Regulation No. 805/68 on the common organisation of the markets in beef and veal, prohibiting taxes of an effect equivalent to customs duties

The Court ruled that the notion of a charge of an effect equivalent to customs duties covered any charge payable on import or by reason of import which, affecting specifically a product imported to the exclusion of a similar Community product, has the same restrictive effect on the free movement of goods as a customs duty. Whatever their amount, therefore, duties imposed in connection with the health inspection of products imported from third countries, and which are determined in accordance with independent criteria which are not comparable with those used to fix charges which may be imposed on similar Community products, should be considered as charges having an effect equivalent to customs duties.

(61) Case No. 28/75, *Baupla GmbH* v. *Oberfinanzdirektion Köln*. Preliminary ruling of September 25, 1975, on request of the *Bundesfinanzhof;* (1975) E.C.R., 989.

In a case concerning the tariff classification of pre-fabricated external wall sections, the Court was asked for a preliminary ruling on the classification of composite products.

The Court ruled that where it appears that a composite product should be classified under two or more headings of the Common Customs Tariff, each relating to materials used in the composite product, no such heading may be considered as more specific than the others on the ground that it gives a more exact or more complete description of the product concerned. Rules 3(b) or 3(c) for the interpretation of the Common Customs Tariff must be applied when classifying such a product.

(62) Case No. 35/75, *Matisa-Maschinen GmbH* v. *Hauptzollamt Berlin-Packhof*. Preliminary ruling of October 23, 1975, on request of the *Finanzgericht*, Berlin; (1975) E.C.R., 1205.

Ruling on the interpretation of the phrase "mechanically propelled" in heading 86.04 of the Common Customs Tariff, the Court held that in the absence of relevant Community provisions on the subject, the explanatory notes and classification opinions provided for by the Convention on Nomenclature for the Classification of Goods in Customs Tariffs are an authoritative source for the purposes of the interpretation of the headings of the Tariff.

(63) Case No. 37/75, *Bagusat KG* v. *Hauptzollamt Berlin-Packhof.* Preliminary ruling of November 11, 1975, on request of the *Finanzgericht,* Berlin; (1975) E.C.R., 1339.

The Court was asked to rule on the tariff classification of cherries put in a mixture of water and ethyll alcohol, and on the validity of Regulation No. 1709/74 of the Commission to the extent that it classifies certain products under subheading 20.06B1 of the Common Customs Tariff.

According to the Court, the Council Regulation No. 97/69 on the nomenclature of the Common Customs Tariff conferred on the Commission, in cooperation with the customs experts of the Member States, a wide discretion as to the choice between two or more headings which come into consideration with regard to the classification of specific goods, with the reservation that the provisions adopted by the Commission do not amend the Tariff. The applicant in the present case had failed to show that the Commission had exceeded the limits of this discretion. The Court therefore declared that Regulation 1709/74 was valid, and that the cherries should in consequence be classified under subheading 20.06B1 of the Common Customs Tariff.

(64) Case No. 38/75, *Douaneagent der NV Nederlandse Spoorwegen* v. *Inspecteur der invoerrechten en accijnzen.* Preliminary ruling of November 19, 1975, on request of the *Tariefcommissie,* The Hague; (1975) E.C.R., 1439.

On a series of questions relating to the classification of a photocopying machine, the Court upheld the validity of an Additional Note to a chapter of the Common Customs Tariff, decided upon by the Council. With effect from July 1, 1968, the Common Customs Tariff has replaced the national customs tariffs, and the Community authorities alone are competent to interpret it and to determine the legal effect of the headings it comprises. With regard to the conflicting classification of the product under the provisions of GATT, the Court held that insofar as the fulfilment of commitments arising under that Agreement are concerned, the Community has replaced the Member States, and the effect in law of these commitments must be determined by reference to the relevant provisions in the Community legal system, and not to those which gave them their previous force under the national legal systems. The same was true in relation to the Conventions of December, 1950, on the Nomenclature for the Classification of Goods in Customs Tariffs and establishing a Customs Cooperation Council.

(65) Case No. 53/75, *Belgian State* v. *J. N. Vandertaelen and D. L. Maes.* Preliminary ruling of December 10, 1975 on request of the Belgian *Cour de Cassation;* (1975) E.C.R., 1647.

In a case concerning the tariff classification of ice-cream, the Court was asked to clarify the term "ice-cream (not including ice-cream powder) and other ices" in terms of the Common Customs Tariff. The Court ruled *inter alia* that for the purposes of the relevant subheadings of the Tariff, the concept of ice-cream refers to substances having as their essential characteristic that they melt at a temperature of approximately 0° C, and that this concept cannot be applied to products, such as that in the instant case, which have a milk-fat content in excess of 15 per cent.

See also *infra,* nos. (68), (76), (77), (79) and (80).

VI. *AGRICULTURE*

(66) Case No. 55/74, *Firma Robert Unkel, Würzburg-Heidingsfeld* v. *Hauptzollamt Hamburg-Jonas.* Preliminary ruling of January 22, 1975 on request of the *Finanzgericht,* Hamburg; (1975) E.C.R., 9.

On a series of questions relating to the granting of export refunds for pigmeat the Court ruled *inter alia* that a control copy delivered at the moment of export of agriculture products and submitted to the department competent to pay export refunds, shows sufficiently the exporter's intention to claim a refund and constitutes therefore an application for the refund within the meaning of Article 15 of Regulation No. 121/67.

Furthermore, the Court ruled that the time limit of six months of Regulation No. 121/67 for lodging the application for a refund is also a time limit for lodging all the other documents enabling the competent authority to verify whether the conditions to which the grant of the refund is subject are fulfilled.

(67) Case No. 31/74, *Publico Ministero italiano* v. *Filippo Galli.* Preliminary ruling of January 23, 1975 on request of the *Pretore di Roma*; (1975) E.C.R., 47.

In this case concerning the compatibility of national conjunctural measures and a common organisation of the market for agricultural products, the Court ruled *inter alia* that although the incompatibility of national measures may be particularly apparent in the case of market organisations comprising a Community price formation system, it is nonetheless true that the very existence of a common market organisation in the sense of Article 40 para 2 sub c has the effect of precluding Member States from adopting in the sector in question unilateral measures capable of impeding intra-Community trade.

(68) Case No. 51/74, *Commanditaire Vennootschap P. J. van der Hulst's Zonen, Hillegom* v. *Produktschap voor Siergewassen, The Hague.* Preliminary ruling of January 23, 1975 on request of the *College van Beroep voor het Bedrijfsleven;* (1975) E.C.R., 79.

On a series of questions concerning a levy imposed by the Dutch authorities on the trade in and export of bulbs, the Court ruled *inter alia* that an internal levy may have equivalent effect to a customs duty on export if it falls more heavily on export sales than on sales inside the country, or where the levy is intended to find activities tending to make the home market more profitable than exports or in any other way to place the product intended for the home market at an advantage compared with the product intended for export.

Furthermore, the Court ruled that an national intervention measure is incompatible with Regulation No. 234/68 insofar as products which do not meet Community quality standards qualify for the intervention.

(69) Case No. 169/73, *Compagnie continental France, Paris* v. *Council.* Judgment of February 4, 1975; (1975) E.C.R., 117.

The applicant, a big exporter of French cereals, had concluded several contracts for the export of barley to the United Kingdom. He did so in reliance on the Resolution of the Council of July 20, 1972 (O.J. 1972, C 86/16) which laid down that such exports would give a right to a compensatory amount. Deliveries were to take place between February and June 1973.

By Regulation No. 229/73 (O.J. 1973 L 27/25) of January 31, 1973 the Council reduced the compensatory amounts, pursuant to Article 55 para. 6 of the Act of Accession, without safeguarding the position of exporters who had already entered into contracts. The applicant claimed compensation under Article 215 (2) for the damage allegedly suffered by him.

The Court held that the omission to make the Resolution subject to the reservation of Article 55 para 6 of the Act of Accession was such as to make the Council liable because it has neglected its task of informing. On the other hand, the Court found that the applicant, being a prudent exporter, was fully informed of the conditions of the market. When the applicant entered into the contracts, the world market prices were already rising and in the view of the Court he should have foreseen as a result of this the lowering of the compensatory amounts.

See also *supra* no. (53), *infra* nos. (72) and (81).

(70) Case No. 64/74, *Firma Adolf Reich, Stuttgart,* v. *Hauptzollamt Lindau.* Preliminary ruling of February 20, 1975 on request of the *Finanzgericht Rheinland-Pfalz;*(1975) E.C.R. 261.

The Firma Reich imported a quantity of fodder maize from France into the Federal Republic on October 3, 1963. It submitted two import licences, which laid down that the firm would be charged a fixed import levy for import during the month of September, and that for imports during the following months the daily rate of levy would apply. The *Hauptzollamt* charged Reich the daily rate of levy for the imports of October 3, 1963. Reich objected, stating that the fact that the imports were delayed was not due to his fault.

On this matter, the Court ruled *inter alia* that a levy fixed in advance under Article 2 paras 1 and 2 of Regulation No. 31/63 continues to apply to such importation, even if it is not effected during the month indicated in the application for the licence, provided the delay is not due to the conduct of the importer or to circumstances that can normally be foreseen, but to *force majeure.*

(71) Case No. 78/74, *Firma Deuka Deutsche Kraftfutter GmbH B. J. Stolp, Düsseldorf* v. *Einfuhr- und Vorratsstelle für Getreide und Futtermittel, Frankfurt/Main.* Preliminary ruling of March 18, 1975 on request of the *Hessischer Verwaltungsgerichtshof;* (1975) E.C.R., 421.

In the main action before the *Verwaltungsgerichtshof* the applicant claimed payment of the high rate denaturing premium for common wheat, despite the fact that the Commission had by Regulation No. 849/70 discontinued the high rate premium in view of possible disturbances of the market for common wheat. The *Verwaltungsgerichtshof* stayed the proceedings and referred a series of questions to the Court of Justice relating to the validity of Regulation No. 849/70 and the effect of the abovementioned discontinuance on pending contracts.

The Court found no ground to declare the Regulation invalid and furthermore ruled, *inter alia,* that it cannot be considered abnormal for a denaturing undertaking to arrange its projects in the light of the entire crop year, and that accordingly, for the sake of legal certainty, the Regulation No. 849/70 has to be applied in such a way that there might still benefit from the system those quantities of goods in respect of which it was established that they were purchased before the coming into force of Regulation No. 849/70, provided the request for the denaturing premium was made to the intervention agency, within the prescribed time-limits.

(72) Case No. 74/74, *Comptoir national technique agricole SA, Paris,* v. *Commission.* Judgment of May 14, 1975, (1975) E.C.R., 533.

In order to avoid disturbances of the market caused by monetary difficulties, the Commission had extended the application of the system of compensatory amounts as laid down in Regulation No. 974/71 to colza seed. This system was also applicable in France. On January 22, 1972 the Commission rescinded the compensatory amounts applicable to the oils and fats sector with effect from February 1, 1972, because it considered that the application of the system was no longer essential in order to avoid disturbances of the market. The applicant considered that the abolition caused serious damage to its interests in disturbing the implementation of current delivery contracts.

The Court ruled *inter alia* that it had not been established that the Commission exceeded the limits of its wide discretionary power when it concluded that the situation on the market in colza and rape seeds was such that the application of compensatory amounts for those products was no longer necessary.

On the other hand, it considered that the application of compensatory amounts avoids the exchange risk, so that a trader, even a prudent one, might be induced to omit to cover himself against such risk. In these circumstances a trader may legitimately expect that no unforeseeable alteration will occur which could have the effect of causing him inevitable loss by reexposing him to the exchange risk.

In the absence of an overriding matter of public interest, the Commission had violated a superior rule of law, thus rendering the Community liable, by failing to include in Regulation No. 189/72, which rescinded the compensatory amounts, transitional measures for the protection of the confidence which a trader might legitimately have had in the Community rules.

(73) Case No. 2/75, *Firma C. Mackprang jun. oHG, Hamburg* v. *Einfuhr- und Vorratsstelle für Getreide und Futtermittel, Frankfurt/Main.* Preliminary ruling of May 27, 1975 on request of the *Bundesgerichtshof*; (1975) E.C.R., 607.

In 1969, after the fall in the exchange rate of the French franc, it was more profitable to offer cereals to intervention agencies of the Federal Republic than to those of France. In order to limit this "intervention trade", the Commission authorised the Federal Republic to limit its intervention in respect of common wheat and barley to cereals harvested in the Federal Republic.

On a question relating to the validity of the Decision authorising the Federal Republic to limit its intervention purchases, the Court ruled that the Decision was also valid in respect of cereals harvested in other Member States of the Community which were already in transit to the Federal Republic and in respect of which an offer in proper form was not made to the intervention agency until after the date of the limitation of intervention.

(74) Case No. 93/74, *Pastificio Triestino, Trieste* v. *Amministrazione delle Finanze.* Preliminary ruling of June 17, 1975 on request of the *Pretore di Trieste*; (1975) E.C.R., 661.

The applicant, an exporter of macaroni, spaghetti and the like *("pasta")*, was charged a compensatory amount for exports at a time when no compensatory amount was levied for the basis product of *pasta, i.e.* durum wheat.

On a series of questions referred to it by the *Pretore di Trieste*, the Court ruled *inter alia* that the compensatory amounts are to be considered as consisting solely of a variable component (*cf.* Case No. 34/74, *supra* no. (25)), and that, when the levy on the basic agricultural products is zero, no compensatory amount may be charged on exports of derived products.

(75) Case No. 5/75, *Firma Deuka Deutsche Kraftfutter GmbH B. J. Stolp, Düsseldorf* v. *Einfuhr- und Vorratsstelle für Getreide und Futtermittel.* Preliminary ruling of June 25, 1975 on request of the *Verwaltungsgericht*, Frankfurt; (1975) E.C.R., 759.

This case is largely identical with Case No. 78/74 (*supra* no. 71). The Court ruled *inter alia* that in exercising its power to adjust the denaturing premium for common wheat during the course of the marketing year, the Commission enjoys a wide discretion.

When examining the lawfulness of the exercise of such freedom, the courts cannot substitute their own evaluation of the matter for that of the competent authority, but must restrict themselves to examining whether the evaluation of the competent authority contains a patent error or constitutes a misuse of power. It concluded that there were no grounds for invalidity of the Regulations of the Commission reducing the said premium.

Furthermore, the Court ruled that in the interest of legal certainty, it is right to apply for the computation of the amount of the denaturing premium, the provisions in force at the time the application was lodged, even if the denaturing is not done until a subsequent date, albeit within the period prescribed by the intervention agency.

(76) Joined Cases Nos. 89/74, 18 and 19/75, *Procureur Général près de la Cour d'appel de Bordeaux* v. *R. J. Arnaud and others.* Preliminary ruling of September 30, 1975, on request of the *Cour d'appel,* Bordeaux; (1975) E.C.R., 1023.

In three cases involving criminal proceedings for the adulteration of wine, the Court was asked for a ruling on the compatibility of Article 8 of the *Code du vin français* and of Article 2 of the *Decret* of January 22, 1974, with Regulation No. 816/70, laying down additional provisions for the common organisation of the market in wine, No. 817/70, laying down specific provisions relating to quality wines produced in specific regions, and No. 1539/71, determining Community methods for the analysis of wines.

The Court ruled that the Community regulations should be interpreted as meaning that a Member State may, under present Community Law, rely, as a normal supervisory measure, on a legal presumption of excess addition of alcohol, based on the ration of alcohol to dry extract determined by the 100° method, provided that this presumption is rebuttable and that it is not applied in such a way as to place wines from other Member States at a disadvantage, whether *de jure* or *de facto,* thus constituting a measure of an effect equivalent to quantitative restrictions.

See nos. (77) and (80) *infra.*

(77) Joined Cases Nos. 10-14/75, *Procureur Général près de la Cour d'Appel d'Aix-en-Provence* v. *P. L. Lahaille and others.* Preliminary ruling of September 30, 1975, on request of the *Cour d'Appel,* Aix-en-Provence; (1975) E.C.R., 1053.

In a series of actions concerning wine frauds, the Court was asked for a preliminary ruling as to whether table wines moving within the Community must not only meet the standards laid down in Regulation No. 817/70, laying down additional provisions for the common organisation of the market in wine, but also conform to national rules and practice. While repeating what it had said in Joined Cases Nos. 89/74, 18 and 19/75, (*supra* no. 76) regarding the presumption of an excess addition of alcohol, the Court held further that table wines need not conform to analytical standards other than those provided for in the Regulation, and that a Member State may not demand an accompanying certificate in respect of wines from another Member State, other than that for which provision is made in Community regulations.

(78) Case No. 23/75, *Rey Soda* v. *Cassa Conguaglio Zucchero.* Preliminary ruling of October 30, 1975, on request of the *Pretore d'Abbiategrasso;* (1975) E.C.R., 1279.

Article 6 of Commission Regulation No. 834/74 imposed the obligation on Member States to adopt measures to avoid disturbances on the market for sugar as a result of the price increases for the 1974-1975 marketing year. Relying on the Italian decree-law adopted in pursuance of that regulation, the *Cassa Conguaglio Zucchero* imposed a tax on sugar stocks held by Italian industrial users of sugar. In the context of the action brought by one of the latter against the Italian authorities, the Court was asked for a ruling on the interpretation of Article 6 of Regulation No. 834/74, and on its conformity with Community Law. Secondly, it was asked to rule on the question whether Article 6 had been illegally adopted inasmuch as such a charge must be expressly authorised by the Council.

The Court held in general terms that where competences are delegated by the Council to the Commission under Article 155, it follows from the context of the Treaty in which the delegation must be placed and also from practical requirements that the concept of implementation must be given a wide interpretation. Where, as in Article 37 (2) of Council Regulation No. 1009/67, the basic regulation relating to the sugar sector, the Council confers wide powers of discretion and action on the Commission, to be exercised according to the procedure of the Management Committee, the limits of these powers must be judged with regard to the basic general objectives of the organisation of the market, and less in terms of the literal meaning of the enabling provisions. Article 37 (2) of the basic regulation could not, however, be interpreted so as to enable the Commission to impose upon the Member States the obligation to draw up, under the guise of implementation measures, essential basic rules which would not be subject to the control of the Council. Under the system established by Article 37 (2) the Commission itself must in such a case determine in a precise manner the essential basic rules. This it had failed to do in relation to Article 6 of its Regulation No. 834/74, and the article was therefore declared invalid.

On a final question relating to the validity of a Member State legislative measure taken for the purposes of implementing an invalid measure of Community Law, the Court ruled that it is first of all for the national authorities to draw the consequences in their legal system of a decision of invalidity made under the Article 177 procedure.

(79) Case No. 30/75, *SpA Unil-It* v. *Amministrazione Finanzaria dello Stato.* Preliminary ruling of November 18, 1975, on request of the *Corte Suprema di Cassazione;*(1975) E.C.R., 1419.

In this case the Court was asked for an interpretation of the Commission Decision of July 17, 1962, taken in implementation of the Council Regulation No. 13/64 (as amended by Regulation No. 82/64) relating to the progressive establishment of a common organisation of the market in milk and milk products. The Decision provided that traders were entitled to pay only the intra-Community levy, so long as they could prove, by production of the certificate DD4, that they had fulfilled the necessary conditions.

The plaintiff company maintained that it had not been able to obtain the necessary certificates from the customs authorities of the countries of export, and that at the time of the import into Italy, no legal provision or internal administrative measure had been adopted imposing the obligation to submit certificate DD4 when importing milk or milk products.

The Court held that a Member State which has not introduced substantive measures to implement a decision imposing the obligation to submit certificate DD4, cannot claim that traders have failed to fulfil that obligation, and that the Member State must provisionally allow other means of proof of origin as are appropriate to the formal requirements in force.

(80) Case No. 64/75, *Procureur Général près de la Cour d'Appel de Lyons* v. *Henri Mommessin and others.* Preliminary ruling of December 9, 1975, on request of the *Cour d'Appel,* Lyons; (1975) E.C.R., 1599.

In criminal proceedings relating, once again, to the adulteration of wine, the Court was asked to rule on the question whether the methods for analysing wine laid down by Regulation No. 1539/71 applied in the fields of research and the prevention of fraud. The Court ruled that the methods of analysis laid down in that regulation were mandatory but not exclusive. It then repeated its ruling of September 30, 1975 (see nos. 76 and 77 *supra*) relating to the use by Member States of a legal presumption of excess addition of alcohol.

(81) Joined Cases Nos. 95-98/74, 15 and 100/75, *Union Nationale des Coopératives Agricoles de Céréales and others* v. *Commission and Council.* Judgment of December 10, 1975; (1975) E.C.R., 1615.

Six French agricultural cooperatives lodged claims with the Court for compensation under Article 215 (2) for loss they claimed to have suffered as a result of a change in the method of calculation of compensatory amounts. Certain of the companies had entered into contracts for export to third countries shortly before the change, and one shortly thereafter, and they had all executed the contracts after the changeover to the new method.

The Court dismissed the applicants' submission based on the violation of vested rights. No provision in Regulation No. 974/71, setting up the system of compensatory amounts, confers on exporters a right to the continuance of a particular method of calculation of the amounts. In any case, under Article 1 of that regulation, the right to benefit from compensatory amounts arises only on the export's taking place, and only from the time that it takes place.

The Court further dismissed the submission of the applicants that the application of the new method of calculation affected the confidence which they were entitled to put in the continuance of the former system. Here the Court distinguished the applicants according to the time of conclusion of the contracts. The company which had concluded after the coming into force of the regulation effecting the changeover could not have been unaware of the new method; and those who had concluded shortly beforehand should have foreseen that a change in the method of calculation was probable.

See also *supra*, nos. (52), (53) and (60).

VII. *FREE MOVEMENT OF PERSONS: ESTABLISHMENT AND SERVICES*

(82) Case No. 68/74, *Angelo Alaimo, Décines* v. *Préfet du Rhône, Lyon.* Preliminary ruling of January 29, 1975 on request of the *Tribunal Administratif, Lyon,* (1975) E.C.R., 109.

In this case, relating to the refusal by the *Préfet* of an educational grant for an Italian migrant worker's child because of its nationality, the Court referred to its judgment of July 3, 1974 in Case No. 9/74 *Casagrande* v. *Landeshauptstadt München,* (1974) E.C.R. 773; 12 C.M.L. Rev. 1975, 109 no. (30), and ruled that Article 12 of Regulation No. 1612/68 must be interpreted as ensuring for the children referred to an equal position with regard to all the rights arising from admission to educational courses.

(83) Case No. 67/74, *Carmelo Angelo Bonsignore, Köln,* v. *Oberstadtdirektor* of *Köln.* Preliminary ruling of February 26, 1975 on request of the *Verwaltungsgericht Köln,* (1975) E.C.R., 297.

After the conviction of Mr. Bonsignore for an offence against the German Firearms Law and for causing death by negligence, the *Oberstadtdirektor* of *Köln* decided to deport him for reasons of a general preventive nature. Bonsignore appealed against this decision to the *Verwaltungsgericht,* which stayed the proceedings in order to put a series of questions to the Court of Justice.

The Court ruled that Article 3 paras 1 and 2 of Directive No. 64/221 on the coordination of special measures concerning the movement and residence of foreign nationals which are justified on grounds of public policies, public security or public health prevents the deportation of a national of a Member State if such deportation is ordered for the purpose of deterring other aliens.

See also *infra,* no. (85).

(84) Case No. 32/75, *Anita Cristini* v. *Société Nationale des Chemins de Fer Français.* Preliminary ruling of September 30, 1975, on request of the *Cour d'Appel,* Paris (1975) E.C.R. 1085.

Mrs. Cristini, widow of an Italian migrant worker and resident in France, was refused her request for the issue of a reduction card for large families for herself and her children. The S.N.C.F. gave as grounds for the refusal the absence of French nationality and/or absence of reciprocal arrangements in the land of origin. In the context of the action brought by Mrs. Cristini against the S.N.C.F., the *Cour d'Appel* referred to the Court of Justice the question whether the reduction card issued to large families constitutes a "social advantage" within the meaning of Article 7 of Regulation No. 1612, which a national of a Member State shall enjoy in the territory of other Member States.

In its judgment of September 30, the Court answered this question in the affirmative, referring also to Regulation No. 1251/70 of the Commission concerning the right to workers and their dependents to remain on the territory of a Member State after completing employment there.

(85) Case No. 36/75, *Roland Rutili* v. *Minister of the Interior.* Preliminary ruling of October 28, 1975, on request of the *Tribunal administratif de Paris;*(1975) E.C.R., 1219. *Cf* Case No. 41/74, 12 C.M.L. Rev. 1975, 109 no. (33).

In a case involving an Italian national, banned on account of his trade-union activities from residing in four French départments, the Court was asked for a ruling on the scope of the exception of public policy in Article 48 (3) of the EEC Treaty.

The Court ruled that the exception related not only to laws and regulations adopted by Member States, but also to individual decisions adopted in pursuance of such. Since the exception amounted to a derogation from the fundamental principles of equality of treatment and free movement of workers, it should be interpreted strictly and in such a way that its scope could not be determined unilaterally by the Member States without control by the Community institutions. Community Law imposes on Member States the obligation to base measures restricting the entry, residence and movement of Member State nationals for the purposes of public policy on the individual conduct of the person concerned, and not to use such measures for purposes unconnected with public policy, such as in order to interfere with the exercise of trade-union rights. Further, in order to safeguard the rights of the person concerned, the reasons for the restrictive measures should be communicated to him without delay.

Finally, the Court ruled that a person could not be banned from part of the territory of a Member State on grounds which discriminated against nationals of other Member States.

See also *supra,* no. (83).

(86) Case No. 39/75, *R. G. Coenen and others* v. *Sociaal-Economische Raad.* Preliminary ruling of November 26, 1975, on request of the *College van Beroep voor het Bedrijfsleven;* (1975) E.C.R., 1547.

The Court was here asked to rule on the compatibility with Articles 59 and 60 of the EEC Treaty of Article 5 (1) (f) of the Dutch *Wet Assurantiebemiddeling* which provides that a natural person intending to act as an insurance intermediary in the Netherlands must reside in the Netherlands.

The Court held that the provisons of the Treaty, and in particular Articles 59, 60 and 65, must be interpreted as meaning that national legislation may not, in order to ensure that professional rules are complied with, impose a requirement of residence on persons residing in other Member States, when less restrictive measures could be employed to achieve this end.

VIII. *SOCIAL SECURITY*

(87) Case No. 66/74, *Alfonso Farrauto, Racalmuto,* v. *Bau-Berufsgenossenschaft, Wuppertal.* Preliminary ruling of February 18, 1975, on request of the *Bundessozialgericht;* (1975) E.C.R. 157.

Article 56 para 2 of Regulation No. 4 provides that, in the case where a worker who is resident in the territory of one Member State has applied for a pension from an institution of another Member State, the competent institution should "notify the claimant of its decision directly" and send a copy to the liaison body of the country in which the claimant lives. A German lower court held that this rule did not lay down the form of notification, and that this should therefore be done according to the relevant German legislation, *i.e.* through the German consular services. The *Bundessozialgericht* referred to the Court the question on the interpretation of Article 56 para. 2.

The Court ruled *inter alia* that the interpretation made by the German lower court was not in accordance with the objective and the purpose of the provision in the context of Community rules on social security for workers.

In an *obiter dictum* it held that the national courts of the Member States must take care that legal certainty is not prejudiced by a failure arising from the inability of the worker to understand the language in which a decision is notified to him.

(88) Case No. 7/75, *Mr. and Mrs. F.* v. *Belgian State.* Preliminary ruling of June 17, 1975 on request of the *Tribunal de Travail,* Nivelles; (1975) E.C.R., 679. See also Case No. 187/73, 12 C.M.L. Rev. 1975, 110 No. 35.

The plaintiffs, of Italian nationality, had applied for an ordinary benefit for their 100% handicapped son under the provisions of Belgian law. This application was refused by the Ministry of Social Security on the grounds that the minor was not of Belgian nationality and had not since the age of 20 resided for at least 15 years in Belgian territory. Mr. and Mrs. F. appealed against this refusal to the Tribunal de Travail, which stayed the proceedings and referred as series of questions to the Court.

The Court ruled that the provisions of Regulation No. 1408/71 must be interpreted as meaning (a) that they include a national legislative system which provides a legal protected right to benefits for the handicapped; (b) that in applying such a system the handicapped child of a worker must not, as compared with the nationals of the State of residence, be less favourably treated by reason only of he fact that the does not possess the nationality of that State; (c) that in the case of the handicapped child who from his minority fulfils the conditions required to qualify for benefits for the handicapped as an member of a employed person's family, the equality of treatment cannot cease at the end of his minority if the child by reason of his handicap is himself prevented from acquiring the status of an employed person within the meaning of the Regulation.

(89) Case No. 8/75, *Caisse primaire d'assurance maladie de Sélestat, Sélestat* v. *Association du footballclub d'Andlau, Andlau.* Preliminary ruling of June 24, 1975 on request of the French *Cour de Cassation;* (1975) E.C.R., 739.

In France, affiliation to social insurance schemes is compulsory for public performers, whatever their nationality. The *Caisse* claimed payment of social security dues from the *Association* as the employer of a music band which it had contracted for three dances. The band worked only occasionally in France, the residence of the participants being in Freiburg in the Federal Republic, where they were affiliated to a recognised private social security fund.

On a series of questions regarding Article 13 para 1 sub e of Regulation No. 3, the Court ruled that a worker having his permanent residence in one Member State and who is occasionally employed in another Member State, is subject to the legislation of the State of his permanent residence insofar as he is affiliated as a wage-earner or assimilated worker to the social security scheme of that State, and if he is not so affiliated he is subject to the social security legislation of the Member State where he occasionally works. Furthermore, the Court ruled that in case of an accident at work which happens to a wage-earner or assimilated worker subject to the social security legislation of his permanent residence, and who is occasionally employed in the territory of another Member State, the social security institution of the latter State is only obliged to issue the benefits in kind provided for by its own legislation at the expense of the institution of the competent State.

(90) Case No. 17/75, *Antonio Anselmetti, Loreto Aprutino* v. *Caisse de compensation des allocations familiales de l'industrie charbonnière, Charleroi.* Preliminary ruling of June 25, 1975 on request of the *Court du Travail,* Brussels; (1975) E.C.R., 781.

The applicant, of Italian nationality, received an allowance at an increased rate from the *Caisse de Compensation.* After his return to Italy the *Caisse* stopped as from November 1965 the payment of the increased allowance and continued to pay the allowance at the basic rate. After the entry into force of Regulation No. 1408/71 the *Caisse* recommenced payment of the increased allowance because this new Regulation provides that family allowances may be transferre abroad without reduction or restriction.

The Applicant considered the reduction from 1965 till 1972 to be unlawful. The *Cour de Travail* stayed the proceedings and referred to the Court of Justice a series of questions, mainly regarding the character of the Belgian invalidity allowance. The Court ruled *inter alia* that under a combined sickness/invalidity insurance scheme, cash benefits paid as invalidity benefits, howsoever designated, must be regarded as pensions within the meaning of Article 42 of Regulation No. 3.

(91) Case No. 6/75, *Dr. Ulrich Horst, Hannover Buchholz* v. *Bundesknappschaft, Bochum.* Preliminary ruling of June 26, 1975 on request of the *Bundessozialgericht* (1975) E.C.R., 32.

The applicant in the main action claimed a federal mineworker's disablement pension for diminished capacity to work, partly on the basis of insurance periods completed by him in Algeria from 1960 to 1962. The defendant refused this application. On a series of questions referred to it, the Court ruled *inter alia* that the concept of "accrued rights" mentioned in Article 16 para 2 of Regulation No. 10/65, must be interpreted as meaning that insofar as it is necessary for the acquisition, maintenance or recovery of the right to benefits, insurance periods completed in Algeria before January 19, 1965 must be taken into consideration in order to determine the pensions referred to in Chapters 2 and 3 of Regulation No. 3, even if the risk materialises and the claim for the pension is made after that date.

(92) Case No. 20/75, *Gaetano d'Amico* v. *Landesversicherungsanstalt Rheinland-Pfalz.* Preliminary ruling of July 9, 1975, on request of the *Bundessozialgericht;*(1975) E.C.R., 891.

In a dispute involving the qualification for an early retirement benefit, the *Bundessozialgericht* referred to the Court a number of questions concerning the interpretation of Article 27 (1) of Regulation No. 3 and Article 45 (1) of Regulation No. 1408/71, in order in particular to determine whether a period of unemployment in another Member State can be considered a period of unemployment within the meaning of German law.

The Court ruled that the provisions of these regulations do not prohibit a rule of national law which requires, for the acquisition of the right to an early retirement pension, that the person concerned shall have been unemployed for a certain time and thus available to the employment bureau of the Member State in question.

(93) Case No. 27/75, *Gaetano Bonaffini and others* v. *Instituto Nazionale della Providenza Sociale.* Preliminary ruling of July 10, 1975, on request of the *Pretore d'Enna;*(1975) E.C.R., 971.

The plaintiffs, Italian migrant workers, applied for unemployment benefit on returning to Italy after losing their work in Germany. Their application was refused on the grounds that they had not remained available to the German employment services for the four week waiting period required by Article 69 of Regulation No. 1408/71.

On appeal by the plaintiffs, the *Pretore d'Enna* asked the Court for a ruling on the question whether the terms of Article 69 precluded a worker who had failed to complete the designated waiting period from obtaining unemployment benefit in the Member State to which he belongs, where, in the absence of Community regulations, he would be entitled to such a benefit.

The Court ruled that Article 69 of Regulation No. 1408/71 is intended solely to ensure for the migrant worker the limited and conditional preservation of the unemployment benefits of the competent State, even if he goes to another Member State, and this other Member State cannot rely on mere failure to comply with the conditions prescribed under that article to deny the worker entitlement to the benefit he may claim under the national legislation of that State.

(94) Case No. 24/75, *Teresa and Silvana Petroni* v. *L'Office National de Pensions pour Travailleurs Salariés.* Preliminary ruling of October 21, 1975, on request of the *Tribunal de Travail,* Brussels; (1975) E.C.R., 1085.

In an action brought by the successors of an Italian migrant worker in relation to the calculation of the retirement benefit to which the latter was entitled at the time of his death, the Court was asked for a ruling on the interpretation and validity of Article 46 (3) of Regulation No. 1408/71, concerning the overlapping of benefits, in particular in relation to Article 51 of the EEC Treaty.

The Court held that Article 46 (3) of Regulation No. 1408/71 is incompatible with Article 51 of the Treaty to the extent that it imposes a limitation on the overlapping of two benefits acquired in different Member States by a reduction of the rights which the persons concerned could already enjoy in a Member State by virtue of the application of national legislation alone.

(95) Case No. 33/75, *Benito Galati* v. *Landesversicherungsanstalt Schwaben.* Preliminary ruling of October 30, 1975, on request of the *Sozialgericht,* Augsburg; (1975) E.C.R., 1323.

In a case concerning the completion of the waiting period for entitlement to a disability pension for an Italian worker residing in the Federal Republic, the Court was asked for an interpretation of Article 15 (3) of Regulation No. 574/72, fixing the procedure for the implementation of Regulation No. 1408/71, with the object in particular of determining how the national court should regard insurance periods completed in another Member State.

The Court ruled that if under German legislation a completed insurance period of less than one month is treated as a whole month, then an insurance period completed in accordance with the legislation of another Member State which, on conversion into months for the purpose of aggregation, produces a fraction, must also be rounded up to the next highest figure in months, in order to ensure that migrant workers do not, because of emigration, lose the rights which they have acquired in their country of origin.

(96) Case No. 49/75, *Camilla Borella* v. *Landesversicherungsanstalt Schwaben.* Preliminary ruling of November 20, 1975 on request of the *Sozialgericht,* Augsburg; (1975) E.C.R., 1461.

The widow of an Italian migrant worker applied to the German authorities for a survivor's pension. The application was refused on the ground that the insurance periods completed by her deceased husband under German legislation amounted to less than the twelve months provided for by Article 48 (1) of Regulation No. 1408/71. The deceased had, however, on the basis of the same insurance periods, previously been awarded an occupational invalidity pension which at the time of his death had been converted into a disablement pension. Under German law, where, at the time of death, the deceased was entitled to an insurance pension, the survivors may claim a survivor's pension.

Ruling on the interpretation of Article 48 (1) of Regulation no. 1408/71, the Court held that the exclusion of that article cannot be applied where the right to benefits of a migrant worker or his survivors arise solely from the provisions of the legislation of the Member State in question.

(97) Case No. 50/75, *Caisse de pension des employés privés* v. *Helga Massonet.* Preliminary ruling of November 25, 1975 on request of the *Cour Supérieure de Justice,* Luxembourg; (1975) E.C.R., 1473.

In a case arising from the refusal of the Luxembourg insurance authorities to pay a specially increased survivor's pension to the widow of a Luxembourg citizen who had completed insurance periods in Luxembourg and the Federal Republic, a number of questions concerning the interpretation of Article 51 of the EEC Treaty, and of Articles 12, 27 and 28 of Regulation 3, relating to the aggregation and apportionment of benefits, were referred to the Court of Justice.

The Court established that the widow's entitlement to a specially increased pension in Luxembourg arose not in relation to insurance periods but apart therefrom, and ruled that the aforementioned provisions do not entitle a national insurance institution to reduce the benefits due to a worker or to those untitled under him by virtue of national legislation alone and without recourse to the procedure of aggregation.

(98) Case No. 57/75, *Fernand Plaquevent* v. *Caisse Primaire d' Assurance Maladie du Havre.* Preliminary ruling of December 9, 1975 on request of the French *Cour de Cassation;*(1975) E.C.R., 1581.

In a dispute concerning the calculation of an invalidity pension in a case where the plaintiff had completed insurance periods in both France and the Federal Republic, the Court was asked to rule on the interpretation of Article 28 of Regulation No. 3 concerning the aggregation of insurance periods.

The Court ruled that where in the calculation of an invalidity pension which is due to an insured person who has been subject successively to the legislation of two Member States, it is necessary to take into account the insurance periods completed in one of these Member States, because the insured person does not fulfil the conditions laid down in the other for entitlement, and where under the legislation of the latter State the calculation of benefits is based upon an average wage or average contribution, without regard to the length of the period of employment, then the *pro rata* calculation must be made after aggregation of all the insurance benefits, as provided by Article 28 (1) (b) of Regulation No. 3.

(99) Case No. 93/75, *J. Adlerblum* v. *Caisse nationale d'assurance vieillesse des travailleurs.* Preliminary ruling of December 17, 1975, on request of the *Commission de première instance du contentieux de la sécurité sociale et de la mutualité sociale agricole,* Paris; (1975) E.C.R., 2147.

The Court held that it had no jurisdiction to rule on a question concerning the classification under French social security law of a benefit awarded under the German Compensation Law.

IX. *TRANSPORT*

(100) Case No. 69/74, *Auditeur du Travail, Mons* v. *Jean Pierre Cagnon and Jean Paul Faquet, Amiens.* Preliminary ruling of February 18, 1975 on request of the *Tribunal de Police,* Mons; (1975) E.C.R., 171.

The defendants in the main action were prosecuted for not having observed Article 11 para 2 of Regulation No. 543/69, which lays down that a carriage driver shall have had a rest period of not less than 10 consecutive hours during the 24 hours preceding driving activity. The main argument of the defendants was that this rule amounts to an obligation for the employer, but not for the employee.

Ruling on a preliminary question, the Court held, referring to the aims of the Regulation No. 543/69 and the duties of crew-members as laid down therein, that the provisions relating to daily rest must be observed both by the employer and the crew-members themselves.

X. *COMPETITION*

(101) Joined Cases Nos. 19 and 20/74, *Kali und Salz AG, Kassel and Kali-Chemi AG, Hannover* v. *Commission.* Judgment of May 14, 1975; (1975) E.C.R., 499.

Kali und Salz AG and *Kali-Chemi AG* are the only German producers of straight potash, one of the main nutritive substances necessary to obtain good harvests. The two companies both sell the straight potash and use it to produce other compound potash fertilizers. With an eye on the diminishing share of the fertilizer market for straight potash, *Kali und Salz* and *Kali-Chemi* agreed that the former would buy from the latter its non-marketed production of straight potash.

The Commission began proceedings on its own initiative on May 8, 1973. It decided, after hearing the oral observations of the companies, that the agreement constituted an infringement of Article 85 para 1, and refused the application for an exemption under Article 85 para 3.

The companies brought an action for annulment of this Decision before the Court. The Court held *inter alia* that straight potash and compound potash fertilizers are to be considered as competing products, with the consequence that the alleged agreement did not lead to a restriction of competition within a substantial part of the market. The Court further ruled that it had not been shown that straight potash could be distributed by a sales organisation which markets competing products, *i.e.* compound potash fertilizers. It could not therefore be expected of KC that it market its straight potash by means of its sales organisation for compound potash products. On these grounds the Court annulled the Commission's Decision.

(102) Case No. 71/74, *Nederlandse vereniging voor de Fruit- en Groentenimporthandel* and *Nederlandse Bond van Grossiers in Zuidvruchten en ander Geïmporteerd Fruit "Frubo"*, The Hague v. *Commission.* Judgment of May 15, 1975; (1975) E.C.R., 563.

The applicants, a Dutch association of fruit-importers and an association of fruit wholesalers, had concluded an agreement concerning the organisation of a system of sale by auction for fresh citrus fruit and apples and pears of non-European origin, imported into the Netherlands.

Article 9 of the agreement obliges wholesalers to deal in the products in dispute through the medium of an import auction unless they were bought from an importer-wholesaler established in another Member State of the EEC where the have actually been brought in, unloaded and cleared through customs.

On request of 22 members of the wholesalers' association the Commission declared by Decision of July 25, 1975, that the provisions of Article 9 of the agreement were in breach of Article 85 para 1 of the EEC-Treaty.

Thereupon the associations brought an action for annulment of the Decision before the Court of Justice.

The Court held that Article 85 para 1 applies to associations insofar as their own activities or those of the undertakings belonging to them are calculated to produce the results to which it refers.

Furthermore, the Court held that this clause (Article 9 of the agreement) was liable to interfere with the natural movement of trade and thus to affect trade between member countries, because it restricts the freedom of members to import direct into the Netherlands.

Finally, the Court held that the agreement was not indispensable to obtain some advantages for consumers, *e.g.* reduced transport and marketing costs. Consequently, the Commission's Decision was not in breach of Article 85 para 3.

The application for annulment was dismissed.

(103) Case No. 25/75, *Van Vliet Kwasten- en Ladder Fabriek* v. *Fratelli dalle Crode.* Preliminary ruling of October 1, 1975, on request of the *Gerechtshof*, Arnhem; (1975) E.C.R., 1103.

In an action resulting from the rescission of its exclusive agency agreement with the Dutch firm Van Vliet, the Italian firm Dalle Crode relied on the incompatibility of the agreement with Article 85 (1) of the Treaty, further claiming that it did not qualify for exemption in terms of Regulation 67/67 concerning the implementation of Article 85 (3).

Ruling on the interpretation of Regulation 67/67 in relation to certain categories of exclusive dealing agreements, the Court held that where an exclusive sales agreement between a manufacturer in one Member State and a dealer in another prescribes an obligation on the part of the manufacturer to prohibit intermediaries and consumers established in his State from exporting or causing to be exported the goods in question to the territory covered by the contract, and where it has the effect of making it impossible for intermediaries or consumers in that territory to acquire an appreciable quantity of the goods from the manufacturer's State, then the agreement falls within Article 3 of Regulation No. 67/67 and may not benefit from exemption. The Court further held that this would continue to be the case even if consumers established in the territory covered by the contract had real possibilities of acquiring the goods from elsewhere in the common market.

(104) Case No. 26/75, *General Motors Continental NV* v. *Commission.* Judgment of November 13, 1975; (1975) E.C.R., 1367.

The appellants in this case appealed against a Decision of the Commission of December 19, 1974, imposing on them a fine of 100,000 UC for the abuse of a dominant position in terms of Article 86 of the EEC Treaty. The Commission asserted that the appellants, in their capacity as the sole authorised agent of the manufacturer in Belgium, had abused a dominant position in requiring that parallel importers of Opel cars should pay excessive prices for the technical inspection and administrative costs involved in the issue of certain certificates of conformity and type shields as required by Belgian law.

The Court quashed the Decision of the Commission. The appellants did indeed hold a dominant position, although this was in the nature of a legal monopoly deriving from a public law duty delegated by the Belgian State, but the Commission had failed to establish an abuse. Although the applicants admitted imposing an excessive charge in specific cases, they had shown that the charge was shortly thereafter brought into line with the real costs of the operation, and that they had, moreover, reimbursed the persons affected by the excessive charge before the intervention by the Commission. The Commission's intervention was therefore unjustified in the actual temporal and factual circumstances in which it occurred.

(105) Case No. 73/74, *Groupement des fabricants de papiers peints de Belgique and others* v. *Commission.* Judgment of November 26, 1975; (1975) E.C.R., 1491.

The appellants asked for the annulment of the Decision of the Commission of July 23, 1974, in which it declared that a series of decisions and agreements of the *Groupement* were incompatible with Article 85 (1), ordered its members to bring the infringements to an end, and imposed fines in connection with a collective boycott of a wallpaper supplier. While upholding the Decision of the Commission in relation to the infringement of the Treaty, the Court annulled that part of the Decision which imposed fines on the members of the *Groupement,* because the Commission had failed to adequately state its reasons for considering that the decisions and agreements in question were liable to affect trade between Member States. Where a decision of the Commission goes further than previous decisions, it must give an account of its reasoning, under the general obligation imposed by Article 190 of the EEC Treaty.

(106) Joined Cases Nos. 40-48, 50, 54-56, 111, 113 and 114/73, *Coöperatieve Vereniging "Suiker Unie" UA* v. *Commission.* Judgment of December 16, 1975; (1975) E.C.R., 1663.

Sixteen undertakings, representing the main producers and marketers of sugar in the

Community, requested the Court to annul the Decision of the Commission of January 2, 1973, which required them to put an end to certain concerted practices in breach of Articles 85 and 86 and imposed fines on them.

In a lengthy judgment, the Court upheld the Decision of the Commission in relation to the majority of the firms, but annulled it in relation to the Italian firms because the Commission had failed to take proper account of the severe limitations on competition in this sector in Italy as a result of national regulations, and in relation to one German firm, where insufficient evidence of concerted action was adduced. The Court further reduced the fines of all the remaining firms because of the fact that the Commission, in determining the seriousness of the infringements, had not taken sufficient account of the fact that competition between undertakings was already restricted by the common organisation of the market for sugar, which imposes a system of national production quotas.

XIV. *EXTERNAL RELATIONS*

(107) *Advisory Opinion* No. 1/75 of November 11, 1975, under Article 228 of the EEC Treaty, relating to the "Understanding on a Local Cost Standard"; (1975) E.C.R., 1355.

Article 228 (1) of the EEC Treaty provides that the Commission, the Council or a Member State may obtain beforehand the opinion of the Court as to whether an international agreement envisaged by the Community is compatible with the provisions of the Treaty. Where the Court's opinion is adverse, the agreement may enter into force only in accordance with Article 236. On July 14, 1975, the Commission made the first request to the Court for an opinion of this kind, concerning the compatibility with the Treaty of the draft "Understanding on a Local Cost Standard", relating to aids for exports, which had been drawn up under the auspices of the O.E.C.D. The Commis sion asked whether the Community had the power to conclude the said Understanding, and if so, whether that power was exclusive.

In its Opinion, the Court held, *inter alia,* that the subject-matter of the Understanding necessarily falls within the field of the Common Commercial Policy and that in the course of measures to implement that policy, the Community is empowered not only to adopt internal rules of Community Law, but also to conclude agreements with third countries. Moreover, the Common Commercial Policy is conceived of in the context of the operation of the Common Market, for the defence of the common interests of the Community, and the provisions of Article 113 and 114 concerning the conditions under which agreements on commercial policy must be concluded, show clearly that the exercise of concurrent powers by Member States in this area is impossible.

The Court therefore concluded that the Community has power to participate in the Understanding, and that this power is exclusive.

B. NATIONAL CASE LAW

The Application of Community Law in Italy in 1974

Following the judgment of the Constitutional Court of December 27, 1973 which was widely commented on by writers [1] and summarised in last year's report,[2] decisions of Italian courts were not particularly plentiful in 1974. A number of judgments are, however, worthy of mention.

1. First, the judgment of the Constitutional Court of July 10, 1974 should be mentioned, even though it is connected only indirectly with Community Law.

In its judgment of April 30, 1974 [3] the Court of Justice of the European Communities was required to examine a series of questions which had been referred to it by the *Tribunale di Biella* concerning the interpretation *inter alia* of Article 37 of the Treaty of Rome. Mr. Sacchi, the owner of an unauthorised television relay firm *(Tele-Biella),* against whom proceedings had been instituted for failure to pay the licence fee on receivers for television relay, alleged that, insofar as cable television was concerned, the Italian system, under which television is a monopoly granted by the State to *Radio Audizione Italiana,* which involves on the one hand a monopoly of televised commercial advertising, and on the other hand a prohibition on any other person or undertaking from receiving for retransmission audio-visual signals transmitted either from national territory or from foreign stations, did not comply with the EEC Treaty. The Court of Justice decided that "the transmission of television signals, including those in the nature of advertisements, comes as such, within the rules of the Treaty relating to services" and that Article 37 applies to trade in goods and cannot therefore relate to a monopoly in the provision of services.[4]

Mr. Sacchi was more fortunate in the Italian Constitutional Court. In the course of criminal proceedings, which had also been instituted against Mr. Sacchi, the *Pretore* of Biella held that the plea of the unconstitutionality of Article 195 of Decree No. 156 of 29 March 1973, on the basis of which proceedings had been instituted against Mr. Sacchi, was not unfounded. The Constitutional Court considered that the questions raised by the *Pretore* affected in a general way the principle by which the State has an exclusive right to install and operate cable television. The Court pointed out that the most significant practical difference between cable and radio television was the fact that the number of channels that could be obtained using the radio diffused system was limited, whereas an unlimited number of channels could be obtained using the cable system. Insofar as the installation and operation of radio networks and limited range cable television was concerned, the Court noted that there were no grounds of public interest by virtue of which the allocation to the state of a reserved power in this respect could be based on Article 43 of the Constitution.

---

1. A detailed list of authors who supported this judgment is provided in P. de Caterini's article in (1975) *Cahiers de droit européen,* 123 *et seq.*

2. 12 C.M.L.Rev. 1975, 431-442.

3. Case 155/73, *Sacchi* (Judgment of April 30, 1974), (1974) E.C.R., 409.

4. This point of view, which was also shared by the German and Italian Governments, the Commission and the Advocate-General Reischl, was strongly criticised in W. Donà-Viscardini, "Il regime della televisione italiana e il diritto comunitario", (1974) *Il diritto degli scambi internazionali,* 89-100.

13 C.M.L. Rev. 1976, 524-539

The Constitutional Court considered, therefore, that the activity in question could not be placed beyond the initiative of private individuals and declared unconstitutional Articles 1, 185 and 195 of Decree No. 156 of March 29, 1973 insofar as they related to cable television services.

2. Last year's report contained a lengthy summary of the judgment of the Constitutional Court of December 27, 1973.[5] It is to be hoped that the Constitutional Court's decision has brought to an end an entire series of subtle arguments, and in particular infringements—such as the reproduction of Community laws in national legislative instruments—by the Italian authorities. One problem which remained to be solved was to discover how an Italian Court could avoid applying a national legal provision which was enacted subsequent to, but which was contrary to Community Law. Could it decide directly not to apply it or must it refer the matter to the Constitutional Court which alone would be competent to eliminate it from national law?

The same report also contained a long summary of the vicissitudes of the case of *Società Industrie Chimiche Italia Centrale (ICIC) v. Ministero Commercio Estero* (Ministry for Foreign Trade). The decisions of the *Tribunale di Roma* and of the Rome Court of Appeal seemed to us to be open to strong criticism. The case was brought before the Court of Cassation which by order adopted on December 23, 1974 in joint session by all chambers, stayed the proceedings and requested the Constitutional Court to give a detailed ruling on the question referred to above. The question raised was as follows:

> "The question of the constitutionality of the second and third paragraphs of Article 13 of Decree Law No. 59 of 20 February 1968, which was embodied without amendment in Law No. 224 of 18 March 1968, which reproduces *inter alia* Community Regulation No. 120/67/EEC, whose entry into force was thus postponed and made conditional in disregard of the principle of the immediate and direct applicability of Community rules, is when read in conjunction with the first paragraph of Article 10 and Article 11 of the Constitution, not without foundation".[6]

The order of the Court of Cassation is interesting for several reasons.

a) The grounds of judgment of the Court of Cassation bear witness to the cooperation which has been established between the Court of Justice and Italian courts:

> "Reproduction of the provisions of EEC Regulations in national rules is an infringement of the second paragraph of Article 189 of the Treaty. It is unnecessary to ask the Court of Justice of the Communities to give its interpretation in respect of this matter since it has already done so in its Judgment of February 7, 1973 in Case 39/72."

b) The Court of Cassation believes that the question of how to deal with national rules, that are contrary to Community Law, does not come within the jurisdiction of the Court of Justice of the European Communities but is a matter subject to national law.

> "The operation of the European Economic Community undoubtedly requires that the direct and immediate applicability in all Member States of Community rules should not be diminished, delayed, hindered or absorbed by national rules which are

---

5. 12 C.M.L.Rev. 1975, 431-442.

6. (1974) *Giurisprudenza italiana,* I, 1, 426, with a note by M. Berri; (1975) *Diritto comunitario e degli scambi internazionali,* 622; (1974) *Foro Padano,* 425; (1975) *Giustizia Civile,* III, 78, containing the submissions of the *Procuratore generale,* who had requested that the action be admitted on the basis of the judgment of the Court of Justice of March 10, 1971; and (1975) *Giustizia Civile,* III, 225, with a note by A. Palmieri. See also M. Berri, "Sulla soluzione del delicato dilemma causato dalle leggi interne illegittime per aver riprodotto regolamenti comunitari direttamente applicabili", (1975) *Revista di diritto europeo,* 131.

contrary to or replace them; the question of the legal validity of such national rules is, however, a matter subject to national law, regarding which an interpretation cannot be requested of the Community Court of Justice."

c) The Court emphasised the dilemma faced by the Constitutional Court: such national rules were either void (in which case there would be no problem of constitutionality), or unconstitutional.

d) The reference to academic writing. In order to show that the question was not unfounded the Court of Cassation recalled the dissenting opinions which had emerged among writers.

The Constitutional Court gave its ruling in Judgment No. 232 delivered on October 30, 1975 which will be commented on in the 1975 report. It held, as is known, that under the Constitutional system in force in Italy, the court cannot avoid applying a subsequently enacted law which is contrary to Community Law but must refer it to the Constitutional Court in order that it may declare such law unconstitutional *erga omnes.*

3. It is likely that the judgment of the Constitutional Court, referred to above, will check the trend that was developing in Italian case law and which tended to acknowledge the precedence of Community law over national law, including national laws enacted subsequently, in line with the interpretation of the Court of Justice of the European Communities.[7]

Examples that may be quoted are the decision of March 18, 1974, of the Court of Appeal of Naples and the decision of April 4, 1974, of the Tribunal of Milan.

The Court of Appeal of Naples had to give a ruling in a dispute between importers and the finance authorities.[8] The former were seeking reimbursement of sums which they had had to pay as statistical duty and for administrative services provided for in Law No. 447 of June 24, 1971. The Court relied on the decisions of the Court of Justice of the European Communities in stating that such duties constituted taxes having an effect equivalent to customs duties [9] and consequently could no longer be levied on products covered by Regulation 120/67, Article 18 (2) of which prohibits "the levying of any customs duty or charge having equivalent effect" as from the date of its entry into force, *i.e.* July 1, 1967. As a result of the precedence of Community Law and of decisions of the Court of Justice of the European Communities, national Law No. 447 of June 24, 1971 could not, therefore, be applied.

> "On the basis of these premises, Article 18 (2) of Regulation No. 120/67, which provides that in trade with third countries it is prohibited to levy any customs duty or charge having equivalent effect, must be regarded as having been incorporated directly in the national law of the Italian state, with the result that from the date on which it entered into force, July 1, 1967, it is prohibited in Italy to demand payment of statistical duties and charges for administrative services which, undoubtedly, have an effect equivalent to customs duties . . . Law No. 447 of June 24, 1971 seems, therefore, to have been adopted on the basis of a non-existent condition (namely the failure to apply the Community Regulation within the state); although the effect of such Law

---

7. The development of Italian case-law in comparison with Community Law has been analysed in a very thorough study by M. Capurso, "Le ideologie giuridiche dello Stato nazionale moderno e l'ordinamento comunitario nella giurisprudenza italiana", (1975) *Studi parlamentari e di politica costituzionale,* No. 29/30.

8. *Corte di Appello di Napoli, Ministero delle Finanze v. Società Rocco,* (1974) *Rivista di diritto internazionale privato e processuale,* 623.

9. Case 24/68, *Commission v. Italy* (Judgment of July 1, 1969), (1969) *Recueil,* 193; Case 8/70, *Commission v. Italy* (Judgment of Nov. 18, 1970), (1970) *Recueil, 961.*

may, therefore, be to confirm the regulation it can never repeal it nor even less so, have retrospective effect, since this could be an infringement of the undertaking given under international law . . ."

The Court of Appeal illustrated all its arguments by frequent references to decisions of the Court of Justice of the European Communities.

The Tribunal of Milan was required to give a decision in proceedings brought by importers of cheese from other EEC Member States against the finance authorities, in which the applicants claimed that the charge paid pursuant to Law No. 30 of January 23, 1968 for the health inspection of milk products and the sum payable to the Italian administrative authorities were contrary to Articles 9 (1), 12, 13 and 95 of the Treaty of Rome.[10]

After having pointed out that Community regulations are directly applicable in the legal systems of the Member States of the Community and that, just as they may impose obligations on Member States and private individuals, they may also confer subjective rights on the latter that must be protected by the national legal courts, the court said:

"The Community system is therefore above and outside the national legal systems of the States which by signing the Treaty and incorporating it in their own legal system waived in the areas governed by the Treaty their sovereignty, and in particular their power to legislate independently in those areas. It follows that were a national law is contrary to Community provisions, it must be regarded as being void by reason of its incompatibility with the Community system and thus inapplicable both as regards Member States and nationals of Community countries. This outcome of the conflict between national law and the Community system occurs both where the national law exists prior to the Community rule (in such a way that the former will no longer be effective in relation to the Member States on account of the entry into force of the latter) and also where the conflict arises out of the adoption of a provision of national law relating to a matter which has been set aside for and already covered by Community provisions. In the second case, the fact that the Member State legislates is an infringement of its waiver of sovereignty in favour of the common system and creates a conflict which in view of the primacy of the common system must be settled by the fact that the national law is ineffective against the Community system.

Some people wonder whether in these circumstances such ineffectiveness immediately renders inapplicable the rule of national law . . . or whether it is necessary for the national legislator to take measures to repeal it independently . . .

The court believes, for the reasons outlined above, that the second alternative must be ruled out, but adds that where a provision of national law overtly infringes Community provisions, the national court must, even where it is not expressly provided that such provision shall not apply to the Member States, regard such inapplicability as being implicit and rule out the possibility, where it is certain that there is no intention to the contrary, that the legislator ("pacta sunt servanda") wished to implement a rule which was clearly incompatible with the obligations under international law which it had undertaken by ratifying a multilateral treaty agreed to on a basis of reciprocity, as in the case of the Treaty establishing the EEC."

The Tribunal held, therefore, that it was illegal to levy the tax known as the health inspection charge and ordered the authorities to refund amounts levied on this account.

4. Community rules relating to agriculture were referred to in two cases. The Tribunal of

10. (1975) *Diritto comunitario e degli scambi internazionali*, 445.

Ancona was concerned with the premium granted to olive oil producers [11] and the Court of Appeal of Potenza had to deal with the premium granted to durum wheat producers.[12]

The interesting aspect of the first case is the objection entered by AIMA *(Azienda di Stato per gli interventi nel mercato agricolo)* that the integration of the producer price of olive oil into a system, whose object is the common organization of European agriculture, would meet a general need but could not be described as a subjective right of a private individual. Only a subjective right entitles an individual to bring proceedings in an ordinary court. The distinction between a subjective right, which is guaranteed protection by the ordinary courts and a lawful interest, whose protection is assured by the administrative courts, had already been raised in the *Salgoil* case in the Court of Justice of the European Communities.[13] The Tribunal of Ancona acknowledged that it had jurisdiction in this case, *i.e.* that the plaintiff had a subjective right to receive the integration premium, and decided in its favour. The Court quoted accurately Regulation 136/66 on the establishment of a common organization of the market in oil and fats,[14] and the right provided thereunder to grant aid to olive oil producers "where the production target price is higher than the market target price ruling at the beginning of the marketing year, such aid being equal to the difference between these two prices." It pointed out clearly that this aid was defined "in accordance with the procedure and criteria laid down by the Council". In actual fact, however, the court based its decision on the Italian law, Decree Law No. 912 of November 9, 1966 which conferred on AIMA responsibility for paying the aid and specified the procedure and necessary checks.

AIMA was also the defendant in the second case. Again it entered a plea *inter alia* of lack of jurisdiction of the ordinary court. The Tribunal of Potenza correctly rejected the plea and held that Community regulations created subjective rights. The Court of Appeal upheld the ruling of the Tribunal on this point but after having drawn attention to the Community legislation, particularly Article 10 of Regulation 120/67 and Article 3 of Regulation 135/67, it relied on national provisions adopted to implement these regulations in order to reject the plea. The excessively long grounds of judgment are drafted in pompous language which, unfortunately, is fairly frequently the case with certain Italian legal decisions and which is contrary to the duty imposed on judges by the Code of Civil Procedure which states that grounds of judgment must be concise.

5. In view of decisions of the Court of Justice of the European Communities concerning the restrictions introduced by Community Law on national rules governing the selling prices of agricultural products,[15] it is interesting to recall decision No. 265 of the Council of State, *(Consiglio di Stato)* of September 25, 1974. The Council of State stated that the measure adopted by the *Comitato interprovinciale dei prezzi* fixing a compulsory producer price for milk was void for lack of competence since the price fixed by the Community had to be applied in all the Member States; the measure was also void by reason of its being *ultra vires:*

---

11. *Tribunale di Ancona, Mercuri v. AIMA* (Judgment of Sept. 21, 1974), (1975) *Foro Italiano,* 442.

12. *Corte d'Appello di Potenza, AIMA v. Tataranni* (Judgment of Dec. 13, 1974), (1975) *Foro Italiano,* 692.

13. Case 13/68, *Salgoil* (Judgment of Dec. 19, 1968), (1968) E.C.R., 662.

14. J.O. p. 3025/1966.

15. Case 31/74, *Galli* (Judgment of Jan. 23, 1975), (1975) E.C.R., 47, 12 C.M.L.Rev. 1975, 418 *et seq.;* Case 65/75, *Tasca,* and Cases 88-90/75, *SADAM* (Judgments of Feb. 26, 1976), (1976) E.C.R. 291 and 323.

> "The President of the Council of Ministers—*"Comitato interministeriale dei prezzi"*—stated very clearly in circular No. 2987 of April 9, 1973 that as far as the producer or import prices of milk were concerned "no decision or measure relating to prices can be taken by the Member States since this matter is subject to Community rules" and that only the subsequent stages come within the competence of the Member States "which may fix the maximum margin to be added to the original price in order to obtain the consumer price." This circular has not been complied with by the measure that is being challenged and consequently, from this point of view, the measure is void by reason of its being *ultra vires.*" [16]

This decision of the Council of State introduced, therefore, in advance, the distinction between the rules governing prices at the wholesale and production stages and those at the retail stage on the same lines as were later to be followed in point 34 of the grounds of judgment in the *Galli* judgment.

6. In conclusion attention should be drawn to the Judgment of 18 March 1974 of the Tribunal of Varese which was to give rise to Case 65/74.[17] In May 1973, a number of employees referred to as *"appaltati"* of the Cemi and Commont firms to whom the Joint Nuclear Research Centre of Euratom (JRC) had entrusted the maintenance and cleaning of buildings and installations of the establishment at Ispra, brought proceedings against their respective employers and Euratom in the Tribunale di Varese claiming that the court should:

a) declare that by reason of Article 1 of the aforementioned law they were officials of Euratom in Categories C/3 and C/2 (or, in the alternative, establishment staff) from the time when they started work;

b) in the alternative, order Euratom and the aforementioned firms, in accordance with Article 3 of the Law, to pay to the plaintiffs with retrospective effect, the salary and emoluments equal to those received by officials or, alternatively, by establishment agents in the categories mentioned;

c) in the further alternative, declare that they were local staff.

Accepting the arguments put forward by Euratom, the Tribunal of Varese delivered a judgment on March 18, 1974, in which he dismissed claims (b) and (c) as unfounded on the grounds that on the one hand Law No. 1369 did not apply to Euratom, which was an organisation other than an undertaking (the law in question applies only to undertakings), and on the other hand that the Agreement between Euratom and Italy concerning the setting up of the Ispra establishment contains a provision creating an exception to Article 3 of Law No. 1369 (the Agreement places the Commission under an obligation to ensure that, in contracts with firms, staff employed by the contractor shall receive only such advantages as are as favourable as those applied in industries in the same region).

The Court ruled that claim (a) was admissible and referred in this connection to the general principles of law governing simulation under which simulated and fictitious situations must be brought to an end and replaced by the actual situations which they conceal.

However, in view of the plea of lack of jurisdiction of the national court raised by Euratom (the disputes in question being within the jurisdiction of the Court of Justice pursuant to Article 152 of the Euratom Treaty), the Tribunal of Varese referred the matter

16. *Società ILCA v. Comitato provinciale dei prezzi di Pescara*, (1975) Giurisprudenza italiana, III, 380; (1975) *Giustizia civile*, II, 166; (1975) *Diritto comunitario e degli scambi internazionali*, 622.

17. Case 65/74, *Porrini v. Euratom and Comont* (Judgment of March 11, 1975), (1975) E.C.R., 319.

to the Court for a preliminary ruling pursuant to Article 150 of the Treaty on those questions which had to be examined by the Court of Justice in Case 65/74 referred to above.[18]

The Application of Community Law in Italy in 1975

A. *The judgment of the Constitutional Court of October 30, 1975*

1. An analysis of Italian legal decisions during 1975 must begin with Judgment No. 232 of the Constitutional Court of October 30, 1975 which is of special importance.[1] The order of the Court of Cassation of December 23, 1974 [2] which afforded it the opportunity of ruling on the constitutionality of the laws dealt with in the cases involving ICIC and the Ministry for Finance was referred to in the review of Italian legal decisions of 1974.[3]

The laws in question reproduced a Council regulation stipulating the provision of securities. They also delegated the executive power to adopt implementing orders. These orders reproduced a Commission regulation. What was therefore peculiar to these cases was that the national legislation was not in substance contrary to the relevant Community regulations but reproduced them almost to the letter. However, the court of first instance, followed by the Rome Court of Appeal, had considered it necessary to apply the national legislation only and to leave out of account the Community regulations and the inter-

---

18. It should be pointed out that the effects of the judgment of the Court of Justice in Case 65/74 are as follows:
a) Claims to the status of officials or establishment staff will not be admissible in the Italian courts; they could, where appropriate, be brought before the Court of Justice on the basis of the Staff Regulations.
b) The alternative claims to the status of local staff or to the same salary as that granted to officials and establishment staff fall, however, within the jurisdiction of the national courts. They were dismissed, however, on the merits both by the Labour Commissioner and recently by the Court of Appeal of Milan.

1. (1976) *Giustizia Civile,* IV, p. 3, with note by M. Berri; (1975) *Diritto comunitario e degli scambi internazionali,* 635, with a note by F. Capelli: "Norme nazionali posteriori confliggenti con quelle comunitarie"; (1975) *Giurisprudenza italiana,* I, 1, 209; (1975) *Foro italiano,* I, 2405, with a note by R. Monaco; (1976) *Foro Italiano,* I, 542, with a note by B. Conforti; (1975) *Giurisprudenza agraria,* II, 599; (1975) *Foro Padano,* III, 117; (1975) *Rivista di diritto europeo,* 343.

2. The Constitutional Court gave a ruling at the same time on a order made by the Rome Court of Appeal. The Court of Cassation sitting in joint session also requested the Constitutional Court to give a ruling on the conformity with the first paragraph of Article 10 and Article 11 of the Constitution, of Articles 9 and 10 of Decree Law No. 59 of Feb. 20, 1968 which was converted into Law No. 224 of March 18, 1968 by order No. 594 of Oct. 2, 1975. The text of the order and the submissions of the Attorney General, M. Berri,—who has published numerous studies and commentaries on Community legislation and case-law—are reproduced in (1975) *Diritto comunitario e degli scambi internazionali,* 627 *et seq.*; (1975) *Giurisprudenza italiana,* p. 1777 and IV, 113.

3. See above, p. 525 *et seq.*.

pretation of the latter by the Court of Justice [4] which had been requested by a German court and a Netherlands court.

In its Judgment No. 232 of October 30, 1975, the Constitutional Court laid down the following principles:

– Any subsequent national provisions adopted in a field already governed by a Community regulation are incompatible with the principles of the EEC Treaty and consequently with Article 11 of the Constitution not only if they are contrary to Community rules but also if they do no more than reproduce them (Sections 5 and 8).

– In the case of legislative provisions, the court hearing the proceedings does not itself have the power to declare them inapplicable, but must refer the matter to the Constitutional Court, which is responsible for declaring them unconstitutional on the ground of infringement of Article 11 (Section 6).[5]

On the one hand this judgment confirms Judgment No. 183 of December 27, 1973 [6] and thus supports the reverse trend already begun in relation to Judgment No. 14 of March 7, 1964.[7] In the latter judgment the Constitutional Court affirmed that since the EEC Treaty had been given effect in Italy by an ordinary law, it did not have supremacy over that source of law and that, consequently, where a law enacted subsequently was contrary to the Treaty, one could only apply the principle of *lex posterior derogat priori.* It had therefore considered that it was unnecessary to examine whether the law nationalising electricity, called into question by Mr. Costa, was incompatible with the Treaty.

This judgment provoked strong reaction in European circles and a rebuff from the Court of Justice in its judgment in *Costa v. ENEL* (Case 6/64) of July 15, 1964.[8] The Court held that Italy had not infringed the Treaty by nationalizing electricity but made a point of proclaiming the principle of the primacy of Community Law.

The Italian Constitutional Court did not, however, modify its approach to the problem of the relationship between Community Law and national law until its Judgment no. 183 of December 27, 1973 in which it acknowledged the "supranational" nature of the Community and the transfer to it of sovereign powers, in particular legislative powers. This transfer was made possible by Article 11 of the Constitution which allowed Italy to join international organisations that ensured peace and justice. The Court emphasised the need to give full weight to the principle of the direct applicability of regulations and several passages of the judgment were based on the principle of the primacy of Community Law.

The Court did not, however, specify how a subsequently enacted law which was incompatible with a regulation should be dealt with and in particular did not indicate:

–whether it is for the Constitutional Court to declare the subsequently enacted law unconstitutional on the ground of infringement of the abovementioned Article 11, or

–whether any court in proceedings in which it is shown that there is such incompatibility has the power to rule that the subsequent law shall not be applied.

The Constitutional Court in its Judgment No. 232 adopted the first solution.

---

4. See survey of Italian case law in 10 C.M.L. Rev. 1973, 340-351, at 348 and 12 C.M.L. Rev. 1975, 431-442, at 439.
5. In the case of rules adopted by the executive power pursuant to *ad hoc* delegation by the legislature, the court would also have to refer the matter to the Constitutional Court for it to declare such delegation to be unconstitutional; only then could the Court decide not to apply the rules in question (Section 7).
6. 12 C.M.L.Rev. 1975, 431.
7. (1974) Giur. Ital. I, 1, 516.
8. (1964) *Recueil,* 1158-1160.

"Insofar as subsequent national rules adopted in the form of laws and instruments having the effect of ordinary laws are concerned, the Constitutional Court believes that the legal system in force does not empower the Italian court to rule that they shall not be applied on the assumption that Community Law takes general precedence over national law. The proposed solution, which has been rejected by the Court of Cassation, of declaring void the subsequently enacted national law is certainly unacceptable since it must be ruled out that the outcome of transferring to the Community institutions the power to adopt laws on the basis of a precise criterion of allocating powers in certain fields "in order to carry out their task and in accordance with the provisions of the Treaties" (see Article 189 of the Treaty of Rome) is to emasculate entirely the sovereignty of the legislative bodies of the Member States, even where such sovereignty is exercised in areas set aside by the Treaties for Community regulation; such a transfer, on the contrary, raises the different problem of the constitutionality of various legislative instruments.

Furthermore, it does not seem possible to envisage inapplicability as resulting from the choice that the Italian court would occasionally be authorized to make between the Community rule and the national rule after having assessed their respective values. On this assumption, the Italian court would have to be regarded as not being empowered to choose between several applicable rules, but rather as being empowered to choose the only rule validly applicable, which would amount to admitting that it had the power, if only in certain restricted areas, to establish and declare that our legislator was totally lacking in competence, a power which is certainly not attributed to it under the legal system now in force.

It follows that, faced with a situation created by the adoption of Italian laws which have incorporated and converted into national law directly applicable Community regulations, the Court must question the constitutionality of such laws."

2. From all points of view, with one exception, this judgment, even more so than the 1973 judgment, follows the line adopted by the Court of Justice of the European Communities. It condemns not only subsequent laws that are incompatible with the provisions of Community regulations but also those which simply reproduce them more or less to the letter.

Although the former are relatively rare, there are many instances of the latter in Italy. Their main aim, at least in the beginning, seems to have been to facilitate awareness of Community rules and to provide those concerned with the opportunity of seeing the rules and the national implementing measures combined in a single text. They would not, therefore, have caused any serious problems if, in accordance with this aim, they had been interpreted as being merely of a declaratory nature.

However, they eventually came to be regarded as an invitation to the administrative and judicial authorities to apply their provisions in place of the Community regulations reproduced and thus as a denial of the principle of direct applicability.

Thus the practice of "reproduction" was condemned by the Court of Justice in Case 39/72, *Commission v. Italian Republic*,[9] and in 34/73, *Variola v. Ministry for Finance*.[10]

The main point of interest in Judgment No. 232 of 1975 lies in the fact that it supplements Judgment No. 183 of 1973 by stating which *penalty under national law* applies to an infringement of Community Law by a subsequent national law. This penalty will be a declaration of unconstitutionality by the Constitutional Court to which the matter is

9. Case 39/72, *Commission v. Italy* (Judgment of Feb. 7, 1973), (1973) E.C.R., 101.

10. Case 34/73, *Variola v. Italian Ministry of Finance* (Judgment of Oct. 10, 1973), (1973) E.C.R., 981.

referred by the court hearing the primary proceedings. This declaration not only permits the latter to take no account of the law complained of in the case in point, but is also valid *erga omnes* because, in accordance with Article 136 of the Constitution, "where the Court declares a provision of law to be unconstitutional, that provision shall cease to have effect from the day following the publication of the judgment".

Article 136 does not mean that a declaration of unconstitutionality has only an *ex nunc* effect. On the contrary, it is interpreted as meaning that from the day following publication of the judgment, the provision must be considered as no longer forming part of the legal system in force; in other words, every court will be obliged to discontinue applying it.[11]

Nevertheless, it remains true that this judgment, by holding intervention by the Constitutional Court to be the sole means of invaliditing a subsequent law which is contrary to or concurrent with Community Law, denies the court hearing a case the power not to apply such a law without having to refer the matter to the Constitutional Court.

It is regrettable, for the reasons described below, that Italy has not endorsed the principle of the non-application by the court of the law complained of, which is now accepted by the Supreme Courts of several Member States (including Germany which has a Constitutional Court similar to the Italian Court) and which is the only one which takes full account of the primacy of Community Law.

3. The merit of this judgment, and of the 1973 judgment, is that it has put and end to fine-spun arguments which have been going on for years. It is now firmly established:
—that the Treaties of Paris and Rome are lawful according to the Italian Constitution;
—that Community Law may be directly applicable;
—that Community provisions which are directly applicable take precedence over earlier national provisions;
—that such precedence also applies to subsequent national provisions.

On all these points the decisions of the Italian Constitutional Court are entirely in agreement with those of the Court of Justice of the European Communities. A single point remains at issue, *i.e.* the method of ensuring the precedence of Community Law over subsequent national law. According to judgment No. 232, it is for the Constitutional Court alone to declare such law unconstitutional for infringement of Article 11.

4. It must be admitted that the solution to this problem provided by the Constitutional Court corresponded with the wishes of prevailing Italian legal writing. It was disturbing and unthinkable that judges hearing a case, who, according to Article 101 of the Constitution "are subject only to the law", could decide not to apply a law *"tanquam non esset"*.[12] There were, however, a number of dissenting opinions on the matter and since they are rare, it is worth mentioning the most recent of them.[13]

---

11. Only acts which have been definitively settled under this law (period of limitation, preclusion, judgment which has the force of *res judicata*) will not be capable of being called into question.

12. A list of authors favouring this solution is provided by M. Capurso "Le ideologie giuridiche dello Stato nazionale moderno e l'ordinamento comunitario nella giurisprudenza italiana", (1975), *Studi parlamenti e di politica costituzionale,* No. 29/30, footnote 79.

13. F. Capelli, "Conflitto tra norma comunitaria e norma nazionale posteriore", (1975), *Foro Padano,* I, 241; "Norme nazionali posteriori confliggenti con quelle comunitarie", (1975) *Diritto comunitario e degli scambi internazionali,* 640-653; M. Capurso, "Le ideologie giuridiche dello Stato nazionale moderne e l'ordinamento comunitario nella giurisprudenza italiana", (1975) *Rivista studi parlamentari e di politica constituzionale,* No. 29/30; Criteri ermeneutici in ordine all'applicazione di norme communitarie, conven-

The solution to this problem provided by Judgment No. 232 of the Constitutional Court is unsatisfactory for many reasons which may be summarised as follows.

What is special about the Treaty of Rome is that the rights and obligations arising under it are not defined by the contracting parties but by the Court of Justice which, according to Article 164, "shall ensure that in the interpretation and application of this Treaty the law is observed". To be precise, the Court has said on a number of occasions,

> "According to the terms of Articles 189 and 191 of the Treaty, Regulations are, as such, directly applicable in all Member States and come into force solely by virtue of their publication in the Official Journal of the Communities, as from the date specified in them, or in the absence thereof, as from the date provided in the Treaty;
> Consequently, all methods of implementation are contrary to the Treaty which would have the result of creating an obstacle to the direct effect of Community Regulations and of jeopardizing their simultaneous and uniform application in the whole of the Community."[14]

And again:

> "The direct application of a Regulation means that its entry into force and its application in favour of or against those subject to it are independent of any measure of reception into national law.
>
> By virtue of the obligations arising from the Treaty and assumed on ratification, Member States are under a duty not to obstruct the direct applicability inherent in Regulations and other rules of Community Law.
>
> Strict compliance with this obligation is an indispensable condition of simultaneous and uniform application of Community Regulations throughout the Community.
>
> More particularly, Member States are under an obligation not to introduce any measure which might affect the jurisdiction of the Court to pronounce on any question involving the interpretation of Community Law or the validity of an act of the institutions of the Community, which means that no procedure is permissible whereby the Community nature of a legal rule is concealed from those subject to it.
>
> Under Article 177 of the Treaty in particular, the jurisdiction of the Court is unaffected by any provisions of national legislation which purport to convert a rule of Community Law into national law."[15]

The Court stressed in conclusion that the rule for solving conflicts between Community Law and national laws cannot be laid down by national constitutions since they would be unable to ensure the uniform authority of Community Law throughout the Community:

> "Recourse to the legal rules or concepts of national law in order to judge the validity of measures adopted by the institutions of the Community would have an adverse effect on the uniformity and efficiency of Community Law.

---

zionali e derivate, confliggenti con norme primarie di diritto interno", (1975) *Rivista trimestriale di diritto pubblico,* 1057-1096; G. Marenco, "La contrarietà della legge al diritto comunitario è una questione di costituzionalità?", (1975) *Diritto comunitario e degli scambi internazionali,* 300-307; R. Monaco, "Norma comunitaria e norma di legge interna successiva", (1975) *Foro Italiano,* I, 2662.

See also the list provided by M. Capurso in the first article quoted above, footnote 81.

14. Case 39/72, *Commission v. Italy* (Judgment of Feb. 7, 1973), (1973) E.C.R., 113.

15. Case 34/73, *Variola,* as n. 10. See also Case 14/68, *Walt Wilhelm* (Judgment of Feb. 13, 1969), 15 *Recueil* 1969, 14; Case 11/70, *Internationale Handelsgesellschaft* (Judgment of Dec. 17, 1970), 16 *Recueil* 1970, 1125; Case 84/71, *Marimex* (Judgment of March 7, 1972), 18 *Recueil* 1972, 89; Case 93/71, *Leonesio* Judgment of May 17, 1972), 18 *Receuil,* 287; Case 39/72, *Commission v. Italy* (Judgment of Feb. 7, 1973), (1973) E.C.R., 101.

The validity of such measures can only be judged in the light of Community Law.

In fact the law stemming from the Treaty, an independent source of law, cannot, because of its very nature, be overridden by rules of national law, however framed, without being deprived of its character as Community Law and without the legal basis of the Community itself being called in question.

Therefore the validity of a Community measure or its effect within a Member State cannot be affected by allegations that it runs counter to fundamental rights as formulated by the Constitution of that State or the principles of a national constitutional structure."[16]

It is, moreover, precisely to implement and properly apply these principles that courts of the various Member States have agreed that the courts should not apply national law which is incompatible with Community Law.[17] It is regrettable therefore that the precedence of Community Law can be guaranteed only by the Constitutional Court. Such regret cannot be countered with the argument that the solution of the "declaration of unconstitutionality" may have an advantage over that of "non-application" in that it gives rise at the stage of primary proceedings to a judgment which is valid *erga omnes* and which removes definitively all legal effect from the law complained of.

The fact remains, however, that from the point of view of principles, the approach adopted is based on a too restricted view of the primacy of Community Law, since the ordinary or administrative court does not have the power to draw the necessary inferences directly from it but has first of all to solicit a ruling from the Constitutional Court.

From a practical point of view, the introduction of an additional step (proceedings before the Constitutional Court) is likely to further complicate the procedure that has to be followed by those concerned to secure application of Community Law.

5. The drawbacks of the solution adopted by the Constitutional Court are even more obvious where the national law which is incompatible with Community Law does not simply reproduce a Community regulation but is openly in conflict with it. This is not a purely hypothetical question as the two examples below show.

a) In case 31/74 the Court of Justice stated:

"... in sectors covered by a common organization of the market—even more so when this organization is based on a common price system—Member States can no longer

---

16. Case 11/70, *Internationale Handelsgesellschaft*, as n. 15. See on this point Zweigert, quoted by M. Capurso in the article referred to in n. 13, published in (1975) *Rivista trimestriale di diritto pubblico*, 1063, note 12.

17. In the case of Belgium, see judgment in *"Fromagerie Le Ski"* of May 22, 1971, of the Court of Cassation, (1971) Rev.Trim.Dr.Eur., 494, and conclusions, 423; (1971) *Cahiers de droit européen*, 561, note by P. Pescatore; (1971) *Journal des Tribunaux*, 509 and 529, note by S. A. Salmon. In the case of France, see judgment in *Dir. Gen. des Douanes v. Soc. des Cafés Jacques Vabre* of the Court of Cassation of May 24, 1975; (1975); *Recueil Dalloz-Sirey, Jurisprudence*, 497-507; 95 *Gazette du Palais* 175, 2-7, nos. 194-196; 90 *Journal des Tribunaux* 1975, 496-501, n. 4922; 11 Rev.Trim.Dr.Eur. 1975, 336-357; (1975) *Cahiers de droit européen*, 631, with note by R. Kovar; 13 C.M.L.Rev. 1976, 128-132, note by G. Bebr. In the case of the Federal Republic of Germany, see judgment of June 9, 1971, of the Constitutional Court; 24 *Die Offentliche Verwaltung* 1971 No. 22, 77; 24 *Der Betrieb* 1971 No. 35, 1651-1652; 17 A.W.D.B.B. 1971 Nos. 8-9, 418-420; 87 *Deutsches Verwaltungsblatt* 1972 No. 7, 271-274; 25 *Monatschrift für Deutsches Recht* 1971 No. 10, 903-904; (1975) *Cahiers de droit européen*, 149, note by G. Cohen Jonathan.

interfere through national provisions taken unilaterally, in the machinery of price formation as established under the common organization."[18]

Mr. Galli, who had been charged by the *Pretore* of Rome with having contravened the Decree Laws adopted in July 1973 by the Italian Government to combat inflation, by reason of the fact that he had not submitted price scales and had invoiced agricultural products at prices higher than he had declared, was subsequently acquitted by the same *Pretore*.[19]

If the *Pretore* of Rome had taken as a prcedent the recent judgment of the Constitutional Court, he would have been unable to acquit Mr. Galli, but having received the opinion of the Court of Justice in Luxembourg, would have had to refer the matter to the Constitutional Court so that it could declare unconstitutional the national provisions under which Mr. Galli had been charged.

b) More recently, the Court of Justice, in reply to questions referred to it by an Italian Court, stated that Article 6 of Commission Regulation No. 834/74 was invalid.[20] It was on the basis of this provision that the Italian Government had adopted Decree Law No. 255 of July 8, 1974 which required all persons who held certain quantities of sugar on July 1, 1974 to pay a certain charge.

In these circumstances the Italian court, having learnt thus that the legal basis was unfounded, could, prior to the ruling of the Constitutional Court, have ordered the defendant to reimburse what it had improperly levied. Now it will have to suspend the proceedings anew and wait until the Constitutional Court has declared the Italian law in question to be contrary to Article 11 of the Constitution. The provision will thus continue to be applied until the date of any future judgment.

6. A list of the drawbacks arising from the judgment of the Constitutional Court could be summarised as follows:

—the primacy of Community Law is certainly acknowledged but is secured only by a "long march" through tortuous legal proceedings;

—until the Constitutional Court gives a ruling the national law will continue to be applied at the expense of Community Law. It may be asked what is to become thus of the primacy of Community Law and its simultaneous and uniform application in the Community;

—a ruling of the Constitutional Court has in principle, *"ex nunc"* effect and consequently does not satisfactorily guarantee the principles inherent in Community Law;

—it may even be asked whether rulings of the Constitutional Court do not affect other aspects of decisions of the Court of Justice of the European Communities. Recent judgments of the Court,[21] under which certain proceedings brought under the second paragraph of Article 215 of the Treaty against the Commission have been declared inadmissible, with the applicants having to have recourse to the national courts, become less convincing if the protection of rights in the national courts is subject to long delays.[22]

---

18. Case 31/74, *Galli* (Judgment of Jan. 23, 1975), (1975) E.C.R., 47, at 66.

19. See below, B, no. 4.

20. Case 23/75, *Rey Soda v. Cassa Conguaglio Zucchero* (Judgment of Oct. 30, 1975), (1975) E.C.R., 1279.

21. Case 99/74, *Grands Moulins v. Commission* (Judgment of Nov. 26, 1975), (1975) E.C.R., 1531; Case 46/75, *IBC v. Commission* (Judgment of Jan. 27, 1976), (1976) E.C.R., 65; Joined Cases 67 to 85/75, *Lessieur Cotelle and others v. Commission* (Judgment of March 17, 1976), (1976) E.C.R., 391.

22. See opinion of Mr. Advocate-General H. Mayras in Case 43/72, *Merkur v. Commission*, (1973) E.C.R., 1079.

B. *Other important judgments in 1975*

1. The Constitutional Court, in Judgment No. 232 of October 30, 1975,[23] declared to be plainly unfounded the question of the constitutionality of the Italian provisions under which the issue of import licences for agricultural products was made subject to the giving of a security or the provision of a bank guarantee to secure performance of the transaction.

The Constitutional Court followed on this point the principles laid down in the judgments of the Court of Justice.[24]

2. Without going into technical details, it is interesting to draw attention to another decision of the Court of Cassation regarding agricultural levies.[25] The Court considered that the date to be taken into consideration for determining the amount of the levy applicable to imports of certain agricultural products covered by the common organisation of the market is the date of authorization to remove the goods and not the date of acceptance by the customs authorities of the importer's declaration of intention to make the goods available for consumption. The interest lies in the regrettable fact that the Court of Cassation did not make use of the procedure under Article 177 to allay the doubts which could legitimately have existed. The Tribunal of Genoa was more prudent on this question and referred to the Court of Justice of the European Communities questions which are currently *sub judice*.[26]

3. The Court of Cassation, following the line adopted in Judgments Nos. 1772 and 1773 of June 8, 1972, referred to in the review for 1972,[27] analysed in Judgments No. 2 of January 4, 1975 [28] and 10 of January 7, 1975,[29] Article III (2) of GATT [30] and Article 95 of the Treaty of Rome. It was thus able to declare that a charge differentiating between imported brandy and nationally produced eau-de-vie, where it existed prior to Law No. 295 of April 5, 1950,[31] which implemented GATT in Italy, was compatible with that Agreement even though such differential treatment was incompatible with Article 95 of the Treaty of Rome, the first paragraph of which is directly applicable from January 1, 1962:

> "It must be made clear that the principle of fiscal parity laid down in Article 95 of the EEC Treaty must be interpreted as meaning total fiscal parity in the same way as the similar provision in Article III of GATT, but with the difference that Article 95 is not

23. (1975) *Foro Italiano*, 2551. A similar ruling was made by the Constitutional Court in Judgment No. 86 of June 19, 1973, (1973) *Foro Italiano*, 2370.

24. Case 11/70, as n. 15 above; Case 25/70, *Einfuhr- und Vorratstelle Getreide v. Köster*, 16 *Recueil* 1970, 1161.

25. C. Cass, Dec. 3, 1975, No. 4004, (1976) *Giustizia Civile*, I, 22, with note by M.B.

26. Case 113/75, *Fracassetti v. Administration des Finances de l'Etat.* See now Judgment of June 15, 1976, not yet published.

27. 10 C.M.L.Rev. 1973, 344.

28. (1975) *Diritto comunitario e degli scambi internazionali*, 267, with note by G. Venturini.

29. *Ibid.*, 281; (1975) Riv.dir.int.proc.e.priv., 76.

30. Article III (2):

> "The products of the territory of any contracting party imported into the territory of any other contracting party shall not be subject, directly or indirectly, to internal taxes or other internal charges of any kind in excess of those applied, directly or indirectly, to like domestic products. Moreover, no contracting party shall otherwise apply internal taxes or other internal charges to imported or domestic products in a manner contrary to the principles set forth in paragraph 1."

31. *Gazzetta Ufficiale* of June 9, 1950, No. 130 (suppl.).

subject to the standstill clause, since it is directly applicable from January 1, 1962 and takes precedence over national law without being subject to any limitation or condition of compatibility with pre-existing law. It is precisely this difference which is responsible for the practical interest of importers in invoking the Community provision rather than the corresponding GATT one. In fact, where the State duty on eau-de-vie is concerned, the reasoning followed above led to the conclusion that the unfavourable treatment of imported brandy may be justified in that such treatment existed previously (October 10, 1949) but may only hold good in the case of Article III of GATT. It cannot be aplied to Article 95 of the EEC Treaty which prohibits even partial differential treatment. . .".

4. It was stated above that the *Pretore* of Rome, after having received the replies of the Court of Justice to the questions referred to it in the *Galli* case,[32] acquitted the defendant. In a judgment of April 15, 1975, the *Pretore* applied the principles contained in the judgment of the Court of Justice. Since Member States can no longer intervene in the machinery of price formation of products covered by the common organisation of the market, Mr. Galli, was not obliged to comply with the relevant Italian provisions and had to be acquitted because the matter with which he had been charged does not constitute an offence.[33]

5. A trader in Naples was also ordered by a decree of the *Pretore* of Naples to pay a fine for infringement of the same Decree Law No. 425 of July 24, 1973. He appealed against the decree and was finally acquitted on the basis of the decision of the Court of Justice in the *Galli* case referred to above.[34] A trader in Voghera suffered the same mishap with the same favourable result.[35]

6. Applying the principle of the primacy of Community Law over national law, the *Pretore* of Castellammare di Stabbia, in a judgment of May 2, 1975, acquitted a producer of spaghetti and similar products which on analysis were discovered to contain 10% of common wheat.[36] The judge held that under Regulations 30/62, 120/67, 768/69 and 1492/71 a percentage of this order was permitted by Community rules. The *Pretore* would have been wiser to refer the matter to the Court of Justice for a preliminary ruling since the scope of the Community and the national provisions could have been different. It is interesting nevertheless to point out that the *Pretore*, acting on the basis of the primacy of Community Law, did not apply the national provision and that this occurred during criminal proceedings, as in the previous case.

7. The conflict between a Community provision and a national provision can be seen rather curiously in the conflicting positions adopted in a judgment of the Tribunal of Milan and in an order of that Tribunal published within a few days of one another, where the same judge acted as rapporteur.

In its judgment of March 6, 1975,[37] the Tribunal acknowledged that the Italian Parliament, following ratification of the Treaty establishing the European Economic

32. Case 31/74, *Galli*, (1975) E.C.R., 47.

33. (1975) *Diritto comunitario e degli scambi internazionali*, 297; (1975) *Foro Padano*, IV, 10; (1975) *Giurisprudenza agraria*, II, 625, and note by V. Metta, 588.

34. *Pretura* of Naples, judgment of April 18, 1975, (1975) *Diritto comunitario e degli scambi internazionali*, 462.

35. *Pretura of Voghera*, judgment of May 22, 1975, (1975) *Diritto comunitario e degli scambi internazionali*, 464.

36. (1975) *Giurisprudenza agraria*, II, 626, with note by V. Metta, 584 *et seq.*

37. (1975) *Diritto comunitario e degli scambi internazionali*, 458; (1975), *Foro Padano*, 241, with a note by F. Capelli.

Community, acting on the basis of Article 11 of the Constitution, had relinquished the right to exercise part of its sovereign powers which it delegated to the Community institutions. Following this renunciation, directly applicable Community rules and national rules do not rank equally, and in view of the fact that the former take precedence in the event of conflict between them, the court must rule that a national rule which is contrary to Community Law, whether it was adopted prior or subsequent to Community Law, is ineffective. It was on the basis of this reasoning that the Tribunal considered that it could leave out of account the question of constitutionality and not refer the matter to the Constitutional Court. In the case in question it was a matter of giving precedence to Community provisions contained in certain regulations introducing a common agricultural policy which prohibited the levying of any customs duty or tax having equivalent effect, over Italian Law No. 447 of June 24, 1971, which had indeed provided for the abolition of statistical duties and charges for administrative services levied on imported goods, but with effect from dates which did not coincide with those laid down in the Community regulations.

A few days later, the same judge, by order of March 13, 1975, held that the conflict between Laws Nos. 30 of January 23, 1968 and 1239 of December 30, 1970 concerning the charge for the health inspection of imported goods, which were contrary to Articles, 9, 12, 13 and 95 of the Treaty and Regulations 13/64 and 804/68, and Article 11 of the Constitution [38] must be submitted to the Constitutional Court.

C. Maestripieri,
Brussels.

38. (1975), *Diritto comunitario e degli scambi internazionali,* 458; (1975), *Foro Padano,* 241, with a note by F. Capelli: "Conflitto fra norma comunitaria e norma nazionale posteriore".

SURVEY OF LITERATURE*

I. *INTEGRATION, ECONOMIC AND POLITICAL*

R. Aron, "The crisis of the European Idea", 11 *Government and Opposition* 1976, 5-20.

L. J. Brinkhorst, "De EEG en de nieuwe internationale economische orde", (1975) *Internationale Spectator*, 325-330.

J. Bryan, Collester and H. Brunham, "Eurocontrol: A reappaisal of functional integration", 13 J. Comm. Mark. Studies 1975, 345-367.

Eurocontrol is used by the authors in order to develop a new variant of the functionalist theories of integration *i.e.* "protofunctionalism". This is a form of functionalism which in some respects closely resembles federalism because it is an integration strategy which is mainly carried out by regional public authorities and benefits the public as a whole rather than particular public or private groups of persons, as is the case with the (neo-)-functionalist strategy. Organisations such as Eurocontrol, which provide international public services, have probably more chance of creating a "spill-over" effect than ordinary international organisations, because the public is directly involved in the services they provide.

David P. Calleo, "The European Coalition in a Fragmenting World", 54 *Foreign Affairs* 1975, 98-112.

According to the author, European integration proceeds not from the desire to hand over sovereignty to supranational communities, but rather out of the tendency to safeguard national sovereignty. The EC is a confederal structure, which by means of economic integration and certain common policies creates the conditions in which the modern, technologically highly-developed state can continue to exist. In the author's opinion, Europe has weathered the oil-crisis well: with their prompt individual actions, the global Mediterranean policy and the Euro-Arab dialogue, the European states have certainly reacted adequately to the situation, and by these means have brought about a more stable and lasting relationship with the Arab states, while also covering themselves on the Atlantic side by participation in the I.E.A. *etc.*

G. Colonna di Paliano, "International private investment problems: European Community-United States", (1975) *Aussenwirtschaft* Heft II/IV, 276-303.

The author discusses the problems created for the process of European integration as a result of direct American investment in the Member States. He further considers the proposals made in this regard by the Commission in the framework of the common industrial policy: no protectionism, but a strengthening of the competitive position of European undertakings.

Claude Evain, "Il faut une Europe politique", (1975) *Les Problèmes de l'Europe* no. 70, 7-16.

I. Fauvre, "La normalisation des produits sidérurgiques dans la Communauté européenne", (1975) R.M.C. no. 189, 457-463.

* See for the classification of subjects and list of abbreviations, 12 C.M.L.Rev. 1975, 115-117.

13 C.M.L. Rev. 1976, 541-554

L. A. Geelhoed, "De Europese Unie", 23 SEW 1975, 431-436.

S. Patijn, "De Europese Unie", 23 SEW, 655-668.

Contributions to the discussion on European Union written for the Netherlands Association for European Law. Geelhoed's report, drawing largely on German literature, goes thoroughly into the questions of coordination and judicial remedies, whereas that of Patijn treats rather the institutional aspects of the European Union.

M. Hirsch, "Influence without power: small states in European politics", 32 *The World Today* 1976, 112-188.

M. Hirsch, "Die Logik der Integration. Ueberlegungen zu Aussenbeziehungen westeuropäischer Kleinstaaten", 29 E.A. 1974, 447-456.

M. Hirsch, "La situation internationale des petits Etats", 24 Rev.fr. de sc.polit. 1974.

These three studies consider the problems encountered by small states in the wider European context. The approach to these problems is more theoretical in the French and German articles, more factual in the English article.

J. H. Leurdijk, "Nederland en de Europese veiligheid: het civiele Europa in discussie", 29 *Internationale Spectator* 1975, 554-565.

A discussion of the reports of the advisory committees—Spierenburg and Röling—in the wider context of the issue of European security.

J. Lodge, "Toward the European Political Community: EEC summits and European Integration", 19 *Orbis, a journal of world affairs* 1975, 626-652.

An analysis of the summit conferences of 1972, 1973, 1974 with regard to their significance for the Community decision-making process. A new institutional balance has been created whereby the role of the intergovernmental organs, such as the COREPER, has been strengthened, whereas that of the Commission has been weakened. The significance of the creation of the European Council is only briefly treated in the conclusion.

G. Møller, "Metoder til harmonisering og unifikation i Norden, EEC og USA", 44 *Nordisk Tidskrift for International Ret* 1974/75, 229-263.

Michael Palmer, "EEC: the road to better political co-operation", 32 *The World Today* 1976, 25-30.

The author expresses the fear that in direct negotiations with Comecon the EEC may be led to make concessions in the area of commercial policy, without obtaining in return concessions in the field of human rights and arms reduction. The EEC must therefore broaden its political cooperation, and be prepared to work together to a certain extent with NATO.

J. Pinder, "Europe as a Tenth Member of the Community", 10 *Government and Opposition* 1975, 387-397.

H. Schneider and W. Wessels, "Gestalt und Inhalt einer "Europäischen Union"; Ein Diskussionsbeitrag zur Tindemans-Mission", 30 E.A. 1975, 587-597.

P. H. Scott, "Beyond the Eurogroup: new developments in European defence", 32 *The World Today* 1976, 31-38.

D. P. Spierenburg, "Het Rapport-Tindemans: een kritische beschouwing", 30 *Internationale Spectator* 1976, 143-152.

The author believes that the Tindemans Report gives a correct analysis of the problems of European integration at the present time, but cannot fully support the solutions suggested by Tindemans.

M. van der Stoel, "Europese eenwording: de Nederlandse waardering van idealen en werkelijkheden", 30 *Internationale Spectator* 1977, 39-48.

A clear analysis of the re-orientation of Dutch policy with regard to Europe, which is now strongly based on the ideas of the Spierenburg Report; the EMU as a motor of further integration, and the European Union as an in-between stage on the way to a federal Europe and the old Dutch hobby-horse of increased powers for the European Parliament.

W. Wallace, "Wider but weaker: the continued enlargement of the EEC", 32 *The World Today* 1976, 104-111.

A description of the problems which will arise with the further enlargement of the European Community. Economically weak States, such as Greece and Spain, apply for membership, whereas economically strong States, such as Norway and Sweden, particularly for political reasons, show little interest. This development emphasizes the need for political motivation in the process of European integration.

II. *INTEGRATION, GENERAL LEGAL ASPECTS*

Manfred Zuleeg, "Die innerstaatliche Anwendbarkeit völkerrechtlicher Verträge am Beispiel des GATT und der Europäische Sozialcharta", 35 Zeit.A.O.R.V. 1975, 341-363.

III. *INTEGRATION, TECHNOLOGICAL ASPECTS*

G. Lafferanderie, "Les organisations spatiales européennes", 21 *Annuaire Européen* 1973, 67-81.

A clear review of the re-structuring of ELDO and ESRO to form the European Space Agency (ESA). Mention is also made of the programmes (present and prospective) of these organisations.

IV. *EUROPEAN COMMUNITIES*

A. *COMMON SUBJECTS*

1. *General*

R. Pourvoyeur, "Effects de redistribution des revenues. Approche théorique et reflexions sur ses applications au marché Communautaire", (1975) R.M.C., 565-581.

G. Thompson, "Europe after the British referendum", 28 *Studia Diplomatica* 1975, 621-629.

Carol and Kenneth Twitchett, "The Common Market Referendum in Retrospect", 5 *International Relations* 1975, 917-934.

A critical review of the literature concerning the Community and British membership thereof which appeared at the time of the referendum. The authors conclude that the British people, in spite of the positive result of the referendum, are far from being convinced Europeans.

2. *Institutional*

J. L. Burban, "Les républicains indépendants et l'élection du Parlement européen au suffrage universel", (1975) R.M.C. no. 190, 495-500.

R. Cohen, "De samenwerking van de socialistische partijen in de Europese Gemeenschap", 29 *Internationale Spectator* 1975, 670-679.

J. L. Giraudy, "Le budget des 'Neuf' ne traduit pas une volonté de faire progresser la construction européenne", (1975) R.M.C. no. 190, 491-495.

A critical review of the 1976 draft budget of the European Communities.

W. E. Paterson and A. H. Thomas (ed.), "Social Democratic Parties of the European Community", 13 J.Comm.Mark Studies 1975, 415-503.

R. Pourvoyeur, "Den Europaeiske Beslutningsproces og ens reformering", 44 *Nordisk Tidskrift for International Ret* 1974/75, 39-49.

M. Quintin, "Participation de l'Assemblée parlementaire européenne au déroulement des accords commerciaux", 11 R.T.D.E. 1975, 211-226.

The repeated attempts by the European Parliament to obtain more say by the EEC has led to the creation of a procedure whereby the Parliament has, in comparison with national assemblies, acquired a relatively large competence. But care must be taken that the procedure does not become too unwieldy.

3. *Court of Justice*

L. Dubouis, "Fonctionnaires des Communautés européennes. Commentaire de la jurisprudence de la Cour de Justice des Communautés européennes", 11 R.T.D.E. 1975, 280-307.

Claus Gulmann, "EF-Domstolen 1974", 44 *Nordisk Tidskrift for International Ret* 1974/75, 50-87.

K. Hagel-Sørensen, "Unmittelbart Anvedelig EF-Ret Belijst ved EF-Domstolen Praksis 1974", 44 *Nordisk Tidskrift for International Ret* 1974/75, 88-112.

C. S. P. Harding, "Decisions addressed to member states and Article 173 of the Treaty of Rome", 25 I.C.L.Q. 1976, 15-34.

A critical look at the case-law of the Court of Justice concerning the conditions which must be fulfilled by an individual before he can appeal against a decision which is addressed to another person, including to a Member State.

L. P. Kristensen, C. Køningsfeldt, "AETR-dommen", 44 *Nordisk Tidskrift for International Ret* 1974/75, 160-228.

Mackenzie Stuart, "La Cour de Justice des Communautés européennes et le contrôle du pouvoir discretionnaire", 26 Rev.int.dr.comp. 1974, 61-72.

In this article Lord Mackenzie Stuart, judge at the Court of Justice, compares the possibilities which exist in the different Member States for appeal against administrative decisions. The situation in the United Kingdom is particularly brought to the fore. The United Kingdom could learn much from the case-law of the Court of Justice and of the courts of the other Member States. This kind of interaction is useful, the more so in that the Court of Justice has itself drawn largely on the administrative law of the original six Member States.

J. M. Mössner, "Haftung der europäischen Gemeinschaft für legislatives Unrecht", 22 A.W.D. 1976, 93-95.

A critical analysis of the CNTA judgment (Case 74/74).

W. Van Gerven, "De niet-contractuele aansprakelijkheid van de Gemeenschap wegens normatieve handelingen", 24 S.E.W. 1976, 2-29.

M. Wathelet, "Pratiques concertées et comportements paralleles en oligopole. Le cas des matières colorantes", (1975) R.T.D.E., 663-699.

On the basis of the *Deystruffs* case, the author discusses certain aspects of concerted and parallel behaviour in an oligopolistic market situation.

5. *Relationship between Community Law and national law*

S. AUken, J. Buksti, C. Lehmann, "Denmark joins Europe: Patterns of adaptation in the Danish political administrative processes as a result of membership of the European Communities". 14 J.Comm.Mark.Studies 1975, 1-37.

The authors distinguish between the "scope of integration" (integration by means of international cooperation, which is supported by Denmark) and the "level of integration" (integration by means of increasing supranationality, which is rejected by Denmark). This support of the confederal approach has brought about a centralisation of political and administrative processes as far as the Danish Community policy is concerned.

G. Bebr, "Examen en validité au titre de l'article 177 du traté CEE et la cohesion juridique de la Communauté", 11 C.D.E. 1975, 379-424.

This article gives a review of the case-law of the Court of Justice concerning the control of validity of Community acts in the framework of the Art. 177 procedure. The author investigates the nature and scope of the control of validity, the grounds of invalidity and the consequences of the decisions of the Court. He also investigates the connection with the exception of illegality and the appeal for a declaration of nullity. Bebr concludes that the control of validity is more an objective control of the "constitutionality" of Community acts than a means for the judicial protection of individuals. For that reason it is of the greatest importance that only the Court is competent to control the validity. In this context, the author strongly criticises the judgment of the German Constitutional Court of May 29, 1974 which poses a danger for the legal cohesion of the Community which it is the purpose of Art. 177 to assure.

"Französisches Kassationsgericht Urteil von 24-5-75, n. 115, betr. Vorrang des EWG-Vertrages vor später erlassenem französischen Recht" mit Anmerkung von Roland Bieber, 10 EuR. 1975, 326-334.

Michel Fromont, "Die französische Rechtsprechung zum Gemeinschaftsrecht Januar 1972-December 1974", 10 EuR. 1975, 334-354.

Niels Gangsted-Rasmussen, "Primauté du droit communautaire en cas de conflit avec le droit danois", 11 RTDE. 1975, 700-707.

Carlo Curti Gialdino, "Rapporti fra la legislazione ambientele nazionale e la normativa comunitaria. In margine alle osservazioni della commissione delle comunità europee sulla proposta di legge n. 3193 dettante "norme per la tutela delle acque dell'inquinamento", 15 *Rivista di diritto europeo* 1975, 97-115.

K. Hagel sørensen, "Forholdet mellem EF-retten og de nationale grundlove," 44 *Nordisk Tidskrift for International Ret* 1974/75, 113-145.

J. Leyten, "Wie beslist over de vraag of er een prejudiciële vraag is?" (Article 177 of the EEC Treaty), 50 NJB 1975, 1187-1190.

J. Lodge, "The organisation and control of European integration in the Federal Republic of Germany", 28 *Parliamentary Affairs* 1975, 416-431.

An overview of the organisational structures established in the Federal Republic in order, on the one hand, to create a European policy, and on the other, to implement the policy of the Communities. Beginning with the situation of the 1950's, when the Federal Republic could only carry out a restricted foreign policy, the growing influence of the EC on German institutions is described. The Chancellor's Office and the Ministries of Foreign and Economic Affairs play a particularly important role. This increase in competences made it necessary to set up coordination committees and interministerial workgroups. The role of the two chambers of parliament is mainly limited to the establishment of channels of information and control.

D. D. Miedema, "Prioriteit van Communautair recht?", 10 S.E.W. 1975, 614-618.

Is it possible to demand repayment of a charge which has been declared invalid *"ex tunc"* by the Court of Justice because of conflict with a directly applicable Treaty provision, once the national appeals deadline had gone by? The author expects in the future a good deal of case-law on this question.

F. Sabiani, "L'incidence du droit de la CEE sur la reglementation française des prix", 11 R.T.D.E. 1975, 470-517 and 633-662.

The EEC Treaty contains no specific provisions for the area of prices policy. But the more Community policies come into being in different areas, whereby national competences are transferred to the Community, the more shall the Member States indirectly lose their authonomous powers in the field of prices policy, and will only be competent to implement the Community policy. The French prices policy in the different areas of economic activity is examined in this context.

G. Ubertazzi, "L'impact du droit communautaire dans le procès pénal interne", 11 R.T.D.E. 1975, 196-210.

6. *Adhesion*

Bengt Beutler, "Der Beitritt Grossbritanniens zur Europäischen Gemeinschaft", 24 *Jahrbuch des Offentlichen Rechts* 1975, 1-25.

One must be acuainted both with the heterogeneous basis of Community Law and the British legal system before being able to reach a judgment on the European Communities Act. From the point of view of Community Law, the author discerns several doubtful points in this otherwise impressive document.

John Pesmazoglu, "Greece's proposed accession to the EEC", 32 *The World Today* 1976, 142-151. German version in E.A. 1976, 215-225.

Pesmazoglu, who led the Greek delegation in the association negotiations argues for a speedy accession of Greece to the Community. He demonstrates that Greece is already, through its long period of association, strongly integrated into the Community, that this association (in spite of the maladministration of the Colonels) has had a very positive influence on the development of the Greek economy, and that it is also politically desirable that Greece should join the Community as soon as possible. He rejects the attitude of the Commission on this question. Finally, he discusses the economic, institutional and political aspects of an eventual Greek membership.

David Rudnick, "Spain's long road to Europe", 32 *The World Today* 1976, 134-141.

C. *EUROPEAN ECONOMIC COMMUNITY*

1. *General*

H. Batifol and R. van der Elst, "Projet de Convention CEE sur la loi applicable aux obligations contractuelles et non-contractuelles", 11 R.T.D.E. 1975, 181-195.

There are in fact two articles here, one dealing with obligations arising out of a contract, and the other with obligations arising other than from a contract, as regulated in the draft convention. A short but clear analysis of some of the problems.

"Choice of Law in the field of contracts in the EEC", 12 *Netherlands International Law Review* 1975, 183-203.

Report of the 1975 annual meeting of the Netherlands Association for International Law, concering the EEC Preliminary Draft Convention on the Law Applicable to Contractual and Non-Contractual obligations.

L. Collins, "Contractual and non-contractual obligations—EEC Preliminary Draft Convention", 25 I.C.L.Q. 1976, 15-35.

H. Lesguillons, "L'extension des compétences de la communauté économique européenne par l'article 235 du Traité de Rome", 20 *Annuaire Française de Droit International* 1974, 886-904.

The recent practice of the Council shows an astonishing increase in the resort to Art. 235 EEC in order to create new Community competences in different areas. This development has been made possible by an extensive interpretation of the objectives of the Community. But in spite of its increasing importance, the application of Art. 235 is limited: the object in question must fall within the economic objectives of the Community and the application of Art. 235 may not threaten the decision-making process of the Community nor conflict with the general principles of law enuntiated by the Court of Justice.

W. Van Gerwen, "De niet-contractuele aansprakelijkheid van de Gemeenschap wegens normatieve handelingen", 24 S.E.W. 1976, 2-29.

J. M. Mössner, "Haftung der europäischen Gemeinschaft für legislatives Unrecht", 22 R.I.W./A.W.D. 1976, 93-95.

An analysis of the CNTA judgment (case 74/74).

R. Pourvoyeur, "Effets de redistribution des revenues. Approche théorique et réflexions sur ses applications au Marché Communautaire", (1975) R.M.C., 565-581.

3. *Agriculture*

"Compte-rendu sténographique de la XXVIIIe Table Ronde (Paris 11 et 12 avril 1975 – Thème: "Face aux nouvelles perspectives mondiales repenser la politique agricole commune", 18 *Les Problèmes de l'Europe* 1975, no. 69, 17-145.

A report of the introduction to and the discussion at the 28th *Table Ronde,* organised by the *"Association pour l'étude des problèmes de l'Europe.* The preliminary documents appeared in no. 68 at pp. 17-65. Central theme: sufficient production, stable price levels and fair distribution of income both in the EC and in the world at large.

Peter Kalbe, "Europäisches Agrarrecht, Internationales Verwaltungsrecht im Werden", 90 *Deutsches Verwaltungsblatt* 1975, 753-758.

With references to case-law and practice, this article examines the influence of European agricultural law on national agricultural law, the significance of basic principles and the system of market organisation for the interpretation of the law governing the organisation of the markets. Further, the author goes into a number of questions concerning the administrative agricultural law which is gradually developing at European level. In this respect the author considers the question as to how more unity is to be attained in the implementation of Community Law by the nine national administrations in the cases where the latter are allowed a certain degree of discretion, and the question of the recognition and violability of administrative acts from one Member State to the other. The general scope of this article means that it can be warmly recommended also to the non-specialist in European agricultural law.

J. Lardinois, "Effets de l'élargissement des Communautés sur la politique agricole commune", 21 *Annuaire Européen* 1973, 39-53.

After a description of the *"acquis communautaire"* of the common agricultural policy, the author considers the significance for this policy of the enlargement of the Community. The enlarged Community should recognise its responsibility in the world by the granting of preferences to developing countries. He concludes with an evaluation of the first year of the enlarged Community, made exceptionally difficult through the oil crisis and the shortage of raw materials.

4. *Free movement of persons, establishment and services*

A. Fresia, "La libre circulation des personnes et le principe de non-discrimination dans la jurisprudence de la Cour de Justice des Communautés", (1975) R.M.C., 550-565.

There is little national case-law relating to the free movement of persons, apart from in the area of social security, so that it is not possible to draw any conclusions here. But the author's survey does not appear to proceed beyond 1973. There follows a detailed discussion of the case-law of the Court of Justice, with an analysis of the notion of "free movement" and of the principle of non-discrimination on which the notion is based.

Y. Loussouarn, "Droit d'établissement", 11 R.T.D.E. 1975, 518-531.
An overview of the recent judgments of the Court of Justice concerning freedom of establishment and freedom to provide services (cases 2/74, 33/74).

6. *Transport*

R. Rodière, A. Chêmel, "Transport mise en place générale du droit communautaire des transports (Années 1973 et 1974)" 11 R.T.D.E. 1975, 550-560.
After a preliminary slowing-down following the accession negotiations, the transport policy appears to be acquiring a certain impetus again. But the length of the article speaks for itself.

7. *Competition*

J. F. Bellis, "Potential competition and concentration policy; Relevance to EEC Antitrust", 10 J.W.T.L. 1976, 24-50.
The author discusses the notion of potential competition which is also significant in terms of European cartel law, and considers this notion in the light of Articles 85 and 86. The significance of potential competition for an effective competition policy is considered, in particular with reference to concentrations.

Edwin H. Clock and Jin Lee John, "Art. 85 and European antitrust litigation: a search for economic balancing", 27 *Stanford Law Review* 1974/1975, 1275-1301.
The authors discuss the economic policy which they believe lies behind the application of Art. 85 by the Commission and the Court. They distinguish three schools in the practice of recent years, and argue for a more economically-orientated approach to the application of Art. 85. The application in practice of their approach would imply that an optimal competition policy would involve a legally-supervised cost-benefit analysis with respect to vertical agreements and a *per se* prohibition of horizontal agreements.

L. Focsaneaunu, "La jurisprudence de la Cour de Justice des Communautés européennes en matière de concurrence; VI — Les pratiques concertées", (1975) R.M.C., 463-479.

Maurice Kay, "Company Mergers and the EEC", (1975) *Journal of Business Law*, 88-107.
The author's central argument is that there is in the EEC no consistent doctrine concerning mergers. He discusses the means whereby the Commission wishes to encourage mergers in order to fare better against competition from third States: the possibility of transnational mergers and the European Limited Company. Thereafter he discusses the question of the control of mergers, in particular Art. 86 and its application in the *Continental Can* case. The author concludes that the merger phenomenon in Europe is only at a very early stage. He considers it possible that competition provisions which differ according to sector will come into being. Where transnational mergers are difficult to realise, much can also be achieved by less far-reaching forms of cooperation. In particular, the Commission's policy with regard to cooperation agreements gives much scope for experiment.

8. *Taxation*

G. Montagnier, "Fiscalité", 11 R.T.D.E. 1975, 532-549.

W. E. Pool, "Jersey, Guernsey and EC plans for direct taxation", (1975) *Intertax* no. 8, 295-299.

At the moment the Channel Islands are an important tax haven, not only for wealthy Britons but also for international corporations. While the first category may be said to amount to a national problem, the tax evasion and flight of the second category has unfabourable consequences for the whole of the Community. The author discusses the plans drawn up by the Commission to check this practice.

9. *Harmonisation of legislation*

N. Bel, "L'oeuvre communautaire en matière d'harmonisation des législations des produits pharmaceutiques", (1975) R.M.C., 505-515.

M. B. Burgio, "Le nouveau régime fiscal des dividendes en Italie par rapport aux perspectives de l'harmonisation communautaire", (1975) *Intertax* no. 8, 315-321.

The author criticises the new Italian tax on dividends, not only in the context of the Community plans for harmonisation, but also because it is a system which *"pratiquement légalise une sorte d'évasion pour les hauts revenues qui restent anonyme".*

M. Gaudet, "Vers un marché européan de l'assurance", 23 *Annuaire Européen* 1973, 113-141.

A clear review, up to the middle of 1974, of the problems which hinder the establishment of a European insurance market. The author does not discuss the legal and technical side of the draft directives, but gives rather a background analysis.

10. *Economic and Monetary Policy*

A. Carlsen, "Den Økonomiske OG monetaere union: EF", 44 *Nordisk Tidskrift for International Ret* 1974/75, 146-159.

I. C. Leygues, "A la recherche de la convergence des politiques économiques des Etats Membres", (1975) R.M.C., 436-441.

V. Sengeant, "Le droit économique des états membres dans une union économique et monétaire", 11 C.D.E. 1975, 464-479.

R. Triffin, "The Community and the disruption of the world monetary system", *Banca Nazionale del Lavoro Quarterly Review* no. 112, March 1975.

The author argues that the EMU would not only contribute to the solution of the problem of market inflation and the international monetary chaos, but that it is also necessary for the realisation of the eventual economic, monetary and political unification of Europe. He also discusses the measures which, in his view, should be taken in the near future with regard to exchange rates, the European currency and the European Monetary Cooperation Fund.

11. *Regional Policy*

T. Buch, "Regional Policy of European Integration", (1975) J.Comm.Mark.Studies, 368-378.

The author first discusses the kinds of regional problems from a theoretical point of view (though his analysis of the role of price effects in the automatic restoration of balance in the interregional balance of payments is not quite correct). He concludes that regional unemployment is rather a consequence of immobility as between sectors of industry than between regions, for which the solution is government intervention in order to bring about structural changes within the region (e.g. subsidies). The author further discusses the effects of economic integration on the regional problem and explains the regional policy of the EC and the proposal for the establishment of a European Fund for Regional Development.

J. van Doorn, "European Regional Policy: an evaluation of recent developments", (1975) J.Comm.Mark. Studies, 391-401.

A critical analysis of the EC regional policy and of the EFRD. The author considers that no proper criteria have been established for the distribution of the Fund's resources and that no underlying analysis of regional problems has been made. The author investigates the operation of the Fund with regard in particular to the UK and concludes that the establishment of a Regional Development Fund is not so much an instrument to deal with regional disparities as a means to cope with national disparities regarding contributions to and payments from the Community budget.

W. J. Feld, "Subnational regionalism and the European Community", 18 *Orbis, a journal of world affairs* 1975, 1176-1193.

Proceeding from the notion of A. Marc and G. Herard of *"L'Europe des Régions"*, i.e. of a maximum autonomy for all regions as a basis for the process of European integration, the author investigates two factors: firstly, the attitude of leading politicians in particular regions to this idea and, secondly, the attitude of the EC as an institution to regional-national and regional-EC relations.

R. J. Jarrett, "Disincentives; the other side of regional development policy", (1975) J.Comm.Mark. Studies, 37 9-390.

Looks at the regional problem from another angle, namely, the measures taken by various Member States to limit over-development in particular regions.

B. Mennis and K. P. Sauvant, "Describing and explaining support for regional integration: an investigation of German business elite attitudes towards the European Community", 29 Int.Org. 1975, 973-995.

P. Romus, "Les facteurs delocalisation industrielle dans le développement régional de la Communauté européenne", 69 *Cahier Economique de Bruxelles* 1976, 5-19.

14. *Social Policy*

J. Detienne, "La Communauté économique européenne et la lutte contre la pauvreté", (1975) R.M.C., 500-505.

P. Hillery, "European policy—a new face for the Community", 21 *European Yearbook* 1973, 21-38.

An investigation of how more substance could be given to the objectives of the 1974 Social Action Programme.

"Sex discrimination in employment", a comment on Case 43/75, *Defrenne v. SABENA*, 1976 *The Journal of Business Law*, 296-298.

16. *Company Law—Bankruptcy Law*

J. Noel, "Lignes directives du projet de convention de la CEE relative à la faillite", 11 R.T.D.E. 1975, 159-171.
J. Lemontey, "Perspectives d'unification du droit dans le projet de convention CEE relative à la faillite", 11 R.T.D.E. 1975, 172-186.

17. *Recognition of judgments*

J. P. Verheul, "The EEC Convention on jurisdiction and enforcement of judgments of 27 September 1968 in the Netherlands legal practice", 22 *Netherlands International law Review* 1975, 203-213.

Commentary on two judgments regarding the Convention.

18. *Industrial Property*

W. R. Cornish, "The European Patent Conventions", 1976 *The Journal of Business Law*, 112-129.

O. F. van Gamm, "Die Auswirkungen der Rechtsprechung des Gerichtshofs der Europäischen Gemeinschaften auf das Warenzeichenrecht", (1975) G.R.U.R. Int., Heft 6, 185-190.

19. *External Relations*

D. Colard, "L'Europe et le tiers monde: un acte constructif", 18 *Les Problèmes de l'Europe* no. 69, 7-15.

The author sees the Lomé Convention, brought about according to the harmony model, as the first step towards a new worldwide economic order, which should serve as a model to the coming international negotiations.

V. Constantinesco and D. Simon, "Quelques problèmes des relations extérieures des Communautés Européennes", 11 R.T.D.E. 1975, 432-469.

The authors investigate the effect on the internal legal order of the Community of international agreements which bind the Community. These agreements form part of the internal Community legal order on the condition that they do not conflict with primary Community Law which takes priority over international agreements. With regard to secondary Community Law, international agreements take priority where they create rights for individuals which may be relied on in legal proceedings.

Huub Coppens *et al*, "Grondstoffenveiligheid, ontwikkeling en de Conventie van Lomé", 30 *Internationale Spectator* 1976, 113-121.

A. van der Hek, "De Associatiepolitiek van de Europese Gemeenschap", 29 *Internationale Spectator* 1975, 531-535.
W. J. Schuijt, "Commentar", 29 *Internationale Spectator* 1975, 736-740.
A. va der Hek, "Antwoord", 29 *Internationale Spectator* 1975 740-741.

A heated discussion between two Dutch politicians—both members of the European Parliament—on the advantages and disadvantages of the present EC policy of association.

Ernst U. Petersmann, "Auswärtige Gewalt, Völkerrechtspraxis und Völkerrechtsbindungen der EWG", 35 Zeit.A.O.R.V. 1975, 213-281.

A very thorough review of the legal aspects of the external relations of the EEC. The first part looks at the competences of the EEC in the external area, at the association and commercial agreements, at legal relations with other international organisations and at the legal relationship between the Community and the changing law of the other international economic organisations (esp. the IMF and GATT). The second part deals with the relationship between Community Law and international law from the Community point of view, and this leads to a discussion of the "conflict" rules laid down in Arts. 232-234 EEC and in Arts. 4 and 5 of the Act of Accession. Attention is also paid to the judgments of the Court of Justice in the ERTA and GATT cases and to the relationship between Community Law and the treaties concluded by Member States since 1958 (the problem of cooperation agreements).

J. Raux, C. Flaesch-Mougin, "Les accords externes de la CEE" (1-1-73/1-1-74), 11 R.T.D.E. 1973, 227-279.

The first of what is to be an annual review of the external agreements concluded by the EEC (not the ECSC or Euratom). The authors consider the following aspects of the agreements: the legal basis, the manner of conclusion, the object, the content and the institutions.

U. Wasserman, "EEC-Israel Trade Agreement", 10 I.W.T.L. 1976, 92-95.

20. *Environment Policy*

M. Bijwater, "La politique d'environnement de la Communauté", (1975) R.M.C., 545-550.

H. Scheuer, "Aspects juridiques de la protection de l'environnement dans le Marché Commun", (1975) R.M.C., 441-457.

A description of the recent legislation concerning the protection of the environment in the Member States, and an analysis of the principles and legal instruments of a Community environment policy.

VI. *COUNCIL OF EUROPE*

A. *General*

"Célébration du vingt-cinquième anniversaire du Conseil de l'Europe le 6 mai 1974", 21 Annuaire Européen 1973, 3-20.

A. Manin, "La Grèce et le conseil de l'Europe du 12 décembre 1969 au 28 novembre 1974", 20 *Annuaire Français de Droit International* 1974, 875-885.

A discussion of the consequences of the withdrawal of Greece from the Council and its eventual re-accession.

M. Wiederkehr, "La Convention européenne sur l'immunité des Etats du mai 1972", 20 Annuaire Français de Droit International 1974, 924-945.

The Convention concerning the immunity of States has been offered for ratification by the Member States of the Council of Europe. The Convention contains provisions governing the scope of the immunity which a State may enjoy in regard to judicial proceedings in other States and concering the implementation of judgments made against a State. The Convention has not yet come into force. There is also a supplementary protocol concerning a procedure for the resolution of disputes.

B. *Human Rights*

E. A. Alkema, "Gelden grondrechten ook voor militaren", 50 N.J.B. 1975, 1429-1438.
A discussion of the case of *Engel v. The Netherlands* concerning the compatibility of military disciplinary procedures with the European Convention.

E. A. Alkema, "Het Europees Verdrag voor de Rechten van de Mens; Overzicht rechtspraak 1972-1975", (1975) *Bestuurswetenschappen,* 611-627.

R. Pelloux, "L'affaire Ringeisen devant la Cour européenne des droits de l'homme—Arrêts de 16 juillet 1971, 22 juin 1972 et 23 juin 1973", 20 *Annuaire Française de Droit International* 1974, 334-353.

P. Siedel, "Der Rang der Europäischen Menschenrechtskonvention in den Mitgliedstaaten", 90 *Deutscher Verwaltungsblatt* 1975, 747-753.
A very useful review of the status of the European Convention in the different legal orders of the 18 member States.

H. Walter, "Die Rechtsprechung des Europäischen Gerichtshofs für Menschenrechte 195-1974", 24 *Jahrbuch des Oeffentliches Rechts* 1975, 25-61.

BOOK REVIEWS

H. P. Ipsen, *Europäisches Gemeinschaftsrecht.* J. C. B. Mohr (Paul Siebeck), Tübingen 1972, XL and 1092 pp.

The belatedness of this attempt to pay a proper tribute to Professor Ipsen's *"Opus Magnum"* is only matched by the exceptional qualities of this wholly unreviewable book. Indeed, the author has set out on his own to describe and to analyse the whole body of the law of the three European Communities, an enterprise no single author has so far embarked upon with so much success. This book provides the reader not only with an enormous amount of positive legal information, but also with reflexions and discussions of a more theoretical nature on fundamental questions of Community Law. Even to the uninitiated these may be of great value. The reader cannot fail to be impressed by the clarity of vision and the depth of treatment displayed in this book. Ipsen shows himself to be a master at many arms. His book reflects not only his profound knowledge of constitutional and administrative law, but also of the other legal disciplines that play such an important role in the development of the Communities. Moreover, his obvious familiarity with the basic theories and scientific methods of other disciplines (economics, political science) is of great and indispensable help in presenting a comprehensive picture of the legal dimension of the process of European integration.

The book consists of nine Parts and fifty-four sections. Apart from the necessary introductory observations, Part I contains extensive bibliographical and documentary references. Part II deals with the sources of Community Law and with the constitutional provisions of the Member States enabling them to participate in the creation of the Communities (*Verfassungsgrundlagen*). Part III, one of the longest of this book, analyses the relationship between the Member States and the Communities. Parts IV and V deal with the institutional structure of the Communities, with the character and effects of the legal instruments available for Community action and with the decision-making process. Part VI is devoted to the rules relating to the establishment of the common market. Part VII deals with the legal position of private individuals (*Marktbürger*) and centres on the protection of fundamental rights and on the Community system of legal remedies. Part VIII examines the legal foundations for the various Community policies and the measures taken in the various fields. Finally, Part IX, entitled *"Perspektiven"*, contains Ipsen's reflexions on the state of the Communities and their further development.

Ipsen's book addresses itself primarily to the author's countrymen and for that reason may seem less easily accessible to non-Germans. Frequently and inevitably, the approach to various questions of Community Law and the selection of problems that call for analysis and discussion are specifically calculated to present German lawyers with a proper view of what Community Law is and of what it is not. However, since the starting point for the solution of any question involving an element of Community Law is invariably the need to recognize the autonomous nature of the Community legal order, the guidance supplied to German lawyers for the correct appraisal of a legal situation may equally benefit lawyers in other countries. Indeed the latter, in the same way as their German counterparts, are often unable or reluctant to pay heed to the specific Community perspective which in many cases is liable to affect the solution of a legal problem.

It would seem that it is the author's main concern to demonstrate that Community Law is a completely new phenomenon. The Communities fit into no accepted legal category. Their law constitutes neither international law nor municipal law. Any approach to this phenomenon influenced by *"begriffsjuristischer Praejudizierung"* must be firmly rejected.

The Communities cannot be equated with states — federal or confederal — and it would be wrong to play down their unique features so as to permit them to be classified as members of the family of international organisations. The many innovative features of the Communities, in Ipsen's view, make it possible to qualify them as *"Zweckverbände funktioneller Integration"*.

Although the Communities have been established by the Member States, these are not to be regarded as "masters of the Treaties". As members of the Communities they continue to play an essential role in the decision-making processes, but they cannot control the existence of the Communities. Community Law constitutes a specific and autonomous legal order which owes its creation to the parallel decisions by which the participating States have invested a new entity with sovereign rights. However, the contents and essence of this new legal order are in no way affected by the national laws and constitutional doctrines governing the relationship between national law and international law. Whatever the views held in the Member States regarding the legal nature of the (ratification) act by which the State's participation in the Communities was effected, it has entailed an unconditional surrender of sovereign rights for the benefit of the new legal order of the Communities. As far as the legal basis for transferring sovereign power to an external body is concerned, the constitutional position in the Federal Republic is far less confused than in most other Member States (It would be particularly interesting if in a second edition the constitutional basis for a transfer of sovereignty in relation to the new Member States could be discussed more extensively). Article 24 of the Basic Law expresses not a mere declaration of policy, but specifically enables the Federal Republic to part with some of its sovereign attributes and to commit itself to accept the effects which the new entity's exercise of the powers transferred to it will have within its territory. The collective action of the Member States has had the effect of laying down a Constitution of the Communities. It is imperative that it is interpreted and applied in accordance with its own logic, to be derived from its basic objectives, instruments, *etc.* Basic principles underlying this constitutional document are the principle of integration and the principle of supranationality. Closely linked with these basic tenets is the principle of effectiveness. Ipsen convincingly demonstrates that this principle amounts to more than the well-known "implied-powers" rule used in general international law. It is of a very fundamental nature, a qualifying *"Leitsatz"* of Community Law which takes precedence over all conventional rules of interpretation known in domestic and in international law. It is this principle which explains why a national court faced with a conflict between a Community provision enforceable in the courts and a provision of municipal law, is bound to declare the latter inapplicable. The principle is one of the cornerstones in the *Costa* v. *ENEL* judgment and it is also implicit in Article 189, para 2 of the Treaty. Ipsen's treatment of the supremacy question is of great interest not only because his views are largely consonant with those of the Court of Justice (they may even have influenced members of the Court) but also because he describes and refutes the views of those who over the years have sought to defend the supremacy of Community Law on erroneous grounds.

Apart from the discussion on these major themes, Ipsen's book is a veritable treasure trove for students of Community Law. No doubt, the sheer size of the subject and the fact that the author has not shared the burden of writing it with others, account for certain limitations. It is only natural that the treatment of the substantive law of the Communities cannot be so detailed and complete as that achieved, in other treatises of Community Law, by the collective efforts of scores of specialists in the several fields. However, the book is unique because it is so comprehensive and because the fundamental problems are dealt with in a way which emphasizes their relevance for the solution of "micro-problems". It is to be hoped that in future editions the book's unitary character may be maintained.

J. A. Winter

COMMON MARKET LAW REVIEW

AIMS

The Common Market Law Review is designed to function as a medium for the understanding and implementation of Community Law within the nine Member States, and for the dissemination of legal thinking on Community Law matters. It thus aims to meet the needs of both the academic and the practitioner.
For practical reasons, English is used as the language of communication.

EDITORIAL POLICY

The editors will consider for publication manuscripts by contributors from any country. Articles will be subjected to a review procedure. The author should ensure that the significance of his work will be apparent also to readers outside his specific expertise. Special terms and abbreviations should be clearly defined in the text or notes. Accepted manuscripts will be edited, if necessary, to improve the general effectiveness of communication.
If editing should be extensive, with a consequent danger of altering the meaning, the manuscript will be returned to the author for approval before type is set.

SUBMISSION OF MANUSCRIPTS

Manuscripts should be submitted, together with a covering letter, to one of the Editors. At the time the manuscript is submitted, written assurance must be given that the article has not been published, submitted or accepted elsewhere. The author will be notified of acceptance, rejection or need for revision within eight to twelve weeks.
Authors are requested to submit two copies of their manuscript, typed and double spaced, together with a summary of the contents.
Manuscripts may range from 3,000 to 10,000 words.
The title of an article should start with a word useful in indexing and information retrieval. Short titles are invited for use as running heads.
The author should identify himself in print, with a short statement as to his current affiliation.
All references and notes should be numbered in a single sequence in the order in which they are cited in the text, and should be typed, single-spaced, on a separate sheet.

OFFPRINTS

The author will receive one free copy of the issue concerned and twenty-five offprints of his article. He may also order any quantity of additional offprints, with a minimum of 100 copies, at forty cents (Dfl. 0.40) per page per copy. This order must be submitted through the Executive Editor at the time of delivery of the corrected galley-proofs for print.

GPSR Compliance

The European Union's (EU) General Product Safety Regulation (GPSR) is a set of rules that requires consumer products to be safe and our obligations to ensure this.

If you have any concerns about our products, you can contact us on ProductSafety@springernature.com

In case Publisher is established outside the EU, the EU authorized representative is:

Springer Nature Customer Service Center GmbH
Europaplatz 3
69115 Heidelberg, Germany

Batch number: 10830943

Printed by Printforce, the Netherlands

EDITORIAL ADDRESS
Common Market Law Review
Europa Instituut, Hugo de Grootstraat 27,
Leyden, The Netherlands

Orders for subscriptions, advertisements and back issues should be sent either direct to the general distributor:

Academic Book Services Holland, P.O. Box 66, Groningen, The Netherlands
phone: (0)50-162329 telex: 53443

or to
Fred B. Rothman & Company, 57 Leuning Street, South Hackensack, New Jersey, N.J. 17606, U.S.A.
Hammicks - Sweet & Maxwell, 50 West Street, Farnham, Surrey, U.K.
Office International de Librairie, 30 Avenue Marnix, 1050-Bruxelles, Belgique.

Annual subscription price for Volume 13 (1976): Dfl. 125.00/ $ 52.00; single issue: Dfl. 32.00/ $ 13.25.

Originally published by A. W. Sijthhoff International Publishing Company in 1976

COMMON MARKET LAW REVIEW

Volume 13
1976

SPRINGER-SCIENCE+BUSINESS MEDIA, B.V

Published in Cooperation with the British Institute of International and Comparative Law and the Europa Instituut of the University of Leyden

Editorial Address

Common Market Law Review
Europa Instituut, Hugo de Grootstraat 27,
Leyden, The Netherlands

This Review may be cited as *13 C.M.L. Rev. 1976*

ISBN 978-94-015-2075-1 ISBN 978-94-015-3283-9 (eBook)
DOI 10.1007/978-94-015-3283-9

Originally published by A. W. Sijthhoff International Publishing Company in 1976

INDEX VOLUME XIII

I. SUBJECTS

II. CASE LAW

A. COURT OF JUSTICE OF THE EUROPEAN COMMUNITIES

B. NATIONAL COURTS OF THE MEMBER STATES

III. ARTICLES AND SHORTER ARTICLES

IV. LIST OF AUTHORS

Names of authors who have contributed to Volume XIII

V. LIST OF BOOKS REVIEWED

Author/Editor	Book Title	Reviewer	Pages
B. Börner and K. Carstens	*Die Aussenbeziehungen der Europäischen Gemeinschaft*	P. J. G. Kapteyn	443-444
J. Boulouis and R. M. Chevallier	*Grands arrêts de la Cour de Justice des Communautés Européennes*	K. Mortelmans	143-144
J. Rideau, R. M. Chevallier, J.-M. Rainaud, L. Balmond and A. Bailleux	*Droit Institutionnel des Communautés Européennes*	K. Mortelmans	143-144
Studienvereinigung Kartellrecht	*Neue Entwicklungen im EWG-Kartellrecht*	H. W. Wertheimer	445-447
A. von Geusau	*Energy in the European Communities*	R. Barents	444-445
H. P. Ipsen	*Europäischen Gemeinschaftsrecht*	J. A. Winter	555-556

Special Issue

THE ECONOMIC LAW OF THE MEMBER STATES IN AN ECONOMIC AND MONETARY UNION

TABLE OF CONTENTS

EDITORIAL COMMENTS

THE TINDEMANS REPORT

The eagerly-awaited report by M. Leo Tindemans, Prime Minister of Belgium, on the future of European Union was finally published on January 7 last. The report will be subjected to extended critical analysis in articles to appear later in this Volume of the *Review* but it is appropriate now to give first reactions to what is undoubtedly one of the most significant overall surveys of the way ahead for the Communities to be published for a decade. M. Tindemans was asked to define what is to be understood by European Union in implementation of the terms of the last head of the communiqué issued by the Heads of State of Member State Governments after the Paris Summit Conference of October 19 and 20, 1972. In his lengthy report, which contains over fifty positive proposals or policy guide-lines, M. Tindemans has produced primarily a political statement of what he believes, on the best evidence currently available to him, may be both credible and acceptable to the Member Governments of the enlarged Communities at the present time and for the foreseeable future. He has interpreted his terms of reference as a practical politician would; the conflict between his personal ideology and certain of the report proposals can be seen at a number of points, especially perhaps in the clash between his personal commitment to the goal of European federalism and his report recommendations on a "two-speed" approach to the next phases of development toward economic and monetary union. Overall, his report is pragmatic, realistic and fundamentally cautious. This has predictably brought forth a spate of criticism from those who claim that the report is ultra-cautious and does not well serve the "European cause" as a whole, but only the interests of the more powerful forces within the Communities—and notably those of the Federal Republic of Germany. As against this, a powerful endorsement of the report has recently come from the "Congress of Europe", which met at Brussels on February 5, 6 and 7, under the auspices of the European Movement and under the chairmanship of M. Jean Rey.

The report, which was discussed by the "European Council" at their meeting on April 1 and 2, is a subtle text which demands, and repays, careful attention and re-reading. Can it, as its author intended, both revive and re-focus the debate on the future path of the Communities into the nineteen-eighties? Already there are ominous signs that socialist politicians in a number of Member States find many features of the report objectionable—particularly those which deal with the "Atlantic allegiance", the generalisation of majority decision-making, and the future joint action proposed with regard to the "snake" of limited currencies. Above all, in these circles, there appears to be a feeling that the evolution of an economic and monetary union, with a rigid co-ordination of policies, would only aggravate the unequal impact of the crisis between rich and poor areas within Europe.

The parts of the Tindemans report which have attracted the most vehement initial criticism are those which deal with advance toward economic and monetary union and with the development of a new type of economic growth designed to reconcile more thoroughly both economic and political goals. M. Tindemans proposes that the "snake" of linked currencies should be consolidated by joint action on monetary, budgetary and short-term economic policy, but that Member States not yet belonging to the "snake" should be brought into these discussions. Machinery for short and medium-term support, through the European Monetary Co-operation Fund, should be made automatic and strengthened. The "snake" countries should then gradually abolish the remaining barriers to capital movements between them, and "non-snake" countries should be encouraged to join. The report declares that ". . . the machinery of the snake, which has proved itself by maintaining the stability of exchange rates, must be used to seek a convergence of economic and monetary policies *between those States which are in a position to achieve it* (emphasis supplied). The "Community convoy', therefore, is to be divided into two parts, with the gap between them progressively widening. The "snake" would become a Community mechanism with the "weak" countries taking part only as spectators to the action of the "strong" countries. The immediate criticism, of course, is that such a policy would be used to justify the actions of those who think that to live on the outside is convenient for the avoidance of unwelcome constraints.

The path of the prophet is indeed a hard one. At the time of writing, a mere two months after the publication of the Tindemans report, the European currency block appears very near to disintegration. The central banks are being forced to intervene on a massive scale in a desperate attempt to preserve the existing "snake" mechanism, whilst outside it the lira has suffered a decline unprecedented in post-war financial history. Commercial dealings between Italy and Germany were affected within one week by an 8% variation in currency values. France has again withdrawn from the "snake", and, of seven currencies still formally participating, only two (the Deutsch mark and the Swedish crown) actually remain within the specified dealing margins. It remains to be seen for how much longer the weaker currencies still within the "snake" (the Belgian franc and Danish crown) will actually remain there. The present wrigglings of the "snake" appear to make M. Tindemans' proposal for a "two-speed" approach to monetary union untenable and indeed illusory. Yet this proposal, in his view, goes to "... the crux of the internal development of the union".

It is impossible here to make more than a passing reference to the remaining outstanding features of the report. It is of the essence of M. Tindemans' concept of European Union that Europeans must present a united front to the outside world. Stronger institutions are necessary both in order to arrive at, and to display, that united front. Direct elections should be the first step toward giving the European Parliament a new political authority which it should then be enabled (through a Treaty amendment) to exercise over all questions within the scope of the Union, whether deriving directly from the constitutive treaties or not. The Council of Ministers should also, in his view, be given competence outside the Treaties on the authority of the "European Council" with majority voting becoming normal practice. It is not surprising to find him advocating strongly that the Commission should re-assert its freedom and be given more mandates. A new system for the appointment of the President of the Commission, and of his colleagues, with the involvement of the "European Council" of the Heads of Government, and in consultation with the European Parliament, is envisaged, with the term of the Presidency being extended to a full year. The position of the individual citizen is far from neglected. A European Union worthy of the name must afford the fullest protection to the fundamental, consumer and environmental rights of its citizens. A citizen should, he recommends, have the right of direct appeal to the European Court of Justice on matters involving fundamental rights.

Finally, the report has much of interest to say on the external relations of the Union, which must be able to deal collectively and comprehensively with all forms of international negotiation, whether in the political, economic, industrial, financial or commercial fields. The "European Council" should end its present distinction between "economic" and "political" ministerial meetings and should draw up common policy guidelines specifically designed to move on from the present phase of loosely co-ordinated foreign policies. On crises within the European region—a matter of consistent controversy in recent years—he recommends generally that Member States should systematically plan and act together, paying particular attention to European countries with a democratic system similar to their own, and establishing with them informal co-operation that could facilitate later membership. Lastly—and significantly, with the prospects for UNCTAD IV currently engaging our attention—Member States should gradually transfer to the

Community a substantial part of their national aid-giving programmes and take a common stand in multilateral negotiations forming part of the search for a new world economic order.

The Tindemans report is being criticised variously as being too modest and too ambitious. It has been overtaken by dramatic events in the monetary field which will almost certainly dominate the early discussion of its contents, both generally and in the "European Council". Can it help to restore the "*parfum d'aventure*" to the idea of European Union? The price of inaction is ever more apparent as events develop.

THE ECONOMIC LAW OF THE MEMBER STATES

This special issue of the *Review* is very largely devoted to the publication of what the Editors believe to be a very significant and searching group of papers originally presented to an international conference sponsored and organised by the Europa Institute of the University of Utrecht in May 1975. These papers provide a stimulating and varied analysis of the first reports submitted by the group of independent legal experts set up by the Commission to enquire into the legal basis and sources of the existing national economic laws of Member States and to make recommendations on the co-ordination of those national laws in the movement toward Economic and Monetary Union in the Communities. The Utrecht papers which are reproduced here contain much perceptive criticism of, and comment upon, the reports prepared for the Commission. Whilst readers in some Member States will undoubtedly be familiar with their underlying concepts and arguments, it cannot be over-emphasised that, as Professor VerLoren van Themaat points out in his introductory remarks, discussion and debate on the elements of a national economic constitutional order has not proceeded at an equal pace (or with a similar orientation) in each of the Member States—and in some both the argument and the literature is fragmented and dispersed. Professor Daintith has written, in the introduction (at p. xi) to his excellent report on the economic law of the United Kingdom, prepared for the Commission and published separately:[1]

> "The absence of any accepted or authoritative United Kingdom definition of economic law should not come as a surprise: classification and definition are not activities which commend themselves to British lawyers, even academic lawyers, who prefer to base judg-

1. Series: Competition—Approximation of Legislation, No. 20, (Brussels, 1975).

> ment and argument on observation rather than on *a priori* intellectual constructions.
>
> The subject of economic law, uncomfortably poised on the dividing line between existing legal categories like commercial law and administrative law, and whose administration is still largely a preserve of civil servants where even practising lawyers do not enter, has therefore, as one would expect, not been recognised at all."

That this should be the case may well come as a surprise to many; the need for the conspectus sponsored by the Commission requires no further justification and the various national reports themselves contain much that is striking, provocative and novel. The Editors hope that the publication of the Utrecht commentaries will encourage readers to turn again to the basic reports, which deserve very close attention. Inevitably, the underlying question in all our minds must be the conundrum posed by Mr. Brinkhorst at the end of his opening speech at Utrecht—is the Community strong enough in its present state to bear Economic and Monetary Union, or is EMU essential if the Community is to survive? M. Tindemans has left us in little doubt as to his own answer and recent events demand that we face, as a matter of the most acute urgency, both the demands and the implications of the question.

INTRODUCTORY REMARKS ON THE ROLE OF NATIONAL ECONOMIC LAW IN AN ECONOMIC AND MONETARY UNION

by

Pieter VerLoren van Themaat*

1. The problems of an Economic and Monetary Union between the Member States of the European Communities can be studied and have been studied from various points of view. The Werner Committee and two successive groups of independent experts,[1] set up by the Commission of the European Communities, as well as an impressive number of academic studies analysed these problems mainly from the viewpoint of the Communities or as a part of the theory of economic integration, and then mainly from an economic and political point of view. In 1970, however, the Commission charged another group of five independent legal experts to make a comparative law study of the economic law of the Member States, and to give indications on the needs and possibilities of their coordination under the EEC-Treaty in view of the planned Economic and Monetary Union. The legal basis and the legal instruments of all of the national economic policies were covered by this study with an exception for such areas as fiscal legislation on which specific studies had been undertaken. Later on, experts from the three new Member States were added to the group. The first four national reports as well as a provisional general report on the role of national economic law in an Economic and Monetary Union were published in 1975 by the Commission as number 20 of the Study series "Competition—Harmonisation of Legislation". The remaining national reports will be published shortly.

In May 1975 these reports were discussed at an international conference, organized by the Europa Institute of the University of Utrecht, in collaboration with the Commission of the European Communities. The introductory lectures given at that conference are published in this volume. They can very well be read without knowledge of the underlying reports.

* Professor of Economic Law at the University of Utrecht.

1. See: Prof. H. W. J. Bosman *et al, Intégration économique européenne et unification monétaire*, Doc. COM II/520/1/73-E; R. Marjolin *et al, "Union Economique et Monétaire 1980"*, UEM-63, Directorate General for Economic and Financial Affairs (Brussels, 1975).

13 C.M.L.Rev. 1976, 153-158

2. Because of the fact that the group consisted of legal experts who had not been asked to study the problems of an Economic and Monetary Union as such, the series of lectures starts with two general introductory lectures on the reasons and general requirements for an Economic and Monetary Union by Messrs U. Mosca, Director General of the Commission in charge of these problems, and C. J. Oort, one of the leading national government experts in this area. An interesting general introduction was also given by Mr. L. J. Brinkhorst, Netherlands Under-Secretary of State for Foreign Affairs. For the same reason that the problems of an Economic and Monetary Union as such had not been covered by the underlying reports, a second group of three lectures introduced a discussion on the fundamental legal principles—the optimum economic constitution—of an Economic and Monetary Union. General reporter on this subject was Professor U. Scheuner from the University of Bonn. Co-reports were submitted by Professors W. Van Gerven from the University of Louvain and J. D. B. Mitchell from the University of Edinburgh. From among the more specific legal problems, those regarding the need for harmonisation or co-ordination of compulsory national economic regulations, or for their replacement by Community regulations, or for the creation of parallel legal instruments on the Community level were selected for more detailed discussion. This discussion was introduced by Professors R. Savy, dean of the Faculty of Law and Economics of the University of Limoges, K. Hopt from the University of Tübingen, C. M. Schmitthoff from the Universities of London and Kent, and summaries of the national reports on the economic law of Denmark and Ireland were also considered. As the reports themselves will be published in the near future in the mentioned Study-series, these last-mentioned summaries have been left out of this volume. Community officials contributed reports on the Community's tasks relating to the protection of the environment. Other subjects of national economic policy, e.g. the budget policy, state subsidies, direct state participation in the economic process, planning contracts and short-term and medium-term planning in general were mainly dealt with in specific working groups with no basis of discussion other than the underlying provisional general report, already published by the Commission, and reviewed in this volume.

3. After the many important economic studies on the Economic and Monetary Union as such, the publication of the lectures in this volume seems worthwhile not only because of their high quality, but also because they may contribute to make lawyers more conscious of the very important and fascinating legal issues involved in the struggle for an Economic and Monetary Union.

Some of these issues are:

Firstly, the notion of an economic constitution, which has been developed very far in German literature, legislation and jurisprudence and to a lesser extent also in Belgian and French literature, but which is hardly known in any of the other Member States. Some of the basic questions in this respect with regard to the European Economic Community are:

(*a*) To what extent is the EEC Treaty neutral with regard to the "economic order", or in other words: to what extent does it leave room for either a neo-liberal or a more socialist economic system at both the Community and at the national level? What are the institutional implications of the answer to this question, e.g. for the division of powers between the European Parliament, the Commission and the Council of Ministers? If there should be no room for options in this respect, it is clear this would limit the interest of parliamentary control.

(*b*) What is the impact of a federal, confederal or pre-federal nature of the Communities on the possibilities of political choice between the various options of an economic constitution on both the Community and the national level? How far can planning go at the Community level without depriving Member States of all essential parts of their autonomous national economic policy? And how far can planning or state intervention go at the national level without endangering the existence of the Common Market and without conflicting with the legal rules of the EEC Treaty? Some of the recent decisions of the Court of Justice of the European Communities[2] make clear that this last question is far from being only of academic interest.

(*c*) To what extent are the economic constitutions of Member States different from one another, and to what extent is it necessary to harmonise them?

(*d*) What legal guarantees for a sufficient degree of autonomy of Member States could one imagine for the economic constitution of an economic and monetary union? To what extent is a complete transfer of national powers necessary? (e.g. the existing common policies and monetary policy). To what extent are parallel powers of the Community sufficient? (e.g. control of restrictive business practices and regional policy). To what extent are general Community rules of the game sufficient, leaving the Member States free to follow their own policy

2. See for example: Case No. 31/74, *Pubblico Ministero Italiano v. Filippo Galli,* 1975 ECR 49, 12 C.M.L. Rev. 1975, 418; Case No. 70/72, *Commission v. Federal Republic of Germany,* 1973 C.M.L.R. 741, 11 C.M.L. Rev. 1974, 199; Case No. 77/72, *Capolongo v. Maya,* 1974 C.M.L.R. 230, 11 C.M.L. Rev. 1974, 202.

within the framework of these rules? (e.g. the "four freedoms" and general principles of budget policy). To what extent should the co-ordination of national economic policies take the form of the subordination or control of specific types of national measures (e.g. state subsidies) and to what extent should it take the form of "indicative planning", with or without financial Community incentives to further the planned common goals? (e.g. some key industries like coal and steel and other basic industries). To what extent is "co-operative federalism" as indicated in Article 6 of the EEC Treaty, and developed also within the German Federal Republic and the U.S.A., sufficient? To what extent does the Community need new powers of compulsory direct intervention? Is it possible to work out a general hierarchy of priorities in the use of instruments or general principles of subsidiarity, the stronger types of intervention being applicable only if the weaker forms of co-ordination of national economic policies cannot achieve the required common goals? (cf. Articles 5 and 57 of the ECSC-Treaty).
(*e*) Are there any fundamental rights or basic principles such as those elaborated in the lecture of Professor Van Gerven, or a constitutional guarantee for the vital interests of Member States, under control of the European Court of Justice, that should be adopted by a European Union?
Secondly. What other changes of the existing treaties are necessary to make an Economic and Monetary Union workable, both in the field of powers (e.g. in the monetary field, with regard to external economic relations, in the field of the protection of the environment, industrial policy and social policy) and in the institutional field? (e.g. a European Institute for economic analysis and research as proposed recently by the Commission,[3] a federal bank, and a change in the general institutional structure and division of powers at the Community level).
Thirdly. What can the Community learn from the comparative law study of legal instruments and basic legal principles of national economic policy for its own policies?

4. Most of these questions and many others were discussed either in the lectures published in this volume, or in the plenary sessions and working groups of the conference. A complete report of these discussions in their original languages can be obtained from the Europa Institute of the University of Utrecht (Janskerkhof 16, Utrecht). The importance of these questions is not only of a legal nature, but some of them are also of great political impact. For example, it follows from the questions listed

3. Doc. COM (75) 450.

under 3 (*d*) that the Council's Resolution of March 22, 1971 on the Economic and Monetary Union (a "mixed" resolution of the Council and the representatives of the governments of the Member States) simplifies the problems in a politically dangerous way by saying that the most important economic policy decisions should be taken at the Community level and that the necessary powers in this respect should be transferred from the national level to the Community level. In fact there exists an enormous variety of intermediate forms of relationship between Community law and national law between a complete transfer of powers to the Community level and full national sovereignty or autonomy in the various fields of economic policy. These intermediate forms merit careful study, not only by economists but by lawyers as well. Such a study would have to cover all of the types of governmental interventions in the economy, which have been analysed in the underlying reports on the economic law of the Member States. The provisional general report is only the beginning in this respect. In the course of the gradual development of an economic and monetary union it should be followed by many more detailed studies. It is to be hoped that the publication of the reports and of this volume of the Common Market Law Review will contribute to further such research.

5. Finally, it should be stressed once more that the legal character of the study of the role of national economic law in an Economic and Monetary Union is not the only aspect which distinguishes this study from most of the other studies published on the issue of an Economic and Monetary Union. Particularly in the present economic and political climate it is significant that in this study, as in the preceding economic study of Dr. Zijlstra on *Economic policy and problems of competition in the EEC and the Member States* (Study series Competition No. 2, Brussels 1966), the main accent is put on a comparison of national economic policies. As a point of fact, in these days of recession, the attitude of national governments with regard to the further development of the European Communities in the field of co-ordination of economic policies is influenced far more by their national economic problems and policies than by considerations of the necessary implications of economic integration. It is therefore useful to have now at one's disposal an analysis of the goals and instruments of national economic policy of most of the Member States. Even if none of the national reports is quite up to date, they nevertheless give a good idea of what kind of national economic policies exist and what types of national economic policies are not compatible with each other or with the legal rules of the EEC Treaty. The British Industry Act 1975 is one encouraging example of how

Member States can benefit from each others' experience. It takes over the Italian example of a state holding company and the French and Belgian examples of planning agreements. But even if all of the other Member States followed this example of autonomous harmonization of instruments of economic policy, this would not yet solve the problem of how to co-ordinate industrial policies of Member States in such a way that their effect is not neutralised by contradictory policies of the Member States in the use of such instruments, and that they do not violate the EEC Treaty. The same is true for many other essential parts of national economic policies. A comparative law study of national economic law of the Member States and autonomous efforts of harmonization of instruments may therefore constitute a good starting point for better co-ordination of national economic policies. It cannot, however, solve the problem of the necessary co-ordination of the use of these instruments. An analysis of the economic laws of the Member States must therefore be followed by a study of the needs and means of this harmonization or co-ordination. But, there again, in the present state of affairs it may be worthwhile to study this question not only from the point of view of the needs of the Community as a whole, but also from the point of view of the optimum effectiveness of national economic policy. For this reason also it is to be hoped that the fascinating Utrecht lectures contained in this volume, as well as the underlying reports published by the Commission, will encourage some of the readers to do new research work in this field. Much remains to be done!

OPENING SPEECH

by

Mr. Laurens Jan Brinkhorst*

It is certainly an excellent idea to have chosen Utrecht as the place for an international congress on the problems of Economic and Monetary Union, the hard core of an ultimately completely integrated Europe. After all, did not the Abbé de Saint Pierre, in his *Projet de traité pour rendre la paix perpétuelle,* assign this town a very special place in his plan for a European Union? Utrecht, as you know, was to be the capital, the seat of the Senate, the "*ville de la paix*".

This colloquium is going to study the economic and monetary unification of Europe. I believe that we cannot consider this separately from unification problems in general. How far have we come at this point with that of Europe?

This question always solicits violent responses. There are the extreme optimists and the die-hard pessimists, who all put forward good arguments to prove their case. Personally I do not side with either group.

It is clear that Europe is undergoing a gradual process of growth, proceeding sometimes by fits and starts.

There has certainly been progress at the institutional level. The declaration of Heads of Government in December 1974 on direct elections to the European Parliament was an indispensable stimulus to the awakening of European consciousness.

Similarly, greater democratisation in decision-making is developing in relations between the Council of Ministers and the European Parliament. I have in mind, of course, the recent agreements on the budgetary powers of the Parliament and the agreements on the concertation procedure for legislation. Moreover, relations between the European Parliament and Ministers in discussions relating to European political co-operation have improved. Finally, incorporation of the summit conference of Heads of Government in the framework of the Community treaties opens the way to closer control by the European Parliament. I am quite aware that a hard battle will still have to be fought to raise the position of the Parliament from that of an advisory institution to that of a fully-fledged representative body. However, I know from my own experience that in the discussions with the Council on the budget the

* Under-Secretary of State, Netherlands Ministery of Foreign Affairs.

13 C.M.L.Rev. 1976, 159-166

representatives of the Parliament showed themselves to be not just "paper tigers". I have no hesitation in associating myself with the words of the new President of the Parliament, Mr. Spenale, at the celebrations to commemorate the 25th anniversary of the Schumann Declaration: *"L'Europe sera une dêmocratie parlementaire, ou elle ne sera pas".*

This progressive growth is also noticeable in specific policy areas, particularly in relations with third countries. The EEC is putting more and more effort into establishing its position in the world. Until recently these efforts were restricted to action in the field of trade policy, notably in relation to other industrialised countries. The changing pattern of relations in the world is forcing the Community to increasingly defend common standpoints in other fields as well, and towards all countries. The recent Lomê Convention with the 46 ACP countries—welcomed a short time ago by all Commonwealth government leaders—may be seen as a contribution by the EEC to an integrated development policy.

The Convention may provide the impetus for an EEC policy aimed at improving the economic structure of the Third World as a whole.

Another example of growth is provided by the attempts of the EEC to actively contribute to an integrated raw materials policy in the world. The expansion of the EEC's external relations should not, however, be allowed to obsure the fact that the internal cohesion of the Community still leaves much to be desired. It is there, to my way of thinking, that the greatest threat to more far-reaching developments lies. If the Community does not succeed quite soon in strengthening itself at the internal level this will undoubtedly have repercussions on its external position.

I am therefore especially pleased that the plans for Economic and Monetary Union will undergo scientific examination at this colloquium.

After all, it is a subject of vital importance to the future of Europe, which certainly needs careful study.

The idea of an Economic and Monetary Union is not new; a lot of water has already passed under the bridge. In spite of unavoidable disappointments, interest in the idea is still very much alive, as we have been able to see on several occasions in the past few months. I have in mind the confirmation of the desire to achieve an Economic and Monetary Union in the declaration of the Summit Conference in December 1974 in Paris, the speech that the President of the Community, Mr. Ortoli, made to the international press at the beginning of this year, the Marjolin study group report, and finally, the Spierenburg report which was presented to the Minister for Foreign Affairs two weeks ago.[1]

1. 2nd Chamber of the Netherlands States-General, *Rapport van de Advies-commissie Europese Unie,* Doc. 13426 No. 2, 1975-76.

The Netherlands Government is studying this report in detail and hopes to make known its reaction before the summer is out.

And yet, despite all the interest shown in the subject, the scope for discussion is by no means exhausted; there are still a lot of problems that need sorting out, and this is one of the reasons why the systematic study which you will be undertaking in the next few days is very important. The more so perhaps because the results of your discussions will still have time to influence thinking in the legal, economic and political fields, since it is far from certain that a final solution to the problems will be possible in the short term.

I would like briefly to recall a few stages in the development of ideas on EMU. In the 'Sixties, considerable differences in economic growth and price trends between the Member States became clearly apparent; attitudes towards international monetary questions, for example, also differed widely.

With the progressive liberalisation measures, the lack of common policy was felt increasingly strongly in the Community. In the second half of 1969 the situation escalated into a monetary crisis which resulted in, among other things, the devaluation of the French franc and the revaluation of the German mark.

The Summit Conference of December 1969 in The Hague instructed the Commission to work out a plan, to be executed in stages, for the establishment of an Economic and Monetary Union.

The mandate to the working group under the chairmanship of Pierre Werner ultimately led to the adoption of a resolution by the government representatives. An important conclusion in the Werner report, namely that a decision centre for economic policy was necessary for the creation of Economic and Monetary Union, was not, however, accepted by the Council. The Resolution of March 1971 expressed the political willingness to set up an EMU step by step. This solemn declaration was followed by an equally solemn declaration at the end of the Paris Summit Conference in October 1972, which stated that the Member States were firmly resolved to set up the EMU.

Transition to the second stage of the EMU on January 1, 1974 had to be made possible, and the process had to be completed by the end of 1980 at the latest.

We all know that even the first stage was not succesfully completed. It must be admitted that the international economic and monetary situations have not been exactly favourable. The dollar flow to certain Member States hampered efforts to narrow the fluctuation margins of currencies in the Community (during the 'Sixties), inflation continued to increase, the oil price developments in 1973 made the situation even worse, and governments of Member States were fully occupied coping with the problem of unemployment. The cold douche administered by these setbacks was the last thing that people had expected when drawing up all those fine declarations.

Moreover, the political will to arrive at real supranational solutions was obviously lacking; political will is crucial to any system of whatever kind. This political hesitation is undermining all the good intentions with regard to co-ordination and harmonisation in many fields. Although anyone can see for himself that the unification process is scarcely progressing at all in the financial and economic sphere, there are nevertheless a few rays of light—for example, the Community loan facility. This indicates quite clearly that members are prepared to help one another in solving balance of payments problems. Furthermore, the consultations on the international monetary system are resulting in Community action being taken in various spheres.

The aim of expanding and strengthening the Community remains expressly on the programme. The Netherlands hopes too that this strengthening of the Community can be achieved quickly. But does the Community possess the determination to proceed with it under present circumstances?

We must ask ourselves whether the current tensions in Member States and outside them are not deflecting us from our purpose. Are the political constraints too great for really important instruments of national decision to be transferred to Community level? The Marjolin group report, *Economic and Monetary Union 1980*,[2] shows that this group felt it would be impossible to draw up a plan for EMU which would have a sufficient degree of credibility under present circumstances. The group believes that further progress demands a demonstration of political will and that it is the existence of this political will which is uncertain at the moment. And yet, as I have already said, it is of the utmost importance that we formulate the ultimate goal as clearly as possible, so that we do in fact know where we want to go as soon as the way is open for us.

More specifically we may ask ourselves whether the prospects as originally seen accord with present reality, and whether the voluntary step-by-step method of approach must not be counted a failure.

It is a matter for satisfaction that the Spierenburg Committee too focussed its observation on this problem of whether or not a progress towards union should be voluntary. Without anticipating the conclusions of the Netherlands Government, I think the Committee has

2. UEM-63 D.G. for Economic and Financial Affairs (Brussels, 1975).

correctly seen that the present economic and institutional structure of the Community is inadequate for a more far-reaching monetary and economic union. Those who have political responsibility in the Europe of today wil find it difficult to escape the force of this analysis. What is also important is that the Spierenburg Committee did not content itself with setting down on paper the shortcomings of the path followed in the past, but has added a number of very specific and practical conclusions. The committee also wanted to provide an answer to a number of questions which are fundamental to the theme of this colloquium.

The first of these questions is why, in spite of all the setbacks, efforts to establish an Economic and Monetary Union must still be continued. Why must this far-reaching form of integration be retained as the central objective of the European Community?

A common monetary policy and a common policy to safeguard the Community balance of payments positions are, after all, only feasible if national economic policies are extensively harmonised, with all the economic and social and, of course, political consequences that this entails.

Monetary and economic union is not just one of a number of possibilities which present themselves along the road to European union. It is an indispensable link in the chain of events leading to unification, on the one hand because Economic and Monetary Union is the necessary complement to the customs union, which is necessary to maintain the free market, and on the other because the creation of Economic and Monetary Union itself acts as a catalyst to unification in other fields.

Economic and Monetary Union constitutes a necessary complement to the customs union and the common agricultural policy, because there is a risk that the disintegrating forces arising from divergent national economic policies might concievably prove too powerful for what has already been achieved to be preserved.

The disintegration of the system of fixed exchange rates is jeopardising the common agricultural policy, which, after all, is partly based on a common level of prices. Differences in the economic development of Member States entails the risk of countries which are, or imagine themselves to be, in a weaker position taking protective measures that would adversely affect the freedom of intra-Community transit. Greater harmonisation of economic policy is required to promote a healthy development that will provide safeguards against national measures which would undermine the free market in general and the common agricultural market in particular.

Progress in the direction of Economic and Monetary Union also needs to be made on account of the international economic and monetary upheavals. These are not only a challenge to the Community to find an answer on a Community basis, they also represent a serious threat to the harmonious development of policy within the Community.

If, for example, as a result of external effects certain countries are affected more seriously than others, this limits the possibilities for joint action.

Efforts to achieve Economic and Monetary Union are also justified, as I have already said, on the grounds of their catalysing effect on harmonisation of policy in areas on the fringe of economic union. Without it being necessary to go as far as uniformity of budgetary policies, it just is not compatible with the requirements of an Economic and Monetary Union for one of the countries to be so out of line with its spending policy that other countries have to carry the burden this entails, on pain of reversion to a regime of independent exchange rate adjustments.

The spin-off from the creation of an Economic and Monetary Union must, however, not only be thought of in terms of economic factors. Real progress towards Economic and Monetary Union must also provide a political impetus in other fields, notably in the complementary policy areas of energy policy, environmental policy, social policy and—let us not forget!—regional policy. It is inconceivable that Member States would, on the one hand, accept considerable interference in their national economic policies, and yet, on the other, not be willing to accept the idea of Community responsibility in such important fields as these.

In all this we must not lose sight of the ultimate objective of European Union. An Economic and Monetary Union is a step along the road to closer political co-operation, whatever form that may take.

It would be beyond the scope of this brief account to go into all the arguments in favour of the Netherlands continuing unremittingly in its efforts to ensure that the political unification of Europe becomes a reality. About this I would like to say only two things.

First of all, the magnitude of the international problems which have confronted us in the past few years has been so great that only countries and groups of countries representing an economic and political force can make an effective contribution to solving them.

If the Netherlands wanted to pursue a policy independent of other European countries, that policy would, unfortunately, amount to little more than words.

Secondly, there are the many internal problems confronting countries as a result of social reforms and present ideas on such matters. To what extent should such problems be examined nationally—or at a lower level—and to what extent centrally in Brussels. Of course, a proper democratic procedure has to be guaranteed in both instances. I have already stated this emphatically at the beginning of my address. The whole situation can of course lead to tension between two schools of thought, one oriented towards decision-making at a lower level, the other tending to favour decision-making in the Brussels framework. It is my view that potential tension of this kind need not lead to a conflict situation and that integration and decentralisation can go hand in hand.

In any event, it is absolutely necessary for tangible progress to be made in the really important policy areas. Apart from the problems arising from divergence in the Member States a central role is also played by the present world economic and monetary situation. This external situation makes such slow progress by the Community scarcely tolerable. The Community should be in a position to play an important role in bringing about a new Bretton Woods that takes into account among other things of the changed power relationships in the world.

The Community should be able and willing to play a leading role in creating a stable and balanced world—in both the monetary and trade sectors—in which the interests of developing countries are taken fully into account. The successful functioning so far of the bloc of countries participating in the snake arrangement could form a basis for the necessary further stabilisation of international exchange rates. The announcement made by President Giscard d'Estaing that France wished to return to this arrangement—which also involves a system of close consultation on questions of monetary and economic policy— must be judged favourable in this light. But for this to represent a real strengthening there must be no relaxation of the rules as a result of France's return.

The interdependence of countries—not only in the monetary and economic field—is so great that if we want to see lasting and balanced progress with regard to production and employment in the world concrete form and shape will have to be given before long to the policy consultations between the various zones, for instance the United States, Japan, Canada, the developing countries and the oil-producing countries. The Member States of the Community—the largest trading block in the world—will have to make every effort to create the conditions which could lead to this more even distribution of prosperity. The current world situation imposes a heavy responsibility on the Community, a responsibility with which it will have to cope and from which it must not shrink.

The European Community conjures up in my mind the picture of a young bird just hatched from its shell, which is learning to fly while it is still in the nest, the bird has no choice. One day it will have to leave the nest. But meanwhile it does all sorts of exercises, frequently not without risk. One step too far and it is dashed to the ground.

It is the same with Europe. For years now the exercises have been going on which must ultimately lead to Europe taking its place as a fully-fledged member of the international community. As far as its own physique is concerned, the young bird still needs, not only to gain the necessary weight, but also to learn how to use its wings in a proper and self-possessed manner. It has no choice but to go through the growth stage: one fatal step . . . the game is up!

Neither extreme optimism nor extreme pessimism is appropriate in such a situation; great dedication, however, certainly is, and perhaps also a degree of self-confidence.

Is the Community strong enough in its present state to bear Economic and Monetary Union? Or should the question be asked the other way round: is union absolutely necessary to finally enable the Community to leave the nest, and will waiting any longer simply mean that the young bird slowly perishes for lack of food? Your colloquium will undoubtedly be able to make a valuable contribution to answering these questions.

First Theme

THE NECESSITY FOR AN ECONOMIC AND MONETARY UNION AND THE CONDITIONS IT NEEDS TO FULFILL IN ORDER TO FUNCTION PROPERLY

REPORT

by

U. Mosca*

I. WHY AN ECONOMIC AND MONETARY UNION?

The point of departure for European integration was the determination, at the end of the Second World War, of an enlightened minority to create in Europe conditions such that it would become impossible—or, at least, extremely difficult—to unleash afresh a fratricidal conflict.

The fathers of this new Europe, of which the essential vocation was to be economic and social progress and the safeguarding of peace, were conscious that their enterprise could not succeed without the support of a very broadly based consensus of public opinion in all the countries of Western Europe. They were equally convinced that, in order to mobilise public opinion in favour of Europe, it was necessary first to create in a concrete way a factual solidarity between the European nations in establishing common bases for their economic, social and political development.

At this initial stage of integration efforts were concentrated above all on the fusion of essential interests. These efforts then led to a double initiative:

- the creation of the Coal and Steel Community, having as its aim the de-nationalisation of the industrial foundation of the war by integrating the European coal and steel industry into a supranational community;
- the attempt to create a European Defence Community aimed at the de-nationalisation of the military apparatus by integrating it into one supranational defence community.

The second attempt met with failure, but the ECSC has been a remarkable success, which has encouraged the following with even more enthusiasm of the economic road to integration.

It is thus that in order to establish "the foundations of an ever closer union among the peoples of Europe" and "to strengthen the unity of their

* Director-General, Directorate-General of Economic and Financial Affairs, Commission of the European Communities.

The author expresses only his personal opinions.

13 C.M.L.Rev. 1976, 169-177

economies",[1] it was decided to create a European Economic Community, of which the aim was—and remains—to create a zone within which goods and services, persons and capital, could circulate freely and without distortions of competition, without at the same time engendering structural or regional imbalances.

From 1958 onwards, the development of the EEC is broadly known, and notably the realisation of three important stages around the year 1968, namely:

—the achievement of the customs union accompanied by
—the setting-up of a common commercial policy and
—the definition of a common agricultural policy.

Nevertheless, it is broadly felt, and the first monetary upsets at the end of the 1960's confirmed it, that the dynamic nature of the Treaty of Rome requires a very solid framework for these various common policies. It is thus that the Heads of State and Government meeting at The Hague on the first and second of December 1969 "re-affirmed their desire to make more rapid progress with the development necessary for the reinforcement of the Community and for *its development as an economic union...*" towards this end they agreed "...that a plan by stages should be elaborated in the course of the year 1970 *in view of the creation of an economic and monetary union*".[2]

It is in this plan, the "Werner plan", that the fundamental justification for an econimic and monetary union was made clear: "... progressive steps towards integration have the consequence that economic disequilibria have repercussions directly and rapidly on the global evolution of the Community. The experience of recent years has clearly shown that such disequilibria are capable of seriously compromising the integration achieved in the fields of freedom of movement of goods, of services and of capital. This is so in particular for the common agricultural market".[3] In other terms, it was the recognition of the unstable and even explosive character of a partial integration that gave rise to an acceleration of the preparations for an economic and monetary union at the beginning of this decade.[4]

1. See Preamble to the Treaty establishing the European Economic Community.

2. See para. 8 of the final communiqué of the Conference of Heads of State and Government of December 1–2, 1969, at the Hague, J. O. 1970 C136/15.

3. J.O. 1970 C 136/2.

4. See especially the Resolution of the Council and of the representatives of the governments of the Member States of March 22, 1971, concerning the realisation by stages of the economic and monetary union in the Community, J.O. 1972 C 28/1 *et seq.;* and Resolution of the Council and the representatives of the governments of the Member States of March 21, 1972, relating to the implementation of this realisation by stages, J. O. 1972 C 38/3 *et seq.*

One is forced, at the present stage, to admit that the creation of an economic and monetary union has become more necessary than ever. In fact, the problems which the Europe of today has to face are of such complexity that their solution far surpasses the capacity of the nation states. Whether one looks at the question of détente in Europe, or peace in the Middle East, relations with the Third World, or aid for development, disorder in the international monetary system or the petrol crisis, inflation or unemployment, then the experience of recent years demonstrates—should this still be necessary—the impossibility for the states of Europe, when each acts on its own, to go beyond partial and precarious solutions.

It would be by attacking these practical problems in a coherent fashion that the Member States of the Community would be launched effectively and irreversibly along the route of Economic and Monetary Union (EMU).

Despite the explanations which may be advanced for this, and despite the dangers which menace the Community at the present time, *the efforts undertaken since 1969 have led to disappointing results.* Certainly, the negotiations and then the renegotiations of the British were conducted on friendly terms, the Third Association Convention was signed at Lomé, and certain progress of a technical nature has been achieved, notably in the matter of co-operation between central banks, and recently in the field of the re-cycling of capital and in regional policy. In general, however, it must be admitted that one of the essential axes for the launching of EMU, namely the approximation of national economic policies, is at present in an impasse. In this respect one can only recall that which the Commission had already indicated to the Council of Ministers in its report on the progress of the first stage, published in the month of April, 1973: [5] "concerted action... only works really when the fundamental interests of the Member States converge, or when the problems do not involve in themselves vital conflicts of interest . . .". Even the great problems of the present have not reinforced the cohesion between the Member States. Instead of facing these difficult circumstances together, the Member States have restricted themselves to modest tentative steps such as the Community loan and the definition of a new unit of account, of which the use is still very limited. The opinion expressed by the group considering the problem, entitled *Economic and Monetary Union 1980,* describes in a striking fashion these developments in stating that: "their desire (that of the governments) has not

5. Communication of the Commission to the Council on the progress achieved in the first stage of the economic and monetary union, Suppl. 5/73 to the Bull. of the E.C.

manifested itself as a European will, but as a series of national wills, more or less ignoring each other, each one trying as best it can to emerge from the venture without loss".[6]

Among the explanations of this failure, the Marjolin group has pointed to "an insufficient comprehension of what EMU amounts to, and of the conditions which must be fulfilled for such a union to see the light of day and to be able to function".[7]

An editorial of the "Europe" Agency has recently remarked that it is possible to share the opinion of the group, provided that it is made clear to whom this lack of comprehension should be imputed. It is perhaps worthwhile remembering that the Werner report had indicated very clearly, back in 1970, that the EMU should not be considered as a mere "gadget" or a technical expedient, because it involved an enterprise which implied from the very beginning the will of the Member States to launch themselves resolutely on the road to far-reaching political integration.[8] Unfortunately, the same clarity is not present in the Resolution of the Council of 22 March 1971,[9] nor in the behaviour of the national administrations and of the governments which should have put into operation the directions of their Heads of State and Government and the resolutions of the Council.

II. THE ESSENTIAL CHARACTERISTICS OF THE ECONOMIC AND MONETARY UNION

There is a fairly wide margin of interpretation regarding the conditions which define an economic and monetary union. This can be explained, *inter alia,* by the fact that in some existing unions the degrees of economic and monetary integration are very different. The United States, Canada, Australia and also, in the Community, the Federal Republic of Germany, bear witness to this concerning:

- the systems of taxation,
- the budgetary autonomy of the regional and local public authorities,
- the access of these authorities to the national capital markets and
- the legislation in the social, cultural, technical, medical, pharmaceutical, *etc.,* spheres.

Nevertheless, without pretending to give a complete list, it can be

6. Report of the working group on *Economic and Monetary Union 1980* (Brussels, 1975), the "Marjolin Report".

7. *Ibid.,* p. 3.

8. See especially points B, C and D of the conclusions of the Werner Report J. O. 1970 C136/13.

9. J. O. 1971 C 28/1.

confirmed that *these unions are characterised by a limited number of common criteria*, namely:

(*a*) broad levels of the population share the sentiment of belonging to the union (the feeling of togetherness);

(*b*) by virtue of the social consensus, these unions are equipped with a central decision-making instance, in which are represented the three traditional powers in the process of democratic decision-making: legislative, executive and judicial. In addition, the relations between the three powers are conceived in such a way as to permit the union:

– to react rapidly in the face of changes of situation, and
– to distinguish the interest proper to the union from the sum total of the interests of its component parts;

(*c*) the degree of openness between the regions is very far advanced, in other words, the freedom of circulation of persons, goods, services and capital is assured and, for each region, the share of external trade in production is very high;

(*d*) a single central bank or a centralised system of federal banks is responsible for the management of a single currency;

(*e*) the central authorities are endowed with a relatively important budget (Federal Republic of Germany: the part relative to the expenses of the *Bund*, 13 per cent of GNP; Canada: federal expenses 16-19 per cent of the GNP); [10]

(*f*) some fiscal systems and some social security regimes ensure a certain degree of re-distribution of revenue including re-distribution between the regions;

(*g*) the ownership of the capital of enterprises is widely distributed within the whole of the territory of the union.

These criteria have as their common denominator the fact that they imply a high degree of political and economic interdependence of the regions which compose the union. In addition, and this is particularly important to ensure the cohesion of the union, they require automatic balancing mechanisms for those cases of differentiation which become too pronounced in the course of economic evolution.

To clarify this last point, it would suffice to confront the difficult economic situation in which certain Member States find themselves since the beginning of the year 1974 in the Community, with the hypothetical situation which the application of these criteria would bring about.

In this hypothetical situation, a diminution of economic activity in a country would have been compensated for in part by:

10. The margin is explained by the special features of the Canadian budgetary system.

—a reduction of imports [11]
—a diminution in the payments of dividends abroad
—an augmentation of direct investments in so far as the existence of surplus manpower promises to make this attractive
—an augmentation of transferred payments coming directly from the central budget or from other systems of centralised finance, such as:
- allocations for unemployment
- transfers under regional policy
- budgetary aids to compensate for a diminution in the fiscal receipts of regions

—a diminution in the contributions for the same systems.

The preceding enumeration is drawn largely from the report of the working party entitled *Economic and Monetary Union 1980.*[12] Certainly, the question remains whether this collection of conditions can be considered as sufficient for the realisation of an economic and monetary union. Thus it is fairly striking to have to record that a similar list can already be found in the Werner report,[13] which attributed to the EMU the following characteristics:

—the Community currencies are assured of total and irreversible reciprocal convertibility, without fluctuation in the rates of exchange and with immutable parity ratios or, preferably, are replaced by a single Community currency;
—the creation of liquidity in the whole of the zone, and the centralisation of monetary and credit policy;
—the monetary policy with regard to the rest of the world is within the Community competence;
—the policies of the Member States with regard to the capital market are unified;
—the essential factors regarding the public budgets, and in particular, variations in their volume, the size of balances and the methods of financing or of utilising the latter are decided at the Community level;
—the regional and structural policies do not remain exclusively within the competence of the member countries;
—a systematic and continuous consultation of the two sides of industry is assured at the Community level.

11. According to the calculations made by the Commission services, made on the basis of the input-output tables, a diminution in exports of a given total would bring a diminution of imports of 56% for Belgium, 50% for the Netherlands, 20% for Italy and 18% for France, of this total. The two first parts of this are in fact comparable with those taken as an indicator of the "openness" of a region in other publications.

12. *Op. cit.* n. 6, at p. 27 *et seq.*

13. *Op. cit.* n. 3.

It is clear from this that the Werner report puts the emphasis more on the establishment of common policies, and to a lesser extent, on the automatic balancing mechanisms mentioned by the Marjolin report.[14]

There is, however, a considerable similarity between the two reports.

To summarise, it appears that *the monetary and economic union requires, from the traditional point of view of competences and institutions:*

—as regards the *repartition of competences*
- a common economic policy,
- a common monetary policy,
- a common social policy;

—in the area of *institutions:*
- a decision-making centre at the level of the union, with competence to operate in the economic and social spheres and capable of operating with a substantial budget;
- a Community central bank or a system of central banks charged with the European monetary policy;
- democratic control by a European parliament elected by universal suffrage and endowed with real legislative powers.

This list of the essential characteristics of the EMU merits some comments. In fact:

—concerning the *competences,* it is necessary to distinguish the decisions which will have to be made at the level of the union from those which will remain within the jurisdiction of the national or local authorities. The responsibilities of the national government will still be very important, because the complexity of the economic and social life of the Member States would not lend itself to excessive centralisation;

—regarding *institutions,* it will be necessary to define their powers and their composition; also, the reciprocal relations between the institutions and the procedures of legitimation.

The analysis of these different problems would go beyond the limits of this present exposé, all the more so because they present political choices which will not be capable of being made except in the light of a democratic process of discussion and decision.

III. HOW TO ADVANCE TOWARDS AN ECONOMIC UNION

The extent of the undertaking required by the economic and monetary union requires a fairly long period of realisation, putting aside the hypothesis of a sudden transformation of political will in the immediate

14. *Op. cit.* n. 6, at p. 27 *et seq.*

future. It is for this reason that the Werner report advocated an approach by stages, of which the first contained modest steps in the sense that it did not require modifications of the Treaty of Rome. On the other hand, these steps were still very ambitious because they necessitated a convergence of economic and monetary policy much more pronounced than those of earlier years. In this respect, the narrowing of the margins of fluctuation between the currencies of the Member States, known as the "snake in the tunnel", represented the most dramatic of these steps, which required essentially a continual *rapprochement* of national policies.

A similar approach is found in the report of the working party *Economic and Monetary Union 1980,*[15] that is to say, that short-term actions and the first steps towards the economic and monetary union are there described in a very precise fashion (for example: creation of an exchange stablisation fund and a community system of unemployment benefits); but that report equally lacks a definition of the entire route which should be followed from this initial phase right up to the point where the union is realised.

The explanation for this gap is simple. It is already evident in part from one of the key phrases of the conclusions of the Werner Report,[16] namely: "the economic and monetary union signifies that the main decisions of economic policy will be taken at the Community level ... These transfers of responsibility and the creation of the corresponding Community institutions represents a process of fundamental political significance which involves the progressive development of political co-operation. . ." Given the difficulties of this political process, a precise description of the first stage only amounts to nothing other than a *definition of a test of the political will of the governments.*

It is to the merit of Robert Marjolin, President of the working party on "Economic and Monetary Union 1980" that he stated in clear terms the necessity of such a test.

In any case, this test of political will can be conceived of in a very different fashion. The approach chosen up to now consisted of proposing some series of actions of an economic and monetary nature, while conscious that the success of these actions would require important political changes. Thus, the question arises whether *the recognition of present failure does not result essentially from the fact that these political changes are always deferred until later.*

15. *Op.cit.* n. 6.
16. *Op.cit.* n. 3, p. 13.

Perhaps it is time to adopt a new method, and require, as a test of the political will to create one Europe:

– the granting to the European Parliament of real legislative powers, and elections by universal suffrage,
– the extension of the FECOM into a system of European central banks with their own monetary reserves,
– the creation of a decision-making centre for economic policy, particularly responsible for everything concerning the budgetary policy of the Community.

This alternative type of test would certainly be more painful than the first. Nevertheless, it involves the advantage of putting at the disposition of the Community the structure for democratic and effective decision-making which is necessary for it to face up to crisis situations and to assure its development.

CONCLUSIONS

The essential content of the necessary conditions for the realisation of an economic and monetary union has been known since the beginning of this decade. Their realisation involves at all stages changes which are sometimes painful, because the EMU is in fact only an aspect of political union. Thus each plan directed towards the establishment of an economic and monetary union is a sort of test of the present political structures of the Member States. In principle this test could be conceived either as a collection of measures of an economic and monetary order (this is the method which has been followed by both the Werner and the Marjolin reports), or as a transfer of the powers of decision from the national level to the Community level, or, indeed, as a combination of the two methods.

Finally, what is indispensable, and which has been lacking up to the present, is that the problem of choice between the different approaches should be presented without reticence to European public opinion.

REPORT

by

C. J. Oort*

1. INTRODUCTION

Some of you will remember the famous song by Tom Lehrer about the fate of Senator, later Vice-President, Hubert Humphrey. It goes something like this:

Whatever became of you, Hubert?
Has anyone heard a thing?
Are you sad, are you cross, are you gathering moss while you wait for the boss to ring?

Until recently, references to the Economic and Monetary Union always reminded me of that song, and I even made up a variation:

Whatever became of you, EMU?
Has anyone heard of her?
Are you dead, are you bust, are you gathering dust while you wait for the snake to stir?

That was until recently. Since then, there has been something of a revival of interest in the EMU. An international study group under the chairmanship of M. Marjolin has just published its report on *Economic and Monetary Union 1980.*[1] At about the same time, a committee of independent persons in this country has published a report on the elusive concept of "European Union", a report in which the EMU plays a central role.[2] Undoubtedly, other countries have engaged in similar studies in connection with the decision of the 1972 European Summit to charge the Belgian Prime Minister, Mr. Tindemans, with the task of submitting a report on European Union by the end of this year.

On the basis of that revived interest in Economic and Monetary Union, I would like to present a few ideas on what I believe we can and should do to bring that final goal closer to realization. I have no illusion whatever—and I do not suppose anybody has—that we can accomplish

* Treasurer-General, Netherlands Ministry of Finance.

1. Brussels, 1975.

2. The "Spierenburg report", *Rapport van de Adviescommissie Europese Unie,* 2nd Chamber of the Netherlands States-General, Doc. 13426 No. 2, 1975-76.

13 C.M.L.Rev. 1976, 179-187

full Economic and Monetary Union by 1980, but I do think it is worthwhile working for it, even if it will take considerably longer.

Since I have only little time, what I want to do is to concretrate on the final goal of full monetary union, i.e. a situation in which exchange rates between Community currencies are irrevocably fixed at a certain level, and payments between Community countries are free of all restrictions whatever. This is equivalent to having a single currency.

I do not want to go through the reasons for wanting full monetary union. Instead, I want to jump immediately to the question of how we can go about realizing that goal. In doing so, I shall make a distinction between three major areas in the national economy which directly affect the balance of payments, and therefore the exchange rate. They are:
—first: the money and foreign exchange markets,
—second: the total demand in the national economy,
—third: the development of production costs and productivity.

I shall go through each of these areas in turn and see what policy instruments we have to regulate developments, and how we could begin to harmonize policies so as to steer developments in the different economies on to parallel course.

2. MANAGEMENT OF THE MONEY MARKET AND THE FOREIGN EXCHANGE MARKET

Management of the money market and the foreign exchange market is the most important policy instrument to regulate the exchange rate in the short run. By contracting or expanding the liquidity of the banking system, which can be done very easily and at very short notice, the central bank can influence short term interest rates. This in turn immediately affects the exchange market, for a reduction of short-term interest rates at home will induce banks to transfer their short-term assets abroad, so as to profit from higher interest rates there. Conversely, a rise of short-term rates at home will induce banks to move funds back, or to borrow abroad, in order to profit from the higher interest rate at home. This technique of money market management, sometimes supported by direct intervention in the exchange markets, is the main instrument which ensures from day to day that exchange rates in the European "snake" stay within the prescribed narrow margins around the so-called "central rates" which express the agreed relationships between the "snake" currencies.

What institutional arrangements do we need in order to make this area of policy, the day-to-day management of the exchange rate, evolve towards full monetary union? It is clear that the one essential policy issue involved is the level at which exchange rates must be maintained. Given these levels, the management of money and foreign exchange markets is a purely technical matter, which requires close technical co-operation between central banks, but does not involve any major policy decisions.

In the past far too much attention has been given to these technical monetary matters and far too little to the real policy issue: that of finding appropriate procedures for deciding on the fevels of the exchange rates, both within the Community and with respect to the dollar. I shall come back to that very important matter at the end of my comments.

3. DEMAND MANAGEMENT

We all know that a monetary union cannot work if each individual country keeps full control over the total level of demand in its economy, i.e. over the total of all claims on resources exerted by the country's citizens, firms and public bodies taken together. To put it very simply: if a country is allowed to spend more than it earns plus what it is capable of borrowing, it will run a balance of payments deficit which sooner or later will force it to depreciate its currency. In a completed monetary union, where exchange rate adjustments are no longer possible, such overspending would take the form of the country appropriating a disproportionate share of the total resources of the Community, including its external reserves. Obviously, this model of the monetary union cannot work. Without some central control over demand management in the separate countries, a monetary union cannot be evolved, nor can it be maintained once established.

From the abundant literature on the subject, one thing is clear: it is essential as a minimum that there should be a measure of central control over two strategic policy targets: the size of public budget deficits and the rate of liquidity expansion in the exonomy. The latter includes in particular the liquidity created by short-term financing of public budget deficits.

I do not want to bore you with the immense technical problems that arise already at the stage of defining the relevant concepts. These are highly complex and there are in the various countries very different relationships between the budget of the central government and the finances of local authorities, public bodies, nationalized industries, social security systems, institutional investors, etc. Also, a budget constraint can be circumvented in a great many ways with which Ministers of finance are only too familiar. For example, public investment in buildings can be channelled outside the budget by renting instead of paying for them outright; public activities can be realized outside the budget *via* agencies or private bodies which receive public guarantees, *etc.* I do not mention these complications in order to conclude that it is impossible to impose a meaningful budget constraint on national governments, but only to indicate how difficult the process is and how much detailed agreement on accounting and financing methods is necessary before such constraints can be made meaningful. We all know this from experience of the relationship between our central governments and the local authorities. It will take a long time and a great deal of hard work before we can reach the same degree of sophistication in the relationship between the Community and member countries, as we have reached between the central government and local authorities.

Assuming that these difficult technical problems can be solved, the really important question we are left with is the institutional and political one. The loose co-ordination, such as we have practised so far in the Community, is simply not enough. We all know that in practice the Commission does not propose directives unless they are in every detail acceptable to national governments; we know that the Council will not approve a directive unless it is acceptable to all; we know that a country will not follow the directive unless it is acceptable to it; and, finally, we know that nothing is done or can practically be done to ensure that a directive, once adopted, is followed-up by appropriate national policies.

I am not saying that the periodic consultations between the Ministers of Economics and Finance are a charade: they serve a very useful purpose of transmitting information and reaching mutual understanding. As such, they have a very real significance for policy. But they do not serve to impose the kind of constraints on national policies which are needed to evolve an Economic and Monetary Union.

I agree with those who argue that we need a political and institutional quantum jump, if we really want to forge ahead in this area. I do not want to elaborate on this, since others are better qualified to do so than I am. That it would involve a very real transfer of authority from national capitals to Brussels and Strasbourg is quite obvious. I simply want to state, as my personal opinion that, both for technical reasons and on political grounds, we are still a very long way off from making the required jump. In the meantime, I believe that we should try to focus our discussions, consultations, and reviews more and more on a few major policy variables such as the public sector deficit and the rate of liquidity creation, rather than dissipate our efforts on wide-ranging reviews of all economic indicators.

This would require a major effort at making these concepts transparent and coherent—a job that is not very dramatic and politically not very rewarding. But it is an absolutely necessary technical prerequisite for the political quantum jump, if and when it comes. So the Commission had better get cracking!

4. COSTS AND PRODUCTIVITY

The last, and in the long run by far the most important condition for full monetary union, is that cost conditions in the different countries stay roughly in line with each other. In particular labour costs, as determined by the rise of wages and of productivity, should not diverge so much or for so long a period that competitive relationships between countries change significantly. If they do, exchange rates must sooner or later be adjusted to correct the imbalance that results from the weakening competitive position of some countries and the strengthening position of others. If we look at exchange rate developments in the last five years, for example, we find that they have in fact moved roughly in line with the changes in national cost levels: the effective depreciation of the pound sterling since 1971, by about 25 per cent, is roughly in line with the extent to which production costs in the UK have risen more than in competing countries. This is natural and inevitable.

I now come to the fundamental question that should receive far more attention that it ussually does in discussions on monetary union: can we bring costs into line by active, co-ordinated policy measures? My own answer to that question is based on two simple observations:

—first: we manifestly do not have sufficient instruments to achieve our national policy goals in this area, a statement that unfortunately needs no further comment;

—second: it is utterly absurd to believe that we could do on a Community level what we cannot do domestically.

Under these circumstances, and as long as they prevail, the attempt to irrevocably fix exchange rates is bound to fail, because it will lead to shifts in relative competitive positions which neither the weaker nor the stronger countries can afford in the long run. The weaker countries would price themselves out of the market; they would run increasing balance of payments deficits and suffer increasing unemployment in their export industries. The stronger countries would build up excessive external surpluses and would suffer increasing inflationary pressures, imposed on them from outside.

One could argue, and it has in fact been argued, that it is precisely this feed-back mechanism which is needed to bring wage costs into line with each other. Unemployment in the one country would lead to wage restraint, and overemployment in the other to higher wage demands. We know from experience that the first is not true, or at least not without a long time-lag, and then only very imperfectly. The latter, the inflationary effect in surplus countries, works only too well, but it is not likely to be accepted with any enthusiasm. In short, it really is quite absurd to believe that governments will enter into a firm commitment to irrevocably fix their exchange rates or, if they were stupid enough to enter into such a commitment, that they would keep to it under pressure of the events I have just described. No national government will allow such a situation to develop; no government is willing to let the classical gold standard mechanism operate in the hope that the threat of unemployment will restrain excessive wage demands or, conversely, will accept that the development of excess demand will raise the rate of domestic inflation to that in the partner countries.

What does this mean? Does it mean we can never achieve full monetary union? That we might as well forget about it and limit ourselves to implementing and perfecting the common market? Of course it does not, for the evidence is there of monetary unions that have worked and still do: the Belgo-Luxembourg monetary union, the *de facto* Irish-British monetary union and, last but not least, the monetary union of the 12 federal reserve districts in the US. What all these succesful monetary unions have in common is highly integrated labour and capital markets, with sufficient actual or potential mobility to ensure that wages and the returns on capital will autonomously move roughly in line in the different parts of the union. The same development will tend to occur in the Community, provided we give it a chance—a point I shall come back to in a minute.

How long will it take for these structural developments to have advanced far enough to be able to irrevocably fix the exchange rates at a certain level? I do not have the faintest idea. Nor does it matter very much: as these developments occur, the exchange rate relationships will tend to settle down in a fixed pattern, establishing the monetary union by actual fact rather than official act. What I do know is that it would be rather ridiculous to set a fixed date in advance, no matter whether that date be 1980 or 1990. Where policy is not the major determinant of an event, setting a date for the event is an empty gesture. Sometimes, such gestures are needed as a spur to action but when they have been proved empty before and when they are as obviously hollow as this one, I very much doubt their political force.

In my opinion, it is far more important that the interpenetration of markets is given as good a chance as we can give it. This implies that we do not disrupt the freedom of movement by restrictions on trade, on migration, on investment across borders, or on payments both for current and for capital transactions. It is my firm conviction, based on observation as well as on the opinions of those who make business decisions, that nothing is so disruptive to economic relationshipts, that nothing will so frustrate the process of interpenetration, as the imposition of direct restrictions, no matter how temporary, or even the threat that such restrictions can be imposed. No firm can afford to become too dependent on foreign markets, if they can be cut off by administrative action. No firm will establish an integral part of his production process abroad, if the lines can at any time be severed by controls. No worker will easily move abroad, if his work permit can at any time be cancelled.

Going back to monetary matters, I therefore believe that the establishment of full convertibility is an essential step on the road to monetary union. When I say full convertibility, I mean the unconditional right of all citizens and undertakings to exchange one Community currency into another at all times, for all purposes, and without limit. I know that there are a great many hurdles to be taken before we can achieve full convertibility, but I believe that this is what we shall have to work for, rather than the ephemeral goal of fixed exchange rates, which I have shown to be largely out of reach of policy actions anyway.

To the extent that there is conflict between convertibility and exchange rate stability—a situation that can easily occur, since payments restrictions are a familiar instrument to "defend" the exchange rate—the Community should accept a very strong presumption in favour of "open circuits" and against exchange controls. It seems to me that a very good case can be made for treating exchange restrictions as we treat trade restrictions: they should be banned in principle, and permitted only by positive consent on the part of the Commission or the Council.

5. THE EXCHANGE RATE REGIME IN THE COMMUNITY BEFORE MONETARY UNION

I now turn to the management of exchange rates in the Community an issue to which I want to devote the last part of my comments. From what I have said on exchange rates so far, one conclusion is clear, namely that for some time to come there must be room for adjustment of exchange rates within the Community. No measure of "political will" which is so often profferred as the ultimate solution of Community problems, can change these economic realities.

This is perhaps unfortunate from some points of view, in particular for the common agricultural policy. But we cannot change the inevitable, nor can it be accepted that the long-run development of the Community is endangered by exchange restrictions in a futile attempt to shield the agricultural sector from overall developments in the economies of member countries. That would be letting the tail wag the dog—and a rather small and scrawny tail at that.

In my opinion, the real question to be discussed is not *whether* we shall have adjustments of exchange rates within the Community, but rather *how* we can organize the decision-making process on two distinct although closely linked aspects of the exchange rate issue, namely:

1. intra-Community exchange rate relationships, and
2. exchange rate relationships between the Community currencies as a group and the dollar.

In terms of the "snake" mechanism, two questions take the form of:

1. the adjustment of central rates within the "snake", and
2. the adjustment of the position of the "snake" as a whole in relation to the dollar.

It seems to me that for some time ahead we will have to leave individual countries considerable freedom in managing their exchange rates. Community influence should be gradually increased, but we should avoid procedures which would tend to make exchange rates even more difficult to change than they are already in the context of the national decision-making process. In other words, as long as we are not willing to accept positive Community action on exchange rates, we should not go too far in imposing formal Community procedures which could act as a drag on national decisions. There should be no bias in favor of inaction on exchange rates!

If we accept that for some time countries will retain some degree of national autonomy on exchange rates, how can we develop a common policy vis-à-vis the outside, in particular the dollar? The experience in the "snake" has already given some ideas of how this might work: countries would be relatively free in adjusting their rate within the "snake", while there would be a fairly stringent common procedure for managing the level of the "snake" as a whole in relation to the dollar.

An intriguing next step has been suggested in the report of an independent study group on Economic and Monetary Union, published by the European Commission in 1973 under the title *European economic integration and monetary unification.*[3] The authors propose setting up a two-tier decision mechanism by introducing the concept of a European monetary unit, which for convenience I shall refer to as the "Europa". The individual countries of the Community would express their exchange rates in terms of Europas, and they would manage their rates by intervention exclusively in Europas.

The exchange rate between the Europa and the dollar would in turn be

3. Prof. H. W. J. Bosman *et al.*, Doc. COM II/520/1/73-E.

managed exclusively by intervention in dollars against Europas. The dollar policy would be carried out on the Community level, by a European version of the American Federal Reserve Board. This scheme would accomplish the institutional separation between the management of intra-European exchange rate policy, which for the time being would remain largely a national affair, and the common dollar policy of the Community carried out on the Community level.

If the "Europa" sounds rather futuristic, let me point out that we have already Europas of a kind, namely in the form of an accounting unit in the EMCF and, with a different definition, in the EDF. The only major step which the authors of the report propose is that the private sector, in particular the banking system, should be allowed to hold Europas, which could take the form of short term liabilities of the EMCF. I do not want to go into the monetary mechanism by which Europas would be created, nor can I go into the wider implications of the Europa concept.

Since the Europa would shield the holder from the larger exchange rate risks on any one individual currency, it might well become an important new reserve asset and an alternative to the dollar and to other currencies presently held as reserve assets. It might also provide a change to reduce the importance of the Eurodollar market and to prevent its drawbacks, by keeping the Europa creation firmly under the monetary control of the Community.

It seems to me that the Europa approach is a promising one. It responds immediately to a real need of the international community-witness the private loans expressed in "baskets" of European currencies. Also, it is based on the sensible thought that even the loosest monetary arrangement among member countries requires a common dollar policy.

The two-stage intervention technique of the Europa approach is perfectly suited to bring about this separation of responsibilities between national and Community authorities. It avoids the impasse in which the supposedly gradual and pragmatic program of the plan for Economic and Monetary Union has been and will continue to get bogged down, whenever countries are not able or willing to accept the consequences of a solidifying exchange rate structure.

Second Theme

THE OPTIMAL ECONOMIC CONSTITUTION OF THE EUROPEAN COMMUNITY WITH REFERENCE TO THE ECONOMIC CONSTITUTIONS OF THE MEMBER STATES

REPORT

by

Ulrich Scheuner*

1. THE ECONOMIC AND MONETARY UNION AND THE ECONOMIC SYSTEM OF THE MEMBER STATES

1.1. *The aim of an effective Economic Union*

The European Community has remained, since its inception as the ECSC, in constant motion towards a remote goal. With the realisation of the customs union, of the common market, it was evident that the intended full economic exchange between the Member States had not been attained to the extent hoped for. The removal of all obstructions, in the area of admission to and qualification for various professions (Article 57 of the EEC Treaty),[1] and the harmonisation of economic legislation have not yet been effected, and in the field of common policies, with the exception of agriculture, no substantial result has to date been achieved. It is clear that, for a full realisation of economic unity, further steps are necessary, above all in the area of economic and monetary policy. Far-reaching objectives of this kind, aimed at the establishment of full economic integration, are contained in the programme for an Economic and Monetary Union (hereafter called the EMU) laid down by the Resolution of the Council and the representatives of the governments of the Member States of March 22, 1971.[2]

The establishment of a full economic union is at the present time more difficult than in the nineteenth century, when it was attained for substantial areas, as the German Reich and Italy. In those days it was necessary to proceed on the basis of a mainly agricultural population, with little inclination to migrate, and of an industry which was just in the process of being built up, and with this the likelihood of considerable regional fluctuations in wages and the standard of living. Nowadays the population is mobile and less inclined to put up with regional differences in wages and living standards. Industrial development is now largely

* Professor of law, University of Bonn.

1. Articles without further reference indicate the articles of the Treaty of Rome.
2. J.O. 1971, C29/1

13 C.M.L.Rev. 1976, 191-213

completed, and poses location problems for all countries. Economic and monetary policy are still nationally orientated, in so far as the much-increased state involvement in these areas is concerned.

1.2. *Crisis in the unification of Europe*

The first steps in the direction of EMU were taken at no propitious point in time. After the accession of the United Kingdom, economic development in Europe entered a period of stagnation. In addition, there were external difficulites, and in 1973 the fixed exchange system between the European currencies, together with the international flexible exchange system were dissolved. Through the introduction of flexible exchange rates, the efficacy of the agricultural market was considerably prejudiced. Problems of unemployment, budgetary deficits and balance of payments arose, the combatting of which lies within the national competence. The European Community has only been able to develop its own policy to a limited extent. Even if there is no disagreement between the Member States concerning the outstanding goals of prosperity and growth, a differing attitude to questions of stability and inflation, and an increasingly nationalistic tendency is making itself manifest. At the present time, the fate of every democratic government in elections depends on its economic policy. This encourages the inclination not to leave the instruments in this area to supranational authorities, and especially to deploy monetary policy as a national instrument. Arguments of this kind have been mentioned by those who favour British withdrawal from the European Community; the British trade unions, for instance, are anxious about a diminution of national flexibility in this area. The economic crisis we are now faced with can only to a small degree be traced back to the burden of increased oil prices,[3] and it calls for critical reflection as to the aims of an EMU, and as to the next steps to be taken in the direction of economic unity.[4]

Without wishing once again to embark on the controversy between the economists and the monetarists, I think that we can today proceed from the assumption that a monetary union is not conceivable without the accompaniment of a co-ordination of the economic policies of the Member States.[5] The foundations of a common monetary policy can

3. On December 11, 1974, Commissioner Haferkamp stated in the European Parliament that of an inflation rate of 15-20% in some countries only about 4% could be attributed to the effect of the rise in oil prices; 1974 O.J., Suppl. No. 183, at. p. 154.

4. On April 24, 1974, Commission President Ortoli spoke in the European Parliament of a crisis in the Community, 1974 O.J., Suppl. No. 175, at p. 98.

5. Ortoli, *loc. cit.*, p. 99.

only be established in a lasting fashion in conjunction with an ever-growing agreement on economic matters. Further, the time limits mentioned in the Werner report and the Council Resolution of 1971 will have to be based on more realistic estimates. It follows from this consideration, and here I agree with the conclusions of Professor VerLoren van Themaat,[6] that it is as important to direct one's attention to the actual steps which are necessary to bring about closer economic agreement between Member States, as to have solely in view the ultimate objective of a monetary union. This report, too, will concern itself less with the abstract portrayal of the ultimate ideal situation, as with the necessary steps to be taken in the establishing of a common economic order and common economic policy. I therefore understand the theme which has been put to me—namely, the optimum economic constitution of the European Community—in this sense, that I should direct my efforts towards the description of the basic features of the economic constitution to be established for the Community. The research which has been carried out for the national reports concerning the economic organisation in the Member States will form the primary basis for this undertaking.[7]

It is gratifying to note, in concluding these introductory remarks, that the Heads of State and Government of the Nine, meeting in Paris in December 1974, re-stated their commitment to the aim of Economic and Monetary Union. The recent return of France to the linking of European currencies is a further confirmation of the will to resolve the crisis and to strengthen common efforts.[8]

1.3. *Putting the question*

This study will concern itself more with the question of economic union and its foundations than with the question of monetary union, particularly because I lack special knowledge of the monetary aspects. In comparison with the idea of a monetary union, which is expressed in terms of the irreversible tying of exchange rates, or even the creation of

6. "Wirtschaftspolitische und rechtspolitische Aspekte einer Währungsunion mit unbefristeter Ubergangszeit", (1975) EuR, p. 20 *et seq.*, esp. at pp. 26 and 41.

7. In the series "Competition—Approximation of Legislation", No. 20 (Brussels, 1975), appear the studies on France (Fromont), Italy (Sacchi Morsiani), The Federal Republic (Zacher), the Netherlands (VerLoren van Themaat); the United Kingdom (Daintith); those on Ireland (McMahon), Belgium (Schrans) and Denmark (Koktvedgaard and Lando) are in draft. See also the Interim Report by Professor VerLoren van Themaat, in the same series (Brussels, 1973).

8. Communiqué of December 10, 1974, (1975) E.A., D. 43.

a unified Community currency, the concepts of economic union seems to be less precisely circumscribed.[9] The concept means, in a pragmatic definition, the state of affairs in which the economic systems of the participating states exhibit a far-reaching conformity with one another, and in which open and unhindered economic intercourse between them is possible. This state of affairs is supported and assured by means of a co-ordination of their economic policies. An effective, common economic policy is therefore required, which goes beyond the four freedoms mentioned in the Treaty of Rome to cover also the areas of budgets, credit, taxation and other instruments for influencing economic activity, supplemented by increasing convergency in the area of social policy. Such a common policy also implies agreement as to the objectives or, better still, the priorities among these objectives, in order to exercise an effective short- and medium-term influence on economic development.

From these considerations arise the following questions:

(a) on the basis of what common principles and aims will an agreement between Member States take place?

(b) in which areas do the economic systems of the Member States show agreement, and in which areas is a resolution of differences, or the development of common legal regulation, required?

(c) in what areas can the Community secure the requisite conformity by means of co-ordination and to what extent must it dispose of autonomous powers? What role has decentralisation, of a regional type, to play?

In seeking an answer to these questions, we will first consider the common economic foundations of the Community, and then the objectives and basic legal principles of a common economic policy. Thereafter, we shall review the instruments of economic policy and the question of their uniform application, and, finally, take a look at the functions of a future further co-ordination of the systems of economic law.

2. COMMON FOUNDATIONS OF THE ECONOMIC SYSTEM

2.1. *The market and planning*

Behind the concrete aims of the Community as formulated in Articles 2 and 104, lie very definite conceptions relating to the kind of economic system to which the Community adheres. The whole idea of a Common Market rests upon the idea of an open economic system which makes free exchange possible. The unity of the market is to be obtained not

9. In this sense see also VerLoren van Themaat (1975) EuR, 24.

through state coercion, but by means of the mechanism of the market itself, on the basis of certain regulatory principles. It was clear from the outset, and is today even more strongly recognised, that this free exchange of goods, capital, persons and services, also requires the supervisory assistance of the Member States or of the Community. The bare setting-aside of restrictions is not enough; a common overall guidance is also required. In the Member States this realisation has been more slowly attained. Whereas France and the Netherlands were from the outset already inclined to the use of pluriannual plans, the Federal Republic first adopted planning provisions in 1967, and the foundations of planning were laid only later in Italy, Belgium and Ireland.[10] In effecting this fundamental reorganisation of their economic systems, that is, in bringing about the co-existence of a market economy, based on competition, with central direction from the state and the Community, the Member States have adjusted to each other. In view of the developments in different countries, it is clear that neither aspect of this mixed system can be abandoned by the Member States without serious repercussions on the Community. Going over to completely liberal methods is hardly in question, but a changeover in a Member State to a system of comprehensive direction by the state, with control over all business decision-making, nationalisation of basic industries *etc.* is conceivable. Such a development would necessarily cancel out the effects of free competition, create centrally-steered discriminations on a national basis, and eventually become totally inflexible in the face of Community economic policy. The Community would be shaken to its core. This transformation of the economic systems of the Member States must, therefore, remain within a fixed framework. Within this framework they may effect certain variations, with regard, for instance, to the system of property ownership (Article 222 EEC), but they may not venture beyond its limits.

2.2. *Limits of State competence*

In order that they may be effectively realised in a unified economic area, the four basic freedoms of the Common Market, the free movement of goods, capital, persons and services attach a fundamental significance to the freedom of private decision. This freedom of decision can be

10. For the five-year plan in France, see Fromont, p. 22 *et seq.*; for planning in the Netherlands, see VerLoren van Themaat, p. 25 *et seq.* and p. 28 *et seq.*; for the transition to planning in Italy, see Sacchi Morsiani, p. 23 *et seq.*; for the changeover in 1958 in Belgium, see Schrans, and for the situation in Ireland, see report on Ireland, Ch. II, II, 2, *op. cit.*, n. 7.

restricted by binding state or Community measures, or can be influenced by means of various instruments, and yet it alone, in conjunction with certain regulatory factors, is capable of bringing about integration by means of free exchange. There are limits here, too, to both state and Community short-term economic policy. Far-reaching policy prescriptions of a binding character could distort competition.[11] This is also valid for the public sector, without taking into account the reservation as to the system of property (Article 222 EEC). The problem is approached in Article 90 EEC. A sector and, according to current views, this may be a substantial part of the economy of a country, can be allocated to publicly-owned enterprises. But these must remain open to competition, and not exceed a certain proportion of the economic structure, as otherwise the economy would become more dependent on national planning than on the principle of free exchange.

2.3. *Co-ordination of economic policy*

The establishment of an economic union is based upon a co-ordination of those institutions and factors which determine the economic development of the Member States. For the realisation of the four freedoms, and the removal of obstacles to their operation whether in the form of differences between the legal systems, discriminations of every sort on the basis of nationality, or distortions of competition, the instruments of economic control must be standardised and applied according to common guidelines. The Werner plan and the Council Resolution of March 22, 1971, accept the necessity for a wide-ranging assumption of competences by the Community. Putting the question in a different way, one might ask which of the common elements of economic policy require the assumption of competences by the Community, and in which areas a mere co-ordination would suffice. This question cannot be answered in terms of general formulas. The fact should, however, not be ignored that certain individual Member States, as, for example, the United Kingdom, insist upon the retention of national competence in the areas of industrial and regional policy.[12] There can be no doubt that the method of mere co-ordination throughout the Community represents a weaker form of integration. But, for many years to come, we shall have to proceed from the fact that the Member States will seek to retain a substantial independence in their internal economic policy.

11. *Cf.* the Interim Report by VerLoren van Themaat (henceforth referred to as the Interim Report), p. 12a.

12. Declaration of Mr. Wilson in the House of Commons on March 3, 1975, (1975) E.A., D. 172.

A common economic policy must, above all, also leave room for a meaningful degree of decentralisation. The Community can always draw up programmes and, where necessary, lay down binding rules for fiscal and monetary policy. But it must always leave the detailed elaboration of policy regarding investment, direction of individual assistance and regional aids to the Member States. The argument for decentralisation is reinforced by the fact that individual Member States also leave room for regional economic policy in their own area—in Germany, to the *Länder* and municipalities, in Italy, the regions, and in the Netherlands, the municipalities.[13] Central direction of all economic matters by the Community is not a practicable solution. The Community will have to, above all later on in the area of monetary policy, assume certain mandatory decision-making powers; but as far as the establishment of a common economic policy is concerned, resort will have to be had to a large extent to measures of co-ordination.

Such measures would include:

(*a*) The drawing up of medium-term plans and programmes, supplemented by short-term actions. These programmes will contain indicative provisions, but also binding provisions relating to the budget, as well as to money and credit policy;

(*b*) The arrangement of the budget, and the other instruments for influencing the economic situation of the Member States will have to be harmonised. In the first place, account must here be taken of the fact that certain Member States employ the system of pluriannual plans, accompanied by incentives (tax reliefs, subsidies, programme contracts); one thinks here of France, Italy and Belgium. On the other hand, other Member States use the budget primarily as a kind of non-systematic method of planning and direction; here one may refer to Germany, the United Kingdom and Ireland.

(*c*) Common policies, such as energy and protection of the environment, also come into consideration as a means to unification, but only for certain sectors. They can be supplemented by means of Community funds (as in regional policy, social affairs).

(*d*) Of continuing importance remain efforts directed towards the harmonisation of laws relating to the structure of enterprises, professional qualifications, *etc.* Significant also remains the Community competition policy, but supplemented by more strongly harmonised national rules of competition. These are today less developed in France, Italy and Belgium than in other countries. In this area a fundamental unification within the framework of the Community has already been attained by

13. For the problem of decentralisation see VerLoren van Themaat (1975) EuR, 36.

means of uniform regulation (Article 85 EEC). But the support of comparable regulation in the national sphere is necessary.
(*e*) Among the means of achieving unification, the renunciation of the use of monetary policy as a means of compromise or evasion within the national framework must be counted; monetary policy should rather be placed exclusively at the service of the monetary union.[14]

This short review shows that co-ordination stands in the foreground in certain areas, but that in others certain objectives can only be secured by means of common measures of a mandatory nature.

2.4. *The scope of Community competences*

Limits to the assumption of decision-making powers by the Community proceed from the Treaty itself, which only in certain areas foresees compulsory regulation by the Community. Article 103 permits the mandatory regulation of short-term economic policy. With regard to economic policy, Article 105 provides a legal foundation for co-ordinative programming, but not for mandatory regulation, so long, of course, as one does not wish to fall back on Articel 235.[15] One may assume that economic policy is something of a medium-term character, but it should be noted that in some Member States the distinction between medium and short-term programming is not very developed (*e.g.* the United Kingdom), whereas in others short-term measures are inserted in the pluriannual plan (*e.g.* France and Italy). Article 107 EEC provides only scanty powers with regard to exchange rates, though these powers may, if the occasion arises, be supplemented by means of support measures where balance of payments difficulties arise—Article 108 (2) EEC.[16] For the creation of common policies in the areas of energy and protection of the environment, a foundation in the Treaty must first be provided. Community competences in the social field also do not extend beyond the power to co-ordinate of Articles 117 and 118 EEC; the significance of this will be referred to later. The fact that for the near future at least a revision of the Treaty in order to extend the competences of the Community cannot be envisaged, limits the possibilities of assumption of powers by the Community, and points to co-ordination as the best

14. *Cf.* Fromont, p. 61 *et seq.*; Sacchi Morsiani, p. 85 *et seq.*, Schrans, p. 18, *op. cit.*, n. 7.

15. On the lack of clarity in the distinction between conjunctural and economic policy in Arts. 103 and 105 EEC, see Everling, *"Die Koordinierung der Wirtschaftspolitik in der Europäischen Gemeinschaft also Rechtsproblem"*, 1964 at p. 19 *et seq.*; on the limitation of competences under Art. 105, ibid, p. 20 *et seq.*; see further C. D. Ehlermann, (1972) EuR, 14 *et seq.*

16. For the procedure under Art. 108, see Bramkamp, (1974) EuR, 305 *et seq.*

interim method. Article 235 may to some extent be of assistance here, especially since the Council has expressly referred to it as a stop-gap measure.

3. AIMS AND LEGAL PRINCIPLES OF THE ECONOMIC ORDER

3.1. *The economic constitution of the Member States*

After a short review of the foundations of a common economic system, and of the methods for the attainment of greater economic unification, we turn our attention now to the legal definition of economic objectives and of the other principles of economic development. Particular problems of unification are posed in this area because the systems of the Member States are different from one another in a number of respects. It is, however, clear that within the legal orders of the Member States there exists a certain agreement on a number of important points. This is the case, for instance, regarding the common adoption of a mixed economic system, combining free exchange and intervention. This system has now been adopted in all the Member States considered, though not, of course, always to the extent of adopting fixed pluriannual plans, on a statutory basis, as in France, Italy and Belgium. This is also the case regarding the legal, or in any case, factual guarantee of the economic and professional freedom of the individual. The Member States are also in agreement in basically leaving the fixing of the level of prices and wages to the market or to the free collective bargaining of the parties. To be sure, Italy and Belgium go in for a certain marginal control of prices,[17] in the Netherlands a strong influence is exercised on prices and wages,[18] and Denmark has an index-related arrangement;[19] and the United Kingdom in 1973 finally introduced the possibility of a more far-reaching control of prices.[20]

There are on the other hand, certain points of difference, relating especially to the instruments of economic direction. In contrast to the systematic planning on the statutory basis carried out in France, Italy and Belgium, planning in the Federal Republic of Germany, the United Kingdom and Ireland is not binding upon citizens, but only upon the State internally. The systems for granting subsidies are also varied. Whereas in Italy this is governed by legislation, in other countries, such

17. See Sacchi Morsiani, p. 73; Schrans, p. 13, *op. cit.*, n. 7.
18. See VerLoren van Themaat, at pp. 30 and 82, *op. cit.*, n. 7.
19. See Koktvedgaard, p. 25, *op. cit.*, n. 7; price control was also introduced in 1971.
20. See Daintith, p. 117, and on the price regulation of 1973, p. 110 *et seq.*, *op. cit.*, n. 7.

as the United Kingdom, the Federal Republic and the Netherlands, it is fixed by the budget. Further, in some Member States the regional authorities, such as the *Länder* in Germany, the regions in Italy and the municipalities in the Netherlands are involved in decision-making by virtue of their limited autonomous competences. The problems which arise from this must not, however, be over-emphasised. The fact that economic policy is laid down within a national framework determines its most decisive lines, so that no deviations from the basic guidelines can result from this regional autonomy. In the Federal Republic, in fact, the relation between the *Bund* and the *Länder* has become a privileged sphere of planning, which ensures to the *Bund* a significant influence.[21]

Looking generally at the economic systems of the Member States, the French system, more strongly based on an overall plan, although its role has recently diminished, and also the Italian system, are thrown into relief as against the system of the Federal Republic which is more strongly orientated towards the free market economy. The Netherlands system exhibits stronger socio-political aspects, while planning in the United Kingdom and Ireland is still little developed. Differences also appear, as will shortly be indicated, in the legal definition of basic economic objectives, and in the establishing of economic principles in the constitution. A differing attitude is evident regarding the expansion of public ownership, as also in the evaluation of the various instruments of state influence on the economy. Where the plan does not stand in the foreground as a legally fixed foundation, the budget gains a great significance, as in the United Kingdom and the Federal Republic. The influence of parliament on economic policy is everywhere slight. However, the systematic establishment of a plan requires parliamentary approval, whereas the discretion permitted to the administration in the United Kingdom, Ireland and the Federal Republic could be described as more far-reaching than in those countries where the plan is the main economic instrument.[22]

3.2. *Objectives of economic policy*

Only in a few of the Member States are the aimed-for objectives of economic policy transcribed in the constitution. In the Federal Republic this is done by means of norms establishing fundamental legal rights, and

21. See Zacher, pp. 27 and 72 *et seq., op cit.*, n. 7.

22. With regard to those basic features of the economic constitutions of the Member States which exhibit a certain conformity, and those exhibiting differences, *cf.* VerLoren van Themaat, Interim Report, p. 16a *et seq.*

in Ireland, by means of Article 45 of the Constitution which lays down an entire social programme.[23] The other Member States do not have such specified economic objectives. In the Community, the objectives of economic policy are laid down in Articles 2 and 104 EEC: Article 2 speaks of growth, stability and the raising of living standards; Article 104 mentions the level of employment, a stable price level and equilibrium in the balance of payments. The German Stability and Growth Law speaks of the stability of price levels, a high level of employment, a balance of external trade and growth in the framework of overall economic equilibrium.

It is not really important here how the different provisions are formulated; the declared objectives, especially those of growth, full employment, equilibrium in the balance of payments and stability, amount to concepts which even in those Member States with no specified economic objectives are currently recognised as the most important goals of economic policy. There is therefore no need to formulate further economic objectives for the Community. One may assume that, where the national legal systems specify certain economic objectives, these are not inconsistent with those of the Community, and that where this is not the case, the Member States concerned have adopted the underlying principles of Articles 2 and 104 EEC. One problem may, however, arise in this context, namely, as to whether question of social policy, which are becoming increasingly important, will be adequately covered by the formula of the highest possible level of employment, normally taken to mean full employment.

The real difficulty lies at another level. Ideally, the objectives mentioned above should be capable of simultaneous achievement, but in practice such a harmonious result is not so easy to bring about. A rigorous stabilisation policy can lead to unemployment a primary emphasis on growth, such as France has followed for many years, will bring inflationary tendencies into play; and the safeguarding of employment in the sense of full employment can also encourage inflation. Consequently, it is not the affirmation of these objectives which is decisive, but rather the question as to their order of importance, and this may also vary according to the actual economic situation. Basically, an important ingredient in the establishing of a Community economic policy consists in the laying down of an order of priority with regard to these objectives. In laying down, for example, indicative or imperative

23. In addition to the fundamental rights and the "welfare state" clause of Art. 20 G.G., specific economic aims were introduced into the Constitution (Art. 109 (2) GG) by the financial reforms of 1967-1969, and also in the *Stabilitätsgesetz* of June 8, 1967, para 1. On the situation in Ireland, see McMahon, p. 6, *op cit.*, n. 7.

rules regarding budgetary or monetary policy under Articles 104 and 105 of the Treaty, it will be necessary to have in mind a certain order of priority relating to the fundamental objectives of economic policy. It is precisely in the different setting of priorities, illustrated by the fact that the Federal Republic, the Netherlands, and recently again, France, give to stability a prominent place, whereas others, such as England or Italy, give priority to the employment situation, that the decisive differences of economic policy lie which, with their repercussions on monetary policy, have brought about the breakdown in the European monetary system and the tendency to divergent development in the Member States. At this juncture it therefore seems that the establishment of agreed priorities is a necessary ingredient of a Community policy.

It is not necessary at this point to undertake a detailed investigation of the legal situation in the Member States, since the fundamental recognition of common objectives appears to have been secured. For a common economic policy, an understanding as to the respective importance of these objectives is, however, necessary.

3.3. *Constitutional basic norms of the economic system*

Of great importance for the unifying of the foundations of economic policy are the constitutional law principles which, in some Member States, in a certain sense normatively lay down the elements of the economic system. These principles usually take the form of basic norms, or of declarations of the aims of the state. Such established norms are lacking in the United Kingdom and in the Netherlands. In France, the principle of nationalisation and that of economic freedom are mentioned, but only in general terms, in the preamble to the Constitution of 1958,[24] while in Belgium the principle of the freedom of trade can be traced back to a widely-interpreted article of a law of 1791.[25] In Denmark, economic freedom and ownership are protected, and in Ireland these basic liberties are more strongly embedded in a welfare state context by Article 45 of the Constitution.[26] Finally, the Federal Republic and Italy guarantee basic legal freedoms, among which property and economic freedom, and in these countries these normative rules are regarded as fundamental to all economic legislation.[27] In this sphere

24. See Fromont, p. 15, *op. cit.*, n. 7.
25. See Schrans, p. 1, *op cit.*, n. 7.
26. See Koktvedgaard, p. 2; McMahon, p. 6, *op. cit.*, n. 7.
27. Sacchi Morsiani, p. 11 *et seq.*; next to the right of private initiative (Art. 41) the right of property is assured (Art. 42), but nationalisation is also permitted (Art. 43); for the Federal Republic see Zacher, p. 25 *et seq.*, *op. cit.*, n. 7.

also there can hardly be any question of an assimilation of national principles, and these in any case exhibit a substantial level of agreement. Moreover, alterations in the constitution are difficult to bring about in most Member States, and it would therefore be unrealistic to reckon with them.

It would appear that the problems which arise in this area cannot be solved by the mere harmonisation of national regulations. In their principle features, the national systems show a certain degree of agreement, with differences of emphasis. The freedom to conduct a business (*liberté de commerce*) and the freedom of choice of occupation are generally accepted. The right to property, the regulation of which is expressly left within the national competence by the Treaty of Rome (Article 222) is respected, although of course the modern social, or socialist, tendency is to place a growing emphasis on restrictions in the interest of the common good. Some systems, as in France and Italy, stress this feature, as well as emphasising the power to nationalise for the general welfare. Here again the difficulty appears to lie rather in the fixing of an order of priority; where does the boundary lie between private economic freedom and state control, and what is the right proportion of private to public enterprises? It is probably more important to develop the Community's own principles in this area than to attempt an almost impossible harmonisation of national principles. This solution is also to be preferred for another reason. In those Member States which possess a rigid constitution, sanctioned by a constitutional court, the propensity has recently shown itself, especially in the decision of the German Constitutional Court of May 29, 1974, to accord the preservation of national fundamental economic rights priority over Community Law.[28] Here again, the remedy can only lie in the formation of principles within the framework of the Community, which would protect the basic economic rights of the subjects of the Member States. Fortunately, the European Court of Justice has for some years recognised this necessity, and has striven to establish such a set of basic principles.[29] Interestingly enough, the conference of Heads of State and Government in Paris in December 1974 also recognised this problem, and set up a working party to consider the question. A development in

28. This judgment (BVerfGe 37, p. 271 *et seq.)* met in the main with criticism in the Federal Republic. Here I refer *inter alia* to H. P. Ipsen, (1975) EuR, 205 *et seq.*; W. Hallstein in *Festschrift für Franz Böhm,* 1975, p. 205 *et seq.;* U. Scheuner, 100 AöR 1975, 30 *et seq.;* Pescatore, (1974) C.D.E., 499 *et seq.*

29. See: Case No. 29/69, *Stauder,* 15 Rec. 1969, 415; Case No. 11/70, *Internationale Handelsgesellschaft,* 16 Rec. 1970, 1135; case No. 4/73, *Nold,* 20 Rec. 1974, 491. See here also Pescatore, *The Law of Integration,* 1974, p. 74 *et seq.*

this direction certainly appears desirable, in order to overcome the obstacles which could otherwise result from the existence of different constitutional norms and traditions.

4. INSTRUMENTS OF THE COMMON ECONOMIC POLICY

4.1. *Means of economic direction at present*

In the formation of a common economic policy, the next factor to be considered after the basic principles is the very important role of the instruments of economic direction employed by the modern state with a mixed economic system. These also indicate the ways in which the Community could exercise its influence, be it through the exercise of its own powers or through co-ordination. The shaping of these methods therefore represents, for the economic constitution of the Community in the construction of an economic union, a crucial area of unification and co-ordination. This summary review cannot indicate all the problems bound up in the application of the individual instruments; it can only outline the existing differences in national practice. It is nevertheless clear that it is in this area that the decisive steps will be taken in the transition to a common economic policy. Let us proceed to a brief description of these instruments:

(*a*) national budgets, with the determination of public expenditure and of measures of assistance;

(*b*) taxation, the level of which can influence the extent of investment and consumption; the granting of advantages, or imposition of disadvantages can also influence certain economic decisions;

(*c*) Measures of assistance provided by the law, the budget or the overall plan, which both provide incentive to investment and influence its direction;

(*d*) money and credit policy, along with interest policy, which control the amount of and the yield for the available capital;

(*e*) public enterprises, in so far as they are used as a means of state influence;

(*f*) planning in its various forms and intensities;

(*g*) currency policy, the repercussions of which on the common Community line of policy could be particularly great;

(*h*) competition policy, which it is only possible to mention with reservations, since the very nature of competition is directed precisely at the interplay of free exchange; such a policy only exists to the extent that a state pursues active methods of ensuring competition.

The detailed application of these instruments in the different Member

States is very varied; even their relative importance as against each other is very differentiated. For example, the budget forms the central instrument in those countries where systematic planning is not developed, as in the United Kingdom, Ireland and the Federal Republic; here the budget regulates the level of public expenditure, measures of assistance and, where necessary, anti-cyclical influence on the level of economic activity. Control effects are sometimes produced in the United Kingdom through quick changes of the tax rates and of the kinds of taxation.[30] Little importance is attached to the budget in Italy, in view of the further legislative enactments which follow it.[31] In France and Italy, the pluriannual plan largely supersedes the functions of the budget. Adaptations of the tax system follow each other rapidly in the United Kingdom, but have little importance as a means of action in Italy or the Federal Republic where more significance is often attached to social considerations.[32] In the Federal Republic, the United Kingdom and the Netherlands, public enterprises are increasingly being accorded independent management, so that they are less important as a means of exercising influence. In France the circumstances are somewhat different, and in Italy the much-expanded public sector itself exercises an important influence on economic decisions.[33] The lessening or overcoming of these differences will form an important part of the tasks of an economic union.

4.2. *Budget and taxation*

According to certain statements in the Werner plan, the budgets will have an important part to play in a common policy if, through Community planning, certain control functions are withdrawn from them. On the basis of Article 103 or 105 EEC the Community can acquire influence over the national budgets by means of a determination of their anti-cyclical use, or by laying down rules governing the overall extent of the budget or deficits. A pre-condition of this is a harmonisation of the structure and composition of the budgets. The direction of the utilisation

30. See Daintith, p. 13 *et seq., op. cit.*, n. 7.
31. See Sacchi Morsiani, p. 33 *et seq.;* Koktvedgaard, p. 8; *op. cit.*, n. 7.
32. See Sacchi Morsiani, p. 39 *et seq.;* Zacher, p. 51 *et seq.; op. cit.*, n. 7.
33. *Cf.* for the Federal Republic, Zacher, p. 57; for the United Kingdom, Daintith, p. 40 *et seq.;* for the Netherlands the Zijlstra report, *Economic Policy and Problems of Competition in the EEC and its Member States*, Brussels 1966, Study Series Competition. No. 2; for Denmark, Koktvedgaard, p. 12; the reverse is true in France, see Fromont p. 34 *et seq., op. cit.*, n. 7.

of revenue and capital by the national public authorities will be of paramount importance for a common economic policy.

On the other hand, it will be very much more difficult to exercise influence over taxation policy. Influence will be limited to turnover and consumption taxes, since a common policy may not interfere with the social aspects of income taxation. But it is exactly in this area that considerable points of difference are manifest. The viewpoints of the Member States with regard to the relationship of direct to indirect taxation are just as differentiated as with regard to the level of value-added tax. But in the first stages of development it will have to suffice to bring under control the effects on the overall equilibrium resulting from taxation.

4.3. *Measures of assistance*

An approximation of the different systems of assistance, which range from appropriations through legislation or the budget, to the building into plans or (as in the Federal Republic) specific arrangements, will be effected essentially in the course of medium-term planning and stabilisation policy. Those areas will be included in the approximation which do not involve special sectoral problems. In the course of harmonisation, strict observance of Article 92 EEC will be important, just as with taxation. Apart from the Community's own aid policy as seen in its Regional Fund, a proliferation of Community funds does not appear desirable.

4.4. *Money, credit and exchange rate policy*

One of the primary instruments of economic control is the money and credit policy.[34] Progress in the area of co-ordination is therefore of fundamental importance here. Without a co-ordination of the amount of lending and of the rates of interest, neither a medium-term nor a short-term policy is feasible. It is important, however, to stress that the goal here cannot be one of complete uniformity, since the cyclical developments of the economies of the different Member States are not uniform,[35] and it is, indeed, even desirable that this should be the case. The relevant factors here must, however, be made to conform to an

34. See VerLoren van Themaat, Interim report, p. 47a.

35. For example, at the end of 1974, the business cycle was receding in the Federal Republic whereas in France and Italy no setbacks were yet evident. *Cf.* here the Economic Report of the Commission of Sept. 20, 1974, Bull. of the E.C., 1974 No. 9, 37.

overall guideline, although it is difficult to see how this could be effected without a mandatory establishment of what these factors are.

On the other hand, one of the basic requirements of an EMU is that the use of the currency, of exchange rate manipulations, as an instrument of national economic policy must be excluded. Without an uncompromising adherence to this principle, every thought of a monetary union is unrealistic.

The differing legal status of the central banks, among which the German Federal Bank enjoys considerable influence, whereas in most Member States the state influence is paramount, will not require approximation so long as the harmony between them—and this has long been the case—can be assured through co-ordination.[36]

4.5. *Public enterprises*

The fact, as stated above, that state influence on public enterprises takes many different forms, would seem to indicate that they should not be regarded as a significant element in the direction of economic activity. Here the fact should also be taken into account that the overall extent of the public sector differs substantially from one Member State to another, and the approximation of laws in this area, in particular where it would produce effects in the sphere of central institutions or the legal formation of enterprises, would affect very sensitive areas of the economic system of the individual Member State. It can, of course, follow that in the context of a plan, stronger obligations might be imposed on public enterprises. But is would certainly not be acceptable to all Member States if the extension of the public sector were seen as a means of furthering planning and control, and if this were accordingly favoured. For if one considers Article 85 and the following articles, as well as Article 90, it is clear that the existence of a strong public sector does create the danger of a reduction of competition, which often thereby gives rise to monopolistic positions, thus whittling down the market.[37]

4.6. *Planning*

The formation of a plan for the Community, together with the harmonisation of the forms of planning in the Member States will be a central feature of further development. It is impossible to deal with this wide

36. On the position of the Federal Bank, see Zacher p. 54 *et seq.*, *op. cit.*, n. 7.; further on the question of approximation, Interim Report, p. 29a *et seq.*

37. The Zijlstra report, *op. cit.*, n. 33, also refers to these drawbacks.

field thoroughly here; only certain indications are possible. In particular, there can be no question here of comment on the different types of planning,[38] nor of an evaluation of the existing Member State systems. In any case, a full approximation of the internal planning methods of the Member States is not necessary so long as they may resort to other adequate means of control in order to conform to the binding rules laid down by the Community. It will, however, be necessary to develop forms of medium-term planning in all Member States which will lay the foundations for Community programming.[39] This means that the Community too must make use of the plan as an instrument of common economic policy, and this applies as much to medium-term planning as to short-term policy. In this connection, it is to be recommended that the Community furnish itself with adequate bases for its own forecasts by means of a greater resort to independent expert consultation.[40] In the past, medium-term forecasts have not always turned out to be correct—I am thinking here of those with regard to the energy situation, or the rate of inflation —and several Member States regard these forecasts with a growing scepticism.

The literature concerning Community planning is frequently inspired by the example of French planning. Here I should like to express some reservations. The individual state can develop a plan as detailed as this, but not the Community, which must also respect the autonomy of the Member States with regard to industrial, regional and social policy. We should think rather in terms of measures of co-ordination. These may merely lay down general guidelines, since certain results may already be achieved in this way, but with regard to the budget (the fixing of the total volume, deficits, *etc.*) it would be difficult to refrain from mandatory regulation. A far-reaching co-ordination of national planning methods would be very difficult to achieve. On the other hand, it is possible to envisage a certain harmonisation of the instruments for exercising influence on the economy, such as subsidies or competition policy. It should be noted that, in terms of medium-term policy, a harmonised and agreed short-term policy will not in any way be necessary, so long as the different national policies are fundamentally in tune with one another. Short-term measures should, however, be adapted to the objectives of medium-term programming.[41]

Without being able to go further into the institutional problems, I

38. *Cf.* here Zijlstra report, *op. cit.*, n. 33, at pp. 33-34.
39. Thus, Interim Report, p. 33.
40. *Id.* at 31a *et seq.*
41. *Id.* at 35a *et seq.*

agree with the report of Professor VerLoren van Themaat that in the formation of this policy, a close co-operation with social interest groups will be necessary.[42]

The common policies of the Community also belong in the area of planning since they will be shaped according to the uniform plan. This does not apply to agriculture. Transport policy, it seems to me, has been thus far pursued in accordance with an inadequate statement of aims. In view of the strength of the public sector in this area, and its problems on the national level, it is not conceivable that all areas of transport will be capable of regulation in terms of free competition. In fact the only result so far achieved in these terms is with regard to long-distance freight traffic.[43] With regard to energy and environment policy, a legal basis must first be provided in the Treaty, so far as these policies may not be realised by means of harmonisation.

4.7. *Wages and prices*

These constitute a particularly problematical area. To look first at wages: the constitutional law of all Member States leaves the fixing of wages to the free collective bargaining of employers and employees. In the Netherlands, where for a long time the state could exercise a certain influence on wages, this influence has recently wholly receded.[44] The question which arises here is not limited to the free fixing of wage levels, but goes very much deeper. The question is, namely, whether an incomes policy could be successfully brought into an economic plan, and I would regard this question as decisive, and not only for the future of economic and monetary policy. For there arise here also problems of a constitutional law nature which are typical of modern democracies, and which limit the freedom of action of the legislator. Practice both in the past and present proceeds from the assumption that a certain level of income, once attained, cannot then be reduced, unless it be by a high level of inflation, which will thus not necessarily be regarded as running counter to the interest of trade unions. The collaboration of the two sides of industry in an advisory and informative capacity in the planning of the economy (*konziertierte Aktion*) has shown itself to be of little usefulness in the Federal Republic.[45] Only partial success, at the most, can be attributed to the British "Social Contract", and the same is true for the

42. *Id.* at 36.
43. *Cf.* my statement in *Festschrift für Jahrreis*, 1974, p. 209 *et seq.*
44. See VerLoren van Themaat, p. 30 *et seq.*; in contrast to Zijlstra report, *op. cit.*, n. 33, at p. 60 *et seq.*
45. See Zacher, p. 109, *op. cit.*, n. 7.

British experiment of an incomes policy.[46] One can wonder if it is possible to bring about, by means of mere consultation, an adjustment of incomes and prices movements to the circumstances and needs of general economic development. In reply to the suggestion that the public sector is particularly suited for this purpose, the German experience constitutes a warning.[47] The problem of the development of an incomes policy has hardly been approached yet, even at the national level.[48]

The same is true for a prices policy. In several Member States, such as the Netherlands, and especially, the United Kingdom, both formerly and currently attempts at price control, and even price fixing, have been made.[49] Without the complement of an incomes policy such efforts remain, in the long term, ineffective. In any case, a far-reaching price regulation would lastingly prejudice the functioning of the market. Price-fixing, in the form in which it exists at present, is of lesser significance. A more far-reaching control of prices would not only have to develop side by side with an incomes policy, but would also, with a view to the protection of the market, have to be subject to scrupulous limitation. Here too, forms of collaboration with interested parties exist as an alternative to mandatory regulation.[50]

4.9. *Reserved areas*

To conclude this section, mention should be made of the fact that there exist areas for which, owing to their nature, the institution of a Community policy is barely conceivable. I include here:

(*a*) The exploitation of natural resources. The demand for regulation on a national basis is necessarily here so strong, and the undertakings required so determined by local factors, that there is little prospect of instituting common rules.

(*b*) House-building. Here also the outcome is so strongly determined by local factors that there can be no question of free competition.

(*c*) Town and country planning. Here the policy of the Community must be limited to the prevention of discriminatory effects.

46. See Daintith, p. 116, *op. cit.*, n. 7.
47. See Zacher, p. 109, *op. cit.*, n. 7.
48. *Cf.* Zijlstra report, *op. cit.*, n. 33, at p. 60 *et seq.*; Interim Report, p. 36 *et seq.* The particular importance of the fixing of price levels is referred to in Triffing, *Integration durch Währungsunion?*, Institut für Weltwirtschaft (Kiel, Symposium, 1971), p. 25.
49. See VerLoren van Themaat, *op. cit.*, n. 7, at p. 30 *et seq.*; and Daintith, p. 116 *et seq.*
50. See Zijlstra report, *op. cit.*, n. 33, at p. 61 *et seq.*

5. ECONOMIC LEGISLATION AND APPROXIMATION OF LAWS

5.1. *Harmonisation of economic legislation*

For the perfection of the common market, there is still a significant area of the economic legislation of the Member States remaining to be unified, namely that concerning occupational qualifications, admission to certain professions, and the freedom of establishment. It is not possible, however, to go into details here.

5.2. *Multinational enterprises*

New problems can arise from the efforts to control the multinational enterprises, since these can produce effects on the free movement of capital and goods, not to mention the possibility of discriminatory prescriptions. In any case, this is an area which can only be effectively regulated on a common basis, and which, also because of its repercussions on external trade, should be subject to Community jurisdiction.

5.3. *The outlook*

Finally, I would like to summarise some conclusions.

1. The picture of the ideal, definitive economic and monetary union can, at the present stage of development, not yet be drawn. It can, however, be expected that its establishment will require a longer period than was seen to be necessary in the decisions of the years 1971-1972. Priority should therefore be given to the laying-down of basic guidelines for the development of the Community in the direction of a common economic policy, without which a monetary union is also not capable of lasting realisation.
2. In the course of construction of a common economic policy, the Community will have to exercise certain autonomous powers, especially in the area of money, credit and exchange rate policy. For action in the areas of medium and short-term economic policy, the Treaty provides a legal foundation, but for the assumption of full responsibility for monetary policy, supplementary provisions would be necessary. The detailed realisation of unifying measures will be effected to a large extent by means of co-ordination, which leaves a large degree of autonomy to the national economic policy.
3. The construction of an economic union assumes the existence of a common basic economic system in all Member States. This basic system

may be described in terms of the mixed economy, founded upon the idea of a free market, controlled by regulatory measures, and in which the state intervention and planning looks after the further development of integration. The state or supranational authority must, however, be aware of definite limits, deriving from the principle of the open market, to the degree of intervention and the extent of the public sector. Without respect for these limits, further development in the direction of economic union is not possible.

4. The common objectives of the economic system—stability, growth, securing of the level of employment and balance of payments equilibrium, should be recognised by the Member States. These objectives need consistent application, and this could be assured through the setting of agreed priorities by the Community. At the same time, differences in cyclical fluctuations between the Member States would create no problem, so long as there was agreement on certain basic principles.

5. Instead of a unification of the basic constitutional rules relating to the economy in the Member States, which would be difficult to achieve, the Community should build up its own legal principles, in particular those relating to fundamental rights, and these should become part of Community Law. This will also surmount the danger of a conflict between national concepts and the Community legal order.

6. A harmonisation of the instruments of economic policy appears necessary insofar as they are exercised by the Member States. As far as the preservation of the autonomy of the Member States is concerned, the means for medium-term planning, and the instruments for influencing the economy will be at their disposal. Upon this foundation, the Community medium-term policy will be built up, and with it the means of short-term regulation.

This harmonisation will have to cover, in the first place, the composition of the budgets, and also the instruments of monetary and credit policy. The systems of assistance, too, and that of indirect taxation, will require progressive approximation, in particular in order to ensure that national barriers may not be created here which might affect the operation of the market.

At all events, the development towards a monetary union must lead to the abandonment of monetary policy as an instrument for the setting of national economic and budgetary objectives. Monetary policy cannot remain an instrument of national economic policy.

7. The common economic policy will have to be supplemented by means of sectoral Community policies, such as agriculture, transport and, in future, energy. The protection of the environment, also requires a common orientation.

8. Regional policy. Apart from the existence of certain Community organs, such as the Regional Fund, this will remain a matter for the Member States within the framework of a common economic policy, as will also town and country planning and other branches of the economy which are strongly conditioned by local factors, such as house-building and the exploitation of natural resources.

9. A common economic policy will also have to pay special attention to a simultaneous further development of social factors in the Community. Co-operation with social groups and forces will be necessary.

An effective, common economic policy will also, in the long term, require an orientation of wages and prices policies, obtained through agreement with the parties. However, even at national level, only preliminary moves in this direction have been made.

REPORT

by

W. Van Gerven*

The aim of this colloquium is to promote an exchange of ideas concerning the reports, and in particular the Interim Report which, at the request of the Commission, have been edited under the direction of Professor VerLoren van Themaat, on the economic law of the Member States in an economic and monetary union.[1] In order to stimulate the discussion it is unfortunately necessary to direct our attention above all to those aspects of the Interim Report which seem to be the most open to criticism. Because of this there is a risk that the positive aspects of the Report may be overlooked. Before proceeding we should, therefore, express our appreciation to the reporters for the considerable work which they have undertaken in a branch of comparative law, namely, comparative economic law, which up to the present has not attracted all the attention which it would seem to deserve.

My report will confine itself to the subject of the second theme, that is, to determine the optimal economic constitution of the European Community. It seems to me that it is exactly on this point that the Interim Report could be improved. The observations which I would like to make on this subject can be summarised as follows. As is stated at page 7 of the Interim Report, this report is intended as the legal complement of the economic report which, in 1966, was drawn up by Professor Zijlstra on the economic policy of the Community and its Member States.[2] In other words, it is intended that the legal report should give an indication of the means to a legal implementation of the optimal economic order which Professor Zijlstra described in his earlier report. It seems to me that this approach is not without risk and cannot, therefore, be approved without reservations. In fact, the optimum legal system is not necessarily subject to the same imperatives as the optimum economic system. In fact, it seems to me that both the optimal economic system and the optimal

* Professor in the Faculty of Law, University of Louvain.

1. P. Verloren van Themaat, *The Economic Law of the Member States of the European Communities in an Economic and Monetary Union,* Commission of the European Communities, Studies: Competition—Approximation of Legislation, Series No. 20 (Brussels, 1973).

2. J. Zijlstra en B. Goudzwaard, *Economic Policy and Problems of Competition in the EEC and the Member States,* EEC Studies Competition, Series No. 2 (Brussels, 1966).

13 C.M.L.Rev. 1976, 215-221

legal system should reflect a certain conception of man and society. It is with regard to this fundamental conception that we should first seek agreement, at least with respect to its main outlines. Consequently, if you wish to prevent the law from being placed unconsciously at the service of an economic system of which the political and ethical foundations have not necessarily been sufficiently well examined, the legal report is no more than the legal complement of the economic report. But it should also constitute the legal complement of a general conception of man and the society of which it forms a part. It is to the necessity of elaborating such a general conception of man and society that I wish to dedicate the various observations below.

In his report,[3] Professor Zijlstra postulates in principle that the optimal economic system of the Community must be a mixed economy system, of which the accepted basis is a market economy, and in which the role played by the state is essentially complementary. He adds, however, that such a preference finds its origin in considerations which are not economic in nature: the choice, he considers, between an economy managed by a central authority and a free market economy, is essentially of a meta-economic order. Professor VerLoren van Themaat in the general legal report agrees with this approach, but not without supplementing it as regards the instruments and the objectives of economic policy to be pursued. This point is important because it demonstrates that the legal report, despite what it says, attempts to be more than the complement pure and simple of the economic report. Professor VerLoren van Themaat estimates, in fact, that the evolution which has taken place since the drawing-up of Professor Zijlstra's report appears to indicate that the co-ordination and the programming of economic policy should be further developed than is recommended in the economic report. In fact, he says, the attempt to simultaneously increase freely disposable private incomes, private investment and public expenditure has brought about considerable inflation, while the hope of seeing overall growth automatically outstrip public expenditure has not been realised. A greater degree of co-ordination is thus necessary, co-ordination which should take into account and quantify not only the classic objectives of economic policy on questions of growth, employment, evolution of prices and the balance of payments, but also the general social objectives to which priority is accorded in all the Member States, such as the improvement of social amenities (to the detriment of the growth of private consumption), the protection of the environment, a greater equality in matters of education and training, a more equitable

3. Op. cit., n. 2.

distribution of incomes and capital, the extension of social security, a balanced regional policy, and aid to developing countries.[4]

It is evident that the definition of these objectives and, above all, the quantification of the resources to be assigned to each of these objectives, require decisions which are not of an economic or legal nature, but which, on the contrary, are political decisions taken in furtherance of a particular existing conception of man and society. However, it seems to me indispensable that in a report relating to the legal bases of the Community system the different options which may exist on this subject should be formulated in clear and precise terms, so that the taking of political decisions may be facilitated. Certainly, it is not the task of jurists to take the decisions on this subject—they should be taken by a European parliament worthy of the name, or, in the absence of such a parliament, by the national parliaments—but it is the business of the jurist to prepare the way for political discussion, with an analysis of the different possibilities, and of the ways in which these possibilities are realised in the legal system of one or other of the Member States.

Let us try, therefore, to sketch the fundamental ideas of a common conception of man and society so far as these ideas are capable of being transformed into legal rules of a kind which may figure in the economic constitution of the Community.

If an analysis of the national laws does not permit the formulation at this stage of a common system of precise legal rules, it does permit us all the same, to catch a glimpse of certain guidelines which are present in the law of all the Member States, even though their degree of realisation may differ from one State to another. To this end we must take the idea of economic law in a broader sense than that used in the Interim Report,[5] namely, in the sense of a law comprising all the legal rules concerning the structure and the internal functioning of enterprises, the relations between enterprises, and between them and the state authorities, and even with regard to their relations with consumers. We can group the common fundamental principles which emerge from an analysis of the economic law of the Member States around the three basic ideas of liberty, equality and fraternity. In other words, it seems to me that these notions continue to reflect this day to the fundamental value judgments on which rests the conception which we in the Western democracies have of man and society.

First let us consider the idea of *liberty*. It is certainly not difficult to indicate the ways in which the law embodies this primordial social value,

4. See Interim Report, pp. 26—29.
5. See Interim Report, p. 9a.

as much in private relationships as in the relationships of enterprises with public authorities. In the context of private relationships one may point to subjective rights such as the right to property, freedom of contract, the freedom of trade and of publicity, which incorporate individual freedom on the legal plane. In relationships with public authorities, this same liberty is protected, above all in matters which concern acts of the executive power, by the rule according to which the subjective rights may be regulated but not suppressed. It is a matter for the civil tribunals, and occasionally of the administrative courts, to see to it that these liberties are respected.

Up to the beginning of this century, however, the idea of liberty was understood as being strictly individual, so that it was forbidden to the economically weak to associate together in order to increase their influence on the market for goods or employment. It was because it was considered as being contrary to individual liberty, itself strictly part of the *"ordre public"* that the liberty of association or combination was so severely restricted. It was only through the influence of the trade unions that one came to realize the fact that the liberty of some could unreasonably limit the liberty of others. The notion of *equality,* according to which each person has the right to a certain measure of liberty, thus began to become an object of legal protection, and that also in the context of private relationships.

With regard to the public authorities, the principle of equality is expressed in the obligation not to discriminate between comparably-situated businessmen or enterprises when it is a matter of distributing advantages (state aids, fiscal exemptions) or of imposing public burdens (maximum prices, production or import quotas). So far as private relationships are concerned, the legal order of each of the Member States contains innumerable provisions which were promulgated after the economic crisis of the 'Thirties and during the post-war period, and which are intended to protect competition, consumers and savers. The desire to protect the economically weak is expressed also in civil or commercial case-law which, in support of general ideas such as public policy, good faith, abuse of right, or abuse of economic power, has invalidated certain commercial practices, particularly those practised by firms in a dominant position, such as boycotts or certain clauses of non-competition or exclusivity, which were by nature a restriction on the liberty of competitors to carry on business or the liberty of consumers to supply themselves as they wished.

In the third place, there is the concept of *fraternity,* or of solidarity between the different groups of the population. According to this notion, which to some extent amounts to the continuation and realisation of the idea of equality on the collective plane, certain groups should be prohibited from acquiring disproportionate advantages at the expense of others, above all at the expense of the least privileged groups. In the area of the economic law (and social law), this notion indicates the necessity of concerted action and of co-ordination; co-ordination in the main on the part of the public authorities which, as is underlined in the Interim Report,[6] have the task of programming and quantifying the different economic and other objectives of economic policy, and in particular those which have been enumerated above (improvement of collective amenities, protection of the environment, equality in education, extension of social security, regional policy and aid to developing countries). These objectives reflect a solidarity between the different groups of the population within and also outside the Community. Concerted action between the public authorities and the individual enterprises (public or private) is also necessary, in order to associate the latter with the realisation of the objectives pursued. In this area, furthermore, it is the duty of the public authorities to institute organs and planning procedures in order to promote negotiations between representatives of the two sides of industry and also with consumers.

It may be apparent from this brief survey that the Interim Report should have been able to detach from this common fund of legal principles some fundamental rules which could serve as a basis for an economic constitution for the Community. Let us recall these principles: individual liberty of enterprises in economic matters, as much in their relations with each other as with the public authorities; equality of enterprises with regard to public benefits and burdens; protection of the freedom of competition, especially with regard to small- and medium-sized enterprises; protection of the freedom of the consumers to consume and, more importantly, not to consume; the necessity for the public authorities to promote solidarity between the groups of the population for the benefit of the least privileged groups, and to programme and quantify the objectives of a social and economic policy which aim to implement such solidarity; and the necessity to set on foot negotiating organs and procedures in order to associate individual enterprises with the realisation of these objectives.

It seems to me that a formulation of these principles would be extremely useful, so that they might form the object of discussion between jurists of the Member States. It seems to me also that, sooner or later, these principles (or others) should be formally declared to constitute an economic constitution for the Community; thus they may

6. See Interim Report, p. 25a *et seq.*

guide the Court of Justice in its role of ensuring respect for the general principles of law, and may also help to establish the primacy of the Community legal system, even in the field of constitutional rules.

So long as one remains on the level of principles it is not difficult to achieve a certain *consensus ad idem.* Matters become more difficult when it is a question of defining the degree of freedom, of equality, and, above all, of solidarity, and thus the degree of co-ordination, of programming and concerted action, which one wishes to realise in a society and in the legal and economic system applicable to it. This is all the more true because agreement upon a certain degree of freedom, equality, programming and concertation, will have a profound influence on the solution of other very important questions such as, to mention the most obvious, the degree of autonomy which is to be permitted to enterprises of production and distribution. It will also profoundly influence the effectiveness of the regulation of cartels and dominant positions, not to mention the extent of the more or less discretionary powers which are accorded to the executive in the definition of the economic policy, and also the extent of legal protection for enterprises and for individuals with respect to interventions by public authorities.

The importance of the divergencies regarding these different questions can be illustrated in the light of that part of the Interim Report which is dedicated to the "principal characteristics of the national systems of economic law".[7] It appears from the outline which is given there that the German system differs profoundly from the French system, or at least did so at the time when the Interim Report was drawn up. In German law the emphasis is put upon the functioning of a market economy. Programming remains global, and does not seek a uniform regulation of the numerous interventions of the authorities in particular affairs, or of the different individual decisions taken by enterprises. On the other hand, the importance attached to fundamental rights such as human dignity, freedom and equality, and to the idea of the Rule of Law is very great in Germany, as is also the degree of judicial protection. The German system has thus obviously opted for an economic system directed by the individual enterprises, and it is also on the level of the enterprises that negotiation and agreement with the workers is organised. Competition between the enterprises in Germany is maintained at a very high level, owing to a very active policy on cartels. The French system, in contrast, is characterised by a far-reaching prior planning of economic growth, which even allows for detailed interventions. The cartel laws, as well as the short-term economic policy, are employed in France as instruments

7. See Interim Report, Ch. II, p. 15 *et seq.*

for the realisation of the objectives of the Plan. To achieve these objectives, the government has been granted extensive powers, whereas the role played by parliament in this area has been very limited. The notions of fundamental rights and of the Rule of Law, as well as of judicial protection in economic matters, are much less developed than in Germany, and participation of the two sides of industry in the preparation and execution of economic policy is organised rather at the national or regional level.

Because of these differences, it does not seem to be possible to propose at the present moment common principles concerning the concrete organisation of economic life. However, given that the Interim Report contains sufficient material relating to the different options adopted in each national system on the subject of the fundamental questions which have just been mentioned, it ought, in my opinion, to have better formulated these questions, for example at the end of the second chapter, and should also to have indicated the different solutions which are possible, as they appear from the description of the national systems. The Interim Report would thus have better prepared and facilitated the discussion of these questions and fundamental choices. These may be of a political nature, but a solution of them will nonetheless be necessary if it is wished, sooner or later, to formulate sufficiently concrete constitutional rules.

REPORT

by

J. D. B. Mitchell*

There is an initial absurdity in inviting anyone from the United Kingdom to speak on this subject. Let me define that frivolously. It is said that Scotland has no climate, only weather, or in the alternative that while all the world has four seasons, Scotland is peculiar in having them all within twenty-four hours. Frivolity should not be taken as such, because at greater length Professor Daintith has demonstrated the same thing in his Report, if you substitute the words "economic constitution" for climate and the word "politics" for weather. That circumstance may matter in any discussion of the United Kingdom attitudes, in general, to this problem.

I will also confess to great difficulty in writing this intervention. There have been many drafts, and at the end unease remained. One problem was a reconciliation of the theme announced "the general legal principles (economic constitution) of an Economic and Monetary Union between Member States with different economic systems", and the definitions, as I understood them in the Interim Report in particular at page nine (in the passage headed "Summary").[1] The first is larger and more fundamental than the second.

I have finally chosen to treat at this stage the first definition rather than the second. It was not ambition which led to that choice, nor was it in any way disrespect for the various national reports and for the *rapport de synthèse*. For these I have great respect, and above all for the latter. That remark is not simply one of courting in this house, but the distillation of the essentials of the other reports into a general one was a remarkable work, which indeed added to my difficulties. In drawing conclusions it said so many things with which I agreed, that one might have been tempted to have stopped at that.

One could not thus stop for a number of reasons. The first and obvious one is the importance of the subject. There is a sort of sound barrier which must be penetrated. I no longer believe that there is a straight and necessary continuum from a customs union, even with the addition of the

* C.B.E., Salvesen Professor of European Institutions, University of Edinburgh.

1. *The Economic Law of the Member States of the European Communities in an Economic and Monetary Union*, Study Series Competition—Approximation of Legislation, No. 20 (Brussels, 1973).

13 C.M.L.Rev. 223-230

four freedoms, to an economic union. I must distinguish the word *necessary*. Manifestly, if the former is to endure, in fact, the second must occur, but on the other hand the second does not follow "of necessity", even if it follows logically, from the first. It does not follow in the peculiar logic of politics. The reason for that is that political considerations which in time or practice affect one or the other stage of organisation differ. Political considerations, by which I mean the organisation of polity, assume far greater importance for the second than they do for the first, that being much more technical. That question is accentuated in importance by considerations of time.

This argument leads to the second reason which moved against a simple agreement. In a sense the reports seem to me to be dominated by the atmosphere of the Werner report. There can be no criticism of that on the intellectual plane. But it is not only events, but it also thought which has changed that atmosphere since that report was written. On the one side let me cite from a recent report from the Institut für Weltwirtschaft on *The Economic Policy for the European Community*. "If monetary union were pushed through prematurely, without being re-inforced by complementary policies and without complementary powers and common institutions to give effect to these policies, the result might well be needless unemployment and waste of resources and the breakdown of the Union."[2] Perhaps that sentence gives the reasons which accounted for the somewhat unenthusiastic account which the Commission was forced to give of the results of the first stage of monetary union.

Facts also have turned against us, but not absolutely. In one sense facts were against M. Schuman, but not entirely, since there was still time to make certain necessities perceived. Conditions now are similar in some respects but are more complicated. The perception of economic reality is perhaps not as widespread, as was the perception of other threats of which he could, and did, speak. Even if it should be as widespread it must also be said that the perception is deeply marked by political folklore or mythology. It is unfortunately true that in the matters fundamental to this debate there is a diversification of Europe which is in a sense deeper than the older nationalism. We are talking of the legal foundations of an economic constitution for Europe at a time when one Member State can control inflation at five per cent and hopes to reduce it to two per cent or less, another is manifestly in difficulty in attempting to control it at

2. Cairncross *et al.* (London *etc.*, 1974), at p. 59. It is then clear that it is unreasonable to blame British attitudes or circumstances too much for the changes in the timing of proposals for arriving at a monetary union. Just as important are changes in ways of thinking.

twenty per cent. That is not the only point of difference, one could go further. There are those who regard growth as a primary aim, and some, welfare. These differences have not diminished since the Treaty of Rome, they have perhaps grown. In themselves they are deeply rooted in history, even if it be modern. Inter-war crises left one Member State, overall (as far as an outsider can judge) with a total fear of inflation. This may be sane, but in a sense it is what I call the folklore of politics. In another, a similar crisis resulted in a comparable total fear of unemployment. I do not defend either of these extreme views as such. I merely say that these things are part of the factual background against which the constitution must be constructed and the principles of law must find their grip. If I sound depressing, let me merely say that I have never thought that if life is difficult it is therefore impossible.

These elements had already been underlined even at the stage of the Commissions' *Third Programme of Medium Term Economic policy.*[3] But they both find their reflection in and also an intensification through the political structures of the Member States. Perhaps in relation to one particular Member State the precise constitutional base is not of primordial importance. What does matter are factors of a derivative order, the place of parliaments in this process and their relationship to the whole governmental process and the relationships of the different parts of the governmental machine to each other, and folklore enters once again with regard to these matters. At one extreme there is perhaps my own state, where everything is centred on Westminster, the political forum. In contrast there stands out in the report (p. 31) the place that can be given in Germany or the Netherlands to relatively neutral bodies. Such differences do not exist only on the surface, or as matters of technique. When the report speaks (p. 73) of the principle that "la banque centrale devait toujours disposer d'un minimum des pouvoirs propres", this is not a simple thing. Almost in living memory (I had only to have been born two years earlier) the Treasury could be said to be the West End Branch of the Bank of England. Now the Bank is the City Office of the Treasury. Even a partial reversal of that position is a major undertaking and would cause reaction. Any Governor of the Bank when (which happens rarely) speaking his mind in public, tends to evoke storms in political quarters.

This of course relates to the entrenched forms of activity. Here I draw particular attention to the case *Crédit Foncier*[4] referred to by Professor Fromont. There M. Bernard in a passage in his *conclusions* which begins *"Mais comme une réglementation de cette sorte . . ."* goes on to indicate

3. J.O. 1971, L 49 *et seq.*, para. 41.
4. C.E. December 11, 1970, R 750, at 753.

that in this economic field governments must have instruments of a suppleness which might not be tolerated in other fields, but nevertheless the Courts in accepting this must play, and adapt, their traditional role with a similar suppleness. Properly regarded this is not a denial, I believe, of *sécurité juridique* but again it challenges accepted ideas in many Member States. It is convenient, but not necessary, to choose my own where a former Lord Chancellor has in effect recently said that even a constitutional court must be rejected because this would lead to political judges. My own comments on that I pass over *sous silence*, but it is a typical attitude.

I have started at this point to emphasize that in a quite different way we come up against political structures and unconscious political attitudes. One could cite Mr. Macmillan criticizing Monnet and Schuman for what he called their absurd "constitution-making" or alternatively one could emphasize that, (as someone has recently pointed out) one reason for the failure of Keynesian economics with us was the refusal to institutionalize it and create the constitution in which a genuine debate could occur. It was thought that old ways would suffice. For this reason it seems to me that one must say clearly that the technical adjustments of legal techniques, while important as a basis cannot themselves create a constitution, which cannot in essence be simply a cumulation of rules. Nor is it likely that the straight transfer of rules from a national to a Community level will suffice, any more than it is likely that we will build a Community regional policy out of the summation of national ones or of their methods. The levels of activity import differences. Clearly the Community budget does not play the economic role which a national budget must, nor, granted the history of the debate on industrial policy, is it likely that effective methods at the national level, such as the *contrats de programmation* will be admitted or have the same result at Community level.

Indeed, I believe that even at this stage it is necessary to put the rules in a setting, as they are in a nation state. Raymon Aron has said [5] that the term constitution "a manifestement une compréhension plus riche que dans son emploi strictement juridique". To define too closely is to impose a burden of intellectual evasion upon our successors, and perhaps if one looks at the reports and especially that of Professor Zacher [6] one cannot go further than to say that we are concerned with a mixed economy within the liberal political tradition of Western Europe. In fact even the

5. Commenting on Hayek's *The Constitution of Liberty* in *Archives européennes de sociologie* (1961) II 2.

6. At p. 46; see for reference p. 193 of this vol., n. 7.

use of the term "mixed economy" does impose limits, though variable ones which will need definition by the Court, just as perhaps the German Constitutional Court will need to decide, at some time in the future, when co-operative federalism has stopped being federalism. If there is generality in that there must also be generality in the determination of Community-State relations. These depend on economic evolution, as the constitutional history of, for example, Germany, Australia or the U.S.A. demonstrates. There must be room for responsive shifts, and I am doubtful how far the traditional technique of a timetable will work even in this particular setting.

I believe equally strongly that the economic constitution cannot at this time be regarded as separate from other elements of evolution. That was the point of the first quotation. It is one of the basic points of the Marjolin report.[7] Perhaps indeed these concepts of such a constitution must be swallowed in the idea of European Union in the Tindemans proposals when they emerge. Unless there is a base of acceptance, the *couche assez large* of which M. Mosca spoke,[8] the economic constitution will not survive, and this generalization will help to create that base better than a narrower approach would.

To secure that base of acceptance will require more than one level of activity. Much of the essential debate (whether it is about economic law in a narrow sense, or in a broader sense in which budgetary or conjunctural policy enters into the debate) will occur within the Member States. After all it is there, so long as the Community budget remains one with limited economic consequences, that the budgets with more specific economic impact will have to be adopted, and that adoption will require comprehension of the general picture. It is there too that rules, relating *eg.* to industrial policy, will have to be applied and the acceptance of those rules will have to be gained. It is for that reason that the common purpose will have to be explained. It follows that while I accept what is said in the report of an enlarged role for the European Parliament, and of the social partners on the European level, I regret that I must also say that, perhaps, too much must not be hoped from the European Parliament alone. It is isolated from the political arenas in which conjunctural policy will have to be fought over, and fought over in a quite different way from the way in which law can work in the more specific fields. That law would not work as well were the European Court isolated. I regret also having to say, that similarly, for the reasons which

7. *Union Economique et Monétaire 1980,* UEM-63, D.G. for Economic and Financial Affairs (Brussels, 1975).

8. See above, p. 193 of this volume, n. 7.

I have indicated, and with both respect and sympathy for Mr. Patijn, that in this field direct elections will not alone suffice to change the whole pattern.

At the end of the day what may matter is to examine the internal rules of the Member States which relate to their own economic constitutions, not simply as such but as means of institutionalizing the essential debate so that there are genuine debates. It is in this respect that one Member State which I could most easily name has been singularly deficient. It is in this way that one can look at the law. It is easy to say that, with regard to economic law in a narrow sense, law is the primary instrument, and then to fall back in conjunctural policy upon harmonisation or co-ordination. The division is too sharp. The law has two characteristics. As well as being an instrument for organizing debate, it is an instrument for imposing discipline. It is true that the law as such cannot play the same part in conjunctural policy, but even at this stage the simple acceptance of co-ordination seems to me to be too weak, and that for two reasons. First, that we are not clear what we are co-ordinating. There are not merely the difficulties of finding comparable statistics and of agreeing upon definitions of unemployment, but, if all those are left aside, there remain other substantial problems. A recent British report looked at the forecasts of public expenditure from 1970.[9] The figures left out of account, among other things, fluctuations in investment grants, regional development grants and aids to shipbuilding which are not insignificant, but the fluctuations are enormous. They are however, as the Committee noted, changes in a *forecast* level of expenditure which actually did not happen. It had earlier remarked "to announce sudden cuts which do not occur is misleading to the public and to all those who are endeavouring to plan investment projects or other expenditure".[10] Hence that Committee drew the inference, which is relevant here, that in planning the management of the economy changes in public expenditure should only be an instrument of last resort. That is not the primary point which I wish to make. That primary one is the very simple point that co-ordination or harmonization is pointless, unless it is, as near as can be, co-ordination of reality and not of fiction. With that reserve one can accept co-ordination provided that it is not left as such, but is ultimately supported by some discipline. The only sort of discipline which can parallel the law in a sense is an extension of Community support facilities, related to this co-ordination. It is through the terms of support that the discipline can be brought to bear, and that in a traditional way.

9. *Third Report from the Expenditure Committee*, 1974-5, H.C., 278.
10. *Ninth Report from the Expenditure Committee*, 1974 H.C., 328.

On the other hand, I would suggest that, apart from elements which clearly affect the free movement of goods, we do need to know, or find out, what degree of variation is acceptable. This is particularly true of those further elements suggested in § 9 of the principal recommendations. I doubt if lessons from elsewhere will help. The conditions of Europe are specific. The point is made in the more general remarks. If one looks at, say, regional policy, or indeed the objects of the Community, they impose specific obligations which, to maintain its legitimacy (in political science terminology), the Community has to carry through. On the other hand, the U.S.A. was not born with a professed purpose of solving the poverty in Arkansas. The obligation has arisen by the pressure of events. We do not yet know what levels of regional disequilibria are acceptable. There is a chance that we will know a little more when the work of the Committee for Regional Policy bears fruit. I certainly do not believe that the size of the discrepancy of technique between that of the U.K. and the rest of the Member States should long endure. The change must then be an educational process.

In that process Community instruments can help. On the one hand, now that there is a regional fund there is a possibility of expanding the role of the Community budget on the re-distributive side. Just as there remains a possibility still of Community instruments being increasingly used. What does disturb me is the concepts of the two levels. Two points lead me to think that the key may be to contemplate not so much co-ordination or harmonization which may come too late, but interpenetration. The *Third Programme of Medium-Term Economic Policy* [11] spoke of seeking a larger place for the Community in the elaboration of national plans. The same point is also made by Professor Zacher where,[12] paradoxically, he speaks of the budgetary autonomy of the German *Länder* and the *Bund* as the starting point. He continues in the text which I have "une evolution remarkable s'est aussi produite, c'est précisément la structure fédérale qui est venue constituer le principal, voire le seul, moyen de planification qu'offrent les dispositions économiques de la constitution et c'est précisément grace à la structure fédérale de la R.F.A. qu'on trouve des organes de l'Etat spécialement voués à des tâches de politique économique". It is not the word federal upon which I insist. It is rather the concept of the distribution of powers and then of their organisation. It is that which I mean by interpenetration. It should not be thought that when I spoke of the importance of the national level, that in this field I wanted to risk the erosion of common institutions. Far

11. *Op. cit.* n. 3, para. 104.
12. At p. 30 in his report; ref. as at n. 6 above.

from it. Nor, however, can I easily accept, because of the fundamental political background, the two levels as distinct entities. Already the initial purity of that system has been compromised in many ways, out of necessity, as has the original purity of the German Constitution. If one looks there, and at the Netherlands, in Community terms it seems to me one must look more to an expansion, adaption and evolution of what one might loosely call the techniques of *comités de réglementation* and in that way to promote mutual comprehension.

That must be done, and certainly within a framework, which is, finally, the law. The burdens upon the court under any such mixed system are considerable because it will have to hold a balance which will itself be changing with conditions. It is only by some such means that one will be able, I believe, to begin to eliminate the differences in national method, and without that the Union will not be easily workable.

Third Theme

THE NECESSITY OF CO-ORDINATING OR APPROXIMATING ECONOMIC LEGISLATION, OR OF SUPPLEMENTING OR REPLACING IT BY COMMUNITY LAW

REPORT

by

Robert Savy*

INTRODUCTION

In my opinion, reflections on the necessity to co-ordinate or approximate the economic laws of the Member States in an economic and monetary union, or to supplement or replace them by Community law, must proceed on the basis of the three following propositions:

1. That there is agreement in all the Member States as to a certain composite of political and social values, even if profound differences exist regarding the form of political institutions or the conception of social organisation. It is the common intention of all nine Member States to adhere to the principle of political democracy, as it was constructed in the nineteenth century on the basis of the British experience and the philosophy of 1789; political liberalism, universal suffrage, the existence of a number of different political parties, and the alternation of political power, are all manifestations of this concept, as are also individual liberties and equality before the law. And this heritage is not seriously questioned either by governments at present in power, or by opposition parties which stand to attain that power. Furthermore, there exists in all Member States the growing desire to further enrich this concept of political democracy by means of the recognition, as much for individuals as for groups, of new economic and social rights. It is upon the realisation of these rights that "... social and economic progress..." and "... the constant improvement in the conditions of life and work..." of which the Preamble to the EEC Treaty speaks will depend.
2. The conception of the economic role of the state in the different Member States is, by way of contrast, less homogeneous. For some Member States, remaining broadly faithful to the neo-classical economic model, the state should content itself with a surveillance of the essential macro-economic equilibria, and should allow the principal role to be played by the market. Other states, concerned at the growing economic power of certain enterprises, and at their increasing influence on the market, are more inclined to think that the state should constitute

* Dean of the Faculty of Law and Economic Science at the University of Limoges.

13 C.M.L.Rev. 1976, 233-243

a democratic counterbalance to private economic power; they therefore accord to the state a more active role in the management and direction of the economy. When speaking of a mixed economy, or of the necessary combination of the market and of programming,[1] one cannot avoid this essential ambiguity. There are those for whom the market is the essential reality, and they have inspired the economic policy of recent years. But there are others who, without entirely abandoning the idea of the market, believe in the necessity of a planned economy in the general interest; the influence of the later group is growing as a result of the present economic crisis.

3. When one looks at the balance sheet of the first fifteen years of the Community—in so far as that is at present possible[2]—these differences of approach come all the more strongly to the fore. It is clear that the EEC has succeeded in all its efforts directed to the creation of a large market: the obstacles to increased freedom of movement have been eliminated, and a specialisation in activities is starting as between the Member States. On the other hand, no-one can deny that the Community has been a failure with regard to those activities which require an active intervention in the affairs of private economic agents, such as town and country planning, energy policy, computer services, organisation of territory, *etc.* It is conceivable that, in the absence of a resumption of effective initiatives by the Community in these essential areas of economic life, this active intervention could only be undertaken by the public authorities of those Member States who are willing to undertake it. The danger of this obliteration of the Community aspect is, however, that it will raise the problem of the compatibility of national economic policies with Community regulations.

Starting from these premises, the national reports and the Interim Report provide a remarkable basis for reflection. They provide not only a progress report of exceptional richness, but also an analysis of the principal orientations which the economic law could follow. It is not my intention here to question the conclusions of these reports; my intention is, indeed, more modest than that.

It would seem to me that the sole function of economic law is to define in terms of rights and obligations on the part of private economic agents and public authorities the objectives of economic policy which are laid down by the political authorities. The function of the jurist is thus to

1. See J. Zijlstra and B. Goudzwaard, *Economic Policy and Problems of Competition in the EEC and the Member States,* EEC Studies Competition, Series No. 2 (Brussels, 1966).
2. See Maillet, *La Construction Européenne* (Paris, 1975).

furnish the political authorities with the technical instruments for the formulation and normative realisation of their decisions. We might, in our subsequent discussion, usefully consider whether the economic law is actually in a position to properly fulfil this role.

Leaving aside the question of the choice of economic policy by the national and Community authorities, because as such it does not concern the jurist, one may enquire into the efficacity of the economic law at the two levels where it may be brought to bear:

- —at the micro-economic level, where the discretionary powers of the economic administration are of such a kind that they may represent a threat to the Rule of Law;
- —at the macro-economic level, where the assimilation of economic policies into the national or Community legal system may cause difficulties.

1. DISCRETIONARY POWER AND THE RULE OF LAW

The economic section is probably the one where state intervention involves the greatest possibilities of arbitrariness. This intervention is by nature selective: it assists the initiatives of sectors and enterprises which are held to further the general economic interest, and it can penalise the others. The danger exists of arbitrary discrimination between economic agents, and that the administration may neglect its duty of impartiality. The rules governing administrative discretion are, in fact, very imprecise and, as the national reports show, the administration enjoys in many areas a very great liberty of appreciation.

The principle of the Rule of Law is an element of that common political heritage to which Europe adheres. This principle means that the administration, too, is subject to law, that the subjects of law must be equal before the law; further, failure to adhere to this principle can be sanctioned by the courts.

It would seem that, at the present stage of its evolution, the economic law of the Member States is undergoing a crisis of legality, to which common solutions should be sought.

The crisis of economic legality

What is meant here is the excessive development of the discretionary power of the administration, which itself brings about a loss of effective control by the courts.

The discretionary power of the economic administration has not been taken as a theme of specific studies by the reporters. It appears, however, in the following areas: unilateral public measures of assistance, and those foreseen in programming contracts;[3] in a number of compulsory dispositions;[4] in sectoral legislation;[5] and, finally, in the application of sanctions,[6] which is also often a matter of discretion. One could quote many examples from the internal law of each of the Member States.

The existence of this state of affairs means that the principle of the Rule of Law is not fulfilling its traditional function properly in economic matters. The application of the principle certainly permits the attribution of some power to the economic administration, but, at the same time, should lay down on what conditions and subject to what limits such powers should be exercised. As it is, for reasons deriving from the complexity and fluidity of economic situations, the Rule of Law no longer regulates the activities of the administration. For instance, in administrative practice, the aim of public interventions is not indicated, or only in a very imprecise manner. Further, the choice of the means of intervention from the wide range provided for by legislation is also left to the discretion of the administration. Generally speaking, the economic authorities are free to determine where and how they act, since there exists no legal restriction on the discretionary character of their power.

The crisis of judicial control is the necessary consequence of this state of affairs. The role of the judge is to state the law, that is to say, to reconcile the administrative decision with a legal rule. If the rule has lost all precision, then the intervention of the judge ceases in turn to be effective.

The national reports have made an inventory of the difficulties of judicial protection.[7] They have rightly called attention to uncertainties relating to the repartition of competences, the degree of specialisation in administrative jurisdiction, and the kind of legal acts which can be referred to the courts. But these are perhaps not the essential problems: in France, where the discretionary power of the administration is in question, the judge will limit himself to the control of manifest errors in the appreciation of the facts; in Italy, the concrete interpretation of the public interest is not a matter for the judge;[8] and in the United Kingdom "... the judges are not qualified to decide questions of economic policy,

3. See Interim Report, Chs. III and IV, *op. cit.* p. 193 of this volume, n. 7.
4. See Interim Report, Ch. V.
5. See Interim Report, Ch. VI.
6. See Interim Report, Ch. VII.
7. See Interim Report, Ch. VIII.
8. See report made to the Utrecht colloquium by Sacchi Morsiani at p. 140, ref. as n. 3.

and such questions are by their nature not justiciable".[9] In the Netherlands, moreover, a number of administrative decisions may not be referred to the courts at all.[10] This state of affairs could be worrying if the risk exists that the administration may use its discretionary power to treat enterprises in a different way, on the basis of criteria which are, perhaps, suspect. It would be interesting to know if, in the opinion of the reporters, this risk exists. Information concerning the volume of litigation in economic matters would be equally valuable: its rarity would no doubt signify that the business community has ceased to have confidence in the law and in the courts to regulate its relations with the administration.

The means of re-establishing the Rule of Law in economic affairs

If one adheres to the view that the economic administration should be subjected to previously-established rules of law, and if one admits that this is at present not the case, then it is necessary to investigate the means of re-establishing, or at least, of safeguarding, the Rule of Law in economic affairs. This undertaking should be directed to the strengthening of the role of law in economic matters, and may lead to a harmonisation, or to a parallel evolution, of national economic laws. The crisis of judicial control will itself be diminished if economic law is made more precise. But it would be vain to hope that the discretionary power of the administration will recede: economic reality is too diverse and changeable to allow itself to be enclosed by rigorous norms. This is why the re-establishment of economic legality will be effected probably more by means of a reinforcement of the rules of form and procedure (external legality) than by a refinement of the fundamental rules (internal legality).

The rules of internal legality will necessarily remain imprecise. It is not possible to decree in advance the objective conditions in which the national authorities decide on price regulation, or action regarding the money supply, or on assistance to some enterprise or sector; they will have to preserve a certain margin of interpretation. But this necessity will not prevent the subjection of administrative activity to a minimum legal framework which would derive from the ability which the administration possesses to limit its own discretionary power.

One method of this kind, already initiated in German law,[11] consists of

9. See report made by Prof. Daintith, at p. 224, quoting from *Charles Roberts and Co. Ltd. v. B.R.B.*, (1965) 1 W.L.R., 396, ref. as n. 3.

10. See report made by Prof. VerLoren van Themaat, at p. 180, ref. as n. 3.

11. See Auby et Fromont, *Les recours contre les actes administratif dans les pays de la C.E.E.*, Paris, 1971.

the acceptance by the administration that it is bound by its own practice, and in particular that it is bound to observe administrative circulars relating to the exercise of discretionary power. The administration may not depart from this established practice without valid reasons.

Another method, in some respects fairly similar, is that of the "*directives*", the existence of which has been recognised by the French *Conseil d'Etat* on different occasions in recent years. These "*directives*" exercise a "power of orientation" regarding the taking of individual decisions by the competent authorities; the authorities must respect the content of the "*directives*", except where the general interest or the specific needs of the situation in question justify a different approach. The concept of the "*directive*" is particularly interesting in that it can be applied both to internal circular letters to the administration and to prospective economic norms, such as plans, concerted programmes, *etc.*

We have two examples of rules which are well adapted to the requirements of economic intervention. They are sufficiently rigid to avoid arbitrary decisions, but also flexible enough to permit, where necessary, the adaptation of administrative action to concrete reality. The conference of the highest administrative authorities of the EEC countries, held in 1970, also recommended that the reinforcement of legality should be sought in this direction.[12]

The rules of external legality could be considerably developed without serious inconveniences. These rules respect the liberty of decision of the administration, and avoid all shifts of responsability; but they do require the administration to explain the way in which it exercises its powers, and thus facilitate democratic control and make the temptation of arbitrariness more remote.

Before an administrative decision is taken, it might be considered desirable to associate in its preparation the representatives of the diverse interests affected. This practice is known as "*concertation*" in France, a term which is legally imprecise. What is mainly involved here is the development of consultative procedures in order that the administration is conducted in such a way that publicity is given to the essential factors which determine its decisions. It is, for example, unlikely that, in connection with the allocation of a public grants, the same decisions would be taken in the same way if the employers' organisations, trade unions and local authorities were informed of the contents of the relevant administrative dossiers. Arbitrary discrimination is furthered by administrative secretiveness. Any methods which might persuade the

12. See *Etudes et documents du Conseil d'Etat* (Paris, 1971).

administration to avoid the temptation of secretiveness should be encouraged.

It is also desirable that, once the decision has been taken, it should be possible to demand the reasons for it. Certainly, it is generally admitted that the administration should reveal the reasons for its decisions to the courts. But this, in my view, is not enough. As is the case in German and Italian law, the reasons for all individual discretionary decisions should also be communicated to the interested parties. Apart from its educative value, this motivation would give the individuals concerned the chance to form their own opinion of the correctness and lawfulness of the reasons invoked, and the opportunity to take proceedings to challenge the decision. It would be interesting to have particulars concerning the application of this rule, and to know whether the guarantees which it provides for the impartiality of the administration broadly compensate for the increase in work which it requires.

It is in my opinion very important to make manifest the insufficiencies of economic legality and of judicial control. The task of our present discussion is, therefore, to consider the dangers which have been indicated here, and to consider which may be the best means of combating them.

2. ECONOMIC POLICIES AND THE LEGAL ORDER

Individual economic decisions, the usual instrument of micro-economic intervention, pose in particular the question of the equality of administered persons before the law. The legal formulation of macro-economic decisions raises even more delicate problems, of which the national reports and the Interim Report give a very complete list. The Interim Report comes to the conclusion that an overall harmonisation of the macro-economic policies of the Member States, co-ordinated by the Community, is necessary.[13] Without wishing to question the correctness of this conclusion, it should be noted that it touches on the very essence of the debate on the political future of Europe, and that it takes for granted the agreement of the partners concerning the subtle equilibrium to be maintained between Community and Member State competences.

In my view, the jurist should certainly not refuse to concern himself with political choices: the Rule of Law has no meaning if it is divorced from the objectives it is designed to serve. But one of the jurist's preoccupations, as a legal technician, should be to ask himself if the economic law is capable of fulfilling the functions which the economic

13. See Interim Report, p. 73a *et seq.*

authorities expect from it. His reply will be positive if he can establish:

- —on the one hand, that the economic law of the Member States permits the realisation of the macro-economic policy decided upon by the Community authorities;
- —on the other hand, that Community economic law does not prohibit the realisation of those economic experiments which the Member States are, in the name of the principle of political democracy, entitled to undertake.

Community policy and national laws

It is hardly necessary to repeat or add to the observations made in the national reports and the Interim Report. If agreement between the Member States is achieved with regard to a Community co-ordination of macro-economic policy, then the economic law of the Member States must provide the legal instruments necessary for this policy, and also the means of assuring its coherent implementation.

As far as short-term economic policy is concerned, the legal instruments of national intervention in conformity with Community orientations are available in each Member State.[14] A legal basis exists for the regulation of prices, of credit and of economic relations with foreign countries. The central authorities are, in addition, empowered to command respect from the decentralised or federalised authorities for their chosen policy, notably in budgetary matters.

The situation in the Member States with regard to medium-term economic policy (encouragement or control of investment, structuring of the market, and physical planning, *etc.*) which should adapt the structure of the productive process to those economic objectives which are considered desirable, is less homogeneous.[15] Some Member States, more attached to the fundamental role of the market, confine themselves in the main to interventions assuring sufficient competition; this is the case, for example, in the Federal Republic of Germany. Others hesitate less to intervene in the affairs of private economic agents; consider, for example, the French system of public aid for private investment, or the British legislation relating to the location of industry. It appears desirable that the national authorities in all countries should be endowed with those means of intervention which they at present lack. This does not mean that the authorities will necessarily make use of those means; but if the objective laid down by the Community authorities render an inter-

14. See Interim Report, p. 46 *et seq.*
15. See Interim Report, p. 50 *et seq.*

vention useful, the means to carry it out will be available. Thus the law fulfils the function assigned to it: to be the instrument for the execution of a policy decided upon by the competent authorities. Moreover, the evolution of French economic policy in the last quarter century demonstrates that the existence of legislation permitting state intervention in all areas of economic life does not constitute an obstacle to a progressive disengagement of the state in economic affairs.

The coherence of public interventions, in view of the interactions between economic phenomena, is sometimes difficult to ensure. This coherence presupposes a concentration of economic power, and as far as the essential economic choices are concerned, does exist in fact in all the Member States. On the other hand, the carrying-out of economic decisions, in which a great number of private and public economic agents participate, fairly often gives rise to discord.[16] Briefly, two solutions to this problem may be considered.

In the first place, it may be desirable to create co-ordinating structures at the different levels at which the public authorities intervene: interministerial committees, regional or provincial conferences, *etc.* On the other hand, the activities of public enterprises must be effectively harmonised with the policy defined by the state but according to procedures which permit diversity. Further, the periodic consultations of those responsible, on the public and private level, for the running of the economy may succeed in becoming institutionalised. National traditions, of a political and administrative nature, broadly control the solution to these problems, but their importance should not be underestimated.

The resort to medium-term programming is also a means of giving cohesion to the economic law, and I subscribe to the conclusions of the general reporter on this point.[17] But it may, perhaps, at the same time be advisable to give some common thought to the place to be given in the legal system to the prospective economic norms to be contained in these plans or programmes. It is not a question of moving towards a generalised obligatory planning; but a programme containing only guidelines will be ineffective. The national medium-term plans or programmes should be compatible with possible future Community plans. They should also be binding to a certain extent on the national public authorities. The French idea of the "*directive*", which is different from the Community concept designated by the same word, could usefully provide an indication as to the legal significance to be attributed to these plans or programmes.

16. See Interim Report, p. 30.
17. See Interim Report, p. 33.

The Community legal order and national policies

This problem has scarcely been considered, for it does not seem to be of current interest. In actual fact, the same neo-liberal philosophy has inspired, at one and the same time over the past fifteen years, both Community and Member State economic policy, and the Interim Report rightly underlines this convergence.[18] But one cannot be sure that this community of views will last to the point where it appears as a constant feature of western European nations, and one may well wonder how the economic law would respond to a state of affairs in which these policies diverged from one another.

The problem is not merely hypothetical. It does indeed seem difficult to admit that there exists such a thing as an optimum economic system for the EEC, the "mixed economy" system, of which the economy of the market forms the basis, and where the public authorities intervene to ensure the conditions of effective competition.[19] Consideration of political theory, of the law and of reality, lead to a rejection of this postulate. Accession to the EEC could not have the consequence of depriving a State of the right to adopt the economic system of its choice; this is a fundamental requirement of political democracy. The fundamental legal principles of the economic systems of the Member States at no point prohibit economic experiments of socialist inspiration, which reduce the liberty of action of private economic agents in the general economic interest. Political developments showed, at the time of the French presidential elections of 1974, that the possibility of an important change in the orientation of the economic policy of a Member State cannot be excluded; other countries may experience comparable situations.

Preventive solutions must be sought to the kind of difficulties which such a state of affairs would cause for the proper functioning of the common market. The Interim Report suggests the institution of preventive consultations regarding the consequences of the exceptional measures which Member States may adopt on the basis of Article 224 EEC.[20] These consultations could be usefully extended to cover the hypothesis raised here. It is, indeed, of fundamental importance for the future of the EEC to establish that European co-operation is not bound to a pre-established economic system, but that it is a manifestation of a far more profound requirement of the European peoples.

18. See Interim Report, p. 25a.
19. See Interim Report, p. 25a *et seq.*
20. See Interim Report, p. 50.

I do not pretend to be able to say here how such difficult problem may be solved, a problem, moreover, in which the law plays only a minor part; economists and politicians will also have to take part in the necessary deliberations. The objective is to make the rules and mechanisms of the EEC compatible with an original economic experiment. The search for a solution may be undertaken in two ways. In the first place, the Community authorities and the Member States should observe an "economic neutrality", that is to say, they should observe a strict impartiality, and sould refrain from all acts capable of hindering the development of the experiment. Correspondingly, the State where the economic experiment is in progress should, in the spirit of Article 225 EEC, adapt the measures which it wishes to take to the rules of the common market. The plan is ambitious, but if matters are simply left to sort themselves out when the crucial moment arives, the danger exists of a slowing-down of European construction.

The material furnished by the national reports and the Interim Report was so rich as not to render arbitrary a choice of directions to propose for our discussions. Many other directions were possible, and remain so. Those suggested here appeared to me, while remaining in the field of the most rigorous legal technique, to have some bearing on important political questions. It is for this reason that in preference to others, I draw them to the attention of the participants in this colloquium.

REPORT

by

Klaus J. Hopt*

Since my esteemed colleague, Savy, has prepared the way with a report covering the fundamental aspects of this theme, I shall be able to restrict my discourse to three more specific questions, which, however, may be said to be crucial to a consideration of economic law in an economic and monetary union.

The Interim Report which was submitted to us points in a striking fashion to the increasing resort to a legal regulation of economic policy in the various Member States, particularly in Belgium and Germany, but also in Italy and the Netherlands.[1] One can only agree with the final recommendation of the Report that this development should be encouraged, and also from the point of view of the co-ordination of the economic policy of the Member States, because of the greater transparency which it brings about. However, even in the Federal Republic itself, a phenomenon which runs contrary to this tendency has in recent years become apparent. This phenomenon has recently attracted comment and criticism in legal and economic literature.[2] I refer here to the so-called voluntary self-control of the economy. It is a question here of the replacement of binding economic law by legally indefinable gentlemen's agreements between the state and the economic circles concerned.

Among the outstanding examples of this phenomenon are the self-restricting agreements, such as the Coal and Oil Agreement. In this agreement the mineral oil companies committed themselves, under pressure from Bonn, to adherence to fixed maximum production levels together with floor prices. These measures were intended to supplement the efforts of the Federal Government in its structural policy for a

* Professor of law, University of Tübingen.

1. P. VerLoren van Themaat, *The Economic Law of the Member States of the European Communities in an Economic and Monetary Union,* Commission of the European Communities, Studies: Competition - Approximation of legislation, Series 20 (Brussels 1973), at Ch. II, 10, 2a; Ch. IV, 1 (6).

2. From a legal point of view, see e.g. Hopt, *Der Kapitalanlegerschutz im Recht der Banken,* Munich 1975, pp. 147-158; for the economic aspects, see Tuchtfeld, "Moral Suasion in der Wirtschaftspolitik", in *Konzertierte Aktion,* ed. Hoppmann, Frankfurt 1971, pp. 19-68.

13 C.M.L.Rev. 1976, 245-251

solution of the coalmining crisis. At the same time, in 1966-1967, the German department stores agreed together voluntarily to halt expansion in towns with less than 200,000 inhabitants. The intention here was to bring some relief to the critical situation of the small and medium-sized specialised retailers. For such cases the German law against restraint of competition provides for the possibility of a so-called "ministerial cartel", which, in exceptional cases, allows for the legalisation of agreements which, although restricting competition, are necessary in the overriding interests of the economy in general and of the common good. However, ressort to this possibility of legalisation occured only at the outset, and later no further use was made of it.

The attempts which have been made to justify these clear violations of the law on the grounds of the principle of the Welfare State (*Sozialstaatsprinzip*), of the weighing of intersts, or merely on grounds of practical necessity, are not at all convincing. It clearly makes a difference whether such cartels are allowed according to the formal and material requirements of the law, or whether they may be practised without the need for preliminary permission. Before such permission is, by way of exception, granted by the Minister, the economic parties concerned must, among other procedures, first be allowed to state their views. A certain publicity regarding the cartels is thus guaranteed, and there is a continuous watchfulness against abuse. However, according to present practice, the whole situation remains conveniently obscure, conveniently, that is, both for the State and for the cartel members, and the Federal Ministry for Economic Affairs has, in a directive to this effect, forbidden the Federal Cartel Office to clarify the position in specific instances.

In a formal sense, the history of the much-discussed German reform of the Stock Exchange law resembled the cases just discussed, but essentially it gives rise to even more serious reservations. The preliminary phase of this reform process was concluded with the amending Act of April 28, 1975. Traces of the original proposal for legislation of 1967, which, *inter alia,* contained provisions for periodic publicity, can barely be found in the Act of 1975. Due to the severe criticism of banks, exchanges and business associations, drastic cuts were made in the plans for reform. Thus, in spite of the widespread public demand, no regulation of the "insider problem" was introduced into the law. Nor were the private dealings of Stock exchange brokers curtailed; and even the representation of investors in the Stock Exchange governing body, a reform which had long been called for, remains optional. The reform of the Stock Exchange does, however, amount to more than just the few provisions of the amending Act of 1975, which are aimed principally at strengthening the self-administration of the exchanges. Many important partial reforms were also put through on a voluntary basis. These reforms included the concentration of the most important share transactions, with the exception of block dealings, on the Stock Exchange, a certain degree of publicity of the Stock Exchange turnover, and a strengthened interim publicity regarding the enterprises with securities quoted on the Exchange. The voluntary guidelines for insider dealings are, on the other hand, barely worth mentioning; informed opinion regards them as no more than a vain attempt to solve the problem.[3] But it is interesting to note that the Stock Exchanges have called for a voluntary solution on the English model, which, apparently, has proved a brilliant success. However, in so doing they overlook or ignore the fact that this solution has recently become the object of broad criticism in England from economic and journalistic quarters; here I need only to refer to my esteemed colleague, Schmitthoff.[4]

It would be easy to illustrate the trend towards self-regulation by reference to further examples. In the banking sector, for instance, the reform of the law protecting depositors has become a political issue since the spectacular bankruptcy of the Herstatt Bank in Cologne. Or in the sphere of foreign trade where a critical problem—and one not confined to Germany—is posed by the buying-up, partially and even totally, of national companies by oil-producing countries. In both these instances, the Federal Government has refrained from the introduction of legislation, and contented itself with a certain degree of voluntary accommodation on the part of the banks.

This method of consensual settlement of problems relating to the reform of economic policy by means of gentlemen's agreements between the state and the economic spheres concerned, creates considerable problems for an economic and monetary union.

This method should not be adopted at Community level in the creation of the Community's own economic law, or in the course of the harmonisation of national economic law. Certainly, and this argument is repeated in the Interim Report, the part played by the two sides of industry in the co-ordination of economic policy should be increased.[5] A merely advisory function, on the lines of the Dutch Economic and Social Council, will not suffice. However, although such a co-operation on the

3. E.g. Hopt & Will, *Europäisches Insiderrecht* (Stuttgart 1973), pp. 111-119; P. Ulmer, "Rechtspolitische Probleme des Insidershandels", (1975) *Juristenzeitung* 625-628.
In the meantime, the guidelines have been very much improved.

4. Schmitthoff, *"The Merits and Disadvantages of Voluntary Regulation in Britain"*, in *Les Emissions de Titres de Sociétés en Europe et aux Etats-Unis* (Brussels, 1970), pp. 255-262.

5. VerLoren van Themaat, Interim Report, Chap. II, 10 2b, Chap. IV, 2(3).

part of management and labour is thoroughly desirable, it need not take the form of voluntary self-restriction without any legal regulation or extraneous control by the state. As the German experience shows, the main characteristic of voluntary self-control is a decided lack of clarity. Not only is it lacking in clear standards, of the kind that binding economic regulation would necessarily ensure, but, which is more serious, it is not subject to any effective control on the part of parliament or the press, which is not otherwise the case when legal reforms in the field of economic policy are carried out. This pattern of voluntary self-control points, furthermore, to a certain functional incapacity on the part of the state. In other words, the state does not insist upon the realisation of its reform projects, but, faced with a certain degree of voluntary accommodation on the part of industry, is content to settle for a compromise regarding precisely the most incisive and far-reaching aspects of its reform plans. What it obtains in exchange is often barely worth mentioning, as in the case of the guidelines for insider trading. And, finally, there is the danger of the closed shop. The conclusion and the terms of a gentlemen's agreement are determined by the parties. The interests of third parties are not articulated, and all too often come off badly. There is no legal protection against a gentlemen's agreement, such as a claim for the observance of the promised self-control, or an action to compel legislative action. For the state, this is all very convenient, since thus the worst inconveniences may be removed without the need for a legal regulation of the economy. In fact, the absence of legal regulation is the price the state has to pay, and here lies, moreover, one of the factors which distinguish this type of economic control from the so-called planning agreements, such as are known particularly to French law. This state of affairs is also very welcome to industry, since thus it is spared legal rules, controls and sanctions.

From the Community point of view, this method of extra-legal bargaining between the state and industry is problematical, even if it is only practised on a national level. In the first place, it makes it extremely difficult for an outside observer to find out what exactly the situation is in the country concerned. In contrast to written economic law, the gentlemen's agreements, in view of their limited clarity, their non-binding nature and the possibility of informal alteration, very easily evade interference from outside. Further, this trend towards operating outside the legal order renders more difficult the co-ordination and harmonisation of the economic laws of the different Member States. In fact, paradoxical as it may sound, I think that this practice creates more problems for harmonisation than the differing rules brought about by legal regulation. For in the latter case at least the uncontrolled activity in the economic sphere concerned is to some extent canalised, and it is easier to alter, relax or intensify this degree of control in the course of the harmonisation of national law, than to attempt to impose a degree of control in the first place. In other words, it is easier to alter already-existing economic regulations than to attempt to apply those same regulations to a new problem for the first time.

In concluding the discussion of my first point, I would like once again to stress that the two sides of industry should be more closely involved in the co-ordination of economic policy and in projects for the reform of economic law. This would ensure that the binding legal regulation of the economy would not only bear more relation to practice, but would also be more effective, because not handed down by the state to the other parties in a one-sided fashion. It is not feasible to dispense altogether with legal regulation of the economy. This obviously does not mean that each and everything must be regulated by the law, or that all the differing national provisions should be standardised. But without a minimum of procedural guidelines, or of material minimum standards, a mere voluntary self-control can be a very valuable first step, but in the long run cannot suffice in the context of an economic and monetary union.

The second point which I would like to discuss concerns the application of binding economic law. According to the German conception, a series of largely independent superior federal authorities are involved in this process. Since recently, wholly independent commissions of experts have also been brought in. The best-known example of the first-mentioned group is the Federal Cartel Office, and of the latter group, the Monopolies Commission established by the Cartel Law of 1973.

Point of departure for the discussion of this point is the recognition that harmonisation of national laws, no matter how satisfactory the result, alone cannot suffice. Each system of economic law is only so good and so compelling as the instruments for application and enforcement which accompany it. In the past, in my opinion, the danger existed of giving too much attention in the process of harmonisation to the original regulations, and not enough to their implementation. It is, therefore, all the more welcome that the Interim Report does go into the question of the implementation of economic law, even if only briefly.

The obvious solution here seems to lie in entrusting the Commission, or some other newly-created Community authority, with the application and enforcement of harmonised law. Thus, for example, the creation of a Shares Office at Community level has been suggested, a kind of European Securities and Exchange Commission. I must confess that I have certain reservations with regard to this suggestion. The different national authorities could be entrusted with comparable powers, and would probably be less overburdened and also better acquainted with the special features of the Member States concerned, a factor which can be decisive for effective implementation. But one cannot assume that the setting-up of similar kinds of authorities in the different Member States will be enough to settle the matter. The example of the German Stock Exchange supervision by the State Commissioners *(Länderbörsenaufsicht)* provides an illustration of this. Despite extensive powers, their practical significance, even according to the members of the Stock Exchanges, remains very slight indeed. It is, therefore, seriously worth considering whether the primary implementation by national authorities should not be supplemented by a subsidiary power of intervention on the part of a Community organ. This doubling of functions would combine the advantage of a greater proximity to the facts with that of a better control of enforcement.

In view of the complexity of the problems involved, I do not think that the first step should consist of the immediate co-ordination or approximation of national economic law and of the procedures for its enforcement. As a first step, a close exchange of information should be instituted between the different specialised authorities, and, where necessary, between these and the Community organs. In this connection, I would like to allude to the fact that the first impetus to an investigation of the fatal foreign currency transactions of the Herstatt Bank was given by information transmitted to the Federal Bank from abroad. But the action which was taken on the basis of this, in particular by the Federal Office for the Supervision of Credit Institutions (*Bundesaufsichtsamt für das Kreditwesen*) came, unfortunately, too late. The European Commission thus chose the right approach when, in December 1974, it proposed that a contact committee for the different national authorities charged with the supervision of the banking sector should be created before any move was made to approximate the different national laws relating to this area. An awareness of common problems, and of the difficulties experienced in all Member States in the solution of certain problems, should in itself further the actual harmonisation of laws, and prepare the way for it; it may even, to a certain extent, actually bring it about. A properly functioning exchange of information should lead almost of its own accord to close co-operation in dealing with inter-state economic affairs. The problem of the independence of supervisory authorities or commissions of experts thereby loses its acuteness. This very independence may appear as a hindrance to a state which is engaged in the harmonisation of law, but as I see it, the Member States have a better chance of growing together from the bottom up, that is, from the level of the specialists who are confronted daily with the same problems of economic regulation. And this chance will be all the better if these experts enjoy a certain degree of factual independence from the intervening Member State in working towards the objectives of economic regulation.

Owing to the passage of time, I can only go very briefly into my third point. Here I would like to stress the primordial importance of a harmonised law with regard to capital markets and the supervision of the banking sector. The importance of this goes far beyond the law relating to freedom of establishment, and this has been rightly accentuated in the national reports and in the Interim Report, particularly with regard to capital market and credit policy. Also of great importance is the role played in economic policy and law by the micro-economic surveillance of banks and exchanges. One should not overlook the fact that the protection of depositors and investors, which this supervision aims to ensure, exists not just for the benefit, or even for the primary benefit, of groups of creditors. More importantly, the function of this protection of individuals is to ensure that the "run-situations", so typical of the international banking crisis of the 'Thirties, and which can so easily produce the most disastrous effects, will not occur again. It also seeks to encourage public confidence in the bank and exchanges, so that on the basis of this confidence the money and capital markets may carry out their function undisturbed, a function which is of fundamental importance for the economic system and for the economic and monetary union. The protection of individuals and of functions here coincides, as also in the question of the restriction by the economic law of the power of banks and enterprises. I would even go so far as to say that such interdependencies and mixtures of functions are characteristic of modern economics, but that because of this the economic lawyer is faced with very difficult, but at the same time very fascinating, tasks.

REPORT

by

Clive M. Schmitthoff* and Alan C. Page**

A. ECONOMIC AIMS AND ECONOMIC LAW

1. *Introduction*

In an earlier article it was stated that "the fact that a concept does not exist in a particular legal system does not allow the inference that the legal regulations which that concept is supposed to systematize do not exist; if only allows the conclusion that the factual situation has not, or not yet, progressed to academic systematisation".[1] Now, as then, the object is to continue the process of systematisation.

That object is best achieved through an examination of the development in the forms of economic law during the last decade. That development cannot be divorced from the changes in economic policy which have occurred during that period. Furthermore, the accession of the UK to the European Economic Community requires that the wider European aspect be taken into account.

Municipal economic law has been defined as comprising "the regulation of state interference with the affairs of commerce, industry and finance".[2] As such its underlying philosophy was described as "economic *dirigisme*" i.e. the idea that the paternalistic state may limit the autonomy of the parties in the public interest. Furthermore "as state planning asserts itself in a constantly more consistent pattern, economic law develops into the discipline which reflects the transition to a planned and directed free market economy".[3] This latter factor represents an important element in the present analysis although it should be emphasised that not all economic law can be subsumed under its aegis.

* LL.M., LL.D., Dr. Jur., Barrister; Visiting Professor in International Business Law at the City University and the University of Kent at Canterbury; Hon. Professor in Law at the Ruhr-Universität Bochum.

** LL.B. (Hons) (Edinburgh).

1. C. M. Schmitthoff, "The Concept of Economic Law in England", (1966) J.B.L. 309-310.
2. *Ibid.*, at p. 315.
3. *Ibid.*, at p. 315.

13 C.M.L.Rev. 1976, 253-277

The search for logically concise definitions of one's subject-matter does, however, carry with it its own dangers, in that one may lose sight of the field which one is attempting to analyse. Clearly any realistic definition of a study like economic law must run primarily in terms of the concrete problems which it adopts as its subject-matter: it must be a definition by type rather than delimitation. Thus, in seeking to understand the relationship of economic policy and law as a means of implementing that policy it is necessary to turn to the background of that relationship, namely the economic policies pursued in the United Kingdom during the last decade in general, and changes in those policies in particular.

2. *Changes in United Kingdom domestic economic policy during the 'Sixties and 'Seventies*

A detailed description of the changes in economic policy during that period is obviously beyond the scope of this paper. Developments can, however, be conveniently summarised in terms of the attitudes of individual administrations to the economy and some of the more important factors influencing the implementation of their policies.

The policy of the Conservative administrations during the 1950's had been one perhaps best described by the phrase "holding the ring". Not that there was no state intervention in the economy. The interwar period had seen a great expansion in the scope and nature of state intervention. Writing in 1939 the *Economist* remarked "since 1932 the state has no longer appeared to industry solely in the guise of monitor or policeman; it has had favours to dispense", "the attitude of industry to the state" has been revolutionised and "the policeman has turned Father Christmas".[4] The postwar period had, however seen a sufficiently large extension of the economic functions of the state as to make it a qualitative dividing line with the past. This extension was not so much marked by direct control over or participation in industry but rather by the extension of the public sector and particularly by the extension of state expenditure, the utilisation of which was capable of exercising considerable influence over the economy.

It was not, however, until the early 1960's that any attempt was made to bring together the disparate elements of public expenditure into one coherent forecast.[5] This development was only part of a reversal of attitudes which led to a more aggressive attitude towards the economy as

4. *The Economist*, March 18, 1939.
5. *Public Expenditure in 1963-4 and 1967-8*, Cmnd. 2235, 1963.

a whole, not only within government but also, importantly, within individual ministries. The same period saw, firstly, the setting-up of the National Economic Development Council as a central planning organisation, and, secondly, the internal reorganisation of the Treasury. Although this reorganisation was the result of internal reform,[6] it identified the necessity of firstly placing government expenditure on a long-term basis, and secondly of machinery for the reconciliation of competing demands in relation to public expenditure.

In addition there was recognition of the potential influence of the volume of economic activity controlled by public authorities over specific sectors of the economy, and furthermore that the underlying problems of the British economy could only be solved on a long-term basis and not through the use of stop-go measures.

This significant reversal in attitudes within the United Kingdom government was further prompted by negotiations then going on for entry into the EEC. The possibility of agreeing to common regulations for such diverse areas as agriculture and the taxation of consumer goods, lent significant impetus to the re-examination which was going on.

The election of a Labour Government in 1964 saw an expansion and continuation of the new approach to the role of the state as outlined above. Although the policy of the Labour Government of 1964-1970 can be divided into several distinct phases, it is perhaps best illustrated by the example of the Industrial Reorganisation corporation which was set up in 1966.[7] The IRC represents an important parallel with present developments in economic law.[8]

The object of the Corporation was "to promote industrial efficiency and profitability and to assist the economy of the United Kingdom through the promotion of assistance of the re-organisation or development of any industry,"[9] It was additionally "to have the power to do anything . . . which is calculated to facilitate the discharge of its functions."[10] It is too early to assess whether the Corporation was successful in achieving its goals, but general reaction to its operation seems more favourable than unfavourable.

However, the Conservative government elected in June 1970 came to office with a broad commitment to "less government". The Corporation

6. *Control of Public Expenditure*, Cmnd. 1342—the publicised version of the Plowden report.

7. Industrial Reorganisation Corporation Act 1966.

8. *Infra*, Part B, S. 6.

9. S. 2(1) of the 1966 Act.

10. *Ibid.*, S. 2(3).

was dismantled,[11] and there was a general change in attitude towards state intervention. That change was, however, short-lived, and did nothing to alleviate the underlying problems of the United Kingdom economy. Mounting unemployment, the failure of capital investment to increase and the continued serach for expansion resulted in a *volte-face* marked, *inter alia,* by the White Paper "Industrial and Regional Development" [12] followed soon after by the Industry Act 1972. That Act provided, *inter alia,* for the provision of capital grants in assisted areas[13] and selective financial assistance in the United Kingdom generally.[14] What had started out as a policy of disengagement had resulted in the broadest commitment yet to state intervention in the economy.

What have been the net results of the various interventionary policies pursued to date? What lessons can we draw from their operation for present and future forms of economic law in the United Kingdom? The intervention of the last decade has not generally achieved the goals it had been set. That failure is the result of many factors, both internal and external, but two problems in particular have been identified as crucial to that failure. Firstly, there is the problem where intervention is achieved through the taking into public ownership of enterprises. Nationalisation is perceived as having comparative disadvantages in that the values of commercial independence and relative flexibility are lost. It should, however, be pointed out that these comparative disadvantages may be equally attributable not to nationalisation *per se* but rather to the policies pursued by central government in relation to the public sector.

Given these disadvantages, the alternative approach is seen as operating directly through the private sector. This is regarded as being doubly advantageous in that it may be possible to achieve results far more quickly than could be attained otherwise, and this is of political value.

Operation through the private sector, however, poses problems as well. The problem is one of ensuring compatibility between the objectives of individual undertakings and those of the government. The objectives pursued by both need not necessarily coincide. The very notion of a private enterprise bears out that possibility. An enterprise in this sense is a private institution fulfilling a social function, and although a link will be established between the ends pursued by an enterprise and

11. Industry Act 1971, S. 1.
12. Cmnd. 4942.
13. Industry Act 1972, Part 1.
14. *Ibid.,* Part II.

the pursuit of those ends regarded as legitimate by society generally, the self-interest pursued by the enterprise need not coincide with that of the state. For if it were otherwise, the separate nature of the private enterprise would disappear and it would become a mere extension of the state. Thus, a decision to operate through the private sector must recognise this possibility of conflict. Intervention therefore ceases to be a temporary thing but rather involves continuous monitoring to ensure that goals are being met. It involves a close relationship between government and the private sector.

Where an industrial policy is based on consent then that policy is always open to frustration because the independence of individual companies may engender resistance to the attempts of government to influence decision-making. The problem is one of ensuring the maximum impact on the decision-making of individual enterprises.

Present and future policy is at present then directed, firstly, to the extension of public ownership, without the undesirable effects of previous nationalisation ventures and, secondly, towards ensuring the maximum impact of government policy on the decision-making process within individual enterprises. This element of control over the economic aims pursued by individual companies is thus an important aspect of the present development of economic law.

3. *The relationship of economic policy and law as a means of implementing economic policy* [15]

In examining the use of law as a means of implementing economic policy we should recall the existence of both the public and private sectors. The distinction between the two, other than the purely legal one, may, however, be obscured, in that, as we have seen, the overall management of the economy has as its basis not only control over the public sector but also increasingly control over the ends pursued by the private sector. There is thus a basic interdependence between the two which is fundamental to any study.

Furthermore, there are two aspects to the role of law in economic policy. Law provides both the framework for the management of the economy and, secondly, one of the means for the implementation of policy[16] and it is with this latter aspect we are concerned here. The

15. P. VerLoren van Themaat, *The Economic Law of the Member States of the European Communities in an Economic and Monetary Union* (Brussels, 1973), p. 29 *et seq.*

16. Daintith, "Public view and Economic Policy", (1974) J.B.L. 9

importance of the former should not, however, be ignored and the questions raised by it have important repercussions for the latter. Two questions of particular importance may be identified which are related to both the framework for the formation of policy and the implementation of that policy. Firstly, there is the question of the efficacy of parliamentary institutions in relation to the bussiness of government; the necessity of ensuring that Parliament plays a meaningful role in relation to government. Secondly, there is the question of how to protect the individual against the necessarily discretionary power of the executive. As can be seen, the two cannot be divorced, control may be both political and legal.

As regards the implementation of economic policy three distinct approaches can be identified in the operation of government. Firstly, there is indicative planning or the provision of information, the quality of the analysis of which convinces the decision-makers involved. Secondly, there is the bargaining of affected interest groups out of which some consensus may be expected to emerge. Both of these to a large extent are extra-legal, the existence of consensus *e.g.* renders the use of law unnecessary but the implementation of policy by these means has consequences for the framework of policy-making. Whilst there may be a need to reform Parliament and to make the excercise of discretionary power more visible, there is equally a pressing need to bring into the open the necessarily intimate relationship between public authorities and private interest groups which may determine the shape and scope of legislation before it has received its first reading.

Thirdly, and finally, the implementation of economic policy may be achieved by the use of legal controls, and it is with this aspect of implementation that we are concerned.

There is thus a dual aspect to economic law within the framework of the overall management of the economy. On the one hand, there is the use and control of the public sector and, on the other hand, the aspect of control over the private sector.

4. *Avoidance of conflict between the United Kingdom economic policy and the EEC*

There is, however, another aspect of economic policy which must be taken into account and that is the accession of the United Kingdom to the European Communities on January 1, 1973. Other than in such specific sectors as agriculture, coal and steel which are the subject of common policies within the Treaties, domestic economic policy must in general be pursued in harmony with the provisions of the Treaties and the rules developed therefrom.

Membership of the Communities clearly entails a detailed and far-reaching set of constraints on the formation and execution of economic policy, enforceable through the supervisory role of the Commission and the conferment of directly enforceable rights on individuals through Section 2(1) of the European Communities Act 1972.

These restrictions will ultimately cover all major areas of the economic policies of the Member States. Article 2 provides for the achievement of the Community's goals through the establishment of a common market *and the progressive approximation of the economic policies of Member States.*

One of the cardinal principles of the establishment of the common market is the securing of free movement of goods. The difficulties created by the existence of public enterprises for free movement of goods is recognised by Article 37. The problem of public enterprises is further dealt with in Article 90 in the chapter of the Treaty regulating competition.

Article 37 applies to state monopolies of a commercial character as a special case of arrangements which may produce effects equivalent to quantitative restrictions. They are defined as any body through which a Member State, in law or in fact, either directly or indirectly supervises, determines or appreciably influences imports or exports between Member States.[17]

Such monopolies are to be progressively adjusted either through their complete abolition or by the removal of their discriminatory aspects so that when the transitional period is over no discrimination regarding the conditions under which goods are procured and marketed exist between nationals of Member States.

Furthermore, there is a directly applicable standstill measure precluding the introduction of any new measure contrary to the above principles.[18]

There has been considerable debate over whether Article 37 envisages the complete abolition of such monopolies or only the removal of their discriminatory aspects.[19] An examination, however, of Article 37 in conjunction with Article 90, against the general background of public enterprises within Member States, would seem to indicate that Article 37

17. See: Case No. 6/64 *Costa v. ENEL,* 12 Rec. 1964, 41. 1964 C.M.L.R. 425; Case No. 13/70, *Cinzano v. HZA Saarbrücken,* 16 Rec. 1971, 1089, 1971 C.M.L.R. 374.

18. Art. 37(2).

19. See 1st Competition Report pp. 148-157 for the views of the Commission.

does not prohibit the continuance of commercial monopolies after the end of the transitional period and that in fact Article 90 presupposes their continued existence. The position would thus seem to be that Article 37 (2) excludes new measures and thus new monopolies to the extent that they violate *inter alia,* Article 37 (1).

The purpose of Article 90 is not to subject public enterprises to the rules of competition, but rather, through an understanding of the relationship between the state and the public sector, to preclude Member States, for example, from dictating to public undertakings behaviour which would, if undertaken by private companies, be contrary to the Treaty provisions. Thus, although it would cover relationships between public enterprises and the private sector it would also serve to prevent the granting of tax exemptions or subsidies by the state to public enterprises, thereby avoiding the prohibitions on aids to industry.

Paragraph 2 of Article 90 does, however, contain an important exception in that the rules of the Treaty shall only apply to undertakings entrusted with the services of general economic interest or having the character of a revenue-producing monopoly. To the extent that the application of the rules does not prevent the performance in law or in fact of the particular tasks assigned to them, subject to the proviso that the development of trade must not be affected to such an extent as would be contrary to the Community interest.

The rules of the Community are thus not only designed to regulate behaviour within the private sector but also, as we have seen, between the public sector and the state. The extension of the public sector and the utilisation of it by government in attempts to control the economy have thus important implications for these rules, and these are rules within the context of which United Kingdom economic policy must be formulated.

5. *Does the EEC Treaty accommodate different phases of economic policy?*

There is one last question which should be examined; one which is of particular importance at present. It may be argued that the economic substratum of the Treaty of Rome has since 1958 been progressively altered so that it is in danger of losing relevance to the economies with which it is concerned. It may be argued that the institutional and legal framework designed to serve six relatively homogeneous economies, each enjoying some rate of growth, is irrelevant to a larger community, containing within it new economies which in certain cases have differing problems, witness the regional problems of the United Kingdom. The impact of world economic events, a slowdown in the rate of growth, a likely redirection in the development of trade, have substantially altered the economic basis of the Treaty of Rome.

Such an argument, whilst perhaps on the face of it an appealing one, ignores the important question of the capacity for change within the Communities, and in particular the above question.

The Treaty itself provides detailed rules for the formation of a customs union and a broad framework for the achievement of the goals laid down in Article 2 through the progressive approximation of the economic policies of the Member States. The very nature of the goals presupposes a pragmatic approach which will take into account economic realities at the time. Furthermore, co-ordination of economic policies shall be achieved to the extent necessary to achieve Community goals,[20] and short-term economic policy at least is to be treated as a matter of common concern.[21]

There are no final objectives specified in the Treaty of Rome. Objectives can only be defined in terms of a progressive interpretation of the Treaties; the doctrine of "emergent purpose" in Treaty interpretation. The nature of the Treaty itself supposes a development of policies. Speaking of Economic and Monetary Union, the introduction to the 10th General Report on the Activities of the EEC, 1967, observes that the achievement of EMU is a matter of urgency because "the intermediate phase in which the Community is situated—a complete customs union but only a partial economic union—involves a definite risk of imbalance perhaps even of disintegration." Continuous development is thus a precondition of preserving the benefits already achieved.

The development of economic policies must, however, have a legal basis within the Treaties. Thus, in discussing the development of Community policies like regional policies, analysis has centred on the scope of Article 235 of the Treaty of Rome. The equivalent provision in the Treaty of Paris, Article 95, places specific limitations on the powers of decision to attain an objective of the Treaty. Any such decision can only be taken in accordance with the objectives as defined in Articles 2, 3 and 4. No such limitation is contained in Article 235 and one must conclude that this reflects the deliberately flexible nature of the Treaty objectives. Article 235 thus appears not only as a provision covering the lacunae which later may become apparent, but also as an instrument of evolution of Community policies.

It is both the nature of the Community commitment and the non-finite nature of the Treaty provisions that permits the conclusion that the Treaty is intended to accommodate different phases of economic policy.

20. Art. 6.

21. Art. 10 in conjunctions with Arts. 104-109.

B. FORMS OF ECONOMIC LAW

Concentration on the forms of economic law is valuable because these forms reflect the various degrees of control which the state wishes to exercise over the national economy at a given moment, and thereby disclose the policy aims of the state. Indeed, an examination of the various forms of control constitutes the contribution which the traditional method of legal scholarship can make to the exploration of that new phenomenon which we comprise under the name of economic law.[22]

We have said that the underlying rationale of economic law is economic *dirigisme*. Thus we might expect to see the failure of existing forms of control or the desire for greater control to be reflected in the search for new and more effective means of control, and our exposition of the background developments substantiates this.

The forms of economic law concerned with the private sector may be located as a spectrum ranging from the self-regulation of particular groups to nationalisation. Two preliminary points should, however, be made.

Firstly, there is no one set of ends towards which control may be sought. It may be sought in terms of public policy, public interest or more purely economic grounds. This will be reflected in the forms of legal regulation used, e.g. the use of an independent official or a close relationship with a ministerial department. Secondly, more than one form of regulation may be utilised in relation to any one type of economic activity. Most of these forms are not in any sense exclusive of one another, rather their use will reflect the attitudes of different administrations or the different ends pursued. Consequently one may note that the same ends may be achieved by different means and that the element of policy, be it of individual governments or departments, is of importance. Regulations used are thus as much the product of politics, philosophy, historical accident and current administrative practice as of any clear conception or rational evaluation of the effectiveness of each form of regulation.

1. *Self-regulation of interest groups*

The simplest form of regulation is where the private interest group regulates its own affairs and the behaviour of the members both in its own and in the public interest. This self-regulation is essentially applied by *codes of conduct* normally supervised and often enforced by profes-

22. VerLoren van Themaat, *op cit.* n. 15, p. 39 *et seq.*

sional or other interested groups. Emphasis is placed upon the role of the representatives of the organised interest group, and the role of public authorities is minimised or non-existent. Its continued non-existence is, however, dependent upon the continued satisfaction of the public interest through the operation of the representatives of the interest group. Insofar the state exercises a passive, but not an active control. This passive control would be converted at once into an active control if it is felt that the self-regulation fails to protect the public interest. It has been most commonly used in relation to the professions, e.g. doctors and lawyers, where representatives exercise delegated public power to maintain professional standards of conduct and competence, although its use has been advocated in other areas. Value may be seen in the comparative flexibility of this form of regulation in comparison with law and it is in keeping with the consensus approach we outlined.

As an example one can take the voluntary self-regulation of the Stock Exchange through its regulations and the self-discipline maintained by the financial institutions in the City through the City Code on Take-overs and Mergers. The City Code is administered and enforced by the Panel on Take-overs and Mergers, which is a body representative of the financial institutions operating in the City. The governing principle of this voluntary self-regulation is the prevention of discriminatory treatment of shareholders on the occasion of take-overs and flotations. The Code itself does not have the force of law and it is dependent on a common consensus within the group. It represents the collective opinion of those professionally concerned in the field of take-overs and mergers on a range of business standards.[23]

Failure to comply with the provisions of the Code is backed by a range of sanctions. They extend from private reprimand to public reprimand and eventually to a report to the Stock Exchange which may suspend the listing of the shares in question. If the standards are not complied with then "those who do not so conduct themselves cannot expect to enjoy those facilities (of the Stock Exchange) and will find that they are withheld".[24] Although the relative effectiveness of this system cannot be denied, its adequacy in the light of changing economic circumstances requires consideration.

The second example is more complex and exhibits several different characteristics from the regulation of the Stock Exchange. The "social contract" emerged as an agreement between the Labour Party and the Trades Unions Council providing an alternative means of regulating,

23. The City Code on Take-overs and Mergers, as amended June 1974, p. 4.
24. *Ibid.*

inter alia, wage negotiations, although many other political goals were also included in the agreement. It was presented as an alternative policy to that of the previous Conservative government which had been finally in favour of the statutory regulation of prices and incomes. The basis of the social contract is the voluntary adherence by individual unions to the voluntary guidelines laid down by the governing body, i.e. the TUC. There is, however, no clear consensus on the standards to be observed, nor is there any immediate sanction for their non-observance. Furthermore, it represents a development beyond the standard situation in that it is an agreement concluded between Government and the unions, i.e. it involves a commitment on the part of the Government. That commitment was, firstly, to abolish the previous government's control over pay settlements which had been controlled through the Pay Board set up under Section 1 of the Counter-Inflation Act 1973, working within the guidelines laid down by the Treasury Code. This was done under Section 6 of the Prices Act 1974.[25] Secondly, it involved a general commitment to secure control over inflation. This second aspect of the previous government's legislation, control over prices, was thus maintained and reinforced, although the economic basis of that legislation had long since disappeared. It had been introduced when the economic objective was expansion. It was seen as a precondition of this that the annual rate of increase in the retail price index, then running at 8 per cent, be reduced. The annual rate of increase is now in the regions of 20 per cent, control over pay has been replaced by a voluntary system, but the abolition of control over prices would be regarded as an outright breach of the social contract. Thus, although we might see voluntary self-regulation as extra-legal, it is essentially founded on consensus which is one form in which law expresses itself, and in some instances it is even enforced by prestigious interest groups; the possibility of imposing sanctions indicates that we are dealing here with a form of law. The success or otherwise of voluntary self-regulation, in particular in connection with private economic interests, may depend on the maintenance of legal controls in other areas.

2. *Licensing*

The second form in which economic law is expressed is the use of licensing in relation to certain activities. Three points should be made. Firstly, licensing may vary according to the purposes for which it is imposed. Secondly, it may be the sole form of regulation in a particular

25. The Counter Inflation (Abolition of Pay Board) Order 1974 s.l.; 1974 No. 1218.

sector or only part of a more comprehensive system of regulation. Thirdly, licensing systems may be administered by central or local government or by independent statutory bodies.

As regards the first point it may, for example, be imposed on grounds of public policy. The manufacture and wholesale of medicines is controlled by two different sets of licences. Firstly, under Part II of the Medicine Act 1968 a licence granted by the responsible Minister is necessary for engaging in the manufacture or wholesaling of medicinal products. In the decision whether to grant a licence, factors such as the equipment, premises and qualifications of supervising personnel, are taken into account. The Act also regulates the retail sale of medicinal products in that it provides for the registration of chemists' shops.[26] Secondly, individual medicinal products are also covered by a licensing system; product licenses, and these licences are necessary for the manufacture, import or sale of these products. Licensing thus provides a comprehensive, although not foolproof, system of regulation designed to protect the individual.

By contrast, the liquor licensing system seeks to limit the number of outlets both on moral grounds and on the grounds of the amenity of the area for which the licence is sought.[27]

Alternatively, licences may be granted for excise purposes either for the raising of revenue, as with betting excise licences, or for the protection of national revenue by imposing controls on the trade in excisable products.[28]

An area of licensing which contrasts with the voluntary self-regulation of the Stock Exchange is that in relation to the financial sector generally. Once again, standards are imposed for the carrying-on of certain businesses. Thus all dealers in securities are required to be licensed, with certain exceptions, under the Prevention of Fraud (Investments) Act 1958, unless they belong to an exempt class of persons. A licence may be revoked on the grounds that the person has not complied with the provisions of the Act, or refused where the administering body, that is the Department of Trade, does not consider the applicant or holder to be a fit or proper person to hold a licence. Similarly, in the field of consumer credit all credit grantors proposing to give credit to consumers must be licensed.[29]

As regards licensing which represents the sole form of control, we

26. Ss. 74–78.
27. Licensing Act 1964.
28. Customs & Excise Act 1952.
29. Consumer Credit Act 1974.

have seen the example of liquor licensing. Licensing may, however, form part of a comprehensive system of regulation in a specific sector designed to supplant the market mechanism by limiting access to the market and controlling competition within it. Licensing forms an important part of the regulation of the United Kingdom domestic air transport. Not only must pilots and aircrew be licensed and aircraft carry a certificate of airworthiness on grounds of public policy, but additionally an air transport certificate is required by the Civil Aviation Act 1971 for the operation of any aircraft for the carriage of passengers and goods for hire and reward. The licensing authority is a statutory public corporation, the Civil Aviation Authority. In deciding whether to grant or refuse a licence not only must the grounds of public policy be taken into account but also economic considerations relating to the proposed market for the service. The criteria governing these economic considerations are laid down by the responsible Minister.[30] Licensing does not thus only seek to impose conditions on grounds of public policy but also in this instance to regulate competition through the control of access to the market.

The third point is that licences may be administered by local authorities, central government or a quasi-independent body such as the Civil Aviation Authority. Important considerations attach to the administering bodies' knowledge of and expertise in the relevant market conditions. These will be referred to later in consideration of areas subject to comprehensive regulation.

The administration of licences by quasi-independent bodies, however, provides a convenient point for discussion of the third form of economic law.

3. *Interposition of an independent official*

The specific example we wish to consider is the office of Director-General of Fair Trading, instituted by the Fair Trading Act 1973. He is responsible for the administration of the law regulating competition and monopolies and also for the protection of the consumer, both generally under the Fair Trading Act 1973 and in the specific area of consumer credit under the Consumer Credit Act 1974.

The Director-General is subject to the general directions of the Secretary of State,[31] and to certain specific controls.[32] He is not,

30. S. 3(2).
31. Fair Trading Act 1973, S. 12
32. S. 50 (6)

however, directly subordinate to the Secretary of State but is rather in a semi-independent position.

The law governing competition and monopoly is now contained in the Fair Trading Act 1973, The Restrictive Trade Practices Acts of 1956 and 1968 and the Resale Prices Act 1964. There is thus control over monopolies, mergers, restrictive trading agreements and resale price maintenance. The first two had been previously dealt with by a reference from the Secretary of State to the Monopolies Commission followed if necessary, in the event of no voluntary compliance, by a statutory order to enforce its recommendation. The latter two had been dealt with by registration and the bringing of the agreement or reference, in the case of resale price maintenance, before the Restrictive Practices Court for a decision as to their compatability with the public interest. These two procedures are now substantially brought together under the Director-General of Fair Trading. In the case of mergers, however, they can only be referred to the Monopolies Commission by the Secretary of State,[33] but in the case of monopolies the Director-General, in addition to the Secretary of State, is empowered, with certain exceptions, to refer them.[34] He is under an additional duty to keep merger developments under review and to advise the Secretary of State as to possible references, thereby increasing the knowledge of his office in its field of reference.[35]

He has additionally taken over the duties of the Registrar of Restrictive Trading Agreements[36] which involves maintaining a register, making sure that all registrable agreements are in fact registered, and the bringing of such agreements before the Restrictive Practices Court. "These functions, in conjunction with his broad task of consumer protection,[37] give him a unique ability to secure the co-ordinated implementation of regulatory powers over commercial behaviour".[38]

Firstly, a Minister or the Director General may refer any consumer trade practice to a new advisory body, the Consumer Protection Advisory Committee.[39] References may include proposals for recommendations by the Committee as to rectificatory action if it is thought that the practice may be misleading or consuming, create undue pressure on

33. S. 64
34. S. 50
35. S. 76
36. S. 94
37. Parts II and III of 1973 Act.
38. Daintith, *Economic Law in the UK*, p. 119, ref. p. 193 of this vol., n. 7.
39. Ss. 14-16 of 1973 Act.

consumers or cause the transaction to be inequitable.[40] Where no proposals for recommendation are made then the role of the Committee is purely investigatory. If, however, the Committee endorses the proposed recommendation, then the Secretary of State may, if he thinks fit, make an order by statutory instrument (to be approved by both Houses of Parliament) which may prohibit or restrict the practice complained of or take other appropriate steps.[41]

The second means of consumer protection is through proceedings by the Director before the Restrictive Practices Court against anyone persisting in a course of conduct which is detrimental to the interests, economic or otherwise, of consumers, and in, unfair to them in the sense that it involves the contravention of enactments enforceable by criminal proceedings, or breaches of duties, contractual or otherwise, enforceable by civil proceedings. Where such persons refuse to give, or fail to observe, assurances to refrain from such courses of conduct in future[42] then if the court finds that the allegations are made out, and that the trader is unwilling to give an acceptable undertaking to desist, which is unlikely, and that is he likely to continue with that course of conduct or something similar, it may make an appropriate order to prohibit, breach of which is punishable by fine or imprisonment.[43]

The functions of the Director-General were extended by the Consumer Credit Act 1974 to cover, through licensing and other controls, all traders concerned with the provision of credit or the supply of goods on hire or hire purchase to individuals. The Act is an "enabling" Act providing for the licensing of those who carry on the business of granting credit and of ancillary credit, and the development of a comprehensive system of control through the regulations which are to be made from time to time by the Director-General.

He has two broad functions under the Act. Firstly, he is required to administer the licensing system provided for in the Act. Although subject to general direction from the Secretary of State, it is his function to grant, withhold, or revoke licences as he determines, subject to the provisions he lays down, and to maintain a register of all licences.

Secondly, he is to supervise the working and the enforcement of the Act and to review all developments both inside and outside the United Kingdom related to the provision of credit. The emphasis is thus on the provision of a flexible system which will be up to date with business

40. S. 17
41. Schedule 6.
42. Ss. 34-35.
43. S. 37.

practice rather than behind it and thus inadequate for the protection of the consumer.

It is against this background that the proposals for a Director-General of companies and investor protection should be seen.[44]

The proposed Director-General should be in a position of quasi-independence, like the Director-General of Fair Trading. His office should include three sections. Firstly, a section covering companies registration. Secondly, a section covering the present companies section of the Department of Trade, and thirdly an Investor Protection Commission. This section should be largely autonomous and should be constituted by the combination of the Quotations Department of the Stock Exchange and the Take-over Panel.

In the regulation of company behaviour, where the Commission requires its rules to be reinforced by statutory measures, it should be able to apply to the Director-General, who, if he considers that to be proper, will issue statutory instruments within the power conferred on him by the Act.

4. *Special control Regulations for private enterprise*

This form of economic law has been already indicated in our examination of the functions of the Director-General of Fair Trading in relation to consumer credit, that is the situation where an entire area of economic activity is subjected to comprehensive regulation. Such regulation, as we have already indicated, is mainly undertaken in the public interest and serves to guarantee the public interest against the results of failure in that private sector. It represents a guarantee to the public by central government which is realised through the subjection of companies concerned to standards of conduct which are sufficient to guarantee that public interest. It thus raises problems of sufficient flexibility of control which accommodates changes in business practice. The impetus for such a guarantee may be a "bolting the stable door" situation, as for example in relation to insurance, or alternatively may stem from the perceived need to reform the law in relation to a common activity *e.g.* the granting of credit no matter by whom it is granted.

The insurance industry provides a good example of an area in which there has been a shift from almost total non-regulation to what is now the most closely regulated industry in the financial sector.

That shift is a result of the failure of the policy of non-regulation to provide sufficient protection for the policy-holder. Until 1967 there had

44. C. M. Schmitthoff, *The Times*, Monday, January 6, 1975.

been practically no regulation whatsoever. The nature of the industry had, however, changed dramatically with the development of motor insurance and investment-linked assurance policies. Under the 1958 Act the Department of Trade was only able to intervene in a company's affairs and stop it trading if it was visibly insolvent, i.e. when it was too late to protect the policy holder.

The Companies Act 1967 gave the then Board of Trade two important new powers in that it could now investigate a company's affairs and, furthermore, was able to authorise or refuse to authorise the trading of a company. The collapse of Vehicle and General, however, illustrated the problems we mentioned in relation to the use of a quasi-independent official; firstly, the Board had an insufficient knowledge of the industry it was supposed to regulate, and, secondly, the legislation was insufficiently used to achieve its function. Thus, not only are the formal qualities of economic law important, its actual operation is of even greater importance.

The main legislation is the consolidating statute the Insurance Companies Act 1974 and the regulations made thereunder, which are still coming into force. This legislation is being further extended by the new Policyholders Protection Bill 1975.

There are two broad aspects to the intervention. Firstly, the regulations on solvency and the requirements for authorisation generally, the rules regarding trading conduct and the provisions for disclosure of information and intervention by the Secretary of State. Secondly, there is the protection afforded to policyholders by the new Bill.

As regards the rules governing authorisation, no person is allowed to carry on insurance business[45] unless authorised under Section 3 of the Act. For authorisation a person must be a fit and proper person.[46] There must be a sufficient margin of solvency;[47] the requisite paid-up capital requirements must be met and the class of risks must be reinsured.[48]

Other than in providing for the regulation of the general conduct of insurance business,[49] the Act makes provision for the regulation of companies.[50] The rules laid down cover the preparation of accounts and balance sheets, provide for actuarial investigation into the financial condition of companies, and require that copies of accounts be deposited with the Secretary of State.

45. As specified in S. 1 (1) of the 1974 Act.
46. S. 7.
47. S. 4.
48. S. 6.
49. Part III.
50. Part II.

The Secretary of State is also given considerable powers of intervention into the affairs of any company. He may intervene where he is of the opinion that the company may be unable to meet its liabilities, where the company has failed to meet its obligations under the Act, where it has furnished misleading or inaccurate information, where he is not satisfied that adequate arrangements are in force or will be made for the insurance of risk and, finally, where he is of the opinion that there exists a ground upon which he would be prohibited from issuing an authorisation.

He may as a result of his intervention exercise his powers under Section 12, imposing conditions on the company.

The second form of intervention is the proposed use of insurance companies funds for compulsory payment for policyholders of failed insurance companies.

The Bill provides for the setting up of Policyholders Protection Board whose expenditure is to be financed by a one per cent levy on the premium incomes of companies. The members of the board are to be appointed by the Secretary of State and the board will be subject to his overall direction. Further provision is made for the disclosure of information by companies to the Secretary of State.

5. *Provision of state funds subject to special conditions*

So far we have been mainly discussing control over the private sector in the public interest. The forms of economic law we are now going, to discuss are more concerned with the operation of central government through the private sector in the pursuit of specific policy objectives. Two specific situations may be distinguished. Firstly, the situation where government largesse is dispensed to private companies in the furtherance of standard policy objectives and secondly, the provision of state funds in extraordinary circumstances e.g. "rescue" situations. The latter situation will be dealt with in the next section.

In examining the first situation, however, it should be borne in mind that the government may utilise its considerable economic power *e.g.* the power of government to further specific goals. Thus the attitude of government to the construction industry in the 'Sixties favoured the placing of contracts with those companies regarded as being most amenable to the utilisation of new methods, to rationalisation and expansion. The control of this incidental power of the state is, as we have seen, as much a question of an effective political and open administrative process as of specifically legal controls. We may, however, examine the provision of state funds under two headings, regional and industrial policy. To distinguish the two regional policy "relates to the public assistance which the producers of a particular region may obtain no matter what they produce", industrial policy, on the other hand, "relates to the public assistance which may be obtained by the producers of a particular line of product, wherever in a country they may be located".[51]

Such funds may be provided for a bewildering variety of purposes, not all of which are necessarily compatible *e.g.* the maintenance of employment, the reduction of regional inequalities, the restructuring and reorganisation of particular industrial sectors *etc.* and obviously a great deal of other state activity *e.g.* research and development, or provision of information, is relevant to the genereal policy aims.

In the area of regional policy the Industry Act 1972 provides for government assistance to industry in assisted areas in the form of regional development grants which are cash grants to persons incurring approved capital expenditure after March 22, 1972 in connection with manufacture, mining and construction in the assisted areas. They may be paid at the Secreatry of State's discretion towards capital expenditure on new buildings or works or on the adaption of existing buildings, on new machinery or plant, on the construction industry and on mining works. The Secretary of State may, in addition, provide industrial sites or premises, pay regional employment premiums and make grants for the resettlement of key workers.

Section 7 of the Industry Act 1972 also allows the payment of selective assistance to undertakings in the assisted areas and Northern Ireland, the purposes for which such assistance may be given and specified in subsection two. The Secretary of State may provide financial assistance where in his opinion the assistance is likely to provide, maintain or safeguard employment in those areas. Such assistance may be given on any terms or conditions, and in any form, including the making of grants. Where, however, the financial assistance is given through investment by acquisition of loan or share capital then it can only be so done where the Secretary of State is satisfied that it cannot, or cannot appropriately, be so given in any other way, and furthermore any stock or shares acquired can only be acquired with the consent of the company.[52] Subsection five of Section 7 further provides that the Secretary of State shall dispose of the shares or stock as soon as in his opinion it is reasonably practicable to do so. There is no time limit on the power to give assistance, no financial limit on payments, and no provision for parliamentary scrutiny or control. Selective financial assistance for industry generally is provided

51. Cairncross *et al., Economic Policy for the EEC* (London, *etc.*, 1974), at p. 19.
52. Industry Act 1972, S. 3(4).

for under Section 8 of the Industry Act 1972. The Secretary of State may, until December 21, 1977 provide selective financial assistance for industry with Treasury consent and for the same purpose as specified in Section 7, where, in his opinion, it is in the national interest to do so and the assistance is likely to benefit the economy of the United Kingdom or any part or area in the United Kingdom. The same limitations are imposed on the provisions of assistance by way of shares or stock acquisition,[53] except that the acquisition must not be or more than half of the equity share capital of the company. Furthermore no one project shall receive financial assistance of more than £ 5 million without authorisation by resolution of the House of Commons, except in cases of urgency where it would be impracticable to do so.[54]

6. *State participation by means of shareholdings*

The limitations imposed on the acquisition and holdings of stock and shares in companies by Sections 7 and 8 of the Industry Act 1972 raise the whole question of increased control over the private sector. That should be seen not in terms of increased intervention but rather in terms of the effectiveness of intervention. The question of share acquisition should thus be seen both against the background of present practice and of proposed developments in the law reflecting the search for increased control.

Clearly there is a considerable history of state participation in the private sector, which is as much a result of historical accident as of any coherent government attitude. Government may take a majority or minority shareholding in a privately-owned company in return, for example, for the right to appoint its own directors, and it seems clear that such mixed enterprises will have considerable overall economic significance in the economy.[55] The restrictions placed on share acquisition by the Conservatives' Industry Act 1972 in part reflected the fears of accusations of back door nationalisation. Present departmental practice, however, reveals considerable disparities in approach, particularly in "rescue operations". The provision of guarantees by central government against present or future financial difficulties may or may not have conditions attached. The existence of absence of such guarantees, however, appears to depend on the attitude of the departments involved. The recent Burmah Oil company difficulties provide a convenient

53. S. 7.
54. S. 8(7).
55. See: T.C. Daintith in W. Friedman and J. F. Garner (eds.), *Government Enterprise*, Ch. 3.

illustration. In this case the three bodies involved, the Bank of England, the Treasury and the Department of Energy guaranteed the company's £ 270 million overdraft. Such action undoubtedly gave the company the capacity to survive. Any future improvement in its financial position will not, however, involve any benefit for the government and hence the taxpayer. Had the rescue been performed by the Department of Industry then the resulting position would have been different. The approach there, which was approved by the select committee, is that where the taxpayer places risk capital, which is what financial assistance is in these situations, into industry then he is entitled to a proportionate share of any profits accruing in future years.

It is, however, likely that the Industry Act, 1975, will provide the means for a rationalisation of the situation both as regards state participation and the search for increased means of securing control over the private sector. The Act has three main aspects: the establishment of a National Enterprise Board, the institution of a system of planning agreements and the provision for disclosure of information both by the government and companies.

The Act provides for the setting up of a state holding company, the National Enterprise Board, to administer its holdings in the private sector.[56] The Board will also be expected to pursue the functions of the former Industrial Reorganisation Corporation in promoting the nationalisation and modernisation of industry generally. Thus its functions will be the establishment of new industrial enterprises, the promotion of industrial reorganisation, the extension of public ownership into profitable areas of manufacturing industry, the promotion of industrial democracy within its subsidiaries and the administration of shareholdings and other property at present within public ownership.[57]

The Board is, in the pursuit of its functions, partially dependent of the Secretary of State. It may however be required to exercise the powers conferred on the Secretary of State by Sections 7 and 8 of the Industry Act 1972 as amended on a direction from the Secretary of State.[58] The Secretary of State must, however, consult the Board before giving such a direction and all such directions must be laid before parliament and be included in the Board's Annual Report.[59] The restrictions placed on their exercise are, however, removed under the present Act.[60] The Secretary of

56. Industry Act 1975, S. 1(1).
57. S. 2(2).
58. S. 3(1) and (2).
59. S. 3(3) and (6).
60. S. 22 and Schedule 5.

State has in addition a general power to give the Board directions under section 7 subject to the same conditions.

The powers of the Secretary of State in relation to the Board do, however, raise two related problems common to all bodies in a position of quasi-independence, that is, firstly, their insulation from short-term political pressures and, secondly, the establishment of the criteria under which they will operate. The conditions attached to the exercise of the Secretary of State's powers reflect concern over the former problem. In relation to the second problem a distinction is drawn between those operations which are to be governed by commercial criteria and those where other considerations predominate. This is reflected in the procedures laid down for the presentation of the Board's accounts. There is a general requirement that the financial duties of the Board are likely to result in an adequate return on the capital employed by the Board.[61]

Although there is a disagreement as to whether the Board will in fact have the power to acquire companies compulsorily, it may acquire up to 30% of the voting rights in a company, or invest up to £ 10 millions in its shares. Beyond these limits the consent of the Secretary of State will be required.[62] Such decisions, although subject to government control, would not be subject to parliamentary control.

The Act also provides for an important new means of influence over corporate activity, that is, planning agreements. To a large extent it is envisaged that they will simply institutionalise the existing dialogue between companies and government departments. Although they are contracts enforceable at law, they will be given sufficient statutory recognition[63] to allow companies concerned to rely on assistance proposed under them. The basis of the system is an exchange of information between companies and government on "stategic issues" covering *inter alia,* investment plans, productivity, employment, exports and imports and product development. They are thus of considerable importance in ensuring the maximum impact of government policy at the level of the company.

Finally, the Act makes provision for the disclosure of information both by government (S.27) and by companies engaged in the United Kingdom in a manufacturing industry which makes a significant contribution to a sector of such an industry which is important to the United Kingdom economy. Such information is to be communicated to government and, in certain circumstances, to unions.

61. S. 6.
62. S. 10(1).
63. S. 21.

The Act thus provides an oppurtunity for the rationalisation of much government activity in this area. The extent to which that proves to be the case will obviously depend, however, on the interpretation by the Board of its functions and the regard had by the government for the powers provided by the Act.

7. *Nationalisation*

The final form of economic law which we may consider is nationalisation; that is, the taking into public ownership of previously privately-owned assets subject to the payment of compensation. These assets are vested in an invariably, but not necessarily, monopolistic body corporate which stands on an often ill-defined relationship with an individual ministry. Its governing body is appointed by the responsible Minister and is charged with the broad duty of undertaking the day-to-day management of the enterprise.

The impact of the intermediate forms of economic law which seek increased control over the operation of the private sector, and the growth of the public sector to the extent that there is now a basic interdependence between it and the private sector, means that nationalisation has lost much of its former political significance in the sense of capturing the commanding heights of the economy, although it retains considerable emotive and ideological significance.

The development of the public sector and its increased importance in the overall management of the economy has, however, resulted in the emergence of new problems. There is now the necessity of ensuring co-ordination between the disparate branches of the public sector in an area marked by a lack of uniformity of control or legal structure.

Although that lack of uniformity may be attributable to the differing reasons for which particular sectors have been nationalised and the functions which they are regarded as performing, the problems posed by lack of uniformity make the necessity of some uniformity of control no less pressing. That control, however, must rather provide for an overall framework for that operation than extend to their day to day decisions. The temptation to apply political pressure in the interests of short-term political objectives too often precludes the achievement of their long-term objectives.

C. CONCLUSIONS

Three conclusions seem justified. Firstly, and most obviously, as the result of technological progress, changing world conditions and a different evaluation of social and economic factors, economic policy aims are progressively changing. In the United Kingdom a new delimination is taking place at present. The former dichotomy of business into a public and a private sector is losing significance and the interaction and interrelationship between those two types is giving way to a new arrangement, *viz.* a trichotomy of the public sector, a more or less strictly controlled private sector, and an (uncontrolled) private sector. The mixed economy of the United Kingdom thus assumes a new character.

Secondly, the law is sufficiently flexible to regulate these fundamental changes in policy aims. Developments in economic policy, as we have seen, are matched by developments in both the forms and uses of economic law. However, not only the legal form but also the operation of economic law is important. Not enough is known about the efficacy of economic law, both as an instrument of policy and as a means for the control of the exercise of discretionary powers. In the United Kingdom, in contrast with the EEC, too much emphasis is placed upon the "enabling" aspects of legislation rather than its possibilities as a means of control. The forms of economic law exhibit great adaptability to new situations. There is, however, a need to translate their necessary flexibility as an *instrument* into flexibility containing within it a sufficiently defined measure of *control,* unless we are to conclude that certainty, the normal value of the legal process for the carrying on of economic activity, has been supplanted by direct access to government. The authors view such a development with concern because an uncontrolled exercise of governmental power may lead to an abrogation of the concept of law itself, in the traditional sense, in wide areas of economic activity.

Thirdly, we may conclude that the Treaty of Rome does accommodate changes in economic policy and is sufficiently widely-drawn to accommodate regulation of the mixed economy irrespective of whether the accent is placed upon the private or public sectors. Consideration must be given to the greatly increased role of government in relation to Articles 85-94 EEC generally and Articles 37 and 90 in particular. Fortunately the Treaty itself is flexible. If the powers contained therein prove insufficient, recourse may be had to Article 235, for an adjustment of the policy considerations of the Treaty, in order to accommodate the changing balance in the economic policies of the Member States.

COMMON MARKET LAW REVIEW

AIMS

The Common Market Law Review is designed to function as a medium for the understanding and implementation of Community Law within the nine Member States, and for the dissemination of legal thinking on Community Law matters. It thus aims to meet the needs of both the academic and the practitioner.
For practical reasons, English is used as the language of communication.

EDITORIAL POLICY

The editors will consider for publication manuscripts by contributors from any country. Articles will be subjected to a review procedure. The author should ensure that the significance of his work will be apparent also to readers outside his specific expertise. Special terms and abbreviations should be clearly defined in the text or notes. Accepted manuscripts will be edited, if necessary, to improve the general effectiveness of communication.
If editing should be extensive, with a consequent danger of altering the meaning, the manuscript will be returned to the author for approval before type is set.

SUBMISSION OF MANUSCRIPTS

Manuscripts should be submitted, together with a covering letter, to one of the Editors. At the time the manuscript is submitted, written assurance must be given that the article has not been published, submitted or accepted elsewhere. The author will be notified of acceptance, rejection or need for revision within eight to twelve weeks.
Authors are requested to submit two copies of their manuscript, typed and double-spaced, together with a summary of the contents.
Manuscripts may range from 3,000 to 10,000 words.
The title of an article should start with a word useful in indexing and information retrieval. Short titles are invited for use as running heads.
The author should identify himself in print, with a short statement as to his current affiliation.
All references and notes should be numbered in a single sequence in the order in which they are cited in the text, and should be typed, single-spaced, on a separate sheet.

OFFPRINTS

The author will receive one free copy of the issue concerned and twenty-five offprints of his article. He may also order any quantity of additional offprints, with a minimum of 100 copies, at forty cents (Dfl. 0.40) per page per copy. This order must be submitted through the Executive Editor at the time of delivery of the corrected galley-proofs for print.

GPSR Compliance

The European Union's (EU) General Product Safety Regulation (GPSR) is a set of rules that requires consumer products to be safe and our obligations to ensure this.

If you have any concerns about our products, you can contact us on ProductSafety@springernature.com

In case Publisher is established outside the EU, the EU authorized representative is:

Springer Nature Customer Service Center GmbH
Europaplatz 3
69115 Heidelberg, Germany

Batch number: 10830943

Printed by Printforce, the Netherlands